# The Hackett Aquinas

## Robert Pasnau and Jeffrey Hause, General Editors

This series offers central philosophical treatises of Aquinas in new, state-of-the-art translations distinguished by their accuracy and use of clear and nontechnical modern vocabulary. Annotation and commentary accessible to undergraduates make the series an ideal vehicle for the study of Aquinas by readers approaching him from a variety of backgrounds and interests.

# Thomas Aquinas

# The Treatise on Happiness
# The Treatise on Human Acts

*Summa Theologiae* I-II 1–21

Introduction and translation by
Thomas Williams

Treatise on Happiness commentary by
Christina Van Dyke

Treatise on Human Acts commentary by
Christina Van Dyke (QQ6–7, 18–21) and
Thomas Williams (QQ8–17)

Hackett Publishing Company, Inc.
Indianapolis/Cambridge

For further information, please address
  Hackett Publishing Company, Inc.
  P.O. Box 44937
  Indianapolis, Indiana 46244-0937

  www.hackettpublishing.com

Cover design by Brian Rak
Composition by William Hartman


**Library of Congress Cataloging-in-Publication Data**

Names: Thomas, Aquinas, Saint, 1225?–1274, author. | Williams, Thomas, 1967–
    translator writer of added commentary. | Dyke, Christina van, 1972– writer of
    added commentary.
Title: The treatise on happiness. The treatise on human acts : Summa theologiae
    I-II 1/21 / Thomas Aquinas ; introduction and translation by Thomas Williams ;
    Treatise on happiness commentary by Christina Van Dyke ; Treatise on human
    acts commentary by Christina Van Dyke (QQ6/7, 18/21) and Thomas Williams
    (QQ8/17).
Other titles: Summa theologiae. Prima secundae. Quaestio 1–21. English | Treatise
    on human acts
Description: Indianapolis ; Cambridge : Hackett Publishing Company, Inc., [2016]
    | Includes bibliographical references and index.
Identifiers: LCCN 2016009484 | ISBN 9781624665295 (pbk.) |
    ISBN 9781624665301 (cloth)
Subjects: LCSH: Happiness—Early works to 1800. | Human acts—Early works
    to 1800. | Christian ethics—Catholic authors—Early works to 1800. | Act
    (Philosophy) —Early works to 1800. | Philosophy, Medieval. | Thomas, Aquinas,
    Saint, 1225?–1274.
Classification: LCC BX1749 .T515 2016 | DDC 230/.2—dc23 LC record available at
    https://lccn.loc.gov/2016009484

# Contents

## The Treatise on Happiness

# The Treatise on Human Acts

Contents

# Acknowledgments

Christina Van Dyke managed to take several years to write (and then rewrite) her commentary on the Treatise on Happiness; she is deeply grateful to the support from various sources that made this work possible: Calvin College (for a Calvin Research Fellowship in 2013 that provided teaching relief during the project's early stages), the Australian National University (where she was a Program Visitor in Spring 2013), Oxford University (where she was a Visiting Fellow in the *New Insights and Directions for Religious Epistemology* for Hilary Term 2014), and Notre Dame's Center for the Philosophy of Religion (for a Visiting Research Fellowship 2014–2015). She wrote most of her part of the Commentary on the Treatise on Human Acts (QQ6–7 and 18–21) in Thomas Williams's office at the Institute for Advanced Studies in the Humanities (IASH) at the University of Edinburgh and would like to thank IASH for their coffee and Thomas for sharing his space. Her time in Edinburgh was supported primarily by a sub-grant from the *Immortality Project*, directed by John Martin Fischer at University of California, Riverside. This project was made possible, in part, through the support of the John Templeton Foundation. The opinions expressed in this publication are those of the author(s) and do not necessarily reflect the views of the John Templeton Foundation.

Thomas Williams wrote the commentary on QQ8–17 while in residence at the Institute for Advanced Studies in the Humanities at the University of Edinburgh in the fall of 2014, when he was the American Philosophical Association (APA) Edinburgh Fellow. He is grateful for the support of IASH and the APA.

Our joint work was supported by a grant from the Calvin Center for Christian Scholarship, which allowed us to meet in person regularly during the crucial stages of planning and beginning our work on this volume. We are grateful for their support.

On a personal level, there are so many people to thank for their encouragement and support over the course of this project that it seems impossible to suppose either that we will remember the whole roster or that Hackett will let us take the space to list them all. If you are scanning the list for your deserving name and don't see it, know that our appreciation is no less genuine for the unintentional omission.

Christina needs to start at home, with her son, David. Single parenting may never be easy, but with the right child, it can be both fun and a fantastic source of philosophical examples. She also owes an insurmountable debt of gratitude to her parents, both for taking David into their home while she sat and wrote in coffee shops and offices in other parts of the world and for their unending (if sometimes uncomprehending) support. The philosophy department at Calvin College and Notre Dame's Center for Philosophy of Religion deserve thanks for their encouragement and critique of her work, as do the audiences of any number of talks in which she's discussed the issues central to this commentary, which include (but are almost certainly not limited to) audiences at Bethel College, Boston University, the Butler Society and the Philosophy Faculty at the University of Oxford, the Epistemology Reading Group at Cambridge University, the Cornell Colloquium in Medieval Philosophy, the Free University of Amsterdam, L'Abri International Fellowship (in Switzerland), Northwestern University, Princeton University, Southern Evangelical Seminary, the University of Colorado at Boulder, the University of Illinois at Chicago, both the Philosophy Department and the Center for Philosophy of Religion at the University of Leeds, the Society of Christian Philosophers Conference hosted by the University of South Florida, the Centre for Time at the University of Sydney, Wheaton College, and Yale University. She thanks her extended Facebook community, who have patiently endured any number of updates about the progress of this commentary and cheered her on to its completion. Finally, she needs to thank Susan Brower-Toland for insightful comments at an early presentation of these ideas at a Logos conference at the University of Notre Dame, Bob Pasnau for being the academic older brother to whom she runs with her philosophical troubles, and—last but certainly not least—Thomas Williams for his endless and delightful wit, for his insightful comments on all stages of this work, and, finally, for his patience with the highly sporadic nature of the work's progress.

Thomas is grateful above all, in this as in all things, to Marty Gould, who has been his companion, partner, sounding board, and adviser for eighteen years and who has never once complained about hearing (yet again) his assaults on the Bach G-major French Suite. He is grateful to the Right Reverend John Armes, Bishop of Edinburgh, for granting him permission to officiate in the Diocese of Edinburgh during his stay in that wonderful city and to the Reverend Canon Ian Paton and the other clergy and people of Old Saint Paul's Episcopal Church for welcoming and encouraging him in the exercise of his priestly vocation, thus extending to him the hospitality that Scottish Episcopalians have been showing to American Episcopalians since 1784. And he is grateful to Christina Van Dyke for good conversations, for philosophical insight, and for sharing his wonder (in perhaps more than one sense) at the thinking of the Angelic Doctor.

# Abbreviations

ST      *Summa theologiae*
        I       First Part (*Prima pars*)
        I-II     First Part of the Second Part (*Prima secundae*)
        II-II    Second Part of the Second Part (*Secunda secundae*)
        III      Third Part (*Tertia pars*)
art(s).    article(s)
prol.      prologue
Q(Q)     question(s)
resp.      response (to an objection)
supp.     supplement

## Other Works of Thomas Aquinas

| | |
|---|---|
| *Comm. 1 Corinth.* | *Commentary on Paul's First Letter to the Corinthians* |
| *Comm. 2 Corinth.* | *Commentary on Paul's Second Letter to the Corinthians* |
| *Comm. Col* | *Commentary on Paul's Letter to the Colossians* |
| *Comm. De anima* | *Commentary on Aristotle's De anima* |
| *Comm. Ethics* | *Commentary on Aristotle's Ethics* |
| *Comm. Galatians* | *Commentary on Paul's Letter to the Galatians* |
| *Comm. John* | *Commentary on the Gospel according to John* |
| *Comm. Matt.* | *Commentary on the Gospel according to Matthew* |
| *Comm. Metaph.* | *Commentary on Aristotle's Metaphysics* |
| *Comm. On Interpretation* | *Commentary on Aristotle's On Interpretation* |
| *Comm. Philemon* | *Commentary on Paul's Letter to Philemon* |
| *Comm. Philipp* | *Commentary on Paul's Letter to the Philippians* |
| *Comm. Romans* | *Commentary on Paul's Letter to the Romans* |
| *Compend. Theol.* | *Compendium of Theology* |
| *Kingship* | *On Kingship (De regimine principum)* |

| | |
|---|---|
| *On Evil* | *Disputed Questions on Evil (De malo)* |
| *On the Trinity* | *Commentary on Boethius's On the Trinity* |
| *On Truth* | *Disputed Questions on Truth (De veritate)* |
| *Power of God* | *Disputed Questions on the Power of God (De potentia Dei)* |
| *Quodlibet* | *Quodlibetal Questions* |
| *SCG* | *Summa contra Gentiles* |
| *Sent.* | *Commentary on the Sentences of Peter Lombard* |
| *Virtues in General* | *Disputed Questions on the Virtues in General (De virtutibus in communi)* |

# Introduction

Thomas Aquinas says in the preface to the *Summa theologiae* that he wrote it for "the education of those who are just beginning." By this he doesn't mean absolute beginners, however, but rather those who were beginning their advanced studies in theology. Such students would have already had a thorough grounding in Aristotelian philosophy and would have been well acquainted with the style in which the *Summa* is written. For today's readers, however, a bit more orientation is necessary. After a brief overview of Aquinas's life and work, I examine the structure of the *Summa theologiae* as a whole and the place of the Treatise on Happiness and Treatise on Human Acts within it. I then look in more detail at the content of the two treatises and explain how to understand and navigate the format that Aquinas uses in setting forth his views.

## 1. Aquinas's Life and Work[1]

Thomas Aquinas was born around 1225, probably in Roccasecca in the Kingdom of Naples. He was the youngest son of a wealthy family, and, as was typical for boys in his position, he received his early schooling at a monastery. In his case it was the Benedictine abbey of Monte Cassino, where he stayed from the time he was five years old until political troubles involving the monastery prompted Thomas's father to remove the fourteen-year-old to the University of Naples. It was at Naples, where he studied for five years, that he encountered two of the definitive influences on his life and work: Aristotle and the Dominicans. Much of Aristotle's work had been lost to the Latin West for centuries, but beginning in the twelfth century Aristotle's works were recovered and translated into Latin, a process still underway during Aquinas's life. In the Arts Faculty at Naples (think of this as roughly equivalent to today's undergraduate college within a research university) he began his lifelong engagement with Aristotle's philosophy. He also decided to become a Dominican rather than, as his family expected and very much wanted, a Benedictine. Life in the relatively new Dominican order, formally known as the Order of Preachers, was not considered a respectable vocation for the scions of the aristocracy. For fifteen months Aquinas's family tried to convince him to leave the Dominicans. (It is often said that they kept him prisoner. That is an exaggeration, but they did keep a very close watch on him.) Finding, however, that their efforts

---

1. The most detailed study of Aquinas's life and work is Torrell (1996).

were unavailing, they eventually allowed him to rejoin the Dominicans in the fall of 1245.

The Dominicans sent Aquinas to Paris, where he studied with Albert the Great, a formidable thinker, polymath, and commentator on Aristotle. When Albert went to Cologne to teach in the new Dominican house there, Thomas went with him, becoming his academic secretary. In 1252 Aquinas left Cologne to begin his advanced studies in what was then, and would be for some years to come, the preeminent Faculty of Theology in Europe: the University of Paris. There he lectured on the *Sentences* of Peter Lombard, a wide-ranging theological work on which all aspiring theologians had to comment as part of their training. He became a master of theology in the spring of 1256 and then taught in the Faculty of Theology until the end of the academic year 1258–1259.

There was only one Dominican chair in theology at Paris, so in order to give other Dominican theologians the opportunity to teach there, the order moved Aquinas to Italy, where he held various teaching positions from 1259 to 1268, completing the first part of the *Summa theologiae* and the whole of the *Summa contra Gentiles*, among other works. In 1268 he returned to the University of Paris, where he completed his most important works on ethics, including a commentary on Aristotle's *Nicomachean Ethics*, the second part of the *Summa theologiae*, and a set of *Disputed Questions on Evil*. In 1272 he took up a professorship at Naples. Late in 1273 he had an experience while saying mass that prompted him to set aside his work for good. "All that I have written seems to me like straw," he told his secretary, "compared with what has now been revealed to me." A few months later he fell ill while traveling to a church council in Lyon. He was taken to the nearby monastery of Fossanova and died there on March 7, 1274.

## 2. The *Summa theologiae*

The structure of the *Summa theologiae* as a whole is as follows:

Part One (*ST* I)
Introduction: Sacred Doctrine (Q1)

I. God
   A. God's essence (QQ2–26)
   B. The divine persons (QQ27–43)
   C. The procession of creatures from God
      1. The production of creatures (QQ44–46)
      2. The distinction among creatures (QQ47–102)
      3. The conservation and governance of creatures (QQ103–119)

Part Two (*ST* II)
II. Human Beings
    A. The ultimate end of human life (I-II QQ1–5)
    B. Acts through which a human being can reach this end
        1. Human acts in general (I-II QQ6–114)
        2. Human acts in particular (II-II QQ1–189)

Part Three (*ST* III)
III. Christ
    A. Christ himself (QQ1–59)
    B. The sacraments (QQ60– )[2]
    C. Immortal life

As this outline shows, the massive Second Part (*secunda pars*) of the *Summa* is further subdivided into a First Part of the Second Part (*prima secundae, ST* I-II) and a Second Part of the Second Part (*secunda secundae, ST* II-II). The Treatise on Happiness and Treatise on Human Acts comprise the first twenty-one questions of *ST* I-II. (A detailed outline of the whole *secunda pars* may be found at the end of this introduction.)

## 3. The Treatise on Happiness and the Treatise on Human Acts

Aquinas is a thoroughly *teleological* thinker: that is, the notion of an "end" or goal (*telos* in Greek, hence "teleological") is of central importance for him. Everything in the cosmos—the fall of a rock, the spread of a fire, the growth of a tree, the way a bird feeds or a cat grooms itself, the gradual maturing of an infant into an adult human being, even the planets in their courses—is directed toward an end. Each kind of thing has its proper end, as well as some kind of built-in directedness toward that end. Aquinas calls this directedness *appetitus*, for which the translation "appetite" is as inevitable as it is, unfortunately, misleading. We would not speak of things without consciousness as having appetites, for example; but even rocks and planets have an *appetitus*, a built-in purposiveness that accounts for why they move as they do.

    Given the central importance of the notion of an end, it is not surprising that Aquinas begins his treatment of ethics by examining the end for human beings, which, following long-standing philosophical tradition, he calls "happiness" (*beatitudo*). Without a clear understanding of what the end is, we cannot hope to understand either how human beings *in fact* act or

---

2. Part Three was left unfinished; Aquinas had written up to Q90 when he set his work aside for good. After his death, ninety-nine questions' worth of material on the remaining topics was compiled from Aquinas's earlier works; we know this compilation as the *Supplement*.

XX

how human beings *ought to* act. The two things can come apart in our case precisely because, unlike rocks and planets, we do have consciousness. We are not propelled toward our end infallibly by mere appetite. Instead, we can think about our end; we can ask what exactly it is and how we can attain it; and we can, and often do, get those answers wrong. Like everything else in an Aristotelian cosmos, we do have appetite; but ours is an appetite for the end *as it appears to us*, as our reasoning capacities reveal it—or, of course, obscure it. Human beings therefore have not just appetite, but what Aquinas calls *rational* appetite or will. We are directed to our end *as we conceive of it*, and so Aquinas begins by setting forth an account of what our end really is, how we ought to conceive of it.

The discussion in the Treatise on Happiness owes a great deal to the first and last books of Aristotle's *Nicomachean Ethics*, and on a superficial reading one might think that these questions are a fairly straightforward rehash of Aristotle on happiness, enlarged by a bit of material from Christian authors but not differing in any fundamental way from Aristotle's account. But as the commentary shows, this reading would be quite mistaken. Aquinas does think that Aristotle was basically right about what happiness consists in, but he discerns a fundamental ambivalence plaguing Aristotle's account. The only activity that could really meet the criteria that Aristotle sets out—in other words, the only activity that could count as happiness *as Aristotle himself rightly understood it*—seems downright superhuman, unattainable in this life. And so Aristotle (as Aquinas sees it) waffles, not wanting to deny that happiness is attainable but also not wanting to say unequivocally that anything achievable in this life actually meets the criteria for something to count as happiness.

Aquinas solves the problem by making a distinction. (There are very few philosophical problems, Aquinas thinks, that can't be solved by making a distinction.) Happiness is twofold: perfect or complete happiness, and imperfect or incomplete happiness. The criteria that Aristotle sets forth are criteria for *perfect* happiness, and Aristotle was right to think that anything meeting those criteria is superhuman and unattainable in this life; only in the next life, in the vision of the divine essence, is such happiness attained. But there is also *imperfect* happiness, the kind of excellent, flourishing, admirable life about which Aristotle wrote so well. That kind of happiness is attainable in this life.

Aquinas's treatment of the complex relationship between perfect and imperfect happiness illustrates a principle that is crucial for understanding Aquinas's work: the principle encapsulated in the maxim, "grace does not destroy nature, but instead brings it to completion" (*gratia non tollit naturam, sed perficit*). By this principle Aquinas stakes out a distinctive position not merely in his account of happiness but in the larger debates raging in his day about how Christian thinkers can or should make use of non-Christian philosophy and in particular of "the Philosopher" himself, Aristotle. For Aquinas, Christian revelation does not supersede non-Christian philosophy; it does not make it irrelevant or expose it as bankrupt. That is what is meant by saying that "grace"—in this case, supernatural revelation—does not destroy "nature"—the truth as it can be known by the exercise of our natural rational powers. Reason in fact points to its own limits: Aristotle could see what happiness had to be, but he could not see how it could be attained. Revelation brings reason to completion by offering an account of perfect happiness as an activity beyond our natural powers, attainable not by our efforts but by divine grace. And yet the prospect of perfect happiness in the next life does not mean that the imperfect happiness attainable in this life is not really happiness, that in aiming at it we are not aiming at a genuine end, or that the moral and intellectual virtues exercised in such a life are not really virtues after all. For grace does not destroy nature, but instead brings it to completion.

Once he has completed his account of happiness, Aquinas turns to human acts, "since happiness must be attained through certain acts" (Q6 prol.). As I noted before, everything in an Aristotelian cosmos is moved toward an end, and things have a built-in directedness, an appetite, for that end. Human beings, unlike rocks and planets and cats and dogs, have a distinctively *rational* appetite, also known as will: the appetite by which we aim at our end is informed by how we think about our end and about how to attain it. Human acts, as Aquinas understands them, are the acts that result from this distinctively human appetite; we have control over such acts because we have the capacity for complex thought that allows us to shape our behavior. The Treatise on Human Acts explores the many ways in which the exercise of our rational capacities can shape our desires, our choices, and even our conception of the end itself—and how our desires as well as our sub-rational capacities can shape our reasoning.

Aquinas's distinctive take on the relationship between nature and grace, reason and revelation, so fundamental in the Treatise on Happiness, is much less in evidence in the Treatise on Human Acts. For there he is talking primarily about how we can use our own capacities for thought to shape our purposive, end-directed behavior. Our natural capacities cannot direct us to our supernatural end; such direction requires grace, the divinely granted virtues of faith, hope, and charity, and the sacramental life, all of which Aquinas discusses elsewhere. So our supernatural end largely recedes from view in the Treatise on Human Acts, and the discussion is remarkable for its naturalism. I use the word 'naturalism' somewhat warily, since it risks misunderstanding. Aquinas is not a naturalist in his analysis of human acts in the sense that he rejects revelation or treats the physical world as a closed system. (We're talking about someone who seriously entertains the possibility that angels influence human behavior, after all.) Rather, he is a naturalist in the sense that the conceptual and argumentative tools he employs in investigating human acts are the same tools he employs in investigating everything else in nature. Human behavior is not sui generis. Yes, human cognition is more complex

than animal cognition, and human appetite is correspondingly more complex than animal appetite; but the same tools of analysis apply. Thus Aquinas
frequently analyzes human desire by an analogy with the motion of an inani-
mate object or applies general principles about how powers elicit their acts
to elucidate how the will in particular elicits its acts. Since he would explain
the metaphysical structure of a tree or a cat in terms of genus, species, and
difference, or distinguish between matter and form or essence and accident,
he sees no reason not to use the same distinctions to explain the metaphysical structure of an act.

The significance of this kind of naturalism can perhaps be best understood by contrasting it with the approach of the Franciscan philosopher and
theologian John Duns Scotus (1265/66–1308). Writing a generation later
than Aquinas, Scotus says that the will is a completely different sort of power
from everything else—he lumps everything else together under the heading
of "nature"—and so even if some general principle applies to everything in
nature, that is no reason to apply it to the will. It would, in fact, be stupid (*fat-
uum*) to do so. Aquinas would hardly have been able to wrap his mind around
such a determinedly anti-naturalistic approach to human acts.

The Treatise on Human Acts thus asks the same kinds of questions about
human acts and their development that an Aristotelian natural philosopher
would ask about different kinds of organisms and their development. What is
the defining feature or essence of a human act? What features of a human act
are accidental? How does our general orientation toward the end lead to particular concrete acts? How can a particular act be classified in terms of genus
and species, and how does that classification enable us to evaluate an act's
goodness or badness? The answers to these questions provide a rich, complex,
and often intellectually satisfying (if also occasionally mystifying) account of
the ways in which the built-in human directedness toward the good is shaped
by thought and desire, by enduring character and by momentary passion, into
particular acts for which we ourselves are responsible.


# 4. Reading the Treatises[3]

Each of the twenty-one questions begins with a short prologue. Often the
prologues do no more than state the topic of the question and then list the
questions that will be asked in each of the articles, but sometimes (QQ1, 6,
8, 13, 18) they mark important transition points and explain the conceptual
connections that determine the internal structure of the treatises. Each question is then divided into articles, each of which asks and answers a question
(usually, though not quite always, a yes-or-no question). The format within

---

3. This section is drawn largely from Pasnau (2002).

each article derives from the standard procedure for debates within the medieval university. After posing the question, the professor would collect various arguments on each side of the question, present and defend his own solution to the question, and then respond to the initial arguments in favor of the view he rejects. Simplifying and streamlining this format, Aquinas structures each article as shown in the following table, which gives a description of each section in the left-hand column and the standard name for each section in the right-hand column:

| (1) arguments (typically three, though the number varies) for the position that he will reject | objections |
| --- | --- |
| (2) one argument (often drawing on an authority) for the position that he will adopt | *sed contra* (Latin for "but on the contrary") |
| (3) a presentation and defense of Aquinas's own answer to the question | *corpus* (Latin for "body"), or reply |
| (4) responses to the initial arguments for the opposing view | responses to objections |

There are some variations—occasionally, for example, Aquinas will also reject the argument in the *sed contra*—but once you understand this basic structure, you can follow every article in the treatises. Admittedly, however, this order of presentation is not a natural one for contemporary readers. Some readers will find it preferable to read each article in this order:

> *sed contra*
> reply
> objection 1/response to 1
> objection 2/response to 2 (and so on).

But because the initial objections often help give some idea of what is at stake in each article—that is, why anyone would find the question interesting or controversial—some readers may prefer this order:

> objections
> *sed contra*
> reply
> objection 1/response to 1
> objection 2/response to 2 (and so on).

Readers who are new to Aquinas should try out both strategies to see which works best for them. Note that the responses to objections quite often extend or clarify the argument of the reply, so that you miss essential information if you skip them. And the responses make no sense unless you have read the objections, so those are essential reading as well.

# The Structure of the Second Part
# of the *Summa theologiae*

### First Part of the Second Part (*ST* I-II): Human Acts in General

I. Happiness (QQ1–5)

II. Human Acts
  A. In general (QQ6–7)
  B. Will (QQ8–17)
  C. Good and evil (QQ18–21)

III. Passions
  A. In general (QQ22–25)
  B. Concupiscible (QQ26–39)
  C. Irascible (QQ40–48)

IV. Habits
  A. In general (QQ49–54)
  B. Virtue (QQ55–67)
  C. Related to virtue (QQ68–70)

V. Sin
  A. In general (QQ71–74)
  B. Cause (QQ75–84)
  C. Effects (QQ85–89)

VI. Law
  A. In general (QQ90–92)
  B. Eternal (Q93)
  C. Natural (Q94)
  D. Human (QQ95–97)
  E. Old (QQ98–105)
  F. New (QQ106–108)

VII. Grace (QQ109–114)

## Second Part of the Second Part (ST II-II): Human Acts in Particular

# The Treatise on Happiness

## Summa theologiae part I-II, questions 1-5

### Prologue

Human beings are said to be "made into an image of God"; and as Damascene says, what it means for us to be an image is that we are intellectual creatures endowed with free choice and capable of controlling our own acts.[1] So, now that I have discussed the one whom we image—namely, God—and the things that have issued from God's power in accordance with his will, it remains for us to investigate God's image—namely, human beings—insofar as we are the source of our own acts because we possess free choice and have power over what we do.

### Question 1. The Ultimate End of Human Beings

We must first investigate the ultimate end of human life, and then those things by means of which human beings can attain this end or stray from it—after all, our accounts of things that are directed to the end should be derived from the end itself. And because the ultimate end of human life is said to be happiness, we should first investigate the ultimate end in general, and then happiness. There are eight questions concerning the ultimate end in general:

Article 1. Is it characteristic of human beings to act for the sake of an end?

Article 2. Is acting for the sake of an end something that only rational natures do?

Article 3. Does the act of a human being take its species from its end?

Article 4. Is there some ultimate end of human life?

Article 5. Can one human being have more than one ultimate end?

---

1. *On the Orthodox Faith* II.22.

1

Article 6. Does a human being direct everything to the ultimate end?
Article 7. Is there one and the same ultimate end for all human beings?
Article 8. Do all other creatures share that same ultimate end?

*Article 1. Is it characteristic of human
beings to act for the sake of an end?*[2]

It seems that it is not characteristic of human beings to act for the sake of
an end:

1. A cause is naturally prior [to what it causes]. But an end is something
that comes *last*, as the very word implies. Therefore, an end does not fit
5    the definition of 'cause.' Yet human beings do act *for the sake of* something
that is the *cause* of their action, since the words 'for the sake of' express a
causal relationship. Therefore, it is not characteristic of human beings to
act for the sake of an end.

2. Something that is an ultimate end is not for the sake of an end. But
10   in some cases, actions themselves are an ultimate end, as is evident from
the Philosopher in *Ethics* I [1094a4]. Therefore, not every action human
beings perform is for the sake of an end.

3. Human beings evidently act for the sake of an end when they engage
in deliberation. But human beings do lots of things without deliberating—
15   sometimes, even, things to which they give no thought at all, as when someone moves a foot or hand while thinking about something else, or when
someone strokes his beard. Therefore, human beings do not always act for
the sake of an end.

**On the contrary.** Everything in a given class is derived from the prin-
20   ciple of that class. And in the domain of possible human activities, the principle is the end, as is evident from the Philosopher in *Physics* II [200a34].
Therefore, it is characteristic of human beings to do everything for the
sake of an end.

**Reply.** Of the actions that human beings perform, the only ones that
25   are properly called human are those that are distinctive of human beings
*as* human beings. Now human beings differ from non-rational creatures
by being in control of their own actions. For that reason, only those actions
over which human beings have control are properly called human. Now
human beings are in control of their acts through reason and will, which
30   is why free choice is said to be a faculty of will and reason.[3] Therefore,
actions that are properly called human are those that issue from a will that
is informed by deliberation. Any other actions that might belong to human
beings can of course be called "actions of a human being," but they are

---

2. Parallel passages: *ST* I-II.1.2, 6.1; *SCG* III.2.
3. Peter Lombard, *Sentences* II.24.3.

not properly human actions, because they are not characteristic of human beings precisely *as* human beings. Now it is evident that every action that 35 issues from a given power is caused by that power in accordance with the nature of the power's object. And since the will's object is the end and the good, it must be the case that every human action is for the sake of an end.

**Response to 1.** Yes, the end is what comes last in carrying out an act— but it comes first in the agent's intention, and it is in that way that an end 40 fits the definition of 'cause.'

**Response to 2.** If some human action is an ultimate end, it must be voluntary; otherwise it would not be a human action, as I have explained. Now there are two ways in which an act can be called voluntary: because it is *commanded* by the will (for example, walking or speaking) or because 45 it is *elicited* by the will (as is the act of willing itself). It is impossible for an act elicited by the will to be an ultimate end. That is because the object of the will is the end, just as the object of vision is color. So, just as it is impossible for seeing itself to be the first object of vision, since every seeing is the seeing of some visible object, so too it is impossible for willing itself to 50 be the first desirable object, which is the end. If, then, any human action is an ultimate end, it must be an action commanded by the will. And in that case, some action on the part of the human being—the willing itself, at least—is for the sake of an end. Therefore, whatever human beings do, it is correct to say that they act for the sake of an end, even in performing 55 an action that is an ultimate end.

**Response to 3.** Such actions are not properly human, since they do not issue from rational deliberation, which is the proper principle of human acts. And so they have an end set by imagination, but not one that is established by reason. 60

*Article 2. Is acting for the sake of an end
something that only rational natures do?*[4]

It seems that acting for the sake of an end is something that only rational natures do:

1. It is characteristic of human beings to act for the sake of an end, and they never act for the sake of an *unknown* end. But there are many things that do not cognize an end: either because they lack cognition altogether, 5 as is the case for creatures without sensation, or because they do not grasp what it means for something to be an end, as is the case with non-rational animals. So it seems that acting for the sake of an end is something that only rational natures do.

---

4. Parallel passages: *ST* I-II.12.5; *SCG* II.23, III.1, 2, 16, 24; *Power of God* 1.5, 3.15; *Comm. Metaph.* V.16.

10      2. To act for the sake of an end is to direct one's action toward the end.
But directing an action toward an end is something that reason does, so it
is not characteristic of things that lack reason.
        3. The good and the end are the object of the will. Now the will is in
reason, as is said in *De anima* III [432b5]. Therefore, only a rational nature
15   acts for the sake of an end.
        **On the contrary.** The Philosopher proves in *Physics* II [200a34] that
"not only intellect but also nature acts for the sake of an end."
        **Reply.** It is necessary that all agents act for the sake of an end. In a series
of causes that are ordered to each other, if the first cause is removed, the
20   remaining causes are necessarily removed as well. Now the final cause is
the first of the causes. Why? Because matter acquires form only insofar as
it is moved by an agent—after all, nothing brings itself from potentiality
to actuality—and an agent moves something only in virtue of intending
an end. For if an agent were not determined to some effect, it would not
25   do one thing rather than another; so in order to produce a determinate
effect, it has to be determined to something definite that has the character
of an end. In things with a rational nature this determination is made by
the rational appetite, which is called the will; but in other things it is done
through a natural inclination, which is called natural appetite.
30      Even so, it is important to note that there are two ways in which something tends toward an end by its own action or motion. One way is by moving itself to an end, as human beings do; the other way is by being moved
to an end by something else, as an arrow tends toward a determinate end
because it is moved by the archer, who directs his own action toward the
35   end. Things that possess reason move themselves to an end, because they
are in control of their acts through free choice, which is a faculty of will and
reason. By contrast, things that lack reason tend toward an end through natural inclination, as moved by another rather than by themselves, because
they have no cognition of what it means for something to be an end and
40   therefore cannot direct anything to an end, but are merely directed to
an end by something else. You see, as I noted earlier, all of non-rational
nature is to God what an instrument is to a principal agent. Accordingly,
it is proper to a rational nature to tend toward an end by directing or leading itself to the end, whereas it is proper to a non-rational nature to tend
45   toward an end by being directed or led by another—whether toward an
apprehended end, in the case of non-rational animals, or toward an end
that is not apprehended, in the case of things that lack cognition altogether.
        **Response to 1.** When human beings act on their own for the sake of an
end, they cognize the end. But when they are directed or led by someone
50   else (for example, when they carry out someone else's instructions or are
moved to act at someone else's instigation), they need not cognize the end;
and that is how things are with non-rational creatures.

**Response to 2.** Directing something to an end is characteristic of things that move themselves toward their end; by contrast, it is characteristic of things that are moved by another toward an end that they are directed 55 toward an end. That can be true of a non-rational nature, provided that it is directed by something that possesses reason.

**Response to 3.** The will's object is the end and the good *universally.* That is why there cannot be will in things that lack reason and intellect: such things cannot apprehend universals. Instead, they have natural or 60 sensory appetite determined to some particular good. Now it is evident that particular causes are moved by a universal cause: for example, leaders of communities, who aim at the common good, move all the particular officials of the community by their command. And so it is necessary that everything that lacks reason is moved to particular ends by some 65 rational will that aims at the universal good—in other words, by the divine will.

### Article 3. Do human acts get their species from their end?[5]

It seems that human acts do not get their species from their end:

1. An end is an extrinsic cause, but everything gets its species from an intrinsic cause. Therefore, human acts do not get their species from their end.

2. What gives something its species has to exist before the thing itself, 5 whereas an end comes into existence afterward. Therefore, a human act does not get its species from its end.

3. One thing can belong to only one species, but numerically one act can be directed to many ends. Therefore, the end does not give human acts their species. 10

**On the contrary.** In his book *On the Morals of the Church and the Manichees* II [ch. 13], Augustine says, "Our deeds are blameworthy or praiseworthy according to whether their ends are blameworthy or praiseworthy."

**Reply.** Each thing is assigned to its species on the basis of actuality, not potentiality; and so things that are composed of matter and form are estab- 15 lished in their species by their proper forms. And this same criterion is to be applied to their proper motions. For motions can be divided into action and passion, and both kinds are assigned to their species on the basis of actuality: an action gets its species from the actuality that is the principle of acting, whereas a passion gets its species from the actuality that is the 20 terminus of the motion. Thus, the *action* of heating is nothing other than a certain motion that proceeds from heat, and the *passion* of heating is

---

5. Parallel passages: *ST* I-II. 18.6, 72.3; *Sent.* II.40.1; *On Truth* 1.2 resp. 3, 2.3.

nothing other than a certain motion toward heat. In both cases, the definition expresses the nature of the species.

25      Now human acts are assigned to their species on the basis of their end whether we look at them as actions or as passions. And indeed human acts can be looked at in both ways, since human beings *move* themselves and *are moved* by themselves. I said earlier [I-II.1.1] that acts are called human insofar as they proceed from a will that is informed by deliberation. Now

30      the object of will is the good and the end, and so it is clear that the principle of human acts as such is the end; and similarly the end is also the terminus of human acts, since what terminates human acts is what the will intends as an end, just as, in natural agents, the form of what is generated conforms to the form of what does the generating. In addition, moral acts receive their

35      species from their end; for, as Ambrose says in his *Commentary on Luke*,[6] "morals are properly called human." After all, moral acts and human acts are one and the same.

**Response to 1.** An end is not something completely extrinsic to an act, since it is related to an act either as its principle or as its terminus. And

40      this is a matter of the act's very nature: that is, it is essential to an action that it be from something, and it is essential to a passion that it be toward something.

**Response to 2.** Insofar as the end is prior *in intention*, as I have explained [I-II.1.1 resp. 1], it belongs to the will. And it is in this way that it gives a

45      human (or moral) act its species.

**Response to 3.** Numerically one act, as it issues at a given time from an agent, is directed to only one proximate end, from which it gets its species; but it can be directed to more than one remote end, one of which is the end of the others. It is, however, possible for an act that belongs to one

50      natural species to be directed to various willed ends. For example, there is just one *natural* species for the act of killing a human being, but such an act can be directed to the end of preserving justice or the end of satisfying anger; and on this basis the acts will have different *moral* species, since one will be an act of virtue and the other an act of vice. You see, a

55      motion does not get its species from an accidental characteristic of its terminus, but only from what is essential to its terminus; and moral ends are accidental to a natural thing, and (conversely) an end's natural classification is accidental to its moral character. And so there is no reason that acts that belong to the same natural species cannot belong to different moral

60      species, and vice versa.

---

6. In the prologue.

*Article 4. Is there an ultimate end of human life?*[7]

It seems that there is no ultimate end of human life, but instead there is an infinite series of ends:

1. The good by its very nature tends to diffuse itself, as is evident from Dionysius, *On the Divine Names* 4. So if what proceeds from the good is also good itself, it must be the case that one good diffuses itself by pouring 5 out another good, and in this way the series of one good after another goes on to infinity. Now a good has the character of an end. Therefore, there is an infinite series of ends.

2. Things that belong to reason can be infinitely numerous; that is why mathematical quantities go all the way to infinity. It is also why the species 10 of numbers are infinite: given any number, reason can think up a greater number. Well, the desire for an end follows the apprehension of reason, so it seems that ends, too, go to infinity.

3. The good and the end is the object of the will. Now the will can reflect back upon itself an infinite number of times: I can will something, 15 and will that I will it, and so on to infinity. Therefore, the ends of the human will go to infinity, and there is no ultimate end of the human will.

**On the contrary.** The Philosopher says in *Metaphysics* II [994b12] that "those who affirm an infinite series destroy the nature of the good." But the good is what has the character of an end. Therefore, it is contrary to 20 the character of an end that there be an infinite series of ends. We must, therefore, posit a single ultimate end.

**Reply.** If we are speaking of an essential order, it is impossible for there to be an infinite series of ends, in any respect. In all things that are essentially ordered to each other, if the first is taken away, all those that 25 are ordered to the first must be taken away as well. On this basis the Philosopher proves in *Physics* VIII [256a17] that there cannot be an infinite series in moving causes: because if there were, there would be no first mover, and without a first mover there can be no subsequent movers, since subsequent movers cause motion only because they are moved by 30 the first mover.

Now we find two orders in ends: the order of intention and the order of execution; and in both orders there has to be something that is first. What is first in the order of intention functions as the principle that moves the appetite in such a way that, if the principle is taken away, the appetite is 35 not moved by anything. But the principle in execution is the source from which activity begins in such a way that if the principle is taken away, one does not initiate any action. Now the principle of intention is the ultimate end, whereas the principle of execution is the first of the things that are

---

7. Parallel passages: *Comm. Metaph.* II.4; *Comm. Ethics* I.2.

40   for the end. In neither case, then, is it possible to proceed to infinity. For
     if there were no ultimate end, nothing would be desired, no action would
     be directed toward anything, and an agent's striving (*intentio*) would never
     come to rest. And if nothing were first among the things that are for the
     end, no one would initiate action, and deliberation would never reach a
45   conclusion; it would just go on forever.
         By contrast, where there is no essential order, but things are just acciden-
     tally connected with each other, there is nothing to prevent there being an
     infinity, since accidental causes are indeterminate. And in this way there
     can be an accidental infinity both in ends and in things that are for the end.
50       **Response to 1.** It is of the very nature of the good that something
     flows from it, but not that it issues from something else. And so, even
     though it is true that the good has the character of an end, and the first
     good is the ultimate end, this argument does not prove that there is no
     ultimate end, but only that from the first end that is presupposed we pro-
55   ceed downward infinitely through things that are for the end. And that
     would indeed make sense if we confined ourselves to considering the
     power of the first good, which is infinite. But since the first good diffuses
     itself in accordance with intellect, and it is characteristic of intellect to
     impose some determinate form on the effects that come from it, there is
60   a determinate measure employed in the outflow of goods from the first
     good, from whom all other goods have a share in this power of the good
     to diffuse itself. And therefore the diffusion of goods does not go to infin-
     ity; instead, as we read in Wisdom 11:21, God has disposed all things "in
     number, weight, and measure."
65       **Response to 2.** In things that are intrinsically connected, reason begins
     from naturally known principles and progresses to some conclusion. This
     is how the Philosopher proves in *Posterior Analytics* I [72b7] that one does
     not proceed to infinity in demonstrations, because demonstrations follow
     the order of things that are intrinsically, and not merely accidentally, con-
70   nected with each other. But in things that are connected accidentally, there
     is nothing to stop reason from proceeding to infinity. Now it is accidental
     to a quantity or to a given number as such that a quantity or unit is added
     to it, so in those sorts of cases there is nothing to stop reason from proceed-
     ing to infinity.
75       **Response to 3.** This multiplication of acts of a will reflecting on itself
     is related accidentally to the order of ends, as is evident from the fact that,
     with respect to one and the same end, the will is indifferent to reflecting
     on itself once or more than once.

### Article 5. Can one human being
### have more than one ultimate end?

It seems possible for the will of one human being to be simultaneously
drawn to more than one thing as ultimate ends:

1. In *City of God* XIX [ch. 1] Augustine says that certain thinkers held
that the ultimate end for human beings consists in four things: "in pleasure, in rest, in the primary blessings of nature, and in virtue." Obviously 5
that is more than one thing. So one human being can locate the ultimate
end of his or her will in multiple things.

2. Things that are not opposed to each other do not exclude each other.
Now there are in fact lots of things that are not opposed to each other. So
if one thing is held to be an ultimate end for the will, that does not auto- 10
matically exclude other things from being ultimate ends as well.

3. The will does not lose its free power by locating its ultimate end in
some particular thing. Now before it locates its ultimate end in that thing—
say, in pleasure—it had the power to locate its ultimate end in something
else—say, in wealth. Therefore, even after one locates the ultimate end of 15
one's will in pleasure, one can at the same time locate one's ultimate end
in wealth. Therefore, it is possible for the will of one human being to be
simultaneously drawn to more than one thing as ultimate ends.

**On the contrary.** What one rests in as one's ultimate end is the master
of one's affections, because it sets the rules for one's whole life. This is why 20
Philippians 3:19 says of the gluttonous, "their God is their belly": in other
words, they locate their ultimate end in the pleasures of the belly. But as
Matthew 6:24 says, "No one can serve two masters"—meaning, of course,
two masters that are not ordered to each other. Therefore, it is impossible
for there to be more than one ultimate end for one human being if those 25
ends are not ordered to each other.

**Reply.** It is impossible for the will of one human being to have multiple
ultimate ends at one time. We can offer three arguments for this. First,
since everything desires its own perfection, what people desire as their
ultimate end is what they desire as a good that is perfect and brings them 30
to completion. This is why Augustine says in *City of God* XIX [ch. 2], "we
speak now of the end of the good: meaning not that the good is destroyed
so that it does not exist, but that it is perfected so that it is complete." Therefore, an ultimate end must so satisfy a person's whole desire that there is
nothing else outside it left over to be desired. That cannot be the case if 35
anything outside it is required for it to be complete. For that reason, it is
not possible for desire to aim at two things as if both were its ultimate end.

The second argument is that just as reason proceeds from a starting
point—what is naturally known—so too rational appetite, which is will,
proceeds from a starting point—what is naturally desired. And this has to 40

be one thing, since nature tends only to one thing. Now the starting point
from which rational appetite proceeds is the ultimate end. So that to which
the will tends as an ultimate end must be one thing.

  The third argument is that since voluntary actions receive their species
45 from the end, as I maintained above [I-II.1.3], they should receive their
genus from the ultimate end, which is common, in the same way that natural things are assigned to a genus based on a common formal characteristic. So since everything that can be desired by the will belongs, as such,
to a single genus, there has to be a single ultimate end. This is especially
50 so because in every genus there is one first principle, and the ultimate end
has the character of a first principle, as I have said [I-II.1.4]. Now the same
relation that holds between the ultimate end for human beings as such and
the whole human race also holds between some particular person's ultimate end and that particular person. For that reason, just as there is natu-
55 rally one ultimate end for all human beings, it must also be the case that
the will of each individual human being is restricted to one ultimate end.

  **Response to 1.** Those who held that the ultimate end consisted in that
plurality of things understood them as composing a single perfect good.

  **Response to 2.** Even if a plurality of things can be identified that are not
60 opposed to each other, it is opposed to a *perfect* good that there be anything
outside it that is necessary for a thing's perfection.

  **Response to 3.** The will does not have the power to make opposites exist
at the same time. And that is what would happen if it tended toward a plurality of distinct things as ultimate ends, as is clear from what I have said.

*Article 6. Do human beings will everything
they will for the sake of the ultimate end?*[8]

It seems that human beings do not will everything they will for the sake
of the ultimate end:

  1. We consider things that are directed to the ultimate end to be serious
business, because they serve a purpose. But we distinguish jests from seri-
5 ous business. Therefore, human beings do not order to the ultimate end
the things they do in jest.

  2. The Philosopher says at the beginning of the *Metaphysics* [982a14]
that the speculative sciences are investigated for their own sake. But we
cannot say that any of the speculative sciences is the ultimate end. There-
10 fore, human beings do not will everything they will for the sake of the
ultimate end.

---

8. Parallel passages: *Sent.* IV.49.1.3.4; *SCG* I.101.

3. Anyone who orders something to an end thinks about that end. But human beings do not think about the ultimate end in everything they desire or do. Therefore, human beings do not desire or do everything for the sake of the ultimate end.

**On the contrary.** Augustine says in *City of God* XIX [ch. 1], "the end of our good is that for the sake of which other things are loved, whereas it is loved for its own sake."

**Reply.** It must be the case that human beings desire everything they desire for the sake of the ultimate end. There are two arguments that make this evident. First, whatever human beings desire, they desire under the aspect of good. So if something is not desired as the complete good, which is the ultimate end, it must be desired as leading to the complete good. After all, a thing's beginning is always directed to its fully developed state; this is as clear in the workings of nature as it is in the products of art. And so every beginning of a perfection is directed to its fully developed state, which is realized in its ultimate end.

Second, what the first mover is in other motions, the ultimate end is in arousing desire. Now it is clear that secondary moving causes cause motion only because they are themselves moved by the first mover. Hence, secondary objects of desire arouse desire only in virtue of their ordering to the first object of desire, which is the ultimate end.

**Response to 1.** Playful actions are not directed to any external end, but they *are* directed to the good of the person who acts playfully, insofar as they are pleasurable or relaxing. And the fully developed good of human beings is their ultimate end.

**Response to 2.** The reply to the second argument, about speculative science, is similar: speculative science is desired as a good of the ones who possess such speculative knowledge—a good that is included in their complete and perfect good, which is their ultimate end.

**Response to 3.** It is not necessary that people always think about the ultimate end whenever they desire something or act. What matters is that the force of that first intention, the intention of the ultimate end, carries over into every desire for anything whatsoever, even if one is not actually thinking about the ultimate end—just as people who are walking along a path do not have to think of their destination every time they take a step.

### Article 7. Is there one and the same
### ultimate end for all human beings?[9]

It seems that there is not one ultimate end for all human beings:

1. It seems that the ultimate end of human beings is, above all else, an unchangeable good; yet some people turn away from the unchangeable good by sinning. Therefore, there is not one ultimate end for all human
5  beings.

2. The whole of human life is regulated by the ultimate end. So if there were one ultimate end for all human beings, different people would not devote their lives to different concerns. That is obviously false.

3. An end is the terminus of an action, and actions have to do with sin-
10 gulars. Now although human beings all have the same specific nature, they differ in terms of their individual characteristics. Therefore, there is not one ultimate end for all human beings.

**On the contrary.** Augustine says in *On the Trinity* XIII [ch. 3] that all human beings agree in desiring the ultimate end, which is happiness.

15   **Reply.** There are two ways in which we can speak about the ultimate end: in terms of what it means for something to be an ultimate end, and in terms of the thing that meets that description. In terms of what it means for something to be an ultimate end, all human beings agree in desiring the ultimate end because they all desire to attain their own perfection, and
20 that is what is meant by "ultimate end," as I have explained [I-II.1.5]. But in terms of the thing that meets that description, human beings do not all agree in their ultimate end: some desire wealth as their full and complete good, whereas others desire pleasure and others desire something else— just as what is sweet is pleasant to everyone's taste, but some people prefer
25 the sweetness of wine, others the sweetness of honey or some other sweet thing. The unqualifiedly best sweet thing must be the one that someone with the best possible sense of taste finds most pleasant, and similarly the most complete good must be the one that someone with well-disposed affections desires as ultimate end.

30   **Response to 1.** Those who sin turn away from the thing that genuinely meets the criteria for being the ultimate end, but they do not turn away from intending the ultimate end, which they mistakenly seek in other things.

**Response to 2.** People devote their lives to different concerns because
35 they seek the ultimate end in different things.

**Response to 3.** Yes, actions have to do with singulars, but their first principle of acting is nature, which tends to one thing, as I have said [I-II.1.5].

---

9. Parallel passages: *ST* I-II. 1.5; *Comm. Ethics* I.9.

### Article 8. Do all other creatures have the
### same ultimate end as human beings?[10]

It seems that all other things have the same ultimate end as human beings:
1. The end corresponds to the beginning. All human beings have their beginning from God—as do all other creatures. Therefore, all other things share in the ultimate end for human beings.

2. Dionysius says in *On the Divine Names* 4 [§4] that "God turns all things to himself as their ultimate end." But God is also the ultimate end for human beings, since he alone is to be enjoyed, as Augustine says.[11] Therefore, other things have the same ultimate end as human beings.

3. The ultimate end of human beings is the object of the will. And the object of the will is the universal good, which is the end of all things. Therefore, it must be the case that all things have the same ultimate end as human beings.

**On the contrary.** The ultimate end of human beings is happiness, which they all desire, as Augustine says.[12] "But to be happy does not fall to the lot of animals that lack reason," as Augustine says in *On 83 Questions* [q. 5]. Therefore other things do not have the same ultimate end as human beings.

**Reply.** As the Philosopher says in Physics II [194a35] and *Metaphysics* V,[13] there are two senses of 'end': the end "for the sake of which" and the end "by which"—that is, the thing in which the aspect of good is found, and the use or attainment of that thing. For example, we might say that the end of the movement of a heavy body is (as the thing) the lower place or (as attainment) being in the lower place, and a miser's end is (as the thing) money or (as attainment) the possession of money. Now if we are speaking of the ultimate end for human beings in terms of the thing that is the end, then all other things have the same end as human beings, because God is the ultimate end of human beings and of all other things. But if we are speaking of the ultimate end of human beings in terms of the attainment of the end, then non-rational creatures do not share in the end of human beings. For human beings and other rational creatures attain their ultimate end by knowing and loving God, which is not the case for other creatures, which reach the ultimate end insofar as they share in some likeness to God by existing, living, or even cognizing.

---

10. Parallel passages: *ST* I.103.2; *Sent.* II.38.1, 2; *SCG* III.17, 25; *On Truth* 5.6 resp. 4.

11. *On Christian Teaching* I.1.

12. *On the Trinity* XIII.3.

13. In fact Aquinas seems to have in mind *De anima* II.4.

35    And from this the response to the objections is straightforward, since
'happiness' means the attainment of the ultimate end.


## Question 2. The Things in Which Happiness Consists

Next we must investigate happiness. First, we must discuss the things in
which happiness consists; second, what happiness is; third, how we can
attain happiness.

Concerning the things in which happiness consists, there are eight
questions:

Article 1. Does happiness consist in wealth?
Article 2. Does happiness consist in honors?
Article 3. Does happiness consist in fame or glory?
Article 4. Does happiness consist in power?
Article 5. Does happiness consist in some good of the body?
Article 6. Does happiness consist in pleasure?
Article 7. Does happiness consist in some good of the soul?
Article 8. Does happiness consist in some created good?


### Article 1. Does human happiness consist in wealth?[14]

It seems that human happiness consists in wealth:

1. Since happiness is the ultimate end of human beings, it consists in
whatever motivates human beings most powerfully. Now wealth is like that,
since as we read in Ecclesiastes 10:19, "All things obey money." Therefore,
5    human happiness consists in wealth.

2. According to Boethius in *Consolation of Philosophy* III [pr. 2], happiness is "the state that is made complete by the accumulation of all goods."
Now it appears that one possesses everything by possessing money, since,
as the Philosopher says in *Ethics* V [1133b12], currency was invented to
10    serve as a guarantee for acquiring anything one might want. Therefore,
happiness consists in wealth.

3. Since the desire for the supreme good never fails, it seems to be infinite. This infinity is particularly found in wealth, since "the greedy never
have their fill of money," as Ecclesiastes 10:19 says. Therefore, happiness
15    consists in wealth.

**On the contrary.** The human good consists in holding on to happiness
rather than in letting it go. But as Boethius says in *Consolation of Philosophy* II [pr. 5], "the glory of wealth is in giving it away rather than in hoard-
ing it; for greed makes people contemptible, but generosity brings renown."
20    Therefore, happiness does not consist in wealth.

---

14. Parallel passages: SCG III.20; *Comm. Ethics* I.5.

**Reply.** Human happiness cannot consist in wealth. You see, as the Philosopher says in *Politics* I [1257a4], there are two sorts of wealth: natural and artificial. Natural wealth includes the things that help human beings meet their natural needs: for example, food, drink, clothing, means of transportation, shelter, and things like that. Artificial wealth includes things, such as money, that do not help nature in and of themselves, but were developed by human ingenuity to be an easy means of exchange, as a sort of measure of things that can be bought and sold.

Now it is evident that human happiness cannot consist in natural wealth, since natural wealth is sought for the sake of something else—namely, to preserve human nature—and so it cannot be the ultimate end for human beings; rather, human beings are the end of wealth. Accordingly, all these things are inferior to human beings in the order of nature, and they were made for the sake of human beings; as we read in Psalm 8:8, "You have put all things under their feet."

Now the only reason to pursue artificial wealth is for the sake of natural wealth: people pursue money only because they can use it to buy things they can use for the necessities of life. So artificial wealth is much further from the character of an ultimate end than natural wealth is. Therefore, happiness, which is the ultimate end for human beings, cannot consist in wealth.

**Response to 1.** All *bodily* things obey money as far as the ignorant masses go, because they only pay attention to the bodily goods that money can buy. But we should take our judgments about what is good for human beings not from the ignorant, but from the wise, just as we take our judgments about flavors from those whose sense of taste is in good condition.

**Response to 2.** By means of money one can possess anything that can be bought or sold, but not spiritual things, which are not for sale. This is why Proverbs 17:16 says, "What good does it do a fool to possess wealth, since he cannot buy wisdom?"

**Response to 3.** The desire for natural wealth is not infinite, since a determinate amount of natural wealth will satisfy the needs of nature. The desire for artificial wealth, by contrast, is indeed infinite, since artificial wealth serves inordinate covetousness, which has no limit, as is evident from the Philosopher in *Politics* I [1258a1]. But the desire for wealth and the desire for the supreme good are infinite in different ways. You see, the more perfectly one possesses the supreme good, the more one loves it and the less one cares for anything else, because the more one has it, the better one knows it. That is why Ecclesiasticus 24:29 says, "Those who eat me will still hunger." But in the desire for wealth and for temporal goods of any kind, the converse is true: no sooner does one possess them than one ceases to care about them and moves on to wanting other things, as is expressed in the Lord's words in John 4:13: "Those who drink of this

water"—signifying temporal things—"will thirst again." And this is because
65   we recognize their inadequacy more clearly when we possess them. And so
this very fact shows their imperfection and demonstrates that the supreme
good does not consist in them.

### Article 2. Does human happiness consist in honors?[15]

It seems that human happiness consists in honors:
1. Happiness or felicity is the reward of virtue, as the Philosopher says
in *Ethics* I [1099a16]. But honor especially seems to be the reward of virtue, as the Philosopher says in *Ethics* IV [1123b35]. Therefore, happiness
5   consists especially in honor.
2. What characterizes God and those who are most excellent seems
especially to be happiness, which is the perfect good. And honor is like
this, as the Philosopher says in *Ethics* IV [1123b20]. Also, in 1 Timothy
1:17 the Apostle says, "To God alone be honor and glory." Therefore, hap-
10   piness consists in honor.
3. Happiness is what human beings desire most. Now it seems that
human beings desire nothing more than honor, since they will sacrifice
everything else to avoid any loss of honor. Therefore, happiness consists
in honor.
15        **On the contrary.** Happiness is in the one who is happy, whereas honor
is not in the one who is honored but in the one who honors—the one who
shows respect for the one who is honored—as the Philosopher says in *Ethics* I [1095b25]. Therefore, happiness does not consist in honor.
**Reply.** Happiness cannot consist in honor. Honor is shown to people
20   because of some excellence that they possess; in this way, honor is a sign
and an indication of some excellence in those who are honored. But what
makes for human excellence is, above all else, happiness, which is the
complete human good, and the components of happiness, that is, the good
things through which one has some share in happiness. And so honor can
25   indeed be a consequence of happiness, but happiness cannot consist primarily in honor.
**Response to 1.** As the Philosopher says in the same place, honor is not
the reward of virtue in the sense that the virtuous act for the sake of honor,
but in the sense that the virtuous receive honor in place of a reward, since
30   people have nothing greater to give them. The true reward of virtue is happiness itself; it is for the sake of happiness that the virtuous do what they
do. Indeed, if they were acting for the sake of honor, it would no longer be
virtue, but rather ambition.

---

15. Parallel passages: SCG III.28; *Comm. Ethics* I.5.

**Response to 2.** Honor is owed to God and to those who are most excellent as a sign or indication of the excellence that is already in them; the honor itself is not what makes them excellent. **Response to 3.** As I have said, honor is a consequence of happiness; human beings especially desire honor because of their natural desire for happiness. This is why people look to be honored most of all by those who are wise, believing themselves to be excellent or happy because the wise judge them to be so.

### Article 3. Does human happiness consist in glory or fame?[16]

It seems that human happiness consists in glory:

1. Happiness seems to consist in that which is given to the saints for the tribulations that they endure in the world. Glory fits this description, since the Apostle says in Romans 8:18, "the sufferings of this time are not worthy to be compared with the glory that is to come, which will be revealed in us." Therefore, happiness consists in glory.

2. The good tends to diffuse itself, as is clear from Dionysius, *On the Divine Names* 4 [§1]. Now it is chiefly through glory that the human good is diffused by becoming known to others; after all, as Ambrose says, glory is nothing other than "illustrious knowledge accompanied by praise."[17] Therefore, human happiness consists in glory.

3. Happiness is the most stable of goods. Now that appears to be fame or glory, since through fame human beings attain eternity in a way. This is why Boethius says in *Consolation of Philosophy* II [pr. 7], "You seem to generate immortality for yourself when you think of your fame in times to come." Therefore, human happiness consists in fame or glory.

**On the contrary.** Happiness is the true human good. Fame or glory, however, can be false; for as Boethius says in *Consolation of Philosophy* III [pr. 6], "Many people have stolen a great name through the false opinions of the vulgar. What more shameful thing can be imagined than this? Those who receive such false acclaim must surely blush to hear themselves praised." Therefore, human happiness does not consist in fame or glory.

**Reply.** Human happiness cannot consist in human fame or glory. For, as Ambrose says, glory is nothing other than illustrious knowledge accompanied by praise. Now human knowledge and divine knowledge have quite different relations to the things they know: human knowledge is caused by the things that are known, whereas divine knowledge is the cause of the things it knows. That is why the perfection of the human good, which is called happiness, cannot be caused by human knowledge; instead, human

---

16. Parallel passage: SCG III.29.

17. This is actually a quotation from Augustine, *Against Maximinus the Arian* II.13.

30    knowledge of someone's happiness proceeds from, and is in a certain way
      caused by, human happiness itself, whether incipient or complete. So
      human happiness cannot consist in fame or glory.
         But the human good does depend causally on God's knowledge, and so
      human happiness depends causally on the glory that is in the eyes of God,
35    as we read in Psalm 90:15–16: "I will rescue him and give him glory; with
      length of days will I satisfy him, and I will show him my salvation."
         One must also keep in mind that human knowledge is often mistaken,
      especially when it comes to particular contingent matters such as human
      acts. For that reason human glory is frequently mistaken. God, however,
40    cannot be mistaken, so glory in God's eyes is always true glory. This is why
      2 Corinthians 10:18 says, "The one whom God commends is approved."
         **Response to 1.** In this passage the Apostle is not speaking of the glory
      that comes from human beings, but of the glory that comes from God in
      the presence of his angels. For this reason Mark 8 says, "The Son of Man
45    will acknowledge him in the glory of his Father, in the presence of his
      angels."[18]
         **Response to 2.** The good of a particular person that exists in the knowl-
      edge of many people through fame or glory must, if indeed that knowledge
      is genuine, derive from the good that exists in that person; and in this way
50    it presupposes complete happiness, or at least the beginnings of happiness.
      If their belief is false, it does not correspond to reality, and thus the good
      is not found in the person who enjoys fame. Hence it is evident that fame
      can in no way make human beings happy.
         **Response to 3.** Fame has no stability; indeed, it can easily be destroyed
55    by a false rumor. If it does in fact remain stable in some case, that is by
      accident. Happiness, by contrast, has stability intrinsically and always.

*Article 4. Does human happiness consist in power?*[19]

It seems that happiness consists in power:
      1. All things desire to become like God, who is their ultimate end and
first principle. Now human beings who are in positions of power seem to
resemble God the most, because they are like him in power. This is why
5    in Scripture they are called gods, as is evident in Exodus 22:28: "You shall
not speak ill of gods." Therefore, happiness consists in power.
      2. Happiness is a perfect good. Now the most perfect good is for some-
one to be able to rule over others, which is true of those who are in positions of power. Therefore, happiness consists in power.

---

18. This quotation includes words from Mark 8:38 and Luke 12:8.
19. Parallel passages: *SCG* III.31; *Compend. Theol.* II.9; *Kingship* I.8; *Comm. Matt.* 5.

3. Since happiness is the most desirable thing, it is the opposite of what     *10*
most deserves to be shunned. Now human beings shun servitude most of
all, and servitude is the opposite of power. Therefore, happiness consists
in power.

**On the contrary.** Happiness is a perfect good, whereas power is highly
imperfect. That is why Boethius says in *Consolation of Philosophy* III [pr.     *15*
5], that "human power cannot banish the gnawings of anxieties or avoid
the stings of fears." And later, "Do you think someone is powerful when
he goes about surrounded by bodyguards, more afraid of those whom he
bullies than they are of him?" So happiness does not consist in power.

**Reply.** There are two reasons that happiness cannot consist in power.     *20*
The first is that power has the character of a principle, as is clear in *Metaphysics* V [1019a15], whereas happiness has the character of an ultimate
end. The second is that power is for both good and evil, whereas happiness
is the proper and perfect human good. So it would make more sense for
some happiness to consist in the good use of power—which comes about     *25*
through virtue—than in power itself.

But in fact we can give four general arguments to show that happiness
does not consist in any of the external goods that we have discussed. First,
since happiness is the supreme good for human beings, it excludes everything bad. But all of the goods we have discussed can be found both in     *30*
good people and in bad. Second, since it is part of the nature of happiness
that it is self-sufficient, as is clear in *Ethics* I [1097b8], it must be the case
that once happiness has been attained, no good thing necessary for human
beings is missing. But when any one of the goods we have discussed has
been attained, there can still be many goods necessary for human beings     *35*
that are missing: for example, wisdom, bodily health, and those sorts of
things. Third, since happiness is a perfect good, nothing bad can afflict
anyone as a result of happiness. That is not true of any of the goods we have
discussed: Ecclesiastes 5:12 says, for example, that wealth is sometimes
conserved to the detriment of its owner, and similar considerations clearly     *40*
apply to the other three as well. Fourth, human beings are directed to happiness by *interior* principles, since they are directed to happiness naturally.
But each of the four goods we have discussed is instead a result of *exterior*
principles, and in more cases than not they are a matter of good fortune,
which is why they are also called "goods of fortune." For these reasons, it     *45*
is clear that happiness in no way consists in any of the goods that we have
discussed thus far.

**Response to 1.** The divine power is its own goodness, which means
that God cannot use his power in any way other than well. But this is not
the case for human beings. As a result, becoming like God with respect to     *50*
his power is not sufficient for human beings to be happy, unless they also
become like God with respect to his goodness.

**Response to 2.** Just as it is an outstandingly good thing for someone to exercise power well in governing many, so too it is an outstandingly bad
55  thing for someone to exercise power badly. And thus power can be both for good and for bad.

**Response to 3.** Servitude is an obstacle to exercising power well, and human beings naturally shun servitude for that reason, not because the supreme good is somehow found in human power.

### Article 5. Does human happiness consist in goods of the body?[20]

It seems that human happiness consists in goods of the body:

1. Ecclesiasticus 30:16 says, "There is no wealth greater than the health of the body." Now happiness consists in that which is the best thing of all. Therefore, it consists in the health of the body.

5   2. Dionysius says in *On the Divine Names* 5 [§3] that being is better than life, and life is better than the other things that follow from life. But bodily health is required for the being and life of human beings. Therefore, since happiness is the supreme good for human beings, it seems that bodily health is an especially important element of happiness.

10  3. The more general something is, the more it depends on a higher principle, since the higher a cause is, the more things its power encompasses. Now just as we judge the causality of an efficient cause by its influence, so too we judge the causality of an end in terms of desire. Therefore, just as the first efficient cause is the one that has influence over all things, so
15  too the ultimate end is desired by all things. Now being itself is what all things desire above all else. Therefore, happiness for human beings consists above all else in the things that are conducive to their being, such as bodily health.

**On the contrary.** With respect to happiness, human beings excel all
20  other animals. But with respect to bodily goods, many animals surpass human beings: elephants surpass us in length of life, lions in strength, deer in swiftness. Therefore, human happiness does not consist in goods of the body.

**Reply.** There are two reasons human happiness cannot consist in goods
25  of the body. First, if a thing is directed to something else as its end, that thing's ultimate end cannot be the preservation of its own existence. That is why a captain does not intend, as his ultimate end, the preservation of the ship that is entrusted to him, since the ship is directed to something else as its end—namely, to sailing. Now in the same way that a ship is entrusted to
30  a captain for him to direct it, human beings are entrusted to their own will

---

20. Parallel passages: *Sent.* IV.49.1.1.1; *SCG* III.32; *Compend. Theol.* II.9; *Comm. Ethics* I.10.

and reason, as Ecclesiasticus 15:14 says: "God established human beings from the beginning, and he left them in the hand of their own deliberation." Now it is clear that human beings are directed to something else as their end; human beings are not their own highest good. Hence, it is impossible for the ultimate end of human reason and will to be the preservation 35 of human existence.

Second, even if we were to grant that the end of human reason and will is the preservation of human existence, we still could not say that the end for human beings is some bodily good. Human existence is constituted by the body and soul, and although the body's existence depends on the soul, 40 the existence of the human soul does not depend on the body, as I showed above.[21] Also, the body exists for the sake of the soul in the way that matter exists for the sake of form and a tool for the sake of what moves it: in each case, the former exists so that the latter can carry out its activities through it. For this reason all goods of the body are directed to goods of the soul as 45 their end. Hence, happiness, which is the ultimate end for human beings, cannot consist in goods of the body.

**Response to 1.** In the same way that the body is directed to the soul as its end, exterior goods are directed to the body itself. And so the good of the body is rationally preferred to exterior goods—which are what is meant 50 by 'wealth' in this verse—in the same way that the good of the soul is preferred to all goods of the body.

**Response to 2.** 'Being' in an unqualified sense includes every perfection of existence; in that sense being is superior to life and all the things that follow from it, since being (so understood) already includes all those things. 55 And that is the sense in which Dionysius is talking about 'being' here. But if instead we think of being as participated in by one thing or another that does not encompass the whole perfection of being, but instead has imperfect being, as is the being of any given creature, then it is clear that being, understood in that sense, is loftier when some further perfection is added 60 to it. That is why Dionysius says in the same place that things that live are better than things that merely exist, and things that understand are better than things that merely live.

**Response to 3.** Because a thing's end corresponds to its principle, this argument proves that the ultimate end is the first principle of being, in 65 which there is every perfection of being, and whose likeness all things desire, each according to its proper measure: some according to being only, some according to living being, and some according to being that is living, understanding, and happy. This last belongs only to a few.

---

21. *ST* I.75.2, I.76.1 resp. 5 and 6, I.90.2 resp. 2.

*Article 6. Does human happiness consist in pleasure?*[22]

It seems that human happiness consists in pleasure:

1. Since happiness is the ultimate end, it is not desired for the sake of anything else; rather, other things are desired for the sake of happiness. And this is true of delight most of all: "for it is ridiculous to ask someone
5  why he wants delight," as is said in *Ethics* X [1172b23]. Therefore, happiness consists most of all in pleasure and delight.

2. "A first cause makes a more vigorous impression than a secondary cause," as is said in the *Book of Causes* [prop. 1]. Now the influence of an end is judged in terms of the desire for it; thus, what moves desire most
10  of all seems to have the character of an ultimate end. But that is pleasure, as is indicated by the fact that delight is so engrossing to human will and reason that it makes someone spurn any other goods. Therefore, it seems that the ultimate end for human beings, which is happiness, consists in pleasure most of all.

15  3. Since desire is for what is good, it seems that what all things desire is the best thing of all. Now all things desire delight: the wise, the unwise, even things that lack reason. Therefore, delight is the best thing of all; and so happiness, which is the supreme good, consists in pleasure.

**On the contrary.** Boethius says in *Consolation of Philosophy* III [pr. 7],
20  "Anyone who is willing to call to mind his own lusts will understand that pleasures end in sorrows. If pleasures could make people happy, there would be no reason not to say that cattle too are happy."

**Reply.** As is said in *Ethics* VII [1153b33], "Because bodily delights are more familiar to most people, they have monopolized for themselves the
25  word 'pleasures,'" even though there are other, higher, pleasures. But happiness does not primarily consist even in those higher pleasures. The reason is that in any given thing, what belongs to its essence is not the same as its proper accident; for example, in human beings, *rational, mortal animal* is not the same as *capable of laughter*. It is therefore important to note that
30  all delight is a proper accident that follows from happiness or from some part of happiness; after all, people experience delight because they possess some good that is suited to themselves (whether they possess it in fact, in hope, or only in memory). Now if this suitable good is complete, it is human happiness itself; if, however, it is incomplete, it is a sort of share of
35  happiness (whether proximate, remote, or merely apparent). From this it is evident that not even the delight that follows from the complete good is the very essence of happiness, but something that follows from happiness as an essential accident.

22. Parallel passages: *Sent.* IV.44.1.3.4 resp. 3, 4; *SCG* III.27, 33; *Comm. Ethics* I.5.

Bodily pleasure, however, cannot follow from the complete good even in the way just discussed. The reason is that it follows from a good appre- 40 hended by sense, which is a power of a soul that makes use of a body; and a good that belongs to the body—a good that is apprehended by sense— cannot be the complete human good. For since the rational soul exceeds any proportion to corporeal matter, the part of the soul that is not bound to any bodily organ is, in a sense, infinite in comparison with the body itself 45 and with the parts of the soul that are tied to the body—just as immaterial things are, in a way, infinite in comparison with material things, given that form is somehow contracted and made finite by matter, which is why form that is not bound up with matter is, in a way, infinite. This is also why sense, which is a bodily power, cognizes singulars, which are made deter- 50 minate through matter, whereas the intellect, which is a power not bound up with matter, cognizes universals, which are abstracted from matter and contain an infinite number of singulars. From these considerations it is evident that no good suited to the body—no good that causes bodily plea- sure through the apprehension of sense—is the complete good for human 55 beings; any such good is negligible by comparison with a good of the soul. This is why Wisdom 7:9 says that "all gold, by comparison with wisdom, is a speck of sand." Accordingly, bodily pleasure is neither happiness itself nor an essential accident of happiness.

**Response to 1.** There is one explanation that accounts both for why 60 people desire good and for why they desire delight, in the same way that there is one natural power that explains both why heavy things fall and why they come to rest in the lowest place: delight *just is* desire's resting in some- thing good. For that reason, in the same way that what is good is desired for its own sake, delight too is desired for its own sake and not for the sake 65 of anything else, if 'for the sake of' indicates a final cause. On the other hand, if 'for the sake of' indicates a formal cause—or, better yet, a mov- ing cause—then delight is in fact desirable for the sake of something else, namely for the sake of a good. A good is the object of delight and is con- sequently its principle; a good gives delight its form—after all, the whole 70 reason that delight is desired is that delight is a resting in the desired good.

**Response to 2.** The reason our desire for sensory delight is so vigor- ous is that the activities of the senses, which are the starting points of our cognition, are especially perceptible. That is also why sensory delights are desired by so many people. 75

**Response to 3.** All things desire delight just as all things desire the good—and yet they desire delight under the aspect of good; they do not desire good under the aspect of delight, as I have explained. Hence, it does not follow that delight is the greatest good or an intrinsic good; rather, what follows is that every delight follows from some good, and that there is a 80 delight that follows from the greatest, intrinsic good.

*Article 7. Does happiness consist in a good of the soul?*

It seems that happiness consists in a good of the soul:

1. Happiness is a human good, and there are three kinds of human good: external goods, goods of the body, and goods of the soul. Now happiness does not consist in external goods or in goods of the body, as was shown
5  above [art. 4–5]. Therefore, it consists in goods of the soul.

2. When we desire a good for something, we love the thing for which we desire that good more than we love the good that we desire for that thing. For example, we love the friend for whom we desire money more than we love money. Now we all desire every good for ourselves. Therefore, we love
10  ourselves more than we love all other goods. And happiness is what is loved most of all, as is evident from the fact that everything other than happiness is loved and desired for the sake of happiness. Therefore, happiness consists in a good of human beings themselves. Now it does not consist in bodily goods, so it consists in goods of the soul.

15  3. A perfection is something *in* what it perfects. Happiness is a perfection of human beings. Therefore, happiness is *in* human beings. Now it is not in the body, as has been shown [art. 5]. Therefore, happiness is something in the soul, which means that happiness consists in goods of the soul.

**On the contrary.** As Augustine says in *On Christian Teaching* I [ch. 22],
20  "that which constitutes the happy life should be loved for its own sake." But human beings should not be loved for their own sake; instead, whatever is in human beings should be loved for God's sake. Therefore, happiness does not consist in any good of the soul.

**Reply.** As I said above [I-II.1.8], there are two ways in which we can
25  speak about the end: as the thing itself that we desire to attain, or as use—in other words, the attainment or possession of that thing. So if we are speaking of the ultimate end of human beings in terms of the thing itself that we desire as an ultimate end, the ultimate end of human beings cannot be the soul itself or anything in the soul. For the soul, regarded in itself,
30  is in potentiality: it goes from potentially knowing to actually knowing, and from potentially virtuous to actually virtuous. Now since potentiality is for the sake of actuality—as something is for the sake of what completes it—something that in and of itself is in a state of potentiality cannot have the character of an ultimate end. Hence, it is impossible for the soul itself
35  to be its own ultimate end.

Similarly, nothing in the soul—whether power, disposition, or act—can be the soul's ultimate end. After all, the good that is the ultimate end is a complete good that totally satisfies the appetite. Now the distinctively human appetite—the will—is for the universal good. But any good that is
40  present in the soul is a participated good, and consequently a particular

good; and for that reason no such good can be the ultimate end for human beings.

On the other hand, if we are speaking of the ultimate end for human beings in terms of the attainment or possession of the good—in other words, in terms of the use of the thing that is desired as the end—then the ultimate end does indeed involve something in human beings, something in the soul, since it is through the soul that human beings attain happiness. Therefore, the thing itself that is desired as the end is that in which happiness consists and that which makes us happy; but the attainment of this thing is called happiness. For this reason what we should say is that happiness is something in the soul, but that in which happiness consists is something outside the soul.

**Response to 1.** If we understand this threefold division as encompassing all the goods that can be desired by human beings, "goods of the soul" include not only powers or dispositions or acts, but also an object that is external to the soul. And there is nothing to prevent us from saying that in this sense that in which happiness consists is a good of the soul.

**Response to 2.** What matters as far as this objection is concerned is that happiness is loved above all else as the good desired, whereas a friend is loved as that for which one desires good; and it is in this latter way that human beings love themselves. So it is not the same sort of love in both cases. Whether human beings love anything with the love of friendship more than they love themselves is another question; we will have an opportunity to consider that when we discuss charity [II-II.26.3].

**Response to 3.** Since happiness itself is a perfection of the soul, it is a good that is present in the soul. But that in which happiness consists—that which makes people happy—is something outside the soul, as I have said.

*Article 8. Does human happiness consist in any created good?*[23]

It seems that human happiness consists in some created good:

1. Dionysius says in *On the Divine Names* 7 [§3] that divine wisdom "joins the ends of first things to the beginnings of second things." From this we can gather that what is highest for a lower nature is to attain to what is lowest in a higher nature. Now the highest good for human beings is happiness. So, since in the order of nature angels are above human beings, as was shown in the First Part,[24] it appears that human happiness consists in somehow attaining to [what is lowest in] an angel.

---

23. Parallel passages: *ST* I. 12.1; *SCG* IV.54; *Compend. Theol.* I.108, II.9; *Kingship* I.8.

24. *ST* I.75.2, I.76.1 resp. 5 and 6, I.90.2 resp. 2.

2. The ultimate end of any given thing lies in its completeness. Hence,
10  a part is for the sake of the whole, as for the sake of its end. Now the totality
of creatures, which is called a macrocosm, is related to the human being,
who in *Physics* VIII [252b24] is called a microcosm, as complete to incomplete. Therefore, human happiness consists in the totality of creatures.

3. Human beings are made happy through that which satisfies their
15  natural desire. Now natural human desire does not extend to a good that
surpasses human capacity. Therefore, since human beings do not have
the capacity for a good that goes beyond the limits of the whole realm of
creatures, it appears that human beings can be made happy through some
created good; and thus human happiness consists in some created good.

20     **On the contrary.** Augustine says in *City of God* XIX [ch. 26], "As the
soul is the life of the flesh, God is the happy life of the human being. Of
God it is said, 'Happy is the people whose God is the Lord.'"

**Reply.** It is impossible for human happiness to lie in any created good.
For happiness is a complete good, one that totally satisfies appetite; for oth-
25  erwise, if there were still something left to be desired, happiness would not
be the ultimate end. Now the object of the will—that is, of the distinctively
human appetite—is the universal good, just as the object of the intellect is
universal truth. From this it is evident that nothing but the universal good
can satisfy the human will. And the universal good is not found in any
30  created thing, but only in God, since every creature has goodness by participation. For this reason God alone can fully satisfy the human will, as is
said in Psalm 102:5: "He satisfies your desire with good things." Therefore,
human happiness consists in God alone.

**Response to 1.** What is highest in human beings does indeed attain to
35  what is lowest in angelic nature in terms of a certain likeness. But human
beings do not stop there, as though that were their ultimate end; instead
they proceed to that universal fount of good which is the universal object
of happiness for all who are happy, as being an infinite and perfect good.

**Response to 2.** If some whole is not an ultimate end but is directed
40  to a further end, the ultimate end of its part will not be the whole, but
something else. Now the totality of creatures, of which human beings are
a part, is not the ultimate end. Rather, it is directed to God as its ultimate
end. Hence, the good that is the ultimate end of human beings is not the
universe, but God himself.

45     **Response to 3.** As something intrinsic to human beings and inhering in them, a created good does not fall short of the human capacity for
good; but as an object, it does fall short. Human beings have the capacity
for an object that is an infinite good. By contrast, the participated good
that is in an angel, and for that matter in the whole universe, is a finite and
50  restricted good.

## Question 3. What Is Happiness?

Next we must investigate what happiness is [Q3] and what is required for it [Q4]. Concerning the first, there are eight questions:

Article 1. Is happiness something uncreated?

Article 2. Given that happiness is something created, is it an activity?

Article 3. Is happiness an activity of the sensory part or only of the intellectual part?

Article 4. Given that happiness is an activity of the intellectual part, is it an activity of the intellect or of the will?

Article 5. Given that happiness is an activity of the intellect, is it an activity of the speculative intellect or of the practical intellect?

Article 6. Given that happiness is an activity of the speculative intellect, does it consist in speculative thought about the speculative sciences?

Article 7. Does happiness consist in speculative knowledge of the separated substances—in other words, the angels?

Article 8. Does happiness consist only in the speculative knowledge of God by which he is seen in his essence?

### *Article 1. Is happiness something uncreated?*[25]

It seems that happiness is something uncreated:

1. Boethius says in *Consolation of Philosophy* III [pr. 10], "We must acknowledge that God is happiness itself."

2. Happiness is the supreme good, and being the supreme good is characteristic of God. So, since there is not more than one supreme good, it seems that happiness is the same as God. 5

3. Happiness is the ultimate end, toward which the human will naturally tends. But the will ought not to tend toward anything other than God as its end; as Augustine says, God alone is to be enjoyed.[26] Therefore, happiness is the same as God. 10

**On the contrary.** Nothing made is uncreated. But human happiness is something made, since according to Augustine in *On Christian Teaching* I.3, "We are to enjoy the things that make us happy." Therefore, happiness is not something uncreated.

**Reply.** As I said above [I-II.1.8, 2.7], we speak of an end in two ways. 15 In one way, the end is the thing itself that we desire to attain, as money is a greedy person's end. In the other way, the end is the attainment or possession itself—in other words, the use or enjoyment of the thing that is desired; for example, we might say that a greedy person's end is the

25. Parallel passages: *ST* I.26.3; *Sent.* IV.49.1.2.1.
26. *On Christian Teaching* I.5 and I.22.

20   possession of money, and an intemperate person's end is the enjoyment of
     something pleasurable. Accordingly, in the first way, the ultimate end for
     human beings is an uncreated good, namely, God; only God can, by his
     infinite goodness, completely satisfy the human will. But in the second
     way, the ultimate end for human beings is something created that exists
25   in them; this is nothing other than the attainment or enjoyment of the
     ultimate end. Now the ultimate end is called happiness. So if we think
     of human happiness in terms of its cause or object, it is in fact something
     uncreated; but if we think of it in terms of the very essence of happiness,
     it is something created.
30        **Response to 1.** God is happiness through his own essence: he is not
     happy through attaining or participating in some other thing, but through
     his own essence. Human beings, by contrast, are happy through partici-
     pation, as Boethius says in the same place,[27] just as they are also called
     gods through participation. And this participation in happiness, by which
35   human beings are called happy, is something created.
          **Response to 2.** Happiness is said to be the supreme good for human
     beings because it is the attainment or enjoyment of the supreme good.
          **Response to 3.** Happiness is said to be the ultimate end in the sense of
     'end' that means the *attainment* of the end.

### Article 2. Is happiness an activity?[28]

     It seems that happiness is not an activity:
          1. The Apostle says in Romans 6:22, "You have your fruit in sanctifica-
     tion but your end in eternal life." But life is not an activity: it is the very
     being of things that live. Therefore, the ultimate end, which is happiness,
5    is not an activity.
          2. Boethius says in *Consolation of Philosophy* III [pr. 2] that "happiness
     is the state that is made complete by the accumulation of all goods." 'State'
     does not name an activity. Therefore, happiness is not an activity.
          3. 'Happiness' signifies something that exists in the one who is happy,
10   since happiness is the ultimate perfection of a human being. 'Activity,' by
     contrast, does not signify something that remains in the agent, but instead
     something that proceeds from the agent. Therefore, happiness is not an
     activity.
          4. In someone who is happy, happiness is permanent. An activity, how-
15   ever, is not permanent, but transitory. Therefore, happiness is not an
     activity.

---

27. *Consolation of Philosophy* III, pr. 10.

28. Parallel passages: *Sent.* IV.49.1.2.2; *SCG* I.100; *Comm. Ethics* 1.10; *Comm.
Metaph.* IX.8.

5. One human being has one happiness, but many activities. Therefore, happiness is not an activity.

6. Happiness is present without interruption in the one who is happy. But human activities are frequently interrupted: for example, by sleep, by some other business, or by rest. Therefore, happiness is not an activity.

**On the contrary.** The Philosopher says in *Ethics* I [1102a5] that "felicity is activity in accordance with complete virtue."

**Reply.** Insofar as human happiness is something created that exists in human beings themselves, we have to say that human happiness is an activity. Why? Happiness is the ultimate perfection of human beings. Now any given thing is perfect to the extent that it is in actuality; after all, potentiality without actuality is imperfect. Therefore, happiness must consist in the ultimate actuality of human beings. Now it is evident that an activity is the ultimate actuality of the one who acts. That is why the Philosopher in *De anima* II [412a23] calls it "second actuality": something that has a form [which is a first actuality] can be in potentiality to acting, as someone who knows can be in potentiality to attending to what he knows. This is why it is said about other things, too, that each one exists for the sake of its own activity, as is said in *On the Heavens* II [286a8]. Therefore, human happiness must be an activity.

**Response to 1.** We speak of life in two ways. In one way, life is the very being of the thing that lives. In this way, life is not happiness; for, as I have shown [I-II.2.5], the being of a particular human person, whatever that being might be like, is not human happiness. After all, only for God is it true that happiness is his very being. But in another way, 'life' means the activity of the thing that lives, insofar as some principle of life is actualized. This is the sense of 'life' we have in mind when we speak of the active life, or the contemplative life, or the life of pleasure. And in this sense, eternal life is called the ultimate end, as is evident from what is said in John 17:3: "This is eternal life, that they may know you, the one true God."

**Response to 2.** In defining happiness, Boethius was attending to the general notion of happiness. After all, the general notion of happiness is that it is a universal, complete good; and he indicated this when he said that happiness "is the state that is made complete by the accumulation of all goods," which means nothing other than this: the one who is happy is in the state of a complete good. Aristotle, by contrast, expresses the very essence of happiness; he shows what it is through which human beings are in such a state, since they are in that state through some activity. This is why he too, in *Ethics* I [1097a29], shows that happiness is a complete good.

**Response to 3.** As is said in *Metaphysics* IX [1050a30], there are two kinds of action. One kind proceeds from the agent into external matter: for example, burning and cutting. This kind of activity cannot be happiness,

60    since this kind of activity is not an action and perfection belonging to the
      agent; instead, it belongs to the patient, as is said in the same place. The
      other kind of action remains within the agent: for example, sensing, under-
      standing, and willing. This kind of action is a perfection and actuality of
      the agent. This kind of activity can be happiness.

65         **Response to 4.** Since 'happiness' indicates a certain ultimate per-
      fection, there must be various senses of happiness corresponding to the
      different levels of perfection that various things having the capacity for
      happiness can reach. You see, in God there is happiness through his
      essence: his activity is his very being, and by that activity he enjoys him-
70    self and not another. In the happy angels, by contrast, there is ultimate
      perfection through a certain activity by which they are joined to the uncre-
      ated good; in them this activity is unitary and sempiternal. Now in human
      beings under the conditions of this present life, there is ultimate perfec-
      tion through an activity by which they are joined to God; but this activ-
75    ity cannot be continuous, and consequently it cannot be unitary either,
      since after each interruption there is an additional activity. For that reason,
      human beings cannot have perfect happiness in this present life. That is
      why, when the Philosopher says in *Ethics* I [1101a20] that human beings
      can have happiness in this life, he calls it imperfect happiness, conclud-
80    ing (after much discussion) that "we call them happy *as human beings.*"
      But God promises us perfect happiness, when we will be "like the angels
      in heaven," as is said in Matthew 22:30. So as far as that perfect happiness
      goes, the objection fails: in that state of happiness the human mind will
      be joined to God in one continuous, sempiternal activity. But in this pres-
85    ent life, we fall short of perfect happiness to the extent that we fall short of
      the unity and continuity of such an activity. Still, though, there is a cer-
      tain participation in happiness; and the more continuous and unitary the
      activity can be, the greater that participation in happiness is. And so the
      active life, which is occupied with many things, has less of the character
90    of happiness than does the contemplative life, which is focused on one
      thing, the contemplation of truth. Granted, people are not always actually
      performing this sort of activity; but because they are always able to do it
      readily, and because they direct even the interruptions of that activity (say,
      sleep or some mundane business) to the activity itself, that activity appears
95    to be continuous in a sense.

           And on the basis of these considerations the reply to the fifth and sixth
      objections is clear.

## Article 3. Is happiness an activity of the
sensory part or only of the intellectual part?[29]

It seems that happiness consists in an activity of sense as well:

1. The only activity found in human beings that is nobler than an activity of the sensory part is an activity of the intellectual part. But in us the intellect's activity depends on the senses' activity, since "we cannot understand without a phantasm," as is said in *De anima* III [431a16]. Therefore, happiness consists in an activity of the sensory part as well.

2. Boethius says in *Consolation of Philosophy* III [pr. 2] that "happiness is a state made complete by the accumulation of all goods." But some goods are sensible goods, and we attain them through an activity of sense. Therefore, it seems that an activity of sense is required for happiness.

3. Happiness is the perfect good, as is proved in *Ethics* I [1097a15–1098a20]. But it would not be the perfect good if it did not perfect human beings in all their parts, and some parts of the soul are perfected by sensory activities. Therefore, sensory activity is required for happiness.

**On the contrary.** Sensory activities are something non-rational animals have in common with us; happiness is not. Therefore, happiness does not consist in a sensory activity.

**Reply.** There are three ways in which something can pertain to happiness: (1) essentially, (2) antecedently, (3) consequently. Sensory activity cannot pertain to happiness essentially, because human happiness consists essentially in our being joined to the uncreated good, which is the ultimate end, as I showed above [art. 1]; and human beings cannot be joined to the uncreated good by any sensory activity. Similarly, sensory activity cannot pertain to happiness essentially because (as I have shown [I-II.2.5]) human happiness does not consist in bodily goods, and bodily goods are the only things we attain through any sensory activity.

But sensory activities can pertain to happiness antecedently and consequently. They pertain to happiness antecedently as far as imperfect happiness is concerned—the kind of happiness that we can have in this life—because the activity of sense is a necessary precondition for the activity of intellect. But in that perfect happiness in heaven to which we look forward, sensory activities pertain to happiness consequently, because after the resurrection, as Augustine says in the Letter to Dioscorus [118.3], "from the soul's happiness there will be a kind of overflow into the body and the senses of the body, so that they will be perfected in their activities"—this will become clearer in what follows, when we discuss the resurrection.[30]

---

29. Parallel passages: *SCG* III.33; *Compend. Theol.* II.9; *Comm. Ethics* I.10.
30. Not completed, but see *ST* III supp. 82.

But at that time the activity by which the human mind is joined to God will not depend on sense.

**Response to 1.** That objection proves that a sensory activity is required
40  antecedently for imperfect happiness, the sort of happiness that we can possess in this life.

**Response to 2.** Perfect happiness—the sort of happiness that the angels have—includes all goods, because those who have perfect happiness are joined to the universal source of every good, not because such happiness
45  requires every particular good. But imperfect happiness requires an accumulation of goods sufficient for the most perfect activity of this life.

**Response to 3.** In perfect happiness the whole human being is perfected, but the perfection of the lower part comes about through an overflow from the higher part. In the imperfect happiness of this present life,
50  by contrast, the converse is true: the perfection of the higher part proceeds from the perfection of the lower part.

*Article 4. Given that happiness is an activity of the intellectual
part, is it an activity of the intellect or of the will?*[31]

It appears that happiness consists in an act of the will:

1. Augustine says in *City of God* XIX [chs. 10–11] that human happiness consists in peace. That is why Psalm 147:3 says, "He has established peace in your ends." Now peace belongs to the will, so human happiness
5  resides in the will.

2. Happiness is the highest good. Now what is good is the object of the will. Therefore, happiness consists in an activity of the will.

3. The ultimate end corresponds to the first mover. For example, the ultimate end of the whole army is victory, which is the end of the general
10  who moves all the soldiers. Now the first mover toward acting is the will, because it moves the other powers, as will be explained below [I-II.9.1 resp. 3]. Therefore, happiness pertains to the will.

4. Assuming that happiness is an activity, it has to be the noblest activity of human beings. Now love of God, which is an act of will, is a nobler
15  activity than knowledge, which is an activity of intellect. This is evident from the Apostle in 1 Corinthians 13. Therefore, it appears that happiness consists in an act of will.

5. Augustine says in *On the Trinity* XIII [ch. 5] that "those who are happy are those who have everything they want, and want nothing bad."
20  And a little further on he adds, "those who, in whatever they will, will rightly are approaching those who are happy; for good things make people

---

31. Parallel passages: *ST* I.26.2 resp. 2; *Sent.* IV.49.1.1.2; *SCG* III.26; *Quodlibet* VIII.9.1; *Compend. Theol.* 107.

happy, and those who will rightly already have one of those good things: a good will." Therefore, happiness consists in an act of will.

**On the contrary.** The Lord says in John 17:3, "This is eternal life, that they may know you, the one true God." Now eternal life is the ultimate 25 end, as has been said [art. 2 resp. 1]. Therefore, human happiness consists in the knowledge of God, which is an act of intellect.

**Reply.** As I said above [I-II.2.6], two things are required for happiness. One is the essence of happiness; the other is, as it were, the essential accident of happiness, namely, the delight conjoined with it. I therefore say 30 that, with respect to what happiness essentially is, it is impossible for happiness to consist in an act of will. After all, our previous discussion [I-II.2.7; 3.1 and 2] has made it clear that happiness is the attainment of the ultimate end; and the attainment of the ultimate end does not consist in the will's act itself. For the will is drawn both to an absent end, when it desires it, 35 and to a present end, when it rests in the end and consequently delights in it. Now it is obvious that the mere desiring of the end is not the attaining of the end, but a movement toward the end. Delight accrues to the will in virtue of the end's being present. But the converse is not true: the will's delighting in something does not make that thing present. So there must 40 be something through which the end is made present to the will, other than the will's own act.

This is clearly true in the case of sensible ends. If attaining money were merely a matter of the will's act, greedy people would have money from the outset, as soon as they wanted it. But in fact the money is not with them 45 from the outset; they attain it by seizing it with their hand or something like that. Only then do they delight in possessing the money.

So something quite like this is also true in the case of an intelligible end. We will from the outset to attain an intelligible end, but we actually attain it through its being made present to us by an act of intellect; only 50 then does the will rest with delight in the end that has now been attained. In this way, therefore, the essence of happiness consists in an act of intellect; but the delight consequent upon happiness belongs to the will. This is what Augustine means in *Confessions* X [ch. 23] when he says that happiness is joy in truth: joy itself is the consummation of happiness. 55

**Response to 1.** Peace belongs to the ultimate end of human beings, but not as though peace were, essentially, happiness itself. Rather, peace is related to happiness both antecedently and consequently: antecedently, insofar as all disturbances and impediments to the ultimate end have now been removed; and consequently, insofar as human beings who have now 60 attained their end abide in a state of peace because their desire has been satisfied.

**Response to 2.** The first object of the will is not its act, just as the first object of sight is not seeing, but the visible. Hence, from the very fact that

65   happiness belongs to the will as its first object, it follows that happiness
does not belong to the will as its act.

**Response to 3.** The intellect does grasp the end before the will does,
but the movement toward the end begins in the will. And so the final consequence of attaining the end—namely, delight or enjoyment—belongs to
70   the will.

**Response to 4.** Love outranks knowledge when it comes to moving one
toward the end, but knowledge is prior to love when it comes to attaining
the end. After all, only what is known is loved, as Augustine says in *On the
Trinity* X [ch. 1]. And therefore we first attain an intelligible end through
75   an action of the intellect, just as we first attain a sensible end through an
action of the senses.

**Response to 5.** Those who have everything they want are happy in virtue of having what they want, and of course their having what they want
comes through something other than an act of will. But their not want-
80   ing anything bad is required for happiness as the appropriate condition
for happiness. Moreover, a good will is counted among the good things
that make them happy insofar as a good will is an inclination toward those
good things, in the same way that a movement is reduced to the category
of its terminus: for example, an alteration is reduced to the category of
85   quality.

*Article 5. Is happiness an activity of the
speculative or of the practical intellect?*[32]

It seems that happiness consists in an activity of the practical intellect:

1. The ultimate end of any creature consists in becoming like God. Now
human beings become like God through the practical intellect, which is a
cause of things understood, rather than through the speculative intellect,
5   which derives its knowledge from things. Therefore, human happiness
consists in an activity of the practical intellect rather than of the speculative intellect.

2. Happiness is the perfect human good. Now it is the practical intellect that is ordered to what is good, rather than the speculative intellect,
10   which is ordered to what is true. That is also why we call people good, not
because their speculative intellects are perfected—that is a reason for calling them knowledgeable or intelligent—but because their practical intellects are perfected. Therefore, human happiness consists in an act of the
practical intellect rather than of the speculative intellect.

15      3. Happiness is a good of human beings themselves. Now the speculative
intellect is concerned chiefly with things that are outside human beings,

---

32. Parallel passages: *Sent.* IV.49.1.1.3; *Comm. Ethics* X.10–12.

whereas the practical intellect is concerned with things that belong to human beings themselves, namely, with human activities and passions. Therefore, human happiness consists in an activity of the practical intellect rather than of the speculative intellect. 20

**On the contrary.** Augustine says in *On the Trinity* I [ch. 8], "To us is promised contemplation: the end of all our actions and the eternal perfection of our joys."

**Reply.** Happiness consists in an activity of the speculative intellect rather than an activity of the practical intellect, as is evident from three 25 considerations. First, given that human happiness is an activity, it must be the best human activity. Now the best human activity is the activity of the best capacity with respect to its best object. The best human capacity is the intellect, and the intellect's best object is the divine good, which is certainly not an object of the practical intellect but of the speculative 30 intellect. Hence, happiness chiefly consists in such an activity, that is, in the contemplation of divine things. "And since," as is said in *Ethics* IX [1169a1] and X [1178a2], "it appears that all people are that which is the best in them," such an activity is most proper to human beings and most delightful to them. 35

Second, the same conclusion is evident from the fact that contemplation above all else is sought for its own sake, whereas an act of the practical intellect is not sought for its own sake, but for the sake of action; and those actions are in turn directed to some end. Hence, it is evident that the ultimate end cannot consist in the active life, which belongs to the 40 practical intellect.

Third, the same conclusion is evident from the fact that in the contemplative life human beings have something in common with higher beings, namely, God and the angels, and happiness makes them like God and the angels. But even the other animals share with human beings in some way, 45 though imperfectly, in the things that pertain to the active life.

Therefore, the ultimate and perfect happiness for which we look in the life to come consists entirely in contemplation. But the imperfect happiness that can be possessed here consists first and foremost in contemplation but secondarily in the activity of the practical intellect directing human actions 50 and passions, as is said in *Ethics* X [1177a12, 1178a9].

**Response to 1.** The practical intellect's likeness to God is a proportional one: the practical intellect is related to what it knows as God is to what he knows. But the speculative intellect's likeness to God is a matter of being united to God or informed by God, and that is a much greater likeness. 55 Nonetheless, it can be said that with respect to his primary object of knowledge, which is his own essence, God does not have practical knowledge, but only speculative knowledge.

**Response to 2.** The practical intellect is directed to a good that is out-
60    side itself, whereas the speculative has its good—namely, the contemplation
of truth—within itself. And if that good is perfect, the whole human being
is perfected by it and becomes good. The practical intellect, of course, does
not have this good, but directs human beings toward it.

**Response to 3.** That argument would work if human beings were their
65    own ultimate ends; in that case, their attending to and directing their own
acts and passions would be their happiness. But since the ultimate end of
human beings is a good extrinsic to them—namely, God, whom we attain
through an activity of the speculative intellect—human happiness consists in an activity of the speculative intellect rather than an activity of the
70    practical intellect.

*Article 6. Does human happiness consist in*
*thinking about the speculative sciences?*[33]

It seems that human happiness consists in thinking about the speculative
sciences:

1. The Philosopher says in *Ethics* I [1102a5] that "felicity is activity in
accordance with complete virtue." And when he distinguishes the virtues,
5    he names only three speculative virtues—science, wisdom, and understanding—all of which pertain to thinking about the speculative sciences.
Therefore, ultimate human happiness consists in thinking about the speculative sciences.

2. What everyone naturally desires for its own sake is what seems to be
10    ultimate human happiness. And thinking about the speculative sciences
is like that, since, as is said in *Metaphysics* I [980a21], "all human beings
by nature desire to know." And a bit further on we read that the speculative sciences are sought for their own sake. Therefore, happiness consists
in thinking about the speculative sciences.

15    3. Happiness is the ultimate perfection of human beings. Now everything is made perfect to the extent that it is brought from potentiality to
actuality, and the human intellect is brought to actuality by thinking about
the speculative sciences. Therefore, it seems that ultimate human happiness consists in this sort of thinking.

20    **On the contrary.** Jeremiah 9:23 says, "Let not the wise boast in their
wisdom"; and it is speaking of the wisdom of the speculative sciences.
Therefore, ultimate human happiness does not consist in thinking about
them.

**Reply.** As I said above [I-II.2.4], human happiness is twofold: one is
25    perfect and the other imperfect. By perfect happiness we mean that which

---

33. Parallel passages: SCG III.48; *Compend. Theol.* 104.

fully satisfies the true definition of happiness, whereas imperfect happiness does not fully satisfy the definition but participates in a certain particular likeness of happiness—in much the same way that perfect prudence is found in human beings, who have the power of reasoning about the things they can do, whereas there is imperfect prudence in some non-rational animals who have particular instincts for acts that are like the acts of prudence. Perfect happiness, then, cannot consist essentially in thinking about the speculative sciences. In order to see clearly why it cannot, one needs to reflect on the fact that in thinking about a speculative science, we can go only as far as the principles of that science can take us, since the whole science is contained virtually in its principles. Now the first principles of the speculative sciences are received through the senses, as is evident from what the Philosopher says at the beginning of the *Metaphysics* [981a1] and the end of the *Posterior Analytics* [100a7]. For this reason, none of our thinking about the speculative sciences can extend any further than cognition of sensibles can take us. But ultimate human happiness, which is ultimate human perfection, cannot consist in the cognition of sensibles. After all, nothing is perfected by something lower than it unless that lower thing shares in some way in something higher. And it is obvious that the form of a rock, or of any sensible thing, is lower than a human being. Accordingly, the human intellect is not perfected by the form of a rock insofar as it is such a form, but insofar as it shares in some likeness to something that is above the human intellect, namely, the intelligible light or something along those lines. Now everything that is through another is reduced to what is through itself, and for that reason it must be the case that the ultimate human perfection is through the cognition of some thing that is above the human intellect. But we have shown [I.88.2] that one cannot reach the cognition of separated substances, which are above the human intellect, through sensibles. The only conclusion left, then, is that ultimate human happiness cannot lie in thinking about the speculative sciences. But in the same way that the forms of sensibles share a certain likeness to higher substances, thinking about the speculative sciences shares in a way in true and perfect happiness.

**Response to 1.** In the *Ethics* the Philosopher is speaking of imperfect felicity, the kind we can have in this life, as I said above [art. 2 resp. 4].

**Response to 2.** Not only is perfect happiness naturally desired, but so is any sort of likeness of or share in perfect happiness.

**Response to 3.** Our intellect is indeed brought to actuality in some way through thinking about speculative sciences, but not to its ultimate and complete actuality.

*Article 7. Does human happiness consist in the cognition*
*of the separated substances—that is, the angels?*[34]

It seems that human happiness consists in the cognition of the separated
substances—that is, the angels:

1. Gregory says in one of his homilies, "It is of no avail to take part in the
feasts of human beings if we do not take part in the feasts of angels,"[35] by
5    which he means ultimate happiness. Now we can take part in the feasts of
angels by contemplating angels. Therefore, it seems that ultimate human
happiness consists in contemplating angels.

2. The ultimate perfection of any thing is for it to be joined to its origin.
This is why the circle is called the perfect figure: its origin and its end are
10   the same. And human cognition originates with the angels, since the angels
illuminate human beings, as Dionysius says in *Celestial Hierarchy* 4 [§2].
Therefore, the perfection of the human intellect is in contemplating angels.

3. Every nature is perfected when it is joined to a higher nature; for
example, the ultimate perfection of the body is to be joined to a spiritual
15   nature. But in the order of nature, angels are higher than human beings.
Therefore, the ultimate perfection of the human intellect is to be joined
to the angels through contemplating them.

**On the contrary.** Jeremiah 9:24 says, "Let those who glory, glory in this,
that they know and understand me." Therefore, the ultimate human glory,
20   or happiness, consists only in knowledge of God.

**Reply.** As I have said [art. 6], perfect human happiness does not consist in something that is a perfection of the intellect by participation, but
in something that is essentially a perfection. Now it is evident that something is a perfection of some capacity to the extent that the notion of the
25   proper object of the capacity applies to that thing. The proper object of the
intellect is the true. Therefore, when the intellect contemplates something
that is true by participation, the perfection it achieves is not its ultimate
perfection. And since things are with respect to being the same way they
are with respect to truth, as is said in *Metaphysics* II [993b30], everything
30   that has being by participation is also true by participation. Now angels
have being by participation, since only God is his own being and his own
essence, as we showed in the First Part.[36] We can conclude, then, that only
God is truth essentially, and contemplating God makes someone perfectly
happy. But there is no reason the contemplation of angels cannot be a kind
35   of imperfect happiness, and indeed a higher happiness than there is in considering the speculative sciences.

---

34. Parallel passages: *ST* I.64.1 resp. 1; *SCG* III.44; *On the Trinity* 6.4 resp. 3.
35. *Homily* 26.
36. *ST* I.44.1; cf. I.3.4, I.7.1 resp. 3, and I.7.2.

**Response to 1.** We will take part in the feasts of the angels not merely by contemplating the angels, but by contemplating God in their company. **Response to 2.** If one accepts the view of those who hold that human souls are created by angels, it seems rather appropriate for human happi- 40 ness to lie in contemplating the angels, as a joining of us with our origin. But this view is mistaken, as I said in the First Part [I.90.3]. For this reason the ultimate perfection of the human intellect comes from being joined to God, who is the ultimate origin both of the soul's creation and of its illumination. An angel, by contrast, illuminates human beings as a minis- 45 ter, as I argued in the First Part [I.111.2 resp. 2]. Hence, by their ministry they help human beings reach happiness, but they are not the object of human happiness. **Response to 3.** There are two ways in which a lower nature reaches a higher nature. One way is in keeping with the level of the capacity that 50 participates; in this sense, the ultimate human perfection will be in reaching contemplation of the sort that angels enjoy. The other way is as an object is reached by a capacity; in this sense, the ultimate perfection of any capacity is a matter of its reaching the thing in which the notion of its object is fully realized. 55

*Article 8. Does human happiness consist in the vision of the divine essence?*[37]

It seems that human happiness does not consist in the vision of the divine essence:

1. Dionysius says in Chapter 1 of *Mystical Theology* that through what is highest in their intellects, human beings are joined to God as to something utterly unknown. Now what is seen in its essence is not utterly unknown. 5 Therefore, the ultimate perfection of the intellect—in other words, happiness—does not consist in seeing God in his essence.

2. To a higher nature belongs a higher perfection. Now seeing God's essence is the perfection proper to the divine intellect. Therefore, the ultimate perfection of the human intellect does not extend to this, but stops 10 somewhere short of it.

**On the contrary.** We read in 1 John 3:2, "When he appears, we will be like him, and we shall see him as he is."

**Reply.** Ultimate and perfect happiness cannot consist in anything other than a vision of the divine essence. In order to make this evident, we need 15 to consider two things. First, human beings are not perfectly happy as long as something is left for them to desire and seek. Second, the perfection of

37. Parallel passages: *ST* I.12.1; *On Truth* 8.1; *Quodlibet* 10.8; *Compend. Theol.* I.14 and 16, II.9; *Comm. Matt.* 5; *Comm. John* 1.11.

each capacity is determined by the nature of its object. Now the object of
the intellect is what-something-is, that is, the essence of a thing, as is said
in *De anima* III [430b27]. Hence, the intellect attains perfection to the
extent that it knows the essence of some thing. If, then, an intellect knows
the essence of some effect through which the essence of the cause cannot
be known (in other words, through which the intellect cannot know *what*
the cause is), the intellect is not said to reach the cause in an unqualified
sense, even though it can know through the effect *that* the cause is. And
so when human beings know an effect, and know that it has a cause, there
remains a natural desire in them to know what the cause is. That desire is
a kind of wonder, and it causes inquiry, as is said at the beginning of the
*Metaphysics* [982b12, 983a12]. For example, if someone sees a solar eclipse,
he reflects that it has some cause. And because he does not know what
that cause is, he wonders about it, and out of his wondering he proceeds
to inquire. And this inquiry does not come to an end until he arrives at a
knowledge of the essence of the cause. So if the human intellect, through
knowing the essence of some created effect, knows of God merely *that* he
is, the perfection of that intellect has not yet reached the First Cause in an
unqualified sense; instead, there remains in it a natural desire to seek the
cause. Hence, it is not yet perfectly happy. So perfect happiness requires
the intellect to reach the very essence of the First Cause. And in this way it
will have its perfection by being united with God as its object; and human
happiness consists in this alone, as I have said [I-II.2.8; 3.1 and 3.7].

**Response to 1.** Dionysius is speaking of the knowledge of those who are
still on the way, journeying toward happiness.

**Response to 2.** As I said above [I-II.1.8], 'end' can be understood in
two ways. Understood in one way, the end is the thing itself that is desired.
In this way, the end of a higher nature is the same as the end of a lower
nature—the same, indeed, as the end of all things, as I said above [I-II.1.8].
Understood in the other way, the end is the attaining of the thing that is
desired. In this way, the end of a higher nature is different from the end of
a lower nature, in keeping with their different relations to the thing. So in
this way the happiness of God, who comprehends his essence through his
intellect, is in fact greater than the happiness of a human being or angel,
who sees the divine essence but does not comprehend it.

### Question 4. The Things That Are Required for Happiness

Next we have to investigate the things that are required for happiness. Concerning this, there are eight questions:

Article 1. Is delight required for happiness?
Article 2. What is more fundamental in happiness: delight or vision?
Article 3. Is comprehension required for happiness?

Article 4. Is rectitude of will required for happiness?
Article 5. Is the body required for human happiness?
Article 6. Is the perfection of the body required for happiness?
Article 7. Are any external goods required for happiness?
Article 8. Is the companionship of friends required for happiness?

*Article 1. Is delight required for happiness?*[38]

It seems that delight is not required for happiness:
1. Augustine says in *On the Trinity* I [ch. 8] that "vision is the entire reward of faith." But it is happiness that is the prize or reward for virtue, as is clear from the Philosopher in *Ethics* I [1099b16]. Therefore, nothing other than vision is required for happiness.    5
2. Happiness is, in and of itself, the supremely sufficient good, as the Philosopher says in *Ethics* I [1097b8]. And what needs something else is not sufficient in and of itself. Therefore, since the essence of happiness consists in the vision of God, as has been shown [I-II.3.8], it seems that delight is not required for happiness.    10
3. "The activity of felicity" or happiness "has to be unimpeded," as is said in *Ethics* VII [1153b16]. But delight impedes the action of the intellect, since "it corrupts the judgment of prudence," as is said in *Ethics* VI [1140b12]. Therefore, delight is not required for happiness.
**On the contrary.** Augustine says in *Confessions* X [ch. 23] that "happi-    15
ness is joy in truth."
**Reply.** There are four ways in which something is required for something else:

- as a first step or preparation for it, as study is required for knowledge;    20
- as perfecting something, as the soul is required for the life of the body;
- as an external help, as friends are required for doing something;
- as something that accompanies it, as we might say that heat is required for fire.    25

It is in this last way that delight is required for happiness. Delight, you see, is caused by desire's resting in a good attained. Hence, since happiness *just is* the attaining of the highest good, there cannot be happiness without accompanying delight.
**Response to 1.** The bestowing of a reward is precisely what causes the    30
wills of those who have earned the reward to come to rest—and that is

---

38. Parallel passages: *ST* I-II.3.4; *Sent.* II.38.2; *Sent.* IV.49.1.1.2 and IV.3.4.3; *Compend. Theol.* 107, 165; *Comm. Ethics* X.6.

what delight is. So delight is contained in the very idea of a reward that is bestowed.

**Response to 2.** The very vision of God causes delight. For that reason, 35  anyone who sees God cannot be without delight.

**Response to 3.** The delight that accompanies an activity of the intellect does not impede it, but instead strengthens it, as is said in *Ethics* X [1174b23]. After all, the things that we do with delight, we do more attentively and with greater persistence. By contrast, delight that is external to 40  the intellect does impede its activity. Sometimes it does so because it draws our attention away. For, as I have said, we pay more attention to things that delight us; and if our attention is strongly focused on one thing, it necessarily is drawn away from something else. And sometimes delight impedes the intellect's activity by being contrary to it: for example, sensory delight 45  that is contrary to reason impedes the judgment of prudence more than it impedes the judgment of the speculative intellect.

*Article 2. What is more fundamental
in happiness: delight or vision?*[39]

It seems that delight is more fundamental in happiness than vision is:

1. Delight is a perfection of an activity, as is said in *Ethics* X [1174b23]. Now a perfection is more important than the thing that can be perfected by it. Therefore, delight is more important than the activity of the intel- 5  lect, which is vision.

2. That for the sake of which something is desirable is more important [than the thing that is desired for its sake]. Now activities are desired for the sake of delight in them—that is why nature attached delight to the activities that are necessary to preserve the individual and the species, so 10  that animals would not neglect such activities. Therefore, delight is more important in happiness than is the activity of the intellect, which is vision.

3. Vision corresponds to faith, whereas delight or enjoyment corresponds to charity. Now charity is greater than faith, as the Apostle says in 1 Corinthians 13:13. Therefore, delight or enjoyment is more important than 15  vision.

**On the contrary.** A cause is more important than its effect, and vision is the cause of delight. Therefore, vision is more important than delight.

**Reply.** The Philosopher raises this in *Ethics* X [1175a18] and leaves it unresolved. But if one considers the matter carefully, it has to be the case 20  that the activity of the intellect, which is vision, is more important than delight. Delight, after all, consists in the will's coming to rest; and the will comes to rest in something precisely because of the goodness of that in

---

39. Parallel passages: *Sent.* II.38.2 resp. 6; *SCG* III.26; *Comm. Ethics* X.6.

which it rests. Therefore, if the will rests in some activity, the will comes to rest because of the goodness of that activity. And the will does not seek the good for the sake of coming to rest—if that were the case, the will's 25 own act would be the end, which contradicts what I proved earlier [I-II.1.1 resp. 2; 3.4]. Rather, the will seeks coming to rest in the activity because that activity is the will's good. From these considerations it is clear that the activity in which the will comes to rest is a more fundamental good than the will's resting in that activity. 30

**Response to 1.** As the Philosopher says in the same place, "Delight perfects an activity as beauty perfects youth"—the beauty that is a consequence of youth. Hence, delight is a perfection that accompanies vision; it is not a perfection in the sense that it causes vision to be perfect in its species. 35

**Response to 2.** Sensory apprehension does not extend to the general notion of the good but to some particular good that is delightful; that is why animals, which possess only a sensory appetite, seek activities for the sake of delight. The intellect, by contrast, apprehends the universal notion of the good, the attainment of which produces delight. For that reason, its inten- 40 tion of the good is more fundamental than its intention of delight. This is also why the divine intellect, which designed nature, attached delights [to natural activities] for the sake of those activities. And we should of course determine what something is in an unqualified sense, not by attending to the ordering of sensory appetite, but rather according to the ordering of 45 intellectual appetite.

**Response to 3.** Charity does not seek the loved good for the sake of delight; instead, it is a consequence of charity that one delights in having attained the good that one loves. Thus, the end of charity is not delight, but vision: it is through vision that the end is first made present to charity. 50

*Article 3. Is comprehension required for happiness?*[40]

It seems that comprehension is not required for happiness:

1. In his letter to Paulinus *On Seeing God*, Augustine says, "To reach God through the mind is great happiness, but to comprehend him is impossible."[41] Therefore, there is happiness without comprehension.

2. Happiness is a human perfection in accordance with the intellectual 5 part, in which there are no capacities other than intellect and will, as was said in the First Part [I.79ff.]. Now the intellect is sufficiently perfected by seeing God, and the will is sufficiently perfected by delighting in God. Therefore, comprehension is not required as some third component.

---

40. Parallel passages: *ST* I.12.7 resp. 1; *Sent.* I.1.1.1; *Sent.* IV.49.4.5.1.
41. In fact this is a quotation from Sermon 117.3.

10    3. Happiness consists in an activity, and activities are determined by
their objects. Now there are two general objects: the true and the good.
The true corresponds to vision and the good corresponds to delight. Therefore, comprehension is not required as some third component.

**On the contrary.** The Apostle says in 1 Corinthians 9:24, "Run in such
15    a way that you may comprehend." Now the finish line of the spiritual race
is happiness, as the Apostle himself says in the last chapter of 2 Timothy
[4:7–8]: "I have fought the good fight; I have finished the race; I have kept
the faith. From now on there is reserved for me a crown of righteousness."
Therefore, comprehension is required for happiness.

20    **Reply.** Because happiness consists in the attainment of the ultimate
end, the way to figure out what is required for happiness is to investigate
the way human beings are ordered to their end. Now human beings are
ordered to an intelligible end partly through intellect and partly through
will. They are ordered to the end through intellect insofar as some incom-
25    plete cognition of the end preexists in the intellect. They are ordered to the
end through will in two ways: first, through love, which is the will's first
movement toward something; and second, through a real relation of the
lover to what is loved. There are three ways in which this real relation can
obtain. Sometimes the thing loved is present to the lover; in that case, it is
30    no longer sought. Sometimes, however, it is not present; but it is impossible
for the thing loved to be attained. In that case, too, the thing loved is not
sought. Sometimes it is possible for the thing loved to be attained, but it is
beyond the capabilities of the one who is to attain it, so that it cannot be
possessed right away. This is how those who hope are related to what they
35    hope for; this relation alone makes one seek the end.

There is something in happiness itself that corresponds to each of these
three: complete cognition of the end corresponds to incomplete cognition; the presence of the end itself corresponds to the relation of hope; and
delight in the end that is now present follows from love, as I said above [art.
40    2 resp. 3]. And therefore these three things must come together in happiness: vision, which is perfect cognition of the intelligible end; comprehension, which means the presence of the end; and delight or enjoyment,
which means the lover's rest in what is loved.

**Response to 1.** We speak of 'comprehension' in two different ways. In
45    one way, we mean that what is comprehended is encompassed by what
comprehends it. In this sense, everything that is comprehended by something finite is itself finite—which is why God cannot be comprehended in
this sense by any created intellect. In another way, 'comprehension' means
nothing more or less than holding on to some thing that is possessed in the
50    present, as someone who is chasing someone else is said to "comprehend"
him when he gets hold of him. It is in this latter sense that comprehension
is required for happiness.

**Response to 2.** Both hope and love belong to the will, since it is the task of one and the same power both to love something and to strive for it when it is not possessed. And in the same way, both comprehension and delight    55 belong to the will, since it is the task of one and the same power both to possess something and to rest in it.

**Response to 3.** Comprehension is not an activity in addition to vision; rather, it is a relation to an end already possessed. For this reason, even vision itself (or the thing seen insofar as it is present) is an object of    60 comprehension.

### Article 4. Is rectitude of will required for happiness?[42]

It seems that rectitude of will is not required for happiness:

1. Happiness consists essentially in an activity of the intellect, as has been said [I-II.3.4]. But rectitude of will, by which people are called pure, is not required for a perfect activity of the intellect. For Augustine says in *Reconsiderations* [I.4], "I do not approve what I said in my speech: 'God,    5 you have willed that only the pure know the truth.' For one could reply that many who are not pure know many truths." Therefore, rectitude of will is not required for happiness.

2. What is prior does not depend on what is posterior, but the activity of the intellect is prior to the activity of the will. Therefore, happiness, which    10 is the perfect activity of the intellect, does not depend on rectitude of will.

3. If one thing is directed to another as its end, it is no longer necessary once the end has been attained: for example, a ship is no longer necessary once you have reached port. Now rectitude of will, which virtue produces, is directed to happiness as its end. Therefore, once happiness has been    15 attained, rectitude of will is not necessary.

**On the contrary.** Matthew 5:8 says, "Happy are the pure in heart, for they shall see God." And Hebrews 12:14 says, "Pursue peace with everyone, and the holiness without which no one will see God."

**Reply.** Rectitude of will is required for happiness both *antecedently* and    20 *concomitantly.* It is required antecedently because rectitude of will exists through an appropriate ordering to the ultimate end. Now an end is related to what is for the end as form is related to matter. Hence, in the same way that matter cannot acquire form unless it is disposed to that form in the appropriate way, so too nothing can acquire an end unless it is ordered to    25 that end in the appropriate way. And for that reason no one can arrive at happiness without having rectitude of will.

Rectitude of will is required concomitantly because (as I have said) ultimate happiness consists in the vision of the divine essence, which is the

30  very essence of goodness. And so the wills of those who see God's essence
    necessarily love whatever they do love as ordered to God, in the same way
    that the wills of those who do not see God's essence necessarily love what-
    ever they do love under the general notion of good that they have come to
    know. And this is the very thing that makes a will right. Hence, it is evident
35  that there cannot be happiness without an upright will.
        **Response to 1.** Augustine is speaking of a knowledge of truth that is not
    the very essence of goodness.
        **Response to 2.** Every act of will is preceded by some act of intellect;
    nonetheless, some acts of will are prior to some acts of intellect. After all,
40  the will tends toward the final act of intellect, which is happiness. And
    therefore an upright inclination of the will is required as a precondition
    for happiness, in the same way that an arrow must move rightly if it is to
    hit the target.
        **Response to 3.** Not everything that is directed to an end ceases when
45  the end is attained—that is true only of what has some aspect of incom-
    pleteness, as motion does. That is why the means of motion are not neces-
    sary after the end has been achieved, whereas an appropriate ordering to
    the end is necessary.

*Article 5. Is the body required for human happiness?*[43]

It seems that the body is required for happiness:
        1. The perfection of virtue and grace presupposes the perfection of
    nature. Now happiness is a perfection of virtue and grace. And a soul with-
    out a body does not have the perfection of nature, since a soul is naturally
5   a *part* of human nature, and any part separated from its whole is imperfect.
    Therefore, a soul without a body cannot be happy.
        2. Happiness is a perfect activity, as was said earlier [I-II.3.2 and 3.5].
    But a perfect activity follows from perfect being, since a thing operates
    only insofar as it is a being in actuality. Therefore, since the soul does not
10  have perfect being when it is separated from the body (as indeed no part
    has perfect being when it is separated from its whole), it seems that a soul
    without a body cannot be happy.
        3. Happiness is a human perfection, but a soul without a body is not a
    human being. Therefore, happiness cannot be in the soul without a body.
15      4. According to the Philosopher in *Ethics* VII [1153b16], "the activity of
    felicity," in which happiness consists, "is unimpeded." But the activity of
    a separated soul is impeded, since, as Augustine says in *Literal Commen-
    tary on Genesis* XII [ch. 35], "there is in the soul a certain natural appetite
    for governing the body, and because of that appetite the soul is restrained

43. Parallel passages: SCG IV.79 and 91; *Power of God* 5.10; *Compend. Theol.* 151.

in a way from pressing on with all its energy toward that highest heaven,"     20
that is, toward the vision of the divine essence. Therefore, a soul without
a body cannot be happy.

5. Happiness is a sufficient good: it satisfies desire. But that is not the
case for a separated soul, which still desires union with a body, as Augustine
says. Therefore, a soul separated from the body is not happy.     25

6. In happiness, human beings are equal to angels; but a soul without
a body is not equal to angels, as Augustine says. Therefore, a soul without
a body is not happy.

**On the contrary.** Revelation 14:13 says, "Happy are the dead who die
in the Lord."     30

**Reply.** Happiness is twofold. There is imperfect happiness, which is
possessed in this life; and there is perfect happiness, which consists in the
vision of God. Now it is evident that the body is necessarily required for
the happiness of this life. After all, the happiness of this life is an activity
of the intellect (either the speculative intellect or the practical intellect),     35
and there can be no activity of the intellect in this life without a phantasm,
which exists only in a bodily organ, as I argued in the First Part [I.84.6 and
84.7]. And thus the happiness that can be possessed in this life depends
in a way on the body.

Now concerning the perfect happiness that consists in the vision of God,     40
some have claimed that such happiness cannot come to a soul existing
without a body. They said that the souls of the saints that are separated from
bodies do not attain perfect happiness until the day of judgment, when they
take up their bodies again. That, however, is plainly false, both according
to authority and according to reason. According to authority: the Apostle     45
says in 2 Corinthians 5:6–7, "As long as we are in the body, we are absent
from the Lord"; and he explains the nature of this absence by adding, "for
we walk by faith and not by sight." From this it is evident that as long as
people are walking by faith and not by sight, lacking the vision of the divine
essence, they are not yet present to God. But the souls of the saints that     50
are separated from their bodies are in fact present to God, which is why
the passage continues, "But we have confidence, and we would rather be
absent from the body and present to the Lord." From this it is clear that the
souls of the saints that are separated from bodies walk by sight; they see the
essence of God, and in that is true happiness.     55

This is also evident through reason. After all, the intellect needs the
body for its activity only for the sake of phantasms, in which it sees intelligible truth, as I said in the First Part [I.84.7]. But it is clear that the divine
essence cannot be seen through phantasms, as I showed in the First Part
[I.12.3]. Hence, given that perfect human happiness consists in the vision     60
of the divine essence, perfect human happiness does not depend on the
body. And for that reason a soul can be happy without a body.

But it is important to note that there are two ways something can pertain
to a thing's perfection. In one way, something pertains to a thing's perfec-
65 tion because it constitutes the thing's essence; this is the way in which the
soul is required for the perfection of a human being. In another way, what
pertains to a thing's well-being is required for the thing's perfection; this
is the way in which beauty pertains to the perfection of a body and quick-
wittedness pertains to the perfection of a human being. So although the
70 body does not pertain to the perfection of human happiness in the first
way, it does in the second way. You see, because activity depends on the
nature of a thing, the more perfect the soul is in its nature, the more perfectly it will possess its distinctive activity, in which felicity consists. This
is why Augustine in *Literal Commentary on Genesis* XII [ch. 35], having
75 asked "whether that supreme happiness can be granted to the spirits of the
departed without bodies," answers that "they cannot see the immutable
substance in the way that the holy angels see it, whether because of some
other, more obscure cause, or because there is in them a certain natural
appetite for governing a body."
80        **Response to 1.** Happiness is a perfection of the soul on the part of the
intellect, through which the soul transcends the body's organs; it is not a
perfection of the soul insofar as the soul is the form of a natural body. And
for that reason, even if the perfection of nature by which the soul is the
form of the body ceases to obtain, the perfection of nature by which hap-
85 piness is appropriate for the soul remains intact.
         **Response to 2.** The soul does not have the same relation to being that
other parts have. [In the case of other parts,] the being of the whole is not
the being of any of its parts; hence, either the part ceases to exist altogether
when the whole is destroyed, as is true of the parts of an animal when the
90 animal is destroyed, or else, if the parts do continue to exist, they have a
different being in actuality, in the way that the parts of a line have a different being from the whole line. By contrast, human souls retain the being
of the composite after the destruction of the body, because the being of
the form and the being of the matter are one and the same, and this is the
95 being of the composite. Now the soul subsists in its own being, as I showed
in the First Part [I.75.2]. Hence, it follows that after it is separated from the
body it has perfect being, and consequently it can have a perfect activity,
even though it does not have the perfect nature of its species.
         **Response to 3.** It is in virtue of their intellects that human beings are
100 happy; and so as long as their intellects remain, they can be happy—just as
an Ethiopian's teeth, in virtue of which he is said to be white, can be white
even after they are extracted.
         **Response to 4.** There are two ways in which something is impeded by
something else. One way is through contrariety, as cold impedes the action
105 of heat; and this way in which an activity is impeded is incompatible with

felicity. The other way is through some sort of defect, because the thing that is impeded lacks something that is required for its complete perfection. This way in which an activity is impeded is not incompatible with felicity, but only with the complete perfection of felicity. And this is the way in which the soul's separation from the body is said to restrain the 110 soul from pressing on with all its energy toward the vision of the divine essence. You see, the soul desires to enjoy God in such a way that its very enjoyment spills over into the body as much as possible. And so as long as the soul enjoys God without a body, its desire is at rest in what it possesses, yet in such a way that the soul would still want its body to attain to a share 115 in its enjoyment.

**Response to 5.** The desire of a separated soul is totally satisfied as far as the desirable object goes, because the soul has what suffices for its desire. But it is not totally satisfied as far as the one desiring is concerned, because it does not possess that good in every way in which it would want to possess 120 it. And for that reason, when the soul again takes up its body, happiness increases, not in terms of intensity, but in terms of its extent.

**Response to 6.** What Augustine says in the same passage—that "the spirits of the departed do not see God in the way that the angels do"— should not be understood as indicating an inequality of *quantity,* because 125 even now some souls of the blessed have been elevated to the higher orders of angels and see God more clearly than lower angels. Instead, it should be understood as indicating an inequality of *proportion,* in that even the lowest angels have all the perfection of happiness that they will ever have, whereas the separated souls of the saints do not. 130

### Article 6. Is the perfection of the body required for happiness?[44]

It seems that the perfection of the body is not required for perfect human happiness:

1. The body's perfection is a bodily good, but it was shown above [art. 2] that happiness does not consist in bodily goods. Therefore, no perfect condition of the body is required for happiness. 5

2. Human happiness consists in the vision of the divine essence, as has been shown [I-II.3.8]; but the body contributes nothing to this activity, as has been said [art. 5]. Therefore, no condition of the body is required for happiness.

3. The more the intellect is disentangled from the body, the more per- 10 fectly it understands. Now happiness consists in the most perfect activity of the intellect. Therefore, the soul needs to be disentangled from the body

---

44. Parallel passages: *ST* III.15.10; *Sent.* IV.49.4.5.2.

in every way. Therefore, no condition of the body is required in any way
for happiness.

15     **On the contrary.** Happiness is the reward of virtue, which is why John
13:17 says, "You will be happy if you do these things." But what is promised
to the saints as their reward is not only the vision of God and [its attendant]
delight, but also a good condition of the body. After all, we read in the last
chapter of Isaiah [66:14], "You will see, and your heart will rejoice, and
20  your bones will flourish like the grass." Therefore, a good condition of the
body is required for happiness.

    **Reply.** If we are speaking of the sort of human happiness that can be
possessed in this life, it is evident that a good condition of the body is necessarily required for it. After all, according to the Philosopher, this happi-
25  ness consists in an activity of perfect virtue[45]; and it is obvious that bodily
infirmity can impede human beings in every activity of virtue.

    But if we are speaking of perfect happiness, then there are those who
have said that no condition of the body is required for perfect happiness—
indeed, that happiness requires the soul to be separated from the body alto-
30  gether. Along these lines, Augustine in *City of God* XXII [ch. 22] brings in
the words of Porphyry, who said, "In order for the soul to be happy, it must
flee from every body." But that is absurd. It is, after all, natural for the soul
to be united to the body; so it cannot be the case that the soul's perfection
is incompatible with the body's natural perfection.

35     And so we should say that for happiness to be perfect in every way, a
perfect condition of the body is required both antecedently and consequently. It is required antecedently because, as Augustine says in *Literal
Commentary on Genesis* XII [ch. 35], "If the body is such that it is difficult and burdensome to govern, like the flesh that is corrupted and weighs
40  down the soul, the mind is turned aside from that vision of the highest
heaven." From this he concludes that "once this body is no longer animal,
but spiritual, it will be made fitting for the company of the angels; and what
once was the soul's burden will be its glory." It is required consequently
because the soul's happiness will overflow into the body, so that the body
45  will receive its own perfection. This is why Augustine says in his letter to
Dioscorus [118.3], "God made the soul with such a powerful nature that
from the soul's fullest happiness the vigor of incorruptibility will overflow
into the inferior nature."

    **Response to 1.** Happiness does not consist in a bodily good as though
50  such a good were the object of happiness, but a bodily good can contribute
something to the beauty or perfection of happiness.

---

45. *Nicomachean Ethics* I.13, 1102a5.

**Response to 2.** Granting that the body contributes nothing to the activity of the intellect by which God's essence is seen, the body could still impede that activity. And for that reason the body's perfection is required so that the body does not impede the mind's elevation.                                55

**Response to 3.** The intellect's perfect activity requires that it be disentangled from this corruptible body that weighs down the soul, but not from the spiritual body that will be wholly under the control of the spirit. We will discuss the spiritual body in the Third Part of this work.[46]

*Article 7. Are any external goods required for happiness?*[47]

It seems that external goods are also required for happiness:

1. What is promised to the saints as their reward pertains to happiness. Now the saints are promised external goods such as food and drink, riches, and a kingdom: Luke 22:30 says, "You will eat and drink at my table in my kingdom"; Matthew 6:20 says, "Lay up for yourselves treasures in heaven";   5 and Matthew 25:34 says, "Come, blessed of my Father, possess the kingdom." Therefore, external goods are required for happiness.

2. According to Boethius in *Consolation of Philosophy* III [pr. 2], "happiness is the state that is made complete by the accumulation of all goods." Now external goods are in fact human goods, albeit the least such goods, as   10 Augustine says.[48] Therefore, they too are required for happiness.

3. In Matthew 5:12 the Lord says, "Your reward is great in heaven"; and being in heaven signifies being in a place. Therefore, an external *place*, at any rate, is required for happiness.

**On the contrary.** Psalm 72:25 says, "What is there for me in heaven?   15 And besides you, what have I wanted on earth?"—meaning, I want nothing else but what follows next: "My good is to cling to God." Therefore, nothing external is required for happiness.

**Reply.** External goods are required for imperfect happiness, the kind of happiness that can be possessed in this life. It is not that external goods   20 belong to the *essence* of happiness; rather, they are instruments that are of service to happiness, which consists in the activity of virtue, as is said in *Ethics* I [1102a5]. After all, in this life human beings depend on certain bodily necessities both for the activity of contemplative virtue and for the activity of active virtue (the latter also requires many other things, by which   25 one carries out virtuous deeds).

But perfect happiness, which consists in the vision of God, does not require external goods in any way. The reason for this is that all such

---

46. Not completed, but see *ST* III supp. 82–85.
47. Parallel passage: II-II.186.3 resp. 4.
48. *On Free Choice of the Will* II.19.

external goods are required either for the preservation of the animal body
30  or for other activities appropriate to human life that we carry out through
the animal body, whereas the perfect happiness that consists in the vision
of God will be either in the soul apart from the body or in the soul united
to a body that is no longer animal, but spiritual. And so such external goods
are not required in any way for perfect happiness, since they are ordered
35  to animal life. And because in this life contemplative happiness resembles
that perfect happiness more closely than active happiness does, because it
is more like God (as is clear from what I have said [I-II.3.5 resp. 1]), it is less
dependent on such bodily goods, as is said in *Ethics* X [1178b1].

**Response to 1.** All those Scriptural promises of bodily things have to
40  be understood metaphorically, in keeping with Scripture's frequent use of
bodily things to stand for spiritual things, "so that from the things we know,
we might rise up to desire things unknown," as Gregory says in one of his
homilies.[49] Thus, food and drink represent the delight of happiness, wealth
represents God's sufficiency in satisfying human beings, and the kingdom
45  represents the exaltation of human beings to union with God.

**Response to 2.** The goods that are of service to animal life have no
place in the spiritual life in which perfect happiness consists. And yet perfect happiness will still be an accumulation of all goods, because whatever
aspect of good is found in those goods will be possessed in its entirety in
50  the supreme fount of goods.

**Response to 3.** According to Augustine in *On the Lord's Sermon on the
Mount* [I.5], the reward of the saints is not said to be in a physical heaven;
instead, 'heaven' represents the loftiness of spiritual goods. Nonetheless,
there will in fact be a bodily place—the empyrean heaven—for the blessed,
55  not because this is necessary for happiness, but for the sake of fittingness
and beauty.

### Article 8. Is the companionship of
### friends required for happiness?

It seems that friends are necessary for happiness:

1. Scripture frequently uses the word 'glory' to signify our future happiness, and glory is a matter of many people coming to know about a person's possessing some good. Therefore, the companionship of friends is
5  required for happiness.

2. Boethius says that "there is no joy in possessing any good without
fellowship,"[50] and delight is required for happiness; therefore, the companionship of friends is also required.

---

49. Homily 11.
50. This quotation is taken from Seneca, *Epistulae ad Lucilium* 6.

3. Charity is perfected in happiness, and charity encompasses love
of God and of neighbor. Therefore, it seems that the companionship of    10
friends is required for happiness.

**On the contrary.** Wisdom 7:11 says, "All good things came to me with
her," that is, with divine wisdom, which consists in the contemplation of
God. And thus nothing else is required for happiness.

**Reply.** If we are speaking of the felicity of the present life, then as the    15
Philosopher says in *Ethics* IX, the happy person needs friends—not, indeed,
for their usefulness, because a happy person is self-sufficient; and not for
delight, because a happy person has perfect delight in his or her own virtuous activity; but for the sake of good activity. That is, the happy person
needs friends in order to do good things for them, to delight in seeing them    20
act well, and to receive their help in acting well. Human beings, you see,
require the help of friends in order to act well, both in the deeds of the
active life and in those of the contemplative life.

But if we are speaking of the perfect happiness that will exist in our
homeland, the companionship of friends is not a necessary requirement for    25
happiness, since human beings will have the fullness of their perfection in
God. The companionship of friends does, however, contribute to the well-
being of happiness. That is why Augustine says in *Literal Commentary on
Genesis* VIII [ch. 25] that "the eternity, truth, and charity of the Creator
are the only inward aids that help a spiritual creature be happy. If we can    30
speak of external aids, perhaps they are helped only by this: they see one
another, and they rejoice in their fellowship in God."

**Response to 1.** The glory that is essential to happiness is not the glory
that human beings have in the eyes of other human beings, but the glory
they have before God.    35

**Response to 2.** Boethius is talking about a case in which the good that
is possessed is not fully sufficient. That is not the case here, since in God
human beings have the sufficiency of all good.

**Response to 3.** The perfection of charity is essential to happiness as far
as it involves love of God, but not as it involves love of neighbor. For that    40
reason, if there were just one soul enjoying God, it would be happy, without any neighbor to love. But if there is a neighbor, love of that neighbor
follows from perfect love of God. Hence, friendship is a sort of concomitant of perfect happiness.

## Question 5. The Attainment of Happiness

Next we have to investigate the attainment of happiness. Concerning this
there are eight questions:

Article 1. Can human beings attain happiness?

Article 2. Can one human being be happier than another?

Article 3. Can someone be happy in this life?

Article 4. Can happiness, once possessed, be lost?

Article 5. Can human beings attain happiness through their natural powers?

Article 6. Do human beings attain happiness through the action of some higher creature?

Article 7. Are any deeds required of human beings in order for them to receive happiness from God?

Article 8. Does every human being desire happiness?

### Article 1. Can human beings attain happiness?

It seems that human beings cannot attain happiness:

1. In the same way that a rational nature is above a sensory nature, an intellectual nature is above a rational nature, as is evident from what Dionysius says in many places in *On the Divine Names* [4.1–2, 6.1, 7.2]. Now
5   non-rational animals, which have only a sensory nature, cannot achieve the end of a rational nature. Therefore, neither can human beings, who have a rational nature, achieve the end of an intellectual nature, which is happiness.

2. True happiness consists in the vision of God, who is pure truth. But
10   what is natural for human beings is to see truth in material things—that is why they understand intelligible species in phantasms, as is said in *De anima* III [431b2]. Therefore, human beings cannot attain happiness.

3. Happiness consists in attaining the highest good. Now one cannot reach what is highest without going beyond things in the middle. So, since
15   the angelic nature is in the middle between God and human nature, and human beings cannot go beyond angelic nature, it seems that human beings cannot attain happiness.

**On the contrary.** Psalm 93:12 says, "Happy are the human beings whom you have instructed, O Lord."

20   **Reply.** 'Happiness' signifies the attainment of the perfect good. Therefore, anyone who is capable of attaining the perfect good can achieve happiness. Now from the fact that the human intellect can apprehend the universal good and the human will can desire it, it is quite clear that human beings are indeed capable of attaining the perfect good. And so
25   human beings can achieve happiness.

This is also evident from the fact that human beings are capable of seeing the divine essence, as I established in the First Part [I.12.1]; and I have of course said that perfect human happiness consists in the vision of the divine essence [I-II.3.8].

30   **Response to 1.** The way in which rational nature surpasses sensory nature is different from the way in which intellectual nature surpasses

rational nature. Rational nature surpasses sensory nature in terms of the object it cognizes: sense can in no way cognize a universal, which reason does cognize. By contrast, intellectual nature surpasses rational nature in terms of the way in which it cognizes *the same* intelligible truth: an intel- 35 lectual nature apprehends instantaneously the truth that rational nature reaches through rational investigation, as is evident from what I said in the First Part [I.58.3; I.79.8]. And so what intellect apprehends, reason reaches through a sort of motion. Accordingly, a rational nature can attain happiness, which is the perfection of intellectual nature, but in a different way 40 from the angels. The angels attained happiness instantaneously after their initial creation; human beings, by contrast, reach happiness after some time. A sensory nature, however, cannot attain this end in any way.

**Response to 2.** This way of cognizing intelligible truth through phantasms is natural for human beings in the condition of this present life. But 45 after this life, human beings will have a different way of cognizing that will be natural to them, as I said in the First Part [I.84.7; I.89.1].

**Response to 3.** Human beings cannot go beyond the angels in terms of the hierarchy of nature, so as to be superior to angels by nature. But they can go beyond angels through the activity of their intellects, by understand- 50 ing a being that is superior to the angels and makes human beings happy. When they achieve this perfectly, they will be perfectly happy.

*Article 2. Can one human being be happier than another?*[51]

It seems that one human being cannot be happier than another:

1. Happiness is the reward for virtue, as the Philosopher says in *Ethics* I [1099b16]. But everyone receives an equal reward for virtuous deeds. After all, Matthew 20:10 says that all who worked in the vineyard received a denarius apiece, because, as Gregory says, "They were assigned an equal 5 reward, eternal life."[52] Therefore, one human being will not be happier than another.

2. Happiness is the highest good, and there cannot be anything greater than the highest. Therefore, one human being's happiness cannot be greater than another's. 10

3. Because happiness is a perfect and sufficient good, it satisfies human desire. But desire is not satisfied if some good is lacking that could be added. And if there is not anything lacking that could be added, nothing else could be any better. Therefore, either a human being is not happy, or else (if one is happy) there cannot be any other, greater happiness. 15

---

51. Parallel passages: *Sent.* IV.49.1.4.2; *Comm. Matt.* 20; *Comm. John* 14.1; *Comm. 1 Corinth.* 3.2.
52. Homily 19.

**On the contrary.** John 14:2 says, "In my father's house are many mansions"; and as Augustine explains, these many mansions "stand for different
dignities of merits in eternal life."[53] Now the dignity of eternal life that is
given in return for merit is happiness itself. Therefore, there are various

20  degrees of happiness, and not everyone's happiness is equal.

**Reply.** As I said above [I-II.1.8; 2.7], the notion of happiness includes
two things: the ultimate end itself, which is the highest good, and the
attainment or enjoyment of that good. As regards the good that is the object
and cause of happiness, there cannot be any happiness greater than any

25  other, since there is just the one highest good, namely, God, and human
beings are happy through enjoying God. But as regards the attainment
or enjoyment of this good, one person can be happier than another: the
greater one's enjoyment of this good, the happier one is. Now one person
can enjoy God more completely than another in virtue of being better dis-

30  posed or ordered to that enjoyment. And in that way one person can be
happier than another.

**Response to 1.** That there is one denarius signifies that there is one happiness in terms of its object; that there are different mansions signifies that
happiness differs in terms of the different levels of enjoyment.

35  **Response to 2.** Happiness is said to be the highest good insofar as it is
the perfect possession or enjoyment of the highest good.

**Response to 3.** No one who is happy is lacking any desirable good,
since anyone who is happy has the infinite good itself, which is the good
of every good, as Augustine puts it.[54] Instead, one person is said to be hap-

40  pier than another because of their differing participation in one and the
same good. But the addition of other goods does not increase happiness;
this is why Augustine says in *Confessions* V [ch. 4], "one who knows you
and these other things is not happier because of them, but is happy because
of you alone."

### Article 3. Can someone be happy in this life?[55]

It seems that happiness can be possessed in this life:

1. Psalm 118:1 says, "Happy are those whose way is blameless, who walk
in the law of the Lord." Now that can happen in this life. Therefore, someone can be happy in this life.

5  2. Imperfect participation in the supreme good still counts as happiness; otherwise one person would not be happier than another. And human
beings can participate in the highest good, albeit imperfectly, in this life,

---

53. *Tractates on the Gospel of John* tr. 67.

54. *On the Trinity* XIII.7.

55. Parallel passages: *Sent.* IV.43.1.1, 49.1.1.4; SCG III.48; *Comm. Ethics* X.16.

by knowing and loving God. Therefore, human beings can be happy in this life.

3. What many people say cannot be completely false. After all, it 10 seems that what is in many is natural, and nature does not go completely astray. Now many people think there is happiness in this life, as is evident from Psalm 143:15, "They have called the people happy who have these things"—meaning, the goods of the present life. Therefore, someone can be happy in this life. 15

**On the contrary.** Job 14:1 says, "Human beings, born of woman, living but a short time, have their fill of many miseries." Now happiness is incompatible with misery. Therefore, human beings in this life cannot be happy.

**Reply.** One can have some share in happiness in this life, but perfect and genuine happiness cannot be possessed in this life. We can establish 20 this conclusion in two ways. The first way looks at the general notion of happiness. Because happiness is a perfect and sufficient good, it excludes all evil and fulfills every desire; but in this life it is not possible to exclude all evil. Indeed, this present life is beset by many evils that cannot be avoided: ignorance on the part of the intellect, inordinate affection on the 25 part of appetite, and many punishments on the part of the body, as Augustine carefully explains in *City of God* XIX [ch. 4]. And similarly, the desire for good cannot be fully satisfied in this life. You see, human beings naturally desire to retain the good that they have, but the goods of the present life are transitory, since life itself—which we naturally desire and would 30 want to retain forever, since human beings naturally shrink from death—is transitory. For those reasons, it is impossible for anyone to possess genuine happiness in this life.

The second way takes into account the particular thing in which happiness consists, namely, the vision of the divine essence, which human beings 35 cannot achieve in this life, as I showed in the First Part [I.12.2].

From these considerations it is perfectly clear that no one can attain genuine and perfect happiness in this life.

**Response to 1.** Some people are called happy in this life either because they have the hope of attaining happiness in the life to come (as in Romans 40 8:24, "We have been saved through hope") or because they have some share in happiness by enjoying the highest good in some way.

**Response to 2.** There are two ways in which participation in happiness can be imperfect. One way is on the part of the object of happiness, because it is not seen in its essence. This sort of imperfection takes away 45 the character of true happiness. In the other way, participation can be imperfect on the part of the one who participates in happiness, who does indeed attain the object of happiness in itself—that is, God—but imperfectly, by comparison with the way in which God enjoys himself. This sort of imperfection does not take away the genuine character of happiness 50 because, since happiness is an activity, as I said earlier [I-II.3.2], the genuine character of happiness depends on the object that gives the act its species, not on the subject.

**Response to 3.** Human beings think that there is some happiness in this
55   life because there is some likeness to true happiness, and thus they are not
completely astray in their thinking.

*Article 4. Can happiness, once possessed, be lost?*[56]

It seems that happiness can be lost:

1. Happiness is a perfection, and every perfection is in what is perfectible in the way appropriate to that perfectible thing. So, since human beings are by nature changeable, it seems that human beings participate
5   in happiness in a changeable way. And thus it seems that human beings can lose happiness.

2. Happiness consists in an activity of the intellect, which is under the control of the will. Now the will is capable of opposites. Therefore, it seems that the will can stop the activity by which human beings are made happy,
10   and thus a person will stop being happy.

3. The end corresponds to the beginning. Now human happiness has a beginning, since a given person has not always been happy. Therefore, it seems that human happiness also has an end.

**On the contrary.** Matthew 25:46 says of the just that "they will enter
15   eternal life"; and this eternal life, as I have said [art. 2 on the contrary], is the happiness of the saints. Now what is eternal does not fail. Therefore, happiness cannot be lost.

**Reply.** If we are talking about imperfect happiness—the sort of happiness that can be possessed in this life—then yes, it can be lost. This is clear
20   in contemplative happiness, which is lost if memory fails (for example, if someone's knowledge is destroyed by an illness) or even if various occupations completely distract someone from contemplation. The same thing is also clear in active happiness. After all, the human will can change, falling from virtue—and [active] happiness consists chiefly in the activity of
25   virtue—into vice. And even if virtue remains intact, reversals of fortune outside the virtuous agent can disturb such happiness by hindering many acts of virtue (though they cannot destroy happiness completely, since some virtuous activity remains as long as someone endures these adversities in a praiseworthy way). And it is because the happiness of this life
30   can be lost, which appears to be contrary to the concept of happiness, that the Philosopher says in *Ethics* I [1101a19] that some people are happy in

---

56. Parallel passages: *ST* I.64.2, 94.1; *Sent.* I.8.3.2; *Sent.* IV.49.1.1.4; *SCG* III.62; *Compend. Theol.* I.166, II.9; *Comm. John* 10.5.

this life, not in an unqualified sense, but as human beings whose nature is subject to change.

If, on the other hand, we are talking about the perfect happiness that we look for after this life, one should know that Origen, following the error of   35
certain Platonists, held that human beings can become unhappy after having enjoyed ultimate happiness.[57] But it is perfectly clear that this is false, for two reasons. The first is derived from the general concept of happiness. Since happiness is a perfect and sufficient good, it must fully satisfy human desire and exclude every evil. Now human beings naturally desire to keep a   40
good that they have, and to have the assurance that they will in fact keep it. Otherwise they will inevitably suffer from fear of losing it or sorrow over the certainty of losing it. So true happiness requires that human beings have an assured belief that they will never lose the good that they possess. And of course if that belief is true, it follows that they will never lose happiness.   45
If, however, it is false, having a false belief is itself an evil, since falsity is an evil for the intellect just as truth is the intellect's good, as is said in *Ethics* VI [1139a28]. In that case, they are not yet truly happy, since they are still subject to some evil.

The second reason becomes clear if we look at what happiness is in par-   50
ticular. I showed earlier that perfect human happiness consists in the vision of the divine essence [I-II.3.8]. Now it is impossible for someone who sees the divine essence to will not to see it. Why? Because if there is any good that one possesses but wills to be without, either that good is insufficient and one is looking for a more sufficient good to take its place, or else that   55
good has some associated drawback that makes it objectionable. But the vision of the divine essence fills the soul with every good, since it joins the soul to the fount of all goodness; this is why Psalm 16:15 says, "I will be satisfied when your glory appears," and Wisdom 7:11 says, "All good things came to me with her," that is, with the contemplation of wisdom. Simi-   60
larly, the vision of the divine essence has no associated drawback: Wisdom 8:16 says concerning the contemplation of wisdom that "companionship with her has no bitterness and life with her no weariness." Therefore, it is evident that those who are happy cannot abandon happiness by their own wills. And similarly, they cannot lose it because God takes it away from   65
them. For taking away happiness is a punishment, so God, who is a just judge, cannot take it away except for some fault; and no one who sees God's essence can fall into any fault, since rectitude of will follows necessarily from that vision, as I showed earlier [I-II.4.4]. And similarly, no other agent can take happiness away, because a mind joined to God is raised above all   70
other things; and thus no other agent can stop that mind from being joined

---

57. *On First Principles* II.3. Augustine discusses the Platonists' teaching in *City of God* X.30.

to God in that way. For these reasons, it seems absurd that human beings could pass from happiness to misery, or vice versa, through any passage of time, since such changes over time can happen only concerning things
75  that are subject to time and motion.

**Response to 1.** Happiness is complete perfection; it excludes every defect from those who are happy. And for that reason those who attain it receive it without any possibility of change, thanks to the divine power, which exalts human beings to share in the eternity that transcends all
80  change.

**Response to 2.** The will is capable of opposites regarding things that are directed to the end, but they are directed to the ultimate end by natural necessity, as is evident from the fact that human beings cannot help but will to be happy.

85  **Response to 3.** Happiness has a beginning because of the nature of those who participate in happiness, but it lacks an end because of the nature of the good, participation in which makes them happy. Thus there is one explanation for the fact that happiness has a beginning and a different explanation for the fact that it has no end.

### Article 5. Can human beings attain happiness through their natural powers?[58]

It seems that human beings can attain happiness through their natural powers:

1. Nature is not deficient in necessary things. Now nothing is as necessary for human beings as that which they attain the ultimate
5   end. Therefore, that is not lacking from human nature. Therefore, human beings can attain happiness through their natural powers.

2. Since human beings are nobler than non-rational creatures, it seems they must be more self-sufficient. Now non-rational creatures can attain their ends through their natural powers. So we have even better reason to
10  say that human beings can attain happiness through their natural powers.

3. According to the Philosopher, happiness is a perfect activity.[59] Now the undertaking of an activity belongs to the same capacity as the perfecting of the activity. Therefore, since imperfect activity, which is, as it were, the starting point in human activities, is under the sway of the natural
15  power in virtue of which human beings are in control of their own actions, it appears that through their natural powers they can achieve the perfect activity that is happiness.

---

58. Parallel passages: *ST* I.12.4, 12.1; *ST* I-II.62.1; *Sent.* III.27.2.2; *Sent.* IV.49.2.6; *SCG* III.52 and 147.

59. *Nicomachean Ethics* VII.13.

**On the contrary.** Human beings are naturally the origin of their own actions through intellect and will. But the ultimate happiness that has been prepared for the saints outstrips human intellect and will. As the 20 Apostle says in 1 Corinthians 2:9, "Eye has not seen, nor ear heard, nor has it entered into the human heart, what things God has prepared for those who love him." Therefore, human beings cannot attain happiness through their natural powers.

**Reply.** The imperfect happiness that can be possessed in this life can 25 be acquired by human beings through their natural powers, in the same way that virtue, in the exercise of which such happiness consists, can be; I shall speak to this subject below [I-II.63]. But perfect human happiness, as I said above [I-II.3.8], consists in the vision of the divine essence. Now to see God in his essence is above not only human nature, but also the 30 nature of any creature, as I showed in the First Part [I.12.4]. For the natural knowledge of any creature accords with the mode of its substance; as is said of an intelligence in the *Book of Causes* [prop. 8], "it knows the things that are above it, and the things that are below it, according to the mode of its substance." Now any knowledge that accords with the mode of a cre- 35 ated substance falls short of a vision of the divine essence, which infinitely surpasses every created substance. Hence, neither human beings nor any other creature can attain ultimate happiness through their natural powers.

**Response to 1.** Nature did not fail in providing necessary things for human beings, even though it did not give us weapons and coverings as it 40 gave to other animals, because it gave us reason and hands by which we can obtain these things for ourselves. And in the same way, nature did not fail in providing necessary things for us, even though it did not give us any principle by which we could attain happiness; for that was impossible. But it did give us free choice, by which we can turn to God, so that he may make 45 us happy. For as is said in *Ethics* III [1112b27], "what we can do through our friends, we can in a certain way do by ourselves."

**Response to 2.** A nature that can attain a perfect good, even if it requires outside help in order to attain it, is of a nobler status than a nature that cannot attain a perfect good but only attains an imperfect good, even if it 50 needs no outside help in order to attain it, as the Philosopher says in *On the Heavens* II [292a22]. By way of analogy, someone who can attain perfect health, albeit with the help of medicine, is better disposed toward health than is someone who can attain only imperfect health, though without the help of medicine. Therefore, a rational creature, who can attain the per- 55 fect good of happiness, though needing divine help, is more perfect than a non-rational creature, which does not have the capacity for such a good, but attains some imperfect good by its own natural power.

**Response to 3.** When the imperfect and the perfect are of the same species, they can be caused by the same power. But this need not be the 60

case when they are of different species: for not everything that can cause
a disposition of matter can confer its final perfection. Now the imperfect
activity that is under the sway of natural human power is not of the same
species as that perfect activity that is human happiness, since the species
65   of an activity is determined by its object. Hence, the argument is invalid.

### Article 6. Do human beings attain happiness
### through the action of some higher creature?

It seems that human beings can be made happy through the action of some
higher creature, namely, an angel:

1. Two sorts of order are found in things: the order that parts of the
universe have to each other, and the order that the whole universe has to
5   something outside it. As is said in *Metaphysics* XII [1075a12], the first sort
of order is directed to the second sort as to its end, in the way that the parts
of an army are ordered to each other in a certain way for the sake of the
order of the whole army to its commander. Now the order of the parts of
the universe to each other is a matter of the way that higher creatures act
10   on lower creatures, as I said in the First Part [I.19.5 resp. 2, 48.1 resp. 5,
109.2], whereas happiness consists in the order of human beings to a good
that is outside the whole universe—that good is God. Therefore, human
beings are made happy by the action of a higher creature, namely, an angel.

2. What is potentially a certain way can be brought into actuality by
15   something that is actually that way: for example, what is potentially hot is
made actually hot by something that is actually hot. Now human beings
are potentially happy. Therefore, they can be made actually happy by an
angel who is actually happy.

3. Happiness consists in an activity of the intellect, as was said above
20   [I-II.3.4]. And an angel can enlighten a human being's intellect, as was
maintained in the First Part [I.111.1]. Therefore, an angel can make a
human being happy.

**On the contrary.** Psalm 83:12 says, "The Lord will give grace and glory."

**Reply.** Every creature, being limited in its power and activity, is subject
25   to laws of nature; and so what exceeds created nature cannot be done by the
power of any creature. Consequently, if something needs to be done that
is beyond nature, it is done directly by God: for example, raising the dead,
giving sight to the blind, and other things like that. Now I have shown that
happiness is a good that exceeds created nature [art. 5]. For that reason it
30   is impossible for happiness to be conferred by the action of any creature;
rather, human beings are made happy by God's activity alone, if we are
talking about perfect happiness. If, on the other hand, we are talking about
imperfect happiness, then what is true of virtue is true of it, since imperfect
happiness consists in the activity of virtue.

**Response to 1.** In ordered active powers, it often happens that the 35
supreme power is the one whose job it is to achieve the ultimate end,
while lower powers help in the attainment of that ultimate end by causing
an appropriate orientation. For example, a ship is built in order to be used;
the use of the ship belongs to the art of navigation, which is in charge of the
art of shipbuilding. Thus, in the ordering of the universe, human beings 40
receive help from angels in attaining the ultimate end, in terms of certain
preliminaries by which they are oriented toward attaining it; but they attain
the ultimate end itself through the First Agent, who is God.

**Response to 2.** When a form that exists in actuality in something has
perfect and natural being, it can be a source of an action on something 45
else, in the way that a hot thing causes heat through its own heat; but when
a form exists in something imperfectly and not with natural being, it cannot be the source by which it is communicated to something else—for
example, the intention of color that is in the pupil of the eye cannot make
anything else white, and not everything that is illuminated or heated can 50
illuminate or heat other things (otherwise illuminating and heating would
proceed to infinity). Now the light of glory, by which God is seen, is in God
perfectly, with natural being; but in any creature it exists imperfectly, and
with imitated or participated being. For that reason, no happy creature can
communicate its happiness to another creature. 55

**Response to 3.** What a happy angel conveys in illuminating the intellect of a human being, or even of a lower angel, is certain notions of God's
works, but not the vision of the divine essence, as I said in the First Part
[I.106.1]. For in order to see the divine essence, all are illuminated directly
by God. 60

### Article 7. Are any deeds required of human beings in order for them to receive happiness from God?[60]

It seems that no deeds are required of human beings in order for them to
receive happiness from God:

1. God is an agent of infinite power, so he does not require any matter, or
condition in matter, as a prerequisite for acting; he can produce the whole
thing all at once. Now as we have said, human deeds cannot be required 5
for happiness as an efficient cause, so the only way they could be required
would be as conditions. Therefore, God, who does not require conditions as
a prerequisite for acting, confers happiness without any deeds beforehand.

2. God is the author of happiness directly, in just the same way that he
also established nature directly. Now when he first established nature, he 10
produced creatures without any previous condition or action on the part

---

60. Parallel passages: ST I.57.4; *Compend. Theol.* 172.

of a creature; instead, he made each thing all at once perfect in its species. Therefore, it seems that he grants happiness to human beings without any prior actions.

15    3. The Apostle says in Romans 4:6 that happiness belongs to someone to whom God grants righteousness apart from works. Therefore, no works are required for a human being to attain happiness.

**On the contrary.** John 13:17 says, "If you know these things, you will be happy if you do them." Therefore, one comes to happiness through action.

20    **Reply.** As I said above [I-II.4.3], rectitude of will is required for happiness, because rectitude of will *just is* the will's proper ordering toward the ultimate end; that ordering is required for the attainment of the ultimate end in the same way that the proper condition of matter is required for the attainment of form. But that is not enough to show that any action on
25    the part of a human being has to *precede* happiness: God could, after all, simultaneously cause the will both to tend rightly to the end and to attain the end, in the same way that he sometimes simultaneously both conditions matter and induces a form in it.

Yet the ordering of divine wisdom requires that this not happen. After
30    all, as *On the Heavens* II [292a22] says, "Of those things that are apt to have a perfect good, some have it without motion, some by one motion, and some by several motions." Having a perfect good without motion is characteristic of something that has that good *naturally*, and only God has happiness naturally; accordingly, it is proper to God alone that he is
35    not moved to happiness by any preceding motion. Now since happiness outstrips any created nature, no mere creature fittingly attains happiness without a motion, that is, an activity by which it tends toward happiness. But in keeping with the order of divine wisdom, the angels, who are above human beings in the order of nature, attained happiness by a single motion
40    of meritorious action, as I explained in the First Part [I.62.5]; whereas human beings attain happiness by many motions of actions, which are called merits. This is also why, according to the Philosopher, happiness is the reward for virtuous actions.

**Response to 1.** Human actions are required as prerequisites for the
45    attainment of happiness, not because of any insufficiency in God's power to cause happiness, but so that the order of things might be preserved.

**Response to 2.** God produced the first creatures all at once and made them perfect, without any prior condition or action on the part of any creature, because he established the first individuals of the various species so
50    that they would propagate their nature to later individuals. And in a similar way, because Christ, who is divine and human, was to bestow happiness on others (as the Apostle says in Hebrews 2:10, "he had brought many sons and daughters to glory"), his soul was happy from the moment of his conception, without any foregoing meritorious action. But this is unique to him,

since it is Christ's merit that enables baptized infants to attain happiness   55
even though they have no merits of their own, because through baptism
they are made members of Christ.

**Response to 3.** The Apostle is speaking of the happiness of hope, which
one possesses thanks to justifying grace, which indeed is not given on
account of prior works. Grace, after all, is not a term of motion, as hap-   60
piness is; rather, it is a starting point of the motion by which one tends
toward happiness.

*Article 8. Does every human being desire happiness?*[61]

It seems that not everyone desires happiness:

1. One cannot desire what one does not know, since it is the apprehended good that is the object of desire, as is said in *De anima* III [433a27].
And many people do not know what happiness is: as Augustine says in *On
the Trinity* XIII [ch. 4], this is evident from the fact that "some placed their   5
happiness in the pleasure of the body, some in the virtue of the soul, and
some in other things." Therefore, not everyone desires happiness.

2. The essence of happiness is the vision of the divine essence, as has
been said [I-II.3.8]. But some people hold the view that it is impossible
for human beings to see God in his essence, and so they do not desire it.   10
Therefore, not all human beings desire happiness.

3. Augustine says in *On the Trinity* XIII [ch. 5], "They are happy who
have everything they want, and want nothing bad." But not everyone wants
this: after all, some people want bad things, and they want to want bad
things. Therefore, not everyone wants happiness.   15

**On the contrary.** Augustine says in *On the Trinity* XIII [ch. 3], "If the
actor had said, 'You all want to be happy; none of you wants to be unhappy,'
he would have said something that none of you could have failed to recognize in your own will." Therefore, everyone wants to be happy.

**Reply.** One can consider happiness in two ways. One way is in terms   20
of the abstract notion of happiness. And in this way it is indeed necessary
that every human being wills happiness. After all, the abstract notion of
happiness is that it is a complete good, as I have said [art. 3–4]. Now since
the good is the will's object, a person's complete good is what totally satisfies that person's will. Thus, desiring happiness is just desiring that one's   25
will be satisfied—and everyone wants that.

In another way, we can speak of happiness in terms of the particular
description of what happiness consists in. And in this way not everyone
grasps happiness, because not everyone knows the particular thing to which

---

61. Parallel passage: *Sent.* IV.49.1.3.1.

30    the abstract notion of happiness applies. And consequently, in this regard,
      not everyone wants happiness.
         From this the **Response to 1** is clear.
         **Response to 2.** The will follows the apprehension of intellect or reason.
      Now it can happen that reason can consider one and the same thing in
35    various ways, and accordingly it can happen that one and the same thing
      is desired in one way but not desired in some other way. Thus, happiness
      can be considered under the description "final and complete good," which
      is the abstract notion of happiness; and the will naturally and necessar-
      ily tends toward happiness considered in this way, as I have said [main
40    reply and 4.2]. Happiness can also be considered under various particular
      descriptions, involving the activity itself or the active power or its object;
      and the will does not necessarily tend toward happiness considered in that
      way.
         **Response to 3.** This definition of happiness that some have put for-
45    ward—"they are happy who have everything they want" (or, alternatively,
      "who have obtained everything they longed for")—is good and sufficient
      *if you understand it in a certain way*; in another way, however, it is incom-
      plete. For if one understands it simply in terms of all the things that human
      beings desire through their natural appetite, it turns out to be true that
50    those who have everything they want are happy, because the only thing
      that satisfies natural human appetite is a perfect good, which is happiness.
      But if one understands that definition in terms of the things that human
      beings will according to the apprehension of reason, then having every-
      thing one wants is not characteristic of happiness, but rather of misery,
55    since having such things can stand in the way of having everything one
      wills naturally, in much the same way that reason sometimes takes certain
      things to be true that in fact stand in the way of knowing the truth. It is
      because he understands the definition in this way that Augustine adds "and
      wants nothing bad" to complete the definition, although the first part—
60    "they are happy who have everything they want"—would be sufficient if
      interpreted correctly.

# The Treatise on Human Acts

## Summa theologiae part I-II,
## questions 6–21

### Question 6. Voluntariness and Involuntariness in General

So, since happiness must be attained through certain acts, we need to investigate human acts so that we can know which acts are those through which one attains happiness and which acts stand in the way of happiness. Now activities and acts concern singulars; it follows, then, that every kind of knowledge relating to activity requires an investigation of the particular in order to be complete. Accordingly, moral inquiry, since it concerns human acts, should be carried out first in general and then in particular.[1]

Now when it comes to the investigation of human acts in general, the first topic that we need to investigate is human acts themselves [QQ6–48]; the second is the principles of human acts [QQ49–114]. Now some human acts are distinctive of human beings, whereas others are common to human beings and the other animals. And since happiness is the distinctive human good, those acts that are distinctively human are more closely connected with happiness than are acts that are common to human beings and the other animals. For that reason we must investigate, first, acts that are distinctive of human beings [QQ6–21], and, second, acts that are common to human beings and the other animals [QQ22–48]—these are called the passions of the soul.

Concerning human acts themselves, two topics arise that require investigation: first, the nature of human acts [QQ6–17]; and second, their distinction [QQ18–21]. Now since the acts that are called distinctively human are those that are voluntary (because the will [voluntas] is rational appetite, which is distinctive of human beings), we need to investigate acts insofar as they are voluntary. So we should first consider voluntariness and involuntariness in general [QQ6–7]; second, acts that are voluntary as elicited by the will itself, which exist in the will without any intermediary [QQ8–16];

---

1. The discussion of moral acts in general occupies the rest of I-II; the discussion of moral acts in particular is found in II-II.

third, acts that are voluntary as commanded by the will, which belong
to the will through other powers that serve as intermediaries [Q17]. And
because voluntary acts are characterized by certain circumstances, on the
basis of which we make judgments about them, we must first investigate
voluntariness and involuntariness [Q6] and then the circumstances of the
acts in which voluntariness and involuntariness are found [Q7].

Concerning voluntariness and involuntariness in general there are eight
questions:

Article 1. Is there voluntariness in human acts?
Article 2. Is there voluntariness in non-rational animals?
Article 3. Can there be voluntariness without any act?
Article 4. Can violence be done to the will?
Article 5. Does violence cause involuntariness?
Article 6. Does fear cause involuntariness?
Article 7. Does desire cause involuntariness?
Article 8. Does ignorance cause involuntariness?

### Article 1. Is there voluntariness in human acts?[2]

It seems that there is no voluntariness in human acts:

1. What is voluntary has its principle within itself, as is evident from
Gregory of Nyssa,[3] Damascene,[4] and Aristotle.[5] But the principle of human
acts is not within human beings themselves; rather, it is external to them,
5   since the human appetite is moved to action by some external desirable
thing—something that plays the role of an unmoved mover, as *De anima*
III [433b11] says. Therefore, there is no voluntariness in human acts.

2. In *Physics* VIII [253a11] the Philosopher proves that in animals there
is no new motion that is not preceded by some external motion. But *every*
10   act of a human being is new, since no act of a human being is eternal.
Therefore, the origin of every human act is external, so there is no voluntariness in human acts.

3. What acts voluntarily can act through itself. Human beings, however,
cannot act through themselves: after all, John 15:5 says, "Without me you
15   can do nothing." Therefore, there is no voluntariness in human acts.

**On the contrary.** Damascene says in Book II that "voluntariness is a
feature of an act that is a rational activity,"[6] and human acts are rational
activities. Therefore, there is voluntariness in human acts.

---

2. Parallel passage: *On Truth* 23.1.

3. Nemesius, *On Human Nature* ch. 32.

4. *On the Orthodox Faith* II.24.

5. *Nicomachean Ethics* III.1, 1111a23.

6. *On the Orthodox Faith* II.24.

**Reply.** There has to be voluntariness in human acts. To see clearly why that is so, one has to reflect on the fact that the principle of some acts and motions is within the thing that performs the act or undergoes the motion, whereas the principle of other motions or acts is external. For example, when a stone moves upward, the principle of this motion is external to the stone; but when it moves downward, the principle of that motion is within the stone itself.

Now of the things that are moved by an internal principle, some move themselves, but others do not. You see, since everything that acts (or is moved) acts (or is moved) on account of an end, as I established earlier [I-II.1.2], things in which there is an internal principle not merely of being moved but of being moved *to an end* are the ones that are moved by an internal principle in the fullest sense. And in order for something to be done on account of an end, some cognition of the end is required. So anything that acts (or is moved) by an intrinsic principle and has some knowledge of the end has within itself the principle of its own act—not merely of acting, but of acting on account of an end.

By contrast, something that has no knowledge of an end, though it may have within itself a principle of action or motion, nevertheless does not have within itself a principle of acting or being moved *on account of an end*; instead, the principle of its acting or being moved on account of an end is in some other thing that imprinted on it the principle of its motion to an end. For that reason such things are not said to move themselves, but to be moved by other things. By contrast, things that have knowledge of an end are said to move themselves, because they have a principle not just of acting, but indeed of acting on account of an end. And therefore, since both their acting and their acting on account of an end are from an internal principle, their motions and acts are called voluntary—the word 'voluntary' implies that a motion or an act arises from a thing's own inclination. And that is why what is called voluntary, according to the definition given by Aristotle and Gregory of Nyssa and Damascene, is not merely something whose principle is internal; we must include knowledge as well. For that reason, since human beings paradigmatically cognize the end of their actions and move themselves, voluntariness is found paradigmatically in their acts.

**Response to 1.** Not every principle is a first principle. So even though the definition of voluntariness requires that the principle of a voluntary act be internal, it is consistent with the definition of voluntariness for the internal principle to be caused or moved by an external principle, since it is no part of the definition of voluntariness that the internal principle be a *first* principle. Nonetheless, it is important to realize that a given principle of motion can be first in a genus yet not first in an unqualified sense: for example, in the genus of things that can undergo alteration, the first

principle of alteration is a heavenly body, but a heavenly body is not a first
mover in an unqualified sense; rather, it is moved with respect to place
by a higher mover. In this way, then, the internal principle of a voluntary
65    act, which is a cognitive and appetitive power, is the first principle in the
genus of appetitive motion even though it is moved by something external
in terms of other species of motion.

**Response to 2.** There are in fact two ways in which some external
motion precedes a new motion by an animal. One way is for an external
70    motion to present to the animal's sense some sensible object that, when
apprehended, moves its appetite: for example, when a deer's motion brings
it close to a lion, and the lion sees the deer, the lion begins to move toward
the deer. The other way is for an external motion, such as cold or heat,
to inaugurate some natural change in the animal's body; and when the
75    animal's body is changed by the motion of the external body, the sensory
appetite, which is a power of a bodily organ, is also changed accidentally, as
when the appetite is moved to desire something as a consequence of some
alteration in the body. But neither of these is contrary to the definition of
voluntariness, as I have explained, since such motions from an external
80    principle belong to a different genus of motion.

**Response to 3.** God moves human beings to act not only by placing
something desirable before the senses or by causing a change in the body,
but also by moving the will itself, since every motion of both will and
nature proceeds from God as First Mover. And in the same way that it is
85    consistent with the definition of nature that a natural motion be from God
as First Mover, insofar as nature is an instrument of God as Mover, so too
it is consistent with the definition of a voluntary act that it be from God
insofar as the will is moved by God. Nevertheless, natural and voluntary
motions have this in common: by definition, they are from an internal
90    principle.

*Article 2. Is there voluntariness in non-rational animals?*[7]

It seems that there is no voluntariness in non-rational animals:

1. The word 'voluntary' is derived from *voluntas*, 'will.' And since will
is in reason, as *De anima* III [432b5] says, it cannot exist in non-rational
animals. Therefore, voluntariness is not found in them either.

5         2. It is because human acts are voluntary that human beings are said to
be in control of their own acts. Non-rational animals, by contrast, are not
in control of their own acts: "they do not act, but are acted upon," as Damascene says.[8] Therefore, there is nothing voluntary in non-rational animals.

7. Parallel passages: *Sent* II.25.1 resp. 6; *On Truth* 23.1; *Comm. Ethics* III.4.
8. *On the Orthodox Faith* II.27.

3. Damascene says that "voluntary acts give rise to praise and blame,"[9] but the acts of non-rational animals deserve neither praise nor blame. Therefore, there is nothing voluntary in them.

**On the contrary.** In *Ethics* III [1111b8] the Philosopher says that "children and non-rational animals share in voluntariness." And Damascene[10] and Gregory of Nyssa[11] say the same thing.

**Reply.** As I have said [art. 1], the definition of voluntariness requires that the principle of an act be internal, with some cognition of the end. Now there are two sorts of cognition of an end: perfect and imperfect. There is perfect cognition of an end when there is not merely apprehension of the thing that is the end but also cognition of its character as an end and of the connection between that end and what is directed to the end. Only rational natures can have this sort of cognition of an end. By contrast, imperfect cognition of an end involves merely apprehending the end, without the cognition of its character *as* an end or of the connection of the act to that end. This kind of cognition of an end is found in non-rational animals; they have it through sense and natural estimation.

Perfect cognition of an end results in voluntariness in its full sense: upon apprehending an end, someone who deliberates about that end and the things that are for the end can either be moved toward that end or not. Imperfect cognition, by contrast, results in voluntariness in an imperfect sense: the thing that apprehends the end does not deliberate, but is immediately moved toward the end. Thus, voluntariness in its full sense belongs uniquely to rational natures, but in an imperfect sense it belongs to non-rational animals as well.

**Response to 1.** 'Will' is the name of the rational appetite, and so a will cannot exist in things that lack reason. But 'voluntary' is derived denominatively from *voluntas,* 'will,' and can be extended to things that participate in will in some way, through some resemblance to will. And in this way voluntariness can be attributed to non-rational animals insofar as they are moved toward an end through some cognition.

**Response to 2.** Human beings are in control of their own acts because they can deliberate about their acts; after all, it is because reason, in deliberating, is concerned with opposites that the will is open to those opposites. In this respect, however, there is nothing voluntary in non-rational animals, as I have said.

**Response to 3.** Praise and blame follow from an act that is voluntary in the full sense. Such acts are not found in non-rational animals.

---

9. *On the Orthodox Faith* II.27.

10. *On the Orthodox Faith* II.24.

11. Nemesius, *On Human Nature* ch. 32.

### Article 3. Can there be voluntariness without any act?[12]

It seems that there cannot be voluntariness without an act:

1. We call something voluntary if it is from the will. But nothing can be from the will except through an act—at least an act of the will itself. Therefore, there cannot be voluntariness without an act.

5    2. An act of will is our basis for saying that someone is willing; and in the same way, when the act of will stops, we say that someone is not willing. And not willing causes involuntariness, which is the opposite of voluntariness. Therefore, there cannot be voluntariness when an act of will stops.

3. The concept of voluntariness includes cognition, as has been said [art. 10    1–2]; and cognition comes about through an act. Therefore, there cannot be voluntariness without some act.

**On the contrary.** What we are in control of is called voluntary, and we are in control of our acting and not acting, our willing and not willing. Therefore, just as acting and willing are voluntary, so too not acting and 15    not willing are voluntary.

**Reply.** What is from the will is called voluntary. Now there are two ways in which we can say that *a* is from *b*. One way is *directly*, when *a* proceeds from *b* insofar as *b* is acting; this is the way in which heating is from heat. The other way is *indirectly*, in virtue of the fact that *b* is *not* acting; this 20    is the way in which we say that the sinking of the ship is from the pilot, insofar as he stops steering the ship. It is important to realize, though, that the result of inaction is not always ascribed to the agent as its cause on the grounds that the agent did not act; the agent who fails to act is regarded as the cause only when the agent both *could* and *should* act. After all, if the 25    pilot were not able to steer the ship, or if the control of the ship had not been entrusted to him, he would not be held responsible for the sinking of the ship that resulted from his inactivity. So, since the will can—and sometimes should—impede its not willing and not acting by willing and acting, it is held responsible for its not willing and not acting on the grounds that 30    these are from the will. This is how there can be voluntariness without an act: sometimes without an exterior act but with an interior act, as when someone wills not to act; and sometimes even without an interior act, as when someone does not will.

**Response to 1.** It is not just what proceeds directly from the will as act-35    ing that is called voluntary, but also what comes from the will indirectly, as not acting.

**Response to 2.** There are two senses of 'not willing.' In one sense, we take it as, in effect, a single word, a form of the verb *nolo*, "I am not willing." Thus, when I say "I am not willing to read," the sense is "I will not to

---

12. Parallel passages: *ST* I-II.75.5 resp. 2; *Sent.* II.35.3; *On Evil* 2.1 resp. 2.

read"; not willing to read signifies willing not to read. Not willing in this    40
sense causes involuntariness. In the other sense, we take it as a combination
of words; taken in that sense, it does not affirm any act of will. Not willing
in this sense does not cause involuntariness.

**Response to 3.** An act of cognition is required for voluntariness in the
same way that an act of will is: that is, it must be in someone's power to    45
consider, to will, and to act. And so, in the same way that not willing and
not acting, when there is occasion to will and to act, is voluntary, so too
not considering is voluntary.

*Article 4. Can violence be done to the will?*[13]

It seems that violence can be done to the will:

1. Anything can be compelled by something more powerful, and there
is something more powerful than the human will: God. Therefore, the
human will can be coerced by God, at any rate.

2. Every passive power is compelled by the corresponding active power    5
when it is changed by the active power. Now the will is a passive power; it
is, after all, a moved mover, as *De anima* III [433b16] says. So, given that
the will is sometimes moved by the corresponding active power, it seems
that the will is sometimes compelled.

3. A violent motion is one that is contrary to nature. Now sometimes    10
the will's motion is contrary to nature, as is evident in the case of the will's
motion toward sinning, which is contrary to nature, as Damascene says.[14]
Therefore, the will's motion can be compelled.

**On the contrary.** Augustine says in *City of God* V [ch. 10] that if something is done by the will, it is not done from necessity. But anything that    15
is compelled is done from necessity. Therefore, what is done by the will
cannot be compelled; consequently, the will cannot be compelled to act.

**Reply.** The will has two kinds of acts. One kind—willing—belongs to
the will directly, since it is elicited by the will itself. The other kind, by
contrast, is an act of will that is commanded by the will and carried out by    20
means of some other power: for example, walking and speaking, which are
commanded by the will [and carried out] by means of the motive power.
As far as acts commanded by the will are concerned, the will can suffer
violence insofar as the body can be prevented by violence from carrying
out the will's command. But as far as the will's own act is concerned, vio-    25
lence cannot be done to the will. The reason for this is that an act of the
will *just is* an inclination that proceeds from an internal principle that has
cognition, just as natural appetite is an inclination that proceeds from an

internal principle that lacks cognition; whereas something that is com-
30   pelled or violent is from an external principle. Hence, it is contrary to the
defining feature of an act of will that it be compelled or violent, just as it
is also contrary to the defining feature of a natural inclination or motion.
It is possible for a stone to be moved upward by violence, but it is not possible for that violent motion to result from its natural inclination. And in
35   the same way, human beings can be affected by violence, but it is contrary
to the definition of violence for this to issue from their own will.

**Response to 1.** God, who is more powerful than the human will, can
move the human will, as we read in Proverbs 21:1: "The heart of the king
is in the hand of God, and he turns it wherever he wills." But if this were
40   a matter of violence, it would no longer involve an act of will, and the will
itself would not be moved; instead, it would be something contrary to the
will.

**Response to 2.** When a passive power is changed by the corresponding active power, this is not always a violent motion; it is violent when the
45   change is contrary to the internal inclination of the passive power. Otherwise, all alterations, and all generations of simple bodies, would be unnatural and violent. In fact, though, they are natural, because of the natural
internal aptitude of the matter or subject to such a condition. And similarly,
when the will is moved by a desirable object in keeping with the will's own
50   inclination, the motion is not violent, but voluntary.

**Response to 3.** Granted, what the will aims at when it sins is *in fact* bad
and contrary to natural reason; but it is *apprehended* as good and appropriate to nature insofar as it is appropriate to someone because of some sensory
passion or corrupt disposition.

*Article 5. Does violence cause involuntariness?*[15]

It seems that violence does not cause involuntariness:

1. We speak of voluntariness and involuntariness with reference to the
will, and violence cannot be done to the will, as has been shown [art. 4].
Therefore, violence cannot cause involuntariness.
5        2. Something that is involuntary is accompanied by sadness, as Damascene[16] and the Philosopher[17] say. But sometimes a person suffers violence without becoming sad as a result. Therefore, violence does not cause
involuntariness.
3. What is from the will cannot be involuntary, and some things that
10   are violent are from the will, as when someone with a heavy body climbs

---

15. Parallel passages: ST I-II.83.6; *Comm. Ethics* III.I.
16. *On the Orthodox Faith* II.25.
17. *Nicomachean Ethics* III.1, 1111a20.

upward or someone bends a limb in the opposite direction to the way it naturally bends. Therefore, violence does not cause involuntariness.

**On the contrary.** The Philosopher[18] and Damascene[19] say that some things are involuntary because of violence.

**Reply.** Violence is directly opposed to what is voluntary, as it is also opposed to what is natural. You see, what is voluntary and what is natural have in common the fact that both are from an internal principle, whereas what is violent is from an external principle. And because of this, just as violence brings about something contrary to nature in things that lack cognition, so too it brings about something contrary to will in things that have cognition. Now what is contrary to nature is called unnatural; and similarly, what is contrary to will is called involuntary. Hence, violence causes involuntariness.

**Response to 1.** Involuntariness is the opposite of voluntariness. Now I explained earlier [art. 4] that not only an act that belongs directly to the will itself, but also an act that is commanded by the will, is said to be voluntary. So, as far as an act that belongs directly to the will itself is concerned, violence cannot be done to the will, as I explained above [art. 4]; consequently, violence cannot make such an act involuntary. But as far as a commanded act is concerned, the will can suffer violence. And in the case of such an act, violence causes involuntariness.

**Response to 2.** In the same way that what accords with the inclination of nature is called natural, what accords with the inclination of the will is called voluntary. But there are two ways in which something is called natural. In one way, something is called natural because it is from nature as an active principle; this is the way in which heating is natural to fire. In another way, something is called natural in accordance with a passive principle, because the nature has an inclination to receiving the action from an external principle; this is the way in which the motion of the heavens is called natural, on account of the natural aptitude of the heavenly body to such motion, although the mover is voluntary. Similarly, there are two ways in which something can be called voluntary: with reference to action, i.e., because someone wills to do something; and with reference to passion, i.e., because someone is willing to undergo what someone else does to him or her. So when an action is imposed by something external, as long as the one who undergoes it remains willing to undergo it, this is not violent without qualification; for although the one who is acted on does not contribute anything by acting, he or she does contribute something by willing to undergo it. As a result, this cannot be called involuntary.

---

18. *Nicomachean Ethics* III.1, 1109b35.
19. *On the Orthodox Faith* II.25.

50    **Response to 3.** As the Philosopher says in *Physics* VIII [254b14], it does
sometimes happen that an animal is moved contrary to the natural inclination of the body; but although such a motion is not natural to the body,
it is still in a way natural to the animal, since it is natural to the animal to
be moved according to appetite. And so this is not violent absolutely, but
55    only in a certain respect. And we should say the same sort of thing about
the case in which someone bends his or her limbs contrary to their natural disposition. This is violent in a certain respect—namely, as far that particular limb is concerned—but not absolutely, with respect to the person.

*Article 6. Does fear cause involuntariness*
*in an absolute sense?*[20]

It seems that fear causes involuntariness in an absolute sense:
       1. Just as violence concerns what is contrary to the will in the present,
fear concerns a future evil that is repugnant to the will. And violence causes
involuntariness in an absolute sense, so fear also causes involuntariness in
5     an absolute sense.
       2. What is intrinsically *F* remains *F* no matter what else is added to it.
For example, something that is intrinsically hot continues to be hot no matter what it is brought into contact with, provided that it continues to exist.
Now what is done as a result of fear is intrinsically involuntary. Therefore,
10    what is done in a state of fear is also involuntary.
       3. What is conditionally *F* is *F* in a certain respect, whereas what is
unconditionally *F* is absolutely *F*. For example, what is conditionally necessary is necessary in a certain respect, whereas what is unqualifiedly
necessary is absolutely necessary. Now what is done as a result of fear
15    is unqualifiedly involuntary, whereas it is only conditionally voluntary
(namely, as averting something bad that the agent fears). Therefore, what
is done as a result of fear is absolutely involuntary.
       **On the contrary.** Gregory of Nyssa says[21]—and so does the Philoso-
pher[22]—that things done as a result of fear are more voluntary than
20    involuntary.
       **Reply.** As the Philosopher says in *Ethics* III [1110b7]—and Gregory of
Nyssa says the same thing in his book on human nature[23]—things done
as a result of fear "are a mixture of voluntary and involuntary," on the
grounds that something done as a result of fear is not voluntary considered

---

20. Parallel passages: *Sent.* IV.29.1.1; *Quodlibet* V.5.3; *Comm. 2 Corinth.* 9.1;
*Comm. Ethics* III.1 and 2.
21. Nemesius, *On Human Nature* ch. 30.
22. *Nicomachean Ethics* III.5, 1110b7.
23. Nemesius, *On Human Nature* ch. 30.

in itself, but it becomes voluntary in a particular situation in order to avert 25
something bad that the agent fears. But if you think about this correctly, such actions are in fact more voluntary than involuntary: they are voluntary absolutely, but involuntary in a certain respect. After all, something is said to be absolutely what it is in actuality; what it is in the mind, it is only in a certain respect, not absolutely. And what is done as a result of fear is 30
in actuality insofar as it is done—acts, after all, are among singulars, and a singular as such exists here and now. Thus, what is done is in actuality insofar as it exists here and now and under other individuating conditions. Moreover, what is done as a result of fear is voluntary in this way—that is, insofar as it is here and now, because in this situation it forestalls a greater 35
evil that the agent fears. For example, throwing cargo into the sea is done voluntarily during a storm because of the fear of disaster. For this reason, it is clear that it is absolutely voluntary, and that it fits the definition of voluntariness, since its principle is internal. Now if instead one looks at what is done as a result of fear independently of this particular situation, 40
as something repugnant to the will, that is something that exists only in thought. And so it is involuntary in a certain respect, namely, as it would be regarded independently of some particular situation.

**Response to 1.** Things that are done as a result of fear and as a result of force do not differ merely in terms of present and future. There is another 45
difference: in something done as a result of force, the will does not consent; instead, the action is completely contrary to the movement of the will. By contrast, something done as a result of fear is done voluntarily because the will is moved toward it—not, of course, for its own sake, but for the sake of something else: in order to forestall an evil that one fears. For an act to 50
count as voluntary, it is enough that it be voluntary for the sake of something else: what is voluntary is not only what we will as an end, for its own sake, but also what we will on account of an end, for the sake of something else. It is therefore clear that in what is done as a result of force, the will as an interior principle does nothing, whereas in what is done as a result 55
of fear, the will does something. And for this reason, as Gregory of Nyssa says, we define the violent not merely as that whose principle is external, but—in order to rule out things done as a result of fear—we add that the thing acted on by force contributes nothing to the action.[24] For the will of the one who is afraid does in fact contribute something to what is done as 60
a result of fear.

**Response to 2.** Things that are said to be *F* absolutely (for example, hot and white) remain *F* no matter what is added to them, whereas things that are said to be *F* relatively vary as they are compared with different things:

---

24. Nemesius, *On Human Nature* ch. 30.

65  what is big compared to this is small compared to that. Now something is
called voluntary not only in its own right—absolutely, as it were—but also
in view of something else—relatively, as it were. And so it is perfectly possible for something that would not be voluntary compared to one thing to
turn out to be voluntary compared to something else.

70      **Response to 3.** Something that is done as a result of fear is unconditionally voluntary—that is, as actually done—but involuntary under a certain
condition, namely, if such fear were not present. So that argument actually
would give more support to the opposite conclusion.

### Article 7. Does desire cause involuntariness?[25]

It seems that desire causes involuntariness:

1. Just as fear is a passion, so too is desire. And fear causes an act to be
involuntary in some respect. Therefore, so does desire.

2. Fearful people act contrary to the way they had set out to act, as a
5  result of their fear; in the same way, incontinent people act contrary to the
way they had set out to act, as a result of desire. And fear causes an act to
be involuntary in some respect. Therefore, so does desire.

3. Voluntariness requires cognition. But desire destroys cognition: the
Philosopher says in *Ethics* VI [1140b12] that pleasure, or the desire for
10  pleasure, destroys the judgment of prudence. Therefore, desire causes
involuntariness.

**On the contrary.** Damascene says, "What is involuntary deserves mercy
or forbearance, and is done with sadness."[26] Neither of these is true of what
15  is done as a result of desire. Therefore, desire does not cause involuntariness.

**Reply.** Desire does not cause involuntariness; on the contrary, it makes
something voluntary. After all, we call something voluntary because the
will is drawn to it, and as a result of desire the will is inclined to will what
is desired. That is why desire makes it the case that something is voluntary
rather than involuntary.

20      **Response to 1.** Fear is of something bad, whereas desire has to do with
something good. What is bad is intrinsically contrary to the will, whereas
what is good harmonizes with the will. For that reason fear is more suited
to cause involuntariness than desire is.

**Response to 2.** In those who do something as a result of fear, the will's
25  repugnance to the act, considered in itself, remains. But in those who do
something as a result of desire, such as the incontinent, the prior will,
which rejected what is desired, no longer remains; instead, the will changes
to willing what it previously rejected. Consequently, what is done as a result

---

25. Parallel passage: *Comm. Ethics* III.2 and 4.
26. *On the Orthodox Faith* II.24.

of fear is involuntary in a certain respect, whereas what is done as a result of desire is not involuntary in any way. Those who are incontinent as a result of desire act contrary to the way they had originally set out to act, but not contrary to what they will at the time of the action; by contrast, those who are fearful act contrary to what they will for its own sake at the very time they act.

**Response to 3.** If desire totally destroyed cognition, as happens in those who are driven mad by desire, then it would follow that desire destroyed voluntariness. Yet, properly speaking, there would not be involuntariness either in such a case, since there is neither voluntariness nor involuntariness in those who cannot exercise reason. Sometimes, though, in acts that are performed as a result of desire, cognition is not totally removed, because the *power* of cognition is not totally removed, but merely actual consideration of the particular act. And that is still voluntary, since we call voluntary what is in the will's power; just as not acting and not willing are in the will's power, so too is not considering. For the will can resist a passion, as I will explain below [I-II.10.3, 77.7].

*Article 8. Does ignorance cause involuntariness?*[27]

It seems that ignorance does not cause involuntariness:

1. "What is involuntary deserves pardon," as Damascene says.[28] Yet sometimes what is done as a result of ignorance does not deserve pardon, as 1 Corinthians 14:38 says: "If any are ignorant, they will be ignored." Therefore, ignorance does not cause involuntariness.

2. Every sin is accompanied by ignorance, as Proverbs 14:22 says: "Those who do evil are mistaken." So if ignorance causes involuntariness, it would follow that every sin is involuntary. And that is contrary to Augustine, who says that every sin is voluntary.[29]

3. "What is involuntary involves sadness," as Damascene says.[30] But some things are done in ignorance and without sadness: for example, if someone kills an enemy whom he was seeking to kill, though at the time he thought he was killing a deer. Therefore, ignorance does not cause involuntariness.

---

27. Parallel passages: *ST* I-II.76.3; *Sent.* II.39.1.1.4 and II.41.3 resp. 3; *On Evil* 3.8; *Comm. Ethics* III.1 and 3.

28. *On the Orthodox Faith* II.24.

29. *On the True Religion* ch. 24.

30. *On the Orthodox Faith* II.24.

15      **On the contrary.** Damascene[31] and the Philosopher[32] say that some acts
        are involuntary as a result of ignorance.
            **Reply.** Ignorance would have to cause involuntariness by removing the
        cognition that (as I explained earlier [art. 1]) is required for voluntariness.
        But not just any ignorance removes the relevant cognition. For this reason
20      it is important to note that ignorance is related in three different ways to
        an act of will: concomitantly, consequently, and antecedently.
            It is related *concomitantly* when there is ignorance of what is done, but
        even if it were known, it would be done anyway. In such a case, the igno-
        rance does not cause someone to will that this be done, but it just happens
25      that something is simultaneously done and not known—as, in the example
        given, when someone wishes to kill an enemy but kills him in ignorance,
        thinking that he is killing a deer. This kind of ignorance does not cause
        involuntariness, as the Philosopher says,[33] because it does not cause any-
        thing repugnant to the will; but it does cause the act to be non-voluntary,
30      because what is not known cannot be actually willed.
            Ignorance is related *consequently* to the will insofar as the ignorance
        itself is voluntary. And that happens in two ways, corresponding to the two
        forms of voluntariness explained above [art. 3]. One way is for an act of will
        to be aimed at ignorance, as when people will to be ignorant so that they
35      will have an excuse for sin or will not be restrained from sinning, as Job
        21:14 says: "We reject the knowledge of your ways." This is called "affected
        ignorance." In another way, ignorance of something that one could know
        and ought to know is called voluntary, in the same way that not acting and
        not willing are called voluntary, as I explained earlier [art. 3]. Ignorance
40      of this kind comes about either when people do not give actual consider-
        ation to what they can and should consider—this is called "ignorance of
        evil choice" and results from some passion or disposition—or when people
        do not take the trouble to acquire knowledge that they ought to have. In
        this latter way, ignorance of the universal principles of law, which every
45      person is obligated to know, is called voluntary because it results from neg-
        ligence. Now when ignorance is voluntary in either of these ways, it can-
        not cause involuntariness in an unqualified sense. It does, however, cause
        involuntariness in a certain respect, insofar as it precedes a movement of
        the will toward doing something, and that movement would not exist if
50      knowledge were present.
            Ignorance is related *antecedently* to the will when the ignorance is not
        voluntary and is the cause of willing what otherwise one would not will,

---

31. *On the Orthodox Faith* II.24.
32. *Nicomachean Ethics* III.1, 1110a1.
33. *Nicomachean Ethics* III.1, 1110b25.

as when one is ignorant of some circumstance of the act that one is not obligated to know, and as a result one does something that one wouldn't have done if one had known. For example, suppose someone who is pay-  55 ing proper attention, not realizing that someone is passing along the way, shoots an arrow and kills the passerby. Such ignorance causes involuntariness in an unqualified sense.

**Responses.** From these remarks it is clear how to respond to the arguments. The first argument dealt with ignorance of things that one is  60 obligated to know. The second dealt with ignorance of choice, which is voluntary in a certain respect, as I explained. And the third dealt with ignorance that is related concomitantly to the will.

## Question 7. The Circumstances of Human Acts

Next we need to investigate the circumstances of human acts. Concerning this there are four questions:

Article 1. What is a circumstance?

Article 2. Should a theologian pay attention to the circumstances of human acts?

Article 3. How many circumstances are there?

Article 4. Which circumstances are most important?

### Article 1. Is a circumstance an accident of a human act?[34]

It seems that a circumstance is not an accident of a human act:

1. Cicero says in his *Rhetoric* [I.24] that a circumstance is "something through which a speech adds authority and solidity to its argumentation." But a speech gives solidity to its argumentation primarily by means of what belongs to the *substance* of a thing: definition, genus, species, and other  5 things of that sort. Indeed, Cicero himself teaches that orators should draw their arguments from such things.[35] Therefore, a circumstance is not an accident of a human act.

2. The distinguishing feature of accidents is that they exist *in* something, whereas circumstances do not exist in something, but outside it.  10 Therefore, circumstances are not accidents of human acts.

3. Accidents do not have accidents. But human acts are themselves accidents. Therefore, circumstances are not accidents of acts.

**On the contrary.** The particular conditions of any singular thing are said to be its individuating accidents. And the Philosopher, in *Ethics* III  15

---

34. Parallel passages: *ST* I-II.18.3; *Sent.* IV.16.3.1.1.

35. *Topics* ch. 3.

[1110b33], calls circumstances "the particulars," that is, the particular conditions of individual acts. Therefore, circumstances are individual accidents of human acts.

**Reply.** Since words, according to the Philosopher,[36] are signs of under-
20  standings, the order of words has to follow the order of intellectual cognition. Now our intellectual cognition progresses from better-known things to less-well-known things; accordingly, we extend the names for better-known things to signify things that are less well known. That is why, as *Metaphysics* X [1055a9] says, "From things that are in a place, the word
25  'distance' was extended to all contraries"; and similarly, we use words that pertain to local motion in order to signify other motions, because bodies, which are bounded by place, are the things we know best.

That is how the word 'circumstances' came to be extended from things that are in a place to human acts. In talking about things that have a place,
30  we say that something "surrounds" (*circumstare*) a thing if it is external to the thing but nonetheless touches it or is located close to it. And so certain conditions that are external to the substance of an act but nonetheless touch a human act in some way are called circumstances. Now something that belongs to a thing and is external to its substance is called an accident
35  of that thing. Hence, circumstances of human acts should be called accidents of those acts.

**Response to 1.** A speech gives solidity to its argumentation primarily from the substance of the act, but secondarily from the circumstances of the act. Thus, someone is vulnerable to being charged primarily because
40  he committed murder, but secondarily because he did so through deceit, or for hire, or in a holy time or place, or something else along those lines. That is why Cicero expressly says that through a circumstance a speech adds solidity to its argumentation—that is, *adds* it as something secondary.

**Response to 2.** There are two ways in which something is said to be an
45  accident of a thing. One way is because it is in the thing; this is the way in which white is said to be an accident of Socrates. The other way is because it exists simultaneously with that thing in the same subject; this is the way in which white is said to be an accident of the musical, insofar as they come together and are in some way coincident in the same subject. It is in this
50  latter way that circumstances are said to be accidents of acts.

**Response to 3.** As I have explained [resp. 2], an accident is said to have an accident because both come together in the same subject. But there are two ways in which this happens. One way is for the two accidents to be related to the same subject without any order, as white and musical
55  are related to Socrates. The other way is for there to be some order—for example, the subject receives one accident through the mediation of the

---

36. *On Interpretation* I.1, 16a3.

other, as a body receives color through the mediation of its surface. In the latter case one accident is said to be *in* another; we do, after all, say that color is in a surface. Now circumstances are related to an act in both ways. Some circumstances ordered to an act—for example, place and a person's  60 status—belong to the agent without the mediation of the act; others, by contrast—for example, the manner of acting—belong to the agent through the mediation of the act itself.

### Article 2. Should a theologian pay attention to the circumstances of human acts?

It seems that a theologian need not pay attention to the circumstances of human acts:

1. Theologians investigate human acts only insofar as they have the quality of being good or evil. And it does not seem that circumstances can make acts have any such quality, since nothing takes on a quality, formally  5 speaking, from what is outside it, but only from what is in it. Therefore, theologians need not pay attention to the circumstances of acts.

2. Circumstances are accidents of acts. But any one thing has an indefinite number of accidents, which is why "there is no art or science—except a sophistical one—concerning what is accidental," as *Metaphysics* VI  10 [1026b3] says. Therefore, theologians need not pay attention to the circumstances of human acts.

3. Examining circumstances is the job of rhetoric, and rhetoric is not a part of theology. Therefore, examining circumstances is not a job for theologians.  15

**On the contrary.** Ignorance of circumstances causes involuntariness, as Damascene[37] and Gregory of Nyssa[38] say. Now involuntariness excuses someone from blame, and blame is a proper matter for theologians to consider. Therefore, it is also proper for theologians to consider the circumstances of acts.  20

**Reply.** There are three reasons that theologians should pay attention to circumstances. First, theologians consider human acts because human beings are directed to happiness through their acts. Now everything that is directed to an end should be proportionate to that end, and what makes acts proportionate to the end is a certain commensurateness that comes  25 about when the circumstances are as they ought to be. Hence, considering circumstances is a proper task for theologians.

---

37. *On the Orthodox Faith* II.24.
38. Nemesius, *On Human Nature* ch. 31.

Second, theologians consider human acts insofar as they are good and
bad, better and worse; and acts take on these differing qualities in virtue
30    of circumstances, as will become evident below [I-II.18.10 and 11; 73.4].

Third, theologians consider human acts insofar as they are meritorious or demeritorious. Merit and demerit are characteristics of *human* acts,
which have to be voluntary. And a human act is judged to be voluntary or
involuntary on the basis of the agent's knowing, or being ignorant of, the
35    circumstances, as I have explained [I-II.6.8]. Hence, consideration of circumstances is a task for theologians.

**Response to 1.** A good that is directed to an end is called useful, which
implies a certain relation; that is why the Philosopher says in *Ethics* I
[1096a26] that "what is good in the category of relation is useful." Now
40    when we speak of something in terms of a relation, something is denomi-
nated not only from what is in it but also from what is external to it but
closely connected with it, as is evident in the cases of 'right' and 'left,'
'equal' and 'unequal,' and similar words. And so, since acts have goodness insofar as they are useful for an end, there is nothing to prevent their
45    being called good or bad because of features that are external to the act
but closely connected with it.

**Response to 2.** Accidents that are completely accidental are uncertain
and indefinite, so no art includes them. But such accidents do not count
as circumstances, since, as I have explained [art. 1], circumstances are
50    external to an act in such a way that they do somehow characterize the act
and are directed to it. And such *per se* accidents do fall within the scope
of an art.

**Response to 3.** Examining circumstances is a job for moral philosophers, politicians, and rhetoricians. It is a job for moral philosophers
55    because circumstances affect whether the mean of virtue in human acts
and passions is hit or missed. It is a job for politicians and rhetoricians
because acts are made praiseworthy or blameworthy, excusable or culpable, through circumstances—though these two roles are different, since
the rhetorician offers persuasion, whereas the politician makes a determi-
60    nation. But all other arts are in the service of the theologian, so all these
ways of considering circumstances belong to theologians: it is their job to
join with moral philosophers in considering virtuous and vicious acts, and
to join with rhetoricians and politicians in examining acts insofar as they
deserve punishment or reward.

### Article 3. Is the list of circumstances
### given in Ethics III correct?[39]

It seems that the list of circumstances given in *Ethics* III [1111a3–7] is incorrect:

1. By a "circumstance" of an act we mean something that is external to the act. Time and place are like that. Therefore, there are only two circumstances: "when" and "where."  5

2. Whether an act is done well or done badly depends on circumstances. Now being done well or badly has to do with the *manner* of the act. Therefore, all circumstances are included in one: the manner of acting.

3. Circumstances do not belong to the substance of an act, whereas the causes of the act do seem to belong to the substance of the act. Therefore,  10 nothing that derives from the cause of an act counts as a circumstance. Consequently, neither "who" nor "on account of what" nor "concerning what" is a circumstance, since "who" is a matter of the efficient cause, "on account of what" of the final cause, and "concerning what" of the material cause.  15

**On the contrary.** There is the authority of the Philosopher in *Ethics* III.

**Reply.** Cicero, in his *Rhetoric* [I.24], lists seven circumstances, which are contained in this line: "who, what, where, by what helps, why, how, when." You see, in evaluating acts, we have to pay attention to *who* acted, *by what helps or instruments* they acted, *what* they did, *where* they did it,  20 *why* they did it, *how* they did it, and *when* they did it. Now in *Ethics* III Aristotle adds another circumstance—"concerning what"—which Cicero includes in "what."

We can provide a rationale for this list as follows. What we call a circumstance is something that is external to the substance of an act but  25 somehow touches it. Now that can happen in three ways: (1) insofar as it touches the act itself, (2) insofar as it touches the cause of the act, (3) insofar as it touches the effect. (1) A circumstance touches the act either as a measure—as time and place do—or as a quality of the act—as the manner of acting does. (3) Or it touches the effect, as when we consider what some-  30 one did. (2) Now in terms of the cause of the act, "on account of what" is taken from the final cause, "concerning what" from the material cause or (in other words) the object, "who acted" from the principal agent cause, and "by what helps" from the instrumental agent cause.

**Response to 1.** Time and place are circumstances of an act as measures,  35 whereas other circumstances touch an act in some other way but are external to the substance of the act.

---

39. Parallel passages: *Sent.* IV.16.3.1.2 and 3; *On Evil* 2.6; *Comm. Ethics* III.3.

**Response to 2.** "Well" and "badly" are not counted as the "manner of acting" that is one of the circumstances; instead, they are consequences
40  of the totality of circumstances. The particular circumstance that we call "manner of acting" is a quality of the act such as someone's walking quickly or slowly, or someone's striking powerfully or gently, and so on.

**Response to 3.** It is not the characteristic of the cause on which the substance of an act depends that is called a circumstance, but instead some
45  associated characteristic. For example, that the object is someone else's property is not called a circumstance of a theft, since that belongs to the substance of theft; but its being large or small is a circumstance. Analogous considerations hold for the circumstances that derive from the other causes. After all, the end that gives an act its species is not a circumstance; some
50  associated end is. For example, someone's acting courageously for the sake of the good of courage is not a circumstance; but it is a circumstance that someone acts courageously in order to free a city or the Christian population or something like that. And similarly, with respect to the "what," the fact that one washes some person by pouring water is not a circumstance
55  of the washing; but the fact that by washing one cools or warms the person, and heals or harms the person, is a circumstance.

*Article 4. Are "on account of what" and "what the
action is in" the most important circumstances?*[40]

It seems that "on account of what" and "what the action is in" are not the most important circumstances, as *Ethics* III [1111a18] says they are:

1. It would seem that place and time are "what the action is in," and they do not seem to be the most important circumstances, since they are
5  the most external to the act. Therefore, "what the action is in" is not the most important circumstance.

2. An end is external to a thing, so it doesn't seem that the end is the most important circumstance.

3. What is most important in anything is its cause and its form. Now the
10  cause of an act is the person who acts, and the form of an act is its manner of being done. Therefore, these two circumstances seem to be the most important.

**On the contrary.** Gregory of Nyssa says that "the most important circumstances are that for the sake of which an act is done, and what is
15  done."[41]

**Reply.** As I explained earlier [I-II.1.1], acts are properly called human to the extent that they are voluntary. Now the mover and object of the

---

40. Parallel passages: *Sent.* IV.16.3.2.2; *Comm. Ethics* III.3.
41. Nemesius, *On Human Nature* ch. 31.

will is the end, and consequently the most important of all the circumstances is the one that touches an act because of its end, namely, "that for the sake of which"; and the second most important circumstance is the 20 one that touches the substance of the act, that is, "what was done." Other circumstances are more or less important as they are closer to or further from these.

**Response to 1.** By "what the action is in" the Philosopher does not mean time and place; rather, he means things that are attached to the act itself. 25 That is why Gregory of Nyssa, instead of using the Philosopher's expression "what the action is in," says "what is done," as though clarifying what the Philosopher meant.

**Response to 2.** Although the end is not part of the substance of the act, it is nonetheless the most important cause of the act, insofar as it is what 30 moves someone to act. That is why moral acts in particular derive their species from the end.

**Response to 3.** A person who acts is the cause of an act in virtue of being moved by the end, and it is primarily in this respect that the person is directed to the act. Other characteristics of the person, by contrast, are 35 not directed to the act in such an important way. Moreover, the manner of acting is not the substantial form of an act, since an act has its substantial form through the object and terminus or end, whereas the manner is a sort of accidental quality.

## Question 8. The Objects of Will

Next we must investigate the particular acts of the will: first, acts that are the will's directly, as elicited by the will itself [QQ8–16]; second, acts commanded by the will [Q17]. Now the will is moved both to an end and to things that are for the end. We should therefore first investigate the acts of will by which it is moved to an end and then the acts by which it is moved to things that are for the end. Now it appears that there are three acts of will regarding an end: willing, enjoying, and intending. So we will examine, first, willing [QQ8–10]; second, enjoyment [Q11]; and third, intention [Q12]. Regarding willing there are three things we need to examine: first, the objects of will [Q8]; second, what moves the will [Q9]; third, how the will is moved [Q10]. Concerning the objects of will, there are three questions:

Article 1. Is will only of what is good?

Article 2. Is will only of the end, or is will also of things that are for the end?

Article 3. Given that will is, in a certain sense, of things that are for the end, is there a single motion by which the will is moved both to the end and to things that are for the end?

## Article 1. Is will only of what is good?[42]

It seems that will is not only of what is good:

1. One and the same power deals with opposites: for example, vision is of both white and black. And good and bad are opposites. Therefore, will is not only of what is good but also of what is bad

5      2. According to the Philosopher, rational powers are capable of pursuing opposites.[43] Now the will is a rational power; it is, after all, in reason, as *De anima* III [432b5] says. Therefore, the will is capable of opposites. Therefore, it is capable not only of willing what is good, but also of willing what is bad

10      3. Goodness and being are coextensive. And there is will not only of beings, but also of non-beings; after all, we sometimes will *not* to walk and *not* to speak. Also, sometimes we will future things, which are not yet actual beings. Therefore, will is not only of what is good.

**On the contrary.** Dionysius says in *On the Divine Names* 4 that "what 15  is bad is outside the scope of the will" [§32] and that "all things desire what is good" [§10].

**Reply.** Will is a rational appetite. Now there is no appetite for anything but the good. The reason for this is that an appetite is nothing other an inclination of that which has the appetite toward something, and noth-20  ing is inclined toward anything but what is similar to it and fitting for it. Therefore, since every thing, insofar as it is a being and a substance, is a good, it must be the case that every inclination is toward what is good. And that is why the Philosopher says in *Ethics* I [1094a3] that the good is what all things desire.

25      Now it is important to note that since every inclination is consequent upon some form, natural appetite is consequent on a form that exists in nature, whereas sensory appetite, or even intellectual or rational appetite—which is called will—follows an apprehended form. Thus, just as what natural appetite tends toward is a good existing in extramental reality, 30  what animal or voluntary appetite tends toward is an apprehended good. So for the will to tend toward something, it is not required that the thing be good in actual fact, but that it be apprehended as good. That is why the Philosopher says in *Physics* II [195a26] that "the end is the good, or the apparent good."

35      **Response to 1.** One and the same power deals with opposites, but it does not deal with both in the same way. Thus, the will relates to both what is good and what is bad, but it relates to what is good by desiring it and to what is bad by avoiding it. Therefore, the actual appetite for what is good

---

42. Parallel passages: *ST* I.19.9; *Sent.* IV.49.1.3.1; *On Truth* 12.6.

43. *Metaphysics* IX.2, 1046b8.

is called will, in the sense of 'will' that designates an act of the will, which is how we are using the word 'will' in this question. The avoidance of what    *40* is bad is more properly called nilling. Hence, just as willing is of what is good, nilling is of what is bad.

**Response to 2.** A rational power is not capable of pursuing just any opposites, but only those that are included in its appropriate object; after all, no power pursues anything but its appropriate object. Now the object    *45* of will is what is good. Hence, the will is capable of pursuing those opposites that are included in what is good: for example, moving and resting, speaking and keeping silent, and so forth. The will is drawn to one or the other in each pair under the aspect of good.

**Response to 3.** What is not a being in extramental reality is regarded as    *50* a being in reason, which is why negations and privations are called beings of reason. And this is the way in which future things *as apprehended* are beings. Therefore, insofar as they are beings of this sort, they are apprehended under the aspect of good; and that is how the will tends toward them. That is why the Philosopher says in *Ethics* V [1129b8] that "the    *55* absence of what is bad counts as something good."

*Article 2. Is will only of the end, or*
*also of things that are for the end?*[44]

It seems that will is not of things that are for the end, but only of the end:

1. The Philosopher says in *Ethics* III [1111b26] that "will is of the end, whereas choice is of things that are for the end."

2. "There are different powers of the soul for things that belong to different categories," as *Ethics* VI [1139a11] says. Now an end belongs to a dif-    *5* ferent category of the good from things that are for an end, since an end, which is an honorable or pleasurable good, is in the category of quality or action or passion, whereas what is called a useful good, which is for an end, is in the category of relation, as is said in *Ethics* I [1096a26]. Therefore, if will is of an end, it will not be of things that are for the end.    *10*

3. Dispositions are proportionate to powers, since they are perfections of powers. And in the dispositions that are called practical arts, the end belongs to one art and what is for the end belongs to another. For example, the use of a ship, which is the ship's end, belongs to the captain; but the construction of the ship, which is for the sake of the end, belongs to the art    *15* of shipbuilding. Therefore, since will is of the end, it will not be of things that are for the end.

---

44. Parallel passages: *Sent.* I.45.2 resp. 1; *Sent.* II.24.1.3 resp. 3; *On Truth* 22.13 resp. 9.

**On the contrary.** In natural things, it is through one and the same power that something passes through what is intermediate and also reaches
20   its terminus. Now things that are for the end are, as it were, the intermediate things through which something reaches its end, which is like its terminus. Therefore, if will is of an end, it is also of things that are for the end.

**Reply.** 'Will' sometimes means the power by which we will, but sometimes it means the act of the will. So if we are using 'will' to mean the
25   power, then yes, it extends both to the end and to things that are for the end. Any power, after all, extends to everything in which the defining characteristic of its object can in some way be found: for example, vision extends to everything that has some share in color. Now the characteristic of what is good, which is the object of the power of will, is found not only
30   in the end, but also in things that are for the end.

On the other hand, if we are using 'will' to refer strictly to the act, then properly speaking will is only of the end. You see, when an act gets its name from a power, that name designates the simple act of that power: for example, 'understanding' (*intelligere*) designates the simple act of the
35   intellect. Now the simple act of a power concerns that which is in and of itself the object of that power. And it is the end that is good and willed in and of itself. For that reason, will is properly of the end itself. By contrast, things that are for the end are not good or willed in and of themselves, but insofar as they are directed toward the end. Accordingly, the will is drawn
40   to them only insofar as it is drawn to the end; so what the will wills in them is the end. In the same way, understanding, strictly speaking, is of things that are cognized in and of themselves—namely, principles—whereas we do not speak of understanding things that are cognized *through* principles, except insofar as we pay attention to principles in thinking about them.
45   "For what an end is in the realm of appetite, a principle is in the realm of understanding," as *Ethics* VII [1151a16] says.

**Response to 1.** The Philosopher is using the word 'will' in the sense in which it designates a simple act of will, not in the sense in which it designates the power of will.
50   **Response to 2.** There are different powers for things that belong to different categories that are on a par with each other: for example, sound and color are different kinds of sensory objects, corresponding to which are the powers of hearing and sight. But the useful and the honorable are not on a par with each other; instead, they are related as what is intrinsically *F* and
55   what is extrinsically *F*. And things related in this way are always connected with the same power: for example, through the power of vision one senses both color and light, through which color is seen.

**Response to 3.** Not everything that makes for different dispositions also makes for different powers. You see, dispositions are determinations
60   of powers to certain particular acts. Nonetheless, some practical arts deal

with both the end and that which is for the end. The captain's art, after all, deals both with the end and with what is for the end: it carries out the end, and it commands what is for the end. And conversely the shipbuilder's art deals both with what is for the end and with the end: it carries out what is for the end, and it directs its work toward the end. And again, every prac-   65
tical art includes both some proper end and something that is for the end and properly falls within the purview of the art.

### Article 3. Is the will drawn in a single act to both the end and what is for the end?[45]

It seems that the will is drawn in a single act to both the end and what is for the end:

1. The Philosopher says, "Where one thing is for the sake of another, there is only one."[46] Now the will wills what is for the end only for the sake of the end. Therefore, it is moved to both in a single act.   5

2. The end is the basis for willing things that are for the end, just as light is the basis for seeing colors. Now light and color are seen in one and the same act. Therefore, the motion in which the will wills an end is one and the same as the motion in which it wills the things that are for the end.

3. There is numerically one natural motion by which something tends   10
through what is intermediate and to what is last. Now things that are for the end are related to the end in the way that what is intermediate is related to what is last. Therefore, the motion by which the will is drawn toward an end is one and the same as the motion by which the will is drawn to things that are for the end.   15

**On the contrary.** Acts are distinguished by their objects. Now the end and what is for the end (which is called useful) belong to distinct species of good. Therefore, the will is not drawn to both in a single act.

**Reply.** Since an end is willed for its own sake, whereas what is for the end is, as such, willed only on account of the end, it is clear that the will   20
can be drawn to an end without being drawn to things that are for the end; but it cannot be drawn to things that are for the end, as such, unless it is drawn to the end itself. Consequently, there are two ways in which the will is drawn to an end: absolutely, for its own sake; and as the basis for willing things that are for the end. It is therefore quite clear that in one and the   25
same motion the will is drawn both to the end as the basis for willing things that are for the end and to those very things that are for the end. But there is a distinct act by which the will is drawn to the end absolutely. Sometimes that act happens earlier in time: for example, someone first wills health and

---

45. Parallel passages: *ST* I-II.12.4; *On Truth* 22.14.
46. *Topics* III.2, 118a18.

30  afterward, as a result of deliberating about how he might attain health, he
    wills to consult a doctor in order to be healed. This is like what also hap-
    pens in the case of the intellect: first one understands principles in their
    own right, and then later one understands principles in their conclusions,
    in that one assents to the conclusions on account of the principles.

35      **Response to 1.** That argument depends on understanding the will as
    being drawn to an end as the basis for willing things that are for the end.

        **Response to 2.** Whenever color is seen, light is seen in that same act;
    nonetheless, light can be seen without color's being seen. And similarly,
    whenever one wills things that are for the end, one wills the end in that
40  same act; but the converse does not hold.

        **Response to 3.** In carrying out an act, things that are for the end are like
    what is intermediate and the end is like a terminus. For that reason, in the
    same way that a natural motion sometimes stops in what is intermediate
    and does not reach the terminus, sometimes a person carries out what is for
45  the end and yet does not attain the end. But in willing, the converse holds:
    the will passes from the end to willing things that are for the end, in the
    same way that the intellect proceeds to conclusions from principles, which
    are called intermediates. That is why the intellect sometimes understands
    an intermediate and does not move on from that to a conclusion. And in
50  the same way the will sometimes wills an end and yet does not move on to
    willing what is for the end.

        But as for the objection **On the contrary**, it is clear from what I said
    earlier [art. 2 resp. 2] how one ought to respond. You see, the useful and
    the honorable are not coordinate species of good; they are related as what
55  is intrinsically F to what is extrinsically F. For that reason an act of will
    can be drawn to the honorable without being drawn to the useful, but not
    the other way around.

### Question 9. What Moves the Will

Next we must investigate what moves the will. Concerning this, there are
six questions:

    Article 1. Is the will moved by the intellect?
    Article 2. Is it moved by the sensory appetite?
    Article 3. Does the will move itself?
    Article 4. Is it moved by any external principle?
    Article 5. Is it moved by a heavenly body?
    Article 6. Is the will moved by God alone as an external principle?

*Article 1. Is the will moved by the intellect?*[47]

It seems that the will is not moved by the intellect:

1. In commenting on the words of Psalm 118:20, "my soul is consumed with longing for your judgments," Augustine says, "The intellect flies ahead, but the affections follow sluggishly, if they follow at all. We know what is good, and we have no delight in doing it."[48] And that would not be the case if the will were moved by the intellect, since the motion of what is movable follows the motion of its mover. Therefore, the intellect does not move the will.

2. The intellect's relationship to the will is that of pointing out the desirable object, just as the imagination points out a desirable object to the sensory appetite. But the imagination's pointing out a desirable object does not move the sensory appetite. Indeed, sometimes our relationship to the things we imagine is like our relationship to things presented to us in a picture, which do not move us at all, as the *De anima* [427b23] says. Therefore, the intellect doesn't move the will either.

3. One and the same thing is not both mover and moved in the same respect. But the will moves the intellect; after all, we understand when we want to. Therefore, the intellect does not move the will.

**On the contrary.** The Philosopher says in *De anima* III [433b16] that "the understood desirable object is an unmoved mover, whereas the will is a moved mover."

**Reply.** Something needs to be moved by something insofar as it is in potentiality to more than one thing. After all, something that is in potentiality has to be brought into actuality by something that is in actuality, and that is what it is to move. Now there are two ways in which a power of the soul can be in potentiality to diverse things: with respect to acting and not acting, and with respect to doing this or that. For example, sometimes vision is actually seeing, and sometimes it is not seeing; and sometimes it sees white, and sometimes it sees black. A power therefore requires a mover in both respects: that is, both for the exercise or use of its act and for the determination of its act. The exercise of the act depends on the subject, which sometimes acts and sometimes does not act; but the determination of the act depends on the object by which the act is specified.

Now the motion of the subject itself is from some agent. And since every agent acts on account of an end, as I showed earlier [I-II.1.2], the principle of this motion is from the end. That is why the art that concerns the end moves by its command the art that concerns what is for the end, "as the captain's art commands the shipbuilder's art," as *Physics* II [194b5] says.

47. Parallel passages: *ST* I.82.4; *SCG* III.26; *On Truth* 22.12; *On Evil* 6.
48. *Commentary on the Psalms* 118 sermon 8.

And the good in general, which has the character of an end, is the object
40   of the will. That is why, in this respect, the will moves the other powers of
the soul to their acts: we make use of the other powers when we will. After
all, the ends and perfections of all the other powers are included in the
object of the will as particular goods; and in every case the art or power that
concerns the universal end moves to action the art or power that concerns
45   a particular end that is included in that universal end, as the leader of an
army, who looks out for the common good (that is, the order of the whole
army), moves by his command one of his captains, who looks out for the
order of a single company.

By contrast, in determining an act, the object moves in the manner of
50   a formal principle, which in natural things is what establishes the species
of a thing: for example, heating is specified by heat. Now the first formal
principle is universal being and truth, which is the object of the intellect.
And so the intellect moves the will according to this kind of motion, as
presenting the will's object to it.
55   **Response to 1.** That passage is not saying that the intellect does not
move the will, but that it does not move the will by necessity.

**Response to 2.** Imagination of a form does not move the sensory appetite unless it is accompanied by an estimation of something's suitability or
harmfulness; and in much the same way, apprehension of what is true does
60   not move the will unless what is true is conceived as good and desirable.
That is why it is not the speculative intellect, but the practical intellect,
that moves the will, as *De anima* III says.

**Response to 3.** The will moves the intellect with respect to the exercise
of its act, since what is true, which is a perfection of the intellect, is also
65   included in the universal good as one particular good. But with respect
to the determination of an act, which depends on the object, the intellect
moves the will, since what is good is also apprehended according to a particular notion that is contained in the universal notion of what is true. And
in this way it is clear that one and the same thing is not both mover and
70   moved in the same respect.

### Article 2. Is the will moved by the sensory appetite?[49]

It seems that the will cannot be moved by the sensory appetite:
1. "What moves and acts is more excellent than what undergoes," as
Augustine says in his *Literal Commentary on Genesis* XII [ch. 16]. But the
sensory appetite is inferior to the will, which is intellectual appetite, just
5    as sense is inferior to intellect. Therefore, the sensory appetite does not
move the will.

---

49. Parallel passages: *ST* I-II.10.3 and 77.1; *On Truth* 22.9 resp. 6.

2. No particular power can bring about a universal effect. And the sensory appetite is a particular power; after all, it follows from a sense's particular apprehension. Therefore, it cannot cause a motion of the will, which is universal, because it follows from the intellect's universal apprehension.    10

3. As is proved in *Physics* VIII [257b23], a mover is not moved by that which it moves, in such a way that there is reciprocal motion. But the will moves the sensory appetite, insofar as the sensory appetite obeys reason. Therefore, the sensory appetite does not move the will.

**On the contrary.** James 1:14 says, "All are tempted by their own concu-   15
piscence, drawn away and enticed." Now the only way for someone to be drawn away by concupiscence is for that person's will to be moved by the sensory appetite, which is where concupiscence is. Therefore, the sensory appetite moves the will.

**Reply.** As I explained earlier [art. 1], what moves the will as an object    20
is what is apprehended as good and suitable. Now there are two reasons that something appears good and suitable: the condition of the thing that is presented, and the condition of the person to whom it is presented. After all, 'suitable' is a relational expression: it depends on both extremes. That is why what is suitable to one taste is unsuitable to a taste that is in a different    25
condition. Accordingly, the Philosopher says in *Ethics* III [1114a32], "How the end appears to someone depends on what sort of condition he or she is in." Now it is clear that a passion of the sensory appetite changes a person into a certain condition; hence, because one is experiencing a particular passion, one will think something is suitable that would not appear suitable    30
if one were not experiencing that passion. For example, something seems good to one who is angry that would not seem good to one who is calm. And it is in this way—on the part of the object—that the sensory appetite moves the will.

**Response to 1.** There is nothing to prevent something that is more    35
excellent in an unqualified sense, and in and of itself, from being weaker in a particular respect. So the will is more excellent than the sensory appetite in an unqualified sense, but sensory appetite is preeminent with respect to someone in whom a passion is dominant, to the extent that the person is under the sway of that passion.    40

**Response to 2.** Human acts and choices concern singulars. For that reason, the very fact that sensory appetite is a particular power means that it has considerable power to condition people in such a way that things appear this way or that way, with respect to singulars.

**Response to 3.** As the Philosopher says in *Politics* I [1254b5], reason    45
(which includes will) moves the irascible and concupiscible by its command, not with despotic authority, as a master moves a slave, but with a royal or political authority, as a leader governs free people who can nonetheless move in a contrary way. Thus, both the irascible and the concupiscible

50    can move contrary to the will; and so there is nothing to prevent the will
      from being moved by them sometimes.

                          *Article 3. Does the will move itself?*[50]

      It seems that the will does not move itself:
          1. Every mover, as such, is in actuality, whereas what is moved is in
      potentiality; for "motion is an act of what is in potentiality as such."[51] Now
      one and the same thing is not both in potentiality and in actuality with
5     respect to the same thing. Therefore, nothing moves itself, and so the will
      cannot move itself.
          2. Something movable is moved when the mover is present. Now the
      will is always present to itself. So if the will moved itself, it would be always
      in motion. Obviously, that is false.
10        3. The will is moved by the intellect, as has been explained [art. 1]. So
      if the will moves itself, it follows that one and the same thing is directly
      moved by two movers at the same time, which seems absurd. Therefore,
      the will does not move itself.
          **On the contrary.** The will is in control of its own act, and both willing
15    and not willing are up to the will. That would not be the case if the will did
      not have the power to move itself to will. Therefore, the will moves itself.
          **Reply.** As I said above [art. 1], it is the will's job to move other powers
      in virtue of the end, which is the will's object. Now as I noted [I-II.8.2], an
      end has the same role in the domain of desirable things that a principle has
20    in the domain of intelligible things. And it is clear that in virtue of cogniz-
      ing a principle, an intellect brings itself from potentiality to actuality with
      respect to cognizing conclusions; and in that way the intellect moves itself.
      And in a similar way, in virtue of willing an end, a will moves itself to will
      things that are for the end.
25        **Response to 1.** The will is not both mover and moved *in the same
      respect*; accordingly, it is not both in actuality and in potentiality in the
      same respect. Rather, insofar as it actually wills an end, it brings itself from
      potentiality to actuality with respect to things that are for the end, so that
      it actually wills them.
30        **Response to 2.** The *power* of the will is always actually present to the
      will, but the act of the will, by which it wills some end, is not always in the
      will. And it is through its act that the will moves itself. So it does not follow
      that the will always moves itself.
          **Response to 3.** The will is not moved by the intellect in the same way
35    that it is moved by itself. Rather, it is moved by the intellect in terms of

---

50. Parallel passage: *On Evil* 6.
51. Aristotle, *Physics* III.1, 201a10.

its object, whereas it is moved by itself to the exercise of its act, in terms of its end.

### Article 4. Is the will moved by any external principle?[52]

It seems that the will is not moved by anything external:

1. The will's movement is voluntary, and it is part of the concept of voluntariness that what is voluntary is from an internal principle. The same goes for the concept of what is natural. Therefore, no movement of the will is from something external. 5

2. The will cannot undergo violence, as was shown above [I-II.6.4]. And what is violent is "what has an external principle."[53] Therefore, the will cannot be moved by anything external.

3. What is sufficiently moved by one mover does not need to be moved by an additional mover, and the will sufficiently moves itself. Therefore, it 10 is not moved by anything external.

**On the contrary.** The will is moved by its object, as I have said [art. 1]. Now the will's object can be some external thing that comes to the awareness of the senses. Therefore, the will can be moved by something external.

**Reply.** It is clear that the will can be moved by something external 15 insofar as it is moved by an object. But we even have to say that the will is moved by an external principle insofar as it is moved to the exercise of its act. You see, anything that at some times is actually acting but at other times is in potentiality to acting needs to be moved by some mover. And it is clear that a will begins to will something that it was not willing before. 20 Therefore, something has to move the will to willing. And indeed, as I have explained [art. 3], the will moves itself: in virtue of willing an end, it brings itself to will things that are for the end. But this can only happen through some intervening deliberation. For example, when someone wills to be healed, he begins to think about how that might be achieved; as a result of 25 such thinking he comes to the conclusion that he can be healed by a doctor, and he wills that. But since he did not always actually will health, he had to begin to will to be healed; and he began to will it because something moved him. Now of course if the will moved itself to [begin to] will this, it would have had to do so through some intervening deliberation based on 30 some prior will. Now we cannot have an infinite regress in this. So we have to say that the will inaugurates its first movement thanks to the impetus of some external mover, as Aristotle concludes in a certain chapter of the *Eudemian Ethics* [1248a14].

---

52. Parallel passages: ST I.105.4, 106.2, 111.2, I-II.80.1, 109.2 resp. 1; SCG III.89; *On Truth* 22.9; *On Evil* 6; *Quodlibet* I.4.2.
53. Aristotle, *Nicomachean Ethics* III.1, 1110a1.

35      **Response to 1.** It is part of the concept of voluntariness that the principle of what is voluntary is internal, but that does not mean that this internal principle has to be a *first* principle that is not moved by anything else. Thus, even if a voluntary movement has an internal proximate principle, its first principle is still external, in the same way that the first principle of

40  a natural movement—namely, what moves nature—is also external.

    **Response to 2.** For a motion to count as violent, it is not enough that its principle is external; one also must add that "the thing that undergoes violence contributes no power to the motion."[54] That is not what happens when the will is moved by something external, since it is the will itself that

45  wills, though as a result of being moved by something else. The motion would indeed be violent if it were contrary to the motion of the will; but that cannot be the case here, because it would mean that the will both willed and did not will the very same thing.

    **Response to 3.** In one respect, and in its own order, the will does suffi-

50  ciently move itself: namely, as a proximate agent. But it cannot move itself in every respect, as I have shown. And for that reason it has to be moved by something else as its first mover.

*Article 5. Is the will moved by a heavenly body?*[55]

It seems that the human will is moved by a heavenly body:

    1. All varied and multiform motions are traced back to a uniform motion as their cause; as is proved in *Physics* VIII [265a27], this uniform motion is the motion of the heavens. Now human motions are variable and multi-

5  form; they begin after having not existed. Therefore, they are traced back to the motion of the heavens, which is uniform by nature, as their cause.

    2. According to Augustine in *On the Trinity* III [ch. 4], "lower bodies are moved by higher bodies." And the movements of the human body, which are caused by the will, cannot be traced back to the movement of the heav-

10  ens as their cause unless the will too is moved by the heavens. Therefore, the heavens move the human will.

    3. By observing heavenly bodies, astrologers make some correct predictions about future human acts, which come from the will. That would not be the case if heavenly bodies could not move the human will. Therefore,

15  the human will is moved by a heavenly body.

---

54. Aristotle, *Nicomachean Ethics* III.1, 1110a3.

55. Parallel passages: *ST* I.105.4, II-II 95.5; *Sent.* II.15.1.3; *SCG* III.85 and 87; *On Truth* 5.10; *On Evil* 6; *Compend. Theol.* 127 and 128; *Comm. Matt.* 2; *Comm. On Interpretation* I.14; *Comm. De anima* III.4; *Comm. Ethics* III.13.

**On the contrary.** Damascene says in Book II that "heavenly bodies are not causes of our acts."[56] But they *would* be if the will, which is the principle of human acts, were moved by heavenly bodies. Therefore, the will is not moved by heavenly bodies.

**Reply.** It is evident that the will can be moved by heavenly bodies in the 20 same way that it is moved by an external *object*: namely, insofar as external bodies that are presented to sense move the will, and insofar as the organs of the sensory powers are subordinate to the movements of heavenly bodies. Now in terms of the other way that the will can be moved—to the exercise of its act—by an external *agent*, some have gone so far as to claim 25 that heavenly bodies directly make impressions on the human will. But that is impossible. After all, the will is in reason, as is said in *De anima* III [432b5]; and reason is a power of the soul that is not tied to a bodily organ. So it follows that the will is a completely immaterial and non-bodily power. Now it is evident that no body can act on a non-bodily thing, but rather 30 the reverse, thanks to the fact that non-bodily and immaterial things have a more formal and more universal power than any bodily things. For this reason it is impossible for a heavenly body to make an impression directly on the intellect or the will. That is why Aristotle in the *De anima* [427a25] says that those who held that intellect does not differ from sense were of 35 the opinion that the human will is "such as the father of gods and men"— that is, Jupiter, by which they understand the whole heaven—"gives day by day."[57] You see, because all the sensory powers are actualities of bodily organs, they can be moved accidentally by heavenly bodies; that happens when the bodies of which they are actualities are moved [by heavenly bod- 40 ies]. But because, as I have explained [art. 2], the intellectual appetite is moved in a certain way by the sensory appetite, the movement of the heavenly bodies has an effect on the will indirectly, to the extent that the will happens to be moved by passions of the sensory appetite.

**Response to 1.** The multiform movements of the human will are traced 45 back to a uniform cause, but that uniform cause is higher than the intellect and will—which cannot be said of any body, but only of a higher immaterial substance. For that reason the will's movement should not be traced back to the movement of the heavens as its cause.

**Response to 2.** Movements of the human body are traced back to the 50 movement of a heavenly body as their cause insofar as an impression from heavenly bodies in some way disposes the organs so that they are apt to move, and insofar as an impression from heavenly bodies moves the sensory appetite, and, finally, insofar as external bodies are moved in accordance

---

56. *On the Orthodox Faith* II.7.
57. Homer, *Odyssey* XVIII.136.

55  with the motion of heavenly bodies, and as a result of this joint movement the will begins to will or not will something (for example, when the
weather turns cold and someone begins to will to make a fire). But this
motion of the will derives from the external object that is presented to it,
not from an internal impetus.

60      **Response to 3.** As I have said [I.84.6 and 7], the sensory appetite is an
act of a bodily organ. So it is perfectly possible for some people to be prone
to anger or lust or some other passion as a result of an impression from
heavenly bodies, just as they can be from their natural temperament. Now
lots and lots of people follow their passions; only those who are wise resist
65  their passions. And so predictions about human acts that are made on the
basis of considering the heavenly bodies turn out to be true in lots and lots
of cases. Nonetheless, as Ptolemy puts it in *Centiloquium* [prop. 5], "The
wise rule the stars"—meaning that by resisting their passions, they forestall
such effects of the heavenly bodies through their will, which is free and in
70  no way under the control of any movement of the heavens. Alternatively,
as Augustine says in his *Literal Commentary on Genesis* II [ch. 17], "We
ought to acknowledge that when astrologers make correct predictions, they
do so through a highly mysterious impression that human minds receive
without knowing how. Since this happens in order to lead people astray, it
75  is the work of deceptive spirits."

### Article 6. Does only God move the will as an external principle?[58]

It seems that the will is not moved only by God as an external principle:
    1. An inferior is apt to be moved by its superior, as inferior bodies are
apt to be moved by heavenly bodies. Now the human will has a superior
besides God, namely, angels. Therefore, the human will can also be moved
5  by an angel as an external principle.
    2. An act of will follows an act of intellect. Now the human intellect is
brought to its act not only by God, but also by an angel, through illumina-
tions, as Dionysius says.[59] Therefore, by the same argument, the human
will is also brought to its act by an angel.
10      3. God is the cause only of good things: as Genesis 1:31 says, "God saw
all the things he had made, and they were very good." So if the human
will were moved only by God, it would never be moved toward anything

---

58. Parallel passages: ST I.105.4, 106.2, 111.2; *Sent.* II.15.1.3; SCG III.88, 89, 91,
92; *On Truth* 22.8 and 9; *On Evil* 3.3, 6; *Compend. Theol.* 129.
59. *On the Celestial Hierarchy* 4.2.

bad; and yet the will is "that by which one sins and lives rightly," as Augustine says.[60]

**On the contrary.** The Apostle says in Philippians 2:13, "It is God who    15
works in us both to will and to persevere."

**Reply.** The will's movement, like a natural movement, is from within.
Now something that is not the cause of the nature of the thing moved can
move a natural thing, but only what is in some way a cause of the nature
can cause a natural movement. After all, a person, who is not the cause of    20
the nature of a stone, can move a stone upward; but that movement is not
natural for the stone. Its natural movement is caused only by the thing that
is the cause of its nature. That is why *Physics* VIII [255b35] says that the
generating cause moves heavy and light things according to place. In this
way, then, it may happen that human beings, who have wills, are moved    25
by something that is not their cause; but it is impossible for a movement
of someone's will to come from any external principle that is not a cause
of that will. Now there cannot be any cause of the will other than God.
That is clear for two reasons. First, the will is a power of the rational soul,
and only God causes the rational soul through creation, as I explained in    30
the First Part [I.90.2 and 3]. And second, this is clear from the fact that
the will is ordered to the universal good, which means that nothing can
be the cause of the will other than God, who is the universal good. Any
other good, by contrast, is called good by participation and is a particular
good; and a particular cause does not confer a universal inclination. For    35
that same reason, prime matter, which is in potentiality to all forms, cannot be caused by any particular agent.

**Response to 1.** An angel is not superior to a human being in such a
way as to be a cause of a human will, as heavenly bodies are causes of the
natural forms from which the natural movements of natural bodies follow.    40

**Response to 2.** A human intellect is moved by an angel with respect
to its object, which is presented to it for cognizing by virtue of an angelic
light. And in that way the will too can be moved by an external creature,
as I have said [art. 4].

**Response to 3.** God, as a universal mover, moves the human will to    45
the universal object of the will, which is the good. Without this universal movement, human beings cannot will anything. But through reason
human beings determine themselves to will this or that, which is a genuine
or apparent good. Nonetheless, sometimes God specially moves certain
people to will some particular thing that is good, as in people whom he    50
moves through grace, as I shall discuss later [I-II.109.2].

---

60. *Literal Commentary on Genesis* II.17.

## Question 10. How the Will Is Moved

Next we need to investigate how the will is moved. Concerning this there are four questions:

Article 1. Is the will moved toward anything naturally?
Article 2. Is it moved necessarily by its object?
Article 3. Is it moved necessarily by the lower appetite?
Article 4. Is it moved necessarily by its external mover, which is God?

*Article 1. Is the will moved toward anything naturally?*[61]

It seems that the will is not moved toward anything naturally:

1. A natural agent is distinguished from a voluntary agent, as is clear at the beginning of *Physics* II [196b19]. Therefore, the will is not moved toward anything naturally.

5      2. What is natural is always in something, as heat is always in fire. But there is no movement that is always in the will. Therefore, no movement is natural to the will.

3. Nature is determined to one, whereas the will is open to opposites. Therefore, the will does not will anything naturally.

10      **On the contrary.** The will's movement follows an act of intellect. Now the intellect understands certain things naturally. Therefore, the will wills certain things naturally.

**Reply.** As Boethius says in his book *On the Two Natures* [ch. 1] and the Philosopher says in *Metaphysics* V [1014b16], the word 'nature' is used in many senses. Sometimes 'nature' means an internal principle in movable things. Nature in this sense is either matter or a material form, as is clear from *Physics* II [193a28]. In another sense, 'nature' means any substance, or even any being; and in this sense we say that what characterizes a thing in virtue of its substance is natural to that thing. And that is what is in a thing 20 *per se*. Now in all things, whatever is not in a thing *per se* is traced back to something that is in the thing *per se*, as its principle. And so, taking nature in this sense, it must be the case without exception that the principle of whatever characterizes a thing is natural.

This is quite evident in the case of the intellect, since the principles of 25 intellectual cognition are naturally known. And similarly, the principle of voluntary movements has to be something naturally willed. Now this is the good in general, toward which the will tends naturally, just as every power tends toward its object; and it is also the ultimate end, which plays the same role with respect to desirable things that the first principles of demonstra-30 tions play with respect to intelligible things; and it is, in general, all the

---

61. Parallel passages: *ST* I.60.1 and 2; *Sent.* III.27.1.2; *On Truth* 22.5; *On Evil* 6 and 16.4 resp. 5.

things that are suitable to those who will in virtue of their nature. After all, what we desire through the will is not just what pertains to the power of the will; we also desire what pertains to individual powers [other than the will] and to the whole person. Hence, human beings naturally will not only the object of the will but also other things that are suitable to other powers, such as cognition of what is true, which belongs to the intellect, as well as being and living and other such things that bear on our natural well-being. All these things, as particular goods, fall within the scope of the will's object.

**Response to 1.** The distinction between will and nature is a distinction between causes: some things are done naturally, and some are done voluntarily. Now there is a mode of causing that is distinctive of the will, which is in control of its own act, beyond the mode of causing that belongs to nature, which is determined to one. But because the will is rooted in a nature, it has to be the case that the will participates in some respect in the movement characteristic of nature, in the way that a posterior cause participates in what belongs to a prior cause. After all, in every thing, its being, which is from nature, is prior to its willing, which is from the will. And that is how it is that the will wills something naturally.

**Response to 2.** In natural things, what is natural because it follows from just the form is always actually in the thing, as heat is always in fire. But what is natural because it follows from the matter is not always actually in the thing; sometimes it is in the thing only potentially. You see, form is actuality, whereas matter is potentiality. Now motion is "an actuality of what exists in potentiality."[62] So in natural things what pertains to motion or follows from motion is not always in the thing: for example, fire is not always moved upward, but only when it is outside its place. Similarly, it need not be the case that the will, which is brought from potentiality to actuality when it wills something, is always actually willing, but only when it is in some determinate condition. By contrast, God's will, which is pure actuality, is always actually willing.

**Response to 3.** Nature always corresponds to some one thing, but that one thing is commensurate with the nature: what corresponds to nature as genus is one in genus, what corresponds to nature as species is one in species, and what corresponds to individuated nature is some one individual. Therefore, since the will (like the intellect) is an immaterial power, it corresponds naturally to one universal, the good, just as the intellect corresponds to one universal, the true, or being, or what a thing is. But the universal good includes many particular goods, and the will is not determined to any of them.

---

62. Aristotle, *Physics* III.1, 201a10.

*Article 2. Is the will moved necessarily by its object?*[63]

It seems that the will is moved necessarily by its object:

1. The relationship of the will's object to the will is that of a mover to what is movable, as is evident in *De anima* III [433b10, b16]. Now if a mover is sufficient, it necessarily moves what is movable. Therefore, the will can
5   be moved necessarily by its object.

2. Just as the will is an immaterial power, so too is the intellect; and both powers are directed to a universal object, as has been said [art. 1 resp. 3]. Now the intellect is moved necessarily by its object. Therefore, the will too is moved necessarily by its object.

10   3. Everything that anyone wills is either an end or something directed to an end. And it seems that one wills an end necessarily, since an end is like a principle in speculative matters, to which we assent necessarily. Moreover, the end is the basis for willing things that are for the end; thus, it seems that we also will things that are for the end necessarily. Therefore, the will
15   is moved necessarily by its object.

**On the contrary.** According to the Philosopher,[64] rational powers are open to opposites. And the will is a rational power, because it is in reason, as is said in *De anima* III [432b5]. Therefore, the will is open to opposites, which means it is not moved necessarily to either of a pair of opposites.

20   **Reply.** The will is moved in two ways: with respect to the exercise of its act, and with respect to the specification of its act, which derives from its object. In the first way, the will is not moved necessarily by any object, because one can just not think about a given object, and consequently one will not actually will it. As for the second way in which the will is moved,
25   it is moved necessarily by some object but not by every object. You see, when it comes to the movement of any power by its object, one has to take account of the aspect in virtue of which the object moves its power. What is visible, for example, moves sight in virtue of an actually visible color. So if a color is presented to sight, it moves sight necessarily, unless someone
30   looks away—which has to do with the exercise of the act. By contrast, if something were presented to sight that was not actually color in every way, but instead was color in one respect but not in another, sight would not necessarily see such an object: it could attend to that object in the respect in which it is not actually colored, and thus it would not see that object.
35   Now just as what is actually colored is the object of sight, what is good is the object of the will. So if some object is presented to the will that is good universally and no matter how you look at it, the will tends toward it necessarily, if it wills anything at all; it would not be able to will the opposite.

63. Parallel passage: *ST* I.82.1 and 2.
64. *Metaphysics* VIII.2, 1046b8.

But if some object is presented that is not good if you look at it in some particular way, the will is not necessarily drawn to it. And since a deficiency of any good has the aspect of not-good, only the good that is complete and has no deficiency is such a good that the will cannot fail to will it. That good is happiness. Other particular goods, by contrast, can be regarded as not-good insofar as they are lacking some good; thus, depending on how one looks at them, the will can either reject them or approve them, since it can be directed to one and the same object under different descriptions.

**Response to 1.** The only sufficient mover of a power is an object that has, in every respect, the aspect in virtue of which the power is moved. If the object lacks that aspect in any respect, it will not move the power necessarily, as I have explained.

**Response to 2.** The intellect is moved necessarily by an object that is always and necessarily true, but not by one that can be true and false, namely, something contingent—just as I have explained concerning what is good.

**Response to 3.** The ultimate end moves the will necessarily because it is a complete good. The same goes for things that are directed to this end and without which it is not possible to have the end: for example, being, living, and so forth. But one who wills the end does not necessarily will other things, things that it is possible to lack and still obtain the ultimate end, just as someone who believes principles does not necessarily believe conclusions that can be false even though the principles are true.

### Article 3. Is the will moved necessarily by the lower appetite?[65]

It seems that the will is moved necessarily by a passion of the lower appetite:

1. The Apostle says in Romans 7:19, "I do not do the good that I will, but the evil that I hate, that is what I do." He says this with reference to desire, which is a passion. Therefore, the will is moved necessarily by passion.

2. As is said in *Ethics* III [1114a32], "How the end appears to someone depends on what sort of condition he or she is in." Now the will does not have the power to get rid of a passion all at once. Therefore, the will also does not have the power not to will that to which a passion inclines it.

3. A universal cause is not applied to a particular effect except through some particular cause as an intermediary; that is why universal reason causes motion only through particular estimation as an intermediary, as is said in *De anima* III [434a19]. Now as universal reason is to particular estimation, so is the will to the sensory appetite. Therefore, the will is not moved to will any particular except through the sensory appetite as an

---

65. Parallel passages: *ST* I-II.77.7; *On Truth* 5.10, 22.9 resp. 3 and resp. 6.

15    intermediary. So if the sensory appetite is oriented toward something by
      some passion, the will cannot be moved toward its contrary.
          **On the contrary.** Genesis 4:7 says, "Your desire will be under you, and
      you will control it." Therefore, the human will is not moved necessarily
      by the lower appetite.
20        **Reply.** As I explained earlier [I-II.9.2], a passion of the sensory appetite
      moves the will in the way that an object moves the will. That is, insofar as
      one is oriented in a certain way by a passion, one judges something to be
      suitable and good that one would not see as suitable or good if one were not
      undergoing that passion. Now there are two ways a passion brings about this
25    sort of change in someone. In one way, reason is totally incapacitated, so
      that the person cannot employ reason. This is what happens in people who
      are so overwhelmed by anger or lust that they become raving or insane; it
      also happens because of some physical disturbance, since such passions do
      not occur apart from some physical change. What is true of such people
30    is what is also true of non-rational animals: they necessarily follow the
      impulse of passion. You see, there is no movement of reason in them, and
      consequently there is no movement of will either. Sometimes, though,
      reason is not completely overwhelmed by passion; instead, the judgment
      of reason remains free to some extent. In that case, some movement of the
35    will remains. Therefore, to the extent that reason remains free, and not
      under the sway of passion, the remaining movement of the will does not
      tend necessarily to the thing to which passion inclines. Thus, either there
      is no movement of will in a person, and the passion alone is in control,
      or else, if there is in fact some movement of will, the will does not follow
40    passion necessarily.
          **Response to 1.** Even if the will cannot stop the movement of desire
      from arising—that is what the Apostle is talking about in Romans 7 when
      he says "the evil that I hate, that is what I do," meaning, that is what I
      desire—nevertheless, the will can will not to have the desire, or not con-
45    sent to the desire. And thus the will does not necessarily follow the move-
      ment of desire.
          **Response to 2.** Although there are two natures in human beings, intel-
      lectual and sensory, sometimes a person is in a certain condition uniformly,
      as regards the whole soul: either because the sensory part is completely
50    under the sway of reason, as is the case in the virtuous, or conversely
      because reason is completely overwhelmed by passion, as happens in the
      insane. But sometimes, even though reason is clouded by passion, reason
      retains some freedom. In that case, one can either completely expel the
      passion or at least keep oneself from following the passion. In such a con-
55    dition, you see, a person is in different conditions in different parts of the
      soul; things appear one way according to reason but another way accord-
      ing to passion.

**Response to 3.** The will is not moved only by a universal good apprehended by reason; it is also moved by a good apprehended by sense. And so it can be moved to some particular good without any passion of the sensory 60 appetite. After all, we will and do many things without passion, through choice alone, as is especially clear in people in whom reason resists passion.

### Article 4. Is the will moved necessarily by God?[66]

It seems that the will is moved necessarily by God:

1. Any agent that cannot be resisted moves necessarily; and since God is infinitely powerful, he cannot be resisted. That is why Romans 9:19 says, "Who resists his will?" Therefore, God moves the will necessarily.

2. The will is moved necessarily toward the things that it wills naturally, 5 as has been explained. "But what is natural for each thing is what God works in it," as Augustine says in *Against Faustus* XXVI [ch. 3]. Therefore, the will necessarily wills everything toward which God moves it.

3. What is possible is such that when it is posited, nothing impossible follows. But if it is posited that the will does not will something toward 10 which God moves it, something impossible follows—because in such a case God's activity would be ineffective. Therefore, it is not possible for the will not to will something toward which God moves it. Therefore, it is necessary for the will to will it.

**On the contrary.** Ecclesiasticus 15:14 says, "God established human 15 beings from the beginning, and he left them in the hand of their own deliberation." Therefore, God does not move the human will necessarily.

**Reply.** As Dionysius says in *On the Divine Names* 4 [§33], "The role of divine providence is not to destroy the nature of things but to preserve it." For that reason God moves all things in the way appropriate to their con- 20 dition. Thus, the result of God's moving is that effects follow necessarily from necessary causes, whereas effects follow contingently from contingent causes. Consequently, since the will is an active principle that is not determined to one outcome but is indifferent to many, that is how God moves it. He does not determine it necessarily to one outcome; instead, the will's 25 movement remains contingent and not necessary, except in things toward which it is moved naturally.

**Response to 1.** The divine will does not extend merely to something's being done by the thing that God moves, but to its being done in a way that is appropriate for the thing's nature. And so if the will were moved 30 necessarily, which is contrary to the will's nature, that would actually be more contradictory to the divine motion than if it were moved freely, as suits its nature.

---

66. Parallel passages: *ST* I.83.1 resp. 3; *On Truth* 24.1 resp. 3; *On Evil* 6 resp. 3.

**Response to 2.** What is natural for each thing is what God *makes* natu-
35    ral to it: thus, something is suitable for a given thing because God wills
that it be suitable to that thing. But God does not will that everything he
does in things be natural to them: for example, that the dead rise again.
He does, however, will that it be natural for each thing that it be subject
to divine power.
40    **Response to 3.** If God moves the will toward something, it is impossible *given this supposition* for the will not to be moved toward it; but it is
not impossible in an unqualified sense. So it does not follow that the will
is moved by God necessarily.

### Question 11. Enjoyment, Which Is an Act of the Will

Next we need to investigate enjoyment. Concerning this there are four
questions:
Article 1. Is enjoyment an act of an appetitive power?
Article 2. Does it belong only to rational creatures or to non-rational
animals as well?
Article 3. Is enjoyment only of the ultimate end?
Article 4. Is it only of an end that is actually possessed?

*Article 1. Is enjoyment an act of an appetitive power?*[67]

It seems that enjoyment does not belong exclusively to an appetitive power:
1. Enjoyment (*fruitio*) seems to be nothing other than getting hold of
the fruit (*fructus*). Now what gets hold of the fruit of human life, which is
happiness, is the intellect, since (as was shown above [I-II.3.4]) happiness
5    consists in an act of the intellect. Therefore, enjoyment belongs, not to an
appetitive power, but to the intellect.
2. Each power has its own end, which is its perfection. For example, the
end of vision is cognizing what is visible, the end of hearing is perceiving
sounds, and so forth. And the end of a thing is its fruit. Therefore, enjoy-
10    ment belongs to every power, and not exclusively to an appetitive power.
3. Enjoyment implies a certain delight. Now sensory delight belongs to
sense, which delights in its object; and by the same reasoning, intellectual
delight belongs to the intellect. Therefore, enjoyment belongs to an apprehensive power and not to an appetitive power.
15    **On the contrary.** Augustine says in *On Christian Teaching* I [ch. 4]
and *On the Trinity* X [chs. 10–11], "To enjoy is to cleave with love to some
thing for its own sake." Now love belongs to an appetitive power. Therefore,
enjoyment too is an act of an appetitive power.

---

67. Parallel passage: *Sent.* I.1.1.1.

**Reply.** Enjoyment (*fruitio*) and fruit (*fructus*) appear to belong to the same thing, and one is derived from the other. Which is derived from 20 which does not matter for our present question, except that it seems probable that the one that is more evident was named first. Now it is the more sensible things that are first evident to us, so it appears that the word for enjoyment is derived from sensible fruits. Now sensible fruit is what we ultimately look for from a tree and is perceived with a certain sweetness. 25 For that reason enjoyment seems to be a matter of the love or delight that someone has in what is ultimately looked for, which is the end. Now the end and the good is the object of an appetitive power. Thus, it is evident that enjoyment is an act of an appetitive power.

**Response to 1.** It is perfectly possible for one and the same thing to 30 belong to different powers under different descriptions. So the vision of God *as vision* is an act of the intellect, but *as good and end* it is an object of the will. And it is in this latter way that there is enjoyment of the vision of God. Thus, the intellect attains this end as the active power, whereas the will attains it as the power that moves toward the end and enjoys the 35 end once it is attained.

**Response to 2.** The perfection and end of any other power is included in the object of an appetitive power as a particular end included in the end in general, as I said above [I-II.9.1]. For that reason the perfection and end of every power, insofar as it is a good, belongs to an appetitive power. 40 Consequently, an appetitive power moves other powers to their ends, and it attains the end when any other power achieves its end.

**Response to 3.** Delight has two components: the perception of what is fitting, which belongs to an apprehensive power, and pleasure in what is presented as fitting. The latter belongs to an appetitive power, in which the 45 nature of delight is fully realized.

*Article 2. Does enjoyment belong only to rational
creatures or to non-rational animals as well?*[68]

It seems that enjoyment belongs only to human beings:

1. Augustine says in *On Christian Teaching* I [ch. 22] that "we human beings are the ones who enjoy and use." Therefore, the other animals cannot enjoy.

2. Enjoyment is of the ultimate end, and non-rational animals cannot 5 attain the ultimate end. Therefore, they cannot have enjoyment.

3. In the same way that the sensory appetite is below intellectual appetite, natural appetite is below sensory appetite. So if the sensory appetite is capable of enjoyment, it would seem, by parity of reasoning, that the

---

68. Parallel passage: *Sent.* I.1.4.1.

10   natural appetite is also capable of enjoyment. But that is obviously false,
     since the natural appetite is not capable of delight. Therefore, enjoyment
     does not belong to the sensory appetite, and accordingly there is no enjoy-
     ment in non-rational animals.
       **On the contrary.** Augustine says in *On 83 Questions* [q. 30], "It is not
15   absurd to suppose that the beasts, too, enjoy food and any bodily pleasure."
       **Reply.** From what has been said so far [art. 1], we can gather that enjoy-
     ment is not an act of the power that attains the end in the sense of realizing
     that end, but of the power that commands its realization; after all, I have
     explained that enjoyment belongs to an appetitive power. Now things that
20   lack cognition have a power that attains the end by realizing that end: for
     example, the power by which what is heavy tends downward and what is
     light tends upward. But they do not have a power that commands that the
     end be realized; instead, such a power is in some higher nature that moves
     the whole [lower] nature by its command in the way that, in things that
25   have cognition, the appetite moves other powers to their acts. Accordingly,
     it is clear that in things that lack cognition, even if they do attain their
     end, there is no enjoyment of the end; only in things that have cognition
     is there enjoyment.
       Now there are two kinds of cognition of an end: perfect and imperfect.
30   In perfect cognition, not only does one cognize the thing that is the end
     and the good, but one also cognizes the universal notion of end and good;
     only a rational nature can have this sort of cognition. In imperfect cogni-
     tion, by contrast, one cognizes the end and the good in its particularity;
     that sort of cognition is in non-rational animals. Also, the appetitive pow-
35   ers of non-rational animals do not command freely; instead, animals are
     moved by natural instinct to the things they apprehend. Thus, perfect
     enjoyment belongs to rational nature and imperfect enjoyment to non-
     rational animals; in other creatures there is no enjoyment of any kind.
       **Response to 1.** Augustine is speaking of perfect enjoyment.
40     **Response to 2.** Enjoyment does not have to be of the ultimate end in an
     unqualified sense, but just of the ultimate end of a given thing.
       **Response to 3.** Sensory appetite follows from some cognition, but natu-
     ral appetite does not, especially insofar as natural appetite is in things that
     lack cognition.
45     **Response to On the contrary.** Augustine is speaking there of imper-
     fect enjoyment. That is clear from the way he words this: he says that it is
     not so absurd to suppose that beasts, too, enjoy, in the way that it would be
     completely absurd to suppose that they use.

*Article 3. Is enjoyment only of the ultimate end?*[69]

It seems that enjoyment is not only of the ultimate end:

1. In his letter to Philemon [verse 20], the Apostle says, "Yes, brother, may I enjoy you in the Lord." But it is clear that Paul did not locate his ultimate end in a human being. Therefore, enjoyment is not only of the ultimate end.                                                                                    5

2. Fruit is what someone enjoys. Now in Galatians 5:22 the Apostle says, "the fruit of the Spirit is love, joy, peace," and so forth, and those do not meet the definition of ultimate end. Therefore, enjoyment is not only of the ultimate end.

3. Acts of the will are reflected back on themselves: I will my willing    10
and love my loving. And enjoyment is an act of will; after all, "it is by the will that we enjoy," as Augustine says in *On the Trinity* X [ch. 10]. Therefore, one enjoys one's enjoyment. But enjoyment is not the ultimate end for human beings; only an uncreated good, God, is our ultimate end. Therefore, enjoyment is not only of the ultimate end.                                            15

**On the contrary.** Augustine says in *On the Trinity* X [ch. 11], "It is not enjoyment if, when people will something, they will it for the sake of something else." Now it is only the ultimate end that we do not will for the sake of something else. Therefore, enjoyment is only of the ultimate end.

**Reply.** As I have said [art. 1], for something to count as a fruit, two    20
things are required: it must be last, and it must bring the appetite to rest with a certain sweetness or delight. Now what is last can be either unqualifiedly last or last in a certain respect. What is unqualifiedly last is what is not referred to anything else; what is last in a certain respect is the last in a particular series. Therefore, something that is unqualifiedly last, in which    25
someone takes delight as in an ultimate end, is properly called a fruit, and someone is properly said to enjoy it. By contrast, what is not delightful in itself but is desired only with reference to something else, as bad-tasting medicine is desired for the sake of health, cannot be called a fruit in any way. Now if something has some sort of delightfulness in itself, and prior    30
things are referred to it, it can be called a fruit in some sense; but we are not said to enjoy it properly and as a fruit in the fullest sense. That is why Augustine says in *On the Trinity* X [ch. 10] that "we enjoy things known in which the will rests with delight." But the will does not rest unqualifiedly except in the ultimate end, since as long as there is anything further to    35
look for, the will's motion remains in an in-between state, even though it has attained something. It is the same with local motion: any intermediate point in the full sweep of the motion is both a beginning and an end, but it is regarded as an end in actuality only when the object rests there.

---

69. Parallel passages: *Sent.* I.1.2.1; *Comm. Philemon* 2.

40    **Response to 1.** As Augustine says in *On Christian Teaching* I [ch. 33],
"If he had said, 'may I enjoy you' and had not added 'in the Lord,' he would
have appeared to locate his delight in him. But since he did add 'in the
Lord,' he signified that he located his end in the Lord and enjoyed the
Lord." Thus, he meant that he would enjoy his brother not as a terminus,
45    but as an intermediate point.
      **Response to 2.** The relation of a fruit to the tree that produces it is not
the same as its relation to the person who enjoys it. The fruit is related to
the tree that produces it as an effect to its cause, whereas it is related to
the one who enjoys it as the last thing looked for and delighted in. So the
50    things that the Apostle lists here are called fruit because they are effects of
the Holy Spirit in us—that is why they are also called fruit *of the Spirit*—
not because we enjoy them as our ultimate end. Alternatively, one could
say, following Ambrose, that they are called fruit because they should be
sought for their own sake:[70] not of course in such a way that they are not
55    referred to happiness, but because they have within themselves something
that ought to please us.
      **Response to 3.** As I said above [I-II.1.8, 2.7], we speak of an end in two
ways: in one way, it is the thing itself; in the other way, it is the attainment
of the thing. Of course that is not two ends; it is one end considered in itself
60    and as applied to something else. So God is the ultimate end in the sense
of the thing that is ultimately sought, whereas enjoyment is the ultimate
end in the sense of the attainment of the ultimate end. Thus, God and the
enjoyment of God are not distinct ends; accordingly, our enjoying God
is the very same enjoyment as our enjoying the enjoyment of God. The
65    same argument holds for created happiness, which consists in enjoyment.

*Article 4. Is enjoyment only of an end that is actually possessed?*

It seems that enjoyment is only of an end that is actually possessed:
      1. Augustine says in *On the Trinity* X [ch. 11] that "to enjoy is to use
with joy, no longer in hope, but in actual fact." But as long as something
is not possessed, there is no joy in actual fact, but only in hope. Therefore,
5    enjoyment is only of an end that is actually possessed.
      2. As has been said [art. 3], properly speaking there is enjoyment only
of the ultimate end, since only the ultimate end brings the appetite to rest.
Now the appetite does not rest in an end unless the end has been attained.
Therefore, there is no enjoyment, properly speaking, except of an end that
10    is actually possessed.

---

70. From the *Glossa ordinaria* on Galatians 5.22; cf. Peter Lombard, *Sentences*
I.1.3.

3. To enjoy is to get hold of the fruit, and one only gets hold of the fruit when the end is actually possessed. Therefore, enjoyment is only of an end that is actually possessed.

**On the contrary.** "To enjoy is to cleave with love to some thing for its own sake," as Augustine says.[71] And this can be done even for a thing that   15
is not actually possessed. Therefore, there can also be enjoyment of an end that is not actually possessed.

**Reply.** Enjoyment implies a certain relation of the will to the ultimate end, depending on how the will possesses something as its ultimate end. Now there are two ways in which an end is possessed: perfectly and imper-   20
fectly. An end is possessed perfectly when it is possessed not merely in intention but also in fact, whereas it is possessed imperfectly when it is possessed only in intention. Therefore, there is perfect enjoyment of an end that is already possessed in reality, but there is imperfect enjoyment of an end that is not possessed in reality, but merely in intention.   25

**Response to 1.** Augustine is speaking of perfect enjoyment.

**Response to 2.** There are two kinds of obstacles that prevent the will from coming to rest. One is on the part of the object, namely, because the object is not the ultimate end but is directed to something else; the other is on the part of the one who desires the end, who has not yet attained the   30
end. Now the object is what gives an act its species, whereas the manner of acting (whether it is perfect or imperfect) depends on the condition of the agent. That is why the enjoyment of something that is not the ultimate end is improper: it falls short of the species of enjoyment. By contrast, the enjoyment of the ultimate end that is not actually possessed is indeed   35
proper enjoyment, but it is imperfect enjoyment because the ultimate end is not possessed in a perfect way.

**Response to 3.** There are two ways in which someone is said to get hold of an end or to possess it: not only in fact, but also in intention, as I have explained [in the main reply].   40

## Question 12. Intention

Next we need to investigate intention. Concerning this there are five questions:

 Article 1. Is intention an act of the intellect or of the will?

 Article 2. Is intention only of the ultimate end?

 Article 3. Can someone intend two things at the same time?

 Article 4. Is intention of the end the same act as will of what is for the end?

 Article 5. Does intention belong to non-rational animals?

---

71. *On Christian Teaching* I.4.

*Article 1. Is intention an act of the intellect or of the will?*[72]

It seems that intention is an act of the intellect and not of the will:

1. Matthew 6:22 says, "If your eye is simple, your whole body will be full of light." 'Eye,' in this passage, signifies intention, as Augustine says in *On the Lord's Sermon on the Mount* [II.13]. Now since the eye is the instrument
5   of vision, it signifies an apprehensive power. Therefore, intention is an act not of an appetitive power, but of an apprehensive power.

2. In that same passage Augustine says that the Lord calls intention "light" when he says, "If the light that is in you is darkness," etc.[73] Now light has to do with cognition. Therefore, so does intention.

10   3. Intention indicates some sort of ordering toward an end, and it is the job of reason to order. Therefore, intention belongs not to the will, but to reason.

4. There is no act of will other than what concerns the end or what concerns things that are for the end. Now an act of will concerning the end
15   is called will or enjoyment, and the act of will concerning things that are for the end is choice. Intention is not the same as any of those. Therefore, intention is not an act of the will.

**On the contrary.** Augustine says in *On the Trinity* XI [ch. 4] that "the will's intention joins the seen body to sight and likewise the species exist-
20   ing in memory to the gaze of the mind thinking inwardly." So intention is an act of the will.

**Reply.** 'Intention' (*intentio*), as the word itself indicates, signifies tending toward something (*in aliquid tendere*). Now both the action of a mover and the motion of what is movable tend toward something. But the fact that the
25   motion of what is movable tends toward something derives from the action of the mover. For that reason, intention primarily and principally belongs to that which moves something toward an end; that is why we say that an architect, or anyone in authority, by his command moves others toward the things that he himself intends. Now it is the will that moves all the powers
30   of the soul toward an end, as I established above [I-II.9.1]. Thus, it is evident that intention is properly an act of the will.

**Response to 1.** Intention is called an eye metaphorically, not because it belongs to cognition, but because it presupposes a cognition that presents to the will the end toward which intention moves, in the same way that by
35   the eye we see beforehand which way we ought to move with our bodies.

**Response to 2.** Intention is called light because it is evident to the one intending. That is also why deeds are called darkness, because people know

---

72. Parallel passages: *Sent.* II.38.3; *On Truth* 22.13.
73. Matthew 6:23.

what they intend but they do not know what will result from their deeds, as Augustine explains in that same passage.

**Response to 3.** True, the will does not order, but it does tend toward 40 something according to reason's ordering. Thus, this word 'intention' names an act of the will *presupposing* the ordering of reason, which orders something toward an end.

**Response to 4.** Intention is an act of will concerning an end. Now there are three ways in which the will has to do with an end. One way is abso- 45 lutely. In that way, we speak of *will*, insofar as we will health or some such thing absolutely. The second way regards an end insofar as someone rests in it. That is the way in which *enjoyment* concerns the end. The third way regards an end as the terminus of something that is ordered toward it. That is the way in which *intention* concerns the end. You see, we are not said 50 to intend health merely because we will it, but because we will to attain it *through* something else.

### Article 2. Is intention only of the ultimate end?

It seems that intention is only of the ultimate end:

1. In Prosper's *Sentences* [sent. 100], we read that "the heart's intention is a cry to God." Now God is the ultimate end of the human heart, so intention always has to do with the ultimate end.

2. Intention has to do with an end insofar as it is a terminus, as has been 5 explained [art. 1 resp. 4]; and a terminus is something ultimate. Therefore, intention always has to do with the ultimate end.

3. Intention has to do with an end in the same way that enjoyment does, and enjoyment is always of the ultimate end; therefore, so is intention.

**On the contrary.** There is one ultimate end for human wills, namely, 10 happiness, as I have explained [I-II.1.7]. So if intention were only of the ultimate end, there would not be a variety of intentions among human beings. That is obviously false.

**Reply.** As I have said [art. 1 resp. 4], intention has to do with an end insofar as it is the terminus of a motion of the will. Now there are two 15 senses of 'terminus' in the domain of motion: one is the ultimate terminus in which something comes to rest, the terminus of the whole motion; the other is something intermediate, which is the beginning of one part of the motion but the end or terminus of another part. For example, when someone goes from *a* to *c* through *b*, *c* is the ultimate terminus of the motion; 20 but *b* is a terminus, though not the ultimate terminus. And there can be intention of either of the two. Accordingly, though it is true that intention is always of an end, it need not always be of the ultimate end.

**Response to 1.** The heart's intention is called a cry to God, not because God is always the object of intention, but because God knows 25 our intention—or because, when we pray, we direct our intention to God, and thus our intention functions as a cry to God.

**Response to 2.** A terminus is something ultimate, but not always something ultimate with respect to the whole; sometimes it is ultimate with
30   respect to one part.

**Response to 3.** Enjoyment implies rest in the end, and that pertains only to the ultimate end. Intention, by contrast, implies motion toward the end, not rest. So the cases are not parallel.

*Article 3. Can one intend two things at the same time?*[74]

It seems that one cannot intend more than one thing at the same time:

1. Augustine says in *On the Lord's Sermon on the Mount* [II.14, 17] that a human being cannot intend God and bodily advantage at the same time. Therefore, by parity of reasoning, one cannot intend any other two things
5   at the same time.

2. 'Intention' names a motion of the will toward a terminus. But there cannot be more than one terminus for a single motion under a single aspect. Therefore, the will cannot intend many things at the same time.

3. Intention presupposes an act of reason or intellect. And according
10   to the Philosopher, "one cannot understand more than one thing at the same time."[75] Therefore, one also cannot intend more than one thing at the same time.

**On the contrary.** Art imitates nature. Now nature intends two uses for a single instrument: for example, "the tongue is ordered to both taste and
15   speech," as is said in *De anima* II [420b18]. Therefore, by parity of reasoning, art or reason can direct one thing to two ends at the same time. And that is how someone can intend more than one thing at the same time.

**Reply.** By "two things" one might mean two things that are ordered to each other, or two things that are not ordered to each other. Now if we are
20   talking about two things that are ordered to each other, it is quite clear from what has been said up to this point that a human being can intend many things at the same time. After all, as I have explained [art. 2], intention is not only of the ultimate end, but also of an intermediate end. And someone intends a proximate end and the ultimate end at the same time:
25   for example, taking medicine and health.

And even if we are talking about two things that are not ordered to each other, it is still true that a human being can intend more than one thing at the same time. Here is an example that makes this clear: someone selects A in preference to B on the grounds that A is better than B, and one way

74. Parallel passage: *On Truth* 13.3.
75. *Topics* II.10, 114b35.

in which A can be better than B is that A is useful for more purposes than    *30*
B is. Thus, someone can select one thing in preference to another on the
grounds that it is useful for more purposes. And it is clear that, in so doing,
the person is intending more than one thing at the same time.

**Response to 1.** Augustine means that a human being cannot intend
God and this-worldly advantage at the same time as *ultimate ends*, because,    *35*
as I showed above [I-II.1.5], one human being cannot have more than one
ultimate end.

**Response to 2.** There can in fact be more than one terminus for a single
motion under a single aspect if one terminus is ordered to another, whereas
if the termini are not ordered to each other, they cannot belong to a single    *40*
motion under a single aspect. Still, you have to realize that what is not one
in fact can be regarded as one by reason. Now as I have explained [art. 1
resp. 3], intention is a motion of the will toward something that has already
been ordered by reason. And so things that are more than one in fact can
be taken as one terminus of intention insofar as reason regards them as one,    *45*
either because two things come together to make up a whole, as heat and
cold in a proper balance come together to produce health, or because two
things are instances of some general class that can be intended. For example, acquiring wine and acquiring clothing both fall under the general
heading of acquiring wealth, and so there is no reason that someone who    *50*
intends to acquire wealth cannot intend both of those at the same time.

**Response to 3.** As I said in the First Part [I.12.10, 58.2, 85.4], it is possible to understand more than one thing at the same time insofar as they
are in some way one.

*Article 4. Is intention of the end the same
act as will of what is for the end?*[76]

It seems that intending an end and willing what is for the end are not one
and the same motion:

1. Augustine says in *On the Trinity* XI [ch. 6] that "the will to see the
window has as its end the seeing of the window; the will to see the passersby *through* the window is distinct." Now my willing to see the passersby    *5*
through the window is a case of intention, whereas my willing to see the
window is a case of willing that which is for the end. Therefore, the intention of the end is a different movement of the will from the willing of what
is for the end.

2. Acts are distinguished by their objects. Now an end and what is for    *10*
the end are distinct objects. Therefore, intending the end and willing what
is for the end are distinct movements of the will.

---

76. Parallel passages: *ST* I-II.8.3; *Sent.* II.38.4; *On Truth* 22.14.

3. Will of what is for the end is called choice. Now choice and intention
are not the same. Therefore, intention of the end is not the same movement
15  as the will of what is for the end.

**On the contrary.** What is for the end is related to the end as something
intermediate is related to a terminus. Now in natural things it is one and
the same motion that passes *through* what is intermediate and *to* the terminus. Therefore, in voluntary things the intention of the end is the same
20  movement as the will of what is for the end.

**Reply.** There are two ways to consider the movement of the will toward
the end and toward what is for the end. One way is insofar as the will is
drawn to each absolutely and for its own sake. In this way, the will's movements toward each are, in an unqualified sense, two movements. In another
25  way, one can consider it insofar as the will is drawn to what is for the end *for
the sake of* the end. And in that way the will's movement that tends toward
the end is one and the same in subject as the movement that tends toward
what is for the end. For example, when I say, "I will medicine for the sake
of health," I am describing only one motion on the part of the will. The
30  reason for this is that the end is the reason for willing things that are for
the end, and one and the same act deals with both an object and the reason for its being an object—for example, the same act of vision deals with
both color and light, as I said above [I-II.8.3 resp. 2]. Similarly, in the case
of the intellect, if it considers a principle and a conclusion absolutely, its
35  consideration of each is a distinct consideration; but when it assents to a
conclusion on account of principles, there is just one act of intellect.

**Response to 1.** Augustine is speaking of seeing the window and seeing the passersby through the window insofar as the will is drawn to each
absolutely.

40  **Response to 2.** As a *thing*, the end is a distinct object of will from what
is for the end; but as the *reason for willing* what is for the end, it is one and
the same object.

**Response to 3.** A movement that is one in subject can be conceived
as more than one with reference to its beginning or its end: for example,
45  ascent and descent, as is said in *Physics* III [202a16–22]. Accordingly, insofar as the movement of the will is drawn to what is for the end *as ordered to
the end*, that is choice, whereas the movement of the will that is drawn to
the end is called intention *insofar as things that are for the end are acquired
through that movement.* An indication of this is the fact that there can be
50  intention of an end even when one has not yet figured out the things that
are for the end, which are the objects of choice.

### Article 5. Does intention belong to non-rational animals?[77]

It seems that non-rational animals intend an end:

1. The nature of things that lack cognition is more distant from rational nature than is the sensory nature that is in non-rational animals. But even in things that lack cognition, nature intends an end, as is proved in *Physics* II [199b30]. All the more so, then, do non-rational animals intend an end.  5

2. Just as intention is of an end, so too is enjoyment. And enjoyment is characteristic of non-rational animals, as has been said [I-II.11.2]. Therefore, so is intention.

3. Whatever acts for the sake of an end intends the end, since intending (*intendere*) is simply tending toward (*tendere in*) something. And non-  10
rational animals act for the sake of an end; after all, an animal is moved to seek food or something of that sort. Therefore, non-rational animals intend an end.

**On the contrary.** Intending an end implies directing something to an end, and that is a job for reason. So, since non-rational animals do not have  15
reason, it appears that they do not intend an end.

**Reply.** As I said above [art. 1], to intend is to tend toward something, and of course both a mover and what is moved tend toward something. Thus, nature is said to intend an end in the sense in which something that is moved to an end by another is said to intend an end: nature is, as it were,  20
moved to its end by God, as an arrow is moved by the archer. And this is also the way in which non-rational animals intend an end, insofar as they are moved toward something by natural instinct. In another way, intending an end is something a mover does insofar as it directs some movement (whether its own or that of another) toward an end. Only reason can do  25
that. So in this second sense, non-rational animals do not intend an end; and this, as I have said [art. 1], is intending in its proper and principal sense.

**Response to 1.** This argument takes intending in the sense in which it belongs to what is moved toward an end.

**Response to 2.** Enjoyment, unlike intention, does not involve directing  30
something to an end; rather, it means absolute rest in the end.

**Response to 3.** Non-rational animals are not moved to an end as though they were entertaining the thought that by means of some movement they can achieve their end—as is true of someone who properly speaking intends something. Rather, because of a desire for the end that arises from natural  35
instinct, they are moved toward the end as though moved by another, just like other things that are moved naturally.

---

77. Parallel passage: *Sent.* II.38.3.

## Question 13. Choice, Which Is an Act of Will concerning Things That Are for the End

Next we need to examine the acts of will that have to do with things that are for the end. There are three: choice, consent, and use. Now choice is preceded by deliberation. First, then, we need to examine choice [Q13]; second, deliberation [Q14]; third, consent [Q15]; and fourth, use [Q16]. Concerning choice there are six questions:

Article 1. Of which power—will or reason—is choice an act?

Article 2. Does choice belong to non-rational animals?

Article 3. Is choice only of things that are for the end, or is it also sometimes of the end?

Article 4. Is choice only of things that we do?

Article 5. Is choice only of possible things?

Article 6. Do human beings choose out of necessity, or freely?

*Article 1. Is choice an act of will or of reason?*[78]

It seems that choice is not an act of will, but of reason:

1. Choice implies a comparison in which one thing is preferred to another, and comparing is something reason does. Therefore, choice is an act of reason.

5    2. It is the same power that both formulates syllogisms and draws conclusions. Now in the domain of action, formulating syllogisms is something reason does. So, since choice is, as it were, a conclusion in the domain of action (as is said in *Ethics* VII[79]), it seems that choice is an act of reason.

3. Ignorance does not pertain to the will but to a cognitive power. And
10  there is such a thing as ignorance in choice, as is said in *Ethics* III [1110b31]. Therefore, it seems that choice does not pertain to the will, but to reason.

**On the contrary.** The Philosopher says in *Ethics* III [1113a9] that "choice is a desire for things that are up to us." And desire is an act of will. Therefore, so is choice.

15  **Reply.** The word 'choice' implies something that pertains to reason or intellect and something that pertains to will. You see, the Philosopher says in *Ethics* VI [1139b4] that choice is "an appetitive understanding or an intellective appetite." But sometimes, when two things come together to compose a single whole, one of the two is like the formal cause with
20  respect to the other. For that reason Gregory of Nyssa says that choice "is neither appetite as such, nor deliberation alone, but something composed

---

78. Parallel passages: *ST* I.83.3; *Sent.* II.24.1.2; *On Truth* 22.15; *Comm. Ethics* III.6 and 9, VI.2.

79. See *Nicomachean Ethics* III.3, 1113a4.

of both. For just as we say that an animal is composed of soul and body, and is neither the soul as such nor the body alone, but both, so too in the case of choice."[80]

Now in the acts of the soul, it is important to note that an act that belongs essentially to one power or disposition receives its form and species from a higher power or disposition insofar as the lower power is directed by the higher. For example, if someone performs an act of courage out of love for God, the act is materially an act of courage but formally an act of charity. Now it is clear that reason precedes the will in a certain way and directs its act, insofar as the will tends toward its object in accordance with reason's direction, since the apprehensive power is what presents the appetitive power with its object. Thus, the act in which the will tends toward something that is proposed to it as something good is materially an act of will but formally an act of reason, because it is reason that directs the act toward an end. Now in such a case the substance of the act is the matter that is formed and directed by the higher power. Therefore, choice in its substance is not an act of reason but of the will; after all, choice is completed in a movement of the soul toward the good that is chosen. For this reason, it is evident that choice is an act of an appetitive power.

**Response to 1.** Choice implies a comparison that has been made beforehand. Choice is not essentially the comparison itself.

**Response to 2.** The conclusion of the syllogism that is made in the domain of action does indeed belong to reason. It is called a determination or judgment, and choice comes after it. And that is why the conclusion itself seems to belong to choice, as what follows from it.

**Response to 3.** We speak of ignorance in choice, not in the sense that choice itself is a kind of knowledge, but because there is ignorance of what should be chosen.

*Article 2. Does choice belong to non-rational animals?*[81]

It seems that choice belongs to non-rational animals:

1. Choice is "a desire for things on account of an end," as is said in *Ethics* III [1111b27, 1113a11]. And non-rational animals desire something on account of an end—after all, they act on account of an end, and they do so out of desire. Therefore, there is choice in non-rational animals.

2. The very word 'choice' seems to signify that one thing is preferred to others. And non-rational animals prefer one thing to another, as is clear

---

80. Nemesius, *On Human Nature* ch. 33.
81. Parallel passages: *Sent.* II.25.1 resp. 6 and 7; *Comm. Metaph.* V.16; *Comm. Ethics* III.5.

when, for example, a sheep eats one plant and spurns another. Therefore, there is choice in non-rational animals.

10    3. As is said in *Ethics* VI [1144a8], "It is through prudence that someone is good at choosing things that are for the end." And prudence belongs to non-rational animals; that is why, at the beginning of the *Metaphysics* [980b22], it says that "animals that cannot hear sounds, such as bees, have prudence without learning." This is also evident to observation: we see

15    incredible cleverness in what animals such as bees, spiders, and dogs do. When a dog is chasing a stag, if he comes to a three-way fork in the road, he will use his sense of smell to investigate whether the stag took the first or the second path; and if he discovers that the stag did not take either of them, he will confidently take the third path without investigating it, as

20    though arguing by process of elimination that the stag took that path, since he didn't take the other two and there are not any others. Therefore, it is clear that choice belongs to non-rational animals.

**On the contrary.** Gregory of Nyssa says that "children and non-rational creatures do indeed act voluntarily, but not by choice."[82] Therefore, there

25    is no choice in non-rational animals.

**Reply.** Since choice is accepting one thing in preference to another, it must be the case that choice has to do with a plurality of things that can be chosen. So choice has no place in things that are completely determined to one. Now there is a difference between sensory appetite and will, in

30    that (as is clear from what I said earlier [I-II.1.2 resp. 3]) sensory appetite is determined to one particular thing according to the order of nature, whereas the will—though it is indeed determined to one universal thing, namely, the good, according to the order of nature—is indeterminate with respect to particular goods. And so choosing belongs uniquely to the will

35    and not to the sensory appetite. Non-rational animals have only the sensory appetite, and consequently choice does not belong to non-rational animals.

**Response to 1.** Not just any desire for something on account of an end is called choice, but only when the desire involves some discrimination between one thing and another. And that can be the case only when the

40    desire can be drawn toward more than one thing.

**Response to 2.** A non-rational animal prefers one thing to another because its desire is naturally determined to that thing. That is why as soon as sense or imagination shows it something to which its desire is naturally inclined, it is moved to that thing, and only that thing, without

45    any choice. It is the same way in which fire is moved upward rather than downward, without any choice.

---

82. Nemesius, *On Human Nature* ch. 33.

**Response to 3.** As is said in *Physics* III [202a13], "Motion is an act of what is movable, caused by the mover." For that reason, the power of the mover is apparent in the motion of what is movable. Consequently, in all the things that are moved by reason, the direction of reason as mover is 50 apparent, even if the things themselves lack reason. For example, an arrow flies right to the target as a result of the archer's motion, just as if the arrow itself had reason directing it. And the same thing is seen in the movements of clocks and all works of human ingenuity that are produced by skill. Now all natural things bear the same relation to God's creativity that the prod- 55 ucts of human ingenuity bear to human skill. And for that reason order is apparent in things that move according to nature just as it is in things that are moved by reason, as is said in *Physics* II [196b17]. That is how it comes about that the activities of non-rational animals display certain kinds of cleverness, insofar as they have a natural inclination to certain highly 60 organized patterns of action that are directed by God's supreme creativity. It is on these grounds that some animals are even said to possess prudence or cleverness, and not because there is any reason or choice in them—as is evident from the fact that all creatures that have the same nature act in similar ways. 65

*Article 3. Is choice only of things that are for the
end, or is it sometimes also of the end itself?*[83]

It seems that choice is not only of things that are for the end:

1. The Philosopher says in *Ethics* VI [1144a20] that "virtue causes correct choice; but whatever must be done for the sake of that right choice is not the task of virtue but of some other power." Now that for the sake of which something is done is the end. Therefore, choice is of the end. 5

2. Choice implies accepting one thing in preference to another. Well, just as one can accept one thing in preference to another regarding things that are for the end, the same is true regarding different ends. Therefore, there can be choice of an end just as there is of things that are for the end.

**On the contrary.** The Philosopher says in *Ethics* III [1111b26] that "will 10 is of the end, whereas choice is of things that are for the end."

**Reply.** As I have already said [art. 1 resp. 2], choice follows a determination or judgment, which is like the conclusion of an operative syllogism. Accordingly, whatever is in the position of the conclusion of an operative syllogism falls within the scope of choice. Now in the domain of action, 15 the end is in the position of a principle rather than that of a conclusion, as the Philosopher says in *Physics* II [200a20]. Hence, an end as such does

---

83. Parallel passages: *Sent.* I.41.1; *Sent.* II.25.3 resp. 2; *On Truth* 24.1 resp. 20; *Comm. Ethics* III.5.

not fall within the scope of choice. But just as in speculative matters it is
perfectly possible for something that is the principle in one demonstration
20    or science to be the conclusion of another demonstration or science, so too
something that is the end in one action can be directed to something else
as a [more remote] end—and in this latter way it [the proximate end] falls
within the scope of choice. For example, in a doctor's work, health is the
end. Health does not fall within the scope of the doctor's choice; instead,
25    the doctor's choice presupposes health as its principle. But the health of
the body is directed toward the good of the soul; so whether a person is to
be healthy or unhealthy can fall within the scope of choice for someone
who is entrusted with the soul's salvation. For the Apostle says in 2 Corinthians 12:10, "When I am sick, then I am strong." By contrast, just as a
30    first indemonstrable principle cannot be the conclusion of any demonstration or science, so too the ultimate end does not fall within the scope of
choice in any way.

   **Response to 1.** The proper ends of the virtues are directed toward happiness as the ultimate end, and in that way there can be choice of those ends.
35    **Response to 2.** As I maintained above [I-II.1.5], there is only one ultimate end. So whenever there is more than one end, there can be choice
among the various ends insofar as they are directed toward a further end.

## Article 4. Is choice only of things that we do?

It seems that choice is not only about human acts:

   1. Choice is of things that are for the end. But it is not just acts that are
for the end; so are tools, as is said in *Physics* II [195a1]. Therefore, choices
are not only about human acts.
5    2. Action is distinguished from contemplation. But choice has a place
in contemplation as well, in that one opinion is chosen in preference to
another. Therefore, choice is not only of human acts.

   3. People are chosen for various offices, whether secular or ecclesiasti-
cal, by people who do not perform any act concerning them. Therefore,
10    choice is not only about human acts.

   **On the contrary.** The Philosopher says in *Ethics* III [1111b25] that "people choose only what they think they can bring about."

   **Reply.** In the same way that intention is of an end, choice is of things
that are for the end. Now an end is either an action or a thing. When a
15    thing is the end, some human action has to intervene, either insofar as
someone causes the thing that is the end, as a doctor causes health, which
is the doctor's end (which is why we also say that *causing* health is the doctor's end), or insofar as a person in some way makes use of or enjoys the
thing that is the end, as money, or the possession of money, is a greedy per-
20    son's end. And the same should be said of what is for the end: what is for

the end must be either an action, or a thing that involves some action by which one either causes what is for the end or else makes use of it. Thus, choice always concerns human acts.

**Response to 1.** Tools are directed to an end insofar as a person makes use of them for the sake of an end. 25

**Response to 2.** Within contemplation itself there is an act of intellect assenting to this opinion or that. What is distinguished from contemplation is *external* action.

**Response to 3.** Someone who chooses a bishop or ruler for a city chooses to *name* him for such a place of honor. Otherwise, if there were no action 30 he performed to establish that person as bishop or ruler, it would not be within his competence to make the choice. And similarly, we have to say that whenever one thing is chosen in preference to another, there is always some action on the part of the one choosing.

### Article 5. Is choice only of possible things?[84]

It seems that choice is not only of possible things:

1. Choice is an act of will, as has been said [art. 1]. And "there is will of impossible things," as is said in *Ethics* III [1111b22]. Therefore, there is also choice of impossible things.

2. Choice is of things that we do, as has been said [art. 4]. Therefore, if 5 what is chosen is impossible absolutely speaking, or just impossible for the one choosing, that is irrelevant to choice as such. Now we frequently are unable to carry out the things we choose, and thus they are impossible for us. Therefore, there is choice of impossible things.

3. No one attempts to do anything except by choice. And St. Benedict 10 says that if a prelate commands something impossible, we should attempt to do it.[85] Therefore, there can be choice of impossible things.

**On the contrary.** The Philosopher says in *Ethics* III [1111b20] that "there is no choice of impossible things."

**Reply.** As I have said [art. 4], our choices always concern things we do. 15 Now the things we do are possible for us. So we have to say that there is no choice except of things that are possible. Similarly, the basis for choosing something is that it leads to the end; and no one can attain an end by means of something that is impossible. One indication of this is that when people are deliberating and reach something that is impossible for them, 20 they stop, as though unable to go further. This is also abundantly clear from the way reason gets to that point in the first place. Remember, what is for the end (which is what choice is concerned with) is related to the end as

---

84. Parallel passage: *Comm. Ethics* III.5.
85. *Rule of Saint Benedict* 68.

a conclusion is related to a principle. Now it is obvious that an impossible
25   conclusion does not follow from a possible principle; accordingly, it cannot be the case that an end is possible unless what is for the end is possible.
And no one is moved toward what is impossible. Thus, no one would tend
toward an end unless the end appeared to be possible. For that reason, what
is impossible does not fall within the scope of choice.
30   **Response to 1.** Will is the intermediary between the intellect and external action: intellect presents the will with its object, and the will itself
causes an external action. So the principle of the will's movement is found
in the intellect, which apprehends something as good in general, but the
termination or completion of the will's act is identified with reference to
35   its ordering toward action, by which someone tends toward attaining the
thing. The will's movement, after all, is *from* the soul *toward* the thing. And
for this reason a complete act of will requires that there be something good
for someone that can be attained by acting—and this must be something
possible. Therefore, there is complete will only of something that is pos-
40   sible and is good for the one willing. But there is incomplete will of what
is impossible; some people call this "velleity" because someone *would will*
(*vellet*) the thing if it were possible. Now 'choice' designates an act of will
that is already determinate with respect to something that is to be done
by someone. Accordingly, there is no way for choice to be of anything but
45   what is possible.
**Response to 2.** Since the object of the will is the apprehended good,
we must make judgments about the object of the will according to how it
is apprehended. And so, just as sometimes there is will for something that
is apprehended as good but is not actually good, so too sometimes there is
50   choice of what is apprehended as possible for the one choosing but is not
actually possible for that person.
**Response to 3.** The point of this saying is that subordinates should not
rely on their own judgment to determine what is possible; instead, they
should abide by the judgment of their superior.

*Article 6. Do human beings choose out of necessity, or freely?*[86]

It seems that human beings choose out of necessity:
1. The end is related to possible objects of choice in the same way
that principles are related to things that follow from principles, as is clear
in *Ethics* VII [1151a16]. But conclusions are deduced from principles by
5   necessity. Therefore, it is by necessity that one is moved by an end to the
act of choosing.

---

86. Parallel passages: *ST* I.83.1; *Sent.* II.25.2; *On Truth* 22.6, 24.1; *On Evil* 6;
*Comm. On Interpretation* I.14.

2. As has been said [art. 1 resp. 2], choice follows reason's judgment about what is to be done. And in certain matters reason judges by necessity, because the premises are necessary. Therefore, it seems that choice, too, follows by necessity.

3. If two things are altogether equal, a person is not moved to one any more than to the other. For example, if someone who is starving has equally delicious food split into two portions at an equal distance from him, he will not be moved to one any more than to the other; so Plato said in explaining why the earth is at rest in the center, as is said in *On the Heavens* II [295b25]. And if what is taken to be equal cannot be chosen, much less can what is taken to be less be chosen. So if two or more things are put forward, among which one appears greater, it is impossible to choose any of the others. Therefore, the one that appears most outstanding is chosen by necessity. And *every* choice is only of that which appears better in some way. Therefore, every choice is a matter of necessity.

**On the contrary.** Choice is an act of a rational power; and according to the Philosopher, a rational power is open to opposites.[87]

**Reply.** Human beings do not choose out of necessity. The reason is that what possibly is not, is not necessary. Now we can derive an argument for the claim that not-choosing and choosing are both possible by reflecting on the twofold power that human beings have: we can will and not will, act and not act, and we can also will this or that and do this or that. The basis for this twofold power is the very faculty of reason itself. After all, the will can tend toward whatever reason can apprehend as good. And reason can apprehend not only willing or acting as good, but also not willing and not acting. Moreover, in every particular good, reason can pay attention to some aspect in which the thing is good and to a deficiency of good, which has the aspect of evil; accordingly, it can apprehend any such good either as something worthy of choice or as something to be avoided. It is only the complete good, happiness, that reason cannot apprehend as having any aspect of evil or deficiency; and for that reason, human beings will happiness by necessity and cannot will to be wretched or not to be happy. Of course, because choice is not of the end but of things that are for the end (as I have already explained [art. 5]), choice is not of the complete good, happiness, but of other particular goods. And for that reason human beings do not choose out of necessity, but freely.

**Response to 1.** It is not always the case that a conclusion proceeds from principles by necessity, but only when the principles cannot be true if the conclusion is not true. Similarly, it need not always be the case that an end necessitates someone to choose the things that are for the end, because not

---

87. *Metaphysics* VIII.2, 1046b8.

everything that is for the end is such that without it, the end cannot be attained; or, if it is such, it is not always considered under that description.

**Response to 2.** Reason's determination or judgment about what is to be
50   done concerns contingent things that can be done by us; and in such matters conclusions do not follow necessarily from principles that are necessary with an absolute necessity, but from principles that are only conditionally necessary, such as, "If something runs, it is in motion."

**Response to 3.** Even if two things are presented that are equal when
55   viewed in one way, there is nothing to prevent someone from paying attention to some feature in virtue of which one of the two is superior, and thus the will leans more to that one than to the other.

## Question 14. Deliberation, Which Precedes Choice

Next we need to investigate deliberation. Concerning this, there are six questions:

Article 1. Is deliberation an inquiry?

Article 2. Is deliberation about the end, or only about things that are for the end?

Article 3. Is deliberation only about things that we do?

Article 4. Is deliberation about all the things that we do?

Article 5. Does deliberation proceed by analysis?

Article 6. Does deliberation go on infinitely?

### Article 1. Is deliberation an inquiry?

It seems that deliberation (*consilium*) is not an inquiry:

1. Damascene says that "deliberation belongs to desire."[88] But inquiry is not a function of desire. Therefore, deliberation is not an inquiry.

2. Inquiry is something that a discursive intellect does; thus, it has no
5   place in God, whose cognition is not discursive, as was established in the First Part [I.14.7]. Yet deliberation is ascribed to God: after all, it is said in Ephesians 1:11 that "he works all things according to the deliberation of his will." Therefore, deliberation is not an inquiry.

3. Inquiry concerns matters that are in doubt, whereas counsel (*consil-*
10   *ium*) is given concerning things that are assuredly good. Thus, the Apostle says in 1 Corinthians 7:25, "Concerning virgins I have no commandment from the Lord, but I do give counsel." Therefore, counsel is not an inquiry.[89]

---

88. *On the Orthodox Faith* II.22.

89. Here *consilium*, translated elsewhere as "deliberation," is rendered as "counsel" in order to make sense of the passage quoted from 1 Corinthians.

**On the contrary.** Gregory of Nyssa says, "All deliberation is an investigation, but not every investigation is deliberation."[90]

**Reply.** Choice, as I have said [I-II.13.1 resp. 2; 13.3], follows reason's judgment about things to be done. Now there is a great deal of uncertainty in things to be done, since actions concern contingent singulars, which are uncertain because of their variability. And in doubtful and uncertain matters, reason does not make a judgment without some preliminary inquiry. Therefore, there has to be some inquiry on the part of reason before it makes a judgment about what it should choose, and this inquiry is called deliberation. That is why the Philosopher says in *Ethics* III [1113a11] that "choice is a desire for what has been deliberated about beforehand."

**Response to 1.** When the acts of two powers are ordered to each other, each act has something that belongs to the other power, and so each act can take its name from either power. Now it is clear that reason's act of giving direction about things that are for the end, and the will's act of tending toward those things in accordance with reason's direction, are ordered to each other. Accordingly, there is something of reason—namely, order—in the will's act of choice; and in reason's act of deliberation, something belonging to the will appears as *matter*, since deliberation is about things that someone wills to do, and also as *mover*, since it is because one wills the end that one is moved to deliberate about things that are for the end. And so the Philosopher says in *Ethics* VI [1139b4] that "choice is appetitive understanding," thus showing that both [appetite and understanding] concur in choice. Likewise, Damascene says that "deliberation is inquiring desire,"[91] thus showing that deliberation in some way belongs both to the will, which is the subject matter and the mover of the inquiry, and to reason, which conducts the inquiry.

**Response to 2.** When we use words to describe God, we must interpret them in a way that excludes all the deficiencies that are found in us. For example, in us there is knowledge of conclusions through discursive reasoning from causes to effects; but when we ascribe knowledge to God, that signifies certainty concerning all effects in their first cause, without any discursive reasoning. Similarly, deliberation is attributed to God with regard to the certainty of determination or judgment, which in us derives from the inquiry of deliberation. But that sort of inquiry has no place in God, so deliberation is not attributed to God in that regard. And in keeping with this, Damascene says that "God does not deliberate; deliberation is for someone who lacks knowledge."[92]

90. Nemesius, *On Human Nature* ch. 34.

91. *On the Orthodox Faith* II.22.

92. Ibid.

**Response to 3.** It is perfectly possible that wise and spiritual men judge some things to be good with absolute certainty, and yet the majority, or carnal people, are not certain that those things are good. And that is why
55  counsel is given concerning such things.

*Article 2. Is deliberation about the end, or
only about things that are for the end?*[93]

It seems that deliberation is not only about things that are for the end, but also about the end:

1. There can be inquiry concerning any areas about which there is uncertainty. And when it comes to matters of human action, there can be
5   uncertainty about the end, and not only about things that are for the end. So, since deliberation is inquiry concerning matters of action, it seems that there can be deliberation about the end.

2. Human actions are the subject matter of deliberation, and some human actions are ends, as is said in *Ethics* I [1094a4]. Therefore, there
10  can be deliberation about an end.

**On the contrary.** Gregory of Nyssa says that "deliberation is not about the end, but only about things that are for the end."[94]

**Reply.** In the domain of action, the end has the character of a principle, because it is on the basis of the end that we make judgments about things
15  that are for the end. Now a principle is not open to question; rather, in every inquiry principles have to be taken as given. So, since deliberation is a kind of questioning, deliberation is not about the end, but only about things that are for the end. Nonetheless, it can happen that something that is an end with respect to certain things is ordered to some further end,
20  much as something that is a principle of one demonstration is the conclusion of another. And for this reason, something that is taken as an end in one inquiry can be taken as something for the end in another inquiry; and in that way there can be deliberation about it.

**Response to 1.** What is taken as an end is already determinate. So as
25  long as it is treated as something uncertain, it is not being treated as an end. And for that reason, if there is deliberation about it, that will not be deliberation about an end, but about something that is for the end.

**Response to 2.** There is deliberation about human actions *insofar as* they are directed to some end. So if some human action is an end, it is, as
30  such, not something about which there is deliberation.

---

93. Parallel passages: *Sent.* III.35.2.4.1; *Comm. Ethics* III.8.
94. Nemesius, *On Human Nature* ch. 34.

*Article 3. Is deliberation only about things that we do?*[95]

It seems that deliberation is not only about things that we do:

1. 'Deliberation' implies a sort of conferring. Now one can confer with others even about immovable things we can do nothing about (for example, about the natures of things). Therefore, deliberation is not only about things that we do. 5

2. Sometimes people ask for consultation (*consilium*) about matters established by law—that is why such people are called consultants (*iurisconsulti*)—even though the ones who seek such consultation are not the ones responsible for making the laws. Therefore, deliberation (*consilium*) is not only about things that we do. 10

3. Some people are said to deliberate about future events, which are not within our control. Therefore, deliberation is not only about things we do.

4. If deliberation were only about things we do, no one would deliberate about things that someone else is supposed to do. But that is obviously false. Therefore, deliberation is not only about things that we do. 15

**On the contrary.** Gregory of Nyssa says, "We deliberate about things that are within our power and that we can do."[96]

**Reply.** Deliberation, properly speaking, implies several people conferring. The very name indicates this: 'deliberation' (*consilium*) means a sitting-together (*considium*), in that many people sit together in order to 20 confer as a group. One must keep in mind, however, that in particular contingent matters, there are many conditions or circumstances that have to be taken into account if there is to be any certain knowledge. These cannot easily be considered by one person, but they can be more effectively discerned by several people, since one person notices what does not occur 25 to someone else. By contrast, the investigation of necessary and universal matters is more absolute and simpler, so that one person can be more self-sufficient in carrying out such an investigation. That is why the inquiry of deliberation is properly concerned with contingent singulars. Now the knowledge of truth concerning contingent singulars is not so important 30 that it is desirable for its own sake, as is the knowledge of universals and necessary things; instead, it is desired because it is useful for acting, since actions concern contingent singulars. And that is why we should say that, properly speaking, deliberation is about things that we do.

**Response to 1.** Deliberation does not mean just any conferring, but con- 35 ferring about things to be done, as the argument just given shows.

---

95. Parallel passage: *Comm. Ethics* III.7.
96. Nemesius, *On Human Nature* ch. 34.

**Response to 2.** Even if what is laid down by law does not derive from the actions of those who seek advice, it does direct their actions, since the law's requirement is one reason for doing something.

40      **Response to 3.** Deliberation is not only about things that are done, but also about things that are directed toward acting. And that is why we say that people deliberate about future events, because by knowing future events someone acquires direction about what to do or what to avoid.

**Response to 4.** We deliberate about the actions of others insofar as they
45      are in some sense one with us: whether by a oneness of affection—thus, friends are as attentive to things that concern their friends as they are to what concerns themselves—or as an instrument, in the way that a principal agent and an instrumental agent are in effect one cause, because one acts through the other—thus, a master deliberates about things that his
50      servant will have to do.


*Article 4. Is deliberation about all the things that we do?*[97]

It seems that deliberation is about all the things that we do:

1. Choice is a desire for what has been deliberated about beforehand, as has been said [art. 1]. And choice is about all the things that we do. Therefore, so is deliberation.

5      2. Deliberation implies an inquiry on the part of reason. And in whatever we do that is not a result of the force of passion, we proceed from an inquiry on the part of reason. Therefore, there is deliberation about all the things that we do.

3. The Philosopher says in *Ethics* III [1112b16] that "if there is more
10      than one means to do something, we deliberate about which means is easiest and best; if there is only one means, we deliberate about how to carry it out." And for everything that is done, there is either one means or more than one means to do it. Therefore, there is deliberation about all the things that we do.

15      **On the contrary.** Gregory of Nyssa says that "there is no deliberation about actions that are done on the basis of learning or skill."[98]

**Reply.** Deliberation is a kind of inquiry, as I have said [art. 1]. Now we typically inquire about things that are subject to doubt; thus, reasoning that carries out an inquiry—which is called an argument—"brings about
20      certainty concerning what had been in doubt."[99] But there are two ways in which it can happen that something in the domain of human action is *not* subject to doubt. One is when there are determinate ways to get to

---

97. Parallel passages: *Sent.* III.35.2.4.1; *Comm. Ethics* III.7.

98. Nemesius, *On Human Nature* ch. 34.

99. Cicero, *On Invention* I.34.

determinate ends. That is how things are in skills that have fixed ways of operating: for example, a writer does not deliberate about how to form letters; that is determined by the skill of writing. The other is when it does not    25
much matter whether something is done in this way or that way. These are trivial things that offer very little help or hindrance in attaining the end; and if something is very little, reason regards it as though it were nothing. And so we do not deliberate about these two kinds of things, even though they are directed to an end, as the Philosopher says.[100] That is, we do not    30
deliberate about trivial things or about things that have to be done in a determinate way, as is the case in works of skill, apart from "certain skills that call for judgment, such as medicine, business, and such," as Gregory of Nyssa says.[101]

**Response to 1.** Choice presupposes deliberation because deliberation    35
produces a judgment or determination. So when the judgment or determination is obvious without any inquiry, there is no need for the inquiry of deliberation.

**Response to 2.** Reason does not inquire into things that are obvious; it just goes ahead and makes a judgment. And so the inquiry of deliberation    40
is not needed in all the things that we do through reason.

**Response to 3.** When something can be done by one means, but in more than one way, there is room for uncertainty, just as when something can done by more than one means. In such a case, there is a need for deliberation. But when not only the thing but the way of doing it is fixed, there    45
is no need for deliberation.

*Article 5. Does deliberation proceed by analysis?*[102]

It seems that deliberation does not proceed by analysis:

1. Deliberation is about things that we do. And our actions do not proceed by analysis, but more by synthesis, proceeding from simple things to composites. Therefore, deliberation does not always proceed by analysis.

2. Deliberation is an inquiry on the part of reason. Now reason fol-    5
lows the more appropriate order, beginning from what is prior and going on to what is later. So since past things are prior to present things, and present things are prior to future things, it seems that the right way to proceed in deliberation is from present and past things to future things. That is not a process of analysis. Therefore, deliberation does not pro-    10
ceed by analysis.

100. *Nicomachean Ethics* III.3, 1112b9.
101. Nemesius, *On Human Nature* ch. 34.
102. Parallel passage: *Comm. Ethics* III.8.

3. Deliberation is only about things that are possible for us, as is said in *Ethics* III [1112b26, b32]. But whether something is possible for us depends on what we can do, or cannot do, in order to achieve it. Therefore, in the
15    inquiry of deliberation, one ought to begin with present things.

**On the contrary.** The Philosopher says in *Ethics* III [1112b20] that "one who deliberates seems to question and analyze."

**Reply.** In every inquiry one has to begin from some principle. If the principle is prior not only in cognition but also in being, one will proceed
20    not by analysis but by synthesis; after all, proceeding from causes to effects is a process of synthesis, because causes are simpler than their effects. By contrast, if the principle, which is prior in cognition, is posterior in being, there will be a process of analysis; this is how it works when we make judgments about manifest effects by tracing them back to their causes. Now the
25    principle in the inquiry of deliberation is the end, which is in fact prior in intention but posterior in being. Accordingly, the inquiry of deliberation has to proceed by analysis, beginning from the intended aim that is in the future and going on until one reaches what is to be done right now.

**Response to 1.** Yes, deliberation is about actions, but our reasoning
30    about actions is based on the end. And so the order in reasoning about actions is the reverse of the order in acting.

**Response to 2.** Reason begins from what is prior *according to reason*, not always from what is prior in time.

**Response to 3.** We would not ask whether something that is to be done
35    for the sake of an end is possible if it were not congruent with the end. So we need to ask whether something is suitable for attaining the end before we investigate whether it is possible.

*Article 6. Does deliberation go on infinitely?*[103]

It seems that the inquiry of deliberation goes on infinitely:

1. Deliberation is an inquiry about particulars, since action concerns particulars. And singulars are infinite. Therefore, the inquiry of deliberation is infinite.
5    2. Deliberation includes inquiry not only into what ought to be done but also into how hindrances are to be overcome. Now every human action can be hindered, and the hindrance can be overcome through some human reasoning. Therefore, the inquiry into how to overcome hindrances lasts to infinity.
10    3. The inquiry of a demonstrative science does not go on infinitely because one must come to a stop with some self-evident principles that are altogether certain. Such certainty cannot be found in singular contingents,

---

103. Parallel passage: *Comm. Ethics* III.8.

which are variable and uncertain. Therefore, the inquiry of deliberation goes on infinitely.

**On the contrary.** "No one is moved to something that is impossible to attain," as is said in *On the Heavens* I [274b17]. And it is impossible to get to infinity. So if the inquiry of deliberation were infinite, no one would ever start deliberating. That is obviously false.

**Reply.** The inquiry of deliberation is *actually* finite at both ends: both on the side of the principle and on the side of the terminus. You see, the inquiry of deliberation has a twofold principle. One is its proper principle, which belongs to the domain of action, and that is the end: there is no deliberation about the end, but instead it is presupposed in deliberation as a principle, as I have said [art. 2]. The other principle is, as it were, taken from another domain, in much the same way that, in demonstrative sciences, one science takes certain presuppositions from another science and does not inquire into them. Principles of this sort, which are presupposed in the inquiry of deliberation, include anything taken from the senses—such as "this is bread" or "this is iron"—and any piece of universal knowledge taken from another speculative or practical science—such as "Adultery is forbidden by God" or "Human beings cannot live unless they receive appropriate nourishment." One who deliberates does not inquire about these things.

Now the terminus of the inquiry is what is in our power to do right here and now. After all, just as the end has the character of a principle, what is done for the sake of the end has the character of a conclusion. Thus, whatever is to be done first has the character of a final conclusion at which the inquiry comes to a halt. Nevertheless, there is nothing to prevent deliberation from being *potentially* infinite, since infinitely many things can arise for deliberation to inquire about.

**Response to 1.** Singulars are not *actually* infinite, but only *potentially* infinite.

**Response to 2.** Although human action can be hindered, there is not always a hindrance in place. And so there is not always a need to deliberate about how to overcome a hindrance.

**Response to 3.** In singular contingents, something can be taken as certain, even if not unqualifiedly certain, then as certain-for-now, insofar as it is a basis for action. After all, it is not necessary that Socrates is sitting, but it is necessary that he is sitting *so long as he is sitting*, and that can be accepted with certainty.

## Question 15. Consent, Which Is an Act of Will concerning Things That Are for the End

Next we need to investigate consent. Concerning this there are four questions:

Article 1. Is consent an act of an appetitive power or of an apprehensive power?

Article 2. Does consent belong to non-rational animals?

Article 3. Does consent concern the end or things that are for the end?

Article 4. Does consent to an act belong solely to the higher part of the soul?

### Article 1. Is consent an act of an appetitive power or of an apprehensive power?[104]

It seems that consent belongs solely to the apprehensive part of the soul:

1. In *On the Trinity* XII [ch. 12] Augustine attributes consent to higher reason, and 'reason' indicates an apprehensive power. Therefore, consent belongs to an apprehensive power.

5    2. To consent (*consentire*) is to sense together (*simul sentire*), and sensing is something that an apprehensive power does. Therefore, so is consenting.

3. Just as 'assent' indicates an application of the intellect to something, so does 'consent.' And assent belongs to the intellect, which is an apprehensive power. Therefore, consent also belongs to an apprehensive power.

10   **On the contrary.** Damascene says in Book II that "if someone makes a judgment but takes no delight, there is no decision,"[105] that is, consent. And delight belongs to an appetitive power. Therefore, consent also belongs to an appetitive power.

**Reply.** Consent implies an application of sense to something. Now what 
15  is properly called sense is what cognizes things that are present. After all, the imaginative power apprehends likenesses of bodily things, including likenesses of things that are absent; and the intellect, by contrast, apprehends universal notions, which it can apprehend equally well whether singulars are present or absent. And because an act of an appetitive power is 
20  a certain inclination to the thing itself, the appetitive power's application to a thing—its cleaving to the thing—receives, by a kind of analogy, the name 'sense,' to indicate that the appetitive power "experiences" the thing to which it cleaves, insofar as it is pleased with that thing. That is why Wisdom 1:1 says, "Sense the Lord in goodness." Accordingly, consent is an act 
25  of an appetitive power.

---

104. Parallel passage: *ST* I-II.74.7 resp. 1.

105. *On the Orthodox Faith* II.22.

**Response to 1.** As is said in *De anima* III [432b5], the will is in reason. Thus, when Augustine assigns consent to reason, he understands reason as including will.

**Response to 2.** Sensing, properly speaking, belongs to an apprehensive power; but by analogy with a certain sort of experience, it belongs to an appetitive power, as I have explained. 30

**Response to 3.** To assent (*assentire*) is, as it were, to sense toward something (*ad aliud sentire*); thus, it implies some distance from what is assented to. By contrast, to consent is to sense together; thus, it implies a sort of union with what is consented to. For this reason, the will, whose job it is to tend toward the thing itself, is more properly said to consent, whereas the intellect, whose operation does not involve movement toward the thing— but rather the reverse, as I explained in the First Part [I.16.1, 49.2]—is more properly said to assent (though it is not unusual for the words to be used interchangeably). It can also be said that the intellect assents insofar as it is moved by the will. 35

40

*Article 2. Does consent belong to non-rational animals?*[106]

It seems that consent belongs to non-rational animals:

1. Consent implies a determination of the appetite to one thing, and the appetites of non-rational animals are determined to one thing. Therefore, consent is found in non-rational animals.

2. If what is prior is taken away, what is posterior is also taken away. And consent precedes the carrying out of an action. So if there were no consent in non-rational animals, they wouldn't carry out any actions. That is obviously false. 5

3. Human beings are sometimes said to consent to acting from a passion such as desire or anger, and non-rational animals act from passion. Therefore, there is consent in them. 10

**On the contrary.** Damascene says that "after judgment, a human being affirms and loves what has been judged as a result of deliberation, and this is called a determination,"[107] that is, consent. Now deliberation is not in non-rational animals. Therefore, neither is consent. 15

**Reply.** Consent, properly speaking, is not in non-rational animals. The reason for this is that consent implies applying an appetitive movement to doing something. Now only someone who has power over the appetitive movement can apply that movement to doing something. (Here is an analogy: a stick does, in a sense, touch a stone; but only someone who has the power to move the stick can *apply* the stick to touching the stone.) But 20

---

106. Parallel passage: *ST* I-II.16.2.
107. *On the Orthodox Faith* II.22.

non-rational animals do not have any power over the movement of their
appetites; instead, such movement in them results from natural instinct.
Hence, a non-rational animal does indeed have appetite, but it does not
25   apply its appetitive movement to anything. And for that reason it is not
properly said to consent. Only a rational nature, which has power over
its appetitive movement and can apply it, or not apply it, to this or that, is
properly said to consent.

   **Response to 1.** In non-rational animals, appetite's determination to
30   something is purely passive. Consent, however, implies a determination of
appetite that is not purely passive, but instead is active.

   **Response to 2.** When what is prior is taken away, what is posterior *and
properly follows from that alone* is taken away. But if something can follow
from any of a number of things, then what is posterior is not taken away
35   just because one of the prior things is taken away. For example, hardening can be brought about by both heat and cold (fire hardens bricks; cold
hardens ice), so hardening is not automatically taken away just because
heat is taken away. And the carrying out of an act does not follow only
from consent; it also follows from the instinctual appetite of the sort that
40   is in non-rational animals.

   **Response to 3.** Human beings who act from passion have the power not
to follow passion; non-rational animals do not. So the cases are not similar.

*Article 3. Does consent concern the end?*

It seems that consent concerns the end:

   1. If one thing is for the sake of another, the latter counts for more than
the former. And we consent to things that are for the end for the sake of
the end. Therefore, consent has more to do with the end than with the
5   things that are for the end.

   2. The acts of intemperate people are their ends, just as the acts of virtuous people are *their* ends. And the intemperate consent to their own acts.
Therefore, consent can concern an end.

   3. Desire for things that are for the end is choice, as was said above
10   [I-II.13.1]. So if consent were only about things that are for the end, there
would seem to be no difference between consent and choice. This is clearly
false, as we find in Damascene, who says that choice happens after the
affirmation that he calls "determination."[108] Therefore, consent does not
concern only things that are for the end.

15   **On the contrary.** In the same passage Damascene says that determination, or in other words consent, is "when a human being affirms and loves

---

108. Ibid.

what has been judged on the basis of deliberation." And deliberation is only about things that are for the end. Therefore, so is consent.

**Reply.** 'Consent' indicates an application of an appetitive movement to something that is already in the power of the one who makes the applica- 20 tion. Now there is an order in the domain of action. First, there has to be some apprehension of an end, then desire for the end, then deliberation regarding things that are for the end, then desire for the things that are for the end. Now appetite tends naturally toward the ultimate end; as a result, the application of an appetitive movement to the [ultimate] end when it 25 is apprehended does not count as consent but as simple will. By contrast, things that come after the ultimate end, insofar as they are directed to the end, fall within the scope of deliberation; and thus there can be consent to them insofar as the appetitive movement is applied to what has been judged as a result of deliberation. But an appetitive movement toward the 30 end is not applied to deliberation; rather, deliberation is applied to it, since deliberation presupposes a desire for the end. By contrast, the desire for things that are for the end presupposes deliberation, and so the application of an appetitive movement to what is determined by deliberation is consent, properly speaking. Consequently, since deliberation is only about things 35 that are for the end, consent, properly speaking, concerns only things that are for the end.

**Response to 1.** We know conclusions through principles, but when it comes to principles, we do not have knowledge, but something greater: understanding. Similarly, we consent to things that are for the end; but 40 when it comes to the end itself, we do not have consent, but something greater: will.

**Response to 2.** Intemperate people have as their end the *pleasure* in the act; it is for the sake of that pleasure that they consent to the act, rather than for the sake of the act itself. 45

**Response to 3.** Choice adds a certain relation to consent: a preference of one thing over another. For that reason, after consent, there is still room for choice. You see, it can happen that deliberation turns up a number of ways of attaining the end, and if each of them is pleasing, there can be consent to each of them; but of the many that are pleasing, we choose one in pref- 50 erence to the others. If, however, there is only one that is pleasing, consent and choice will not differ in reality, but only conceptually; it will be called "consent" insofar as one finds the prospect of acting in this way pleasing, but "choice" insofar as one prefers it to other ways that are not pleasing.

### Article 4. Does consent to an act belong
### solely to the higher part of the soul?[109]

It seems that consent to an act does not always pertain to higher reason:

1. "Pleasure follows from activity and completes it, as beauty completes youth," as is said in *Ethics* X [1174b31]. Now consent to pleasure pertains to lower reason, as Augustine says in *On the Trinity* XII [ch. 12]. Therefore,
5   consent to an act does not pertain exclusively to higher reason.

2. An action to which we consent is said to be voluntary, and there are many capacities that produce voluntary actions. Therefore, it is not only higher reason that consents to an act.

3. Higher reason "forms intentions by gazing upon eternal things and
10  consulting them," as Augustine says in *On the Trinity* XII [ch. 7]. But quite often people consent to an act, not on the basis of eternal reasons, but on the basis of temporal reasons—or even on the basis of certain passions of the soul. Therefore, consent to an act does not pertain exclusively to higher reason.

15  **On the contrary.** In *On the Trinity* XII [ch. 12] Augustine says, "One cannot definitively make up one's mind to commit a sin unless the mind's intention, which has ultimate authority over moving the limbs to act or restraining them from acting, yields to the evil action and serves it."

**Reply.** A final determination always pertains to the one who is higher,
20  the one whose job it is to make judgments about the others. After all, as long as what is proposed remains to be judged, the final determination has not yet been made. Now it is clear that higher reason has the job of making judgments about all things, since we make judgments about sensible things through reason; and when it comes to things within the scope of human
25  reasons, we make judgments in accordance with divine reasons, which pertain to higher reason. And so as long it is unclear whether, according to divine reasons, something ought to be resisted or not, no judgment of reason counts as a final determination. Now the final determination about matters of action is consent to an act. And so consent to an act pertains to
30  higher reason—though in the sense of 'reason' that includes the will, as I said above [art. 1 resp. 1].

**Response to 1.** Consent to pleasure in an act pertains to higher reason, just as consent to an act does; but consent to pleasure in thought pertains to lower reason, just as consent to a thought does. And yet higher reason
35  does have judgment concerning thinking or not thinking, considered as an action, and likewise concerning the resulting pleasure. But insofar as thinking or not thinking is directed to some other action, it pertains to lower reason. After all, what is directed to something else belongs to a lower art

---

109. Parallel passages: *ST* I-II.74.7; *Sent.* II.24.3.1; *On Truth* 15.3.

or power than does the end to which it is directed. That is why the art that
concerns the end is called "architectonic" or "principal."                    40

**Response to 2.** Actions are called voluntary because we consent to
them; for that very reason, consent has to belong to no other power but
the will, from which the voluntary gets its name. And the will is in reason,
as I have explained [art. 1 resp. 1].

**Response to 3.** Higher reason is said to consent, not only because it    45
always moves to action in accordance with eternal reasons, but also because
it does not dissent from acting in accordance with eternal reasons.

## Question 16. Use, Which Is an Act of Will concerning Things That Are for the End

Next we need to investigate use. Concerning this there are four questions:

Article 1. Is use an act of the will?

Article 2. Does it belong to non-rational animals?

Article 3. Does it concern only things that are for the end, or does it
concern the end as well?

Article 4. What is the order of use with respect to choice?

### Article 1. Is use an act of the will?[110]

It seems that use is not an act of the will:

1. Augustine says in *On Christian Teaching* I [ch. 4] that "to use is to
refer the thing that is used to obtaining something else." Now referring one
thing to another is the task of reason, whose job it is to relate and to order.
Therefore, use is an act of reason; therefore, it is not an act of the will.    5

2. Damascene says that "human beings put forth effort toward acting,
and this is called impetus; then they use [their other powers], and this is
called use."[111] Now acting pertains to an executive power. But an act of the
will does not follow an act of the executive power; instead, the execution
[of the action] is what comes last. Therefore, use is not an act of the will.   10

3. In *On 83 Questions* [q. 30] Augustine says that "all created things
were made for human use, since reason, which was given to human beings,
makes use of all things by making judgments about them." Now to make
judgments about things created by God is the prerogative of speculative
reason; and speculative reason seems to be entirely separate from the will,   15
which is the origin of human acts. Therefore, use is not an act of the will.

**On the contrary.** In *On the Trinity* X [ch. 10] Augustine says, "To use
is to take up something into the power of the will."

---

110. Parallel passage: *Sent.* I.1.1.2.

111. *On the Orthodox Faith* II.22.

**Reply.** To use something means to apply it to some action. Hence, the
20 action to which we apply a thing is called the use of that thing. For example, riding is the use of a horse, and striking is the use of a stick. Now
we apply not only internal principles of acting but also external things to
action: internal principles such as the powers of the soul or the parts of
the body, as we apply the intellect to thinking and the eye to seeing, and
25 external things, as we apply a stick to striking. But it is clear that we apply
external things to action only through intrinsic principles, which are either
powers of the soul, or dispositions of those powers, or organs, which are
parts of the body. Now I showed above [I-II.9.1] that it is the will that moves
powers of the soul to their acts; that is what it is to apply those powers to
30 action. So it is clear that use belongs primarily and principally to the will
as what initiates movement, but to reason as directing action and to other
powers as carrying out action. Reason and other powers are related to the
will, which applies them to acting, as instruments to a principal agent.
And action is not properly attributed to an instrument, but to the principal
35 agent, as building is attributed to builders and not to their tools. Hence, it
is clear that use is properly an act of the will.

**Response to 1.** Yes, reason refers one thing to another, but the will is
what tends toward the thing that reason refers to something else. And that
is what we have in mind when we say that to use is to refer something to
40 another.

**Response to 2.** Damascene is speaking of use insofar as it belongs to
the executive powers.

**Response to 3.** Even speculative reason itself is applied to the work of
understanding, or judging, by the will. And so the speculative intellect,
45 just like the other executive powers, is said to use as something moved by
the will.

*Article 2. Does use belong to non-rational animals?*

It seems that use belongs to non-rational animals:

1. Enjoyment is nobler than use, because, as Augustine says in *On the
Trinity* X [ch. 11], "We use things that we refer to something else that is
to be enjoyed." Now enjoyment belongs to non-rational animals, as was
5 said above [I-II.11.2]. Therefore, all the more so does use belong to non-
rational animals.

2. To apply parts of the body to acting is to use the parts of the body.
And non-rational animals apply parts of their bodies to acting: for example,
they apply their feet to walking and their horns to striking. Therefore, use
10 belongs to non-rational animals.

**On the contrary.** In *On 83 Questions* [q. 30] Augustine says, "Only an
animal that has a share in reason can use something."

**Reply.** As I have said [art. 1], to use is to apply some principle of action to acting, just as to consent is to apply an appetitive movement to desiring something, as I have said [I-II.15.1–3]. Now only something that has judg-   *15* ment concerning a thing can apply that thing to another, and such judgment belongs only to something that has the knowledge to refer one thing to another, which is a function of reason. And so only a rational animal consents and uses.

**Response to 1.** Enjoyment implies an absolute movement of the appe-   *20* tite to its object, whereas use implies a movement to something as ordered to something else. Consequently, if use and enjoyment are compared in terms of their objects, enjoyment is indeed nobler than use, since what is desirable absolutely is better than what is desirable only as ordered to something else. But if they are compared in terms of the apprehensive power   *25* that precedes them, greater nobility is required for use, since ordering one thing to another is a function of reason, whereas even sense can apprehend something absolutely.

**Response to 2.** Animals act through the parts of their body by natural instinct, not because they have cognition of how the parts of their body are   *30* ordered to those actions. For that reason they are not properly said to apply the parts of their body to acting, or to use the parts of their body.

*Article 3. Can use also concern the ultimate end?*[112]

It seems that use also concerns the ultimate end:

1. Augustine says in *On the Trinity* X [ch. 11], "Everyone who enjoys, uses." And someone enjoys the ultimate end. Therefore, someone uses the ultimate end.

2. "To use is to take something up into the power of the will," as is said   *5* in the same passage. And nothing is taken up by the will any more than the ultimate end. Therefore, there can be use of the ultimate end.

3. Hilary says in *On the Trinity* II [ch. 1] that "eternity is in the Father, beauty is in the Image," that is, in the Son, and "use is in the Gift," that is, in the Holy Spirit. And the Holy Spirit, being God, is the ultimate end.   *10* Therefore, there can be use of the ultimate end.

**On the contrary.** In *On 83 Questions* [q. 30] Augustine says, "God is not rightly used, but enjoyed." Now God alone is the ultimate end. Therefore, the ultimate end is not to be used.

**Reply.** As I have said [art. 1], use means applying one thing to another.   *15* Now what is applied to something else has the character of something that is for the end. And that is why use is always of what is for the end. Accordingly, things that are suitable for an end are called "useful," and usefulness

112. Parallel passage: *ST* I-II.1.8.

itself is sometimes called "use." But it is important to note that there are
20   two ways of talking about the ultimate end: simply, and with respect to a
particular person. For since, as I have explained [I-II.1.8, 2.7], we speak of
an end sometimes as the thing itself and sometimes as the attainment or
possession of the thing (for example, a greedy person's end is either money
or the possession of money), it is clear that, speaking simply, the ultimate
25   end is the thing itself. After all, the possession of money is good only
because money is good. But speaking with respect to a particular person,
attaining money is the ultimate end: a greedy person seeks money solely in
order to have it. Therefore, speaking simply and properly, particular people
*enjoy* money because they locate their ultimate end in money; but insofar
30   as what they have in view in dealing with money is possessing it, they are
said to *use* money.

**Response to 1.** Augustine is speaking of use in a general sense, as indicating the ordering of an end to the enjoyment of that very end, the enjoyment that someone seeks concerning the end.

35   **Response to 2.** An end is taken up into the power of the will so that the
will might come to rest in it. Hence, this very resting in the end, which is
enjoyment, can, in this sense, be called a use of the end. By contrast, what
is for the end is taken up into the power of the will not only with an ordering to the use of what is for the end, but with an ordering to some other
40   thing in which the will comes to rest.

**Response to 3.** In Hilary's statement, 'use' is understood as resting in
the ultimate end, taking 'use' in the general sense in which someone is said
to use an end in order to obtain it, as I have explained [in the main reply].
Hence, in *On the Trinity* VI [ch. 10] Augustine says that "this delight, plea-
45   sure, felicity, or happiness is called 'use' by Hilary."

### Article 4. Does use precede choice?

It seems that use precedes choice:

1. The only thing that comes after choice is execution. And since use
pertains to the will, it precedes execution. Therefore, it also precedes
choice.

5   2. What is absolute is prior to what is relative. Therefore, what is less
relative is prior to what is more relative. Now choice implies two relations:
what is chosen is related both to the end and to the other things to which
it is preferred. Use, by contrast, implies only a relation to the end. Therefore, use is prior to choice.

10   3. The will uses the other powers insofar as it moves them. Now as has
been said [I-II.9.3], the will also moves itself. Therefore, it also uses itself
by applying itself to acting. But it does that when it consents. Therefore, in

that very consent there is use. And consent precedes choice, as has been said [I-II.15.3 resp. 3]. Therefore, so does use.

**On the contrary.** Damascene says that "after choice the will provides 15 impetus for action, and afterward, use."[113] Therefore, use follows choice.

**Reply.** The will has a twofold relation to what is willed. It has the first relation insofar as what is willed is, in a certain sense, *in* the one who wills, thanks to a certain proportion or order to what is willed. Accordingly, things that are naturally proportionate to some end are said to desire that 20 end naturally. But to have an end in this way is to have it imperfectly. And whatever is imperfect tends toward perfection. And so both natural appetite and voluntary appetite tend toward having an end in reality, which is to have it perfectly. And that is the second relation of the will to what is willed.

Now what is willed includes not only the end but also what is for the 25 end. The last thing that belongs to the will's first relation, with respect to what is for the end, is choice; after all, in choice the will's proportion is completed, so that it completely wills what is for the end. Use, by contrast, pertains to the will's second relation, by which it tends toward attaining the thing willed. Hence, it is clear that use follows choice—provided that we 30 take 'use' with reference to the will's using an executive power by moving it. Now since the will also moves reason in a certain way, and uses reason, we can also understand 'use' as concerning what is for the end, insofar as the reason of the person who refers it to the end attends to it. And use in this sense precedes choice. 35

**Response to 1.** The movement by which the will moves [the executive powers] to execute an action precedes the execution of the action, but it follows choice. And thus, since use pertains to that movement of the will, it is intermediate between choice and execution.

**Response to 2.** What is essentially relative is posterior to what is abso- 40 lute, but something to which relations are attributed need not be posterior. Indeed, the greater the priority of a cause, the more relations it has to numerous effects.

**Response to 3.** Choice precedes use if they are related to the same thing. But there is no reason that the use of one thing cannot precede 45 the choice of something else. And since the will's acts are reflected upon themselves, in any given act of the will we can find consent and choice and use: we might say that the will consents to its choosing, and consents to its consenting, and uses itself for consenting and choosing. And in every case, the acts that are ordered to what is prior are themselves prior. 50

---

113. *On the Orthodox Faith* II.22.

## Question 17. Acts Commanded by the Will

Next we need to investigate acts commanded by the will. Concerning this there are nine questions:

Article 1. Is command an act of the will or of reason?
Article 2. Does command belong to non-rational animals?
Article 3. What is the order of command and use?
Article 4. Are command and the commanded act a single act, or distinct acts?
Article 5. Is an act of the will commanded?
Article 6. Is an act of reason commanded?
Article 7. Is an act of the sensory appetite commanded?
Article 8. Is an act of the vegetative soul commanded?
Article 9. Is an act of the parts of the body commanded?

*Article 1. Is command an act of the will or of reason?*[114]

It seems that command is not an act of reason, but of the will:

1. Commanding is a kind of moving. After all, Avicenna says that there are four kinds of moving: perfecting, disposing, commanding, and advising.[115] And it is the will's role to move all the other powers of the soul, as
5    was said above [I-II.9.1]. Therefore, command is an act of the will.

2. Just as being commanded is proper to what is subordinate, commanding seems to be proper to what is preeminently free. Now the root of freedom is preeminently in the will. Therefore, it is the will's role to command.

3. An act follows immediately after a command. But an act does not
10   follow immediately after an act of reason; after all, it is not the case that anyone who judges that something is to be done, immediately does it. Therefore, command is not an act of reason, but of the will.

**On the contrary.** Gregory of Nyssa says—and so does the Philosopher— that the appetitive power obeys reason.[116] Therefore, it is reason's role to
15   command.

**Reply.** Command is an act of reason but presupposes an act of the will. In order to see clearly why this is, it is important to note that because acts of the will and of reason can be directed to each other—reason reasons about willing, and the will wills to reason—it can turn out that an act of the
20   will proceeds from an act of reason, and vice versa. And since the power of

---

114. Parallel passages: *ST* II-II.83.1; *On Truth* 22.12 resp. 4; *Quodlibet* IX.5.2; *Sent.* IV.15.4.1.1 resp. 3.

115. Avicenna, *Sufficientia* I.10.

116. Nemesius, *On Human Nature* ch. 16; Aristotle, *Nicomachean Ethics* I.13, 1102b26.

the prior act remains in the subsequent act, it sometimes happens that the will acts in virtue of retaining something of the power of a prior act of reason—as I said about use [I-II.16.1] and choice [I-II.13.1]—and, conversely, that reason acts in virtue of retaining something of the power of a prior act of the will. Now command is essentially an act of reason, since one who commands gives direction, by declaring or announcing, to the one who is commanded to do something; and to give direction by means of some sort of declaration is a job for reason.

Now there are two ways in which reason can declare or announce something. One way is absolutely. This kind of declaration is expressed by a verb in the indicative mood, as when someone says to another, "You must do this." Sometimes, by contrast, reason declares something to someone by moving that person toward it. And that kind of declaration is expressed by a verb in the imperative mood, as when someone says, "Do this." Now, as I explained above [I-II.9.1], among the powers of the soul, the will is the first mover in carrying out an act. So, since a secondary mover moves only by the power of the first mover, it follows that the very fact that reason moves something by commanding it derives from the power of the will. So we can conclude that command is an act of reason, but it presupposes an act of the will: by the power of the will, reason, through its command, moves something to carry out an act.

**Response to 1.** Commanding is not just any kind of moving; it is a kind of moving that works by declaring and announcing something to another. And that is a job for reason.

**Response to 2.** The will is the root of freedom in the sense that it is the *subject* of freedom; but reason is the root of freedom in the sense that it is the *cause* of freedom. You see, the reason that the will can be freely drawn to various things is that reason can have various conceptions of the good. And that is why philosophers define free choice as free judgment on the part of reason, implying that reason is the cause of freedom.

**Response to 3.** This argument shows that command is not an act of reason absolutely, but only with a certain motion, as has been explained [in the main reply].

*Article 2. Does command belong to non-rational animals?*

It seems that command belongs to non-rational animals:

1. According to Avicenna, "The power that commands movement is appetitive, and the power that carries out movement is in the muscles and nerves."[117] And both powers are in non-rational animals. Therefore, command is found in non-rational animals.

---

117. *Liber de anima* I.5.

2. Part of what it means to be a slave is to be commanded. And the body is to the soul as a slave is to a master, as the Philosopher says in *Politics* I [1254b4]. Therefore, the body is commanded by the soul, even in non-rational animals, who are composites of soul and body.

10    3. Through command a person causes an impetus toward an act. And impetus toward an act is found in non-rational animals, as Damascene says.[118] Therefore, command is found in non-rational animals.

**On the contrary.** Command is an act of reason, as has been said [art. 1]. And reason does not exist in non-rational animals. Therefore, neither

15  does command.

**Reply.** To command is simply to direct someone to do something, moving the one commanded through some sort of declaration. Now directing is distinctively an act of reason. Hence, it is impossible for there to be any sort of command in non-rational animals, who lack reason.

20    **Response to 1.** An appetitive power is said to command movement insofar as it moves reason, which commands. But that happens only in human beings. In non-rational animals, by contrast, the appetitive power does not, properly speaking, command, unless we take 'command' in a very broad sense as meaning "move."

25    **Response to 2.** In non-rational animals the body does indeed have the wherewithal to obey, but the soul does not have the wherewithal to command because it does not have the wherewithal to direct. And so non-rational animals do not fit the definition of commander and commanded, but merely of mover and moved.

30    **Response to 3.** The impetus toward act that is found in non-rational animals is different from the impetus found in human beings. You see, human beings bring about an impetus to act through the direction of reason, and that is why in human beings this impetus fits the definition of command. But in non-rational animals the impetus to act comes about

35  through natural instinct, because their appetite is naturally moved to pursue or flee from something as soon as they apprehend something suitable or unsuitable. Thus, they do not direct themselves to act; they are directed by another. And so there is impetus in them, but not command.

*Article 3. What is the order of command and use?*[119]

It seems that use precedes command:

1. Command is an act of reason that presupposes an act of the will, as was said above [art. 1]. Now use is an act of the will, as was said above [I-II.16.1]. Therefore, use precedes command.

---

118. *On the Orthodox Faith* II.22.
119. Parallel passage: *ST* I-II.16.4.

2. Command is one of the things that are directed to an end, and use 5
concerns things that are for an end. Therefore, it seems that use is prior
to command.

3. Every act of a power moved by the will is called use, because the
will uses the other powers, as was said above [I-II.16.1]. Now command is
an act of reason as moved by the will, as has been said [art. 1]. Therefore, 10
command is a kind of use. Now a genus is prior to its species. Therefore,
use is prior to command.

**On the contrary.** Damascene says that impetus to action precedes use,
and impetus to action is brought about by command.[120] Therefore, command precedes use. 15

**Reply.** The use of what is for an end, insofar as it is in the reason of the
one who refers it to the end, precedes choice, as I said above [I-II.16.4]. All
the more so, then, does it precede command. But the use of what is for an
end insofar as it is under the control of the executive power follows command, because the act of use is inseparably connected with the act of the 20
power that is used. For example, you do not use a stick before you in some
way do something with the stick. Command, by contrast, is not simultane-
ous with the act of what is commanded; rather, the command is naturally
prior—and sometimes temporally prior—to the command's being obeyed.
Thus, it is obvious that command is prior to use. 25

**Response to 1.** Not every act of the will precedes the act of reason
that is command. Rather, there is an act that precedes it—choice—and
another act that follows it—use. After deliberation has reached its conclusion, which is the judgment of reason, the will chooses; and after choice,
reason commands the power through which what has been chosen is to be 30
carried out. Then, finally, the will begins to use something, thus carrying
out reason's command. Sometimes, in fact, it is someone else's will, when
a person commands someone else; and sometimes it is the will of the one
commanding, when one commands oneself.

**Response to 2.** Just as acts are prior to powers, so are objects prior to 35
acts. Now the object of use is what is for the end. So the fact that command
itself is for the end actually supports the conclusion that command is prior
to use, rather than that it is posterior.

**Response to 3.** Just as an act of the will making use of reason for commanding precedes command itself, so too it can be said that some com- 40
mand of reason precedes the will's use of reason, insofar as the acts of these
powers are reflected back on each other.

---

120. *On the Orthodox Faith* II.22.

## Article 4. Are command and the commanded
act a single act, or distinct acts?[121]

It seems that the commanded act is not the same act as the command itself:

1. Distinct powers have distinct acts. And the commanded act and the command itself belong to distinct powers, since the power that commands is distinct from the one that is commanded. Therefore, the commanded act is not the same act as the command.

2. Things that can be separated from each other are distinct, since nothing is separated from itself. And sometimes the commanded act is separated from the command, since sometimes command comes first and then the commanded act does not follow. Therefore, command is a distinct act from the commanded act.

3. Things that are related as prior and posterior are distinct, and command is naturally prior to the commanded act. Therefore, they are distinct.

**On the contrary.** The Philosopher says that "where one thing exists on account of another, there is just one thing."[122] Now the commanded act exists only on account of the command. Therefore, they are one.

**Reply.** It is perfectly possible for things to be many in one respect and one in some other respect. In fact, *all* things that are many are one in *some* respect, as Dionysius says in the last chapter of *On the Divine Names* [13.2]. Nonetheless, it is important to note this difference: some things are many in an unqualified sense but one in a certain respect, whereas for other things the converse is true. Now 'one' and 'being' are said in the same way. And a being in an unqualified sense is a substance, whereas a being in a certain respect is an accident, or even a being of reason. And so things that are one according to substance are one in an unqualified sense and many in a certain respect. For example, a whole in the category of substance, composed of its integral or essential parts, is one in an unqualified sense; for a whole is a being and a substance in an unqualified sense, whereas its parts are beings and substances *in the whole*. By contrast, things that are distinct according to substance, and one in some accidental way, are distinct in an unqualified sense and one in a certain respect. For example, many human beings are one people, and many stones are one pile. This is the unity of composition or of order. Similarly, many individuals that are one in genus or species are many in an unqualified sense, but one in a certain respect; after all, to be one in genus or species is to be one as regarded in a certain way by reason.

121. Parallel passage: *ST* III.19.2.
122. Aristotle, *Topics* III.2, 117a18.

Now in the domain of natural things, a whole composed of matter and form—as a human being is composed of soul and body—is one natural being even though it has a multiplicity of parts. And in the same way, in human acts, the act of a lower power is related as matter to the act of a higher power insofar as the lower power acts in virtue of the higher power's moving it; for in this way the first mover's act serves as the form of the instrument's act. From this it is clear that command and the commanded act are one human act in the way that a whole is one, but it is many in terms of its parts.

**Response to 1.** If the powers were distinct and not ordered to each other, their acts would be distinct in an unqualified sense. But when one power is the mover of another, their acts are one in a way; after all, "the act of a mover and the act of what is moved are the same," as is said in *Physics* III [202a15].

**Response to 2.** The fact that command and the commanded act can be separated from each other shows that they are distinct *parts*. After all, the parts of a human being can be separated from each other, and yet they are one in the whole.

**Response to 3.** In cases where there are many parts that make up one whole, there is no reason one thing cannot be prior to another. For example, the soul is in a certain way prior to the body, and the heart is prior to the other parts of the body.

*Article 5. Is an act of the will commanded?*[123]

It seems that an act of the will is not commanded:

1. Augustine says in *Confessions* VIII [ch. 9], "The mind commands the mind to will, but it does not do it." And willing is an act of the will. Therefore, an act of the will is not commanded.

2. What can be commanded is what can understand a command. Now the will cannot understand a command; the will is, after all, distinct from the intellect, and the intellect is what understands. Therefore, an act of the will is not commanded.

3. If any act of the will is commanded, then by parity of reasoning all acts of the will are commanded. But if all acts of the will are commanded, there would have to be an infinite regress, since an act of the will precedes reason's act of command, as has been said [art. 1]. So if that act of will is in turn commanded, yet another act of reason precedes that command, and so on to infinity. And it is absurd for there to be an infinite regress. Therefore, an act of the will is not commanded.

123. Parallel passage: *Comm. Ethics* I.20.

**On the contrary.** Everything that is in our power is subject to our command. And an act of the will is preeminently in our power, since all of our acts are said to be in our power precisely to the extent that they are voluntary. Therefore, an act of the will is commanded by us.

20    **Reply.** As I have said [art. 1], command is nothing other than an act of reason that, presupposing some motion, directs something to act. Now it is clear that reason can direct an act of the will: just as it can judge that it is good to will something, it can also, by commanding, direct someone to will it. From this it is clear that an act of the will can be commanded.

25    **Response to 1.** As Augustine says in this very passage, when the mind commands itself *perfectly* to will, it does indeed will. That the mind sometimes commands and does not will comes about because it does not command perfectly. And an imperfect command comes about because reason is moved by different considerations to command or not to command, and
30    so it fluctuates between the two and does not command perfectly.

**Response to 2.** Among the parts of the body, a given part does not act only for itself, but for the whole body; thus, the eye sees for the whole body. And the same is true for the parts of the soul: the intellect does not understand only for itself, but for all the powers; and the will does not will only
35    for itself, but for all the powers. And so human beings command an act of will for themselves insofar as they have both understanding and will.

**Response to 3.** Because command is an act of reason, only acts that are subject to reason are commanded. Now the will's first act is not directed by reason, but instead by natural instinct or a higher cause, as was said above
40    [I-II.9.4]. And so there is no need for an infinite regress.

*Article 6. Is an act of reason commanded?*[124]

It seems that an act of reason cannot be commanded:

1. It seems absurd for something to command itself, and reason is what commands, as was said above [art. 1]. Therefore, an act of reason is not commanded.

5    2. What is *F* essentially is distinct from what is *F* by participation. Now a power whose act is commanded by reason is reason by participation, as is said in *Ethics* I [1102b13, b26]. Therefore, an act of the power that is reason essentially is not commanded.

3. An act that is commanded is one that is in our power. But knowing
10   and judging what is true, which are acts of reason, are not always in our power. Therefore, an act of reason cannot be commanded.

---

124. Parallel passage: *Virtues in General* 7.

**On the contrary.** What we do by free choice can be done by our command. And acts of reason are carried out through free choice; after all, Damascene says that "it is by free choice that human beings inquire, examine, judge, and dispose."[125] Therefore, acts of reason can be commanded.    15

**Reply.** Because reason reflects on itself, it can direct its own act just as it directs the acts of other powers. Consequently, reason's own act can be commanded. But it is important to note that an act of reason can be considered in two ways. One way is in terms of the exercise of the act. And in this way an act of reason can always be commanded, as when someone is    20
instructed to pay attention and use reason. The other way is in terms of the object; and we can note two acts of reason with respect to an object. The first is apprehending the truth about something. That is not in our power, since it comes about through the power of some natural or supernatural light. And so the act of reason with respect to apprehending the truth is not    25
in our power and cannot be commanded. The other act of reason is assenting to what reason apprehends. If, then, the things that are apprehended are the sort of things to which our intellect assents naturally, such as first principles, assent to them (or dissent from them) is not in our power, but a matter of the natural order. And so, properly speaking, they are not subject to command. By contrast, some things that are apprehended are not    30
so convincing that the intellect cannot either assent or dissent, or at any rate suspend assent or dissent, for some reason. And in those cases assent or dissent is in our power and is subject to command.

**Response to 1.** Reason commands itself in the same way that the will    35
moves itself, as was explained above [I-II.9.3]: each power reflects on its own act and tends from one act toward another.

**Response to 2.** Because of the diversity of objects that are subject to an act of reason, there is nothing to keep reason from participating in itself, in the way that cognition of conclusions participates in cognition    40
of principles.

**Response to 3.** The response to the third objection is clear from what has been said [in the main reply].

*Article 7. Is an act of the sensory appetite commanded?*[126]

It seems that an act of the sensory appetite is not commanded:

1. The Apostle says in Romans 7:15, "I do not do the good that I will," and the Common Gloss explains that human beings will not to desire, and

---

125. *On the Orthodox Faith* II.22.

126. Parallel passages: *ST* I.81.3; I-II.56.4 resp. 3, 58.2; *On Truth* 25.4; *Virtues in General* 4.

yet they desire.[127] Now desire is an act of the sensory appetite. Therefore,
5   an act of the sensory appetite is not subject to our command.

2. Corporeal matter obeys God alone when it comes to formal transmutation, as was established in the First Part [I.65.4, 91.2, 110.2]. And an
act of the sensory appetite involves a formal transmutation of the body,
namely, heat or cold. Therefore, an act of the sensory appetite is not sub-
10  ject to human command.

3. The proper mover of the sensory appetite is what is apprehended by
sense or imagination, and it is not always in our power to apprehend something by sense or imagination. Therefore, an act of the sensory appetite is
not subject to our power.

15  **On the contrary.** Gregory of Nyssa says that "the part that obeys reason
is divided into two: the desiderative and the irascible";[128] and these belong
to the sensory appetite. Therefore, an act of the sensory appetite is subject
to the command of reason.

**Reply.** An act is subject to our command insofar as it is in our power,
20  as I said above [art. 5 on contr.]. And so in order to understand how an act
of the sensory appetite is subject to the command of reason, we need to
investigate how such an act is in our power. Now you need to know that
the sensory appetite differs from the intellectual appetite, which is called
the will, in that the sensory appetite is a power of a bodily organ, whereas
25  the will is not. And every act of a power that makes use of a bodily organ
depends not only on the power of the soul but also on the disposition of the
bodily organ. For example, seeing depends on the power of sight and on the
condition of the eye, which either helps or hinders the power of sight. So
an act of the sensory appetite also depends not only on the appetitive power
30  but also on the disposition of the body. Now the aspect that depends on
the power of the soul follows apprehension; and because the imagination's
apprehension is particular, it is ruled by reason's apprehension, which is
universal, as a particular active power is ruled by a universal active power.
And so as far as this aspect goes, an act of the sensory appetite is subject
35  to the command of reason. By contrast, the condition and disposition of
the body is not subject to the command of reason. And so because of this
aspect the movement of the sensory appetite is not totally subject to the
command of reason. It also sometimes happens that a movement of the
sensory appetite is suddenly incited by something apprehended by imagi-
40  nation or sense, and then that movement is outside the command of reason, although reason could have stopped that movement if it had foreseen

---

127. The *Glossa ordinaria*, a twelfth-century compilation of patristic and medieval
glosses on the Bible.
128. Nemesius, *On Human Nature* ch. 16.

it. That is why the Philosopher says in *Politics* I [1254b5] that reason does not preside over the irascible and concupiscible appetites with dictatorial authority, like that of a master over his slave, but rather with constitutional or royal authority, which is exercised over free people who are not totally    45
subject to command.

**Response to 1.** That someone wills not to desire, and yet desires, results from the disposition of the body, by which the sensory appetite is prevented from totally obeying reason's command. That is why in the same passage the Apostle adds, "I see another law in my members, fighting against the    50
law of my mind." This also happens because of a sudden movement of desire, as I have explained [in the main reply].

**Response to 2.** There are two ways in which the condition of the body is related to an act of the sensory appetite: antecedently, as someone's body is disposed in such a way as to make that person especially susceptible to    55
this or that passion; and consequently, as when someone becomes flushed because of anger. An antecedent condition of the body is not subject to the command of reason, since it is either from nature or from some previous movement that cannot be instantaneously stopped. But a consequent condition does follow the command of reason, since it follows the local    60
motion of the heart, which is moved in various ways in keeping with the various acts of the sensory appetite.

**Response to 3.** Since a sense's apprehension requires an external sensible object, it is not always in our power to apprehend something by sense, but only if the object is present; and whether the object is present is not    65
always in our power. When an object is present, however, human beings can use their senses whenever they want, unless there is something wrong with the sense organ. By contrast, imagination's apprehension is subject to the direction of reason, according to the strength or weakness of the imaginative power. If someone cannot imagine the things that reason is    70
considering, this is either because they are not imaginable (for example, incorporeal things) or because of the weakness of the imaginative power, which results from some indisposition of the organ.

*Article 8. Is an act of the vegetative soul commanded?*[129]

It seems that acts of the vegetative soul are subject to the command of reason:

1. Sensory powers are nobler than the powers of the vegetative soul. Now the sensory powers of the soul are subject to the command of reason. Therefore, much more so are the powers of the vegetative soul.    5

---

129. Parallel passages: *ST* II-II.148.1 resp. 3; *ST* III.15.2 resp. 1, 19.2; *On Truth* 13.4; *Quodlibet* IV.11.1; *Sent.* II.20.1.2 resp. 3.

2. A human being is called a microcosm because the soul is in the body
in the same way that God is in the cosmos. And God is in the cosmos in
such a way that everything in the cosmos obeys his command. Therefore,
everything in a human being is subject to reason's command, even the
10   powers of the vegetative soul.

3. Praise and blame are applicable only to acts that are subject to the
command of reason. And there can be praise and blame, and virtue and
vice, in acts of the nutritive and generative powers, as is obvious in the case
of gluttony and lust and the virtues that are opposed to them. Therefore,
15   acts of these powers are subject to the command of reason.

**On the contrary.** Gregory of Nyssa says that "that which is not persuaded by reason is the nutritive and the generative."[130]

**Reply.** Some acts proceed from natural appetite, but some acts proceed
from animal or intellectual appetite: for you see, everything that acts has,
20   in some way, an appetite for an end. Natural appetite, however, does not
follow from any apprehension, as animal and intellectual appetite do. But
it is as an apprehensive power that reason issues commands. And so acts
that proceed from intellectual or animal appetite can be commanded by
reason, but not acts that proceed from natural appetite. And acts of the
25   vegetative soul are the kinds of acts that proceed from natural appetite,
which is why Gregory of Nyssa says that the generative and the nutritive
are called natural.[131] Accordingly, acts of the vegetative soul are not subject
to the command of reason.

**Response to 1.** The more immaterial an act is, the nobler it is, and
30   the more it is subject to the command of reason. So the very fact that the
powers of the vegetative soul do not obey reason shows that they are lowly.

**Response to 2.** The analogy holds in one respect—namely, that just
as God moves the cosmos, the soul moves the body. But it does not hold
in every respect. After all, the soul did not create the body from nothing,
35   as God created the world from nothing—which is why the world is totally
subject to God's command.

**Response to 3.** Virtue and vice, praise and blame, do not apply to the
acts of the nutritive or generative power, which are digestion and the forming of a human body. Rather, they apply to the acts of the sensory parts
40   that are directed toward acts of the generative or nutritive power, namely,
in desiring the pleasure of food and of sexual relations, and making use of
them in the right or wrong way.

130. Nemesius, *On Human Nature* ch. 22.
131. Nemesius, *On Human Nature* ch. 22.

### Article 9. Is an act of the parts of the body commanded?[132]

It seems that the parts of the body do not obey reason in their acts:

1. It is uncontroversial that the parts of the body are more distant from reason than are the powers of the vegetative soul. And the powers of the vegetative soul do not obey reason, as has been said [art. 8]. Therefore, much less do the parts of the body obey reason. 5

2. The heart is the principle of an animal's movement. And the heart's movement is not subject to the command of reason; after all, Gregory of Nyssa says that "the pulsative cannot be persuaded by reason."[133] Therefore, the movement of the parts of the body is not subject to the command of reason. 10

3. In *City of God* XIV [ch. 16] Augustine says that "the movement of the genital members is sometimes inopportune, happening when it is not desired; and yet at other times it abandons someone who longs for it, and though the mind is hot with lust, the body is cold." Therefore, the movements of the parts of the body do not obey reason. 15

**On the contrary.** In *Confessions* VIII [ch. 9] Augustine says, "The mind commands and the hand moves, and with such ease that one can scarcely distinguish the command from the obedience."

**Reply.** The parts of the body are organs of the powers of the soul. Accordingly, however the powers of the soul stand in relation to obeying 20 reason, that is how the parts of the body also stand. So, since the sensory powers are subject to the command of reason but the natural powers are not, all the movements of parts of the body that are moved by sensory powers are subject to the command of reason, whereas the movements of parts of the body that follow upon natural powers are not subject to the 25 command of reason.

**Response to 1.** The parts of the body do not move themselves; they are moved by powers of the soul. And some of those powers are closer to reason than are the powers of the vegetative soul.

**Response to 2.** In matters that pertain to intellect and will, what accords 30 with nature is found first, and other things are derived from that. For example, cognition of conclusions is derived from cognition of naturally known principles, and choice of things that are for the end is derived from the will for what is naturally desired. So too in bodily movements the principle is from nature. Now the principle of bodily movement is from the move- 35 ment of the heart. Hence, the heart's movement is from nature, not from will. You see, it follows as an essential accident of life, which comes from

---

132. Parallel passages: *ST* I.81.3 resp. 2; *ST* I-II.56.4 resp. 3; 58.2; *Power of God* 3.15 resp. 4; *Sent.* II.20.1.2 resp. 3.

133. Nemesius, *On Human Nature* ch. 22.

the union of soul and body, in the same way that the movement of heavy and light things follows from their substantial form, which is why the Phi-
40   losopher in *Physics* VIII [255b35] says that such things are moved by what generates them. That is why the movement of the heart is called "vital." Hence, Gregory of Nyssa says that just as the generative and the nutritive do not obey reason, neither does the pulsative, which is vital. Now "pulsa-tive" is what he calls the movement of the heart, which is made evident in
45   the pulsing of the veins

**Response to 3.** As Augustine says in *City of God* XIV [chs. 17, 20], the fact that the movement of the genital members does not obey reason is a punishment for sin: for its disobedience to God, the soul suffers the punishment of disobedience especially in that part of the body through
50   which original sin is transmitted to one's descendants. Yet because (as I will explain later [I-II.85.1 resp. 3]) nature is left to itself as a consequence of the disobedience of our first parents, having lost the supernatural gift that had been divinely bestowed on them, we still need to identify a natural reason why the movement of these parts in particular does not obey rea-
55   son. Aristotle assigns a cause in his book on the causes of the movements of animals. He says that the movements of the heart and the private parts are involuntary because such members are moved by some apprehension in the following way: intellect and imagination represent certain things that give rise to passions of the soul, and those passions in turn produce
60   movements of those members. But they are not moved in accordance with a dictate of reason or intellect. Why not? Because in order for those mem-bers to move, some natural alteration—heating or cooling—is required, and that alteration is not subject to the command of reason. And this happens in these two members in particular because both of them are, in a sense,
65   a separate animal, because they are principles of life, and a principle is the whole virtually. The heart is the principle of the senses; and the seminal power, which is the whole animal virtually, issues from the genital member. And so they have their own movements naturally, since principles have to be natural, as has been explained [resp. 2].

## Question 18. The Goodness and Badness of Human Acts

Next we need to investigate the goodness and badness of human acts: first, how a human action is good or bad; and second, the things that follow from the goodness or badness of human acts, namely, merit or demerit, sin, and fault. Concerning the first there are three things to investigate: first, the goodness and badness of human acts in general [Q18]; second, the good-ness and badness of interior acts [Q19]; and third, the goodness and bad-ness of exterior acts [Q20].

Concerning the goodness and badness of human acts in general, there are eleven questions:

Article 1. Is every act good, or are some acts bad?

Article 2. Does a human act derive its goodness or badness from its object?

Article 3. Does a human act derive its goodness or badness from a circumstance?

Article 4. Does a human act derive its goodness or badness from its end?

Article 5. Is any human act good or bad in its species?

Article 6. Does an act have goodness or badness in species because of its end?

Article 7. Is the species that is derived from the end contained in the species that derives from the object, as in a genus, or the reverse?

Article 8. Is any act indifferent in its species?

Article 9. Is any individual act indifferent?

Article 10. Does any circumstance put a moral act into a good or bad species?

Article 11. Does every circumstance that increases goodness or badness put a moral act into a good or bad species?

## Article 1. Is every human act good?[134]

It seems that every human act is good, and none is bad:

1. Dionysius says in *On the Divine Names* 4 [§20] that what is bad does not act except through the power of what is good. But nothing bad is done by the power of what is good. Therefore, no action is bad.

2. Things act only insofar as they are in actuality. And nothing is bad    5
insofar as it is in actuality, but insofar as some potentiality is deprived of actuality; after all, insofar as a potentiality is brought to completion in actuality, it is good, as is said in *Metaphysics* IX [1051a4, a29]. Therefore, every action is good, and none is bad.

3. What is bad cannot be a cause, except accidentally, as is evident from    10
Dionysius, *On the Divine Names* 4 [§20]. And every action has some effect in its own right (*per se*). Therefore, no action is bad; rather, every action is good.

**On the contrary.** The Lord says in John 3:20, "Everyone who acts badly hates the light." Therefore, some human actions are bad.    15

**Reply.** We should say the same thing about good and bad in actions that we say about good and bad in things, since each thing produces an action that corresponds to what the thing itself is like. Now among things, each thing has as much good as it has being, since good and being are

---

134. Parallel passage: *On Evil* 2.4.

20    convertible, as I said in the First Part [I.5.1, 5.3, 17.4 resp. 2]. And only God
has the complete fullness of his being as something unitary and simple,
whereas every other thing has the fullness of being suitable for it through a
plurality of features. That is how it happens that some things have being in
some respect and yet lack something of the fullness of being that is appro-
25    priate for them. For example, the fullness of human being requires being
a composite of soul and body, having all the powers and instruments of
cognition and motion. Someone who lacks any of these is lacking something of the fullness of human being. So a thing has as much goodness as
it has being, whereas to the extent that it lacks something of the fullness
30    of being, it also lacks goodness and is said to be bad. For example, blind
people have goodness in that they are alive, but their being unable to see
is a bad thing in them. Now if something had no being or goodness, it
could not be called either good or bad. But because fullness of being is
part of the very concept of good, if something lacks anything of the full-
35    ness of being appropriate to it, it will not be called good in an unqualified
sense, but only in a certain respect, insofar as it is a being—whereas it can
be called a being in an unqualified sense, and a non-being in a certain
respect, as I said in the First Part [I.5.1 resp. 1]. So what we should say is
that every action has goodness precisely insofar as it has being; but inso-
40    far as it lacks something of the fullness of being that is appropriate for a
human action, it lacks goodness and is said to be bad: for example, if it
lacks the determinate quantity prescribed by reason, or the appropriate
place, or something like that.

      **Response to 1.** What is bad acts through the power of something that
45    is good but deficient. After all, if there were nothing good there, there
would be no being either, and no action would be possible. But if it were
not deficient, it would not be bad. Accordingly, the action that is caused is
also a deficient good: it is good in a certain respect, but bad in an unqualified sense.

50    **Response to 2.** It is perfectly possible for something to be in actuality—and therefore to be able to act—in one respect, but to be deprived of
actuality—and thus to cause a deficient action—in some other respect. For
example, a blind person has in actuality the power of movement, so that
he can walk; but insofar as he lacks sight, which directs one in walking, he
55    suffers from a deficiency in walking by stumbling when he walks.

      **Response to 3.** Insofar as a bad action has goodness and being, it can
have an effect in its own right (*per se*). For example, adultery causes the
generation of a human being, not insofar as it departs from the ordering of
reason, but insofar as it involves the intercourse of male and female.

## Article 2. Does an action derive its
## goodness or badness from its object?[135]

It seems that an action does not derive its goodness or badness from its object:

1. The object of an action is a thing. But badness is not in things; it is in the use that sinners make of things, as Augustine says in *On Christian Teaching* III [ch. 12]. Therefore, a human action does not derive its good-   5
ness or badness from its object.

2. An object is the matter of an action, whereas a thing's goodness does not derive from its matter, but instead from its form, which is an actuality. Therefore, acts do not have goodness or badness because of their objects.

3. The object of an active power is related to action as effect to cause.   10
Now the goodness of a cause does not depend on its effect, but rather the converse. Therefore, a human action does not derive its goodness or badness from its object.

**On the contrary.** Hosea 9:10 says, "They have become abhorrent, like the things they loved." Now people become abhorrent to God because of   15
the badness of their deeds. Therefore, the badness of a deed comes from the bad objects that people love. And the same reasoning applies to the goodness of an action.

**Reply.** As I have said [art. 1], the goodness and badness of an action, just like the goodness and badness of other things, are a matter of their fullness,   20
or deficiency, in being. Now the first thing that seems to pertain to fullness of being is what gives a thing its species. And just as a natural thing gets its species from its form, an action gets its species from its object, just as a motion does from its terminus. And so just as a natural thing's first goodness derives from its form, which gives the thing its species, so too a moral   25
act's first goodness derives from a suitable object. Some people accordingly call this "goodness in genus": for example, making use of one's own possessions. And as in natural things the first badness is if the thing that is gener-
ated does not attain the specific form (for example, if what is generated is not a human being, but something else in place of a human being), so too   30
the first badness in moral acts is the badness that derives from the object: for example, taking someone else's possessions. And this is called "badness in genus," understanding the word 'genus' as meaning "species," in the same way that we call the whole human species "the human race" (*genus*).

**Response to 1.** Yes, external things are good in themselves, but they   35
are not always properly suited to this or that action. And so, considered as objects of such actions, they do not count as good.

---

135. Parallel passages: *ST* I-II.19.1; *Sent.* II.36.5.

**Response to 2.** An object is not matter from which, but matter about which. Insofar as it gives an act its species, it plays the role of form.

40      **Response to 3.** The object of a human action is not always the object of an active power. After all, an appetitive power is passive in a way, in that it is moved by what is desirable; and yet it is a principle of human acts. Nor are the objects of active powers always effects, but only when they are already transmuted by the active power. For example, food that has been

45      transmuted is an effect of the nutritive power, but food that has not yet been transmuted is the matter on which the nutritive power acts. Now from the fact that an object is in some way an effect of an active power it follows that it is the terminus of the power's action, and consequently that it gives the action its form and species—because a motion gets its species from

50      its terminus. And although the goodness of an action is not caused by the goodness of its effect, it is nonetheless true that an action is said to be good because it can bring about a good effect. And thus this very proportion of the action to its effect is the reason that the action is good.

### Article 3. Is an action good or bad because of a circumstance?[136]

It seems that an action is not good or bad because of a circumstance:

1. Circumstances "stand around" (*circumstant*) an action as something outside it, as has been said [I-II.7.1]. Goodness and badness, by contrast, are in the things themselves, as is said in *Metaphysics* VI [1027b25]. Therefore,

5      an action is not good or bad because of circumstances.

2. The goodness or badness of an act is the main thing considered in the study of morals. But circumstances, which are accidents of acts, seem to fall outside the scope of art, since no art considers what is accidental, as is said in *Metaphysics* VI [1026b4]. Therefore, the goodness or badness of

10      an action does not derive from a circumstance.

3. What belongs to a thing in virtue of its substance is not attributed to that thing *per accidens*. And good and bad belong to an action in virtue of its substance, since an action can be good or bad in genus, as has been said [art. 2]. Therefore, good and bad do not belong to an action in virtue

15      of a circumstance.

**On the contrary.** The Philosopher says in the *Ethics* [1104b26] that "the virtuous act as they should, and when they should, and so on for the other circumstances." Therefore, with respect to each vice, those who are vicious act in a contrary way: they act when they should not, where they

20      should not, and so on for the other circumstances. Therefore, human acts are good or bad because of their circumstances.

---

136. Parallel passages: *On Evil* 2.4 resp. 5; *Sent.* II.36.5.

**Reply.** In natural things, the substantial form that gives a thing its species does not confer the complete fullness of perfection that the thing ought to have; rather, a great deal is added by accidents over and above the substantial form: for example, in human beings, by figure, color, and similar accidents. And if a suitable proportion of any of these accidents is lacking, the result is something bad. The same thing is true in the case of action. The species alone does not give an act complete goodness; items over and above the species, which are like accidents, add something. And appropriate circumstances are such items. So if anything required for the appropriate circumstances is lacking, the action will be bad.

**Response to 1.** Circumstances are outside an action in the sense that they do not belong to the essence of the action, but they are in the action itself as accidents. Similarly, the accidents that are in natural things are outside the things' essences.

**Response to 2.** Not all accidents are related *per accidens* to their subjects. Some are *per se* accidents, and those fall within the scope of the relevant art. And that is how circumstances of acts are considered in the study of morals.

**Response to 3.** Since good and being are convertible, just as we speak of 'being' both substantially and accidentally, so too goodness is attributed to something both in virtue of its essential being and in virtue of its accidental being, both in natural things and in moral actions.

*Article 4. Do goodness and badness in*
*human acts derive from the end?*[137]

It seems that goodness and badness in human acts do not derive from the end:

1. Dionysius says in *On the Divine Names* 4 [§19] that "no one acts with evil in view." So if an act derived its goodness or badness from the end, no action would be bad. That is obviously false.

2. The goodness of an act is something that is *in* the act. An end, by contrast, is an *extrinsic* cause. Therefore, an action is not called good or bad because of its end.

3. It is possible for a good act to be directed to a bad end, as when someone gives to charity for the sake of an empty reputation, and conversely for a bad act to be directed to a good end, as when someone steals in order to give the money to the poor. Therefore, an action is not good or bad in virtue of its end.

---

137. Parallel passage: *Sent.* II.36.5.

**On the contrary.** Boethius says in the *Topics* that "if a thing's end is
15    good, the thing itself is also good; and if a thing's end is bad, the thing
itself is also bad."[138]

**Reply.** Things stand the same way with respect to goodness as they do
with respect to being. Now there are some things whose being does not
depend anything else, and to investigate them it is sufficient to consider
20    their being absolutely. But there are other things whose being does depend
on something else, and to investigate them one must consider the cause
on which they depend. Now a thing's goodness depends on its end in the
same way that a thing's being depends on its agent and its form. Accordingly, in the case of the divine persons, we do not consider any aspect of
25    goodness derived from the end, because their goodness does not depend
on another. Human actions, by contrast, as well as other things whose
goodness depends on another, do derive some goodness from the end on
which they depend, over and above the absolute goodness that exists in
them. Thus, there is a fourfold goodness in a human action that we can
30    investigate. First, there is goodness in genus, insofar as it is an action,
because (as I have said [art. 1]) an action has as much goodness as it has
action and being. Second, there is goodness in species, which an action
gets from having a suitable object. Third, there is goodness according to
the circumstances that are, in effect, its accidents. And the fourth is good-
35    ness according to the end, which depends on the action's relation to the
cause of goodness.

**Response to 1.** The good that someone has in view when acting is not
always a genuine good; sometimes it is a genuine good, but sometimes it
is an apparent good. When the end is an apparent good, the act is bad.
40    **Response to 2.** Although the end is an extrinsic cause, the appropriate
proportion and relation to the end inhere in the action.

**Response to 3.** It is perfectly possible for an action to have one of the
goodnesses we have discussed but lack another. That is how it can turn out
that an action that is good in its species or according to its circumstances is
45    directed to a bad end, or vice versa. Nonetheless, an action is not unqualifiedly good unless all the goodnesses concur in it, since "any single defect
causes badness, whereas goodness is caused by a perfect cause," as Dionysius says in *On the Divine Names* 4 [§30].

---

138. *De topicis differentiis* II (1189).

*Article 5. Do good and bad acts differ in species?*[139]

It seems that good and bad moral acts do not differ in species:

1. Goodness and badness work the same way in acts as they do in things, as has been said [art. 1]. And goodness and badness do not make for different species in things: after all, a good person and a bad person are the same in species. Therefore, goodness and badness do not make for different species in acts either.

2. Since badness is a privation, it is a non-being. And a non-being cannot be a difference, according to the Philosopher in *Metaphysics* III [998b22]. Therefore, since a difference constitutes a species, it seems that an act's being bad does not place it in a species. And so goodness and badness do not make for different species of human acts.

3. Acts of diverse species have diverse effects. But a good act and a bad act can produce effects of the same species. For example, both adultery and marital intercourse generate a human being. Therefore, a good act and a bad act do not belong to different species.

4. Sometimes acts are said to be good or bad because of their circumstances, as has been explained [art. 3]. But circumstances are accidents, so they do not give an act its species. Therefore, human acts do not differ in species because of their goodness and badness.

**On the contrary.** According to the Philosopher in *Ethics* II [1103b21], "similar dispositions produce similar acts." And a good disposition differs in species from a bad disposition: for example, generosity and wastefulness. Therefore, a good act and a bad act also differ in species.

**Reply.** Every act gets its species from its object, as I explained above [art. 2]. That means that some difference in the object will make for a different species in the acts. But it is important to note that a difference in the object that makes for a different species in an act when referred to one active principle may not make for a different species when referred to another active principle. Why? Because only what is *per se* constitutes a species; what is *per accidens* does not. And a difference in the object that is *per se* for one active principle is *per accidens* for another principle. For example, the difference between cognizing color and cognizing sound is *per se* for the senses, but not for the intellect. Now we speak of goodness and badness in human acts with reference to reason, because, as Dionysius says in *On the Divine Names* 4 [§32], the good for human beings is to be in accordance with reason, whereas what is bad is to be opposed to reason. After all, what is good for any given thing is what belongs to the thing according to its form, and what is bad is what is opposed to the order of its

---

139. Parallel passages: *ST* I.48.1 resp. 2; *ST* I-II.1.3; *SCG* III.9; *On Evil* 2.4; *Virtues in General* 2 resp. 3; *Sent.* II.40.1.

form. It is therefore evident that the difference between good and bad in
an object is a *per se* difference when considered with reference to reason,
that is, according to whether the object is suitable or not suitable to reason. Now acts are called *human* acts, or *moral* acts, insofar as they are from
reason. Hence, it is evident that goodness and badness make for different
species in moral acts, because *per se* differences make for different species.

**Response to 1.** Even in natural things, the goodness and badness that
are in accord with nature and contrary to nature make for different species in nature. After all, a dead body and a living body do not belong to the
same species. Similarly, goodness, as according with reason, and badness,
as contrary to reason, make for different moral species.

**Response to 2.** Badness implies, not an absolute privation, but a privation with respect to some particular potentiality. After all, an act is said
to be bad in its species, not because it has no object at all, but because it
has an object that does not suit reason: for example, taking away someone
else's possessions. Thus, insofar as the object is something positively, it can
establish the species of a bad act.

**Response to 3.** Marital intercourse and adultery do differ in species
with reference to reason, and they have effects that differ in species, since
one of them deserves praise and reward whereas the other deserves blame
and punishment. They do not, however, differ in species with reference to
the generative power; and, so considered, their effects belong to one and
the same species.

**Response to 4.** Sometimes a circumstance makes for an essential difference of the object as related to reason, and in that case it can give a
moral act its species. And that has to be the case whenever a circumstance
changes an act from good to bad, since a circumstance does not make an
act bad unless it is opposed to reason.

*Article 6. Does the goodness or badness that derives
from the end make for a difference in species?*[140]

It seems that the goodness or badness that derives from the end does not
make for a difference in species for acts:

1. Acts get their species from the object, and the end does not count as
an object. Therefore, the goodness and badness that derive from the end
do not make for a different species of act.

2. What is *per accidens* does not constitute a species, as has been said
[art. 5]. And being directed to a particular end is an accident of an act, for
example, that someone gives to charity for the sake of an empty reputation.

---

140. Parallel passage: *Sent.* II.40.1.

Therefore, the goodness and badness that derive from the end do not make
for different species of acts. 10

3. Acts that belong to different species can be ordered to one end: for
example, acts of different virtues, and of different vices, can be directed to
the end of an empty reputation. Therefore, the goodness and badness that
derive from the end do not make for different species of acts.

**On the contrary.** It was shown above [I-II.1.3] that human acts get their 15
species from the end. Therefore, the goodness and badness that derive from
the end make for different species of acts.

**Reply.** The reason that certain acts are called human acts is that they
are voluntary, as I said above. Now there are two sorts of voluntary acts:
the interior act of will and the exterior act. Each of these acts has its own 20
object. The end is properly the object of the interior voluntary act, whereas
the object of the exterior act is what the act has to do with. So, just as the
exterior act gets its species from the object it has to do with, the interior
act of will gets its species from the end as its proper object. Thus, what
the will does provides the form for the exterior act, since the will uses the 25
bodily members as instruments for the purpose of acting, and the only
reason exterior acts even count as moral is that they are voluntary. And so
the species of human acts are considered formally according to their end,
but materially according to the object of the exterior act. That is why the
Philosopher says in *Ethics* V [1130a24] that "someone who steals in order 30
to commit adultery is, speaking *per se*, more adulterer than thief."

**Response to 1.** The end does indeed count as an object, as has been
said [in the main reply].

**Response to 2.** Even if being ordered to such-and-such an end is an
accident of an exterior act, it is not an accident of the interior act of will, 35
which stands as form to the matter of the exterior act.

**Response to 3.** When acts of several different species are directed to
one end, the exterior acts do indeed belong to various different species, but
there is a single species for the interior act.

*Article 7. Is the species that derives from the
end contained in the species that derives from
the object, as in a genus, or the reverse?*

It seems that the species of goodness that derives from the end is contained
in the species of goodness that derives from the object in the way that a
species is contained in a genus: for example, when someone wills to steal
in order to give to charity:

1. Acts have their species from their object, as has been said [arts. 2, 6]. 5
And it is impossible for anything to be contained in some other species that
is not contained in its own species, since one and the same thing cannot

be in diverse species unless one of those species is subordinate to the other. Therefore, the species that derives from the end is contained in the species

10    that derives from the object.

2. An ultimate difference always constitutes a most specific species. But the difference that derives from the end seems to be posterior to the difference that derives from the object, since an end has the character of something ultimate. Therefore, the species that derives from the end is

15    contained as a most specific species within the species that derives from the object.

3. The more formal a difference is, the more species-determining it is, since a difference stands to a genus as form to matter. Now the species that derives from the end is more formal than the species that derives from the

20    object, as has been said [art. 6]. Therefore, the species that derives from the end is contained within the species that derives from the object, as a most specific species is contained within a subordinate genus.

**On the contrary.** For each genus there are determinate differences. But acts that belong to the same species based on their object can be directed

25    to indefinitely many ends: for example, theft can be directed to indefinitely many good or bad purposes. Therefore, the species that derives from the end is not contained in the species that is derived from the object as in a genus.

**Reply.** There are two ways in which the object of an exterior act can be

30    related to the will's end: as intrinsically ordered toward the end, in the way that fighting well is intrinsically ordered toward victory, or as accidentally ordered toward the end, in the way that taking what belongs to someone else is accidentally ordered toward giving to charity. Now as the Philosopher says in *Metaphysics* VII [1038a9], the differences that divide a genus

35    and constitute the species of that genus should divide the genus intrinsically. If they divide the genus accidentally, the division does not proceed correctly—for example, if someone were to divide *animal* into *rational* and *non-rational* and then divide *non-rational animal* into *winged* and *non-winged*, since *winged* and *non-winged* are not intrinsically determinative of

40    *non-rational*. Instead, here is a correct way to carry out a division: among animals, some have feet and some do not; among animals that have feet, some have two feet, some have four, and some have many—these [the different numbers of feet] are intrinsic determinations of the prior difference [having feet]. So when the object is not intrinsically ordered toward the

45    end, the specific difference that derives from the object is not intrinsically determinative of the difference that derives from the end; nor is the latter intrinsically determinative of the former. Accordingly, neither of these species is subordinate to the other; instead, in such a case a moral act falls within two disparate species, as it were. That is why we say that someone

50    who steals in order to fornicate commits two offenses in a single act.

If, by contrast, the object is intrinsically ordered toward the end, one of the previously discussed differences is intrinsically determinative of the other. In that case, one of these species is contained under the other. But we still need to figure out which difference is determinative of which. In order to see clearly why this is, the first thing to pay attention to is that a 55 difference is more specific to the extent that it derives from a more particular form. Second, the more universal an agent is, the more universal is the form that comes from that agent. And third, the more remote an end is, the more it is the prerogative of a more universal agent: for example, victory, which is the ultimate end of an army, is the end intended by the 60 supreme commander, whereas the direction of this or that regiment is the end intended by one of the subordinate officers. And it follows from these considerations that the specific difference that derives from the end is more general, and the difference that derives from an object that is intrinsically ordered toward such an end is a specific difference of that more general dif- 65 ference. After all, the will, whose proper object is the end, is the universal mover of all the powers of the soul, whose proper objects are the objects of particular acts.

**Response to 1.** In terms of its substance, a thing cannot be in two species neither of which is contained in the other. But in terms of its addi- 70 tional features, a thing can be contained in diverse species. For example, in terms of its color, this fruit is contained in one species, the species of white things; and in terms of its odor, it is contained in another, the species of good-smelling things. And similarly, acts that in terms of their substance belong to one natural species can be assigned to two species on 75 the basis of additional moral characteristics, as I explained above [I-II.1.3 resp. 3].

**Response to 2.** The end is the very last in terms of execution, but it is first in reason's intention, and that is what counts in determining the species of moral acts. 80

**Response to 3.** A difference stands to a genus as form to matter insofar as it makes the genus exist in actuality. But the genus is also understood as more formal than the species insofar as it is more absolute and less contracted. That is why the parts of a definition are placed in the genus of formal cause, as is said in the *Physics* [194b26]. And in this respect, the 85 genus is a formal cause of the species, and the more general it is, the more formal it will be.

*Article 8. Is any act indifferent in species?*[141]

It seems that no act is indifferent in species:

1. Bad is a privation of good, according to Augustine.[142] Now privation and possession are immediate opposites, according to the Philosopher.[143] Therefore, there is no act that is indifferent in its species, as if there were
5    some condition in between good and bad.

2. Human acts get their species from the end or object, as has been said [art. 6]. Now every object, and every end, is either good or bad. Therefore, every human act is either good or bad in species. Therefore, no act is indifferent in species.

10    3. As has been said [art. 1], an act is said to be good because it has the appropriate perfection of goodness, or bad because it lacks something of that perfection. Now it has to be the case that any act either has the complete fullness of goodness or lacks something of that goodness. Therefore, it has to be the case that every act is either good or bad in species, and no
15    act is indifferent in species.

**On the contrary.** Augustine says in *On the Lord's Sermon on the Mount* [II.18] that "some deeds are intermediate; they can be done either with a good mind or with a bad mind. It is rash to judge such deeds." Therefore, some acts are indifferent in species.

20    **Reply.** As I have said [arts. 2, 5], every act gets its species from its object; and a human act, which is called a moral act, gets its species from the object as related to the principle of human acts, which is reason. Accordingly, if the object of an act includes something that is consonant with the order of reason, the act will be good in species: for example, giving charity
25    to someone in need. By contrast, if the object includes something that is incompatible with the order of reason, the act will be bad in species: for example, stealing, which is taking someone else's possessions. But it is possible for the object of an act not to include anything that relates to the order of reason at all: for example, picking up a stick from the ground, walking
30    through a field, and so forth. Such acts are indifferent in species.

**Response to 1.** There are two kinds of privation. One is complete privation. This leaves nothing and takes away everything, as blindness completely takes away vision, darkness completely takes away light, and death completely takes away life. There can be nothing intermediate between
35    this privation and its opposite in a thing that can take on either. The other privation, by contrast, is partial. This is the way in which sickness is a privation of health: sickness does not completely take away health, but it is sort of

---

141. Parallel passages: *ST* I-II.18.2; *On Evil* 2.5; *Sent.* II.40.4.
142. *Enchiridion* ch. 11.
143. *Categories* 10, 12b26.

a step along the road toward the complete destruction of health that death brings about. And so, since this kind of privation leaves something, it is not always immediately opposed to possession. And this is the way in which bad   40
is a privation of good, as Simplicius says in his commentary on the *Categories* [ch. 10], because it does not take away all good, but leaves some. For that reason there can be something intermediate between good and bad.

**Response to 2.** Yes, every object or end has some *natural* goodness or badness; but that does not always imply *moral* goodness or badness, which   45
depends on how the object is related to reason, as I have explained [in the main reply]. And moral goodness or badness is what we are talking about here.

**Response to 3.** Not every feature of an act belongs to its species. So even though an act might not have everything that is required for its complete   50
goodness simply by reason of its species, that does not mean that the act is bad in species, or that it is good. Thus, human beings are neither virtuous nor vicious just because of their species.

*Article 9. Is any individual act indifferent?*[144]

It seems that some individual act is indifferent:

1. Every species does, or at least can, include some individual as a member. And some act is indifferent in species, as has been said [art. 8]. Therefore, some individual act can be indifferent.

2. Individual acts produce dispositions that correspond to those acts, as   5
is said in *Ethics* II [1103b21]. And there is such a thing as an indifferent disposition. After all, in speaking about certain people, such as the even-tempered and the wasteful, the Philosopher says in *Ethics* IV [1121a26] that they are not bad; and yet clearly they are not good either, because they fall short of virtue. And so as far as their dispositions go, they are indifferent.   10
Therefore, some individual acts are indifferent.

3. Moral goodness pertains to virtue and moral badness to vice. But it sometimes happens that a person performs an act that is indifferent in species and does not direct it to an end of either virtue or vice. Therefore, it happens that an individual act is indifferent.   15

**On the contrary.** Gregory says in a homily, "An idle word is one that lacks the usefulness of righteousness, or the reason of just necessity or pious usefulness."[145] And an idle word is bad, since human beings must give an account of an idle word on the day of judgment, as is said in Matthew 12:36. But if a word does not lack the reason of just necessity or pious use-   20
fulness, it is good. Therefore, every word is either good or bad. Therefore,

---

144. Parallel passages: *On Evil* 2.5; *Sent.* I.1.3 resp. 3, II.40.5, IV.26.1.4.
145. Gregory the Great, *Homiliae in evangeliis* I.6.

by parity of reasoning, every other act is either good or bad as well. Therefore, no individual act is indifferent.

    **Reply.** It sometimes happens that an act that is indifferent in species
25  is good or bad taken individually. The reason for this is that a moral act,
as I have said [art. 3], has goodness not only from its object, from which
it gets its species, but also from its circumstances, which are like its accidents, just as an individual human being has certain individual accidents
that do not belong to human beings in virtue of their species. And it has
30  to be the case that every individual act has some circumstance that draws
it toward good or bad, at least on the part of the intention of the end. You
see, since it is reason's job to direct, if an act that proceeds from deliberative reason is not directed to an appropriate end, that very fact makes the
act repugnant to reason, and the act is bad. If, however, it is ordered to an
35  appropriate end, it is consonant with the order of reason and hence is good.
Now, necessarily, an act either is or is not directed to an appropriate end.
So, necessarily, every human act that proceeds from deliberative reason is,
taken individually, either good or bad. On the other hand, if it does not proceed from deliberative reason but from some sort of imagination, as when
40  someone strokes his beard or moves a hand or a foot, such an act is not
properly speaking moral or human, since an act's being moral or human
derives from reason. And thus it will be indifferent in the sense that it falls
outside the genus of moral acts.

    **Response to 1.** There are different ways in which an act can be indif-
45  ferent in species. One way is for an act to be indifferent precisely because
of its species. And for this kind of indifference, the argument succeeds.
But then no act is indifferent in species in this way, because there is no
object of a human act that cannot be directed either to something good or
to something bad through its end or through some circumstance. Another
50  way an act can be indifferent in species is that its species alone does not
make the act either good or bad, and accordingly it can be made good or
bad by something else. It is like the way human beings are not white or
black simply in virtue of their species, but their species also does not make
them not white or not black, so either whiteness or blackness can come
55  upon a human being from a source other than the principles of the species.

    **Response to 2.** The Philosopher says that a bad person, properly speak-
ing, is one who is harmful to other people. And on that basis he says that
wasteful people are not bad, because they do not harm anyone but themselves. And the same goes for all others who do not harm their neighbors.
60  By contrast, we are using 'bad' here in a general sense, for whatever is
repugnant to reason. And in that sense, every individual act is either good
or bad, as I have explained [in the main reply].

    **Response to 3.** Every end intended by deliberative reason pertains to
the goodness of some virtue or the badness of some vice. For example, in

someone who directs his body to the good of virtue, whatever he does in a   65
properly ordered way to sustain or refresh his body is directed to the good
of virtue. And the same thing is clear in other cases.

### Article 10. Does any circumstance determine<br>the species of a good or bad act?[146]

It seems that a circumstance cannot determine the species of a good or
bad act:

1. The species of an act comes from its object. Circumstances are not
objects. Therefore, circumstances do not give an act its species.

2. Circumstances are related to a moral act as accidents, as has been   5
said [I-II.7.1]. And accidents do not determine a species. Therefore, circumstances do not determine any species of good or bad.

3. A single thing does not belong to more than one species, but a single
act has more than one circumstance. Therefore, a circumstance does not
place an act in a particular species of good or bad act.   10

**On the contrary.** Place is a circumstance, and place puts a moral act
in a particular species of bad act: stealing from a sacred place is sacrilege.
Therefore, a circumstance places a moral act in a particular species of
good or bad act.

**Reply.** Just as the species of natural things are determined by natural   15
forms, the species of moral acts are determined by forms as conceived by
reason, as is evident from what I have said thus far [art. 5]. But because
nature is determined to one and there can be no infinite regress (*processus*)
in nature, one must arrive at some ultimate form from which the specific
difference is taken, after which there can be no further specific difference.   20
And that is why in natural things what is accidental to some thing cannot
be taken as a difference that determines a species. By contrast, the working (*processus*) of reason is not determined to some one thing; instead,
whatever point it reaches, reason can still work further. And so, in one act
there can be something that is taken as a circumstance over and above the   25
object that determines the act's species; yet in some further act, reason, in
directing the act, regards that same thing as a central feature of the object
that determines the act's species. For example, the act of taking away someone else's possession gets its species from the description "someone else's
possession"; that is what places the act in the species *theft*. And if, beyond   30
this feature, the act's place or time comes into consideration, it is regarded
as a circumstance. But reason can also give direction concerning place or
time or what have you, and so it can happen that an act's place is regarded
as contrary to the order of reason—for example, that reason directs that no

146. Parallel passages: *ST* I-II.18.5 resp. 4, I-II.73.7; *On Evil* 2.6–7; *Sent.* IV.16.3.2.3.

35    wrong should be done to a sacred place. Consequently, taking someone
      else's possession from a sacred place adds a special repugnance to the order
      of reason. And therefore place, which previously was regarded as a circum-
      stance, is now regarded as a central feature of the object, and one that is
      repugnant to reason. And in this way, whenever a circumstance is relevant
40    to a particular direction of reason, either for or against, it has to be the case
      that the circumstance gives a species to a moral act, either good or bad.
          **Response to 1.** A circumstance gives an act its species insofar as the cir-
      cumstance is regarded as a feature of the object, as I have said [in the main
      reply], and as being, in effect, a specific difference of the object.
45        **Response to 2.** If a circumstance remains in the role of a circumstance,
      it does not give an act its species, because it has the character of an acci-
      dent; but insofar as it is transformed into a central feature of the object, it
      does give an act its species.
          **Response to 3.** Not every circumstance places a moral act in a particular
50    species of good or bad act, because not every circumstance involves some
      harmony or disharmony with reason. And that is why the fact that a single
      act has more than one circumstance need not imply that a single act is in
      more than one species. Of course, there is actually nothing absurd about
      a single moral act's being in more than one moral species, even disparate
55    moral species, as I have explained [art. 7 resp. 1].

                    *Article 11. Does every circumstance relevant to*
                    *goodness or badness give a species to an act?*[147]

      It seems that every circumstance relevant to goodness or badness gives a
      species to an act:
          1. Good and bad are specific differences of moral acts. Therefore, what-
      ever makes a difference to the goodness or badness of a moral act changes
5     its specific difference, and that changes its species. And whatever adds to
      the goodness or badness of an act makes a difference to its goodness or bad-
      ness and therefore changes its species. Therefore, every circumstance that
      adds to the goodness or badness of an act determines a species.
          2. Either an additional circumstance has in itself some aspect of good-
10    ness or badness, or it does not. If it does not, it cannot add to the goodness
      or badness of an act: what is not good cannot make something better, and
      what is not bad cannot make something worse. If, however, it does have
      in itself some aspect of goodness or badness, it thereby has some species
      of good or bad. Therefore, every circumstance that increases goodness or
15    badness determines a new species of good or bad.

      _____

      147. Parallel passages: *ST* I-II.73.7; *On Evil* 2.7; *Sent.* IV.16.3.2.3.

3. According to Dionysius in *On the Divine Names* 4 [§30], "Badness is caused by individual defects." Now every circumstance that increases badness has its own defect. Therefore, every such circumstance adds a new species of sin. And by the same reasoning, every circumstance that increases goodness seems to add a new species of good, just as each unit added to a 20 number makes a new species of number; and the good, after all, consists in number, weight, and measure.

**On the contrary.** More and less do not make for a difference in species. But more and less are circumstances that add to goodness or badness. Therefore, not every circumstance that adds to goodness or badness places 25 a moral act in a species of good or bad act.

**Reply.** As has been said [art. 10], a circumstance puts a moral act into a species of good or bad act insofar as it bears on some particular direction of reason. Now it sometimes happens that a circumstance does not bear on reason's direction about what is good or bad except as presupposing some 30 other circumstance from which the moral act gets its species of good or bad. For example, taking away a lot or a little of something does not bear on reason's direction about what is good or bad except as presupposing some other feature through which the act has badness or goodness—for example, that what is taken away is someone else's possession, which is repugnant to 35 reason. Accordingly, taking away a lot or a little of someone else's possession does not make for a different species of sin. It can, however, make the sin greater or less. And similar considerations hold for other bad or good acts. Hence, not every circumstance that adds to goodness or badness changes the species of a moral act. 40

**Response to 1.** In things that can become more or less intense, a difference in intensity does not make for a difference in species. For example, the difference between more and less white is not a difference in the species of color. And similarly, what causes a difference in the intensity of good or bad does not cause a difference in the species of moral act. 45

**Response to 2.** Sometimes a circumstance that makes a sin worse or increases the goodness of an act does not have any goodness or badness in itself, but only through its connection with some other feature of the act, as I have explained [in the main reply]. And for that reason it does not give the act a new species; it just increases the goodness or badness that derives 50 from that other feature of the act.

**Response to 3.** Not every circumstance causes a particular defect in its own right, but through its connection with something else. And similarly, a circumstance does not always add a new perfection, except through its relationship with something else. And as such, even though it increases 55 goodness or badness, it does not always change the species of good or bad.

## Question 19. The Goodness of the Interior Act of the Will

Next we need to investigate the goodness of the interior act of the will. Concerning this there are ten questions:

Article 1. Does the will's goodness depend on the object?
Article 2. Does it depend *only* on the object?
Article 3. Does it depend on reason?
Article 4. Does it depend on the eternal law?
Article 5. Does mistaken reason oblige?
Article 6. Is a will that follows mistaken reason, contrary to God's law, bad?
Article 7. Does the will's goodness concerning things that are for the end depend on the intention of the end?
Article 8. Does how good or bad the will is follow how good or bad the intention is?
Article 9. Does the will's goodness depend on conformity to the divine will?
Article 10. Must the human will conform to the divine will with respect to what it wills in order to be good?

### Article 1. Does the will's goodness depend on the object?

It seems that the will's goodness does not depend on the object:

1. Will can only be of what is good, since what is bad is outside the scope of the will, as Dionysius says in *On the Divine Names* 4 [§32]. So if the goodness of the will were judged on the basis of its object, it would follow
5    that every will would be good, and no will would be bad.

2. Goodness is found first of all in the end. Hence, an end's goodness, as such, does not depend on anything else. Now according to the Philosopher in *Ethics* VI [1140b6], "a good action is an end, but making is never an end," because making is always directed to the thing made as its end.
10   Therefore, the goodness of an act of will does not depend on any object.

3. Things that are *F* make other things *F*. Now the will's object is good with the goodness of nature, so it cannot confer moral goodness on the will. Therefore, the will's moral goodness does not depend on the object.

**On the contrary.** The Philosopher says in *Ethics* V [1129a9] that jus-
15   tice is that by which some will just things, and by the same logic, virtue is that by which some will good things. And a good will is one that accords with virtue. Therefore, a will possesses goodness because someone wills what is good.

**Reply.** Good and bad are intrinsic differences of an act of will, because
20   good and bad pertain to the will intrinsically, just as true and false pertain to reason intrinsically, and true and false are intrinsic differences of an act of reason, so that we say that an opinion is true or false. Hence, good

will and bad will are acts that differ in species. And as I have explained [I-II.18.5], acts differ in species because of their objects. And so good and bad in acts of will are properly derived from the objects.                    25

**Response to 1.** Will is not always of what is genuinely good; sometimes it is of what is only apparently good. An apparent good does indeed have some aspect of good, but it is not fit to be desired in an unqualified sense. And for that reason acts of will are not always good; instead, sometimes they are bad.                    30

**Response to 2.** Although an act can be the ultimate end for human beings in one sense, such an act is not an act of will, as I explained earlier [I-II.1.1 resp. 2].

**Response to 3.** What is good is presented to the will by reason as an object, and insofar as it is within the scope of reason's direction, it belongs    35
to the domain of morals and causes moral goodness in an act of will. Reason, after all, is the principle of human and moral acts, as I explained above [I-II.18.5].

### Article 2. Does the will's goodness depend only on its object?

It seems that the will's goodness does not depend only on its object:

1. The end is more closely connected to the will than it is to any other power. Yet acts of other powers derive goodness not only from the object but also from the end, as is clear from things said above [I-II.18.4]. Therefore, the will's act likewise derives goodness not only from the object, but    5
also from the end.

2. The goodness of an act is not only from the object but also from circumstances, as was said above [I-II.18.3]. And it can happen that a difference in circumstances makes for a difference in the goodness or badness of an act of will: for example, that someone wills when he should and where    10
he should, and how much he should, and how he should, or as he should not. Therefore, the will's goodness does not depend only on the object, but also on circumstances.

3. Ignorance of circumstances excuses badness in the will, as was maintained above [I-II.6.8]. And that would not be the case unless the will's    15
goodness and badness depended on circumstances. Therefore, the will's goodness and badness depend on circumstances, and not only on the object.

**On the contrary.** As was said above [I-II.18.10 resp. 2], an act does not get its species from circumstances as such. But good and bad are specific    20
differences of an act of will, as has been explained [art. 1]. Therefore, the will's goodness and badness do not depend on circumstances, but only on the object.

**Reply.** In any genus, the more prior something is, the simpler it is, and
25   the fewer things it consists in. For example, the first bodies are simple. And
so we find that things that are first in a given genus are in some way simple
and consist in one thing. Now the principle of goodness and badness in
human acts is from an act of will, so the will's goodness and badness derive
from some one thing, whereas the goodness and badness of other acts can
30   derive from various different things. And the one thing that is the principle
in a given genus is not *per accidens* but *per se*, since everything that is *per
accidens* rests on something that is *per se* as its principle. Consequently, the
will's goodness depends solely on that one thing that is the *per se* cause of
goodness in an act, namely, the object—not on the circumstances, which
35   are accidents of an act.

**Response to 1.** The end is the object of the will, but not of the other
powers. So with respect to an act of the will, there is no difference between
the goodness that derives from the object and the goodness that derives
from the end, as there is in the acts of the other powers, except perhaps
40   accidentally, insofar as one end depends on another end and one will on
another will.

**Response to 2.** If the will's object is good, no circumstance can make
the will bad. So there are two ways to understand the claim that someone
wills something good when he should not or where he should not. One
45   way is to take the circumstance with reference to what is willed. In that
case, the will's object is not good, because willing to do something when
it should not be done is not willing something good. The other way is to
take the circumstance with reference to the act of willing. And in that case
it is impossible for someone to will what is good when he should not, since
50   human beings should always will what is good, except perhaps accidentally,
insofar as by willing *this* good someone is kept from willing some good that
he ought to be willing at that time. And in that scenario, the badness is not
a result of his willing that good, but of his not willing the other good. And
a similar account holds for the other circumstances.

55   **Response to 3.** Ignorance excuses badness in the will insofar as circumstances bear on what is willed—that is, insofar as someone is ignorant of
the circumstances of the act that he wills.

*Article 3. Does the will's goodness depend on reason?*

It seems that the will's goodness does not depend on reason:

1. What is prior does not depend on what is posterior. And the connection between good and the will is prior to the connection between good
and reason, as is clear from what was said above [I-II.9.1]. Therefore, the
5   will's goodness does not depend on reason.

2. The Philosopher says in *Ethics* VI [1139a29] that goodness in the practical intellect is truth in conformity with correct desire. Now correct desire is a good will. Therefore, the goodness of practical reason depends on goodness in the will, rather than the other way around.

3. A mover does not depend on what is moved, but rather the reverse. And the will moves reason and the other powers, as was explained above [I-II.9.1]. Therefore, the will's goodness does not depend on reason.

**On the contrary.** Hilary says in *On the Trinity* X [ch. 1], "The will is always immoderate when it clings stubbornly to what it wills and is not subject to reason." And the will is good precisely when it is not immoderate. Therefore, the will's goodness depends on its being subject to reason.

**Reply.** As has been said [art. 1–2], the will's goodness properly depends on the object. Now the will's object is proposed to it by reason. After all, the understood good is the object that is proportionate to the will, whereas the sensible or imagined good is not proportionate to the will but to the sensory appetite, since the will can tend toward the universal good that reason apprehends, whereas the sensory appetite tends only toward a particular good, which is what a sensory power apprehends. And so the will's goodness depends on reason in exactly the way in which it depends on the object.

**Response to 1.** The will's connection with good qua good—that is, good qua desirable—is prior to reason's. But reason's connection with good qua true is prior to the will's connection with good qua desirable, since the will cannot desire a good unless it is first apprehended by reason.

**Response to 2.** In that passage the Philosopher is talking about practical reason as what deliberates and reasons about things that are for the end; that is the sense in which practical reason is perfected by prudence. Now in things that are for the end, reason is correct when it conforms to desire for an appropriate end. And yet that very desire for an appropriate end presupposes a correct apprehension of the end, and that comes through reason.

**Response to 3.** The will moves reason in one way, and reason moves the will in another way, namely, by presenting its object, as was explained above [I-II.9.1].

### Article 4. Does the goodness of a human will depend on the eternal law?

It seems that the goodness of a human will does not depend on the eternal law:

1. A single thing has a single rule and measure. And the rule for the human will, on which its goodness depends, is right reason. Therefore, the will's goodness does not depend on the eternal law.

2. A measure is homogeneous with what it measures, as is said in *Metaphysics* X [1053a24], whereas the eternal law is not homogeneous with

the human will. Therefore, the eternal law cannot be the measure of the human will in such a way that the goodness of the human will depends
10   on the eternal law.

3. A measure ought to be supremely certain, whereas the eternal law is unknown to us. Therefore, it cannot be the measure of our will in such a way that the goodness of our will depends on it.

**On the contrary.** Augustine says in *Against Faustus* XXII [ch. 27] that
15   "sin is something done, said, or desired contrary to the eternal law." And the will's badness is the root of sin. Therefore, since badness is opposed to goodness, the will's goodness depends on the eternal law.

**Reply.** In all ordered causes, an effect depends more on the first cause than it does on a secondary cause, because a secondary cause acts only in
20   the power of the first cause. Now the fact that human reason is the rule for the human will, in such a way that the will's goodness is measured according to reason, derives from the eternal law, which is divine reason. That is why Psalm 4:6 says, "There are many who say, 'Who will show us good things?' The light of your countenance has shone brightly upon us,
25   O Lord"—as if to say, the light of reason that is in us can show us good things and can regulate our will inasmuch as it is the light of your countenance, that is, the light that is derived from your countenance. Hence it is evident that the goodness of the human will depends on the eternal law much more than it does on human reason; and where human reason falls
30   short, one must have recourse to eternal reason.

**Response to 1.** There is no more than one *proximate* measure for a single thing, but there can be multiple measures when one is subordinate to another.

**Response to 2.** A proximate measure is homogeneous with what it mea-
35   sures, but a remote measure is not.

**Response to 3.** Although the eternal law as it exists in the divine mind is unknown to us, it is made known to us to some degree either through natural reason, which is derived from eternal reason as its proper image, or through some additional revelation.

### Article 5. Is a will that is out of harmony with mistaken reason bad?[148]

It seems that a will that is out of harmony with mistaken reason is not bad:

1. Reason is the rule for the human will insofar as reason is derived from the eternal law, as has been said [art. 4]. But mistaken reason is not derived from the eternal law. Therefore, mistaken reason is not the rule

---

148. Parallel passages: *On Truth* 17.4; *Quodlibet* IX.7.2, III.12.2; *Sent.* II.39.3.3; *Comm. Galatians* 5.1; *Comm. Romans* 14.2.

for the human will. Therefore, the will is not bad if it is out of harmony   5
with mistaken reason.

2. According to Augustine,[149] the command of a lower power does not
oblige if it contradicts the command of a higher power: for example, if a
proconsul commands something that the emperor forbids. Now mistaken
reason sometimes proposes something that contradicts the command of   10
a superior, namely, God, who is the supreme power. Therefore, a dictate
of mistaken reason does not oblige, so a will that is out of harmony with
mistaken reason is not bad.

3. Every bad will can be assigned to some species of badness, whereas
a will that is out of harmony with mistaken reason cannot be assigned to   15
any species of badness. For example, if reason makes the mistake of saying
that one ought to commit fornication, the will of someone who does not
will to commit fornication cannot be assigned to any species of badness.
Therefore, a will that is out of harmony with mistaken reason is not bad.

**On the contrary.** As I said in the First Part [I.79.13], conscience is simply   20
the application of knowledge to some act. And knowledge is in reason. So if
a will is out of harmony with mistaken reason, it is contrary to conscience.
And every such will is bad, since as Romans 14 says, "Whatever is not of
faith"—that is, whatever is contrary to conscience—"is sin." Therefore, a
will that is out of harmony with mistaken reason is bad.   25

**Reply.** Since conscience is in a way a dictate of reason (it is, after all,
the application of knowledge to action, as I said in the First Part [I.79.13]),
asking whether a will that is out of harmony with mistaken reason is bad is
equivalent to asking whether a mistaken conscience obliges. Concerning
that question, some people have distinguished three kinds of acts: those   30
that are good in genus, those that are indifferent, and those that are bad in
genus.[150] Accordingly they say that if reason or conscience says that something that is good in genus should be done, there is no mistake in that case.
And the same holds if it says that something that is bad in genus should
not be done, since bad things are forbidden for the same reason that good   35
things are commanded. By contrast, if reason or conscience tells someone
that human beings are obliged by a commandment to do things that are
in fact bad in themselves, or that things that are good in themselves are
forbidden, then you have a case of mistaken reason or conscience. And
similarly if reason or conscience tells someone that something that is indif-   40
ferent in itself (such as picking up a stick from the ground) is forbidden or
commanded, you have a case of mistaken reason or conscience. So they say
that when reason or conscience makes a mistake about indifferent things

149. *Sermones ad populum* 62.8.
150. See Bonaventure, *Sentences* II.39.1.3.

by either commanding or forbidding them, it obliges in such a way that a
45    will that is out of harmony with such mistaken reason is bad and sinful.
But if reason makes a mistake by commanding things that are bad in themselves or forbidding things that are good in themselves and necessary for
salvation, it does not oblige; accordingly, in such matters a will that is out
of harmony with mistaken reason or conscience is not bad.
50        But that makes no sense. After all, in the case of indifferent acts, a will
that is out of harmony with mistaken reason or conscience is bad in a
particular way because of its object, which is the very thing on which the
will's goodness or badness depends—not, certainly, because the object is
by its very nature bad, but because the object is apprehended accidentally
55    by reason as something that it is bad to do or something that ought to be
avoided. And since, as I have said [art. 3], the will's object is what is presented by reason, the fact that reason presents something as bad means
that the will counts as bad if it is drawn to that thing. And that is true, not
only for indifferent acts, but also for acts that are good or bad in them-
60    selves. After all, it is not only what is indifferent that can become good
or bad accidentally; what is good can take on the character of something
bad, and what is bad the character of something good, thanks to reason's
apprehension. For example, abstaining from fornication is a good thing,
but the will is drawn to this good thing only as reason presents it; so if mis-
65    taken reason presents it as something bad, the will will be drawn to it as
something bad. And that means the will itself will be bad because it wills
something bad—not, of course, something bad in itself, but something
bad accidentally, thanks to reason's apprehension. Similarly, believing in
Christ is good in itself, and necessary for salvation; but the will is drawn
70    to believing in Christ only as that is presented by reason. So if reason presents it as something bad, the will will be drawn to it as something bad,
not because it is bad in itself, but because it is bad accidentally, thanks to
reason's apprehension. And that is why the Philosopher says in *Ethics* VII
[1151a33] that, speaking *per se*, "someone who does not follow right reason
75    is incontinent; but even someone who does not follow mistaken reason is
incontinent, *per accidens*." Accordingly, one ought to say without qualification that every will that is out of harmony with reason, whether reason
is right or mistaken, is always bad.
        **Response to 1.** Although the judgment of mistaken reason is not derived
80    from God, mistaken reason does nonetheless present its judgment as something true and therefore as derived from God, the source of all truth.
        **Response to 2.** What Augustine says applies when someone knows that
the lower power is commanding something that contradicts the command
of the higher power. But if someone were to believe that the proconsul's
85    command was the same as the emperor's command, in scorning the proconsul's command he would also scorn the emperor's command. And

similarly, if someone knew that human reason was dictating something contrary to God's command, he would not be required to follow reason—but then in that case reason would not be totally mistaken. But when mistaken reason presents something as a command of God, then scorning the dictate of reason is the same thing as scorning God's command.

**Response to 3.** When reason apprehends something as bad, it always apprehends that thing as bad for some particular reason: say, because it contradicts a divine command, or because it is a scandal, or for some other such reason. And then a will that is bad in that particular way is assigned to that particular species of badness.

*Article 6. Is a will that is in harmony with mistaken reason good?*[151]

It seems that a will that is in harmony with mistaken reason is good:

1. In the same way that a will that is out of harmony with reason tends toward what reason judges to be bad, a will that is in harmony with reason tends toward what reason judges to be good. Now a will that is out of harmony with reason—even mistaken reason—is bad. Therefore, a will that is in harmony with reason—even mistaken reason—is good.

2. A will that is in harmony with God's command and the eternal law is always good. And the eternal law and God's command are presented to us through the apprehension of reason, even if reason is mistaken. Therefore, a will that is in harmony even with mistaken reason is good.

3. A will that is out of harmony with mistaken reason is bad. So if a will that is in harmony with mistaken reason is also bad, it seems that when someone's reason is mistaken, every act of will will be bad. And in that case, such a person will be in a state of perplexity and will sin by necessity, which is absurd. Therefore, a will that is in harmony with mistaken reason is good.

**On the contrary.** The will of those who killed the apostles was bad, and yet it was in harmony with their mistaken reason: as John 16 says, "The day will come when all those who kill you will think they are offering worship to God." Therefore, a will that is in harmony with mistaken reason can be bad.

**Reply.** Just as the previous question was equivalent to asking whether mistaken conscience obliges, this question is equivalent to asking whether mistaken conscience excuses. Now this question depends on what I said earlier about ignorance. I said above [I-II.6.8] that sometimes ignorance causes involuntariness, but sometimes it does not. And since moral goodness and badness are in an act insofar as it is voluntary, as is clear from our

---

151. Parallel passages: *On Truth* 17.3 resp. 4; *Quodlibet* VIII.6.3, VIII.6.5, IX.7.2, III.12.2 resp. 2.

previous discussions [art. 2], it is evident that ignorance that causes involuntariness removes the character of moral goodness and badness, whereas
ignorance that does not cause involuntariness does not. And I said above
30    [I-II.6.8] that ignorance that is in some way willed, whether directly or
indirectly, does not cause involuntariness. By "directly willed ignorance"
I mean ignorance toward which some act of will is drawn; by "indirectly
willed ignorance" I mean ignorance that results from negligence, in that
people do not will to know what they are obligated to know, as I explained
35    above [I-II.6.8]. Suppose reason or conscience is mistaken owing to an
error on the part of the will, whether directly or through negligence. In that
case, then, because the error concerns something that a person is obligated
to know, such a mistake on the part of reason or conscience does not excuse
a will that is in agreement with mistaken reason or conscience from being
40    bad. But if it is an error that causes involuntariness, one that arises from
ignorance of some circumstance apart from any negligence, such a mistake on the part of reason or conscience does excuse a will that is in agreement with it from being bad. For example, suppose mistaken reason says
that human beings are obligated to have intercourse with other people's
45    wives. A will that is in harmony with this mistaken reason is bad, because
that mistake arises from ignorance of God's law, which one is obligated to
know. By contrast, suppose reason's mistake is that someone believes that
this woman is his wife, and when she asks him to pay the marital debt, he
wills to have intercourse with her. In that case, the will is excused, so that
50    it is not bad, because that mistake arises from ignorance of a circumstance.
Such ignorance excuses, and it causes involuntariness.
     **Response to 1.** As Dionysius says in *On the Divine Names* 4 [§30],
"goodness is caused by a perfect cause, whereas badness is caused by individual defects." And so in order for something toward which the will is
55    drawn to be called bad, it is sufficient for it to be bad by nature or for it to be
apprehended as bad. But in order to be good, it has to be good in both ways.
     **Response to 2.** The eternal law cannot be mistaken, but human rea-
son can be mistaken. And so a will that is in harmony with human reason
is not always right, and it is not always in harmony with the eternal law.
60    **Response to 3.** In syllogisms, if one absurdity is granted, others necessarily follow; and in a similar way, in moral matters, if one unsuitable thing
is assumed, others necessarily follow. For example, assuming that someone
seeks an empty reputation, he will sin if he does what is necessary for him
to achieve such a reputation, and he will sin if he fails to do it. Even so, he
65    is not in a state of perplexity, because he can get rid of his bad intention.
And similarly, assuming a mistake of reason or conscience that arises from
non-excusing ignorance, something bad in the will necessarily follows.
Yet one is not in a state of perplexity, because one can correct the mistake,
since the ignorance is voluntary and can be overcome.

## Article 7. Does the will's goodness
*depend on the intention of the end?*[152]

It seems that the will's goodness does not depend on the intention of the end:

1. It was said above [art. 2] that the will's goodness depends solely on the object. And in the case of things that are for the end, the will's object is not the same as the intended end. Therefore, in the case of such things, *5* the will's goodness does not depend on the intention of the end.

2. Willing to keep God's command is a mark of a good will. But that can be directed to a bad end: for example, the end of an empty reputation, or of greed, when someone wills to obey God in order to obtain temporal goods. Therefore, the will's goodness does not depend on the intention of the end. *10*

3. Goodness and badness distinguish ends just as they distinguish wills. Now the badness of a will does not depend on the badness of the intended end; after all, someone who wills to steal in order to give to charity has a bad will, even though he intends a good end. Therefore, neither does the goodness of a will depend on the goodness of an end. *15*

**On the contrary.** In *Confessions* IX Augustine says that God rewards the intention.[153] And God rewards something because it is good. Therefore, the will's goodness depends on the intention of the end.

**Reply.** Intention can be related to the will in two ways: as preceding the will and as following the will. Intention precedes the will causally when *20* we will something because of our intention of an end. And then the ordering to the end is regarded as a good-making feature of what is willed: for example, when someone wills to fast for God's sake, that fasting counts as good precisely because it is done for God's sake. Accordingly, since (as I explained above [art. 1-2]) the will's goodness depends on the goodness *25* of what is willed, the will's goodness necessarily depends on the intention of the end. By contrast, intention follows the will when it is added to a preexisting will: for example, if someone wills to do something, and then afterward directs it to God. In that case, the goodness of the first will does not depend on the subsequent intention, unless the act of will is repeated *30* with that subsequent intention.

**Response to 1.** When an intention is the cause of willing, that ordering to the end is taken as a good-making feature in the object, as I have said [in the main reply].

**Response to 2.** A will cannot be called good if a bad intention is the *35* cause of the willing. After all, someone who wills to give to charity in order to acquire an empty reputation wills something that is good in itself, but

---

152. Parallel passages: *ST* I-II.19.1–2; *Sent.* II.38.4–5.

153. See *Confessions* XIII.26.

under a description under which it is bad; and so *as willed by him*, it is bad. Hence, his will is bad. If, however, that intention follows the will, the will
40 could have been good; and the subsequent intention does not make the preceding act of will bad. But if the act of will is repeated with that subsequent intention, the intention makes that repeated act bad.

**Response to 3.** As I have already said [art. 6 resp. 1], badness arises from individual defects, but goodness comes from a whole and perfect cause. So
45 if a will is for something that is bad in itself, even under an aspect of good, or for something good but under an aspect of bad, the will will always be bad. By contrast, in order for a will to be good, it has to be for something good, under the aspect of good: that is, it must will what is good, because it is good.

### Article 8. Does how good the will is depend on how good the intention is?

It seems that how good the will is depends on how good the intention is:

1. The Common Gloss on Matthew 12:35, "Those who are good bring forth good things from the good treasure of their hearts," says, "People do as much good as they intend."[154] Now intention gives goodness not only to
5 the exterior act, but also to the interior act, as has been said [art. 7]. Therefore, people's wills are exactly as good as their intentions.

2. If a cause is increased, its effect is increased. And the intention of what is good is the cause of a good will. Therefore, a will is good precisely to the extent that it intends what is good.

10 3. In the case of bad acts, people sin precisely to the extent that they intend what is bad. For example, if someone throws a rock intending to commit homicide, he or she is guilty of homicide. Therefore, by parity of reasoning, in the case of good acts, the will is good precisely to the extent that someone intends what is good.

15 **On the contrary.** It is possible for an intention to be good but the will bad. Therefore, by parity of reasoning, it is possible for an intention to be better but the will less good.

**Reply.** When it comes to an act and the intention of an end, we can judge "how much" in two ways: according to the object, in that someone
20 wills or does a greater good; and according to intensity, in that someone wills or acts intensely (this is a "more" on the part of the agent). So if we are talking about "how much" in terms of the object, it is clear that how good or bad an act is does not follow how good or bad the intention is. In the case of an exterior act, this can happen in two ways. One way is that the

---

154. The *Glossa ordinaria*, a twelfth-century compilation of patristic and medieval glosses on the Bible.

object that is directed to the intended end is not proportionate to that end:     25
for example, if someone hands over $10, he would not be able to achieve
what he intends if his intention is to buy something that costs $100. The
other way is because of obstacles that can get in the way of the exterior act,
which we have no power to remove: for example, someone intends to go
to Rome, but obstacles arise, so that she cannot do so. Now in the case of     30
the interior act of will, there is only one way, since interior acts of will are
in our power, whereas exterior acts are not. The will can, however, will an
object that is not proportionate to the intended end; and thus the will that
is drawn to that object considered absolutely is not as good as the intention
is. Yet because the intention too pertains in a way to the will's act, insofar     35
as it is the ground of that act, how good the intention is overflows into the
will, insofar as the will wills some very good thing as an end, even though
the object through which it wills to attain so great a good is unworthy of
that good.

On the other hand, if we look at how good or bad intentions and acts are     40
in terms of their intensity, then the intensity of the intention overflows into
the interior and exterior acts of the will, since the intention itself stands in
a way as formal cause to both, as is clear from things I said above [I-II.12.4,
18.6]. But in terms of the material cause, it is possible for the interior or
exterior act not to be as intense as the intention is: for example, when some-     45
one does not will to take the medicine as intensely as he wills health. Yet
someone's intensely willing health does overflow formally into his intensely
willing medicine. Even so, it is important to realize that the intensity of an
interior or exterior act can be the object of intention: for example, someone
might intend to will intensely or to do something intensely. And yet that     50
does not mean that such a person in fact wills or acts intensely, since how
good an interior or exterior act is does not follow how good the intended
end is, as I have explained. And that is how it comes about that someone
does not merit as much as she intends to merit, since how much someone
merits depends on the intensity of the act, as I will explain below [I-II.20.4].     55

**Response to 1.** That Gloss is speaking in terms of God's judgment; he
chiefly considers the intention of the end. That is why another Gloss on
the same passage says that "the treasure of the heart is the intention, by
which God judges deeds." After all, as I have said [in the main reply], the
goodness of the intention overflows somehow into the goodness of the will,     60
which makes the exterior act also meritorious before God.

**Response to 2.** The goodness of the intention is not the complete cause
of a good will, so the argument does not work.

**Response to 3.** If the intention is bad, that is sufficient by itself for the
will to be bad; and consequently, the will is at least as bad as the intention     65
is. But that reasoning does not hold for goodness, as I have explained [in
resp. 2].

*Article 9. Does the goodness of a human will*
*depend on its conformity with the divine will?*[155]

It seems that the goodness of a human will does not depend on its conformity with the divine will:

1. It is impossible for a human will to be conformed to the divine will,
as is clear from what is said in Isaiah 55:9: "As far as the heavens are above
5    the earth, so far are my ways above your ways and my thoughts above your
thoughts." So if it were necessary for a human will to be conformed to the
divine will in order to be good, it would follow that a human will could
never be good. And that is absurd.

2. In the same way that our will is derived from the divine will, our
10   knowledge is derived from divine knowledge. But it is not necessary, in
order for us to know, that our knowledge be conformed to divine knowledge; there are, after all, many things that God knows but we do not.
Therefore, it is not necessary for our will to be conformed to the divine will.

3. The will is a principle of action. Now our action cannot be con-
15   formed to divine action. Therefore, neither can our will be conformed to
the divine will.

**On the contrary.** Matthew 26:39 says, "Not as I will, but as you will."
As Augustine explains in the *Enchiridion*, Jesus says this because "he wants
human beings to be right and to be directed toward God."[156] Now the will's
20   rightness is its goodness. Therefore, the will's goodness depends on conformity to the divine will.

**Reply.** As I have explained [art. 7], the will's goodness depends on
its intention of the end. Now the ultimate end of the human will is the
supreme good, which is God, as I said above [I-II.1.8, 3.1]. Therefore,
25   in order for the human will to be good, it has to be directed toward the
supreme good, which is God. And this good is in fact primarily and essentially related to the divine will as its proper object. Now what is first in a
given genus is the measure and standard of all the things in that genus,
and a given thing is right and good to the extent that it attains its proper
30   measure. Therefore, in order for the will to be good, it must be conformed
to the divine will.

**Response to 1.** The human will cannot be conformed to the divine will
by way of equality, but by way of imitation. And that is like the way in which
human knowledge is conformed to divine knowledge, insofar as it knows
35   what is true, and human action to divine action, insofar as it is appropriate
to the agent. This is by way of imitation, not by way of equality.

---

155. Parallel passages: *On Truth* 23.7; *Sent.* I.48.1.
156. See Augustine, *Commentary on Psalms* 32 enarr. 2, sermon 1.

**Response to 2 and 3.** On this basis, the response to the second and third arguments is clear.

*Article 10. Should a human will always be conformed
to the divine will in terms of what it wills?*[157]

It seems that a human will need not always be conformed to the divine will in terms of what it wills:

1. We cannot will what we do not know; after all, the object of the will is the *apprehended* good. And more often than not, we do not know what God wills. Therefore, the human will cannot be conformed to the divine    5
will in terms of what it wills.

2. God wills to damn those who he foreknows will die in mortal sin. So if human beings were obligated to conform their wills to the divine will in terms of what is willed, it would follow that human beings are obligated to will their own damnation. But that is absurd.                10

3. No one is obligated to will something that is contrary to piety. But if a human being were to will what God wills, that would sometimes be contrary to piety: for example, when God wills that someone's father dies, if the son willed the same thing, it would be contrary to piety. Therefore, human beings are not obligated to conform their wills to the divine will   15
in terms of what is willed.

**On the contrary 1.** The Gloss on Psalm 32:1, "It is fitting for the upright to sing praises," says, "One who wills what God wills has an upright heart." And everyone is obligated to have an upright heart. Therefore, everyone is obligated to will what God wills.                20

**On the contrary 2.** The form of an act of will, just like the form of any other act, derives from the object. So if human beings are obligated to conform their wills to the divine will, it follows that they are obligated to conform in terms of the object willed.

**On the contrary 3.** There is incompatibility between [human] wills    25
because human beings will different things. Now anyone who has a will that is incompatible with the divine will has a bad will. Therefore, all who do not conform their wills to the divine will in terms of what is willed have bad wills.

**Reply.** As is clear from what I have already said [art. 3, 5], the will is    30
drawn to its object according to the way reason presents it. Now reason can consider something in a variety of ways, so that it is good when looked at in one way but not good when looked at in another way. And so the will of someone who wills that the thing exist insofar as it is good is good; and the will of someone else, who wills that the same thing not exist insofar as    35

---

157. Parallel passages: *On Truth* 23.8; *Sent.* I.48.2–4.

it is bad, is also good. For example, a judge has a good will when he wills
that a robber be killed, since that is just; yet the will of someone else—say,
the robber's wife or son—who does not want him to be killed, insofar as
killing is by nature bad, is also good.

40      Now since the will follows the apprehension of reason or intellect, the
will is drawn to a more general (*communis*) good insofar as the aspect of
good that reason apprehends is itself more general. That is clear in the
example I have given. The judge has oversight over the common (*communis*) good, which is justice; and so he wills that the robber be killed, because
45   that is a good thing in relation to the general welfare. But the robber's wife
is properly concerned for the private good of the family, and accordingly
she wills that her husband, the robber, not be killed. Now what God apprehends is the good of the whole universe, which he created and governs.
Hence, whatever he wills, he wills under the aspect of the general good,
50   which is his own goodness; that is the goodness of the whole universe. By
contrast, what a creature apprehends, in keeping with its own nature, is
some particular good that is proportionate to the creature's nature. And it
can happen that something is good according to particular reason that is
not good according to universal reason, and vice versa, as I have explained.
55   And so it can happen that some will is good when it wills something considered according to particular reason that, nonetheless, God does not will
according to universal reason, and vice versa. And that is also how it can
happen that different human beings will opposite things, and yet their differing wills are all good, insofar as they will something to be or not be on
60   the basis of different particular reasons.

        Still, when human beings will some particular good, their will is not
right unless they refer that good to the common good as an end; after all,
even the natural appetite of each part of a thing is directed toward the common good of the whole. Now the end supplies what is in effect the formal
65   aspect of willing what is directed to the end. Hence, in order for some will
to be right in willing some particular good, that particular good must be
what is willed materially, but the common, divine good is what must be
willed formally. So the human will is obligated to conform to the divine
will formally in what is willed, because it is obligated to will the divine and
70   common good, but not materially, for the reason already given.

        Yet in a way the human will is conformed to the divine will in both
respects. You see, insofar as it is conformed to the divine will in terms of the
general reason for what is willed, it is conformed to the divine will in terms
of the ultimate end. By contrast, insofar as it is not conformed to the divine
75   will in terms of what is willed materially, it is conformed to the divine will
qua efficient cause, since it is from God as efficient cause that the human
will has this proper inclination consequent on its nature or on the particular apprehension of this object. That is why we typically say that, in this

respect, a human will is conformed to the divine will because it wills what God wants it to will. And there is another kind of conformity in terms of formal causality: a person's willing something out of charity, as God wills. And this conformity is an instance of the formal conformity that derives from the ordering to the ultimate end, which is the proper object of charity.

**Response to 1.** We can know what God wills in terms of its general character, what sort of thing it is. We know, after all, that whatever God wills, he wills under the aspect of good. And so anyone who wills something under any aspect of good has a will that conforms to the divine will in terms of the character of what is willed. True, we do not know the particulars of what God wills, and in that respect we are not obligated to conform our will to the divine will. Yet in the state of glory, all will see, for each and every thing that they will, the order of those things to what God wills. And so they will conform their wills to God not only formally, but also materially.

**Response to 2.** God does not will anyone's damnation qua damnation, or anyone's death qua death, "because God wills that all human beings be saved."[158] Rather he wills these things under the aspect of justice. Hence, concerning such things it is sufficient for someone to will that God's justice and the order of nature be preserved.

From this the **Response to 3** is clear.

**Response to On the contrary 1.** Those who conform their will to the divine will with respect to the *reason* for what is willed are willing what God wills more than are those who conform their wills with respect what is willed. Why? Because the will is drawn more fundamentally to the end than to what is for the end.

**Response to On the contrary 2.** The species and form of an act have more to do with the formal character of the object than with what it is materially.

**Response to On the contrary 3.** When different people will different things under different aspects, their wills are not incompatible. But if there were something that one person willed under one aspect, and some other person willed against it under that same aspect, then you would have a case of incompatible wills. That is not the case here.

## Question 20. The Goodness and Badness of Exterior Acts

Next we need to investigate the goodness and badness of exterior acts. Concerning this there are six questions:

Article 1. Are goodness and badness primarily in the act of the will or in the exterior act?

---

158. 1 Timothy 2:4.

Article 2. Does the goodness or badness of the exterior act depend wholly on the goodness of the will?

Article 3. Is there one and the same goodness and badness for both the interior and the exterior act?

Article 4. Does the exterior act add any goodness or badness beyond that of the interior act?

Article 5. Does a consequence add any goodness or badness to the exterior act?

Article 6. Can one and the same exterior act be both good and bad?

*Article 1. Are goodness and badness primarily
in the act of will or in the exterior act?*[159]

It seems that goodness and badness are primarily in an exterior act and derivatively in an act of the will:

1. The will has goodness in virtue of its object, as was said above [I-II.19.12]. And the exterior act is the object of the interior act of will: we
5    are said to will theft, or to will to give to charity. Therefore, goodness and badness are primarily in an exterior act and derivatively in an act of the will.

2. Goodness belongs primarily to the end, since things that are for the end count as good because they are ordered to the end. Now an act of the will cannot be an end, as was explained above [I-II.1.1 resp. 2], whereas an
10   act of any other power can be an end. Therefore, goodness resides primarily in an act of another power and derivatively in an act of the will.

3. The will's act stands as formal cause to the exterior act, as was said above [I-II.18.6]. And a formal cause is posterior, since a form accrues to matter. Therefore, goodness and badness are primarily in the exterior act
15   and derivatively in an act of the will.

**On the contrary.** Augustine says in the *Reconsiderations* [I.9] that "it is by the will that we sin and live rightly." Therefore, moral goodness and badness reside primarily in the will.

**Reply.** Exterior acts can be called good or bad in two ways. One way is
20   according to their genus and according to their circumstances considered in themselves: for example, giving to charity, assuming all the circumstances are appropriate, is called good. In another way, something is called good or bad because of its ordering to an end: for example, giving to charity for the sake of an empty reputation is called bad. Now since the end is the
25   proper object of the will, it is clear that the character of good or bad that an exterior act has because of its ordering to an end is found primarily in an act of the will, from which the exterior act gets its derivative goodness or badness. By contrast, the goodness or badness that an exterior act has in and

---

159. Parallel passage: *On Evil* 2.3.

of itself, because of its appropriate matter and circumstances, is not derived from the will, but rather from reason. Hence, if the goodness of the exterior 30 act is evaluated in terms of reason's ordering and apprehension, its goodness is prior to the goodness of the will's act; but if it is evaluated as actually carried out, it follows the goodness of the will, which is its principle.

**Response to 1.** The exterior act is the object of the will insofar as reason presents that act to the will as a good that is apprehended and ordered by 35 reason, and in that way it is prior to the goodness of the will's act. But as actually carried out, it is an effect of the will and follows the will.

**Response to 2.** The end is prior in intention but posterior in execution.

**Response to 3.** A form, as received in matter, is posterior to matter in the process of generation, even though it is prior by nature; but the form 40 as it is in the agent cause is prior in every way. And the will is related to the exterior act as efficient cause. Hence, the goodness of an act of will is the form of the exterior act as existing in an agent cause.

*Article 2. Does the goodness or badness of the*
*exterior act depend wholly on the will?*[160]

It seems that the goodness and badness of the exterior act depend wholly on the will:

1. Matthew 7:18 says, "A good tree cannot bear bad fruit, nor can a bad tree bear good fruit." And according to the Common Gloss, we are to understand a tree as the will, and its fruit as the deed. Therefore, it is 5 impossible for the interior will to be good but the exterior bad, and vice versa.

2. Augustine says in the *Reconsiderations* [I.9] that it is only by the will that one sins. Therefore, if there is no sin in the will, there will be no sin in the exterior act. And thus the goodness or badness of the exterior act 10 depends wholly on the will.

3. The goodness and badness we are talking about now are differences of a moral act. And differences divide a genus *per se*, according to the Philosopher in *Metaphysics* VII [1038a9]. So, given that an act is moral because it is voluntary, it seems that goodness and badness are in an act 15 solely because of the will.

**On the contrary.** Augustine says in *Against Lying* [ch. 7] that "there are some acts that cannot be done well, no matter how 'good' the end or the will."

**Reply.** As has already been said [art. 1], there are two ways in which an 20 exterior act can be good or bad: one based on appropriate matter and circumstances, the other based on its order to an end. And of course the one

---

160. Parallel passage: *Sent.* II.40.2.

that depends on its order to an end depends wholly on the will. But the one
that derives from appropriate matter or circumstances depends on reason,
25   and the goodness of the will *insofar as it is drawn to that act* depends in
turn on this second goodness.

Now it is important to note that (as I said above [I-II.19.6 resp. 1]) one
individual defect is sufficient for something to be bad, whereas in order for
something to be unqualifiedly good, one individual good is not enough;
30   instead, complete goodness is necessary. So if the will is good on the basis
of both its proper object and its end, it follows that the exterior act is good.
But the goodness of the will that comes from the intention of the end is
not sufficient for the exterior act to be good; instead, if the will is bad *either*
because of its intention of the end *or* because of the act willed, it follows
35   that the exterior act is bad.

**Response to 1.** A good will, as signified by "a good tree," should be
understood as having goodness because of both the act willed and the
intended end.

**Response to 2.** One sins by the will not only when one wills a bad end,
40   but also when one wills a bad act.

**Response to 3.** It is not only the interior act of the will that is called
voluntary; exterior acts are too, insofar as they issue from will and reason.
Consequently, the difference of good and bad can be found in both kinds
of acts.

*Article 3. Is there one and the same goodness*
*for both the interior and the exterior act?*[161]

It seems that the goodness or badness of the interior act of the will is not
the same as that of the exterior act:

1. The principle of an interior act is an interior apprehensive or appetitive power of the soul, whereas the principle of an exterior act is a power
5    that executes movement. And where you have distinct principles of action,
you have distinct acts. But an act is the subject of goodness or badness, and
one and the same accident cannot exist in distinct subjects. Therefore,
there cannot be one and the same goodness for both the interior and the
exterior act.

10   2. "Virtue is what makes its possessors good and makes their deeds
good," as is said in *Ethics* II [1106a15]. And intellectual virtue in the commanding power is distinct from moral virtue in the commanded power, as
is clear from *Ethics* I [1103a3]. Therefore, the goodness of the interior act,
which belongs to the commanding power, is distinct from the goodness of
15   the exterior act, which belongs to the commanded power.

---

161. Parallel passage: ST I-II.18.6.

3. A cause and an effect cannot be the same, since nothing is its own cause. But the goodness of the interior act is the cause of the goodness of the exterior act, or vice versa, as has been said [art. 1–2]. Therefore, the goodness of the two acts cannot be the same.

**On the contrary.** I showed above [I-II.18.6] that the will's act stands as    20
form to the exterior act. Now what is composed of form and matter is one. Therefore, there is one goodness for both the interior and the exterior act.

**Reply.** As was said above [I-II.17.4], the interior act of the will and the exterior act *regarded as a moral act* are one act. Now an act that is one in subject sometimes has more than one aspect of goodness or badness, and    25
sometimes only one. Thus, the right thing to say is that sometimes there is one and the same goodness or badness for both the interior and the exterior act, and sometimes their goodness or badness is distinct. After all, as I have already explained [art. 1–2], the two goodnesses or badnesses—the interior act's and exterior act's—are ordered to each other. And in the case    30
of things that are ordered to another, it sometimes happens that something is good solely because it is ordered to something else. For example, a bitter drink is good just because it causes health: accordingly, the goodness of the drink is not distinct from the goodness of health; they are one and the same. Sometimes, however, something that is ordered to another has some    35
aspect of good in its own right, even apart from its ordering to that other good. For example, a delicious medicine is good because it is pleasurable, in addition to being good because it brings about health. So when an exterior act is good or bad solely because of its order to an end, the goodness or badness of the will's act, which is intrinsically concerned with the end, is    40
altogether the same as that of the exterior act, which is concerned with the end only through an act of the will. But when the exterior act has goodness or badness in its own right, because of its matter and circumstances, then there is one goodness for the exterior act and a distinct goodness for the will because of its end—though in such a way that the goodness of the end over-    45
flows from the will into the exterior act, and the goodness of the matter and circumstances overflows into the act of the will, as I said earlier [art. 1–2].

**Response to 1.** That argument proves that interior and exterior acts are distinct in the domain of nature. But in the moral domain these two distinct acts come together to constitute something that is one, as I explained    50
above [I-II.17.4].

**Response to 2.** As is said in *Ethics* VI [1144a8], moral virtues are ordered to those virtuous acts that are, as it were, the ends of the virtues. By contrast, prudence, which is in reason, is ordered to things that are for the end. That is why distinct virtues are necessary. But the goodness of right    55
reason concerning the end of the virtues is not distinct from the goodness of virtue, insofar as the goodness of reason shares in a given virtue.

**Response to 3.** When a feature of one thing derives from another by a
univocal agent cause, what is in each is distinct. For example, when some-
60   thing hot heats, the heat of what causes heat and the heat of what is heated
are numerically distinct, though they are the same in species. By contrast,
when a feature of something derives from another according to analogy
and proportion, then there is numerically one thing. For example, health
in medicine and urine derives from the health that is in the body of an
65   animal; there is no health of medicine or urine distinct from the health of
the animal, which medicine causes and urine indicates. And this is the way
in which the goodness of the exterior act derives from the goodness of the
will, and vice versa: according to the order of one to the other.

*Article 4. Does an exterior act add any goodness*
*or badness beyond that of the interior act?*[162]

It seems that the exterior act does not add any goodness or badness beyond
that of the interior act:
1. Chrysostom says in his commentary on Matthew [homily 19], "The
will is what is either rewarded for good or condemned for evil," whereas
5   deeds are the testimonies of the will. Therefore, God does not scrutinize
deeds for his own sake, in order to know how to judge, but for the sake of
others, so that all will understand that God is just. And goodness and badness should be assessed according to God's judgment, rather than human
judgment. Therefore, the exterior act adds no goodness or badness to the
10   interior act.
2. As has been said [art. 3], there is one and the same goodness for
the interior and exterior act. An increase happens by adding one thing to
another. Therefore, the exterior act does not add any goodness or badness
to the interior act.
15   3. The whole goodness of creation adds nothing to the divine goodness,
since it derives from the divine goodness. Now sometimes the whole goodness of the exterior act derives from the goodness of the interior act, and
sometimes vice versa, as has been explained [art. 1–2]. Therefore, neither
of them adds to the goodness or badness of the other.
20   **On the contrary.** Every agent intends to pursue what is good and avoid
what is evil. So if the exterior act added no goodness or badness, it would
be pointless for anyone who has a good or bad will to do a good deed or
refrain from a bad deed. And that is absurd.
**Reply.** If we are talking about the goodness that an exterior act has from
25   the willing of the end, then the exterior act adds no goodness, unless it
turns out that this will itself is made better in those who are good or worse

162. Parallel passages: *On Evil* 2.2 resp. 8; *Sent.* II.40.3.

in those who are bad. And it does seem that that can happen in three ways. The first way is numerically: for example, suppose someone wills to do something for the sake of a good or bad end, and then does not do it, but then later wills it and does it. The act of will is repeated, and so there 30 is a twofold goodness or twofold badness. The second way is in terms of extension: for example, suppose someone wills to do something for the sake of a good or bad end but stops doing it because of some obstacle, whereas another follows through on the will's movement until the deed is completely done. It is clear that the latter sort of will is more persistent in 35 good or bad, and accordingly is better or worse. The third way is in terms of intensity. There are of course some exterior acts that are naturally suited to make the will more or less intense because they are pleasant or troublesome; and it is uncontroversial that the more intensely a will tends toward what is good or bad, the better or worse it is. 40

On the other hand, if we are talking about the goodness that an exterior act has because of its matter and appropriate circumstances, that is related to the will as its terminus and end. And in that way it adds to the goodness or badness of the will, since every inclination or movement is perfected by achieving its end or attaining its terminus. Accordingly, a will is not complete unless it is such that, given the opportunity, it would act. If, however, there is no possibility of acting, but the will is complete in such a way that it would act if it could, the lack of perfection that comes from the exterior act is unqualifiedly involuntary. Now just as what is involuntary does not deserve punishment or reward when someone does what is good or bad, 50 so too when someone's failing to do what is good or bad is unqualifiedly involuntary, that does not subtract anything from punishment or reward.

**Response to 1.** Chrysostom is speaking of a case in which someone's act of will is complete and he fails to act only because he lacks the power to do so. 55

**Response to 2.** That argument is about the goodness that the exterior act has from the willing of the end. The goodness that the exterior act has from matter and circumstances is distinct from the goodness of the will that comes from the end, but not from the goodness that the will has from the act willed; rather, the goodness that the exterior act has from matter 60 and circumstances is the ground and cause of the goodness that the will has from the act willed, as I explained above [art. 1–2].

And from this the **Response to 3** is clear.

### Article 5. Does a consequence add to
### the goodness or badness of an act?[163]

It seems that a consequence adds to the goodness or badness of an act:

1. An effect preexists virtually (*virtute*) in its cause, and consequences follow from an act in the way that effects follow from causes. Therefore, they preexist virtually in acts. And any given thing is judged in terms of its
5    virtue (*virtus*), since virtue is what makes its possessor good, as is said in *Ethics* II [1106a15]. Therefore, consequences add to the goodness or badness of an act.

2. The good things that hearers do are of course effects that follow from the preaching of the learned. And such good things redound to the credit
10    of the preacher, as is evident from what is said in Philippians 4:1, "My most beloved and longed-for brothers, my joy and my crown." Therefore, a consequence adds to the goodness or badness of an act.

3. Punishment is not increased unless guilt grows. That is why Deuteronomy 25:2 says, "The measure of the sin will set the limit of the beating."
15    And punishment is increased because of a consequence; after all, Exodus 21:20 says, "If the ox gored yesterday and the day before, and people warned its owner but he did not lock it up, and it killed a man and a woman, the ox shall be stoned, and they shall kill its owner"—whereas the owner would not be killed if the ox did not kill anyone, even if he did not lock it up.
20    Therefore, a consequence adds to the goodness or badness of an act.

4. If one does something that can cause death, by striking or by pronouncing judgment, and death does not follow, one does not contract irregularity, whereas one would contract irregularity if death did follow. Therefore, a consequence adds to the goodness or badness of an act.

25    **On the contrary.** A consequence does not make a good act bad or a bad act good. For example, if someone gives alms to a poor person who then uses the money to sin, that does not detract from the one who gave alms. And similarly, if someone patiently bears a wrong done to her, the one who did the wrong is not thereby exonerated. Therefore, a consequence does
30    not add to the goodness or badness of an act.

**Reply.** A consequence is either foreseen or not. If it is foreseen, obviously it adds to goodness or badness. After all, when someone realizes that many bad things can follow from his act, and does not refrain from the act in light of that, it is evident that his will is more inordinate as a result. If,
35    however, the consequence is not foreseen, we need to make a distinction. If it follows *per se*, or in most cases, from such an act, the consequence adds to the goodness or badness of the act; it is, after all, clear that an act from which many good things can follow is better in its genus, and an act

---

163. Parallel passages: *ST* I-II.73.8; *On Evil* 1.3 resp. 15, 3.10 resp. 5.

from which many bad things are apt to follow is worse. But if it follows *per accidens*, or in few cases, then the consequence does not add to the good- 40 ness or badness of the act; after all, a thing is not judged according to what it is *per accidens*, but only according to what it is *per se*.

**Response to 1.** The power (*virtus*) of a cause is judged according to its *per se* effects, not its *per accidens* effects.

**Response to 2.** The good deeds of the hearers follow from the preach- 45 ing of the learned as *per se* effects. That is why they redound to the credit of the preacher, and particularly so when they were intended beforehand.

**Response to 3.** The consequence for which the infliction of punishment on the owner is commanded is a *per se* effect of such a cause and is also assumed to be foreseen. That is why it is imputed for punishment. 50

**Response to 4.** That argument would work if irregularity followed from guilt. But it does not; it follows from a deed, because of some defect in a sacrament.

*Article 6. Can one and the same
exterior act be both good and bad?*[164]

It seems that one act can be both good and bad:

1. A movement that is continuous is one movement, as is said in *Physics* V [228a20]. And one continuous movement can be good and bad. For example, someone who walks continuously to church might first intend an empty reputation but then later intend to serve God. Therefore, one act 5 can be good and bad.

2. According to the Philosopher in *Physics* III [202a18], action and passion are one act. And it is possible for a passion (such as Christ's) to be good when the action (such as the Jews') is bad. Therefore, one act can be good and bad. 10

3. Since a slave is in effect an instrument of a master, the slave's action is the master's action, in just the way that a tool's action is the action of the artisan. Now it can happen that a slave's action issues from a good will on the part of the master, and thus is good, but from a bad will on the part of the slave, and thus is bad. Therefore, the same act can be good and bad. 15

**On the contrary.** Contraries cannot be in the same thing. Good and bad are contraries. Therefore, one act cannot be good and bad.

**Reply.** There is no reason something cannot be one as it exists in one genus but multiple as it is referred to some other genus. For example, a continuous surface is one, considered in the genus of quantity, but mul- 20 tiple considered in the genus of color if it is partly white and partly black. And similarly, there is no reason an act cannot be one as considered in the

---

164. Parallel passage: *Sent.* II.40.4.

domain of nature, but not one as considered in the domain of morals, or
vice versa, as I have explained [I-II.18.7 resp. 1]. So continuous walking is
25    one act in the domain of nature, but it can turn out to be more than one
act in the domain of morals if the will of the one who is walking changes,
because the will is the principle of moral acts. Therefore, if by 'one act' we
understand an act that is one in the domain of morals, it is impossible for
one act to be both good and bad, with moral goodness and moral badness.
30    But if we understand it as one act in the domain of nature, and not in the
moral domain, one act can be both good and bad.

**Response to 1.** That continuous motion that issues from different intentions is one with respect to nature, but not one with respect to morals.

**Response to 2.** Action and passion belong to the domain of morals inso-
35    far as they are voluntary. And therefore, since they are called voluntary on
the basis of distinct wills, they are two, morally speaking, and can be good
in one will and bad in another.

**Response to 3.** The slave's act is not the master's act insofar as it issues
from the slave's will, but only insofar as it issues from the master's com-
40    mand. That is why the slave's bad will doesn't make the master bad.

### Question 21. Features That Accrue to Human Acts

Next we need to investigate the features that accrue to human acts by reason of their goodness or badness. Concerning this there are four questions:
    Article 1. Does a human act count as right or sinful simply by being
good or bad?
    Article 2. Does it count as praiseworthy or blameworthy?
    Article 3. Does it count as meritorious or demeritorious?
    Article 4. Does it count as meritorious or demeritorious before God?

*Article 1. Does a human act count as right*
*or sinful simply by being good or bad?*

It seems that a human act does not count as right or sinful simply by being
good or bad:
    1. "Monsters are sins in nature," as is said in *Physics* II [199b4]. But
monsters are not acts; they are things generated apart from the order of
5    nature. Now the products of art and reason imitate the products of nature,
as is said in the same passage [199a16]. Therefore, an act does not count as
a sin simply because it is inordinate and bad.
    2. As is said in *Physics* II [199a33], a sin occurs in nature and art when
the end intended by nature or art is not attained. By contrast, the good-
10    ness or badness of a human act consists above all else in the intention and

pursuit of the end. Therefore, it does not seem that the badness of an act makes it a sin.

3. If the badness of an act made it a sin, it would follow that there would be sin wherever there is something bad. But that is false: punishment, though it is bad, does not count as sin. Therefore, an act does not count as 15 a sin simply because it is bad.

**On the contrary.** As I showed above [I-II.19.4], the goodness of a human act ultimately depends on the eternal law, and consequently the badness of a human act consists in its being out of harmony with the eternal law. And the fact that something is out of harmony with the eternal law makes 20 it a sin, since, as Augustine says in *Against Faustus* XXII [ch. 27], "Sin is something said, done, or desired contrary to the eternal law." Therefore, a human act counts as a sin simply because it is bad.

**Reply.** *Badness* is broader than *sin*, just as *goodness* is broader than *rightness*. After all, any privation of goodness, whatever it is in, counts as 25 bad; whereas sin, properly speaking, is in an act that is done for the sake of some end, when the act does not have an appropriate relation to that end. Now the appropriate relation to an end is measured according to some rule. The rule in things that act according to nature is the very power of nature that inclines to such an end. So when an act issues from a natural power 30 in keeping with its natural inclination to an end, rightness is preserved in the act, since what is intermediate does not depart from the extremes—or more precisely, the act does not depart from the order of the active principle to its end. But when an act diverges from such rightness, it counts as a sin.

By contrast, in things that are done by will, the proximate rule is human 35 reason, but the supreme rule is the eternal law. So when a human act moves toward an end in keeping with the order of reason and the eternal law, the act is right; but when an act diverges from this rightness, it is called a sin. Now it is clear from what I have already established [I-II.18.3–4] that every voluntary act is bad in virtue of diverging from the order of reason 40 and the eternal law, and every good act is in harmony with reason and the eternal law. From this it follows that an act counts as right or as sinful simply because it is good or bad.

**Response to 1.** Monsters are called sins insofar as they are produced by a sin in an act of nature. 45

**Response to 2.** There are two kinds of end: ultimate and proximate. Now in a sin of nature, the act does indeed fall short of the ultimate end, which is the perfection of what is generated; but it does not fall short of some proximate end, since nature works by forming something. Similarly, in a sin of the will, the act always falls short of the ultimate end that is 50 intended, since no voluntary bad act can be ordered to happiness, which is the ultimate end; but it need not fall short of some proximate end that

the will intends and achieves. For that reason, since the intention of this
proximate end is itself ordered to the ultimate end, the intention of such
55    an end can count as either right or sinful.

**Response to 3.** Each thing is ordered to its end through its act. Consequently, since what it means for something to be a sin is for it to deviate
from the order to the end, sin is properly found in an act. Punishment, by
contrast, has to do with the person who sins, as I explained in the First
60    Part [I.48.5 resp. 4].

*Article 2. Is a human act praiseworthy or*
*blameworthy simply because it is good or bad?*[165]

It seems that a human act is not praiseworthy or blameworthy simply
because it is good or bad:

1. "Sin occurs even in things that are done by nature," as is said in *Physics* II [199a35]. Yet natural things are not praiseworthy or blameworthy, as
5    is said in *Ethics* III [1114a23]. Therefore, a human act is not blameworthy
just because it is bad, and consequently neither is an act praiseworthy simply because it is good.

2. Sin in moral acts is analogous to sin in acts of an art, since, as is said
in *Physics* II [199a33], "A grammarian sins by not writing correctly and a
10    doctor by not giving medicine correctly." But the practitioner of an art is
not blamed for doing something bad, because those who practice an art can
make a good product or a bad one on purpose, as they choose. Therefore, it
seems that a moral act as well is not blameworthy simply because it is bad.

3. Dionysius says in *On the Divine Names* 4 [§31] that what is bad is
15    weak and powerless. And weakness and powerlessness either take away or
diminish blameworthiness. Therefore, a human act is not blameworthy
simply because it is bad.

**On the contrary.** The Philosopher says that the deeds of the virtues are
praiseworthy, whereas the contrary deeds are loathsome or blameworthy.[166]
20    Now good acts are acts of virtue, since "a virtue is what makes its possessors
good and makes their deeds good," as is said in *Ethics* II [1106a15]; accordingly, the opposite acts are bad acts. Therefore, a human act is praiseworthy
or blameworthy simply because it is good or bad.

**Reply.** Just as *badness* is broader than *sin, sin* is broader than *blamewor-
25    thiness.* You see, an act is called blameworthy or praiseworthy because it
is imputed to an agent—to praise or blame *just is* to impute to agents the
goodness or badness of their acts. Now acts are imputed to agents when
they are in the agents' power in such a way that they have control over their

---

165. Parallel passage: *On Evil* 2.2 resp. 3.
166. See perhaps pseudo-Aristotle, *On Virtues and Vices* I, 1249a25–30.

own acts. And that is the case in all voluntary acts, since human beings have control over their acts through the will, as is evident from things I said    30
above [I-II.1.1–2]. So we can conclude that goodness or badness makes for praiseworthiness or blameworthiness only in voluntary acts; in voluntary acts badness, sin, and blameworthiness are all the same thing.

**Response to 1.** Natural acts are not in the power of the natural agent, because nature is determined to one. And so, although there is sin in natu-    35
ral acts, there is no blameworthiness in them.

**Response to 2.** Reason works differently in the domain of art from how it works in the moral domain. You see, in the domain of art, reason is ordered to a particular end, which is something thought up by reason. In the moral domain, by contrast, reason is ordered to the general end of    40
the whole of human life. Now a particular end is ordered to a general end. Therefore, since a sin comes about through some divergence from the order to an end, as I have said [art. 1], there are two ways in which a sin can occur in an act of art. One is through a divergence from the particular end intended by the practitioner. That is the sort of sin that is proper to    45
the domain of art: for example, when an artisan intends to produce a good work but produces a bad one, or intends to produce a bad work but produces a good one. The other way is through a divergence from the general end of human life. This is the way in which an artisan sins by intending to produce—and successfully producing—a bad work, by which someone    50
else is deceived. But this sort of sin belongs to the artisan not as artisan, but as human being. Accordingly, for the first sort of sin, the artisan receives blame as an artisan, whereas for the second sort of sin, the human being receives blame as a human being.

In the moral domain, by contrast, the order of reason to the general end    55
of human life is what matters, so sin and badness are judged according to their divergence from the order of reason to the general end of human life. And so for such a sin, human beings are blamed insofar as they are human beings, and insofar as they are in the moral realm. That is why the Philosopher says in *Ethics* VI [1140b22] that "one who sins willingly is more    60
choiceworthy in the realm of art, but less choiceworthy in what concerns prudence, as also in the case of the moral virtues," which it is the job of practical reason to direct.

**Response to 3.** The weakness that exists in bad wills is subject to human control, and so it does not take away or diminish blameworthiness.    65

### Article 3. Does a human act count as meritorious or demeritorious simply because it is good or bad?[167]

It seems that a human act does not count as meritorious or demeritorious simply because it is good or bad:

1. We speak of merit and demerit in connection with recompense, which applies only to acts that affect someone else. And not all human
5   acts are good or bad for someone else; some acts are good or bad for the agent. Therefore, not every good or bad human act counts as meritorious or demeritorious.

2. People do not merit punishment or reward for doing as they please with things over which they have control: for example, someone who
10  destroys his own possession is not punished, as he would be if he destroyed someone else's possession. Now human beings are in control of their own actions. Therefore, they do not merit punishment or reward for acting well or badly.

3. Someone does not merit having someone else do something good for
15  her simply because she acquires something good for herself; and the same reasoning holds for acquiring something bad. And a good act is itself a good thing for the agent, and a perfection of the agent, whereas an inordinate act is a bad thing for the agent. Therefore, someone does not acquire merit or demerit simply because she does a good or bad act.

20  **On the contrary.** Isaiah 3:10–11 says, "Tell the just that things go well for them, because they eat the fruit of their labors. Woe to the impious! Things go badly for them, for what their hands have done will be done to them."

**Reply.** We speak of merit and demerit in connection with recompense
25  that is made according to justice. Now people are recompensed according to justice because they act to help or harm someone else. But it is important to note that everyone who lives in any society is in a way a part and member of the whole society. So whatever anyone does for the good or bad of someone who lives in a society overflows into the whole society, as
30  someone who causes injury to a hand causes injury to the person. Therefore, when someone acts for the good or bad of another individual, the act is meritorious or demeritorious in two ways: first, in that it deserves recompense from the individual who is helped or harmed; and second, in that it deserves recompense from society as a whole. By contrast, when
35  someone orders an act directly to the good or bad of the whole society, the act deserves recompense primarily and principally from society as a whole, but secondarily from all the parts of society. But even when one acts in a way that brings about something good or bad just for oneself, the act still

---

167. Parallel passage: *On Evil* 2.2 resp. 3.

*Question 21. Features That Accrue to Human Acts* 205

deserves recompense insofar as it also affects the whole, since the agent
is part of that whole, though it does not deserve recompense insofar as it 40
is good or bad for the individual person who is the agent—except perhaps
from that very person, by a sort of analogy, since there is such a thing as
justice to oneself.

Thus, it is clear that a good or bad act counts as praiseworthy or blameworthy because it is in the power of the will, as right or sinful because of 45
its order to an end, and as meritorious or demeritorious in accordance with
the recompense demanded by justice with respect to another.

**Response to 1.** Sometimes a good or bad human act, though it is not
ordered to the good or bad of another individual person, is indeed ordered
to the good or bad of another, which is the community itself. 50

**Response to 2.** Yes, human beings have control over their own actions.
But insofar as they belong to another, namely, their community, of which
they are a part, they acquire merit or demerit for acting well or badly, as
they also do if they make good or bad use of other things of their own with
which they ought to serve the community. 55

**Response to 3.** This very good or bad that people do for themselves
through their acts overflows into the community, as has been explained
[in the main reply].

*Article 4. Does a human act count as meritorious or
demeritorious before God simply because it is good or bad?*[168]

It seems that a good or bad human act does not count as meritorious or
demeritorious before God:

1. As has been said [art. 3], merit and demerit imply a relation to some
recompense for help or harm done to another. And a good or bad human
act does not help or harm God himself: as Job 35:6–7 says, "If you sin, what 5
harm will you do to him? And if you act justly, what benefit will you do for
him?" Therefore, a good or bad human act does not count as meritorious
or demeritorious before God.

2. An instrument does not acquire merit or demerit with respect to the
one who uses it, since the instrument's whole action belongs to the one 10
who uses it. And human beings in acting are instruments of the divine
power that is their principal mover. That is why Isaiah 10 says, "Shall the
ax boast against the one who wields it, or the saw magnify itself against
the one who handles it?"—clearly treating human beings as instruments.
Therefore, human beings do not acquire merit or demerit before God by 15
acting well or badly.

---

168. Parallel passage: ST I-II.114.1.

3. Human acts count as meritorious or demeritorious insofar as they are
ordered to another. And not all human acts are ordered to God. Therefore,
not all good or bad human acts are meritorious or demeritorious before
20   God.

**On the contrary.** The last chapter of Ecclesiastes [12:14] says, "God will
bring into judgment everything that is done, whether good or bad." Now
judgment implies recompense, and we speak of merit and demerit precisely
in connection with recompense. Therefore, every good or bad human act
25   counts as meritorious or demeritorious before God.

**Reply.** As has been said [art. 3], an act of any human being counts as
meritorious or demeritorious insofar as it is ordered to another, either by
reason of that other, or by reason of the community. Now our good or bad
acts can be meritorious or demeritorious before God for both reasons. They
30   can be such by reason of the other insofar as God is the ultimate end of
human beings, and human beings ought to direct all their acts to the ultimate end, as I maintained above [I-II.19.10]. Accordingly, someone who
does a bad act that cannot be directed to God fails to treat God with the
honor that is due to the ultimate end.

35       By contrast, human acts can be meritorious or demeritorious before God
by reason of the whole community of the universe because in any community, the one who governs the community is chiefly concerned for the
common good; that is why it is that person's job to make recompense for
the good or bad acts that are done within the community. Now God gov-
40   erns and rules the whole universe, as I showed in the First Part [I.103.5],
and especially rational creatures. Thus it is clear that human acts count as
meritorious or demeritorious with respect to God; otherwise, it would follow that God has no concern for human acts.

**Response to 1.** God cannot acquire or lose anything in and of himself
45   through a human act, but human beings, for their part, do take something
away from God or offer something to him when they preserve, or fail to
preserve, the order that God has instituted.

**Response to 2.** Human beings are moved by God as instruments in a
way that does not rule out their moving themselves through free choice, as
50   is clear from things I said above [I-II.9.6 resp. 3]. And therefore they acquire
merit or demerit before God through their acts.

**Response to 3.** The ordering of human beings to their political community does not encompass everything they are and everything they have, and
so not every human act has to be meritorious or demeritorious in virtue of
55   its ordering to the political community. But everything human beings are,
everything they can do, and everything they have ought to be ordered to
God, and so every good or bad human act counts as meritorious or demeritorious before God by the very nature of the act.

# Commentary on the
# Treatise on Happiness

The Commentary on the Treatise on Happiness follows Aquinas's division of questions and articles. We proceed article by article, first stating the question Aquinas poses in the article and then supplying a one- or two-sentence summary of his answer. After general remarks about the issues raised in the article, the commentary considers the objections and responses and then Aquinas's main reply.

One feature of the commentary worth noting is that it differs from the structure of the original articles in treating Aquinas's response to an objection immediately after presenting the objection (as opposed to having a separate section for responses to objections that comes after the main reply). This reads more smoothly and also allows for a more unified discussion of those exchanges.

## Prologue

As discussed in the Introduction (pp. xix–xxii), the Treatises on Happiness and Human Acts comprise the first twenty-one questions of the Second Part of the *Summa theologiae*. Thomas Aquinas is turning here from his examination of God and God's creatures in the First Part, to the moral life: how human beings are meant to act in light of their status as image bearers of God.

As Aquinas puts it, "now that I have discussed the one whom we image—namely, God—and the things that have issued from God's power in accordance with his will [namely, creatures], it remains for us to investigate God's image—namely, human beings—insofar as we are the source of our own acts because we possess free choice and have power over what we do." The entire Second Part of the *Summa* is devoted to an examination of human beings, then, but as with the First Part the end purpose is to gain a better understanding of God.

It is significant that Aquinas opens the prologue with the comment that human beings are made *into* the image of God, as opposed to their being made simply *in* the image of God. The First Part of the *Summa* focused on the *nature* of God, angels, material creatures, and human beings; the Second Part of the *Summa* focuses on the *actions* of human beings in relation to their final end—imaging God. This imaging is not just a passive matter of being stamped with God's likeness. It is an active process of being made more like God through our good exercise of free choice and our power over our own actions. Aquinas's language here is purposive: the image of God is both the form we possess insofar as we are human and the final end we are headed toward, in the sense that the more complete or perfect we become as human beings, the better we represent God. Imaging God requires shaping our own lives through reason and free choice. (As Aquinas makes clear in the Second Part of the Second Part, however, God's grace is necessary for us to reach this final end.)

One of the most important themes that ties the Treatise on Happiness to the Treatise on Human Acts is Aquinas's interest in what it means for human beings to be "endowed with free choice and capable of controlling our own acts." After all, if human actions weren't under our control in some important sense, the entire Second Part of the *Summa* would just be a narrative of how we do act, rather than an examination of how we should act. Yet, as we'll see, Aquinas is keenly interested in distinguishing acts for which human beings are morally responsible from those for which we aren't.

At the same time, Aquinas brings up our capacity for free action in the context of our relation to God—our First Cause and Final End. His description of human beings as "the source of our own acts because we possess free choice and have power over what we do" should not be read in a radically existential way, where we face unlimited possibilities. Rather, human beings possess various sorts of powers (including sense perception, locomotion, memory, imagination, and reason) in distinctively human ways that limit their exercise. We are able to exercise those powers intrinsically, as opposed to extrinsically (like how a stone's power to change location can only be actualized by something else's picking it up and moving it), but our capacity for free choice is always exercised within the boundaries of human nature as God's creations. And, for Aquinas, our choices are always made within a eudaimonist framework: that is, in a framework in which happiness (in Greek, *eudaimonia*), is the ultimate end or aim of all rational action. What this means, and whether it's philosophically defensible, is the subject of the entire first question of the Treatise on Happiness.

### Question 1: The Ultimate End of Human Beings

*1.1. Is it characteristic of human*
*beings to act for the sake of an end?*

Answer: yes, it is characteristic of human beings to act for the sake of an end.

This whole question is aimed at establishing a premise key to both Aquinas's account of human happiness and his claims about how human actions relate to it—namely, that all human beings share one, final end: knowing and loving God. The first article starts small. Rather than attempting to establish anything about an ultimate end, it simply asks whether acting for the sake of an end (in general) is typical of human action. In his response, Aquinas clarifies what the scope of "human action" is (discounting involuntary actions such as sneezing in favor of actions that involve a deliberate interplay between intellect and will) and argues that all such acts must be aimed at some end. Insofar as we act *as human beings*, we act for the sake of an end.

**Obj. and resp. 1.** The first objection pushes the question of what it means to act for the sake of an end. We appear to act "for the sake of" things that we describe as *causing* our actions, like when I say I went to the coffee shop for the sake of getting a cappuccino, and it seems fair to describe the cappuccino as being the cause of my going to the coffee shop. Causes are the kind of things that come before their effects, though, whereas an end is the kind of thing that comes last (as its name indicates).

In response, Aquinas distinguishes between two senses of what it means for something to be an end of action: an end is the *last* thing achieved in an action in the sense that sipping the cappuccino is the last stage of the process aimed at that end, but it is also the thing that comes *first* in the agent's intention in the sense that I set getting a cappuccino as my end. In the second way, the end counts as the cause of my going to the coffee shop (and ordering and then enjoying it).

**Obj. and resp. 2.** The second objection cuts right to the chase. As will become clear in art. 4, Aquinas is most interested in determining whether all human beings act for the sake of an ultimate end, and this objection focuses on the nature of ultimate ends, claiming that actions that are themselves ultimate ends cannot be performed for the sake of an ultimate end (since they themselves *are* the ultimate end). This objection also explicitly draws on Aristotle's *Nicomachean Ethics*, which is significant because the entire structure of the Treatise on Happiness consciously parallels Aristotle's discussion of happiness in book I of the *Ethics*.

In his response to this objection, Aquinas first notes that any human action that might itself count as an ultimate end must be voluntary (for reasons he explained in the reply—namely, all properly human acts are the result of an interplay between intellect and will). Second, Aquinas says that voluntary acts are either commanded or elicited. Elicited acts involve the will actualizing itself, and this means that elicited acts can't be ultimate ends. Why? Because Aquinas thinks that the end is the object of the will, and he doesn't think that we can take the act of willing itself as an end. That would be like trying to take the act of seeing as itself the object of vision. In the same way that it doesn't make sense to say that what we're trying to see is itself seeing, it doesn't make sense to say that what we want is itself willing. If a voluntary action isn't elicited, however, then it's commanded. And so any action that would itself be an ultimate end must be commanded. But commanded acts (where the will is directed at some object, like walking or speaking) are always aimed at some end. So any action that counts as an ultimate end still counts as an action aimed at an end—where, in that case, its end is itself.

**Obj. and resp. 3.** We don't always think about what we're going to do before we do it, like when we're scratching an itch or jiggling a leg. So it doesn't seem like we always act for the sake of an end.

In response, Aquinas agrees that not everything a human being does is the result of deliberation—but (as he argues in the main reply) all genuinely *human* actions are. When we're absentmindedly scratching an itch, we're unthinkingly responding to sensory input in the same way that non-rational animals also do. (Non-rational animals also have imaginations, which for Aquinas is a way of talking about the ability to store images that we get from our senses, like the way the sun feels on your back or the way freshly mowed grass smells.)

The argument **On the contrary** here also appeals to Aristotle's authority. According to Aristotle, the principle of an action is its end (in the sense of being what the action is aimed at—its cause, in the sense specified in the response to the first objection). And every properly human act—the sort that is intentional and voluntary—has an end as its principle.

**Reply.** In his reply, Aquinas stresses the importance of the actions we perform *as human*—that is, insofar as we are not just animals but are *rational* animals. The difference for Aquinas is that being rational means having control over one's actions, in the sense of being able to imagine various courses of action with different sorts of outcomes and then being able to deliberate between those options and to choose which one we want to pursue. As Aquinas will expand on in the next article, what's most characteristic of human action is this interplay between intellect and will. We can act instinctively, like when I jerk my hand back after accidentally touching something hot, or when you absentmindedly shift position to get more comfortable in a long lecture, but the qualifiers in those descriptions are vital: I'm acting before my brain has time to process the pain sensations my hand is experiencing, and you're moving into a more comfortable position without any conscious thought. Genuinely *human* actions are ones that we choose freely, as the result of interaction between intellect (which presents the will with a specific potential goal or end) and will (which desires that end *as good*).

Aquinas discusses the mechanics of human action, including the role and process of deliberation, in much more detail in the Treatise on Human Acts. Here at the outset of the Treatise on Happiness, he is focused just on what motivates our actions and on making a distinction between the sorts of actions that we have control over and those that we don't. This distinction proves crucial for the rest of both the Treatise on Happiness and the Treatise on Human Acts, for (as he repeatedly remarks) we are only morally responsible for the actions we perform voluntarily—and only voluntary actions will lead to our becoming perfectly happy.

That said, Aquinas's argument here for the claim that all properly human actions are "for the sake" of an end is not immediately transparent. He writes that "Every action that issues from a given power is caused by that power in accordance with the nature of the power's object," but this isn't likely to be very illuminating to anyone who isn't already familiar with medieval metaphysics. Imagine, then, the power of sight. Plugging vision into Aquinas's general framework here, we get the conclusion that seeing is an action that issues from the power of sight and that it is caused by the power of sight "in accordance with the nature of the power's object." The proper object of sight is color. This means that the *action* of seeing is caused by the *power* of sight and aimed at seeing its proper *object*: color. (This is actually the same example he uses in his response to the second objection.) The action of seeing gets its nature from the object of the power of sight.

The same thing is true of human actions. Every action that issues from the will (so, every action that we have control over) is caused by that power (namely, the will) in accordance with the nature of the will's object. What's the will's proper object? According to Aquinas, it is "the end and the good." Put simply, the idea here is that all properly human actions are voluntary and caused by the will for the sake of some desired end—namely, a particular good that will desires.

### 1.2. Is acting for the sake of an end something that only rational natures do?

Answer: all agents act for the sake of an end, but *intentionally* acting for the sake of an end is something that only beings with rational natures (like human beings, angels, and God) do.

This article raises the question: what is distinctive of rational nature? Aquinas is assuming familiarity here with what he's said in the first part of the *Summa*, particularly in the Treatise on Human Nature (QQ75–89). For our purposes, what's most relevant there is his claim that all rational beings have intellects and wills, which we can think of roughly as the capacity to judge the true and the capacity to desire the good.

The difference this makes when we're thinking about actions is that while a stone (Aquinas's paradigmatic example of something non-rational) will naturally fall to the floor when it gets knocked off a shelf, it can't decide that it *wants* to move itself down. Rational beings, on the other hand, can both intend a particular end (as when I get annoyed by my office door blowing shut when I have the window open and decide I want to prop it open with the stone paperweight my son gave me for Mother's Day) and act to realize that end (as when I then take the rock off my desk and put it on the floor in front of my door).

**Obj. and resp. 1.** The first objection begins with an assumption that Aquinas appears to share: human actions don't just aim randomly toward some unknown end—they aim at a particular end that the person has in mind. But this makes it look as though non-rational creatures don't act for the sake of an end. Rocks and trees, for example, don't have minds at all and so can't knowingly act for an end, and non-rational animals (which for Aquinas means all non-human animals) don't have the right sort of minds and so can't *intend* to act for an end in the relevant way. (For Aquinas, a cow might move under shelter during a rainstorm, but it's acting in response to sense perception, not because it's consciously formed the intention to get out of the storm.)

Aquinas's response is to qualify the claim that human beings always act for the sake of an end they have in mind. Sometimes, he says, we act in response to someone else's instructions (as when I'm driving and you give me directions) or instigation (as when you cry "Duck!" and I immediately duck). In those cases, we're don't ourselves cognize the end; we're being directed or moved by someone else. And that's how it always is with non-rational creatures.

**Obj. and resp. 2.** The second objection and response clarify what it means for something to be directed toward an end. The objection states that acting for the sake of an end means directing oneself toward the end, as when I decide to get another cup of coffee and then move myself to do so. Non-rational creatures cannot direct themselves toward an end.

In response, Aquinas stresses one of the distinctions that he lays out in the main reply of the article—namely, that things can be described as acting for the sake of an end insofar as they are directed toward an end. Being directed toward an end can happen either when a thing directs itself toward an end (as with rational beings) or when it is directed toward an end by someone rational. Clearly, self-directed action is going to be the kind of action most relevant to Aquinas's discussion of happiness, but it's important to recognize that he agrees with Aristotle that all things act for the sake of the good.

**Obj. and resp. 3.** The point of this objection is to clarify the will's role in acting for the sake of an end. You might think that since the object of the will is the good (as an end) and the will is a distinctively rational capacity, only beings with a rational nature can act for the sake of an end.

In response, Aquinas argues that—although only rational beings can intentionally act for the good qua good (that is, understood as the universal "good" and not as a particular good like "a cup of coffee" or "getting more comfortable"), because only creatures with a will have a rational appetite aimed at the good as such—nevertheless *all* creatures have natural or sensory appetites that aim at particular goods. Non-rational creatures can't knowingly act for "the good": they are moved toward the good under particular descriptions, as when a cow moves across a pasture to eat a patch of clover or when a stone is naturally inclined to fall "down." Nevertheless, the movement of all non-rational creatures aims at the universal good insofar as those creatures respond to the particular ends that God wills for them. In the Aristotelian framework that Aquinas adopts, everything has a final cause, or end, that it is naturally inclined toward. Aquinas here is just making explicit the idea that God sets those final causes; in that sense, everything is moved by the divine will. Rational creatures are unique in that they are able to set their own ends, and in so doing deviate from their natural inclinations.

**Reply.** The Treatise on Happiness closely mirrors the structure of Aristotle's *Nicomachean Ethics*. When Aquinas says that all agents act for the sake of an end, he is basically paraphrasing the opening sentence of the *Ethics* (namely, that all things act for the sake of the good). It's important to note that by 'agent' Aquinas isn't referring just to *conscious* agents. In this context, an agent is anything that's acting, as opposed to being acted on. When a stone is dropped and it falls, it counts as an agent. And, in falling down, the stone is tending toward its natural end. (Aquinas adopts the four element [earth, fire, wind, water] framework in which earth's natural place is "down," just as fire's natural place is "up.")

The stone doesn't fall knowingly, however—its moving "down" is the result of a natural inclination (which Aquinas also calls a natural appetite) that it has *because of the sort of thing that it is.* Any thing that moves has to be "determined to some effect," according to Aquinas, because if an agent weren't inclined toward one effect over another, it wouldn't do one thing instead of another when it moves. That is, to be an agent, a stone has to be inclined to do *something* when it gets knocked off a shelf. The fact that it falls to the ground rather than rises to the ceiling is explained by its telos, or final cause, as a stone. Non-rational animals are also directed toward natural ends, by the sensory appetite that they possess because of the sort of thing they are. Fish, for instance, will naturally be inclined to swim toward what they sense to be food, and sheep will be naturally inclined to run away from what they sense to be a threat.

For rational beings, it's not a natural or sensory appetite that determines the effect of our action: it's the will, defined as the rational appetite (or desire) for the good as such. We move ourselves toward an end that we intend, and we are naturally moved toward ends that we perceive as good. As Aquinas puts it here, we are in control of our acts "through free choice, which is a faculty of will and reason." We can decide both what particular end we want to pursue and how we want to pursue it. (This, of course, raises a whole host of issues about which ends we choose, how we choose them, and why we choose them. Not surprisingly, this is the general subject of the entire Second Part of the *Summa*—what is the nature of the moral life, and how do we live it?)

### 1.3. Do human acts get their species from their end?

Answer: yes, human acts are placed into different species ("throwing" versus "catching" versus "kicking") by what the end of that action is. What exactly this means is quite complicated and something Aquinas will discuss in much more detail in the Treatise on Human Acts, but the short answer (which is all we need at this point in the Treatise on Happiness) is that human acts are in fact "specified" (that is, lumped into a particular species of action) by their ends.

**Obj. and resp. 1.** The idea behind this objection is that an end is an extrinsic cause, because it is something outside the agent that moves the agent toward it. When you're specifying things, however, you're referring to something intrinsic—after all, specification is all about identifying which category captures something essential to a thing.

Aquinas's reply is that the end of an action isn't completely extrinsic, insofar as the action is for the sake of the end. In fact, an essential part of an action is that it be aimed at an end (either actively, as when an agent moves itself toward the end, or passively, as when an agent is moved toward the end). Thus, it makes sense for human actions to be placed in particular species according to their ends.

**Obj. and resp. 3.** On the Aristotelian theory of species that Aquinas adopts, each thing belongs to only one species: the same thing can't be both a human being and a donkey, for example. But the same act—say, patting someone on the back—can be aimed at a whole variety of different ends. I could be congratulating you for getting a new job; I could be trying to dislodge something from your throat as you choke; I could be patronizing you after you said something stupid. But the action itself could look exactly the same in all three cases.

Aquinas's response to the worry that the same action can have a number of different ends makes a distinction between natural and moral species. For any particular action, such as my patting you on the back here and now, there will be only one end, and that end will give the act its species. That is, any particular time I pat you on the back, that act will be aimed primarily at one end—congratulating, helping, or condescending. Types of action like "patting someone on the back," however, can have a wide variety of possible willed ends insofar as they belong to one *natural* species. Actions are put into different *moral* species by their particular ends, though, not by what type the action is. As Aquinas will argue later in the Treatise on Human Acts (18.8–9), types of actions can be morally neutral, but individual actions never can. This points to an important distinction between natural and moral actions: something's natural classification is accidental to its moral character, and vice versa. What's important when I congratulate you by patting you on the back is that I'm congratulating you, not that I'm patting you on the back; it's also completely accidental to its natural classification that my action of patting you on the back is aimed at congratulating you.

**Reply.** In his earlier Treatise on Human Nature, Aquinas explains that all physical objects are composites of matter and form, where matter should be understood in terms of potentiality and form should be understood as what actualizes that potentiality. (Human beings, for example, are composites of matter and form: our rational souls are the forms that actualize matter into human bodies.) In this article, Aquinas takes this basic framework and applies it to motion. Physical objects get their species from their actualizing form; human beings are rational animals on account of the rational souls that actualize their matter. Motions also get their species from actuality: the *action* of heating gets its species from the actuality that is the principle of the action (so, insofar as the fire is hot, it proceeds to heat what is around it), whereas the *passion* of heating gets its species from the actuality that is the terminus or natural end of that motion (so, insofar as a stone near the fire is disposed to get hot, it is moved toward heat). Whether we're thinking of motion in terms of action or passion, then, it's the actuality of that motion that places it in a particular species.

In the case of human acts, the end determines the act's species, whether we're thinking of them as actions or passions. Human beings move themselves toward ends (action) and are moved toward those ends by themselves (passion). We move ourselves toward an end that we apprehend and intend as a good, and so the end is the principle of that act. At the same time, the end is the terminus of our act: it is what we are moved toward as the act's final cause.

The analogy with generation is meant to help here, although it's not immediately transparent to people who are not familiar with medieval theories of generation and corruption. In generation, the generating form (for example, "hedgehog") acts to create its form in new matter, acting as both principle and terminus. That is, the form is both what is actualizing the matter in ways that make it a hedgehog, and what sets the end goal for that process (a living, breathing hedgehog!). In the case of human actions, the end is both the starting point of the act and the thing that's to be realized by that action. The act's internal end is specified by its intended end, and its external act is specified by the concrete realization of that end. In both cases, we have a single form realized in two different ways: in human acts, we have the form (qua end) first apprehended by reason and then concretely achieved; in generation, we have the form first intended by nature and then actually informing matter.

One final note: Aquinas concludes this discussion with the comment that moral and human acts are one and the same thing, but he doesn't go on to say anything more about this. As we saw in art. 1, however, properly human actions are the result of interaction between reason and will—they are the actions we perform consciously and voluntarily. Their status as voluntary is also what makes them moral, as Aquinas will discuss in much more detail in the subsequent Treatise on Human Acts (QQ6–21).

### 1.4. Is there an ultimate end of human life?

Answer: yes. If there weren't, human action would be impossible.

In fact, the central purpose of the Treatise on Happiness is to first establish that there is an ultimate end of human life and then to identify what that ultimate end is. (The secondary goal—clarifying the mechanics of the actions by which human beings achieve this ultimate end—forms the core of the Treatise on Human Acts.) Aquinas has spent the last three articles arguing that all human actions aim at an end (and that moral actions are classified by that end). With that established, he now leaves an extended discussion of human acts to questions 6–21 and moves here to a discussion of whether human *life* has an ultimate end and, if so, what the ultimate end of human life is—the medieval version of asking what the meaning of life is. This article begins that discussion by addressing whether there needs to be a final end that terminates a series of ends or whether you could have an infinite regress of ends. (Given Aquinas's general metaphysical framework, it's clear that he's not going to allow an infinite regress of ends here; his main point is essentially that you need a prime mover to get things going in the first place.)

**Obj. and resp. 1.** Aquinas is famous for his engagement with Aristotle's philosophy, but he is also influenced by Platonic thought, particularly the Neoplatonic doctrines advocated by Augustine and Boethius and absorbed into the Aristotelian tradition by the Islamic scholars whose commentaries accompanied the translation of Aristotle's texts into Latin in the late twelfth century.[1] This objection appeals to a prominent Neoplatonic figure whom Aquinas knew as Dionysius (and whom we today refer to as Pseudo-Dionysius). One of his central ideas—and one that Aquinas accepts—is that the good by nature "overflows" to everything around it. You can think not just of how water pours out of a fountain but also of how fire spreads and generates more of itself as it spreads.[2] In any event, the idea behind this objection is that if the good by nature pours itself out and generates another good thing, this process looks like it will proceed forever. Since (as Aquinas himself has just argued) the will's object is "the good," qua end, this also makes it look as though there will be an infinite procession of ends.

---

1. See Marenbon (2006) for a good introduction to the transmission of Platonic and Aristotelian ideas in the first half of the Middle Ages.

2. For a detailed discussion of this idea, see Kretzmann (1991).

In response, Aquinas flips the direction of procession. That is, the objection imagines the good continuing to pour itself out infinitely; Aquinas points out that this in no way entails that every good has to itself be poured out from another good. In fact, he believes that this outpouring has to start *somewhere*—and that this somewhere is the first good, or prime mover. So there can be an ultimate end, which would be this first good, from which all other good flows. In addition, he agrees that there *could* be an infinite procession of goods from the first good (namely, God), if we were just thinking in terms of the infinite power that first good possesses. But we also need to think of God as an intellect, and intellects naturally think in determinate terms. That is, God's goodness doesn't just overflow indiscriminately or at random: God's nature is to order and structure the good, and this means that God's goodness overflows in determinate ways and not just mushily into infinity.

**Obj. and resp. 2.** This objection trades on Aquinas's belief that the will desires only what the intellect conceives as good. (For my will to want something—say, walking to the store—my intellect first has to have judged that taking a walk would be a good way to achieve an end, such as buying some milk.) The worry here is that reason can think of an infinite number of things (for example, numbers), and so can also apprehend an infinite sequence of goods, which would seem to imply that we could also desire an infinite sequence of goods.

Aquinas's response is that things that are intrinsically related to each other never involve an infinite progression, because there is some determinate thing that connects them (namely, a particular end). Things that are accidentally related to each other, however, can proceed into infinity. So, for example, you take a number and just keep adding to it forever. But there's no intrinsic relation between the numbers in that sequence, in the way that matters for this discussion.

**Obj. and resp. 3.** This objection refers to the recursive nature of willing. I can not only will to go for a run but also will to will to go for a run, and will to will to will going for a run, etc. It looks like I could keep this process going indefinitely, and this seems incompatible with there being an ultimate end to the process.

Aquinas's response is short and sweet: he points out that it's really the same end you're willing in all those cases (namely, going for a run), and so the fact that you can will to will (to will to will to will) a particular end doesn't say anything about whether ends can be related to each other in an infinite progression.

**Reply.** The question posed at the outset of the article is whether human life has an end, but the question that Aquinas actually answers here is a bit narrower—namely, whether there need to be ultimate ends in general. He takes the next two articles to settle whether there is one particular ultimate end for human life (and whether that end is the same for all human beings). So this article is really just arguing that there need to be ultimate ends in general.

The intuition that this argument relies on is that for any sort of action to get off the ground, there needs to be something that kicks off the whole process. This is essentially Aristotle's famous argument for the Prime Mover: if there were just an infinite series of things moving each other, nothing could explain the motion starting in the first place. Aquinas claims that this need for an ultimate end is common to any essentially connected causal chain. That is, the ultimate end of a chain in which there is some real (as opposed to accidental) connection between the different links provides the unifying/motivating "something" that unites those links. (An accidental sequence, however, can keep going indefinitely, since there isn't one thing that ties the elements of the sequence together and toward which everything else is directed. When I'm thirsty, my deliberation ends once I've come up with a plan for satisfying that thirst, but if I'm rolling a die to determine which way to turn when I get to an intersection, there is, in theory, no reason that sequence should ever end.)

It's important to note that Aquinas is not thinking of an ultimate end in the sense of the "end-all, be-all" of, say, human existence. An ultimate end in its most general form is simply something that is desired for its own sake rather than for the sake of anything further. And Aquinas holds that there needs to be something desired for its own sake to put appetite (rational or sensory) in motion in the first place. Suppose that I am extremely thirsty. I desire the satisfaction of my thirst. In this context—that is, in the situation where my focus is how much I need something to drink—satisfying my thirst is something I desire for its own sake, and it is what ties together and explains an entire sequence of events, such as my getting off the couch, looking around for a glass, walking over to the fridge, etc. The very nature of trying to perform an action would be frustrated if there were an infinite series of ends—there wouldn't be anything that got me moving in the first place.

In this general sense of ultimate end, of course, we can have multiple ultimate ends. The next three articles focus on the specific nature of the ultimate end of human life, which is where happiness finally enters the discussion.

*1.5. Can one human being*
*have more than one ultimate end?*

Answer: no, human beings can have only one ultimate end at any one time.

Although the previous article asked whether there is an ultimate end for human life, it actually focused on the need for ultimate ends in human action. Having argued that for action to kick off, there really does need to be something we desire for its own sake, Aquinas turns in this article to the question of whether we can desire multiple things for their own sake at the same time.

His answer to this question is going to be important insofar as it illuminates his account of the will and its role in moral responsibility. Aquinas gives three separate arguments defending the claim that we can will only one ultimate end at any given time. (Unfortunately, as we'll see later in the Treatise on Human Acts, the way he defends this claim here sets him up for further philosophical difficulties with his theory of the will.)

The objections to this article shift between "ultimate end" in the sense of (1) something that is willed for its own sake rather than for the sake of something further, and "ultimate end" in the sense of (2) *the* ultimate end toward which all the other things we will are aimed. To be fair, Aquinas also shifts between these two senses in this article, which doesn't help in understanding his position.

**Obj. and resp. 1.** This objection trades on the second understanding of ultimate end. If the ultimate end for human beings involves multiple components (such as pleasure, rest, health, and virtue), then it seems as though human beings desire each of those components simultaneously for their own sake.

Aquinas's response doesn't rule out the possibility that the ultimate end of human life is compositional (as opposed to monolithic and consisting in only one activity). As we'll see in 3.5, he believes that our ultimate end, perfect happiness, "consists entirely in contemplation." Here, however, Aquinas simply replies that people who see our ultimate end as compositional still understand the different elements of that composition as being unified into a single perfect good.

**Obj. and resp. 2.** This objection moves back to the first sense of ultimate end, pointing out that it seems as though we can will multiple things for their own sake, as long as those ends are not mutually incompatible.

Aquinas's response makes it clear that he's interested primarily in the second sense of ultimate end (namely, *the* ultimate end toward which all the other things we will are aimed). It might be possible for us to will a variety of things for their own sake, he says—although the body of the article argues that even then it's not possible for us to will them all simultaneously—but the sort of ultimate end that is a *perfect* good contains within it everything that we could want in relation to that thing. Aquinas is relying in this response on what he's said about the relation between an ultimate end and a perfect good in the main reply; the concept of a perfect good becomes increasingly important as he focuses on the sort of ultimate end he thinks could be *the* ultimate end for all human beings.

**Obj. and resp. 3.** This objection appears to be arguing that because human beings have free choice, we can change our minds about what we will as our ultimate end, and so we can have multiple ultimate ends. Even in a case where I've chosen pleasure as my ultimate end (an example that Aquinas borrows from Aristotle's *Nicomachean Ethics* I.3), it still appears open to me to choose wealth as my ultimate end instead. Thus, it seems like I can want more than one ultimate end at a time, in the sense that our wills are not locked into desiring just one particular ultimate end.

Aquinas doesn't disagree with the claim that we can change our mind about what we aim our lives at. What he does disagree with is the idea that this means we can genuinely will more than one ultimate end at the same time. He says the will doesn't have the power to make opposing things exist simultaneously ('*opposita*' here doesn't mean opposites in the hot-and-cold or black-and-white sense of opposite; it means flatly contradictory things, like taking a walk and not taking a walk). This doesn't quite seem to get at the original objection, insofar as pleasure and wealth aren't mutually exclusive, so it's good that this point isn't essential to his overall argument.

**Reply.** Aquinas presents three arguments here against human beings' ability to will multiple ultimate ends simultaneously. The first argument is one that he returns to frequently in the rest of the Treatise on Happiness, because it deals with the nature of perfect happiness, which he will identify with our ultimate end in 1.8. The argument begins with the Aristotelian assumption that "everything desires its own perfection." What 'perfection' means in this context isn't "ideal" or "unable to get any better," although it has a bit of that flavor. The Latin '*perfectio*' has more the sense of "completion" or carrying something through to its logical end. So the claim that an ultimate end is one we desire as a perfect good amounts to the claim that an ultimate end is an end we want because it completes us as human beings. Although Aquinas doesn't make this explicit here, a further assumption that he adopts is that perfection involves the satisfaction of natural tendencies. An acorn, for example, is perfected in this sense when it has developed into a mature, flourishing oak tree. Human beings are perfected when our characteristically human tendencies are actualized. Aquinas explains what this involves in much more detail in the rest of the Treatise on Happiness, but for his purposes in this article, what's important is that the ultimate end that we desire *insofar as we are human* (the second sense) must completely satisfy our most basic desires. If it doesn't, and what we desire as our ultimate end still leaves us wanting something that we naturally tend toward qua rational animals, then there would be something further that we'd desire outside of what we already had, and (the way Aquinas understands it, anyway) we wouldn't be perfected or complete. (As we'll see throughout the rest of this treatise, this stress on our wills coming to rest in the satisfaction of our natural desires is central to Aquinas's idea of perfect happiness. He clearly doesn't share the intuition common to many modern thinkers that one of the features most characteristic of human beings is a restlessness and continual dissatisfaction that keeps us striving for more.)

The second argument Aquinas offers against our being able to will multiple ultimate ends relies on his definition of the will as a *rational* appetite. Just as there is a distinct starting point for our intellectual investigations (what's naturally known, namely, information that we gather from our surroundings or know a priori), there is a distinct starting point for our volitions (our willings): what is naturally desired. Aquinas has already said several times by this point that what the will naturally desires is "the good"; in the first argument, he identified the perfect good for human beings with their ultimate end. So it makes sense for him to conclude (as he does) that our wills naturally desire the ultimate end (in sense [2]). What makes less sense is his claim that this ultimate end has to be one distinct thing, because nature tends to only one thing. Nature tends to one thing in the sense that an acorn tends toward becoming an oak tree, and a stone tends to fall "down." Knowing that the will tends toward the good, however, doesn't seem to guarantee that its starting point must be our ultimate end (as opposed to the good in general).

The third argument here actually picks up on that point. Voluntary actions—ones aimed at a chosen end—are placed into a particular species ("hugging" or "congratulating") by their intended end. Aquinas claims that voluntary actions can, in turn, be placed into a particular genus by the ultimate end that all those specific intended ends have in common. What he says is that everything desired by the will belongs to a single genus insofar as it is desired by the will. (So, hugging, congratulating, grocery shopping, and every other voluntary action belongs in the same genus, namely, things "desired by the will.") That makes it sound as though being "desired by the will" is the nature of the ultimate end for all voluntary actions, but that would be (at best) rather vague as descriptions of ultimate ends go. If, however, we make a connection that Aquinas himself doesn't explicitly make here, and we identify the common nature of all the specific ends desired by the will as "the good" (since everything desired by the will is desired under the description 'good'), then we're on slightly better footing. The ultimate end for all voluntary actions being "the good" seems *too* general, however. If we read the rest of this argument in the most charitable light, we can understand Aquinas as narrowing the scope of "the good" to "the good for human beings." The telos, or final cause, for any and all rational animals is the ideal actualization of their distinctively human characteristics—in particular, intellect and will.[3] Aquinas assumes that this means that all human beings have the same ultimate end, and (thus) that the will of each individual human being is aimed at that general end via its choice of specific ends (whether knowingly or not).

---

3. See, for example, Aquinas's discussion of human nature in the Treatise on Human Nature, or Robert Pasnau's extended discussion of this issue in *Thomas Aquinas on Human Nature: A Philosophical Study of Summa Theologiae*, I.75–89 (2002). Scott MacDonald also provides a helpful analysis of Aquinas's account of ultimate ends in "Ultimate Ends in Practical Reasoning: Aquinas's Aristotelian Moral Psychology and Anscombe's Fallacy," in *Philosophical Review* 100 (1991).

One thing that's worth noting as Aquinas moves forward in the following articles to discuss the specific nature of the ultimate end for human life is that, now that Aquinas has established that there is an ultimate end for human life, he simply assumes that all human actions aim at that end.

### 1.6. Do human beings will everything they will for the sake of the ultimate end?

Answer: yes, but (as Aquinas makes clear in response 3) they don't always have to have the ultimate end in mind when they're willing something.

**Obj. and resp. 1.** The objection here is that actions aimed at the ultimate end (which, from now on, will mean ultimate end in the sense of *the* ultimate end common to all human actions) are serious business, because they are directed toward the ultimate goal of human life. Practical jokes or playful actions don't seem to fit this action, though, and so it doesn't seem as though the person who is just being silly (making a funny face, for example) is willing that action for the sake of the ultimate end.

Aquinas's response takes jokes and playful actions very seriously. He claims that insofar as being silly is relaxing or enjoyable, those actions are aimed at the good of the person who's being playful, because they contribute to the healthy development and complete good of the human being. (There's something both heartening and poignant about Aquinas's reply here—heartening because it reminds us that medieval monasteries would have seen their fair share of laughter and pranksters, and poignant because it strongly conveys the impression that Aquinas would not have numbered amongst the jokesters.)

**Obj. and resp. 2.** This is the first time Aquinas mentions the speculative sciences in the Treatise on Happiness, so it's worth noting that this is a term he's picking up from the Aristotelian tradition. The speculative sciences involve *theoretical* or *speculative reason* and are focused on thinking (speculating) about the truth. They're usually contrasted with the practical sciences, which involve *practical reason* and are focused on deliberating about concerns of everyday living, like what to eat for breakfast and how much to tip your server. (These sorts of deliberations concern our good and shape our moral character.) Put in slightly more complex terms, the practical intellect is responsible for actively synthesizing and processing the information we receive from the sensible world and making decisions on how best to act on the basis of that information, whereas the speculative intellect (also called the theoretical intellect) is responsible for what we might call higher-order thought, or abstract contemplation of the concepts or ideas the lower capacities have made available to it. Speculative sciences are brought up here because investigations into, say, the nature of the movements of the heavenly bodies seem to be aimed at finding the truth for its own sake, not at something further that we find useful, as the practical sciences are. But these sorts of investigations can't be the ultimate end, since we certainly don't will everything else we will for the sake of understanding planetary motion.

Aquinas's response here is that we engage in the speculative sciences because knowledge of the truth is a good that is included in our "complete and perfect" good, or ultimate end. (Note that this seems to indicate that our ultimate end will be compositional, or made up of a number of goods that together complete and perfect us. Later, Aquinas argues that perfect happiness consists solely in contemplation of the divine essence; as we'll see, it's not clear how to reconcile these claims.)

**Obj. and resp. 3.** This objection raises the obvious point that even if human beings do actually aim all their actions at a single ultimate end, that doesn't mean they do it *intentionally*. And intention looks like it's a necessary part of ordering an action toward an end.

Aquinas's response clarifies the nature of the ultimate end and its relation to our other ends. Our ultimate end provides us with the first intention that unifies all our other ends—as he puts it, "the force of that first intention carries over into every desire for anything whatsoever." We don't need to have that ultimate end in mind every time we act for it to serve as the guiding principle for our other actions.

**Reply.** Aquinas gives two arguments here for the claim that everything we desire we desire for the sake of the ultimate end. First he appeals to the doctrine widely accepted from Plato's day through his own that "whatever human beings desire, they desire under the aspect of the good." That is, whatever we want, we want because it seems good to us in some way or other. Even in the case of objectively harmful things (like smoking), what we want from that experience is what we see as good: the nicotine buzz or the social component or annoying our parents. We can be wrong about what is good for us, but that doesn't change the fact that when we desire something, we desire it because it appeals to us. Because Aquinas has identified our ultimate end with the complete good for us, he believes that the fact that we desire everything under the guise of the good entails that our wills are always directed—in one way or another—toward our complete good, which all the other goods lead to. (Again, it's important to note that we don't have to be *right* about what contributes to our complete good for us to want things under that description. Think about the people who direct their actions toward some specific goal, like getting a particular promotion, because *then* they'll finally be appreciated or satisfied or happy. What they desire is their perfect good, even if they're wrong about what it is.)

The second argument refers again to the analogy between the prime mover and the ultimate end familiar from the previous articles. For anything to move, Aquinas holds, there needs to be a first mover who started the motion.

In the same way, for us to desire anything, there needs to be an ultimate end or first object of desire that kicks off the whole desiring process. Put this way, the analogy doesn't seem particularly convincing. It just seems as though we need something to kick desire into gear, where that could be any number of things, not an ultimate end. In general, the case for there being a highest good that is the ultimate end of everything we desire seems to be made more strongly by the first set of considerations Aquinas provides here than the second.

### 1.7. Is there one and the same ultimate end for all human beings?

Answer: yes, all human beings have the same ultimate end.

Here at last Aquinas explicitly addresses a claim he's been implicitly dealing with for the last few articles—namely, that insofar as they are human, all human beings not only possess *a* final end but in fact share *the same* final end. Intuitively, this seems false: human beings both do and want to do any number of different (and conflicting) things, and it's hard to imagine that there is any single thing that all human beings both want and actually act toward in every case. Yet, in this article, Aquinas makes the case that insofar as we're all human (where what it is to be human is to be a rational animal), we all share the same goal. The fact that we can disagree about what our common ultimate end is doesn't show that we don't have one: it just shows that some (perhaps most) people are wrong about what it is.

**Obj. and resp. 1.** The "unchangeable good" that this objection says appears to be the ultimate end of human beings is God. People certainly don't always aim their actions toward that particular ultimate end, however—as when they sin (which is, by definition, turning away from God).

In response, Aquinas points out that people can be mistaken about what the ultimate end is: our actions are aimed at what we *identify* as the ultimate end. But there really is just one ultimate end, and we always intend it.

**Obj. and resp. 2 & 3.** The second and third objections make similar points: If there were just one ultimate end for all human beings, you might expect us to all want to live the same sort of life and do the same sorts of things. But human beings actually differ enough from each other in personality, interests, etc., that it seems hard to see how there could be one ultimate end for all of them, even if they're all rational animals.

Aquinas responds that people can search for their ultimate end via different means. In the same way that anyone who is thirsty looks for a way to satisfy that thirst but can do so in any number of different ways, we all desire our perfect and complete good but (in this life at least) are able to channel that desire in any number of different ways: mountain climbing, military service, academics, etc. In addition, Aquinas reminds us that he's already argued (in art. 5) that nature tends to one thing (as, for example, a stone tends to fall when dropped, and an arrow tends to a particular trajectory when shot), and so human nature provides the first principle for human actions. (A nature in this sense is a set of end-directed powers organized in a teleologically directed way, not a set of characteristics common to a particular kind of thing.)

**Reply.** Aquinas makes a useful distinction here between what it means for something to be an ultimate end (which he's explained in the previous article) and what it is that actually fits that description. Everyone who understands what an ultimate end is should agree that there is one (that's been the point of the last few articles), but that doesn't mean they have to agree on what meets the criteria for being that ultimate end.

The analogy Aquinas provides to illustrate this—"what is sweet is pleasant to everyone's taste"—goes beyond just the point that people can differ in their judgments about the thing that fits the description of the ultimate end; it's also meant to show how we can adjudicate between these competing descriptions. There will actually be one thing that best fits the description of the ultimate end. It will be the "most complete good" that the person with "well-disposed affections" desires as the ultimate end. (This is similar to Plato's argument in book 9 of the *Republic* for philosophical pleasures being the best pleasures.) How to identify the person with well-disposed affections might seem tricky, but Aquinas's metaphysics provides him with a clear answer to this question: it will be the person who is optimally actualizing their nature as a rational animal. Much of the rest of the Treatise on Happiness is aimed at explaining and defending what this sort of person will judge to be their ultimate end.

### 1.8. Do all other creatures have the same ultimate end as human beings?

Answer: yes, in the sense that God is the ultimate end of all things; no, in the sense that human beings attain this end by knowing and loving God, which requires intellective and volitional powers that non-rational creatures do not possess.

**Obj. and resp. 1–3.** This is one of the few articles in which Aquinas agrees with everything in all three objections. He just wants to make a distinction that those comments don't capture. Thus, his answer for each of the three objections (which all amount to the claim that God is the ultimate end for all creatures) is the same: God is an ultimate end that we share with all other things, rational and non-rational, but our means of attaining that end is unique to rational creatures.

The argument **On the contrary** here is notable as the first place where the ultimate end of human beings is identified as happiness. Aquinas himself makes the same identification at the very close of the reply.

**Reply.** Insofar as Aquinas identifies God as the ultimate end of human beings here, it seems obvious that God—the first cause and final end—will also be the ultimate end of the rest of creation, rational or not. Aquinas doesn't want just to make this point, however. Instead, he wants to distinguish between the ultimate end considered in itself (namely, God) and considered in our *attainment* of that end (which he finally identifies here as happiness). This distinction is crucial to the account of happiness Aquinas goes on to lay out in the following four questions; it is also one of the features that make his account of happiness more philosophically plausible than many of its predecessors. (In the *Consolation of Philosophy*, for instance, Boethius claims that happiness is the Highest Good, which is God. This puts him in an awkward position, however, when it comes to explaining how human beings can be happy, since it would seem to require that we become God.)

Aquinas's analogy of the miser is helpful in understanding this distinction. Take Scrooge at the beginning of Dickens's *Christmas Carol*. Scrooge's desire is for money—money is the end (understood as the thing) that guides his actions. At the same time, you can also say that Scrooge's end is possessing money—his *keeping* his money is his end (understood as attainment). Although all of creation has God as its ultimate end (understood as the thing), then, human beings have an end that differs from the end of non-rational creatures (understood in terms of the *attainment* of that end). Our ultimate end must perfect and complete our nature: as rational animals created in God's image with will and reason, our ultimate end must involve loving God with those wills and knowing God with those intellects. And this activity—knowing and loving God—is what Aquinas identifies as happiness.

Although Aquinas does not make this explicit here, he believes that only rational beings can be happy, strictly speaking. In *De Veritate*, for example, Aquinas addresses the question of whether non-rational creatures can be happy and (in 5.6 resp. 4) argues that although non-rational creatures are capable of attaining the ultimate end by participating somewhat in the likeness of God, they lack the rational capacities that would make this participation count as happiness. In particular, they lack the free choice that allows rational creatures to attain (or fail to attain) their ultimate end through their own power. This naturally raises the question of what the nature of happiness is—the very issue Aquinas turns to in the following three questions.

### Question 2: The Things in Which Happiness Consists

Aquinas doesn't explicitly mention happiness until the last article of Q1, where its identification with the ultimate end is mentioned almost in passing. The next four questions of the Treatise are phrased entirely in terms of happiness, however, and develop Aquinas's understanding of happiness as the final end for all rational beings.

Q2 in particular addresses the nature of happiness by considering and eliminating a number of different possibilities of what human happiness might consist in—a brief *via negativa*, as it were. Indeed, given Aquinas's description of the ultimate end in Q1 as "knowing and loving God," it's clear from a quick glance at the topics canvassed in the eight articles of Q2 that none of them are genuine options. Why does Aquinas march through them all in turn, then? One reason is that Aquinas is following the structure of Aristotle's *Nicomachean Ethics*; the first three questions of the Treatise on Happiness essentially form a short commentary on the first book of the *Ethics*, and nowhere is this clearer than Q2. Aristotle takes each of these possibilities seriously, and so does Aquinas. That makes this potentially dull question take on interesting dimensions: in looking at how Aquinas responds to possibilities that Aristotle also explicitly considers, we can see both areas of convergence and important points of possible departure between the two thinkers.

In particular, Aquinas's responses to these questions settle him firmly on the side of those Aristotle interpreters who adopt an exclusivist or intellectualist reading of his account of happiness (on which happiness is identified solely with intellective contemplation) as opposed to an inclusive or comprehensive interpretation (on which happiness might contain intellective contemplation as a dominant component but also includes any number of other goods). In addition, the final two articles of this question develop the sense in which happiness is not something human beings can realistically achieve in this life, thus forcing a distinction between the sort of imperfect happiness human beings can achieve now and the sort of perfect happiness in which our ultimate end consists.

### 2.1. Does human happiness consist in wealth?

Answer: no. Of course not.

**Obj. and resp. 1.** This objection appeals to the motivating power of money, whose seductive power is mentioned more than once in Scripture. What motivates us most, however, must be our ultimate end.

Aquinas responds by commenting that only the "ignorant masses" are most motivated by money, because the only goods they're interested in are bodily goods (fine food, comfort, etc.) that money can buy. Wise people, in contrast, put more stock in goods of the soul (virtue, knowledge, etc.). (Aquinas doesn't actually argue for this claim, but it's one that was almost universally accepted by earlier philosophers and theologians.)

**Obj. and resp. 2.** According to Boethius (who wrote one of the most famous earlier treatises on happiness, the *Consolation of Philosophy*), happiness is "the state that is made complete by the accumulation of all goods." But money was specifically invented in order to purchase goods. Therefore, the ability to buy anything you want is happiness.

Aquinas's response anticipates the Beatles' "Can't Buy Me Love" by a good seven hundred years: you can't buy spiritual things (like wisdom). Aquinas doesn't directly address Boethius's definition of happiness, though, which is a shame. One of the fiercest debates about happiness is whether it involves the possession of all goods (what's sometimes called the "comprehensive" or "inclusive" conception of happiness) or whether it requires the possession of only one dominant or highest good (sometimes called the "exclusive" conception). As we'll see, Aquinas himself appears to vacillate between the two conceptions: on the one hand, happiness is described as union with God, the *summum bonum*, to the exclusion of other types of goods; on the other hand, that union is also described as perfecting human beings in such a way that they then possess all the other goods.

**Obj. and resp. 3.** We always want the supreme good, and we always want money. So, it looks like the supreme good must be money.

This objection is particularly uninspired, but Aquinas makes an interesting claim in response about the nature of our desire for the ultimate end/supreme good: "The more perfectly one possesses the supreme good, the more one loves it and the less one cares for anything else, because the more one has it, the better one knows it." In other words, the more fully we know and love our ultimate end—God—the less we care for anything else. As Aquinas points out, this is different from the normal case of human desire, where once we get what we want, we tire of it. Perfect happiness consists in the possession of the only good where once we get what we want, our enjoyment of it only increases.

**Reply.** No philosopher in the history of the world has actually believed that human happiness consists in wealth, where wealth is understood as money. Aquinas is no exception. The distinction he draws here between natural and artificial wealth is interesting, however. In short, natural wealth includes the things that help human beings meet their natural needs: food, drink, clothing, shelter, etc. Artificial wealth, in contrast, includes things like currency, which human beings exchange in lieu of goods and services for the sake of convenience. Aquinas agrees completely with Aristotle that happiness— the ultimate end of human desire—can't consist in artificial wealth on the grounds that money is only useful for the further things one can buy with it. (For a fuller discussion of the reasons Aquinas doesn't believe artificial wealth can be happiness, see SCG III.30.) Happiness can't consist in natural wealth like the possession of food and drink either, though, because those goods are also directed toward a further end—namely, the preservation and flourishing of human nature.

## 2.2. Does human happiness consist in honors?

Answer: no, human happiness can't consist in honors, because we aren't primarily responsible for whether or not we are honored.

Aquinas's answer to this question is utterly unsurprising, and follows Aristotle's to the letter: honor is something that is given to us by others, and happiness as the highest good can't depend on what others thinks of us. Honor is properly shown to someone who possesses a certain excellence, such as virtue . . . or happiness. Honor can be a consequence of happiness, then, but it can't be happiness itself.

**Obj. and resp. 1.** This is the first place where virtue enters Aquinas's discussion of happiness. Readers familiar with Aristotle's *Nicomachean Ethics* will be expecting this, since Aristotle's famous definition of happiness in *Nicomachean Ethics* I.7 is "the life of activity expressing virtue, that is, expressing reason well" and the bulk of the rest of the *Ethics* concerns what virtue is and how we can achieve it. (As we'll see over the course of the next three questions, Aquinas himself will not connect happiness so closely with virtue.) The actual objection is very weak: it makes the connection that, because happiness is the reward of virtue, and honor is also a reward of virtue, happiness is honor.

Aquinas gently untangles the confusion in this objection, pointing out that although Aristotle does say that both honor and happiness are the reward of virtue, the Philosopher makes it clear that the "true" (in the sense of being a natural consequence) reward of virtue is happiness, whereas honor is the reward of virtue only in a contingent sense. We honor people who display virtue because we don't have anything better to give them. Virtuous people don't do what they do for the sake of honor, whereas they are motivated by the hope of attaining their ultimate end—and rightly so. The next objection and response reiterate this point: we honor God, who possesses happiness to the highest degree, but we honor God *because* of this; honor is not what makes God possess happiness.

**Obj. and resp. 3.** This objection makes the same claim for honor that the objections to the first article made for wealth—namely, that it is what we desire more than anything else.

Aquinas's response is that we are motivated by a "natural desire for happiness," and we desire honor because it is a normal consequence of happiness. That is, we don't desire honor for its own sake; we desire honor, especially from wise people with good judgment, because it is a sign that we have achieved happiness.

**Reply.** This is one of the places that raises the question of whether Aquinas has an inclusive or exclusive view of happiness. He stresses happiness's status as the "complete human good" and mentions its "components," which are the "good things" (note the plural) "through which one has some share in happiness." This suggests a degreed picture of happiness, where how happy someone is depends on how many of the individual components of happiness that person has. Aquinas has not yet made the distinction he will draw in Q3 between perfect and earthly happiness; as we'll see, one of the important differences between perfect happiness (the possession of the beatific vision) and earthly happiness is precisely that earthly happiness has a number of components which can be gained or lost, whereas perfect happiness is singular and complete. Because Aquinas has not arrived at a full account of the nature of happiness yet, though, he is not yet in a position to explain that honor is merely a consequence of happiness, as opposed to a component of the highest good itself.

### 2.3. Does happiness consist in glory or fame?

Answer: no, happiness does not consist in glory—whatever glory is.

**Obj. and resp. 1–3.** The objections here are familiar in form from the previous two articles, and Aquinas's responses are equally unsurprising. The most interesting thing that occurs in them is Aquinas's claim in his response to the third objection that happiness is intrinsically and eternally stable. This notion of the permanent and unchanging nature of happiness becomes increasingly central to his conception of the highest good as something we cannot lose— and that, perhaps, might not even be subject to change in any meaningful sense.

**Reply.** Perhaps the most puzzling thing about this article for the contemporary reader is how fame or glory is meant to differ from honor, the subject of the previous article. In the body of the article, Aquinas gives us a working definition of glory that's (presumably) meant to help us see the distinction: glory is "illustrious" knowledge and corresponding praise. For human beings, happiness can't consist in glory because the sort of shining knowledge that we would praise someone for having, and about which we can be mistaken, is a result of their happiness. That is, we have to first know (or at least think we know) that someone is happy in order to give them glory for it. Like honor, glory is a *consequence* of happiness, not one of its essential components.

This is true only for human knowledge, however. Our happiness *is* causally dependent on *God's* knowledge of our happiness. That is, human happiness does consist (at least in part) in the glory that is God's knowledge and recognition of our blessed state.

As an argument for happiness's not consisting in glory, this seems fine, but this article would be clearer if Aquinas had either defined 'honor' in the previous article or used a consistent definition of 'glory' in his other works. In SCG III.29, for instance, he defines 'glory' as *celebritate famae*, which can be translated literally as "the celebrity of fame" and which drops the knowledge component mentioned in this article altogether (except in the sense of being well known). In *Summa contra Gentiles*, Aquinas also describes glory as essentially being well known, and he claims that we seek it so that we can be honored. This makes the distinction between honor and glory even less clear.

### 2.4. Does human happiness consist in power?

Answer: no. At most, happiness consists in the right exercise of the powers we possess as human beings.

Power is the last of the four external goods that Aquinas considers as candidates for happiness, none of which are meant to seem to us like real possibilities. There's nothing surprising in his answer here, either: it provides several of the classic reasons for thinking that power cannot be the ultimate end of human beings—chief among them, the fact that human beings can use power both well and badly.

**Obj. and resp. 1.** All things desire to become like God, our ultimate end. God, however, is all powerful, and so it's just possible that someone might think that our ultimate end is to be found in ultimate power.

Aquinas responds that—unlike us—God can't use power badly. In fact, he says, "The divine power is its own goodness." According to the doctrine of divine simplicity, God's essence is identical to God's existence, and thus all of the divine attributes that are part of that essence are identical to each other and to God's existence. This entails that God's power is identical with God's goodness; God cannot use power badly. Since we don't exist necessarily and aren't simple beings in this sense, we *can* use power badly, so our happiness can't consist merely in having power. We have to become as good as we are powerful: we have to use our power well.[4]

**Reply.** Aquinas begins his reply by giving two reasons for thinking that happiness is not power. The first is that power is more like a principle than an ultimate final end. This point is clearer in Latin, where the word for power is '*potentia*,' a word that indicates a starting point rather than something complete. (*Potentia* is often translated as "potentiality" or "potency" and contrasted with actuality.) An ultimate end completes and perfects the thing that has it as its end, though, whereas power is just the ability a thing has to start this process. Connected to this is the second reason Aquinas gives against

---

4. For an extended discussion of the doctrine of divine simplicity, see Brian Shanley's commentary to Aquinas's *Treatise on the Divine Nature* (2006); see also Norman Kretzmann's *The Metaphysics of Theism* (1997), which amounts to a commentary on the first book of Aquinas's *Summa contra Gentiles* and a defense of the doctrine of divine simplicity.

power's being happiness: power can be used for good or evil. It is itself neutral, whereas our ultimate end has already been identified as the perfecting good for human beings.

Aquinas goes on to provide four arguments that summarize what's generally wrong with thinking any external good could be our final end. First, happiness is the highest good, but both good and bad people can possess wealth, honor, glory, and power. Second, happiness is complete and self-sufficient: that is, once a human being is happy, she cannot be lacking anything she needs for happiness. None of the candidates discussed so far, however, are complete in the right sort of way. We can have wealth, for example, and still lack health or wisdom. (This intuition about the complete nature of our final end motivates much of Aquinas's account of happiness, especially in his later discussion of the nature of *perfect* happiness.) Third, happiness is a perfect good—it perfects the person who possesses it. The external goods discussed so far, however, can have both good and bad effects on the person who has them. Fourth, Aquinas argues that human beings naturally desire happiness, and this natural desire is an internal (rather than external) principle. Wealth, honor, glory, and power result from exterior principles (forces that work on us), and are completely contingent. We are lucky to have those external goods; we are not *lucky* to attain our ultimate end. That state needs to be the result of exercising our uniquely rational powers.

In his *Compendium of Theology* (2.9), Aquinas reiterates this point, claiming that "Natural human desire rests in this [ultimate] good." As long as something remains to be desired (as it does no matter how amazing an external good is), we have not yet attained perfect happiness. The possession of our ultimate end that characterizes perfect happiness does not involve continuing to change or move toward that end.

### 2.5. Does human happiness consist in goods of the body?

Answer: no. We have bodies insofar as we are animals, but (as we saw Aquinas remark in the Prologue) it is our rational capacities that make us most like God; our ultimate end must involve intellect and will, not just bodily goods.

In the ancient/medieval tradition that Aquinas is drawing on, the primary goods of the body are health, strength, and beauty; health is the paradigmatic good of the body (seen as grounding the others), and the one on which Aquinas focuses in this question. Aquinas is not a traditional substance dualist; he identifies the self and the person with the composite of soul *and* body (rather than just with the soul). At the same time, it's clear from what Aquinas has already said about the ultimate good that it's not going to be purely physical. The main purpose of this article, then, is to establish the basics of Aquinas's account of the body/soul relation before he turns in Q4 to the more complex question of what role the body does play in perfect happiness. (See particularly art. 5 and 6.)

**Obj. and resp. 1.** This objection offers a quote from Scripture and argues that when it says that there is no wealth greater than health, it means that health is the greatest good (and, thus, our ultimate end).

In response, Aquinas offers a different (and more plausible) interpretation of the same passage—namely, that 'wealth' there refers to the sorts of external goods he discussed in 2.1. Bodily goods (and health in particular) are the best external goods and are, in fact, what the other external goods are aimed at. Bodily goods are not the best of all the goods possible for human beings, however, as Aquinas argues in the body of this article. The best goods for us involve what is distinctively human about us—namely, our rational capacities.

**Obj. and resp. 2.** This objection appeals to pseudo-Dionysius's claim that being is better than life, arguing that since bodily health is vital for both, it should be central to human happiness.

In his response to the objection, Aquinas focuses not on the claim that health is vital for happiness but rather on explaining what pseudo-Dionysius meant when he said that "being is better than life." Being, "in an unqualified sense that includes every perfection of existence," is better than life, since being in that sense *includes* life (as one of the perfections of existence). A particular living thing's existing is not better than its being alive, however, because that act of existence is made better by the perfections that come with life.

**Obj. and resp. 3.** Bodily health is described in this objection as one of the things most conducive to the existence of human beings and thus vital to their happiness, since "being itself is what all things desire above all else."

In response, Aquinas invokes the idea that the ultimate end (namely, God) is also the first principle of being, which contains "every perfection" of being. As the structure of the *Summa theologiae* itself is meant to demonstrate, everything naturally tends back toward the source from which it proceeds. (See pp. xviii–xxvi of the Introduction for a brief discussion of the structure of the *Summa*.)[5] All things want to become more like the first principle (God), and so all things desire being—but they desire that perfected being according to what sort of thing they are. (Rocks and trees, for example, desire existence and life in the broad sense of 'desire' that Aquinas discussed in Q1.) For human beings, who are made in the likeness of God (the *imago Dei*), that desire is for existence, life, and happiness, which consists primarily in conformity

---

5. For more detailed discussions of the *Summa*'s structure and aims, see Jordan (1999 and 2003).

of intellect and will to that First Principle. Bodily goods such as health are important for happiness only insofar as they contribute to this greater good.[6]

**Reply.** Aquinas provides two reasons here for denying that happiness consists in goods of the body, both of which depend on metaphysical principles he laid out in the First Part of the *Summa*. The first reason is that human beings are not their own ultimate end—our continued existence is not itself the point of our existence. Bodily goods are aimed at preserving and improving our lives, however, and so they could only be our highest good if the continuation of our life were our ultimate end.

The second reason Aquinas gives for happiness being something higher than bodily goods like health is that we are not purely material beings. Rather, we are form/matter composites who possess a rational soul that animates our physical bodies. (Explaining what this means is the main goal of the Treatise on Human Nature, QQ75–89 of the First Part of the *Summa*.) Aquinas believes that our souls are "higher" than our bodies, in that the purpose of the activities of the body is to preserve life and support human activities, the most paradigmatic of which are activities of the soul such as thinking and willing. In Aquinas's terminology, the body is "for" the soul: it exists primarily so that our intellects and wills can function as they're meant to. In this life, for instance, the body provides the intellect with the phantasms that make cognition (and, thus, decision-making and voluntary actions) possible.[7]

It is worth noting at this point in Aquinas's discussion of being and its relation to our highest good that, for Aquinas (and most medievals), being and goodness are convertible; that is, being and goodness are metaphysically identical. Aquinas accepts the medieval doctrine often referred to as the Convertibility Thesis—namely, that being and goodness are metaphysically identical, or "convertible." (This thesis has been the subject of intense discussion.)[8]

### 2.6. Does human happiness consist in pleasure?

Answer: no. Happiness is pleasur*able*, but pleasure is not what its nature consists in.

Many of the arguments in the objections for happiness consisting in pleasure mentioned are familiar from earlier philosophers, such as Epicurus (who famously defended the claim that happiness is pleasure, or the absence of

---

6. See Appendix 2 for the text of *ST* I.5.1, which directly addresses this topic.

7. For a discussion of the complex relation Aquinas develops between body and soul, see Van Dyke (2009).

8. See Macdonald (1991) for a collection of excellent essays on this topic, and Wippel (2000) for a comprehensive discussion of how this thesis fits into Aquinas's broader metaphysical framework.

pain). As the third objection notes, pleasure motivates us on a more basic level than anything else, and it appears to motivate everything that experiences it: "the wise, the unwise, even things that lack reason." Since Aquinas has already agreed that everything seeks happiness, this gives at least prima facie reason to suppose that happiness is pleasure. Aquinas will agree that happiness *involves* pleasure—he just believes that it involves it as a necessary consequence rather than as an essential component.

**Obj. and resp. 1.** We want happiness for its own sake: that's what it means for it to be our ultimate end. But, as Aristotle notes, human beings seem to want pleasure and delight for their own sake. (One translation issue is worth noting here: although in Latin the word used for pleasure is usually '*voluptas*' and the word used for delight is usually '*delectatio*,' Aquinas uses the two terms interchangeably in this article.)

Aquinas's response is that it's true that we desire delight or pleasure for its own sake—if what that means is that we desire it as a natural part of our final end (happiness). Delight just is "desire's resting in something good"; it follows necessarily on our attaining the good we desire. Insofar as we manage to attain our highest good, then, we will experience pleasure. It is the good itself that we desire for its own sake, though, and that Aquinas says "gives delight its form." The pleasure we experience when we reach our ultimate end isn't a diffuse or general state: it is delight *that we have achieved that particular good*. (Think of someone's happiness on his wedding day: he isn't just generally happy to be getting married—or at least we hope that's not his primary emotion. He's happy to be marrying *this particular person*.)

**Obj. and resp. 2.** The idea of primary and secondary causes or ends is brought in here to support the idea that pleasure, which motivates us more strongly than anything else seems to, must be a primary or ultimate end.

In his response to this objection, Aquinas implicitly addresses the question of why people seem more powerfully motivated by sensory pleasure than higher goods. The reason these pleasures have such a strong hold on us is that they are more immediate ("especially perceptible") to us than higher (intellectual or volitional) pleasures. According to Aquinas, all human cognition starts with sense perception; sensory pleasures and pains naturally occupy more of our attention than the higher pleasures that we have to work to achieve. Many people, in fact, will remain focused on sensory delight rather than turning to pleasures that are more remote and harder to acquire.

**Obj. and resp. 3.** Every living thing wants pleasure, and so it seems like pleasure might be the ultimate end, which everything also desires.

Aquinas agrees that everything desires pleasure. He just claims that we desire delight or pleasure "under the aspect of good," or as a natural component of attaining a good, rather than as an end in itself. Every delight follows from the possession of some desired good, and the possession of the greatest good is no exception.

**Reply.** The first thing Aquinas does in his response to this question is to draw a distinction between "higher" and "lower" pleasures, where "higher" pleasures are those that involve "higher" faculties like intellect and will (a rational appetite for the universal good), and "lower" pleasures are those that involve the "lower" faculties of the nutritive/vegetative and sensory soul, including sense appetite. Given what he's said in earlier articles, it's clear that happiness won't consist in lower pleasures—but Aquinas is quick to argue here that it can't consist in the higher pleasures either. His main argument for this is that pleasure or delight is merely a "proper accident" (*proprium*) of happiness, not one of its essential features.

What's a proper accident? The classic medieval example of a *proprium* is the one Aquinas gives here: risibility, or the ability to laugh. This ability is one that all human beings have, but it is not contained in the essence "rational, mortal animal." Human beings belong to the genus "animal" by virtue of their nutritive and sensory powers, and are placed in the species "human" by their rational capacities. Part of what it means to be an animal is to be mortal, so mortality also belongs to the essence of human being. The ability to laugh or be amused, however, is a capacity that does not belong to all animals. Rational animals alone possess the ability to laugh. Being able to laugh isn't part of the essence of being human, however. It's just something that follows necessarily from that essence. In the same way, although no one is happy without feeling pleasure, that delight isn't part of the essence of happiness itself—it is something that follows necessarily from happiness.

Bodily pleasure can't be our complete or ultimate good in any event. In Aquinas's words, bodily goods are "negligible by comparison" with goods of the soul (wisdom, etc.), since immaterial things are "infinite in comparison" with material things. In SCG III.27, Aquinas goes into much more detail about the nature of bodily pleasures, calling them *"delectationes carnales,"* the chief of which are the pleasures of food and sex. The reason these sorts of physical pleasures can't constitute human happiness is that they're aimed respectively at the preservation of the body and the generation of offspring, neither of which is our final end. In fact, Aquinas sometimes worries that these bodily pleasures impede contemplation, insofar as they distract human beings.

### 2.7. Does happiness consist in a good of the soul?

Answer: no—at least, not if we're thinking of happiness in terms of the thing itself that we desire as our ultimate end. To go back to the distinction Aquinas drew in 1.8, happiness is something in the soul, understood as the attainment of our ultimate end, but the thing we desire and which makes us happy transcends the human soul.

**Obj. and resp. 1.** The first objection appeals to Aristotle's distinction between the three types of goods for human beings: external goods, goods of the body, and goods of the soul. External goods and bodily goods have already been ruled out as candidates for being our ultimate end, and so it looks like we're left with the conclusion that happiness must consist in a good of the soul (like virtue or wisdom).

Aquinas's response to this is that happiness is a good of the soul, but only if we're thinking of "goods of the soul" as including external objects (such as, say, God) that we participate in by means of the power or dispositions of the soul.

**Obj. and resp. 2.** This objection notes that we desire the (ultimate) good for ourselves more than anything else. This might make it look as though happiness consists in a good of human beings, such as a good of the soul.

In response, Aquinas distinguishes between the good as object desired as opposed to whom we want to experience the desired good. We desire happiness for ourselves, but the object we desire is not a good of the soul, like virtue or wisdom. It's God. As Aquinas points out in **resp. 3** (responding to the objection that happiness must be in the soul because it perfects us, and what perfects us can't be something outside us), this also explains how happiness perfects and completes us. It is the activity of happiness, not the ultimate end understood as the thing, that accomplishes this.

**Reply.** Our ultimate end (understood as the thing we desire, as opposed to the attaining or possessing of that thing) can't be the soul, because, Aquinas says, our souls exist in potentiality for being perfected by happiness. But something that exists in potentiality rather than actuality can't be an ultimate end— human beings are meant to be perfected by their possession of their ultimate end, which they wouldn't be if their ultimate end was itself in potentiality for perfection. (This is one of those places where Aquinas appears to be intent on ruling out every possible logical option before finally arriving at his conclusion: it's not clear who would think that our ultimate end was the soul in the first place.)

Aquinas also argues that our ultimate good (understood as the thing we desire) can't be any of the soul's powers, dispositions, or acts. His reason for this is that our ultimate end must be a good that completely satisfies our characteristically human appetite; and the most characteristically human appetite is the will, which is a rational desire for the *universal* good. But our souls don't contain the universal good. Whatever goods are present in the soul are participated, particular goods. The thing desired as our ultimate end, then, must be external to human beings. Understood as the attainment of our ultimate end, however, happiness is an activity of the soul. In other words, the soul is what *attains* happiness rather than the *source* of happiness.

## 2.8. Does human happiness consist in any created good?

Answer: no, human happiness consists in God, not in anything that God has created.

It's clear from the way that Aquinas phrases this question that the answer will be no. The First Cause is the source of all else that exists, and Aquinas has already claimed repeatedly in the previous articles that perfect happiness completely satisfies all human desire—something only the First Cause (which is also the Final Cause) can do. That said, the objections and replies in the article are worth attention insofar as they clarify Aquinas's views about God's created order and the place human beings occupy in that order.

**Obj. and resp. 1.** The first objection draws on the hierarchy of being, which is the ordering of all things from First Actuality (God) down to Pure Potentiality (prime matter). In this hierarchy, human beings fall right at the division between immaterial and material creatures. We have immaterial souls that survive our death, but those souls are the substantial forms of material bodies. What's best for human beings, then, might seem to be to bump up a level in this hierarchy: that is, we could have angelic nature as our ultimate end. (See the Treatise on Human Nature as well as the discussion of human nature in SCG II for Aquinas's most extensive treatments of the nature of this hierarchy and how it relates to who we are, as well as to illuminating the nature of action and virtue.[9])

Aquinas's medieval nickname was The Angelic Doctor, in part because he had so much to say about angels—immaterial creatures with intellects and wills. And, as we'll see in the following three questions, Aquinas does draw a close connection between perfected human nature and the state of the non-fallen angels. He doesn't think our final end is to become angels, however, or that our highest good could be found in any relation to those beings. Instead, he says, human beings desire the "universal fount of good" which is the common object of happiness for *all* rational beings. Even the highest angel has a finite amount of goodness; we naturally seek the infinite and perfect good. (In fact, as Aquinas observes in SCG IV.54, the angels don't experience happiness that is any better than the perfect happiness we're capable of: "God is the only being greater than human beings in the order of happiness, for angels, although they are superior with respect to the condition of nature, are not superior with respect to the order of the end, since they are beatified by the same end.")

**Obj. and resp. 2.** The second objection also focuses on the place of human beings in the created order, this time as a part to the whole (microcosm to

---

9. For an accessible discussion of the hierarchy of being, see the first third of DeYoung, McCluskey, and Van Dyke (2009).

macrocosm). It suggests that creation as a whole might be what satisfies human desire: by knowing and loving all creation, our natures will be fulfilled. Aquinas responds that if the creation were all there is, it might be our ultimate end in this sense. But given that there is a creator from whom all things proceed and to whom all things naturally desire to return (as the very structure of the *Summa* is meant to illustrate), we can't possibly be completely fulfilled by relation to anything less—even the totality of all creation.

**Obj. and resp. 3.** The third objection reminds us that perfect happiness is that which fully satisfies natural human desire, and goes on to suggest that the sort of desires involved in being a rational animal wouldn't extend to a good that completely surpasses created existence. We should naturally desire some *created* good.

In response, Aquinas allows that if we restrict ourselves to things that are intrinsic to and inherent in human beings, it does seem like we would naturally desire some created good as our final end (like satisfaction of all the levels in Maslow's hierarchy of needs). But, he claims, human beings do naturally have the capacity to desire "an object that is an infinite good." Frustratingly, he does not provide an argument for this claim; he appears to assume it falls naturally out of his account of human nature and our intellects' inclination for cognizing the universal true and our wills' inclination for desiring the universal good. In short, the object of human desire can surpass human capacities.[10]

**Reply.** Aquinas argues against the idea that our ultimate end could be anything created by focusing on the sort of completeness that such an end must have. As he observes in the *Compendium of Theology* 2.9: "The proper good of any thing is that which perfects that thing. . . . This good is known by this sign—that the natural desire of a human being comes to rest in it." Our ultimate end must wholly satisfy us, or we would still want more, in which case the happiness would not be complete. The will is a rational appetite for the universal good, however, as we've seen. Only possession of that universal good can fully satisfy it. But God is the universal good, not anything created. Our desire for knowing God is natural, too: as Aquinas says earlier in the *Summa theologiae* (I.12.1), "There is a natural desire in human beings to know the cause whenever they see an effect." God is our ultimate end, understood as the thing we naturally tend toward.

This conclusion raises the question of how human beings can possibly attain this ultimate end, given that it requires reaching far beyond anything our natural capacities can get to on their own. And this is precisely the question that Aquinas addresses in Q5 of this treatise. Before he discusses the mechanics of attaining perfect happiness, however, he needs to get clearer

---

10. Bradley (1997) discusses this dilemma—namely, that we naturally desire a good that we can't possibly attain by natural means—at length.

both on the nature of this end (Q3) and on what human beings require in order to attain it (Q4).

## Question 3: What Is Happiness?

The previous question focused on what happiness consists in; now that Aquinas has settled that our ultimate end is God, understood as the thing we most desire, he devotes this question to a closer examination of our ultimate end, understood as our attainment of the highest good. As with the last question, he marches through a variety of possibilities in order of increasing plausibility before finally arriving at what he thinks is the right answer: our ultimate end is direct knowledge of God's eternal, unchanging essence. This, in turn, sets him up for Q4, which examines the necessary components of that experience.

### 3.1. Is happiness something uncreated?

Answer: yes.

Aquinas has just argued in 2.8 that happiness consists in an uncreated good, considered in terms of its cause or object—namely, God. His real interest in this question, however, is happiness considered in terms of attainment or enjoyment (what Aquinas calls here "the very essence of happiness" for human beings). Happiness in this sense is created and exists in us. (See also *ST* I.26.3, where Aquinas makes this distinction explicitly in terms of the happiness of intellective beings: "The happiness of an intellective nature consists in an act of the intellect, in which two things can be considered: the object of the act, which is the thing being thought about, and the act itself, which is the thinking.")

**Obj. and resp. 1–3.** The objections in this article all focus on the sense in which God is our ultimate end and that in which our happiness consists. Aquinas's response to all three objections is just to point out that—as he's said numerous times already—there is another sense of happiness, too, in which it is the attainment or enjoyment of our highest good. So yes: God is happiness in the truest and best sense of happiness. In fact, as Aquinas says in his response to the first objection, God's very essence is happiness. All other beings, in contrast, are happy only through participation in that essence. (Aquinas shows no qualms here about using the Platonic term 'participation' to describe our relation to God.) Our act of participation, however, is created. It has a distinct beginning, and it exists derivatively rather than through itself.

**Reply.** Aquinas's answer to this question is extremely similar to his reply in 1.8, with the main difference being the explicit identification of our ultimate end here with happiness. God, the *summum bonum*, or highest good, is the thing in which our happiness consists. Understood in terms of use or enjoyment of that thing, however, happiness is something created. In fact, Aquinas claims that this created enjoyment is the "very essence" of happiness. Aquinas's example of the greedy person helps here: if I'm greedy, my intellect and will are focused on getting and retaining and enjoying money, not just on money itself. In the same way, the essence of happiness for human beings is knowing and loving God, not just God.

### 3.2. Is happiness an activity?

Answer: yes, happiness is an activity. In fact, it is the ultimate actuality of human beings' capacities for action.

The number of objections in this article (six, rather than the more usual two or three) lets you know that Aquinas considers this an important topic. Why so important? Because he's finally getting at the heart of happiness. We haven't been surprised to learn that happiness doesn't consist in wealth or power or that it involves knowing and loving God, the First Cause and Highest Good. But what will happiness be like for us? The answer to that question is far from obvious, and this article is the first one to address it.

Why begin by asking whether happiness is an act? For one thing, an activity, by its very nature, seems transitory—an activity tends toward a particular end, and none of the activities that we are familiar with in ordinary life can continue indefinitely: we can only do something for so long before we need to do something else. This makes it seem as though happiness might better be characterized as a state, which is a stable and persisting condition. To overcome this worry, Aquinas distinguishes between the sort of imperfect happiness human beings are capable of in this life, and perfect happiness, which consists in the full and unending actualization of our capacities for knowledge and love of God. Perfect happiness thus has both the stable and persisting nature of a state and the active nature appropriate to our highest, perfecting good.

**Obj. and resp. 1.** The first objection draws on a passage from Romans to argue that our ultimate end is eternal life, and that "eternal life" isn't an activity as much as it is just a way of describing our always existing.

In response, Aquinas distinguishes here between two senses of 'life': being alive, generally speaking, and the kind of life a thing lives, which is characterized by its actualizing certain of that thing's principles. God is the only being for whom existence is identical with happiness. As discussed in 2.4, God is absolutely simple; God's essence is identical with God's existence. Human beings in contrast have a whole host of capacities or "principles of life"—nutritive, sensory, and rational being the main ones—that we can focus on actualizing. That focus is what we're referring to when we say someone is living the "life of leisure" or the "life of contemplation." Perfect happiness is eternal life, understood in this sense: it consists first and foremost in actualizing the rational capacities by which we image God.

**Obj. and resp. 2.** According to Boethius—one of the figures most influential at Aquinas's time in discussions of happiness—happiness is a state: one that "is made complete by the accumulation of all goods." But states and activities are usually understood as separate things, so it seems like happiness can either be a state or an activity, not both.

In his response, Aquinas gives a rather spurious interpretation of Boethius's comment, insisting that Boethius was referring there just to the general idea of happiness as a complete good, so that we should understand him as affirming the claim that someone who has happiness is in a state of possessing a complete good. Aquinas then goes on to invoke Aristotle as the expert in this discussion, since Aristotle agrees that happiness involves being in a state— but a state that is completed and maintained via activity. Someone who is in a state (say, knowing Arabic) with respect to some good only has that good in a "complete" way when she's actualizing that state (e.g., speaking or reading Arabic). Our participation in God's essence, then, can fairly be characterized as a state of *active* participation.

**Obj. and resp. 3.** This objection draws out a point about the nature of activity that will become important later, in the Treatise on Human Acts. As we saw in 3.1, happiness is something that must exist in us—but we typically think of actions as things that are initiated by an agent and are then carried out by that agent on the external world. My action of taking a sip of coffee, for instance, involves my decision to sip the coffee and then the corresponding movement of reaching out my arm, grasping the cup, etc. It's not as typical, however, to imagine happiness being an action. This objection highlights that oddity, arguing that actions naturally proceed "outward" from an agent; happiness couldn't be an action because it's something internal to an agent.

In response, Aquinas introduces Aristotle's distinction between two kinds of action: the first kind is one that moves from an agent outwards, as when fire burns what's around it or a knife cuts a loaf of bread. In these cases, the action centers on the thing being acted upon: the wood that burns, or the loaf that is cut. The second kind of action is the one relevant to human happiness because it involves perfecting or completing the agent in some way (for example, digesting, smelling, thinking, or willing). Happiness is the second kind of action, and so does count as an activity.

**Obj. and resp. 4.** This objection argues that happiness must be continuous and—given that we don't seem capable of continuing to engage in any particular activity without eventually needing a break—thus more likely to be a state than an activity.

Aquinas's response amounts to a small treatise on the nature of perfect happiness as opposed to the nature of imperfect happiness, and contains one of the most detailed descriptions of our ultimate end in the entire Treatise on Happiness. It begins with the observation that there are different senses of happiness that correspond to the different levels of perfection available to the sorts of beings who can be happy (that is, beings with intellects and wills). God, who is pure actuality and contains no potentiality at all, represents the highest level of perfection possible. In this case, the activity of happiness is God's very act of existence, which is eternal; the enjoyment God experiences in that activity is maximally complete. For angels, by contrast, happiness is an intellective and volitional activity through which they participate in God's uncreated goodness. Perfect happiness for angels is perfect—but it remains a lesser sort of perfection than the sort available to God. (As an analogy, think of different brands of chocolate bars. The very best Hershey bar possible is still less good than the best Vosges bar, even though it's perfect for a Hershey bar.)

Aquinas goes on to claim that the activity of happiness for angels is "unitary and sempiternal." God is eternal (and thus atemporal),[11] whereas "sempiternity" is an everlasting state that involves, for example, a beginning. The happy angels weren't always happy: at the first moment of their creation, they turned either toward or away from God. For the ones who turned toward God, this constituted the inception of their happiness. From the moment of its beginning, angelic happiness is a single, unending act.

Finally, Aquinas turns to human beings. In this life, he says, we are perfected by an activity that joins us to God, but this activity is neither unitary nor unending. In other words, our perfecting activity will always remain incomplete during earthly life. The reason for this is that, following Aristotle in *Nicomachean Ethics* X, Aquinas doesn't think there is any voluntary activity we participate in during this life that we can sustain indefinitely. No matter what we're doing or how much we enjoy doing it, eventually we'll need to stop to eat or sleep, or we'll get distracted, etc. Even in the best of situations, we are capable only of the sort of interrupted activity that would qualify as imperfect happiness. That doesn't mean we can't talk about being happy in this life; it just means that we can be happy only to the (limited) extent to which we can carry out the activity of happiness here and now.

Perfect happiness for human beings involves a single, unending activity joining us to God, because any break in that union would mar our happiness. This makes the activity of perfect happiness for human beings look a lot like the activity of angelic happiness just described, and Aquinas indeed claims that we will be like "the angels in heaven" in the union we will have with God. In fact, his appeal to Matthew 22:30 here, that we will be "like the

---

11. See Kretzmann and Stump (1981) for a classic discussion of Aquinas's theory of eternity.

angels in heaven," appears each time that he discusses perfect human happiness.[12] The perfect happiness we are capable of in the next life will be a unified, continuous, and sempiternal activity, unlike the fragmented experience of happiness we are capable of now.

One final thing worth noting about this response is Aquinas's endorsement of the contemplative life (focused on study and reflection) over the active life (consisting primarily in activities such as politics, farming, and/or finance). In the Middle Ages, there was a lively debate about the merits of the active versus the contemplative life; proponents of the contemplative life frequently appealed to the biblical story of Mary and Martha (Luke 10:38–42), in which Jesus rebukes Martha for trying to get Mary to stop listening to Jesus in order to help Martha prepare the dinner for Jesus and the disciples. According to Aquinas, the active life "which is occupied with many things" is further away from perfect happiness for human beings than the contemplative life "which is focused on one thing, the contemplation of truth." As we'll see in 3.8, Aquinas believes that perfect human happiness consists solely in the activity of contemplating the Truth (namely, God's essence). Again, this raises issues about what role the other components of human life as we currently experience it might play in our attainment of the ultimate end; Aquinas addresses these questions at length in Q4.

The argument **On the contrary** affirms Aristotle's definition of happiness as "activity in accordance with complete virtue" without any sort of qualification. Aristotle's account of happiness here isn't *complete*, according to Aquinas, since he doesn't directly connect the activity of happiness with God. At the same time, Aquinas never suggests that there is anything actually incorrect with Aristotle's account. He seems to accept it as an apt description of imperfect happiness and then simply want to add more to it to arrive at the nature of perfect happiness. (It is striking in this connection that there is no mention in this discussion of human happiness of God's grace or general role in our attaining our ultimate end. Aquinas's focus in this Treatise remains entirely on the human side of the story.)

**Reply.** Not surprisingly, Aquinas claims that when we're thinking about the nature of our ultimate end in terms of *attainment*, we should understand it as an activity. Happiness, after all, isn't something that we attain and then just passively possess, like a house. It's more like mastering a language. As Aquinas puts it, the sort of ultimate perfection involved in happiness is what Aristotle calls "second actuality." Someone who knows Arabic but is not currently using that knowledge is in first actuality. Someone who knows Arabic

---

12. This raises questions about the extent to which our ultimate end fulfills human nature as opposed to raising us above it. For a detailed discussion of this, see Christina Van Dyke (2014a).

and is using it (reading, thinking, speaking, etc.) is in second actuality. Perfect human happiness is a second actuality: it is the continued *actualization* of our nature as human beings.

### 3.3. Is happiness an activity of the sensory part or only of the intellectual part?

Answer: happiness is not a sensory act but an activity of only the *intellectual part* of the soul.

Having established in the previous article that happiness is an activity, Aquinas now turns in the remainder of Q3 to an examination of what sort of activity it is. Art. 3–5 address the question of what part of us carries out this sort of activity, and then art. 6–8 focus on the nature of the activity itself. In this article, Aquinas—who takes it for granted that perfect happiness doesn't consist in the ability to take in nourishment, grow, or reproduce (that is, the capacities we share with plants as well as animals)—rules out the possibility that the activity of happiness involves our sensory capacities (which include sense perception and sensory appetite), on the grounds that perfect happiness is union with an immaterial God, whom we can't perceive with our senses.

None of the objections in this article argue that happiness is solely a sensory activity; they attempt to show only that happiness requires or involves sensory activity either as a precursor to intellective activity or as part of the complete good in which our happiness consists. The fact that Aquinas explicitly rejects even these relatively weak sorts of involvement signals how radically intellectualist his conception of perfect happiness is going to be.

**Obj. and resp. 1.** This objection gets to the heart of why one might think that happiness would involve sensory activity on Aquinas's account—namely, because he believes that sensory activity is a necessary precondition for human intellection. In fact, it is the necessary starting point for our mental processes. We gather information through our senses in order to produce "phantasms," or mental images, and then we use these phantasms to arrive at the abstract concepts or "intelligible species" (such as "cup" or "dog") that serve as the building blocks of human cognition. And, according to Aquinas, we "revert," or turn back, to those phantasms when we think.[13] So if our ultimate end is an intellective activity, it looks as though it will involve the sensory as well as the intellective part of our soul.

In response, Aquinas grants that this means that sensory activity is necessary for the sort of imperfect happiness we can attain in *this* life, but he doesn't admit that it plays any role in the activity of perfect happiness.

---

13. For further discussion of Aquinas's theory of cognition, see Scott MacDonald's excellent overview (MacDonald, 1993).

**Obj. and resp. 2.** This objection again refers to Boethius's definition of happiness as "a state made complete by the accumulation of all goods," arguing (reasonably enough) that some goods (such as feeling a hug) require activity of the senses.

In response, Aquinas again distinguishes between perfect and imperfect happiness. Imperfect or earthly happiness requires the accumulation of all the goods necessary for us to know and love God in this life. Perfect happiness, by contrast, is an all-in-one sort of a deal. In the life to come, we don't run around collecting individual goods that contribute to our happiness: we possess all possible goods via our union with God, the highest good and source of all other goods.

**Obj. and resp. 3.** As we've seen before, there's a much closer connection between 'perfect' and 'perfecting' in Latin than in contemporary English usage. When Aquinas refers to something as "perfect," he means that it's complete or finished, not just that it's without flaw. Happiness is the complete good that perfects us: our being happy involves the completion or fulfillment of human nature. This makes it seem plausible that happiness would involve the sensory as well as the intellective part of the soul, since our sensory capacities are integrally involved in the fulfillment of our intellective capacities.

In response, Aquinas again stresses the difference between imperfect happiness and perfect happiness. Here and now, the perfection of our "higher" rational capacities depends on the activities of our "lower" capacities, since we couldn't think about or desire anything without the objects of thought that our perception of the world around us gives us. (That is, contra Plato, Aquinas holds that we couldn't contemplate the nature of beauty if we didn't start off by perceiving beautiful things with our senses.) In heaven, Aquinas says, this order changes, so that our lower physical and sensory capacities are perfected via the perfection of our rational capacities, which are in turn perfected via our contemplation of God's essence.

**Reply.** Aquinas distinguishes here between a thing's contributing to happiness essentially, antecedently, and consequently. He denies that any activity of the senses is essential for perfect happiness, but he allows that human happiness can involve sensory activities both antecedently and consequently.

The first reason Aquinas gives for denying that the senses are essentially involved in the activity of perfect happiness seems right: our happiness consists in union with God, who is immaterial and thus wholly inaccessible to the senses. In this respect, it's not surprising that the activity involved in happiness wouldn't involve the senses. The second reason Aquinas gives seems rather less plausible. He says that sensory activity can't be part of the essence of human happiness because the only goods we can attain through those activities are bodily goods. This, however, seems misleading at best. Bodily goods (such as health, strength, and beauty) might be the only things we can attain *purely* through sensory activities, but Aquinas believes that human cognition requires sensory input of various sorts, and so it seems awfully fast for Aquinas to conclude here that the senses aren't involved in our knowing and loving God.

Aquinas himself brings that very point up in the next paragraph, pointing out that sensory activities are necessary for happiness in this life, since "the activity of sense is a necessary precondition for the activity of the intellect." (Aquinas refers to "sense" (singular) here as opposed to "the senses" (plural) because he's talking about the entire apparatus that deals with sensory input, as opposed to just the individual senses.) So sensory activities are antecedently involved in perfect happiness, insofar as they're a necessary precondition for our cognition (and our happiness) in this life. They are consequently involved in perfect happiness, too. That is, our sensory capacities will be actualized following on the attainment of our final end. The central activity of perfect happiness is an act of unending contemplation of God's essence made possible only through a gift of divine grace (as Aquinas argued in *ST* I.12), but we will possess bodies in the life to come, and the sensory capacities and activities of those bodies will be perfected via our union with God. We will be perfected "inside out," so to speak.

### 3.4. Given that happiness is an activity of the intellectual part, is it an activity of the intellect or of the will?

Answer: happiness is an activity of the intellect, although the will is involved insofar as we naturally delight in and enjoy the attainment of our ultimate end.

Aquinas has just argued that the activity of happiness belongs entirely to the intellectual part of the human soul. Here he begins to get clearer on the nature of this intellective activity. The question of whether it is an activity of the intellect or the will sounds strange to modern ears, however. We're not used to thinking of the will as intellective. Aquinas defines the will (in 1.2) as a *rational* appetite for the universal good, though, and the fact that there are five objections rather than the usual three in this article indicates that Aquinas takes this question very seriously. In this article, although he argues that the activity, or *essence*, of perfect happiness belongs primarily to the intellect, he acknowledges that the *delight* of happiness is something our wills can experience as the result of attaining our heart's desire. (He will return to this issue in the first two articles of Q4.)

**Obj. and resp. 1.** This objection argues that human happiness consists in peace—a claim to which Aquinas is extremely sympathetic. Peace is, for him, the will's resting in enjoyment of the object of its desire, and so it seems that the primary activity of happiness might be this enjoyment.

Aquinas's response is to claim that perfect peace *follows on* happiness, but that peace is the result of the activity that constitutes happiness, not the

activity itself. (He also says that peace is antecedent to the activity of happiness, in the sense that when we have reached the afterlife, anything that might
impede the activity of perfect happiness [such as disease or the need for sleep]
has been removed.)

**Obj. and resp. 2.** This objection is both straightforward and extremely reasonable: the will's object is the good, and the highest good is happiness. Therefore, it seems as though happiness should consist in an activity of the will.

Aquinas's response distinguishes between the object of the will and its
activity. The example he gives here—namely, that the first object of sight is not
seeing but the visible—is not likely to be very illuminating to contemporary
readers, though. The comparison he's trading on is that sight is a power of the
sensory capacities (just as the will is a power of the rational capacities), and
we're meant to recognize that the object of sight is the visible world around
us, not the activity of seeing. (That is, we don't see *sight*. We see things.) So
the object of the will is the good, but that doesn't mean that happiness (our
highest good) is going to be an activity of the will.

**Obj. and resp. 3.** The will is responsible for moving us toward our final end,
and so one might think that it also plays the key role in the activity that is our
final end.

Aquinas highlights the interaction between intellect and will to respond
to this objection. Sure, the will moves us toward the end—but it's an end
presented to it by the intellect. The intellect also attains the ultimate end via
contemplation of God's essence (as we'll see in art. 8) prior to the will, since
Aquinas holds that we need to know God in order to love God. The intellect's activity is primary in happiness, then, in the sense that it comes first
and is a necessary precondition for the "final consequence" of attaining our
ultimate end.

**Obj. and resp. 4.** This objection argues that love is higher than knowledge
(Paul, after all, says that "the greatest of these is love" in his famous discussion in I Corinthians 13), and that the primary activity of happiness must thus
belong to the will rather than the intellect.

Aquinas's response is to repeat his claim that knowledge is prior to love in
attaining an end (you have to know what it is you're loving), and that we thus
attain perfect happiness through the activity of the intellect before we experience the enjoyment and peace of that attainment. This doesn't really seem
to establish that happiness is an activity of the intellect rather than the will,
though. The activity of the intellect might come first, but the activities of
both intellect and will seem like indispensable components of that happiness.

**Reply.** In 1.8, Aquinas claimed that our ultimate end consists in knowing
God with our intellects and loving God with our wills. In this article, Aquinas
argues that the "knowing" component of that end is the primary activity of

happiness, and that the enjoyment we experience in attaining our final end is an "essential accident" of happiness, not happiness itself. In short, Aquinas appears to believe that some acts of will (such as desiring the good and delighting in acquiring it) are the wrong sorts of acts to be perfect happiness, and thus *no* act of the will can be the activity of perfect happiness. In addition, because the intellect is what supplies the will with the object of its desire, Aquinas holds that the intellect's activity is primary in perfect happiness.

One is tempted to ask in response, "Where is the love?" After all, as Aquinas himself points out in other contexts, the devil and the fallen angels all *know* God, but they certainly don't experience perfect happiness. Indeed, in other contexts (such as the Treatise on Charity), the love of God is portrayed as more central to the beatific vision—but love is not the focus here. Within the Treatise on Happiness, he takes up the importance of love in 4.3.

### 3.5. Is happiness an activity of the speculative or of the practical intellect?

Answer: Happiness is an activity of the speculative (not the practical) intellect. Our intellective capacities are the best capacities we have, and the speculative is the best of the intellective capacities; its exercise is thus the best activity of which we are capable.

This aim of this article (as with the previous two) is to locate the activity of perfect happiness more precisely within the human soul. Aquinas has just established that this activity belongs first and foremost to the intellect (rather than the will), so the next question is what part of the intellect is responsible for carrying out this activity. Given that the two options are "practical" and "speculative," and that we already know from 3.2 resp. 4 that happiness involves unending contemplation of the divine essence rather than practical actions, it's not going to come as a shock when Aquinas goes with the speculative, or theoretic, intellect. The main interest of this article, then, is what it tells us about the nature of that speculative activity (and its role in the imperfect sort of happiness we're capable of in this life).

**Obj. and resp. 1.** This objection's force depends on the reader's knowledge of the difference between the practical and speculative intellect. (See the commentary on 1.6, obj. and resp. 2.) The practical intellect deals with what ought to be done or made, as opposed to truth; it can be thought of as the *cause* of the things in the world that we think about, as opposed to the speculative intellect, whose job it is to know those things. (So, for example, I decide via the practical intellect that I should knit a sweater and then use my practical reason in making it. My speculative intellect just thinks about it.) Insofar as God is the first cause of everything, one might then think that the activity of the practical intellect makes us more like God than the speculative intellect, and that its activity will be perfect happiness.

As Aquinas points out in his response, however, in perfect happiness we are made like God by being *united* to God—and it is our speculative intellect (whose role it is to contemplate unchanging, necessary truths) that performs this uniting activity, not our practical intellect.

**Obj. and resp. 2.** One of the central features that distinguishes the speculative and the practical intellect is what they are aimed at: the speculative intellect's end is the truth, and the practical intellect's goal is the good. Happiness is the highest good, though, and it might seem that the activity of the practical intellect is better suited to it than the speculative.

As Aquinas points out in his response, however, the practical intellect may be ordered to our attaining the good (and is, thus, the primary part of the intellect involved in our moral lives), but the speculative intellect's activity is contemplating the truth. And, as we've already seen, the primary activity of perfect happiness is contemplating the Divine Truth.

**Obj. and resp. 3.** This objection focuses on the distinctively *human* nature of our final end. Practical intellect is focused on the active, moral life of human beings, and so human happiness might be thought to involve the work of the practical intellect more than that of the speculative intellect, which is focused on grasping abstract truths.

As Aquinas notes in his response, though, this argument would be a lot more plausible if human beings were their own end. Given that our end is God, though, the speculative intellect is better equipped for the activity of participating in the divine essence.

**Reply.** Aquinas's response here is not surprising: the primary activity of perfect happiness is an activity of the speculative intellect, which is (after all) the highest capacity of the human being—that to which all other capacities are subordinate, and which all their activities are designed to support. The whole point of nutrition, growth, sense perception, imagination, and even practical thought is to get human beings to the point where they can contemplate the essence of the First Cause. Aquinas backs up this claim by appealing (again) to Aristotle's *Nicomachean Ethics* X, where Aristotle argues that contemplation is the best and most delightful activity available to human beings. Aquinas goes on to support this claim with two arguments: (1) contemplation is the only activity that's sought for its own sake, since even the acts of the practical intellect are aimed at actions that achieve some further end; and (2) contemplation (*not* practical thought) is an activity we share with the only other beings that can achieve happiness: the angels and God. (Although angels and God participate in contemplation, they don't have bodies, and so they don't have to deal with the practical sorts of concerns involved in animal life.)

What is surprising about this reply, perhaps, is the bold claim that Aquinas makes at its end—namely, that perfect happiness consists *entirely* in the activity of contemplation. He allows that imperfect, earthly happiness involves the activity of the practical as well as speculative intellect (insofar as the practical intellect directs the moral life), but he states that contemplation is the only activity in which perfect happiness consists. This puts him decidedly in the "intellectualist" or "exclusive" camp of Aristotle interpreters and, as we'll see in the remainder of the Treatise, has important ramifications for his account of the afterlife.

### 3.6. Does human happiness consist in thinking about the speculative sciences?

Answer: no, perfect happiness does not consist in contemplating the speculative sciences.

Now that Aquinas has identified happiness exclusively with the activity of the speculative intellect, he spends three articles getting clearer about the nature of that activity. Knowledge of the speculative sciences (theoretical knowledge of things like mathematics, metaphysics, and theology; see the commentary on 1.6 obj. and resp. 2) is the highest intellective activity we're capable of via our own powers. Yet, as Aquinas points out, this can't be the activity of perfect happiness; even the highest cognition of theology in this life is limited by our dependence on the senses for the objects of thought. We simply can't reach full knowledge of the First Cause and Highest Good by means of the senses. Thus, although knowledge of the speculative sciences is the best sort of activity available to us now, the activity of perfect happiness that completes and fulfills us must reach beyond that—beyond anything accessible to the senses.

**Obj. and resp. 1–3.** In this connection, Aquinas doesn't actually disagree with anything said in the objections: he just thinks they're true of the activity of imperfect rather than perfect happiness. As he repeatedly says in his replies, thinking about the speculative sciences is the highest activity available to us in this life, but for us to reach our ultimate end we require more than the knowledge available to us via the senses. It will become increasingly clear in the following articles that perfect human happiness requires divine intervention.

**Reply.** The argument here for why perfect happiness can't consist in knowledge of the speculative sciences relies on the medieval idea of *scientia*, which originally just meant "knowledge" and only takes on the contemporary sense of "science" toward the end of the Middle Ages.[14] In the thirteenth century, a science was understood to be a subject of study that begins from certain

---

14. For a discussion of the development of this central medieval concept, see Pasnau (2010).

"first principles." These first principles are a priori (known in themselves, without appeal to experience) for a given science. Thus, physics was understood as a science that takes the conclusions of geometry as its first principles and proceeds from them to reach conclusions about the material world. Our knowledge of these first principles, however, requires sense perception. As Aquinas points out here, even our knowledge of the first principles of theology is sparked by sense perception: we perceive the external world and begin to wonder what its cause is, and then we realize that everything must have a cause, and that there must be a First Cause of existence.

Perfect human happiness—our ultimate end—completes us. If we could be perfected and completed by any sort of knowledge we could gain from sense perception, however, we would be able to achieve perfect human happiness in this life. Given that we can't (as Aquinas has argued in various places, but most particularly in 3.2 resp. 4), happiness must consist in contemplating something "higher" or "better" than the sensible world. In particular, it must consist in comprehension of our ultimate end: God.

Aquinas grants that what happiness *is* available to us in this life comes from engaging in the speculative sciences, however. When we contemplate the truth of mathematics or metaphysics (the study of "being qua being"), our objects of thought are as close to the truth of God's essence as we're capable of getting without divine assistance.

### 3.7. Does happiness consist in the cognition of the separated substances—that is, angels?

Answer: no. Perfect happiness consists entirely in contemplating God, who "is truth essentially."

This seems like another pro forma question, since we already know that happiness is going to consist in the cognition of the divine essence, but Aquinas likes to canvass all his options, and so instead of jumping straight from the speculative sciences to God, he stops to consider the middle option—intellective substances, or the angels. Aquinas's answer grants some validity to this option, however. Happiness can't consist *essentially* in contemplation of the angels, because our intellects are properly perfected only by something that is itself essentially perfect; but insofar as the angels participate in God's essence, contemplation of them can contribute to our happiness. Intellective union with God, however, is what it takes for us to reach our final end in the fullest way, the way that will ultimately complete and perfect us.

**Obj. and resp. 1.** The first objection reads the exhortation of Gregory of Nyssa (an early church father) to "take part in the feasts of angels" as involving contemplation of the angels.

Aquinas responds that we won't take part in the feasts of the angels by contemplating *them*, but by contemplating *God* in their company. In other words, we will be present with the angels when we're engaging in the activity of perfect happiness—there's no need to identify that activity with focusing on the angels when God is in the picture.

**Obj. and resp. 2.** In the Neoplatonic and Arabic tradition, "separated" or "immaterial" substances are the intermediaries that God uses both to create the material world and to illuminate lower intellects (that is, angels lower on the hierarchy of being, as well as human beings).[15] This objection maintains that, insofar as we're illuminated by angels, our final end should consist in their contemplation, as contemplation of the source of our knowledge.

Aquinas does not deny that angels illuminate our intellects. In fact, he claims that they do help our intellection in certain ways.[16] Instead, Aquinas denies that the angels *create* us.[17] Our ultimate end must consist in intellective contemplation not merely of what illuminates our intellect but of what is also the *cause* of those intellects.

**Obj. and resp. 3.** The objection as stated doesn't seem very plausible: it suggests that all it takes for a human being to be perfected is for it to be joined to a nature higher than itself—which seems far too low a bar, given everything Aquinas has said so far in the Treatise.

In his response, Aquinas states that there is a sense in which human nature will reach a higher nature, insofar as the activity of perfect happiness will be of the same nature in us as it is for angels. For both us and the angels, however, that activity will consist solely in contemplation of God, the only thing that could fully actualize our capacity for intellectual perfection.

**Reply.** The activity of perfect happiness completes and perfects human beings. We can't be perfected, however, via contemplation of something that is, itself, only perfect through participation. That would be like saying that once one human being—say, Bob—attained perfect happiness, all other human beings could become perfectly happy just by contemplating Bob. The proper object of our intellects is the true; only the activity of contemplating what is True *in itself* could be the activity of perfect happiness. That said, Aquinas does allow not just that contemplating the angels can be a component of imperfect happiness but that it actually yields a better sort of imperfect happiness than the contemplation of speculative sciences.

---

15. See Goris (2012) for a good discussion of this.

16. The question of Aquinas's position on angelic illumination of human intellects remains the subject of active debate. See, in particular, Pegis (1974) and Wippel's 2002 response.

17. See *ST* 1.90.3, and also *ST* 1.44 for a discussion of Aquinas's account of God's unique role as Creator.

### 3.8. Does human happiness consist
### in the vision of the divine essence?

Answer: yes, human happiness consists in intellective vision of God's essence. In fact, the answer to this question is so non-controversial that Aquinas gives it only two objections instead of the usual three.

**Obj. and resp. 1.** This objection appeals to Pseudo-Dionysius's claim that God remains "utterly unknown" to us even when we are joined to God. And it does seem plausible to worry about the ability of our finite intellects to cognize God's essence.

Aquinas's response is that Dionysius is talking about the sort of mystic union with God that we might be fortunate enough to achieve in this life. The intellective activity by which we are joined to God in the next life does involve our knowing God's essence in itself. (Although, as he is careful to point out in his response to the next objection, we will never know the divine essence to the extent that God knows it.)

**Obj. and resp. 2.** Intellective vision of the divine essence sounds like it might be too much for us. After all, *God's* happiness consists in contemplation of the divine essence. Surely, we can't share in the same sort of perfection God does, even in the life to come.

Aquinas's response distinguishes—again—between our ultimate end understood as the thing which we most desire and understood as the attaining of that desired end. All beings capable of happiness are the same in having God as their ultimate end in the first sense. When it comes to attaining that happiness, however, God has an infinitely greater level of perfection. Human beings and angels are capable of *contemplating* the divine essence (although, as we'll see, even this requires divine assistance), but we are not capable of fully *comprehending* that essence in the way that God can.

**Reply.** Aquinas builds his argument that the activity of perfect human happiness consists in direct intellective vision of the divine essence on two central considerations. First is the intuition that human beings cannot be perfectly happy if there is still something left for them to want. (This is just the point that our ultimate end must be complete and self-sufficient, as argued in Q1.) The second consideration is that what it takes to perfect a capacity depends on what it is a capacity *for*—its proper object. Human beings are able to meet most of our needs in this life, but what we need for our complete and unending satisfaction is the fulfillment of the desires of our highest part (namely, the speculative intellect). And, as we've seen earlier, the speculative intellect's object is the true. So our highest capacity can only be satisfied by the true. But, Aquinas argues here, complete knowledge of the true requires knowing not just *that* something is, but *why* it is. When we see a solar eclipse, for example, we know *that* it is the sun's light being blocked, but this naturally stirs the desire to know *why* it's being blocked. (Aquinas further follows Aristotle in identifying this sort of curiosity as the starting point for intellectual investigation of all kinds, and being distinctive of rational creatures.)

The highest knowledge of God we can reach in this life is based on sense perception, which gets us only to the conclusion *that* God exists (as First Cause). But this leaves us with the natural desire to understand the very essence of the First Cause—the why and how of it. The only thing that could satisfy this desire, however, would be the sort of union with the First Cause that could allow us to grasp its essence. And, once started, that union would have to be unending, so that our desire would remain satisfied. Thus, Aquinas concludes that the activity of perfect happiness must be unending and direct intellective contemplation of God's essence.

### Question 4: The Things That Are Required for Happiness

In the first article of this question, Aquinas gives four ways in which something can be required for something else: (1) as *preparation* for it, (2) as *perfecting* it, (3) as *assisting* it, and (4) as *necessarily accompanying* it. Each of the things he considers in this question—delight, comprehension, rectitude of will, the body, external goods, and friendship—will meet at least one of those criteria. Art. 1–4 address the will's role in our final end. We know from Q3 that the activity of happiness consists first and foremost in the speculative intellect's contemplation of God's essence. Our final end was defined at the end of Q1 as "knowing *and loving* God," however, and the first half of this question spells out in more detail the way in which the will is also involved in the activity of perfect happiness. Art. 5–8 work their way outward from intellect and will. As we saw in Q2, Aquinas follows Aristotle in dividing human goods into three categories: goods of the soul, goods of the body, and external goods. Having settled how the goods of the soul are involved in perfect happiness, Aquinas now returns to the second two categories to consider what role—if any—bodily and external goods play in the activity of our ultimate end. The extremely qualified role he grants them both underscores the radically intellectualist nature of his account of happiness and raises questions about the extent to which perfect happiness is the fulfillment of our nature as rational animals.

### 4.1. Is delight required for happiness?

Answer: yes. We always feel delight upon attaining a desired good, and happiness is our highest good.

Delight is, by definition, the enjoyment the will feels in attaining the object of its desire. It seems fairly obvious, then, that delight is going to be involved in the will's attaining the ultimate object of its desire: the universal good.

At the same time, Aquinas has already denied in the previous question that the activity of perfect happiness is an activity of the will. In this article, Aquinas explains that the intellect's activity of contemplating God's essence entails delight rather than consisting in delight. For an analogy, think of fire. The essence of a fire isn't heat—it's burning. You can't burn something without generating heat, however, and in the same way, you can't contemplate God's essence without experiencing delight.

**Obj. and resp. 1 & 2.** The first two objections in this article both stress the all-sufficient nature of perfect happiness. If vision of God's essence is what perfect happiness consists in, then that vision must be sufficient all by itself. If delight were also necessary, intellective vision alone wouldn't be sufficient.

Aquinas's response is to claim that delight can be integrally involved in our vision of God's essence without itself being part of what happiness consists in. Delight is not something added above and beyond the activity of contemplating God's essence: it is a necessary *consequence* of it.

**Obj. and resp. 3.** This objection appeals to the well-known power of pleasure to distract our intellects, particularly its power to lure our practical intellect away from making good judgments.

In response, Aquinas explains that the pleasure of delight affects our intellective activities differently, depending on its source. The delight that comes with or from an intellective activity, for instance, actually strengthens that activity. If you enjoy mathematics, for instance, you're likely to concentrate harder, work longer, and do better at it. This kind of delight is, obviously, the sort that accompanies (and enhances) our vision of the divine essence. Pleasure "external to the intellect" and whose source is non-intellective activity, however, does interfere with our ability to cognize. Our attention is naturally drawn to things we find pleasant, and so the delight we find in non-intellective activities, such as eating a delicious dinner, naturally focuses us on the meal and draws our attention away from contemplation. Some sorts of pleasure are even what Aquinas calls "contrary to" certain activities of the intellect, because they are directly opposed to them. The pleasure we get from eating a great meal, for instance, directly interferes with our ability to make a prudent choice about how much to eat, much more than it interferes with, for instance, our ability to work out how much of the bill we're responsible for.

**Reply.** Aquinas's distinction here between the four ways in which something can be required for something else (see the general introduction to this question) is clearly meant to set up his replies to all eight articles in this question. (The examples he provides here, for instance, are all cases he discusses later in this question.) There's really not much more Aquinas needs to say: delight is the enjoyment we feel when our wills rest in the attainment of the good they've sought, and perfect happiness—which just is attaining the very highest good possible for rational creatures—thus necessarily entails delight.

### 4.2. What is more fundamental
### in happiness: delight or vision?

Answer: *vision* is more fundamental.

We already know the answer to this question. Aquinas has argued several times in the previous three questions that the intellect's vision of the divine essence is the primary activity in which perfect human happiness consists. So what's going on in this article, then? In short, it appears that Aquinas wants to provide a definitive reply to this question, which—as he points out—Aristotle leaves unanswered at the end of the *Nicomachean Ethics*. That said, what Aquinas says here merely summarizes points that he's made in earlier questions.

**Obj. and resp. 1.** This objection quotes Aristotle as claiming that delight is a perfection of an activity; in response, Aquinas quotes Aristotle right back (also from book X of the *Nicomachean Ethics*). Delight is a perfection in the sense that it follows naturally from an activity and is, in that way, a completion of the activity. It is not a perfection in the sense that it is necessary to complete or perfect our vision of the divine essence itself.

**Obj. and resp. 2.** This objection gets at the fundamentally motivational nature of delight or pleasure. Don't we desire to participate in activities for the pleasure that comes from them? In fact, isn't that why nature made activities necessary for animal survival (such as eating and having sex) pleasurable— that is, so that we would be motivated to participate in them?

**Obj. and resp. 3.** This is (rather surprisingly) the first place in the Treatise on Happiness where charity is mentioned explicitly. The objection refers to Paul's famous statement in I Corinthians 13: "And these three remain: faith, hope, and charity [usually translated today as 'love'], but the greatest of these is charity." Faith is a virtue that relates to the intellect's vision, whereas charity is a virtue that relates to the will that culminates in the delight the will experiences in attaining its desired object; if charity is greater than faith, it seems that delight should be greater than vision.

Aquinas argues in response that the real goal of charity—which he defines in II-II 23.1 of his Treatise on Charity (QQ23–46) as "the friendship of human beings for God"—is attaining the good that we desire. The pleasure or delight we get from loving God is not what motivates our will to seek the good. It is a necessary consequence of attaining that good, not the end goal itself. The end of charity is the activity through which God is made present to both intellect and will: contemplation of God's essence, which perfects the friendship we can have for God.

**Reply.** Aquinas states here that the intellect's activity of contemplating the divine essence is more important than the will's delight in that activity. His argument for that claim, however, is not particularly strong. Delight, he says, consists in the will's resting in the enjoyment of possessing a desired good. If the will rests in an activity (like the contemplation of the divine essence), then, it is because of the goodness of that activity. And the will seeks coming to rest in that activity because that activity is the good the will is aimed at, not because the will is after the delight that the activity entails. For (and here things start to look rather circular), if the will were aimed at delight, then delight would be the activity of perfect happiness. But, Aquinas says, delight is *not* the activity in which happiness consists, and so it can't be what the will is aimed at.

### 4.3. Is comprehension required for happiness?

Answer: yes—where comprehension is understood not as the sort of complete grasp of God's essence that only God can have, but rather in the sense of the good that we know and love actually being present to us.

At first glance, it looks as though Aquinas is backtracking here and asking whether *intellective* comprehension is required for perfect human happiness. Instead, this article is focused on comprehension in a sense closer to what modern readers probably think of as "apprehension" or "possession." In this sense, we comprehend an end or a good when it is present to us, in the same way that our ultimate good is present to us when we contemplate the divine essence. Aquinas has concentrated so far in this question on the enjoyment or delight the will experiences upon attaining perfect happiness; in this article, he finally discusses the role of love (which, after all, one might think is the primary activity of the will).

**Obj. and resp. 1.** This objection quotes Augustine as claiming that although we can reach God's essence via intellective cognition, it's impossible for any created being to *comprehend* him.

In response, Aquinas distinguishes between two different sorts of comprehension: (1) full possession or encompassing knowledge of the loved thing by the person who loves it—a sort of relation finite beings clearly can't have to an infinite being like God, even with God's assistance, and (2) simply holding onto something that is present to you, which is the sense in which we are able to comprehend God's essence.

**Obj. and resp. 2.** This objection states that because human happiness involves the intellective or rational capacities—intellect and will—the perfection of these capacities need involve only two activities: (1) vision of God's essence for the intellect and (2) delight in this vision for the will. Comprehension (whatever it is) seems like a third, unnecessary component.

In his response, Aquinas draws on the three theological virtues (faith, hope, and love [the Latin here is *amor* rather than *caritas*, or charity]) to argue that there are actually three components to perfect happiness: vision (which is the completion or fulfillment of faith), comprehension (which is the fulfillment of hope), and delight (which is the fulfillment of love). Faith involves the intellect, whereas hope and love involve the will: as Aquinas says in his reply to this article, we have love for the desired object (God, the highest good) and hope that we will attain it (via intellective vision). In perfect happiness, that desired object is present to us—this is comprehension—and our wills rest in our attainment of it (delight).

**Obj. and resp. 3.** Our intellects aim at the true, and our wills aim at the good, and perfect happiness consists in our vision of the true and our delight in our possession of that good. It's not clear from this picture that comprehension is needed, or where it would fit as a third component.

Aquinas's response is that the one real activity of human happiness is contemplation of God's essence, as he's argued in Q3. Comprehension isn't an activity separate from that vision any more than delight is. Instead, delight is a natural and necessary result of that vision, and comprehension just is our possession of that vision—it is the relation between us (who desire that vision as our final end) and the final end that we have desired above all else and now possess.

**Reply.** Aquinas begins his reply here by commenting that the way to figure out what's required for happiness is to look more closely at how human beings are ordered to their end, which, he says, happens partly through intellect and partly through will. (Note that he again focuses here exclusively on our rational capacities, putting aside the sensory and nutritive capacities that are part of our animal nature.)

The intellect's end is the true. We are ordered or moved to that end via an incomplete grasp of that truth: we seek to know and understand fully what we first grasp only in part. So, to use Aquinas's eclipse example from 3.8, we first notice that there are times when the sun gets obscured during the day and we get curious as to what's happening; then we pay attention and realize that this event happens at predictable times that correspond to the movements of the moon and grasp what an eclipse is. This knowledge then motivates us to search for an even more complete grasp of the truth that would include *why* an eclipse happens (all of which eventually moves us toward investigating the true nature of the First Cause).

The will's end is the good. We are ordered or directed toward that good in two ways: (1) through love, the desire of the will for the perceived good and the starting point for all acts of will, and (2) through "a real relation" of the lover to what is loved. We can have this relation to what we love in any of three ways: (a) we can possess the object of our desire, as when I love my friend, want to see him, and he's sitting right in front of me; (b) we can want something that is not only not currently present to us but actually impossible for us to have, as when I love my grandmother, want to see her, but can't because she died last year. In both of these cases, Aquinas says, we don't search for the object of our desire: in the first case, because we already have it, and in the second case, because we *can't* have it. (This echoes Meno's Paradox about inquiry, from Plato's *Meno*.) There is a third case, however: (c) we can want something that we are able to attain but aren't able to attain at that point, as when I love my brother, want to see him, but can't at the moment because he lives in Hong Kong and I live in Chicago. This third kind of relation of the lover to what is loved, Aquinas says, is the one in which we hope for the fulfillment of our desire and look for ways to attain that end—I might check for cheap flights to Hong Kong, say, or accept a conference invitation there.

Having described these three ways in which human beings are ordered to their end (the one way in which intellect is ordered to its end, and the two ways in which will is ordered to its end), Aquinas finally returns to the main subject of the article—comprehension. Perfect human happiness involves the fulfillment of all three kinds of ordering: complete cognition fulfills the incomplete knowledge we start off with; the presence of the loved end in that vision fulfills the lover's hope for what she loves; and the delight we experience in our possession of that desired end is a fulfillment of the love we have for that object. Comprehension is the presence of our ultimate end (God), which we see via intellective union and delight in possessing.

### 4.4. Is rectitude of will required for happiness?

Answer: yes. Having a will that is rightly ordered to the ultimate end is both necessary for us to attain happiness in the first place and part of the activity of perfect happiness itself.

This is another question that's likely to look puzzling to a modern audience, given that "rectitude of will" is not exactly a phrase that comes up often, even in contemporary conversations. It has a long and illustrious history in medieval philosophy, though, and is an idea developed in detail in Anselm.[18]

In its most basic form, which is what's relevant for Aquinas's purposes in this article, rectitude of the will is the will's being rightly ordered toward its proper object. Our wills are rational appetites for the good considered as such, and they are naturally ordered toward that good—but they are also capable of going astray and desiring things that only *appear* good. I can, for instance, develop a strong passion for a show like *Doctor Who* and order my entire life around my being able to watch the entire series over and over again, neglecting friends, family, and my job in the process. I'm doing so because I love the show and consider it the most important thing in my life. In this situation, though,

---

18. See Anselm's *On the Fall of the Devil*. For detailed discussions of the doctrine of rectitude of the will, see Boler (2010), and Visser and Williams (2009).

I do not have rectitude of will: *Doctor Who* (wonderful as it is) is not the highest good, and my will is not ordered appropriately when my life's activities are focused around it. I have rectitude of will when my will is rightly ordered—focused appropriately on what is actually the highest good (God)—and all my other activities are appropriately ordered toward that love. Once we understand what rectitude of the will is, then, it's going to be fairly clear that it is involved in our perfect happiness. And Aquinas claims here that it is necessary both as an *antecedent* requirement (we can't attain our final end if we're not ordered to it appropriately) and as a *concomitant* requirement (our will's being rightly ordered to the good just is part of what it is to know and love God).

**Obj. and resp. 1.** Rectitude of will—having one's will ordered rightly with respect to its proper object—is equated with purity, in the sense of the "pure in heart" mentioned in Jesus's Sermon on the Mount (Matthew 5–7). This objection argues that because Augustine explicitly modifies his earlier statement about the pure in heart in order to make it clear that even those who are not pure can know the truth, it must be possible for someone to know the True through vision of God's essence even without purity of heart.

In response, Aquinas explains that Augustine is talking not about our knowledge of the truth that is our highest good, but rather of knowledge of a lesser sort of truth, like physics or shoemaking or mathematics. Even thoroughly wicked people can have knowledge of those sorts of truths and be properly ordered to the truth in that respect.

**Obj. and resp. 2.** As Aquinas will explain in more detail in the Treatise on Human Acts (QQ6–21; see especially 9.1 and 3), the activity of the intellect is prior to an activity of the will—our wills don't have anything to move toward or away from until our intellects present them with a specific object. Since perfect happiness is exclusively an activity of the intellect, though, one might think that there is no action of the will that is required for that activity's performance. (One might especially think this, given how vehemently Aquinas has argued in Q3 against the activity of happiness being anything other than intellective contemplation of the divine essence.)

In response, Aquinas stresses the antecedent nature of rectitude of the will: every act of the will requires an act of the intellect to get started, but that doesn't mean that *all* acts of the intellect precede *all* acts of the will. In particular, working toward a long-term goal—such as one's ultimate end—requires a complex series of interactions between the intellect and the will. Becoming a generous person, for instance, involves repeated acts of one's intellect and will engaging with each other; what's required for living the moral life as a whole requires a whole host of such interactions. Our wills naturally tend toward our highest good, but (as we are painfully aware from personal experience) we are capable of being wrong about what that good consists in and of going for the easy option rather than right one. Our will's being ordered or aimed toward the perfect good in such a way that it can actually attain that end (which is, after all, just what rectitude of will *is*) is thus a necessary precondition for perfect happiness. Although this all seems true, it's also worth noting that Aquinas rather dodges the issue of whether rectitude of will is required for the activity of perfect happiness itself, although in the body of the article he allows that rectitude of will *is* part of the activity of happiness.

**Obj. and resp. 3.** The third objection picks up on this: granted that rectitude of will is necessary for attaining perfect happiness, is it required for the activity of happiness itself?

In response, Aquinas claims that our wills don't cease to be directed rightly toward their ultimate end simply because we now possess that end. That would be true only if this case involved a certain sort of incompleteness, as with motion. Motion is directed toward an end, but once that terminus is achieved, the motion ceases. Love is not essentially incomplete in this way, however: we don't stop loving something when we attain it (well, at least we don't if the object of that love turns out to meet our expectations—and, in this case, we're talking about the Highest Good, which completely satisfies all desire). To use a slightly irreverent analogy, we park our car when we reach our desired destination, but we don't park the love when we get to heaven. In fact, Aquinas claims that rectitude of will is *enhanced* by the possession of the end toward which it is ordered. We want the good even more, and for even more of the right reasons.

**Reply.** In 3.3, Aquinas made a distinction between three ways in which something can pertain to happiness: *essentially, antecedently,* and *consequently.* In this article, Aquinas adds *"concomitantly"* to this list. Rectitude of the will is required antecedently because being ordered appropriately to our ultimate end is a necessary pre-condition for our attaining that end and concomitantly because contemplating God's essence involves ordering all our desires toward that essence.

The analogy Aquinas provides here to explain the *antecedent* requirement is helpful if hylomorphism (the Aristotelian doctrine that all physical substances are composites of matter and form) is your primary metaphysical framework; the analogy will be somewhat obscure otherwise. His basic point is that the relationship between form and matter is similar to the relationship between our final end and "what is for the end" (in this case, the will). As Aquinas argues in his commentary on Aristotle's *De anima* (I.8.316–63), matter can't acquire just any form whatsoever—it can acquire only a form that it's appropriately disposed toward. A rock can't acquire a human form, for instance, because stone isn't disposed toward carrying out characteristically human activities such as loving and thinking: a rock lacks the sort of capacities that would make such activities possible. In the same way, a will that's disposed only toward love of, say, *Doctor Who* will not be able to acquire the activity of perfect happiness. Our wills need to be disposed appropriately toward the love of God and the vision of the divine essence in order for us to attain perfect happiness. Rectitude of the will just is that sort of disposition.

This also helps explain why perfect happiness requires rectitude of the will *concomitantly.* Our final end is the vision of God, the Highest Good. When we're actively participating in that intellective vision, we naturally order all our other loves to that highest love—in fact, as Aquinas says, we "necessarily love whatever [we] love as ordered to God." Again, that's just what it is to have rectitude of the will, and so anyone participating in perfect happiness will have rectitude of will.[19]

### 4.5. Is the body required for human happiness?

Answer: the body is *not* required for the activity of perfect happiness, which consists entirely in the contemplation of the divine essence. It *is*, however, required both for imperfect happiness in this life and for the complete perfection and well-being of the resurrected human being.

This is perhaps the longest and most controversial article in the Treatise on Happiness. One sign that this is an issue of importance is the fact that there are six objections, in contrast with the usual three. Another is the length and complexity of Aquinas's reply. This is also an article where, surprisingly/puzzlingly/interestingly, all six objections seem entirely in line with things that Aquinas himself has argued in other places. According to Aquinas's account of human nature, a human being is essentially composed of body and soul, matter and form. As we've seen, the definition of 'human being' is 'rational animal,' which entails physicality as well as rationality. Yet, Aquinas argues in this article, the body is *not* required for human happiness; human souls are capable of happiness without being joined to bodies.

In this connection, it's important to see that one of the issues driving Aquinas here is the question of whether "separated" human souls (souls in the nonembodied intermediate state between death and the bodily resurrection) are happy. Christian doctrine advocates the resurrection of the body: our souls will be joined again to matter at the Final Resurrection. Standard Catholic teaching in the thirteenth century, however, held that our eternal rewards and punishments begin at the moment of death. Aquinas accepts this teaching, and so he argues here that the souls of the saints are happy already while everyone else's souls are in purgatory or hell. If souls separated from bodies can be capable of happiness, though, those bodies must not be required for perfect happiness.

---

19. See the commentary on 5.7 below for further development of the relationship between happiness and rectitude of will.

**Obj. and resp. 1.** As Aquinas himself argues in *Summa theologiae* I.75.4, a human being is necessarily composed of form and matter, or soul and body. The human soul is part of human nature, not the whole of it, and so it seems as though the activity of perfect happiness—which involves complete virtue and grace—also requires the soul's union with the body.

Aquinas's response to the objection that perfect happiness presupposes the perfection of that thing's nature (in the case of human beings, 'rational animal') is to claim that the relevant perfection of nature in this case is the perfection of the intellect, which transcends the body and (as we've seen) doesn't require the body for its highest activity. Thus, although the soul is not complete or perfect in this state insofar as it's not serving as the form of a body, it can be complete or perfect with respect to the relevant activity (namely, contemplating God's essence).

**Obj. and resp. 2.** We already know that happiness is an activity (3.2); this objection draws on that feature of happiness to argue that something "incomplete in being"—that is, existing imperfectly in some respect—can't operate perfectly. Separated from matter, however, the soul has imperfect being (because it isn't carrying out its essential function as substantial form of actualizing a human body and thus exists as a part in separation from the whole), so it seems it can't carry out the activity of perfect human happiness in that state. In other words, perfect human happiness requires the body as well as the soul.

In response, Aquinas makes a distinction between the way in which the soul is a part of the human being and the way something like a hand is a part of the human being. The physical parts of an animal cease to exist when the whole ceases to exist: in hylomorphic metaphysics, this means that if a human being dies, the physical parts of that human being cease to exist as such, even before they begin decomposing. The hand of a human being is no longer a hand once the human being dies: it becomes a collection of particles that *used* to be a hand. A human eye ceases to be an eye at the human being's death: it becomes a collection of particles that used to be an eye.[20] The soul is a part of the human being in a radically different sort of way from a hand or an eye, however. As the substantial form of the body, the rational soul is what gives being to the entire composite: the rational soul is what makes the composite of matter and form exist *as a human being*. In the case of other matter/form composites (plants, animals, etc.), the substantial form doesn't survive the destruction of the composite. The human soul is unique in this respect, though, because its proper function is intellective contemplation,

---

20. For extended discussion of this doctrine, see Shields (1999).

which doesn't necessarily depend on physical organs.[21] Not only can the soul survive the death of the body, then, but its continued existence entails the continuation of the "being" of the human being. In virtue of this, Aquinas argues, the soul can carry out the activity of perfect happiness (contemplation of the divine essence) even in separation from matter.

**Obj. and resp. 3.** This objection cuts right to the heart of the matter: "a soul without a body is not a human being." Aquinas himself maintains this in a number of places, including the Treatise on Human Nature (I.75.4), his *Commentary on the Sentences* (IV.43.1.1.1 resp. 2), his commentary on Paul's discussion of the bodily resurrection in 1 Corinthians 15, his commentary on Job (Lectio 2), and *SCG* II. How can the activity that Aquinas has claimed is the ultimate end of *human* nature not require the existence of the whole human being (as opposed to just one of its parts)?

Aquinas's response to this objection is brief and involves an example that appears to completely miss the point (as well as being distinctly creepy). He claims that a human being is happy in virtue of her intellect's engaging in the activity of perfect happiness, and so as long as that intellect exists and is engaging in that activity, the human being gets to count as happy even in the absence of the body. The example Aquinas gives to illustrate this point is that an Ethiopian counts as white in virtue of his teeth, which stay white even if they're extracted. But this example actually highlights what seems troubling about Aquinas's defense of perfect happiness not requiring a body. If Aquinas just wants to make the claim that human beings count as happy so long as their intellects engage in the activity of happiness, the parallel claim in the example he provides should be that the Ethiopian still counts as white because his teeth stay white after they're extracted. But that doesn't seem plausible at all! In fact, this example just underscores what Aquinas seems to be overlooking: even if we grant that the intellect can be happy apart from the body, that doesn't amount to the *human being*'s being happy, in the same way that granting that someone's teeth remain white when they're pulled out doesn't amount to that person's being white in virtue of those extracted teeth. (What makes this worse is the fact that Aquinas has just finished arguing in his response to the previous objection that a human hand doesn't count as a hand in separation from the human being. Human teeth don't even count as *teeth* once they've been pulled out.)

**Obj. and resp. 4 & 5.** Aquinas has already argued (see 3.2 resp. 4) that the activity in which our ultimate end consists must be unimpeded—wholly free from distractions or interruptions—and an activity that wholly satisfies all of

---

21. See Pasnau (2002) for a discussion and defense of this claim, which is central to Aquinas's argument for the immortality of the human soul.

our natural desires. The soul separated from the body retains a natural desire for union with that body, though (see *SCG* IV.79), and so it seems that the disembodied soul has an unfulfilled natural desire that would get in the way of the perfection or completeness of its happiness.

In response, Aquinas makes a rather delicate distinction between perfect happiness *simpliciter* and the complete perfection of perfect happiness. Aquinas says that the separated soul that is cognizing God's essence has perfect happiness because it possesses the ultimate object of its desire. It lacks the complete perfection of that happiness, however, insofar as it continues to long for union with matter so that its enjoyment can, so to speak, "spill over" into the body and perfect the soul's act of actualizing that body.

Aquinas appears here to be relying on the difference he drew originally in 1.8 between our ultimate end understood as the thing toward which all our actions aim and our ultimate end understood as our attaining of that thing. As long as we attain cognition of our desired end, he seems to be saying, we count as perfectly happy because we possess the thing in which our happiness consists. This doesn't necessarily imply that our attainment of that object is completely perfect, though: in his words, "as far as the one desiring is concerned, it does not possess that good in every way in which it would want to possess it."

In the last sentence of resp. 5, Aquinas gives another way of understanding the claim that the separated soul can be happy even if it still longs for union with the body: happiness increases at the bodily resurrection, not in intensity but, rather, in extent. In short, it's not that we become more happy when our souls are reunited with matter—rather, there's simply more of us to be happy.

To say that this response to the original objections seems unsatisfactory is to put things mildly. First, as objection three pointed out, our separated souls aren't *us* in separation from the body. Aquinas is committed to the view that human beings are composed necessarily of form and matter. As we saw, his response to this objection (involving the Ethiopian's teeth) seemed tangential to its central concern. Perhaps as a result, his response to these objections seems uncharacteristically off as well. Regardless, Aquinas's claim that we have perfect happiness insofar as our intellects cognize God's essence even if there are some natural desires left unsatisfied (namely, our soul's natural desire to serve as the form of a human body) seems to conflict with his repeated emphasis on how perfect happiness involves the fulfillment of human nature in such a way that no desire is left unsatisfied. In addition, Aquinas's appeal to the intensity and the extent of happiness ignores the rather strong intuition that if an impediment to the completion of perfect happiness has been removed (because our soul's natural desire to inform a human body has been satisfied), we would become more happy.

Not surprisingly, Aquinas's account of the separated soul and the identity and happiness of human beings is the subject of significant controversy.[22]

**Obj. and resp. 6.** Aquinas has quoted Matthew 22:30 ("We will be like the angels in heaven") approvingly in a number of places already; this objection picks up on that, appealing to Augustine's authority to argue that a human soul without a body isn't equal to angels, and so the soul can't be happy if it's not united to the body.

Aquinas's response relies on the distinction he's just made in resp. 4 between perfect happiness and the complete perfection of perfect happiness. The souls of the saints are already participating in the activity of perfect happiness at the level of the higher angels, he says, and already see God more clearly than the lower angels. (He'll return to this point in Q5; for now, it's worth noting that human beings do *not* become angels when we die. We remain human, and after the Final Resurrection, we experience the afterlife in embodied form.) Those separated souls count as happy insofar as they are contemplating God's essence. Their happiness does not yet reach the complete perfection of perfect happiness, however, for reasons described in resp. 4 & 5 above.

**Reply.** The first part of the reply is exactly what Aquinas's Treatise on Human Nature would lead you to expect: the body is definitely required for earthly happiness. Imperfect happiness is an intellective activity (the speculative intellect being focused on the True, and the practical intellect on living the moral life aimed at attaining the Good), and no intellective activity is possible in this life without a phantasm that is preserved in a physical organ. So the body is essential for any sort of cognition (and therefore happiness) in this life.

The second part of the reply is where Aquinas ventures into new territory. It is also the first place in the Treatise on Happiness where we see him support his answer explicitly by appeal to both Scripture and reason—another sign that he realizes this is a controversial topic. Aquinas holds that human beings are composites of soul and body, so it seems reasonable to suppose initially that he would be on the side of the people he cites who claim that the beatific vision doesn't begin until the final judgment and bodily resurrection. Furthermore, the reference to the body in the Scripture passage quoted here seems to the modern reader to be highly metaphorical: we are "in the body" here and now, and we're "absent from the body" at death. Aquinas, however, takes it literally and says that it indicates that the souls of the saints already "walk by sight" after their death, meaning that they already enjoy the beatific vision. (It is, however, worth noting that Aquinas doesn't refer to "the saints"

---

22. See Toner (2009) for both an overview of relevant literature to that point and a defense of Aquinas's position; for more recent debate about the best way to read Aquinas on this topic, see Jeffery Brower (2014) and Van Dyke (2014b).

here, but rather to "the souls of the saints." Aquinas takes pains in SCG IV.96 to argue that there are two separate moments of reckoning after death: the first involves our separated souls at the moment of our death, and the second involves our resurrected selves at the moment of the final judgment. For further discussion of these issues, see the works cited in the discussion of resp. 4 & 5 above.)

Aquinas goes on to claim that reason also supports the idea that perfect human happiness does not require a body *per se*: happiness consists entirely in the vision of the divine essence, and such a vision is not something that sense perception or phantasms would help us with. Aquinas does allow that the body is important for human happiness insofar as it pertains to a thing's "well-being," but it is not completely clear what he means. The examples he provides (beauty for the perfection of the body and quick-wittedness for the perfection of a human being) suggest a sort of icing-on-the-cake model, however. In other words, perfect happiness should be thought of as "complete in species" or having a certain essential nature rather than as requiring that our experience of it be ideal. The soul can be perfectly happy, then, as soon as it begins to cognize God's essence, since that activity is our ultimate end. Reunion with the body is just the icing on the cake that allows that activity to reach its fullest expression. (As Aquinas writes in resp. 5, being rejoined to the body doesn't increase the intensity of our happiness but only its extent.)

### 4.6. Is the perfection of the body required for happiness?

Answer: yes. Given that we're going to have resurrected bodies in the afterlife, they definitely need to be *perfected* bodies in order for us to enjoy perfect happiness.

Having just argued that the body itself is not required for happiness, Aquinas nevertheless goes on in this article to argue that the perfection of the body *is*. The main reason for this prima facie confusing shift is that Aquinas has moved from considering whether the separated soul can be happy in the period between death and the bodily resurrection to considering the sort of body to which our souls will be joined after the bodily resurrection. In that light, it's not surprising that he argues that our heavenly bodies will need to be perfect, although he says far less here about the exact nature of that perfection than he does in other places (most notably, SCG IV.81–88).

**Obj. and resp. 1.** This objection identifies bodily perfection with the sort of bodily good (health, beauty, etc.) that Aquinas has already said happiness doesn't consist in.

In his response, Aquinas simply comments that something's being required for happiness is different from that thing's itself being what happiness consists in. Bodily perfection may not be our ultimate end, but it can enhance (or at least not impede) the activity of perfect happiness. (Given this sense of what it means for something to be required for happiness, however, it looks like Aquinas should have agreed that the body is required for happiness.)

**Obj. and resp. 2.** Aquinas has already argued that the body is not necessary for perfect happiness, since the body does not contribute directly to the activity of cognizing the divine essence. It doesn't seem, then, that it should matter what sort of body we have in heaven.

Aquinas's response is that although the body doesn't actively contribute anything to that activity, it could still impede it. The sorts of post-resurrection bodies we have must in no way detract from our unending contemplation of the divine essence. They need to be perfected so that they will not get tired, for example, or hungry, or sick.[23]

**Obj. and resp. 3.** According to this objection, the intellect is better able to carry out its work—cognizing God's essence—the more it is "disentangled" from the body (a very Platonic sentiment!), and so for the intellect's activity to be perfected, it should be disentangled completely from the body.

In response, Aquinas distinguishes between the corruptible, "fallen" body that distracts the intellect with its needs and wants, and the perfect, "spiritual" body of the life to come. (Although Aquinas doesn't mention this here, our resurrected bodies count as spiritual not because they're somehow immaterial, but rather because they're incorruptible and completely responsive to the soul or spirit's commands.)

**On the contrary.** Interestingly, this argument doesn't appeal to any of the classic bodily resurrection passages (e.g., 1 Corinthians 15; Job 19:26), but rather to a passage from Isaiah that refers to our bodies flourishing in the kingdom of God.

**Reply.** Aquinas divides his reply between imperfect and perfect happiness but claims that the perfection of the body is required for both. First, a "good condition" of the body is required for imperfect happiness because the moral life is aimed at acquiring virtue, and physical imperfections can get in the way of our attaining virtue (the central element of earthly happiness) by preventing us from performing the actions necessary to become virtuous. (Both Aristotle's and Aquinas's views involve a strong component of moral luck and ableism in acquiring earthly happiness: your physical condition as well as your external circumstances might prevent you from being able to perform the sorts of actions that will allow you to become wise, say, or brave.)

With respect to perfect happiness, Aquinas argues that because the soul is naturally united to the body as its substantial form, the perfection of that

---

23. See Van Dyke (2014a) for further discussion of what Aquinas believes our new, improved bodies will be like.

soul can't be incompatible with the perfection of that body. (Note that this is a rather weak claim that in no way suggests that the body is necessary for the activity of perfect happiness.) In fact, he says, our bodies require perfection *antecedent* to the activity of perfect happiness—so that our bodies don't impede their intellects' vision, and our bodies will also have perfection *consequent* to that activity, via the soul's perfection in the beatific vision. In rather poetic terms that echo Pseudo-Dionysius, Aquinas says that the soul's happiness "will overflow into the body, so that the body will receive its own perfection."

### 4.7. Are any external goods required for happiness?

Answer: no, we do not require any external goods (like food or drink) for perfect happiness.

The last two articles of this question seem rather anticlimactic: clearly, if the *body* isn't required for happiness, external goods (including friends) aren't going to be required. This and the following article represent Aquinas's exhaustive consideration of the various options and serve as a bit of a wrap-up for some of the issues that have arisen in the previous articles.

**Obj. and resp. 1.** This objection cites a number of gospel passages which describe our enjoying external goods in heaven, such as eating and drinking at the Lord's table, having treasure, and inheriting the kingdom of God.

In response, Aquinas claims that these passages should be taken metaphorically, not literally.

**Obj. and resp. 2.** Aquinas has already responded several times to Boethius's definition of complete happiness as "the state made complete by the accumulation of all goods," and that definition is brought up again here, since external goods appear to fall under the scope of "all goods."

Aquinas's response is a bit perplexing. First, he says that external goods (food, drink, wealth, etc.) will play no role in the life to come because those goods are aimed at fulfilling the needs of "animal" life, and we will no longer have the needs those goods satisfy. (Our incorruptible bodies will never, for example, get hungry.) He then goes on to claim, however, that perfect happiness *does* involve the accumulation of all goods, insofar as whatever was good about those external things exists in God as the fount and source of all goods. This, however, seems rather like telling someone who really loves chocolate that their desire for it will be perfectly satisfied in heaven because there will be all the chocolate they ever wanted there . . . in God's mind. (Aquinas's actual point is more nuanced—he says that whatever was *good* about chocolate exists in the Supreme Good, and so our desire for that good will be satisfied. Still, if you think that there is anything about external goods whose goodness is integrally related to their existence as, say, physical objects, this goodness will not be preserved.)

**Obj. and resp. 3.** This objection comes from a slightly different angle, arguing that heaven must be a physical place. (It will, after all, contain our physical bodies.) Insofar as heaven is an external thing that is good, then, it looks like heaven itself must be an external good that we require for perfect happiness.

Aquinas agrees that heaven will be a physical place—not because external goods are required for happiness, however, but "for the sake of fittingness and beauty."[24]

**Reply.** Again, Aquinas distinguishes in his reply between what's required for imperfect and perfect happiness. External goods are necessary for our both attaining and maintaining imperfect, earthly happiness; the category of external goods, after all, includes all the things we need for physical functioning and the active moral life, as well as things like the books and teachers that we need for the contemplative life. Not surprisingly, though, Aquinas denies that external goods are required for perfect happiness. External goods are aimed at supporting the active life of corruptible bodies, and perfect happiness is an activity that either doesn't involve the body at all or that involves our new-and-improved, incorruptible bodies that no longer require external assistance for their flourishing.

### 4.8. Is the companionship of friends required for happiness?

Answer: not really. The companionship of friends will "contribute to the well-being of happiness" in the afterlife, but is not strictly necessary.

Aquinas's answer to this question is perhaps less enthusiastically in favor of friendship than one might hope, but exactly what we should expect at this point in his discussion of happiness. We need friends for imperfect happiness, insofar as they help us lead the moral life, but our contemplation of God's essence is all we need for perfect happiness.

**Obj. and resp. 1.** This objection returns to the role of glory in happiness (see 2.3). If our future happiness involves glory, and glory involves a number of people knowing that you possess a good, then it looks like perfect happiness involves friends who know and honor us for our attaining our highest good.

In response, Aquinas explains that the sort of glory involved in perfect happiness is just the glory we have in God's eyes, not in the eyes of others.

---

24. The question of the location of heaven is a rather vexed issue in medieval discussions. For a general overview that includes illustrations, see McDannell and Lang (2001).

(This essentially just repeats what he says in the reply of 2.3.) The glory of the saints, then, consists not in our glorifying them but rather in God's recognition of the good they possess.

**Obj. and resp. 2.** Boethius claims that we need friends to enjoy the goods that we have.

Aquinas responds that Boethius is thinking here of a good that's not itself fully sufficient, and that the beatific vision contains "the sufficiency of all good." We might need friends to help us enjoy our birthday cake, but we don't need friends to help us enjoy intellective contemplation of God.

**Obj. and resp. 3.** Jesus's first Great Commandment is to love God, and the second is to love our neighbor as ourselves. As this objection points out, however, that makes it seem as though the love of neighbor and companionship of friends is necessary for the fulfillment of happiness.

In his response, Aquinas emphasizes the first commandment—love of God—as what's essential to perfect happiness. His reason is that even if there were just one soul in heaven (presumably one of the blessed, prior to the bodily resurrection), that soul would be perfectly happy without anyone else there. Furthermore, even if there were other souls there, our love for our neighbor would follow from our love for God. That is, our love for our neighbor would be the natural outflowing of our love for God.

**Reply.** Aquinas's explanation of what we need friends for in this life denies that we need them for utility or pleasure—the first two of the three types of friendship Aristotle discusses in the *Nicomachean Ethics*—but allows that we do need them for the exercise of virtue. He claims that we need friends to live both the active and the contemplative life well: they encourage and support us, we encourage and support them, and part of the formation of our virtue is in our actions toward them (and vice versa).

Perfect happiness, however, is the unending and unchanging culmination of the moral life, and so friendship can't be needed in heaven as it is on earth. Our vision of God will fulfill all our needs. Even so, Aquinas grants friends the same role in heaven that he grants our bodies: they will "contribute to the well-being of happiness." Aquinas quotes Augustine approvingly as saying that *if* there is any external good that plays a role in our possession of perfect happiness, it would be the companionship of friends as we share the beatific vision. Seeing our loved ones and rejoicing together in our shared vision of the divine essence will enhance our experience of happiness, then, even if we would be lacking nothing essential without this.

## Question 5: The Attainment of Happiness

In this final question of the Treatise on Happiness, Aquinas moves from discussing the nature of happiness to more practical questions about human beings attaining it. We know now what perfect happiness is, what it isn't, and what it requires. As Aquinas would say, it remains for us to examine what the chances are for human beings becoming—and remaining—perfectly happy.

The two central issues at stake in the eight articles of this question are (1) whether human beings are the sort of creatures who are capable of perfect happiness (and if so, when and for how long) and (2) to what extent our attaining the state of perfect happiness is under our control. Can we attain happiness through the exercise of our own powers? Does our becoming happy require good deeds on our part?

This second set of issues (namely, the degree to which human happiness is voluntary) forms the bridge to the subsequent Treatise on Human Acts (QQ6–21), which focuses on the interplay of intellect, will, and external factors in voluntary human actions.

### 5.1. Can human beings attain happiness?

Answer: yes. Insofar as we are capable of knowing and loving God, we are capable of attaining perfect happiness.

This article poses a question with an obvious answer: if Aquinas hadn't thought that human beings could attain happiness, he wouldn't have made the Treatise on Happiness the starting point for his extensive discussion of the moral life. As with other questions that appear to have obvious answers, then, we need to ask ourselves what's really motivating this discussion. In this case, it's the peculiar nature of human beings as the highest of material and lowest of intellectual creatures. As Aquinas has argued in his Treatise on Human Nature (ST I.75–89), human beings are the only intellectual creatures who are composed of matter: we are, therefore, the only creatures capable of abstract thought who also rely on sense perception. (See, for example, I.76.5.) God's essence is (obviously) imperceptible, however, and so you might wonder whether the perfect happiness that consists in unending intellective vision of God's essence is something that rational *animals* can attain.

Aquinas dispenses with this worry by noting that insofar as the human intellect is capable of apprehending the universal good and insofar as the human will is capable of desiring it, we are thus capable of the twin components of the activity of perfect happiness: knowing and loving God. Human beings can't cognize the universal good in its perfect form (God) in their *natural* state, however. We need grace both to be able to receive God's essence as the object of our cognition and to contemplate that object. So human beings can attain happiness, yes, but not without significant supernatural assistance.[25]

**Obj. and resp. 1.** This objection relies on—and also clarifies—the hierarchy of being that is central to Aquinas's metaphysics. To the traditional levels of beings with vegetative, sensory, and rational natures, Aquinas adds the level of intellective natures. Beings with rational natures (such as human beings) use discursive reasoning; that is, they move from one premise to another in order to reach a conclusion. Creatures with intellectual natures, however, can grasp an entire demonstration as a whole and don't need to work through each individual premise to see the truth of the conclusion. In the same way that non-rational creatures can't attain the end of rational creatures because they lack the relevant higher-order capacities, then, it might seem that human beings can't attain the end of intellectual creatures because we lack the relevant higher-order capacities.

In his response, Aquinas claims that the way in which rational creatures surpass non-rational creatures is relevantly different from the way in which intellectual creatures surpass rational creatures—namely, non-rational and rational creatures do not share the same objects of cognition. In particular, human beings can cognize universals (for example, "red"), whereas non-rational creatures can grasp only objects of sensory cognition ("this red ball"). This means that human beings can think about the good considered as the good, and not just about particular good things, as non-rational animals do. Rational and intellectual creatures, on the other hand, do share the same object of cognition: universal truth. The difference between their natures is the way in which they grasp that truth: rational creatures arrive at knowledge through a process of investigation that begins with sense perception and moves through abstraction from phantasms to a grasp of the truth. Intellectual creatures, by contrast, apprehend or grasp the same truth instantaneously. The difference between these two modes of cognition explains why the angels either fell or were beatified in the first instant of their creation: they immediately grasped all the relevant truths and made their choice. Human beings, by contrast, remain on a journey toward knowledge—and, hopefully, happiness—for their entire earthly lives. It takes time (and a lot of sense perception, experience, and thought) for them to reach the truth.

**Obj. and resp. 2.** This objection stresses the fact that human beings naturally cognize the truths they can reach via their experience of the material world,

---

25. Some scholars have expressed concern that this entails that the ultimate end of human nature is something that human beings can't naturally attain. See, for example, Denis Bradley, who describes this as the "natural endlessness" of human beings—the "vision of God, which nature demands but cannot provide" (Bradley 1997). Aquinas himself appears to see nothing troubling about this conclusion.

reminding us that human beings continue to require phantasms (mental pictures, so to speak, that are stored in sensory organs) when engaging in abstract thought. It thus seems clear that human beings can't reach perfect happiness through natural means.

Aquinas, of course, grants this—and claims that in the life to come, "human beings will have a different way of cognizing that will be natural to them." In other words, God's direct illumination of our intellects as they contemplate the divine essence will become the new normal for human cognition. This implies that human nature itself will change in the life to come, in the sense that we will no longer rely on the process of cognition that involves sense perception, but rather rely entirely on our intellective vision of God's essence. Aquinas himself doesn't address the implications of this shift, perhaps because not only does he believe that although our present state of cognition is suitable for human nature in the limited and imperfect circumstances we're in right now, it was always built into human nature to cognize the Truth via God's essence in the ideal circumstances we'll exist in after the Final Judgment.

**Obj. and resp. 3.** Aquinas's description of perfect happiness for human beings makes frequent reference to the angels (and angelic cognition), in large part because angels constitute a template for what our beatified state might be like. They are the only other sort of creatures capable of happiness, but they exist above us on the hierarchy of being. This objection raises the issue of how we rank compared to angels. The worry is that perhaps our powers of intellection can't reach all the way to God, and so we can only go as far as contemplating angelic natures, and thus are unable to attain perfect happiness via contemplation of God's essence.

In reply, Aquinas points out that perfect happiness doesn't require human nature to transcend angelic nature—it just requires us to be capable of the same intellective activity the happy angels engage in, namely, contemplating God's nature. We don't have to *be* something higher than the angels, then. We just have to *know* something higher than the angels.[26]

**Reply.** We are capable of seeing the divine essence, Aquinas says. We can grasp the universal good with our intellects, and we can desire that good with our wills. Thus, he argues, we are by nature *capable* of attaining the highest good—perfect happiness. And that is all he is attempting to demonstrate in this article.

---

26. Although Aquinas doesn't discuss this here, he holds that God's assistance is essential to any being's engaging in this sort of contemplation. See, e.g., *ST* I.12.4, as well as 56.3 reply and resp. 2.

## 5.2. Can one human being be happier than another?

Answer: yes. Although every human being who contemplates the divine essence is perfectly happy, a human being can be better or worse disposed to enjoy that good (and, therefore, more or less happy).

This is a curious article: at first glance, it seems that the answer will be "Yes, of course, in this life, but not in the life to come, when we will all be perfectly happy"—but that's not the direction Aquinas takes. Instead, he relies on the distinction he's drawn now several times (see, for example, 1.8) between happiness understood in terms of the ultimate end itself (God, the highest good), which is the same for all beings, and the *attainment* or *enjoyment* of that end (the activity of happiness that only rational beings can experience). According to Aquinas, although everyone who participates in the activity of happiness will be focused on the same object (namely, the divine essence), we can differ with respect to the degree to which we enjoy contemplating that object. (Presumably, although Aquinas does not make this explicit, because our wills can be disposed differently toward God—one person can love God more than another.) In short, although everyone in heaven will experience perfect happiness, they will each experience that happiness only to the degree to which they're able.

**Obj. and resp. 1.** The Biblical parable of the workers in the vineyard (Matthew 20)—all of whom are paid exactly the same wage although they've worked a different number of hours—is often referenced in arguments for an egalitarian view of heaven, as it is here.

In his response, Aquinas references another gospel passage (John 14:2)—where Jesus says, "In my Father's house, there are many mansions"—to argue that although each person receives the same reward in terms of its object (unending contemplation of God's essence) there will be different levels of enjoyment of this one reward (as there are many different mansions).

**Obj. and resp. 2.** The second objection makes the reasonable assumption that, if happiness is the *highest* good (that is, there can't be anything higher than it), it doesn't seem to be the sort of thing that admits of degrees. It is already as good as things get—you can't have more or less of it.

Aquinas's response to the second objection is quite brief, but that's because he's done the work of answering it in the main reply. Perfect happiness is the highest good because it involves possessing and enjoying the highest good (namely, God). The fact that different human beings can enjoy possession of that highest good to greater or lesser degrees doesn't change the fact that they are all enjoying the highest good. God's enjoyment of his own essence, for instance, is far greater than anything human beings or angels could even manage, but that doesn't mean that human beings and angels can't be perfectly happy simply because they can't meet God's level of happiness.

**Obj. and resp. 3.** If our happiness in heaven is really a *perfect* good, it completely satisfies all our desires: nothing else could be added to make it better. (This is a point for which Aquinas has already argued at various places in the Treatise.) This objection makes the reasonable claim that if one human being can be happier than another when enjoying the beatific vision, it looks as though the less happy person's enjoyment could be better and, thus, wasn't perfect to begin with.

Aquinas stands his ground in his response, claiming that the person who enjoys the vision of the divine essence less than someone else does not, in fact, lack any thing they could possibly desire, because they possess the "infinite good itself" (God). Once someone possesses the highest good, Aquinas argues, there is no other good that could be added to that experience that would increase their happiness. (Knowing that you are the happiest human being in heaven, for instance, would not increase your happiness. Only a greater disposition for knowing and loving God could make you happier.)

**Reply.** Aquinas implicitly relies here on the distinction between the activity of contemplation (which belongs to the intellect) and the corresponding enjoyment (which belongs to the will). Everyone who attains perfect happiness shares the same object—the highest good (namely, God)—and in that respect everyone's happiness is exactly alike. That said, Aquinas claims that human beings are nevertheless able to enjoy our possession of that good to different degrees, insofar as we are disposed differently toward that enjoyment.

But what does it mean to be differently disposed toward enjoyment? Imagine that my brother (who is a professional musician) and I both listen to an orchestra flawlessly perform a beautiful piece of music. Both of us participate in the same act: listening to the performance. Both of us enjoy it to the greatest extent possible—for us. The highest level of enjoyment available to the professional musician, however, seems much higher than my own. Although I am completely entranced by the music, my brother can appreciate aspects of the performance of which I am completely ignorant (the perfect balance between different sections of the orchestra, for instance, or the careful nuance created by changing tempos). It would be wrong to say that I am not fully satisfied with my concert-going experience. I enjoy it every bit as much as I am able, given my dispositions. There's nothing I want from that performance that I am not getting. My brother is also fully satisfied with his experience and enjoys it every bit as much as he is able—he is just able to enjoy it to a greater degree. The experience of different human beings in the afterlife is meant to be similar: everyone who experiences the beatific vision is perfectly happy, but one person can have greater enjoyment of it than another. Although Aquinas doesn't explain here why that would be the case, in *Summa theologiae* I.12.6 he explains that one intellect can have a greater ability to see God's essence than another—and that the difference comes down to who has greater charity, or love for God, because greater love disposes us to receive the object of our love (in this case, the divine essence).

## 5.3. Can someone be happy in this life?

Answer: no—at least not perfectly happy.

Aquinas's reply to this question is, again, interesting primarily for the grounds he gives for his answer. Human beings can, of course, have some measure of happiness in this life, but they cannot possess perfect happiness until they have unending experience of the beatific vision (which Aquinas has argued in *ST* I.12.2 happens only after death). The interesting part of this article is Aquinas's claim that happiness as a perfect and sufficient good "excludes all evil and fulfills every desire," which clarifies a question about which sorts of goods we'll have in the afterlife. Clearly, we can't avoid all evils in this life. Ignorance, for one, is an unavoidable lack in this life which, given Aquinas's acceptance of the Convertibility Thesis (being = goodness), counts as an evil. All physical ills fall into this category as well, since they involve a lack of health. But we also can't fully attain our desire for happiness in this life because the goods of this life—up to and including life itself—are transitory. By contrast, all the goods involved in perfect happiness are everlasting. (See, e.g., *SCG* IV.83, where Aquinas writes that "All the occupations of the active life, which seem ordered to the use of food and sex and those other things that are necessary for corruptible life, will cease. Only the activity of the contemplative life will remain after the resurrection.")

**Obj. and resp. 1 & 3.** Someone who lives blamelessly is perfectly happy, and it seems at least possible for this to occur on earth. (It was fairly standard doctrine in the thirteenth century, for instance, that Mary, the mother of Jesus, lived a sinless life.)

In response, Aquinas repeats that people in this life are called happy only to the extent to which they imperfectly know and love God or because they have the hope of attaining perfect happiness after death. The third objection and response are a variation on this same theme: we consider people happy in this life insofar as they have some share in the activity in which perfect happiness consists, but they cannot possess perfect happiness here.

**Obj. and resp. 2.** The idea behind this objection is that if one human being can be happier than another with respect to perfect happiness (namely, to the extent that they are better or worse disposed to enjoy that good), then people participate imperfectly in that highest good. But human beings participate imperfectly in the highest good in *this* life to the extent to which they manage to know and love God. So it seems that if we call the people participating imperfectly in the highest good in the next life happy, we should call the people imperfectly participating in this highest good in this life happy, too.

In response, Aquinas distinguishes between (1) imperfection with respect to someone's grasp of the object of happiness—the case where someone does not see the divine essence clearly—and (2) imperfection with respect to the person doing the grasping—the case where someone who does have intellective vision of the divine essence nevertheless participates in that activity imperfectly. The first sort of imperfection is not compatible with perfect happiness. Perfect happiness (as we've seen) requires direct vision of God's essence. The second sort, by contrast, is the lot of everyone who experiences the beatific vision and enjoys perfect happiness, with the exception of God (because only God is disposed to enjoy contemplation of the divine essence to the highest degree, as Aquinas has already argued in 3.8 resp. 2).

**Reply.** Aquinas's reply to this article underscores several of the points he's been making so far in the Treatise. Perfect happiness is complete and sufficient, and no state we can possess in this life meets those criteria; we can't control for the vagaries of fate, and all the goods we can possess in this life are transitory. Even intellection ceases when we fall asleep or get distracted. Most importantly, we are not able to directly cognize God's essence in this life. Thus, the best we can do here is imperfect participation in the highest good.

### 5.4. Can happiness, once possessed, be lost?

Answer: no, perfect happiness cannot be lost (although, of course, imperfect happiness can be).

This is another article that gets its bite from the central issue driving this question: what is experiencing happiness like *for human beings*—creatures who are subject to change? In this life, we change in ways that prevent us from attaining perfect happiness. We eat but then get hungry again, sleep but then get tired again. We never remain in a state of perfect rest. Because of this, you might think that human beings are the sort of thing that by nature change, and thus remain by nature able to lose perfect happiness even in the afterlife. Aquinas's (lengthy) response indicates that the transformation involved in our beatification entails a dramatic shift in human experience that prevents us from changing in a way that would threaten our possession of the beatific vision. He claims that human beings will not be subject to change once they attain perfect happiness, because "such changes over time can happen only concerning things that are subject to time and motion." According to Aquinas, God is perfectly simple and does not undergo change: our vision of God's essence will mirror this. Human beings' experience of the beatific vision will not be subject to time or motion; it will be unending and it will not involve intellectual or volitional change.

Will human beings experience change or movement in other ways, though, such as change in sense perception or physical motion? Aquinas leaves that an open question here, since his focus is exclusively on the activity of perfect happiness (which he has made clear consists entirely in cognition of the divine essence). Moreover, it's not clear entirely what his answer to that question would be. There would certainly not be any need for such motion or change: all of our desires are satisfied, so we won't need to perceive things and/or move to acquire them to reach our ends. If there is change in sense perception or motion in heaven, then, it would seem to have to be the result of an outflow from our inner experience of God's essence. Perhaps we will move our bodies as a way of expressing our joy, or to enjoy what we perceive around us as a fulfillment of God's purposes. (Again, for an extensive discussion of what our resurrected bodies will be like, see *SCG* IV.79–89.)

**Obj. and resp. 1.** This objection draws its force from human nature: human beings are by nature rational animals and thus changeable; it seems, then, that they should participate in happiness in a changeable way, as suits their nature.

Aquinas's response is that happiness is the sort of complete perfection that excludes *every* defect—including the possibility of losing that happiness. Our animal nature will lose its corruptibility: God "exalts human beings" to a state that "transcends all change." What this means in practical terms is that human beings will cease to exist in time as we currently experience it, since "time" as Aquinas understands it is a measure of motion.[27]

**Obj. and resp. 2.** Because human beings have changeable wills that are "capable of opposites"—that is, willing and not willing the same thing at different times—it might seem that human beings can cease being happy in the life to come, if their wills change.

In response, Aquinas reminds us that the will is a rational appetite for the good qua good and is thus necessarily directed toward our ultimate end. We can only will opposites when it comes to means to our ends ("things that are directed to the end"), such as when I will in the morning to go to the gym for the sake of my health but will against going to the gym when it comes time to go because I am hungover. Since perfect happiness is our ultimate end, once we actively possess it we are incapable of willing not to have it.[28]

**Obj. and resp. 3.** This objection relies on the general principle that "the end corresponds to the beginning"—that is, that because human happiness has a determinate starting point (namely, the moment of beatification), it will also have a determinate ending point.

---

27. See, for example, *De Veritate* 8.4, where Aquinas discusses the relation between time, change, and cognition in beatified angels and human beings.

28. Aquinas has a great deal more to say about the distinction between willing ends versus willing things for an end, in the Treatise on Human Acts. See, for example, 10.2 and 13.6.

Aquinas's response is that human happiness has a beginning because we are the sort of creatures who need to move toward their happiness over time, but our happiness doesn't have to have an end because the good that we attain in perfect happiness has an unending nature. This should come as no real surprise. Aquinas has argued extensively in the Treatise on Human Nature that although human souls have a determinate beginning to their existence (namely, the moment at which God infuses the rational soul into the pre-existing fetal body [see also SCG II.87]), those souls are immortal and will never cease to exist (see also SCG II.79).

**Reply.** Everyone agrees that *imperfect* happiness can be lost. Indeed, as Aquinas pointed out in article three, this is one of the central reasons it counts as incomplete. The real question for this article is whether human beings can lose *perfect* happiness, as Origen and "certain Platonists" held.

Aquinas offers two arguments in favor of the permanence of perfect happiness. First, he says that any state truly deserving the title of "happiness" has to be permanent, because fearing the loss of a good is (as Augustine pointed out in *On Free Choice of the Will*) itself an evil. In short, if we're worrying about losing our perfect happiness, we're not yet perfectly happy. So perfect happiness must include "an assured belief" that we will always be happy. That belief, however, is either true or false. If it's true, we will retain our happiness forever. If, on the other hand, it's false, then human beings are still subject to evil, because holding false beliefs is an evil for the intellect (whose final end is truth). Perfect happiness excludes every evil, though, and so we couldn't be wrong about the permanence of happiness and be perfectly happy. Thus, Aquinas concludes, once we become perfectly happy, we will always remain so.

Second, Aquinas argues that it is impossible for anyone who sees the divine essence clearly to will not to see it. (You might wonder about the fallen angels. Aquinas's account is extremely complicated, in part because of the nature of sempiternity. For our purposes, what's relevant is that Aquinas holds that the angels who fell at the first moment of their creation did not comprehend the divine essence clearly enough to be unable to will against it [see I.62.2]. Only God can see God's essence perfectly; the angels who didn't fall received the beatific vision from God once they chose him and thus now count as blessed, but not to a higher degree than beatified human beings are capable.) Possession of the beatific vision is the possession of our highest good—the very thing our wills are naturally turned toward—and Aquinas says that we can't *not* want this good once we get it. The only other option would be for God to take perfect happiness away from us. But this option is ruled out on the grounds that such an action on God's part would be a punishment (indeed, the greatest punishment imaginable), and anyone who is already enjoying the beatific vision has already been judged worthy. No other being could possibly interrupt our experience of the beatific vision, since God is directly responsible for our vision of the divine essence. This vision can't fade over time, either, because "such changes over time can happen only concerning things that are subject to time and motion," and (as mentioned above) our experience of the beatific vision won't be subject to time and motion.

### 5.5. Can human beings attain happiness through their natural powers?

Answer: we are able to become imperfectly happy through the exercise of our natural powers, but we cannot attain perfect happiness on our own.

Aquinas gives precisely the answer to this question that we'd expect at this point in the Treatise. Yes, we can attain some version of imperfect happiness in this life through our own powers (to the same extent that we're able to acquire virtue through our own powers, anyway—Aquinas distinguishes between acquired and divinely infused virtues, and discusses the extent to which acquired virtues can make us happy in I-II.63). No, we can't become perfectly happy through our natural powers, though, since perfect happiness requires direct vision of the divine essence, and that sort of intellective activity surpasses the natural capacities of all created things. God must both give us the divine essence as an object for our cognition and give us the grace to understand what we see. (See, e.g., *ST* I.12.4, or *SCG* III.51, where Aquinas writes that in the beatific vision, "the divine essence must be both what is seen and that by which it is seen.")

**Obj. and resp. 1.** The first objection relies on the principle that "nature is not deficient in necessary things." In other words, a member of a natural kind will possess the sorts of features and capacities required for it to reach its natural end. The example Aquinas provides in his response is how animals are naturally provided with the means for their defense and protection: claws, tough hide, swiftness, etc. It seems, though, that our ability to reach our final end would be more necessary than anything else for human beings, and thus we must be naturally equipped to reach that end.

Aquinas maintains that nature *has* given us the means to attain perfect happiness—in the same indirect sense that it provided us with the means to defend and protect ourselves. That is, although we can't attain perfect happiness purely on our own, we naturally possess the free choice that allows us to turn to God, who does possess the ability to make us perfectly happy. (Aquinas appears to recognize that this move might not seem satisfactory, for he further appeals to Aristotle's theory of friends as "other selves" to support his point, claiming that having a friend do something for us is, in a way, the same as doing it for ourselves.)

**Obj. and resp. 2.** This objection appeals to the hierarchy of being, in which human beings are the highest of material beings, and argues that human beings should thus also be the most self-sufficient of physical creatures. Non-rational animals can attain their ends via their own powers; therefore, a fortiori, human beings should be able to attain their final end (happiness) through their own powers.

In response, Aquinas distinguishes between perfect and imperfect goods, and claims that the sort of thing that is able to attain a perfect good is better than the sort of thing that can attain only an imperfect good—even if (a) that thing is able to attain that imperfect good perfectly, and (b) the other being can only attain the perfect good imperfectly. The fact that non-rational animals can attain their natural ends via their own powers is a case of (a) above. Human beings may require divine assistance to reach their final end, but that final end is a perfect good, and so the fact that they cannot reach this end through their own powers isn't a mark against them.

**Obj. and resp. 3.** Happiness is an activity—and perfect happiness is a perfect activity. This objection uses this idea to argue that because our natural capacity for free action (which will be discussed at length in the subsequent Treatise on Human Acts) is what allows us to undertake the imperfect activity of happiness, it is also what allows us to achieve the perfection of that activity in perfect happiness.

Aquinas's response is to claim that this would be true only if the activities of imperfect and perfect happiness belonged to the same species; he then denies that the actions of imperfect and perfect happiness belong to the same species, on the grounds that species of activities are determined by their objects. As Aquinas makes clear in his response to this question, the object of imperfect happiness is the fulfillment of our natural capacities, realized in virtuous activities, whereas the object of perfect happiness is the fulfillment of our status as *imago Dei*, realized in the beatific vision.

**Reply.** Sometimes, it sounds as though the difference between imperfect and perfect happiness is just a matter of degrees: we know and love God better in the life to come, but we can make a pretty good start here, etc. In this article, however, Aquinas reminds us that perfect happiness is an activity completely surpassing anything we are naturally capable of. The reason for this is that natural knowledge corresponds to "the mode of its substance." We are finite substances with limited capacities, and as such, whatever knowledge of God we are capable of is correspondingly limited. The vision of God's essence in which perfect happiness consists requires going far beyond our natural powers of cognition.

### 5.6. Do human beings attain happiness
### through the action of some higher creature?

Answer: no, human beings cannot attain perfect happiness (intellective vision of the divine essence) though angelic intervention.

This article goes out to all the Neoplatonists who believe in the emanation of being and hold that the "intelligences" or angels were involved in the creation of all physical beings. As we saw in 3.7, Aquinas has no in-principle objection to the thought that we might be illuminated by angels. (Indeed, obj. 3 affirms that angels can illuminate human intellects.) There's no real question for him of whether we can attain our vision of the divine essence from another creature, though. As he makes clear in his response to the third objection, the most angels can illuminate human intellects about are "certain notions of God's works." Aquinas does leave open the possibility that we are aided by higher creatures (both the intelligences that move the planets and the whole echelon of created immaterial substances) in attaining imperfect happiness in this life, however. (According to *ST* I.111, for instance, higher creatures do aid us in acquiring virtue by, for example, rousing the passions, moving the imagination, effecting physical changes such as making the blood boil around the heart, etc.)

**Obj. and resp. 1.** This objection distinguishes between two sorts of order: (1) the order that parts of the universe (creatures) have to each other and (2) the order that the universe as a whole has to God. The argument is that the first sort of order includes higher creatures (angels, say) assisting lower creatures (human beings, say), and this entails ordering us to our ultimate good (God). Because our happiness consists in our being correctly ordered toward God, it thus appears that angels make us happy.

Aquinas essentially responds by distinguishing between necessary and sufficient conditions for happiness. He allows that angels can *help* us achieve happiness—and even appears to agree that they in fact do so insofar as they dispose us toward attaining our ultimate end—but he insists that God alone (described in this response as both the supreme power and the First Agent) is responsible for actualizing that disposition and actually making us happy.

**Obj. and resp. 2.** This objection trades on the general principle that something in potentiality can be brought into actuality by something that is actually already that way. So, for instance, water (which is potentially hot) can be made hot by something (for example, a fire) that is actually hot. Human beings are potentially happy, however, insofar as they are human, and so it seems that they can be made actually happy by a happy angel.

Sadly, Aquinas disagrees that happiness is infectious in this way. He modifies the general principle as stated in the original objection so that something in potentiality can be brought into actuality only by something that has that form in actuality *"with perfect and natural being."* That is, although water can be made hot by fire, which has the form of heat with perfect and natural being, it doesn't follow that the water that has been heated by that fire can in turn communicate its heat to more cold water in the same way. (It will either heat up the water imperfectly, or, if the other water is cold enough or there is enough of it, it will fail to heat up the water at all.) In the same way, the perfect happiness of God cannot be shared with us via the happiness of another creature (which has that happiness in imperfect form), but only via God.

**Obj. and resp. 3.** Angels can illuminate human intellects; happiness is an activity of the intellect; therefore, angels can make human beings happy.

This is not a strong objection, for reasons we've seen above. Angels can illuminate human intellects only with respect to God's works, not with respect to vision of the divine essence itself.

**Reply.** All creatures are limited in power and are subject to the laws of nature. Vision of the divine essence goes far beyond anything we are naturally capable of, however—and, for that matter, goes beyond anything the angels are capable of. Only God can directly accomplish what goes beyond nature, and so only God can make us perfectly happy. (Imperfect happiness, of course, is a different story. Because angels can assist us in becoming virtuous, they can assist us in becoming imperfectly happy.)

*5.7. Are any deeds required of human beings*
*in order for them to receive happiness from God?*

Answer: yes—human beings need to develop rectitude of will, and this development requires any number of actions (as detailed in the Treatise on Human Acts and the entire rest of the Second Part of the *Summa*, as well as already having been discussed in 4.4).

Rectitude of will is the single activity required for human beings to attain perfect happiness in the life to come, since rectitude of will is itself simply the will's being ordered in the right way toward its ultimate end (God). But Aquinas argues that activities are a necessary part of this life for the purpose of attaining perfect happiness in the life to come. Only God possesses a perfect good (namely, knowledge of the divine essence) without having to do anything to attain that good; we and the angels, as imperfect creatures, have to move toward perfection, and such motion requires acting—and acting toward the right end. The angels, who exist in sempiternity, require only one motion toward attaining the perfect good (namely, choosing God); we, who exist in time, need to keep moving toward the good through meritorious actions. This also is a vital part of how we dispose our individual wills toward the enjoyment of the ultimate good (as discussed in art. 2).

**Obj. and resp. 1.** God has infinite power and can, as this objection puts it, "produce the whole thing all at once" without any pre-existing dispositions. It seems, then, that God should be able to produce happiness in us without any pre-existing disposition toward that happiness in us.

Aquinas here again affirms that God *could* bring about perfect happiness in us without any pre-existing dispositions toward it, but argues that certain human actions are nevertheless required for that proper order of things. (In other words, God could but won't violate the order of things as God created them.)

**Obj. and resp. 2.** This objection appeals to God's nature as Creator: when God first brought creatures into being, he made them ex nihilo—without their having any previous dispositions or actions. They each came into being complete and perfect in species. Thus, the objection claims, God could make human beings perfectly happy without their having any previous dispositions or taking any particular actions toward that happiness.

Aquinas's response to this objection involves appeal to the only human being who was created perfectly happy, namely, Christ. God created the first creatures in every species perfect and ex nihilo, because they needed to pass their natures on to their descendants, and the first human beings had perfect *natural* happiness. Only Christ, however, had the sort of perfect happiness that requires no dispositions or virtuous actions. (Infants who die after baptism and before they are able to merit happiness on their own are able to gain perfect happiness only via being members of the body of Christ.) This response doesn't actually address the question of whether God could make human beings happy generally without any action on their part, but perhaps Aquinas considers that question answered by the previous response.

**Obj. and resp. 3.** Paul writes in Romans 4:6 that God grants righteousness— and, thus, happiness—to human beings apart from their actions or works.[29]

Aquinas's response is to claim that the happiness referred to in this passage is merely "the happiness of hope," which is given to us by justifying grace in order for us to be able to work toward perfect happiness.

**Reply.** Aquinas allows that God *could* make human beings happy without their performing any actions on their own; although rectitude of will (namely, the will's being properly ordered toward its ultimate end) is required for happiness, God could bring about rectitude of will in a person at the same moment he gives them perfect happiness.

At the same time, however, Aquinas argues that "the ordering of divine wisdom" means that God will not actually do this. The only sort of being who can have a perfect good (such as happiness) without any sort of motion

---

29. This passage assumes a great deal of importance in the Protestant Reformation, which objects to the idea of "works righteousness."

toward that good is a being who has that good naturally. And, of course, only God has perfect goodness as a natural part of his essence. Angels, which are higher than human beings, can attain happiness by means of one single motion (namely, choosing God); human beings, on the other hand, attain happiness by means of many motions—namely, virtuous activities. (Aquinas does not here discuss the fact that the sort of happiness virtuous action can bring human beings is only imperfect happiness, or why this motion is necessary for God's granting us the perfect happiness of the beatific vision. The assumption, however, appears to be that God will not grant perfect happiness to any creature who hasn't moved itself toward that happiness, for reasons of fittingness. Only God is the sort of being who *should* have perfect happiness without any motion toward that end; therefore, only God is the sort of being who *will* have perfect happiness in that manner.)

### 5.8. Does every human being desire happiness?

Answer: yes, every human being wants to be happy (although they can be wrong about what will make them happy).

The Treatise on Happiness ends with the question of whether every human being desires happiness: it both sums up the nature of perfect happiness as Aquinas has described it so far and begins the closer examination of the will that continues in the Treatise on Human Acts. Everyone trivially desires happiness, considered as an abstract notion, because the abstract notion of happiness is simply "the final and complete good which everyone desires." (This is, of course, not at all how most people today think of happiness, but it was the dominant conception of happiness for millennia and is the one undergirding everything Aquinas says on this topic.) The nature of happiness considered as a *particular* notion, however, is what Aquinas has been explicitly discussing for the last five questions and is a topic of contention. (Is happiness just pleasure, as Epicurus thought? Is it the life of activity expressing reason well, as Aristotle believed? Is it identical to virtue, as Socrates argued?) Thus, although every human being desires happiness under its general description, individual human beings can be ignorant of the particular nature of happiness or can have knowledge of that nature and yet reject it to pursue happiness under a different description.

**Obj. and resp. 1.** This objection trades on exactly the distinction just mentioned above, which Aquinas himself makes in the reply to this question. Because some people are ignorant of the true nature of happiness, it says, and we can desire only what we know (in a loose sense of 'know'), not everyone desires happiness.

Aquinas's response is clear: everyone does desire happiness, taken in the abstract sense. Nevertheless, anyone can be ignorant of the particular thing to which the general notion applies.

**Obj. and resp. 2.** Aquinas has been arguing that the best particular description of happiness is "seeing God's essence." This objection accepts that, but worries that some people who believe that this sort of vision is impossible do not desire it—and, therefore, do not desire happiness.

Aquinas's response to this is that reason can consider the same thing in different ways: it's true that some people do not desire happiness under the description "seeing God's essence," but even those people still desire happiness under the general description "final and complete good."

**Obj. and resp. 3.** This objection quotes Augustine's claim that people who are happy have everything they want and do not want anything bad. But, it goes on to argue, some people not only want bad things but also want to want bad things. If this is true, then not everyone desires to be happy (because they don't desire the good).

Aquinas responds that the description of happiness as having everything we want is only a good description if "everything" is taken to refer to "all the things that human beings desire through their natural appetite" and not if it's taken to refer to "the things that human beings will according to the apprehension of reason"—that is, everything we desire because we think it's good. The only thing that ultimately satisfies our natural appetite (the will) is the perfect good of happiness. In cases where we're wrong about what's good for us, having everything we want wouldn't be happiness because it would conflict with having what we should will.

**Reply.** The abstract or general notion of happiness is that it is a complete good, and a person's complete good is what totally satisfies that person's will. In that sense, everyone desires happiness because it consists in getting what we want. Happiness taken as a particular notion of the good, however, is not something everyone desires, because some people are ignorant of what that good is.

This question does not address whether we could still reject the supreme good if we knew what that good was, but that is presumably because our highest good is intellective vision of the divine essence, which Aquinas has already claimed we couldn't reject if we actually had it.

# Commentary on the Treatise
# on Human Acts

The Commentary follows Aquinas's division of questions and articles. We proceed article by article, first stating the question Aquinas poses in the article and then supplying a brief summary of his answer.

The structure of the commentary on individual articles is determined by logical rather than textual order: that is, we do not typically follow the order in which Aquinas presents his material but instead organize the material as we judge most conducive to understanding. Thus the commentary on each article (especially in QQ8–17) is meant to be read as a whole, as an essay structured internally according to logical (and pedagogical) order, rather than paragraph by paragraph.

Nonetheless, in order to facilitate finding the commentary on particular subdivisions of each article, we have set such references as 'obj. 1,' 'reply,' and 'resp. 1' in boldface.

### Overview of the Treatise on Human Acts

Aquinas concludes in the Treatise on Happiness that (1) happiness is our ultimate end and (2) happiness both consists in and is attained through action. It makes sense, then, for him to turn next to a discussion of human acts, "so that we can know which acts are those through which one attains happiness and which acts stand in the way of happiness." The next sixteen questions—which Aquinas describes as "moral inquiry," and which begin the lengthy discussion of ethics that continues through the entire Second Part of the *Summa theologiae*—comprise the Treatise on Human Acts.

It is worth noting at the outset that the Treatise on Human Acts is only one small part of Aquinas's discussion of actions in the *Summa theologiae*: it is, in fact, just the beginning of a two-volume investigation. (See the Introduction [pp. xviii–xix] for an overview of the structure of the *Summa*.) Aquinas divides his discussion broadly between human acts in general and human acts in particular; human acts in general occupy what's known as the "First Part of the Second Part," often abbreviated as I-II, or 1a2ae (from the Latin '*Prima Secundae*'), whereas human acts in particular occupy the whole of the "Second Part of the Second Part" (II-II, or 2a2ae, from '*Secunda Secundae*'). Aquinas further subdivides his discussion of human acts in general into an examination of the *nature* of those acts (QQ6–48, the first half of I-II) and an examination of the *principles* of those acts (QQ49–114, the second half of I-II).

290 Commentary on the Treatise on Human Acts

The Treatise on Human Acts is the first half of this discussion of the nature of human acts in general. Aquinas refers to these as the acts "distinctive of human beings," as opposed to the sorts of acts human beings have in common with other animals; Aquinas is focused on moral inquiry in the *Summa theologiae* I-II and II-II, and so the general acts such as locomotion and sense perception that human beings and non-rational animals share are relevant only insofar as they have potential moral significance. (Aquinas goes on to further distinguish in this treatise between the *general* nature of distinctively human acts [QQ6–17] and the *specific sorts* of such acts [QQ18–21].)

Aquinas believes that investigation into the general nature of human acts needs to begin with an examination of which acts are voluntary and which acts are involuntary. Voluntary acts are the ones most distinctive of human beings—and, not incidentally, the ones most closely connected to our happiness.

The word 'voluntary' comes from the Latin *voluntas*, the word for the will (which Aquinas describes in 1.2 of the Treatise on Happiness as a rational appetite for the good). We've already seen in the Treatise on Happiness (1.1) that intellect and will are the two essential principles of any human act. The Treatise on Happiness focuses on the intellect, since its activity is the central activity of perfect happiness. Because we're now turning to the actions aimed at that happiness, however, the Treatise on Human Acts focuses on the will.

The treatise begins with a distinction between voluntary and involuntary acts (both generally [Q6] and in terms of their circumstances [Q7]) and then turns to a close examination of "pure" acts of will—those acts "elicited by the will itself"—in QQ8–16 before turning in Q17 to voluntary acts that are commanded by the will but carried out through "intermediaries" (for example, bodily acts). The treatise concludes with a discussion of the goodness and badness of human acts (QQ18–21), which sets the stage for the extended treatment of morality in the remainder of the Second Part.

## Question 6: Voluntariness and Involuntariness in General

In the same way that the first few questions in the Treatise on Happiness are heavily influenced by book I of Aristotle's *Nicomachean Ethics*, the first two questions of the Treatise on Human Acts are heavily influenced by book III of the *Ethics*, in terms of both general structure and content. In particular, Aquinas draws heavily on Aristotle in his discussions of what conditions cause involuntariness, and the circumstances of human acts (the where, what, why, etc.).

Q6 is focused entirely on the nature of voluntary versus involuntary actions. Art. 1–2 address whether there are voluntary actions at all (in human beings and non-rational animals, respectively) and art. 3 whether omissions can be voluntary. Art. 4–5 address the effects of violence on the will. Art. 6–8 focus on three other potential causes of involuntariness: fear, desire, and ignorance.

Of these, the relation between ignorance and involuntariness is by far the most complicated (and the most interesting), for the real question underlying all the discussions of potential causes of involuntariness is "Under what circumstances we are morally culpable for our actions?" Violence, fear, and desire present relatively straightforward cases for Aquinas's account, but ignorance presents a mixed bag (as it does for Aristotle); most sorts of ignorance do not make related acts involuntary, but at least one kind of ignorance does. By the end of Q6, then, the reader is meant to have a sense for which of her actions she can be held morally responsible for—and, thus, which actions are directly leading her toward or away from her own happiness.

### 6.1. Is there voluntariness in human acts?

Answer: yes, there is voluntariness in human acts.

Of course Aquinas is going to claim that there is voluntariness in human acts. If there weren't, there would be no point to the entire rest of the Second Part of the *Summa*, because the moral life would be impossible (on his way of thinking). In fact, Aquinas doesn't even bother to argue for the possibility of some human acts being voluntary: he just explains what it means for an act to be voluntary (namely, to be moved by an internal principle toward a cognized end) and then observes that this is paradigmatic of properly human acts, as he's already discussed at length earlier. (See Question 1 of the Treatise on Happiness.)

**Obj. and resp. 1.** This objection immediately brings up the distinction between internal and external principles of motion, a distinction that will be crucial in Aquinas's reply. Voluntary acts must come from a principle internal to the actor; if an actor is moved from an external source, the action is involuntary. Yet, the objection worries, the will is defined as a rational appetite for the good and is, thus, moved by a good *external* to it.

Aquinas's response to this worry—namely, that our wills are necessarily moved by goods external to them—is to distinguish between different levels of the sorts of principles at stake in this discussion. An action's being voluntary requires that it stem from an internal principle, but that internal principle doesn't have to be a first principle. That is, it's enough for an internal principle to be *a* source of an action: it doesn't need to be the ultimate or only source of that action. (On Aquinas's picture, of course, God is the Prime Mover, the First Cause, and the sustainer of everything in existence. As such, God is the ultimate source of every action.) For creatures, like human beings, that possess an awareness of the ends toward which they can move, the first principle of appetitive motion just is the internal principle of a voluntary act. The fact that it's the first principle of appetitive motion (namely, motion toward something we desire), however, doesn't entail that it's an ultimate first principle.

Thus we can talk about voluntary actions as being caused by internal principles of motion without denying that such actions are also caused by external principles in a different sense.

**Obj. and resp. 2.** The force of this objection will probably not be clear to most contemporary readers. It appeals to Aristotle's discussion in the *Physics* of causes and animal motion, and its main point is that because animals are constantly being acted on by and responding to external forces, every new motion of an animal is preceded by some external motion. So, for instance (to use the examples Aquinas provides in his response), when a deer moves close to a lion, the lion senses it and begins to move toward the deer; when the sun heats my head, I become thirsty. On this framework, human beings (who are, after all, rational animals) are always acting in response to some external motion. But, the worry is, this means that the origin of those acts is external to the human being, and thus non-voluntary (since voluntariness requires an internal ground of motion).

In response, Aquinas allows that external motion does precede a new motion by an animal—either by moving its appetite in response to sensory perception (such as when a plump young deer wanders close to a lion and the lion's perception of the deer moves its appetite and motivates it to move closer to its prey), or by causing natural changes in the animal's body (as when my face is heated by the sun, causing me to become thirsty). Aquinas denies, however, that this gets in the way of voluntary action. Drawing on his response to the previous objection, he claims that the deer's motion which draws the lion's attention and the sun's heating which causes my thirst both count as external principles of action in a different sort of way than the sort relevant to the discussion of voluntary versus involuntary acts. Of course we respond to the motions of the world around us! Those movements would only count as external principles of motion, however, if they were the primary source of our action (like when we're standing in the ocean and a wave knocks us off our feet). Insofar as our appetite for the good is what moves us toward action, that action is voluntary.

**Obj. and resp. 3.** This objection appeals to John 15:5, "Without me you can do nothing," to claim that since voluntary actions require acting from an internal principle (through itself) and since we can do nothing without God, we are unable to act voluntarily.

The relation between God's will and our own is a notoriously tricky topic in Christian theology. For one thing, God's status as First Mover doesn't just mean that he tipped over the first domino that started the cascade of other dominoes. It means that God sustains all things in every moment of their existence. According to Aquinas, this also means that God moves human beings to act by putting desirable objects in the range of our senses and by causing natural changes in our body (like when the sun makes me dehydrated and, thus, thirsty). Aquinas responds here that God even moves the human will. Yet, Aquinas maintains, the way in which God moves our wills doesn't interfere with the voluntariness of our acts any more than the fact that a natural motion (such as a stone's falling when dropped) is caused by God as First Mover violates that motion's being natural. Every motion—whether of will or nature—proceeds ultimately from God as First Mover. That does not, however, prevent us from saying that voluntary (and natural) motions also proceed from more proximate internal principles of motion (like the will).

**On the contrary.** The comment of Damascene quoted here—namely, that voluntariness is an intrinsic feature of any rational act—is one Aquinas accepts. Since Aquinas has already argued that what is distinctive of human acts is that they are rational acts, he will also agree that there must be voluntariness in rational acts.

**Reply.** Aquinas is, not surprisingly, insistent that there is voluntariness in human acts. He has already established in the Treatise on Happiness that human acts are directed toward some end. In fact, he argues in Q1 that all human acts are directed toward an ultimate end, happiness. In this article, rather than argue for the voluntary nature of human acts (since he sees that feature as intrinsic to what it is for human acts to be human acts in the first place), Aquinas simply explains in general terms what it is for an act to be voluntary.

To do this, he distinguishes between internal and external principles of motion: a stone lifted up by a curious child is moved by a principle of motion external to that stone, but when the child loses interest and drops the stone, its motion downward is due to a principle of motion internal to that stone: what Aquinas, following the science of the day, would have thought of as earth's "natural inclination" to be "down." (Ancient and medieval physics had the notion of weight rather than gravity. The stone falls when dropped not because of gravitational forces of attraction between two bodies but because of the stone's weight, which gives it a natural inclination to fall down.)

There is a further distinction between things with internal principles of motion: those that move themselves (such as dogs, cats, and human beings) and those that do not (such as rocks). Things that move themselves are things that are moved by an internal principle of motion toward a cognized end. This requires both an internal principle of motion and an awareness or knowledge of a particular end. A cat, for instance, notices a sunbeam and is moved toward it by its desire for warmth. As Aquinas notes, the definition of 'voluntary' given by Aristotle, Gregory of Nyssa, and Damascene includes both that a thing's motion stems from its own internal inclination (for, say, warmth) and also that the thing has some knowledge of the end toward which it's inclined (the warm sunbeam). Voluntary acts involve internal rather than external principles of motion.

As Aquinas will explain in more detail in the following article, human beings are the paradigm case of creatures who both know the end of their actions and move toward that end via an internal principle of motion, for human beings are the only animals who can recognize something as an end (via the intellect) and be motivated toward or away from it under that description (via the will).

### 6.2. Is there voluntariness in non-rational animals?

Answer: yes, there is voluntariness in non-rational animals, although their acts are not voluntary in the strongest sense.

Careful readers will have noticed that Aquinas's description of voluntary acts in art. 1 involves simply having an internal principle of motion toward a known end, where what it means for an end to be "known" is left wide open. In this article, Aquinas explicitly acknowledges that voluntariness comes in degrees, depending on the degree to which the end is cognized. The acts of non-rational animals can be voluntary to an extent—namely, the extent to which the animal apprehends an end (for example, a warm sunbeam) and is correspondingly moved toward that end. Acts where the end is not merely apprehended but also understood as an end are more voluntary. Acts in which there is perfect cognition of an end as an end, in which there is deliberation about that end and the considerations in favor of and against that end, and—most importantly—in which the agent can either be moved toward that end or not are voluntary in the fullest sense. That is, the most voluntary acts are the ones where the agent consciously considers the end as such, considers reasons for and against that end, and then is either moved toward that end (or not) as a result of her deliberations.

**Obj. and resp. 1.** This objection reminds us that the word 'voluntary' comes from the Latin for 'will,' a faculty that non-rational animals lack by definition (since the will is defined as a *rational* appetite for the good), and concludes that the acts of non-rational animals cannot be voluntary.

In reply, Aquinas claims that both 'voluntary' and 'will' are terms that can be extended to things that resemble them, as (in this case) the acts of non-rational animals resemble the acts of creatures with reason and will—namely, by also being moved toward an apprehended end via some kind of cognition. If you look at a dog and a teenager heading for the kitchen when you call them for dinner, for instance, it's clear that their actions bear a strong resemblance to each other. The primary difference, as Aquinas will go on to argue, is that the teenager can consider the prospect of dinner under more than just the sense appetite's urging toward tasty things. He can think of it as a means of bulking up, or a chance to put off doing homework, and he can desire it under those descriptions of the good.

**Obj. and resp. 2.** One of the reasons human acts are considered voluntary is that human beings seem to be in control of our actions; that is, we can contemplate various courses of action and refrain from simply following the urging of our sense appetite (which tells us, for example, how lovely it would be to take a nap right now). Non-rational animals, however, seem driven by instinct alone. This objection concludes that there is, then, nothing voluntary about the actions of non-rational animals.

Aquinas agrees that in this sense there is nothing voluntary about the actions of non-rational creatures. It takes the intellect's ability to canvass opposite possibilities in order for the will to have those opposing possibilities as potential motivators. Yet this doesn't mean that there is nothing voluntary about the acts of non-rational animals in the broad sense he's outlined in 6.1, for non-rational animals are still self-moved toward an end that they are aware of. (Again, the dog moves itself enthusiastically toward its dinner.)

**Obj. and resp. 3.** Another feature of voluntary acts is that we praise and blame people for them. If I, for instance, attend a friend's lecture and decide to crunch loudly away at an apple during it, my friend has the right to blame me for this behavior in a way that he doesn't if the horse I brought with me does the same thing. (He does have the right to complain about my bringing the horse, of course.) Aquinas simply points out—again—that praise and blame don't accrue to all voluntary actions, but only to fully voluntary actions. So, for instance, my friend will blame me more if I decide to take a nap in the middle of his lecture after carefully considering all the available options than he will if I doze off after fighting hard to stay awake.

**Reply.** Aquinas has already explained that voluntariness comes in degrees. Here, he returns to the "imperfect" versus "perfect" distinction, familiar from the Treatise on Happiness, to characterize the difference between the acts of non-rational and rational animals. Voluntariness requires some sort of awareness or cognition of an end. Human beings can have this awareness in a complete or perfect sense. That is, we are capable of cognizing an end as such, as well as of being aware of how the act in question is related to that cognized end. (I can, for instance, know both that warming up in the sun is a potential goal and that moving toward the sunbeam currently falling on the couch would achieve that goal.) Non-rational animals, by contrast, have awareness of an end and motivation toward that end only via their senses and what Aquinas calls "natural estimation" (see the Treatise on Human Nature for a fuller discussion of estimation in animals). The cat cannot, on Aquinas's theory, deliberate about the various pros and cons of moving toward the sunbeam; it is naturally motivated by its perception of the sunbeam and its estimation that bathing in it is warm and pleasant.

What is new to this article is the introduction of the idea of deliberation: Aquinas does not describe this process in any detail, contenting himself merely with noting that it is an important step in most fully voluntary acts, as well as an essential component of perfect cognition of an end. Human beings, who are capable of such complete cognition, can thus have acts that are voluntary in the fullest sense; the acts of non-rational animals can be voluntary, but in a weaker, incomplete sense.

### 6.3. Can there be voluntariness without any act?

Answer: yes, there can be voluntariness without either an internal or an external act.

To this point, the discussion of voluntariness has been cast primarily in terms of acts. In this article, Aquinas considers the important question of whether we *have* to talk about voluntariness in terms of acts. This is important because there are numerous—and, often, highly controversial—cases in which the relevant factor is what the agent has *not* done. Aquinas is careful to note that there are, in fact, two distinct categories of cases in which there can be voluntariness without an external (that is, visible) act: (1) situations in which someone wills not to act and (2) situations in which there is voluntariness without an internal act. Which situations are these? The first category is relatively straightforward. We're all familiar with cases in which we will not to act: we hear someone call our name when we want to be alone, for instance, and will not to respond. The second category is more complicated. As will be discussed in much more detail in later questions, Aquinas sees human acts as complex interactions of intellect and will: the intellect considers various options, and the will (as rational appetite for the good) responds to those options insofar as they appear good. Although Aquinas says nothing at all about the intellect in this article, the category of voluntariness in the absence of any act of the will corresponds to the cases where the will simply does not respond to the options presented to it. This includes, for instance, cases where we consider getting up to go for a walk versus staying on the couch and taking a nap, and end up willing neither. It also includes cases where we simply fail to will something we should have: for example, we are in such a hurry to meet a friend for lunch that we don't notice the bus heading straight toward the person crossing the street in front of us and thus fail to warn them.

**Obj. and resp. 1.** It seems strange to call something voluntary if it doesn't actually involve an act of some sort. After all, it seems that to be voluntary is to come from the will; how can *not*-acting come from the will?

In response, Aquinas points out that, insofar as not acting sometimes also involves the will, inaction can proceed from the will (albeit indirectly) and can thus be voluntary.

**Obj. and resp. 2.** This objection gets into the semantics of voluntariness. We say that someone is willing when she performs an act of will, and when that act of will stops, we say that she is not willing. So it looks as though if we're not willing an act, it is involuntary. If we haven't seen each other in a while, for instance, and you give me an enthusiastic hug while I do not will to give you a hug, it looks as though that hug is involuntary on my part.

Aquinas responds by distinguishing "not willing" from "willing not to." If I simply haven't willed anything with respect to hugging you, because I'm weighing that option against giving you a kiss hello instead (in which case I might be perfectly happy to be hugged), that's different from my willing not to hug you (and thus being unhappy to be caught up in a hug). Aquinas states that only the second sense (where I will not to be hugged) involves an involuntary action. The first case isn't voluntary or involuntary, because there was no act of will involved at all on my part.

**Obj. and resp. 3.** This objection appeals to the role of the intellect in human acts, reminding us that complete voluntariness requires cognition of the end as an end. Cognizing an end is an activity, though, and so it seems that voluntariness in the fullest sense will always involve an act.

Aquinas's response is helpful in illuminating the scope of voluntariness without an act, particularly the second sort (voluntariness without even an interior act): he says that for voluntariness to be involved, it has to be *in our power* for us to consider, will, and act. So, he says, if we are in a situation where we could (and should) will to act but don't, this is voluntary—as is failing to consider our options in that situation. If I'm bustling down the street to meet a friend for lunch, for instance, and simply fail to pay attention to the bus about to run down the person in front of me, I do not perform an act of cognition, I do not perform an act of will, and I do not act. But, Aquinas argues here, my not considering my options, my failing to will, and my not acting are all voluntary in this case because I could (and should) have attended to the relevant features of the situation I'm in.

**Reply.** Aquinas defends the claim that there can be voluntariness without an act by distinguishing between two ways in which one thing can proceed from another: (1) directly, where *a* proceeds from *b* insofar as *b* is acting, as when my car avoids a pothole because I steer it away from it, and (2) indirectly, as when *a* proceeds from *b* because *b* is *not* acting, as when my car bottoms out in a pothole because I fail to steer it away.

When we're thinking of voluntary acts, we're usually thinking of the first sort of case. Indirect cases are also voluntary, though, according to Aquinas: it's fair to say that the captain crashed his ship, for instance, when the reason the ship runs into the iceberg is that the pilot has stopped steering it (to, say, take a bathroom break or get a cup of coffee). What makes situations like this involve voluntariness on the part of the pilot, Aquinas says, is the fact that the pilot both could and should be steering the ship. A passenger below deck on the *Titanic*, for example, is not in any way responsible for the ship's sinking,

because it's not their job to direct the ship. If the pilot at the helm is not incapacitated (by a heart attack or a stroke, say), fails to steer the ship, and it sinks,
we (rightly) hold him responsible for the ship's sinking, even if he did not will
the ship to sink.

In fact, Aquinas claims, there are at least two ways in which the ship's sinking could be indirectly voluntary on the pilot's part: first, the pilot could see
the iceberg in the distance and just will not to steer the ship away from it (a
case where there is an interior act of will without any exterior act, as the pilot
simply stands there watching the iceberg approach); second, the pilot could
be preoccupied (perhaps by thoughts of how wonderful it will be when the
*Titanic* arrives in port for the first time) and fail to will anything regarding the
approaching iceberg (a case in which there isn't even an interior act).

### 6.4. Can violence be done to the will?

Answer: no, violence cannot be done to the will, strictly speaking.

Insofar as the will *just is* an inclination that proceeds from an internal principle toward a cognized end (as it was defined in art. 1 and 2), and insofar as
violence is by definition something that comes from an external principle, it
is conceptually impossible to do violence to the will. That said, it is possible
to thwart an act of the will's being carried out, as when a parent straps his
toddler into her car seat while she yells, "No! Want to WALK!" Violence here
should be thought of as affecting the will on the level of its commands (say,
to the body) rather than on the level of the will itself. No external principle
can force the will to will something.

**Obj. and resp. 1.** This objection jumps straight to the trump card: God. Anything can be forced to act by something more powerful than it, and God is
more powerful than the human will. Surely *God* could coerce our wills, then.

In response, Aquinas maintains that God can move our wills, but he argues
that if God were to do actual violence to our wills by forcing us to will something we don't want to will, the resulting action wouldn't be an act of will
on our part at all but something contrary to will. In this case, God would be
using us as mere instruments for his purposes and we wouldn't count as voluntary agents. (It's worth noting, in fact, that the formulation of "forcing us
to will something we don't want to will" is actually incoherent on Aquinas's
account: for us to will is just for our wills to move toward a particular object.
The movement of the will is the source of voluntariness. Strictly speaking,
God couldn't violate our wills by forcing them to move toward something
they don't want at the time that they are moving toward it. God could move
our will toward an end that we had previously been opposed to, but that's a
slightly different phenomenon.)

**Obj. and resp. 2.** This objection trades on the fact that the will is an appetite and thus a passive power that is actualized by something else. Insofar as the will is activated in response to its proper object, though, isn't the will compelled by that object? That is, isn't the will *forced* to will the good?

In response, Aquinas points out that this would only count as violence against the will if the will's being moved by a desirable object were contrary to its natural inclination. But, of course, the will is a rational appetite for the good—it is a passive power that is specifically meant to be moved by the good. The will's being so moved, then, is hardly a case of its being coerced but rather of its functioning as it's meant to.

**Obj. and resp. 3.** The definition of a violent motion, this objection claims, is a motion that is contrary to nature. The will is a rational appetite for the good, and yet sometimes it goes against the good by sinning. This seems to imply that sinning is a violent motion—something that goes against the will's inclination.

As Aquinas points out in his response, however, even when we are sinning, we still direct our wills at what *appears* to us to be good. When I tell a lie to avoid going to a lengthy faculty meeting, for instance, this is a voluntary act because it is aimed at what I'm perceiving as good: avoiding a long and boring meeting. It's not actually good to tell a lie, even if it does get me out of the meeting, but my act is not involuntary because of that.

**Reply.** Violence can't be done to the will itself, Aquinas argues, because an act of will just is an inclination from an internal principle, and violence necessarily involves an external principle acting on an agent or thing. Violence can adversely impact the effects of an internal act, then, but can't itself be the cause of the internal act. Thus, direct acts of the will (that is, the movement of the will itself) cannot be coerced. *Indirect* acts of the will—that is, acts commanded by the will and then carried out by some other power, such as my willing to stand up and stretch my legs on a long flight—can be interfered with, however. The flight attendant can run over and prevent me from standing when I unbuckle my seat belt because of dangerous turbulence, or I might have someone next to me who is sleeping soundly and too large for me to get around. In these situations, Aquinas says, human beings are affected by violence, but violence isn't being done directly to their will. (The flight attendant might hold me down if I try to stand up and it's too turbulent, but my will is still willing my body to stand up.)

### 6.5. Does violence cause involuntariness?

Answer: yes, violence causes involuntariness in commanded acts of the will.

Given what Aquinas has just said in the previous article about the nature of violence, his answer to this question should be clear: any violence that prevents us from carrying out commanded acts of will causes involuntariness. If a flight attendant is holding me down on a bumpy flight and preventing me from standing, my sitting is involuntary, and I cannot be held responsible (and, thus, either praised or blamed) for sitting.

**Obj. and resp. 1.** The objection trades on the fact that we are usually referring to the will's acts when we talk about something's being voluntary or involuntary, arguing that since violence can't be done to the will, violence can't cause involuntariness. But Aquinas has just argued in the previous article that both acts of will and acts commanded by the will fall under the category of "voluntary" and "involuntary" acts—and here he repeats what he said there, namely, that violence can't be done to the will's act of willing, but can be done to the acts commanded by the will, and that such violence makes those acts (such as sitting when I will to stand) involuntary.

**Obj. and resp. 2.** One of the hallmarks of involuntary action, according to this objection (and Damascene) is that it makes us sad: we didn't want to do what we did. And yet, sometimes someone undergoes violence without experiencing that feeling of sadness. Take, for example, my action of going to the dentist to have a root canal. I don't want the dentist to be poking around in my face, but I also don't feel sorrow over it. Thus, the objection goes, violence does not always cause involuntariness.

Aquinas's response is that there are both voluntary actions and voluntary 'being-acted-upons' (which he calls passions, from the Latin for "to suffer or undergo"). The dentist performs a voluntary action in performing my root canal; I perform a voluntary being-acted-upon by climbing into the chair and letting her work on me. In short, being willing to undergo something that someone else does to us is not a case of involuntariness (and, thus, doesn't cause sadness). As long as the person undergoing the action is willing to undergo it, the action isn't violent in a way that would lead to involuntariness. (The sort of violent action that would cause involuntariness would be, for example, if the dentist strapped me down, injected me with a paralytic, and then performed a root canal on me while I am unable to struggle.)

**Obj. and resp. 3.** This objection also trades on vagueness in our concept of violence. Imagine a heavy body climbing upwards, like Thomas Aquinas climbing a tree to get away from an attacking dog, or someone bending their fingers back toward their wrist. These acts seem violent, insofar as they involve going against natural inclinations of those bodies, but we can decide to perform them, and so they don't seem involuntary.

Aquinas agrees that these actions aren't involuntary—but he also claims that they are not paradigm examples of violent action. Although a heavy body's moving upwards goes against such a body's inclination to stay "down," it is still natural for animals to be moved by their appetites (in this case, Aquinas's desire to avoid being bitten). In the same way, although it is not natural to our fingers to bend backwards toward our wrists, it can still be natural for someone to desire to do so (to win a bet, say, or to demonstrate their flexibility). In both of these cases, the act itself is voluntary even though it goes against nature in certain respects, and there is no violence being done to the person performing that act.

**Reply.** Violence is opposed both to the voluntary and to the natural, Aquinas claims. As he has already remarked earlier in this question, both voluntary and natural acts come from internal principles, whereas violence necessarily involves an external principle. For things that lack cognition, like stones, a violent act is one that brings about something contrary to that thing's nature, as when someone lifts a stone up when the stone's natural inclination is to be "down." For things with cognition, a violent act is one that brings about something contrary to that thing's desire or will—as when I restrain my dog so that she can't jump on and lick visitors, or when a parent straps his struggling toddler into her car seat. What is contrary to nature is, by definition, unnatural; what is contrary to will is, by definition, involuntary. (What Aquinas does not mention in the reply here but makes clear in his responses to the objections are the different ways in which something can be contrary to the will.)

### 6.6. Does fear cause involuntariness in an absolute sense?

Answer: no, fear does not cause complete involuntariness in human actions.

The fact that this article phrases the issue in terms of "absolute" involuntariness gives the reader a rather strong hint that the answer to the question will be negative. Fear causes us do things we wouldn't otherwise want to do, but Aquinas (following Aristotle in *Nicomachean Ethics* III) argues that acting from fear is still acting according to what seems good to us at the time and under those circumstances. In this respect, he says, "such actions are in fact more voluntary than involuntary."

**Obj. and resp. 1.** This objection draws on the conclusion of the last article and argues that just as violence causes involuntariness by going against our commanded act of will in a present situation, fear causes involuntariness because it concerns a future evil that we do not desire.

In his response, Aquinas distinguishes between things that are done as a result of violence or force and things that are done as a result of fear in terms of what is happening now as opposed to what we are worried about happening in the future. He also stresses another difference between cases of violence and cases of fear: the will never consents in the case of what's done by violence, whereas the will is moved toward the thing done in the case of actions motivated by fear. The toddler being strapped into her car seat against her wishes continues to protest (loudly) while being strapped in, whereas the captain on a boat in danger of sinking willingly, if not enthusiastically, throws the cargo overboard in hopes of keeping the ship afloat.

For an act to be voluntary, Aquinas says, the will can be moved toward an end for the sake of something else, not necessarily for that end's own sake. After all, we will many things for an end that is for the sake of something else: for instance, we will to wake up earlier than normal to give a friend a ride to the airport or to go running. Those actions aren't involuntary just because they're willed for the sake of some further end. In fact, if they were, the vast majority of our actions would be involuntary, for Aquinas has argued in the Treatise on Happiness that we will everything for the ultimate end of happiness. Involuntary acts are ones in which the person's will contributes nothing at all to the act. Acts done from fear are still acts where the will *does* contribute something.

**Obj. and resp. 2.** The objection here makes the argument that what is done from fear is *intrinsically* involuntary, and that anything done in a state of fear is thus also involuntary. The idea is that anything intrinsically F stays that way no matter what: if a fire is intrinsically hot, for instance, or if ice is intrinsically cold, it will remain that way as long as it exists, no matter what it is brought into contact with. (Put an ice cube on a fire, and the fire will stay hot as long as it burns; the ice will also remain cold as long as it remains ice.)

In response, Aquinas allows that there are cases where things are said to be F absolutely, but points out that other things can be called F relatively speaking, and that the extent to which they are F will depend on what they are being compared to. He then claims that even when we can call something absolutely voluntary in one respect, we can still think of that same act as relatively voluntary from another point of view. It's possible, then, for something that would not be considered voluntary in comparison to one situation to be voluntary when compared to something else.

This is all quite vague as Aquinas puts it here, and it also seems to conflict with his claim in the reply that acts done from fear are voluntary absolutely. The appeal to relativity, however, accommodates our intuition that there really is something involuntary about what we do from fear, even if we understand why those acts are going to be generally categorized as voluntary. The captain of the ship chooses to throw the cargo overboard, but only in a situation where the relevant alternatives include "let the ship sink" and "throw passengers and crew overboard." In a situation where the relevant alternatives include "watch the sunlight sparkle on the waves" and "enjoy a nice chat with the bosun," the captain would not voluntarily throw the cargo overboard. Regardless, in the actual set of circumstances in which the ship is about to go down, the captain's act of throwing cargo overboard is voluntary: he consciously acts for a cognized end that he desires. The fact that he wouldn't desire that end in different circumstances is beside the point when it comes to judging the voluntariness of that particular act. (The confusion created by the various circumstances in which we find ourselves performing actual actions is why Aquinas turns next to a discussion of circumstances, in Q7.)

**Obj. and resp. 3.** This objection stresses the same sort of point made in the previous one. If we do something from fear that we would only ever do because that act prevents what we fear from coming to pass, it seems like this action is unconditionally involuntary and conditionally voluntary: it is not an act we would want to perform, were the situation different.

In response, Aquinas claims that this gets the order of "conditional" and "unconditional" exactly wrong: insofar as an act done out of fear is what is actually willed in a particular set of circumstances, it is unconditionally (or absolutely) voluntary. In contrast, it counts as involuntary only when we consider its particular condition—namely, that it is an act we wouldn't have chosen to perform in other circumstances.

**Reply.** Aquinas begins by quoting Aristotle, who describes acts performed from fear as involving a mixture of the voluntary and the involuntary, but after paying lip service to the Philosopher, Aquinas then immediately goes on to claim that "if you think about this correctly" you can see that acts performed from fear are more voluntary than they are involuntary.

What's driving Aquinas's claim here is his belief that an act performed out of fear satisfies the definition of "voluntary action" he's given above. Suppose that in the midst of a severe storm, a captain orders his crew to throw all the cargo overboard to avoid the ship's sinking, despite the loss of profits this will entail. Aquinas argues that the captain's act counts as voluntary because it is an act willed "here and now," and it is specifically aimed at avoiding an even worse evil that the captain fears—namely the loss not just of the cargo but also the ship and the lives of everyone on board. That is, the captain actively wills throwing the cargo overboard, where that is cognized as an end directed to a further end (namely, safety or survival). In this sense, what the captain does fits every part of the definition of 'voluntary.'

Aquinas grants that there is a sense in which the captain's act counts as involuntary, but he maintains that it is not a sense that renders the act involuntary in any significant way, since it is a sense existing only "in the mind" or "in thought"—that is, the sense in which the agent wishes he didn't have to do what he is doing. If the captain were considering "throwing the ship's cargo overboard" as an end abstractly and in separation from the particular situation in which the act takes place, she would not will that end. But in the situation of a severe storm, she does will to throw her cargo overboard, and so her action is voluntary, even if there is an element of the involuntary in the neighborhood.

### 6.7. Does desire cause involuntariness?

Answer: no, desire does not cause involuntariness. Not even a little bit.

Aquinas's answer to this question is essentially, "Um, no." The thought that desire might make an act involuntary is supposed to gain its force from the overpowering nature of the passions: swamped with love, I am compelled to write a sonnet; overwhelmed by the taste of the crème brûlée, I eat my friend's portion as well as my own. (See Aquinas's further discussion of this topic in 10.3.) Aquinas's response, however, is to point out that the paradigm case of a voluntary action is precisely one in which we will something because we desire it and are drawn toward it. Our desire for an end is what makes willing that end voluntary in the first place.

**Obj. and resp. 1.** Fear is a passion, and desire is a passion. Fear causes an act to be involuntary in at least some respect, though, and so desire should also cause an act to be involuntary in some respect.

Aquinas's response is to emphasize the difference between the object involved in fear and the object involved in desire. Fear is of something bad, he says, whereas desire is of something good. That is, when we act from fear, we are motivated by our desire to avoid something bad and thus contrary to our will. When we act from desire, however, we are motivated by our desire for what we perceive as good, period. Although actions from fear and from desire both involve the passions, the way in which those passions affect the will are quite different: fear moves us to perform an action that we do not want in a whole-hearted sense; desire moves us to perform an action that we want quite intensely.

**Obj. and resp. 2.** People who act on desire are often incontinent—that is, they originally intend to do one thing (such as eat only their own crème brûlée and no one else's), but they end up acting in a way contrary to their original intention (and eat their friend's dessert as well). This is similar to the way in which people who act from fear end up doing something contrary to what they originally intended to do. Thus, because fear can cause an act to be involuntary in some respect, desire can also cause an act to be involuntary in some respect.

In response, Aquinas points out that in acts done from fear, the involuntariness arises from the sense in which the agent doesn't really *want* to be doing what she does, although she still wills to do it in those particular circumstances. In acts motivated by desire, however, our wills move from desiring one thing (eating only our own dessert) to desiring another thing (eating all the desserts). Even if we later regret that action and the fact that it differs from what we originally intended to do ("Ugh . . . I'm so full. I can't believe I did that!"), when we act from desire, we are, at the time of our acting, doing what is very much in accordance with our will. Thus our act fits the definition of voluntary in the fullest sense.

**Obj. and resp. 3.** The definition of voluntariness laid out in earlier articles in this question includes cognition of the end as such. This objection appeals to Aristotle's authority to claim that extreme desire destroys such cognition: strong pleasure, or even sometimes just a strong enough desire for pleasure, interferes with our cognitive faculties to such an extent that we are no longer able to exercise practical reason. Thus, actions performed in such a condition are not, properly speaking, voluntary actions.

Aquinas allows that desire can affect our cognitive capacities, but he strongly denies that this results in the corresponding act's being involuntary. In the extreme case of the person who is driven mad with desire, Aquinas denies that the person is acting involuntarily because, he says, in this situation the person ceases to act rationally at all; thus, neither the term 'voluntary' nor the term 'involuntary' applies to their actions. In more moderate cases, where, driven by desire, we act thoughtlessly but retain the capacity to cognize, Aquinas stresses the agent's continuing ability to consider the various options open to her. What is lost in cases of passionate desire, he claims, is just actual consideration of the particular act in question, not the ability to think *per se*. Because the agent maintains the ability to cognize and to will various ends even when viewing them through a haze of desire, she is responsible for the actions she performs in that haze (in the same way that she is responsible for not acting or willing in cases she should have attended to, as described in 6.3). As Aquinas goes on to explain in 10.3 and 77.7, the will always retains the ability to resist such passions.

**Reply.** This is perhaps Aquinas's briefest reply to any article in either the Treatise on Happiness or the Treatise on Human Acts. It simply doesn't need a long answer: desire can't cause involuntariness, because desire is what makes an action voluntary in the first place. We call something voluntary precisely because the will (*voluntas*) is drawn to it.

### 6.8. Does ignorance cause involuntariness?

Answer: only antecedent ignorance causes complete involuntariness; other sorts of ignorance do not.

This is the most complicated article in Q6, because the relation between ignorance and involuntariness is quite complex. As Aquinas takes pains to point out, there are different kinds of ignorance, and they have different consequences for the voluntariness or involuntariness of an act. In particular, there is (to break from Aquinas's own order) *antecedent* ignorance, *concomitant* ignorance, and *consequent* ignorance. Only antecedent ignorance makes an act unqualifiedly involuntary. Consequent ignorance causes involuntariness only in a certain respect (the act is done from ignorance, but the ignorance itself is voluntary, either because the agent wills to be ignorant or because the agent is ignorant of something she could and should know), and concomitant ignorance makes an act *non*-voluntary rather than *in*voluntary. The reader should note that although these distinctions appear to have clear implications for the moral status of the acts done from different sorts of ignorance, Aquinas himself is not yet interested in discussing moral responsibility and/ or praise and blame: he waits to address that issue until the last question of the Treatise on Human Acts (Q21).

All of the objections in this article present reasons to think that not all cases of ignorance cause involuntariness. Aquinas himself agrees, and so his responses simply map the distinctions he makes between different sorts of ignorance in the main reply onto the cases presented in the objections (the first two objections involve the two types of consequent ignorance; the third objection involves concomitant ignorance).

**Reply.** For ignorance to cause involuntariness, it must "[remove] the relevant cognition." As Aquinas states repeatedly in the earlier articles of this question, voluntariness requires both an internal principle of motion and the cognition of the desired end as an end. In this discussion, Aquinas takes pains to distinguish between different ways in which ignorance might interfere with our cognition of the desired end. As he notes, not all types of ignorance render the corresponding acts of will involuntary.

The first sort of ignorance Aquinas discusses, concomitant ignorance, is one in which an agent does not know what they are actually doing (in the sense of acting toward a clearly cognized end) but would have wanted to do it if they had known. The example Aquinas provides of concomitant ignorance—someone kills an enemy under the mistaken impression that he is killing a deer—sounds a bit strange to the modern ear. Yet if we imagine the medieval feudal context in which Aquinas is writing, this example makes perfect sense. Imagine two feuding fiefdoms, where the yeomen in both fiefs have standing orders to kill the yeomen from the other fief on sight. Suppose one of these men is in the forest hunting deer, sees what he thinks is a deer and shoots it, and then is pleased to discover that he has actually shot and killed one of the yeomen from the rival fief. This kind of ignorance, Aquinas says, does not cause involuntariness, because the act performed was not contrary to the will of the person who performed it. To be involuntary, the will would have to be opposed to what was done, and this is a case where the yeoman is delighted to discover that he killed one of his enemies. The act is, instead, *non*-voluntary: the agent didn't will the act insofar as he was ignorant of what he was doing, but the action was in line with what he would have willed. In fact, the term 'concomitant' itself comes from the will's being "for" the act committed from ignorance.[1]

---

1. For an excellent discussion of this passage and of Aquinas's account of non-voluntary actions in general, see Hause (2006).

The second kind of ignorance Aquinas discusses is consequent ignorance, or ignorance that is the result of a previous willing (or failure to will). In the case of consequent ignorance, the ignorance itself is voluntary: the agent doesn't know precisely what she is doing, but the reason for that is her previous willing (or lack thereof). Aquinas divides consequent ignorance into two kinds: (1) affected ignorance, where the agent actively wills not to know something so that she can do something she would otherwise not do, and (2) ignorance of something an agent both could and ought to know. Imagine a situation where you're at a party, you meet someone you find very attractive, and you clearly have the chance to hook up with them. When you don't ask the person whether they're dating anyone so that you can make out with them without feeling guilty, you are "affecting" ignorance. (You can truly say, "Hey—I didn't know that she had a partner!") This is not enough to make the act involuntary, strictly speaking, though, because your ignorance is itself voluntary.

The second kind of consequent ignorance (where you remain ignorant of what you could and should know) is also voluntary in a crucial sense. Aquinas divides this sort of ignorance into two further kinds: (2a) situations where you do not actively consider what you should consider (and are able to consider), which he calls "ignorance of evil choice," and (2b) situations where you do not bother to acquire knowledge you should have had (for example, the traffic laws in the foreign country where you've just rented a car). Aquinas says the latter (2b-type cases) are cases of voluntary ignorance, because everyone is responsible for knowing the universal or general principles of the law. Suppose I'm pulled over in England for driving on the right side of the road, and I say, truthfully, "But I didn't know that I was supposed to drive on the left side of the road here!" In this situation, it's fair for the police officer to say, "Yes, but you *should* have known; in fact, it was your duty to know that before you got on the road here!" and to give me a ticket. Situations involving "ignorance of evil choice" (2a-type cases)—where you have the relevant information at hand but don't attend to it for some reason—are also situations of voluntary ignorance. As Aquinas pointed out in 6.3, we can be held responsible for *not* knowing, acting, and willing. If I'm listening to music in my car and drive right through a stop sign because I'm so caught up in singing along, I have failed to notice what I could and should have noticed: my ignorance is voluntary. All actions performed in cases of consequent ignorance, however, are involuntary in the sense that the will would have willed otherwise if full knowledge had been present. (I would have willed to stop at the stop sign, for example, or to drive on the left side of the road, or to not make out with someone who has a partner.)

The final type of ignorance Aquinas discusses is the only sort that causes involuntariness in the full sense: antecedent ignorance. Antecedent ignorance involves those cases in which the ignorance itself is not voluntary (and so the agent is not responsible for her not knowing the relevant features of the situation) and in which the agent would not have willed what she willed if she had possessed knowledge of the relevant circumstances. The example Aquinas gives is a variation on the example for concomitant ignorance. A hunter who is paying proper attention to his surroundings aims his bow at a deer that is clearly visible in the distance, but as he releases the arrow, someone the archer could not have seen earlier and could not have expected to be passing along walks into the clearing and is killed by the arrow. In this case, Aquinas says, the archer is not responsible for his ignorance. Furthermore, insofar as the archer would not have willed his action if he had been aware of the relevant circumstances, the act carried out (killing the passerby) is in opposition to the archer's actual volition, and so Aquinas designates it as a case in which ignorance causes involuntariness.

As Aquinas moves from the discussion in Q6 of the general nature of voluntary and involuntary acts to the discussion in Q7 of the circumstances of voluntary acts, it's important to note that the range of actions which count as involuntary (and for which we are off the moral hook) is quite small. There is only one sort of ignorance, for instance, that actually renders an act properly involuntary (and thus not under our control in the way relevant for moral responsibility). Fear doesn't make actions involuntary, nor does desire, and violence can't be done to our wills—it can only be done to the acts our wills command our bodies to carry out. It will be vitally important to understand the circumstances in which we perform our acts, then, for a full evaluation of their moral status.

## Question 7: The Circumstances of Human Acts

Q7 is relatively short and continues Q6's pattern of closely following Aristotle's discussion in *Nicomachean Ethics* III. Its main focus is the nature of the circumstances of human action: what are they, how many are there, and which are the most important. Aquinas devotes an article, though, to the question of why the theologian should pay attention to the circumstances under which an act takes place, reminding us there that the whole point of the Treatise on Human Acts is its relation to the Treatise on Happiness and our attainment of the ultimate end. (The minutiae surrounding the evaluation of human actions get a bit overwhelming here, so it's rather nice to have this reminder.)

### 7.1. Is a circumstance an accident of a human act?

Answer: yes, a circumstance counts as an accident (rather than an essential part) of a human action.

This article focuses on the nature of the circumstances of human acts—in particular, whether they should be understood as part of the substance of an act or as accidents of that act. Roughly put, the difference is that whatever is part of the substance of an act is essential to it (what Aquinas will go on to refer to as the "species" of an act, which he describes in much more detail in QQ18–21). This article makes it clear that whatever circumstances are, they are not part of the substance of a human action. According to Aquinas, the substance of an act involves aspects such as the definition, genus, and species of the action. We will, for example, *to throw cargo overboard*: "throwing cargo overboard" is the end that our intellect cognizes and presents to the will as a good and that our will then desires as good. We do not will to throw the cargo overboard *frantically, at midnight,* or *off the stern of the boat.* Circumstances, Aquinas tells us, are those conditions that are "external to the substance of an act but that nonetheless touch a human act in some way." They are the contingent conditions that relate to, or surround, the substance of an act.

**Obj. and resp. 1.** This objection appeals to the authority of Cicero (the first-century Latin orator), who in his discussion of circumstances in the *Rhetoric* observes that circumstances are part of what gives a speech its argumentative authority.

In his response, Aquinas agrees but also distinguishes between things contributing to a situation primarily and secondarily. Someone is brought to court primarily because she committed murder, he says, and only secondarily because the murder was done by means of deceit, or for money, etc. Circumstances can certainly add to the action, but they do not define it.

**Obj. and resp. 2.** The second objection appeals to the nature of accidents themselves, which are usually defined as existing *in* something (as white exists in a piece of paper, or heat exists in my coffee). Circumstances do not exist in an act in this way, however—they are by nature what "stand around" (a literal translation of the Latin *'circum-stare'*) an act.

In response to this objection, Aquinas makes yet another distinction: this time, between the sort of accident that (a) inheres in a substance as white inheres in paper, and the sort of accident that (b) "exists simultaneously with that thing in the same subject." His (admittedly not very helpful) example is the way white is said to be an accident of the musical, "insofar as they come together and in some way are coincident in the same subject." Aquinas is referring here to an example from Aristotle's explanation of change in *Physics* I.7, in which Socrates is the subject, or substance, in which both "white" and "musical" exist. That is, Socrates is a man who is pale and who is also musical. "White" is said to be an accident of "musical" insofar as Socrates is both white and musical: those accidents that exist simultaneously in the same subject (Socrates). Relating this all back to the question of whether circumstances are accidents of human actions, the point is that circumstances *are* accidents in this second (b) way, because human actions are themselves, properly speaking, accidents of the human beings (like Socrates) who perform them. (The relation between "white" and "musical" in Socrates seems completely contingent, however, as opposed to the way that "in stormy seas" is supposed to be related to "throwing the cargo overboard." Fortunately, Aquinas addresses this in his response to the next objection.)

**Obj. and resp. 3.** The third objection draws on the fact that, as just noted, human acts are themselves accidents. It doesn't seem that accidents can have accidents, though, and so circumstances cannot be accidents of the accidents that are human acts.

In response, Aquinas claims that some accidents *are* said to have accidents, because both are found together in the same subject (see category [b] discussed above). He goes on to distinguish between two sub-categories within this category: (b1) accidents that inhere in the same subject without any intrinsic order or relation between them (e.g., the way that white and musical both exist in Socrates) and (b2) accidents that have an intrinsic order or relation to each other, as when we say that the surface of a ball (which Aquinas thinks of as an accident) is blue (an accident that inheres in the ball by virtue of inhering in its surface). Circumstances can be related to human acts in both these ways: (b1)-type circumstances are accidents that belong to an agent independent of the act an agent performs (where the agent is, for instance, or what state the agent is in when performing an act—angry, sleepy, etc.), whereas (b2)-type circumstances are accidents that belong to the agent in virtue of the act being performed (the manner in which the agent performs the act, for instance—hastily, deliberately, etc.).

**Reply.** Aquinas begins this response with a brief discussion of semantics to explain how the word 'circumstances' (which, again, means "standing around" in Latin) applies to the accidents of human acts. As Aristotle is famous for saying, when we are trying to understand something, we move from what is better known to what is less well known. So, the word 'circumstances'—which used to refer only to what is external but near to or touching a particular body in a particular place—gradually gained an extended sense, and now it also applies to conditions that are external to the substance of a human act but nonetheless "touch" that act in some way (like place, manner, duration, etc.).

### 7.2. Should a theologian pay attention to the circumstances of human acts?

Answer: yes, of course a theologian should pay attention to the circumstances of human acts.

Aquinas appears to include this discussion here to remind the reader that the point of the Treatise on Human Acts is not purely theoretical. The issues under discussion—including these complicated questions about circumstances—bear a direct relation to our ultimate end (happiness) as well as to goodness, badness, merit, and blame.

**Obj. and resp. 1.** This objection claims that theologians should consider human acts only insofar as they're good or evil. Circumstances can't make an act good or bad, however, because they are external rather than intrinsic to that act.

In response, Aquinas argues that circumstances can have that sort of effect on a human act. Acts themselves are called good or bad insofar as they are more or less useful for attaining a particular end. The relation of "useful" between the act and the end becomes important here, for relations involve not just what is intrinsic to something (like, say, "whiteness"), but also what is external but closely connected to that thing (like, say, "right" and "left," where those terms denote the position of something in relation to the things immediately surrounding it). Acts are counted as good insofar as they are useful for an end, but both whether a particular act will be useful for an end and how useful it is can definitely vary depending on the circumstances of an act. (I want to break my personal best record for a race on Saturday, but instead of drinking lots of water the night before the race I go out with friends and drink nothing but beer. In other circumstances, my drinking nothing but beer that evening is fine—maybe even good, insofar as my consumption is moderate enough and contributes to my enjoying time out with my friends. In the circumstances where I'm racing the next morning, though, my act of drinking beer rather than water the night before detracts from my end of setting a new personal best.)

**Obj. and resp. 2.** The previous article concluded that circumstances are accidents; this objection points out that any substance has an indefinite number of accidents. My laptop, for instance, has any number of accidents, including its proximity to the Queen of England and to the Swiss Alps). Theologians can't be expected to pay attention to all these accidents, however, and so perhaps they should just focus on the substance of human acts and not their circumstances.

Aquinas responds that the sort of accidents that are completely or wholly accidental (like my laptop's proximity to the Queen) can be safely ignored. The circumstances that surround a particular action are not like that, however, because they both help characterize an act and form part of how that act is directed toward its end.

**Obj. and resp. 3.** The first article of this question discussed Cicero's *Rhetoric*; this objection claims that rhetoric—and not theology—is the proper place for discussing circumstances, and thus that theologians can safely ignore circumstances.

Aquinas's response underscores the medieval doctrine that theology is the "queen of the sciences." All the arts, too, such as rhetoric and poetry, are ultimately in the service of theology.[2] Theologians are thus responsible not just for examining circumstances insofar as they affect whether human acts are virtuous or vicious (the purview of the moral philosopher) but also insofar as they relate to whether an act deserves punishment or reward (the purview of politicians, who determine such things for legal purposes, and of rhetoricians, whose job it is to make persuasive speeches about them).

**Reply.** Aquinas is emphatic that theologians should take circumstances into account in their study of the "divine science" (theology, the study of God), and provides three reasons for this. First, the whole point of human acts is to direct us toward our ultimate end, happiness. Whether an act is actually appropriately ordered to its end, however, depends in part on whether the circumstances that surround that act are appropriate. Suppose I ought to thank you, for instance, for giving me your seat on a crowded train when I've got a broken foot. If I thank you too softly for you to hear or only after you've already moved away, I haven't performed the act appropriately. So the study of circumstances is relevant for theology, which includes consideration of our final end. Second, theologians are quite interested in the relative goodness or badness of human acts, and (as Aquinas will go on to describe in detail below) circumstances affect whether acts are good or bad.[3] Third, theologians are concerned with whether human acts deserve reward or punishment—in Aquinas's words, whether they are "meritorious" or "demeritorious." Whether an act deserves reward or punishment depends in part on whether it's voluntary, and Aquinas has already argued in 6.8 that an agent's awareness of certain circumstances directly affects whether an act is voluntary or involuntary.

### 7.3. Is the list of circumstances given in Ethics III correct?

Answer: yes, Aristotle's list of circumstances in the *Nicomachean Ethics* is correct.

This is one of the places where Aquinas explicitly refers to the text that is obviously guiding this entire discussion of circumstances in Q7: Aristotle's *Nicomachean Ethics*, book III. In *Ethics* III, Aristotle gives a list of eight circumstances relevant to human acts: who, what, where, by what instruments, why, how, when, and concerning what. Aquinas isn't going to disagree with Aristotle on this topic. Indeed, the extent to which Aristotle is considered an authority on this subject is made clear by the 'on the contrary' in this article, which could be fairly paraphrased as: "The list of circumstances given in

---

2. See the discussion of *scientia* and the sciences in the commentary on 3.6 in the Treatise on Happiness.

3. See Q18, art. 10 and 11 for further discussion of how they do this.

Aristotle's *Ethics* is, after all, *Aristotle's* list. He isn't called 'the Philosopher' for nothing." In this article, Aquinas simply groups Aristotle's circumstances into three categories meant to illuminate how circumstances can "touch" human acts and affect the act's relation to its end.

**Obj. and resp. 1.** This rather flat-footed objection gives a literal reading to the claim that circumstances are external to an act and argues that time and place must be external to an act because they are external to human beings as a whole in a way that other circumstances aren't. After all, it's 7:30 in the evening in the Potting Shed in Edinburgh whether I'm there happily typing away on my laptop or not. All of the other circumstances on the list appear to directly involve the agent in some way or another, however, and so Aristotle was wrong to include time and place in his list of circumstances.

Time and place are "measures," which Aquinas grants is a different category of circumstance than the others. The way time and place "measure" an act can be understood if you think about measuring as giving a particular spatio-temporal index to an act: time and place distinguish otherwise identical acts from each other and thus give us a way to measure them. We can distinguish my waking up on Monday morning in Ghent, for instance, from my waking up on Thursday morning in Edinburgh by the time and/or place of those acts of awakening. Aquinas denies, however, that this means that time and place can't be circumstances. Measuring an act is, after all, hardly the only way something can be external to the substance of an act.

**Obj. and resp. 2.** Circumstances determine whether an act is done well or badly—that is, whether that act was the right or the wrong thing to do. This objection says that because whether an act is done well or badly depends entirely on the *manner* in which we act, we can collapse Aristotle's list of circumstances into just that one circumstance: the manner of acting.

Aquinas dismisses this objection by observing that it relies on a misunderstanding of what it means for an act to be done well or badly, and what the "manner of acting" is. The manner of our acting is simply the quality of that act, such as "quickly" or "slowly." Whether an act is done well or badly, however, is a broader issue that depends on the sum total of that act's circumstances taken together with the act, not just the manner in which that act was done.

**Obj. and resp. 3.** Causes of an act seem central to that act: why, then, should they count as accidental circumstances and not part of the substance of an act itself? To make its case, this objection draws on Aristotle's account of the four causes (material, formal, efficient, and final), identifying "who" as the efficient cause of an act; "on account of what" as the final cause toward which the act is directed; and "concerning what" as the act's material cause.

The reason "on account of" and "who'" get counted as circumstances rather than as part of the substance of an act, Aquinas says, is that they are "associated characteristics" of the relevant cause, rather than the substance of that cause. So, for instance, "on account of" counts as a circumstance because it refers to contingent features of the final end—like walking home *to spend time with my family* or acting courageously *to free a city*. The same thing applies in the case of the circumstance "what"—it refers to the contingent features of the act, like walking home *through a cemetery* or washing someone's forehead *in order to cool them down*. The confusion that motivates this objection is natural, though: Aquinas goes on in the next article to explain that "on account of" and "what" are, indeed, the two circumstances most important to an act.

**Reply.** Aquinas accepts Aristotle's list as correct and provides further rationale for the particular items on the list by dividing them into three separate categories: *Category 1* circumstances that touch the act itself—time and place (which "measure" an act, as discussed in his response to the first objection) and manner (which qualifies the act, as discussed in his response to the second objection); *Category 2* circumstances that touch the cause of the act—"on account of what" (which relates to the final cause of the act), "concerning what" (which relates to the material cause or object of the act), "who acted" (which relates to the principal agent or efficient cause), and "by what means or instrument" (which relates to the instrumental agent cause); *Category 3* circumstances that touch the effect of an act—the consequences of the agent's action.[4]

To see how this categorization is supposed to work, take the act of my heading home at the end of a long day of work. *Category 1* circumstances would include the time and place of my heading home, as well as whether I was doing it quickly, slowly, reluctantly, etc. *Category 2* circumstances would include the reason I'm walking home (perhaps to spend time with my family or eat dinner), the route I take to get home, the person doing the walking (me), and by what means I'm getting there (for example, walking on my own two feet, using a scooter, getting a piggyback ride, etc.). *Category 3* circumstances would include my improved mood and elevated heart rate (supposing I walk).

### 7.4. Are "on account of what" and "what the action is in" the most important circumstances?

Answer: yes, the reason for our acting and what is done are the most important circumstances in evaluating an action.

This is another article that focuses explicitly on Aristotle's treatment of circumstances in *Nicomachean Ethics* III and in which Aquinas is content to follow the Philosopher's lead. Both because it summarizes much of what's gone before and because Aquinas will address the relevant issues discussed here in much greater detail elsewhere (see especially 18.3, 9–10), not much

---

4. Aquinas explains why this is not part of the substance of an act in resp. 3.

needs to be said about this article. First, Aquinas claims "that for the sake of which" is the most important circumstance for a human action. After all, as he points out in his response to the second objection, the end for which something is done is what moves someone to act in the first place. Our reason for acting is what motivates everything that comes after it. Aquinas also argues that the second most important circumstance is the full description of "what is done"—which, as he points out in response to the first objection, is a better way of describing the circumstance also called "what the action is in."

## Question 8: The Objects of Will

According to most scholarship, in QQ8–17 Aquinas lays out a series of steps or components that make up a complete human act. There is interpretive debate about how many steps there are and in what sequence they come as well as philosophical debate about whether Aquinas was right to identify so many steps or to distinguish certain components from others.[5] But does Aquinas actually intend to set forth a sequence of discrete act-components that compose a single complete human act? He certainly never says that this is what he is doing, and the order in which he treats the various acts—which is not at all the sequence prescribed by any of the standard interpretations—is quite baffling if we assume that such was his intention.

Our commentary instead presents Aquinas as doing what he says he is doing: analyzing the various acts of will. It happens that certain kinds of acts of will presuppose others, and in those cases the acts will be sequential; but in general Aquinas is interested in the different ways in which the human capacity for intellectual desire—the capacity he calls "will"—is related to various objects and to the kinds of purposive activity in which this capacity of will allows human beings to engage.

Aquinas sets forth the outline of the material in the introductions to QQ8 and 13. The first division is between acts *elicited* by the will—acts that the will itself performs—and acts *commanded* by the will—acts performed by capacities other than the will but at the will's direction. This crucial distinction will be treated in much greater detail as we go forward, but a rough example might be helpful at this stage. My choosing to raise my hand to ask a question is an elicited act; the movement of my hand is a commanded act. Why call a movement of my hand an act of will at all? Consider the difference between two reasons my hand might go up: (1) I raise my hand to ask a question; (2) a scientist causes my hand to go up by stimulating electrodes she has hooked up to my brain. (1) is an act of will in a sense that (2) obviously is not, because in (1) the movement of my hand expresses and carries out what I want. This

---

5. See appendix 1 for an overview of competing interpretations.

is what Aquinas means by calling such purposive acts of capacities other than the will *commanded acts* of the will.

Aquinas discusses elicited acts in QQ8–16 and commanded acts in Q17. The discussion of elicited acts is further subdivided into acts of will concerning an end, QQ8–12, and acts of will concerning what is for an end, QQ13–16. There are three acts of will concerning an end—will itself (QQ8–10), enjoyment (Q11), and intention (Q12)—and three acts of will concerning what is for an end—choice (Q13), consent (Q15), and use (Q16). Aquinas also includes a question on deliberation (Q14). As an activity of intellect rather than will, deliberation might initially seem out of place here; but in fact deliberation is driven by the will's intention of an end and precedes the will's act of choice, so the analysis of deliberation is appropriately included in this section.

**Acts of will**

| elicited acts | concerning an end | will | Q8 objects of will |
| --- | --- | --- | --- |
| | | | Q9 what moves the will |
| | | | Q10 how the will is moved |
| | | enjoyment | Q11 enjoyment |
| | | intention | Q12 intention |
| | concerning what is for an end | choice | Q13 choice |
| | | deliberation* | Q14 deliberation |
| | | consent | Q15 consent |
| | | use | Q16 use |
| commanded acts | | | Q17 acts commanded by the will |

*not strictly an act of will, but driven by the will's intention of an end and (often) presupposed by the will's act of choice

The discussion of will in QQ8–10 plays two different roles, because Aquinas uses the word *voluntas*, "will," to name both the *capacity* of will and one particular kind of *act* of that capacity, its most generic or basic act. In English we can easily keep the two distinct by calling the capacity "the will" and the act "will," but Latin has no articles and so there is no obvious way for Aquinas to mark the distinction. Thus, in the first question, "Is will only of what is good?" Aquinas could be asking whether the capacity of will has only what is good as its object, or he could be asking whether this particular act of that capacity has only what is good as its object. He in fact slides back and forth between the two, as Latin allows him to do, and without confusion, because the answer to both questions is the same—yes—and it is precisely because the object of the *capacity* is exclusively what is good that the object of the *act* is exclusively what is good. In general, his focus in QQ8–10 is the capacity rather than the act—yet another reason, incidentally, to reject the sequence-of-acts reading of QQ8–17: the *act* "will," as a discrete act with a particular place in some elaborate sequence, is not a focus of Aquinas's account.

### 8.1. Is will only of what is good?

Answer: Will is only of what is apprehended as good.

The first two objections focus straightforwardly on the capacity or power of will (rather than a particular act of that power). **Obj.** 1 makes a point about powers in general: they deal with opposites. We see both white and black; we feel both smooth and rough. So it seems reasonable that we should will both good and bad. **Obj.** 2 focuses on a particular class of powers, the ones that Aristotle calls rational powers. Such powers can actually pursue opposites, and because "the will is in reason," and therefore a rational power, it can pursue not only good but also evil.

**Obj.** 3 invokes the standard medieval view that goodness and being are coextensive: that is, whatever has being is good and whatever is good has being. We can obviously will non-being—I will *not* to walk or *not* to speak—and since what lacks being also lacks goodness, we can will what lacks goodness, and not only what has goodness. I can also will that something happen in the future, and what is still in the future is not yet a being.

In his **reply** Aquinas continues the focus on the power of will. He first reminds us that will is rational appetite. (See commentary on 1.2.) The *appetite* part of "rational appetite" is crucial in the first paragraph and the *rational* part in the second. Appetite is a built-in directedness. Remember that we are in an Aristotelian universe here, and an Aristotelian universe is purposive. Forget everything you were taught about inertia. Aristotelian objects are naturally dynamic, rather than static; and their internal dynamism is not indiscriminate. It is aimed at some definite purpose or "end," as Aquinas calls it. In particular, a thing is directed to "what is similar to it and fitting for it." Given that being and goodness are coextensive, whatever *is* is *good* and is therefore directed toward what is good; so every appetite is for what is good.

This appetite for what is good is *rational* appetite, and in the second paragraph of the reply Aquinas explains how the rational character of rational appetite plays a role. Appetites or inclinations depend on a *form*, and there are three different kinds of forms that are relevant here: natural, sensory (or animal), and rational (or intellectual). A natural form exists in nature, and the inclination that results from such a form, called "natural appetite," is toward something that exists (or can exist) in nature. By contrast, sensory and rational forms exist in the mind, not in extramental reality; they are *apprehended* forms. The sensory and rational appetites therefore incline toward what is apprehended as good. Human reason can be mistaken, apprehending something as good that is not actually good; in such a case, rational appetite will be directed to something *as* good, though not to something good.

In **resp.** 1 Aquinas clarifies that the *power* of will does deal with opposites, but in opposite ways: it desires what is good but avoids what is bad. The *act* of will is the act of desiring what is good; we really should use a different word, he says, for the act of avoiding or rejecting what is bad. Aquinas suggests 'nilling'—'*noluntas*,' formed from '*non*,' "not," plus '*voluntas*,' "will"—though in fact the word *noluntas* appears nowhere else in his works.

**Resp.** 3 relies further on the point made in the reply that the inclination of rational appetite is to *apprehended* forms. A negation (e.g., not speaking) or privation (e.g., silence) is not a thing in extramental reality, but they are things in the mind, "beings of reason," as are future things. Thus they are apprehended as beings, and it is how things are apprehended that matters for rational appetite.

### 8.2. Is *will* only of the end, or also of things that are for the end?

Answer: The *power* of will concerns both the end and things that are for the end; the *act* of will concerns the end.

**Obj.** 1 simply appeals to the well-known Aristotelian dictum that we will ends and choose things that are for the end. **Obj.** 2 relies in a more complicated way on Aristotle's theory of categories. There are different powers for things that belong to different categories, and the end belongs to a different category from things that are for the end, so the power that concerns the end must be a different power from the one that concerns things that are for the end.

To follow **obj.** 3 it is important to know how Aquinas understands power and habits. A power is a capacity for acting. A habit is a characteristic that a power acquires when it is developed so that it acts more readily and reliably in some particular way. For example, I have the power to speak; my practiced ability to speak eloquently and persuasively is a habit that perfects that power. The objection argues that in the case of certain habits, the ones that are called "practical arts," the art that considers the end is a different art from the one that considers what is for the end. Ships are for sailing: the art of shipbuilding concerns what is for the end, the art of navigation concerns the end. So given that there are different habits regarding the end and what is for the end, there must also be different powers (since habits belong to powers); thus, given that the power of will concerns the end, some power other than will must concern what is for the end.

Unusually, the argument **On the contrary** does not cite an authority but introduces a new argument. Though the argument is a perfectly general one about powers, it is easiest to understand if we think specifically about the power to move from one place to another. (This has the added benefit of setting up a comparison that Aquinas will use again and again in the Treatise on Human Acts: the analogy of the "movement" of the will to local motion.) Suppose I walk from my starting-point, A, to my destination, B; along the way I pass through C. The power of walking that I use in order get from A to C is obviously the same power of walking that I use to get from A to B. The end in willing is analogous to the destination in walking, and things that are for the end are analogous to the intermediate places through which I walk. So, by analogy, it is the same power—will—that concerns both the end and things that are for the end.

In his **reply** Aquinas distinguishes again between the power and the act. The power of will concerns both the end and things that are for the end, because any power extends as far as its object is found. The proper object of sight, for example, is color; so everything that "has some share in color" can be seen. The proper object of will is what is good, so everything that is good can be willed. And things that are for the end are good, precisely because they are for the end, which in turn is good in its own right.

The act of will, by contrast, is only of the end. Aquinas's argument is as much terminological as it is conceptual, so in order to understand the argument it is important to know his terminology. In the domain of cognition, certain truths are self-evident—Aquinas calls these "principles"—whereas others become evident only through argument from those self-evident truths. We are said to *understand* (*intelligere*) principles but to have *knowledge* or *science* (*scientia*) of the conclusions derived from them. Principles are cognized in their own right and have truth in their own right; conclusions are cognized in virtue of principles and have truth in virtue of principles. Note that the power of intellect or understanding (*intellectus*) gives its name to its simplest or most basic act (*intelligere*), and that act is directed at what has the object of the power (truth, in this case) in its own right. Aquinas asserts that this relationship holds whenever an act gets its name from a power. So will (the act) must be the simplest and most basic act of will (the power), and that act is directed at what has the object of the power in its own right. The object of the power of will is what is good, and the end is what is good in its own right. What is for the end is good in virtue of the end, not in its own right. So the act of will, strictly speaking, is only of the end, just as the act of understanding is only of principles. Just as we do not speak of understanding conclusions (unless we are thinking about conclusions in light of principles), we do not speak of willing things that are for the end (unless we are thinking about things that are for the end in light of the end: "what the will wills in them is the end"). This analogy between the realm of appetite and the realm of cognition will keep coming back; it is one of the most important ways in which Aquinas develops his account of action.

The distinction between the act of will and the power of will takes care of objection 1. In **resp.** 2, Aquinas says that things that are for the end are not different from the end in a way that would require different powers, as sound and color are different kinds of sensory object and therefore require different sensory powers. Rather, they are related as what has a certain characteristic in its own right ("intrinsically *F*") and what has that same characteristic in virtue of something else ("extrinsically *F*"), and things related in this way are connected with the same power. Aquinas could have illustrated the point at least as well using the example of principles and conclusions from his reply: principles have truth in their own right, conclusions have truth in virtue of principles, but it is the same power, the intellect, that concerns both. Instead he uses another sensory analogy: light is visible in its own right, color is visible in virtue of light, but it is the same power, vision, that concerns both.

**Resp. 3** breaks down the too-sharp separation between ends and what is for the end; some arts deal with both. The captain's art both carries out the end and commands what is for the end; you need someone who understands how navigation works to instruct the shipbuilder about what makes for a good ship. And the shipbuilder's art carries out what is for the end but directs its work toward the end; it builds the ship for the sake of navigation and therefore builds it in a way that will make it seaworthy (and not just in a way that would make it impressive to look at, for example).

### 8.3. Is the will drawn in a single act to both the end and what is for the end?

Answer: Yes, if the will is drawn to what is for the end at all.

The objections all invoke the close relationship of the end and things that are for the end: things for the end are willed *for the sake of* the end (**obj. 1**), the end is the *basis* or *reason* on account of which one wills things for the end (**obj. 2**), and things for the end are the intermediate points along the way to the end (**obj. 3**; note how this argument picks up on the analogy with motion introduced in art. 2 On the contrary). Given this close relationship, the will's motion toward the end should include its motion toward the things that are for the end.

The argument **On the contrary** should seem surprising at this point, because it makes exactly the kind of sharp distinction—a distinction in species—between ends and things that are for the end that Aquinas just rejected in art. 2 resp. 2. And indeed Aquinas will make that very point in his response. The end and what is for the end do not belong to different species of good, as the argument On the contrary supposes, but instead are related as what has a certain characteristic in its own right ("intrinsically *F*") and what has that same characteristic in virtue of something else ("extrinsically *F*").

Aquinas's **reply** builds on the previous article. Recall that an end is willed for its own sake, whereas what is for the end is, as such, willed for the sake of the end. (That "as such" is meant to rule out a case in which something that can be for an end can also be willed as an end. I might will to go for a run for the sake of my health, but if I happen to enjoy running, I might also will to go for a run for its own sake. Aquinas is here analyzing only the first kind of case, in which I will running—what is for the end—for the sake of health— the end.) What that means, then, is that an end is the right sort of thing to move the will in its own right, whereas what is for the end can move the will only in virtue of its connection with the end. So if I will what is for the end, I do so only because I will the end, and that whole willing is a single motion. One might think of it in this way: my willing of what is for the end is not a separate act from my willing of the end precisely because it is, so to speak, *powered by* my willing of the end. (Or think of the analogy with motion: on my road trip from Tampa to Tallahassee I pass through Ocala; there is no separate trip to Ocala.)

So it is not possible to will things for the end without willing the end, but the converse is not true. I can will an end "absolutely," that is, without relating it to any other things that might help me attain that end. I can will health without yet willing to take any particular steps to attain health. If I later deliberate (see Q14 on deliberation) about how I might attain the end, and I come to will some particular way of attaining it (such as consulting a doctor), I am now willing the end in a new way: no longer absolutely, but as the basis for willing what is for the end.

Aquinas does not make a great deal here of this distinction between being drawn to the end absolutely and being drawn to the end as the basis for willing things that are for the end, in part because he's going to assign *intention* as the term for the latter, and intention will get a whole question to itself (Q12). Here he just says enough about the distinction to make two points: (1) one can will the end without willing things that are for the end, and (2) willing the end as the basis for willing things that are for the end is the same motion as willing the things that are for the end. Note that "one motion" need not mean "a single act" as we might normally think of an act. There is a temporally extended process, at the very least. The point is that the willing of the things that are for the end flows from, is powered by, the willing of the end (in the second, non-absolute way) without interruption and without the need for some fresh assessment of the worthiness or desirability of the end. (By "without interruption" I mean without *requiring* interruption. Of course you could will the end of health as something that could be attained by taking certain steps, but then think "Mmm, look, cookies!" and get off track.) Until we have looked at both intention and deliberation, we will not have the full picture of how this "one motion" really goes.

*De veritate* 22.14, which asks this same question, makes the oneness of the "one motion" more clearly dependent on how the end is *regarded*, and thus on the intellect's consideration of the end. It is a very slight difference in emphasis, not, it appears, a difference in teaching.

The **responses** to the objections and to the argument On the contrary all follow straightforwardly from what Aquinas says in the reply.

### Question 9: What Moves the Will

#### 9.1. Is the will moved by the intellect?

Answer: The intellect moves the will in terms of specification; the will moves the intellect in terms of exercise.

Aquinas begins his **reply** by explaining what is meant by 'move.' To move something is to bring it from potentiality to actuality. (Notice, then, that 'move' has a much broader sense in Aquinas's philosophical vocabulary than it does in contemporary English.) The will is in potentiality, so it needs something to move it. And there are two different ways in which the will, like other powers of the soul, is in potentiality: (1) with respect to acting and not acting, which Aquinas calls the *exercise* of the act; and (2) with respect to doing this or that, which Aquinas calls the *specification* or *determination* of the act. This distinction between exercise and specification is crucial throughout Q9, so it is important to have it quite clear from the outset. Aquinas gives a helpful example in the first paragraph of his reply. Thinking provides another example: I can think or not think (exercise), and I can think about x or think about y (specification).

We look first at exercise. A power of the soul acts because some agent moves it to act. And every agent acts on account of an end, as we saw in 1.2. So ultimately it is an end that moves a power to exercise. Something is an end because it is good. Now the object of the will is not just this good or that good; it is the good in general. This means that *every* end falls within the scope of the will's object. As Aquinas puts it, "the ends and perfections of all the other powers are included in the object of the will as particular goods." So, given that agents move powers to exercise their acts for the sake of some end, and the ends of all the powers of the soul are included in the will's object, it follows that the will moves the other powers of the soul to the exercise of their acts. (Yes, but does the will move *itself* to the exercise of its act? Aquinas leaves this question hanging for now; he takes it up in art. 3.) In terms of exercise, then, the will is not moved by the intellect. Quite the contrary: the intellect is moved by the will. In terms of specification, however, the intellect moves the will. The intellect is what presents the object—remember the crucial point that will is *intellectual* appetite, and so we will things *as apprehended*—and the object is what "specifies" the act. That is, willing *x* is a different *kind* (species) of act from willing *y*. So the specification of the act comes from the intellect.

Aquinas also uses the language of the four Aristotelian causes to make these points. A *formal* cause is what "makes" something the kind of thing it is, in the sense of 'make' that I use when I say that the shape of a piece of metal is what makes it a key and a certain biological structure is what makes something a cat. (Aquinas's somewhat obscure example should be explained in this same way: it is heat that makes a given motion a case of heating, as opposed to a case of turning blue or a case of getting fat.) The object is a formal cause of an act of will: it makes the act the kind of act it is. By presenting the object, then, the intellect supplies the formal cause of an act of will and thereby specifies the act. The exercise of the act, by contrast, depends on an *efficient* (or *agent*) cause, which brings about the act for the sake of some end. (Ends are *final* causes, though Aquinas does not use that expression here.) As we have already seen, the will's scope as agent cause is, at least in theory, unlimited, because its object is the good in general, which includes the goodness of every end. In the same way, the intellect's scope as formal cause is also, again in theory, unlimited, because its object is being and truth in general, which includes the being and truth of every object.

**Obj. and resp. 1** and **obj. and resp. 2** clarify a few further details. To the objection that the will does not move the intellect, because if it did, we would always gladly do what we know to be right—which is contrary to Augustine and, alas, to personal experience—Aquinas replies that this merely shows that the intellect does not move the will *by necessity*. **Resp. 2** is important because it makes clear that it is not just any presentation of an object by the intellect that moves the will: it is a presentation of the object *as good and desirable*. This is what we should expect, given that the object of the will is the good in general. If the intellect presents an object as, say, true (or yellow, or three-sided, or whatever), but not as good, the object does not fall within the scope of the will and so the will is not moved.

All of this general theory—about exercise and specification, about formal and agent causality, about the respective objects of the will and the intellect—will continue to be important as Aquinas answers further questions. But at this point he has applied that theory only to show that the intellect moves the will in terms of specification and the will moves the intellect in terms of exercise. We have yet to see what moves the will in terms of exercise, and there remains the possibility that other things besides the intellect also move the will in terms of specification.

## 9.2. Is the will moved by the sensory appetite?

Answer: Yes, in terms of specification, when the sensory appetite makes something appear suitable.

**Reply.** That Aquinas is talking about specification and not exercise is clear from the fact that he begins by speaking of what moves the will "as an object." We have already learned that it is the intellect that presents the will with its object, so it might seem that there is nothing for the sensory appetite to do in terms of specification. But Aquinas's understanding of human psychology is more subtle than that. What moves the will, he notes, is what is apprehended as good and suitable. And 'suitable' is a relational expression: object *x* is suitable for person *y*. So whether something is suitable, or apprehended as suitable, will depend not only on the object but also on the person. (The "extremes" of a relation are simply the things that are related. For example, if Socrates is similar to Plato, Socrates and Plato are the extremes of this relation of similarity.) Hence Aristotle remarks that "how the end appears to someone depends on what sort of condition he or she is in." The relevant condition might be a fairly stable state of character, but it could also be the more transient sort of condition that Aquinas calls a passion. Passions—for example, anger, fear, sorrow, joy—belong to the sensory appetite, but they can affect the way we see things. As Aquinas says, "something seems good to one who is angry that would not seem good to one who is calm." Thus, because the passions of the sensory appetite can affect our judgment of what is suitable, and our judgment of what is suitable provides the object that specifies the will, the sensory appetite can move the will in terms of specification.

The first two objections are especially important because they rely on contrasts between the sensory appetite and the intellectual appetite, or will, that Aquinas himself clearly accepts. **Obj. 1** notes that sensory appetite is inferior to will, just as sense is inferior to intellect, and argues from Augustine that what is inferior does not move what is superior, but vice versa. In **resp. 1** Aquinas agrees that the will is more excellent than the sensory appetite in an unqualified sense, but when someone is experiencing a passion, the sensory appetite is "preeminent." As we will learn in 10.3, he does not mean that the sensory appetite overrides the will or that it prevents the intellect from considering the object in a more reasonable, less passionate way. But the sensory appetite does strongly color the way in which someone experiencing a passion apprehends an object, and it is much easier to judge, and therefore to will, in the way that sensory appetite inclines than to consider an object dispassionately when one is in under the sway of a passion.

**Obj. 2** notes that sensory appetite, like sense, is concerned with particulars, whereas intellectual appetite, like intellect, is concerned with universals, and argues that as a particular power, the sensory appetite cannot bring about a universal effect, such as a motion of the will. Again, Aquinas agrees with this way of distinguishing sense and its appetite from intellect and its appetite; but he argues in **resp. 2** that this distinction actually tells in favor of the influence of sensory appetite over acts of will, because human acts and choices concern particulars. So sensory appetite, which can affect the way we think about the very particulars that our acts and choices deal with, "has considerable power to dispose people in such a way that things appear this way or that way."

In I-II.77.1 Aquinas says that a passion of the sensory appetite can also affect the movement of the will by, in effect, draining the soul's resources. "All the powers of the soul," he explains, "are rooted in a single essence." Consequently, "when the act of one power is particularly intense, the act of another power must become less intense or even be impeded altogether. . . . [So] when a movement of the sensory appetite is strengthened by a passion, the proper motion of the rational appetite, which is the will, must become less intense or even be impeded altogether."

### 9.3. Does the will move itself?

Answer: Yes. By willing the end, the will moves itself to will what is for the end.

Aquinas now takes up the question he left hanging in art. 1: does the will move itself? **Obj. 1** explains why self-motion should be impossible—not just for the will but for anything. Movers are in actuality; things moved are in potentiality. And by definition nothing is both in potentiality and in actuality with respect to the same thing at the same time.

But "with respect to the same thing" is crucial here. There is no absurdity in something's being in potentiality in one respect and in actuality in some other respect: at the moment I am in potentiality with respect to translating Scotus and in actuality with respect to commenting on Aquinas. The will that moves itself is in actuality with respect to willing an end and is in potentiality with respect to willing things that are for the end; by actually willing an end, it brings itself from potentially willing things that are for the end to actually willing them. How exactly this self-motion on the part of the will works is not further explained here; it will turn out to involve important contributions from the intellect, particularly in the form of deliberation (art. 4, and at length in Q14) and judgment (13.1 resp. 2).

In his **reply** Aquinas reminds us that the will moves other powers in virtue of its object, the end. Oddly, he does not argue directly from this that the will also moves itself in virtue of the end. Rather, he returns to his analogy between the domain of appetite and the domain of cognition. An end is to appetite what a principle is to cognition. In the domain of cognition, it is clear that the intellect moves itself from cognizing principles to cognizing conclusions that are derived from the principles. (You might think this is actually not clear at all. For surely the will has to contribute something by directing the intellect to draw those conclusions; otherwise every intellect that cognized a principle would inevitably cognize the conclusions as well, which is clearly false. "We understand when we want to," as we read in 9.1 obj. 3, and we also derive conclusions when we want to. But Aquinas's point is simply that cognition of conclusions is in a sense "contained in" cognition of the principle, and so it is in virtue of its cognition of the principle that intellect brings itself to cognize conclusions.) In the same way, the will moves itself from willing the end to willing what is for the end. (And just as the will has something to contribute to the intellect's self-motion, the intellect has something to contribute to the will's self-motion.)

In art. 1 and 2 Aquinas was concerned with what moves the will in terms of specification; here he finally addresses what moves the will in terms of exercise. In the argument **On the contrary** he makes it clear that the will *must* have the power to move itself to the exercise of its act; otherwise it would not be in control of its own act. Note, however, that Aquinas's reply argues only that the will moves itself with respect to willing what is for the end, which means that at this point he has established only that the will is in control of its willing what is for the end. Is it also in control of its willing the end itself? For the answer to this we must wait for art. 6.

### 9.4. Is the will moved by any external principle?

Answer: Yes. The will is moved by an external object in terms of specification; it is also moved by God in terms of exercise, because God gives the will its initial impetus toward what is good.

**Obj. 1 & 2** make the important contrast between an internal principle (source of motion) and an external principle. By definition, what is voluntary is from an internal principle (6.1); and obviously the movement of the will (*voluntas*) is voluntary (*voluntarius*). By contrast, what is violent is from an external principle, and it has already been established that no violence can be done to the will (6.4). So it seems that the source of the will's motion can only be internal to the will, not external. **Obj. 3** argues that the will's own self-motion is sufficient; the will needs no other mover.

In the argument **On the contrary** Aquinas notes the (by now) well-established fact that the will is moved by its object, and obviously the will's object can be something external that comes to the awareness of the senses. So it follows straightforwardly that the will can be moved by something external. This is movement with respect to specification. But Aquinas goes further in his **reply**, arguing that the will is also moved by an external object with respect to exercise. The will is not always actually willing—in other words, not always actually exercising its act—and we know that whatever goes from potentiality to actuality requires a mover. So the will needs something to move it from potentially willing to actually willing. In the case of willing what is for the end, we know that the will moves itself to its exercise (art. 3); as Aquinas now tells us, this requires intervening deliberation. I will health; I deliberate about how to achieve health and conclude that I can be healed by a doctor; as a result I will to consult a doctor. But what about my willing of the end? There too I have gone from potentiality to actuality; I was not always willing health. What moved me to will health? Perhaps my will did: in the same way that my will moves itself from willing the end of health to willing a consultation with the doctor as something for that end (a means to the end), perhaps it moved itself from willing some larger end—say, a life that is satisfying on the whole—to willing health as something for that end (a component or ingredient of the end). Possibly. But then what moved me to will that larger end? We cannot have an infinite regress of deliberation and self-movement; there has to be some initial mover. So, Aquinas concludes, "the will inaugurates its first movement thanks to the impetus of some external mover," which in art. 6 he will identify as God.

How can Aquinas acknowledge an external source of motion—whether the object, in terms of specification, or God, in terms of exercise—without running afoul of the worries about voluntariness and violence raised in the first two objections? He argues in **resp. 1** that voluntariness requires only that there be a *proximate* source of motion in the will, not that the will be the *ultimate* or *exclusive* source of motion. And he says in **resp. 2** that a violent motion is not merely one with an external principle, but one in which the thing moved contributes nothing to the motion. Yes, the will is moved by something external, but it contributes something to the motion: it actually does the willing. Furthermore, a violent motion is one that is contrary to the natural inclination of the thing moved; but when the will wills something, it always wills in accordance with its natural inclination to what is good.

As for **resp. 3**, we have already seen that the will cannot be its own sufficient mover. As something that is brought from potentiality to actuality, it requires something else to move it.

### 9.5. Is the will moved by a heavenly body?

Answer: Yes, but only with respect to specification.

However odd this question might sound to us—is Aquinas really worried about something like astrology?—he takes it very seriously, as the large number of parallel discussions in other works attests. To understand this question better, it is helpful to have an overview of the medieval cosmos. I take these descriptions, first of the structure of the medieval cosmos and second of its operation, from C. S. Lewis's *The Discarded Image*,[6] an indispensable resource for anyone who wishes to understand "the harmonious mental Model of the Universe"[7] that shapes philosophy, theology, and literature in the Middle Ages:

> The central (and spherical) Earth is surrounded by a series of hollow and transparent globes, one above the other, and each of course larger than the one below. These are the 'spheres', 'heavens', or (sometimes) 'elements'. Fixed in each of the first seven spheres is one luminous body. Starting from Earth, the order is the Moon, Mercury, Venus, the Sun, Mars, Jupiter and Saturn; the 'seven planets'. Beyond the sphere of Saturn is the *Stellatum*, to which belong all those stars that we still call 'fixed' because their positions relative to one another are, unlike those of the planets, invariable. Beyond the *Stellatum* there is a sphere called the First Movable or *Primum Mobile*. This, since it carries no luminous body, gives no evidence of itself to our senses; its existence was inferred to account for the motions of all the others.[8]

> All power, movement, and efficacy descend from God to the *Primum Mobile* and cause it to rotate. . . . The rotation of the *Primum Mobile* causes that of the *Stellatum*, which causes that of the sphere of Saturn, and so on, down to the last moving sphere, that of the Moon. . . . Besides movement, the spheres transmit (to the Earth) what are called Influences—the subject-matter of Astrology. . . . The statement that the medieval Church frowned upon this discipline is often taken in a sense that makes it untrue. Orthodox theologians could accept the theory that the planets had an effect on events and on psychology, and, much more, on plants and minerals.[9]

What the Church fought against, Lewis says, were three things: "the lucrative, and politically undesirable, practice of astrologically grounded predictions," "astrological determinism," and "practices that might seem to imply or encourage the worship of planets."[10] The discussion in this article, then, reveals Aquinas to be well within the mainstream of orthodox medieval theologians, willing to acknowledge considerable influence from the heavenly bodies but steadfastly opposed to astrological determinism.

In the **reply** Aquinas acknowledges two ways in which heavenly bodies can move the will in terms of specification. The first is "insofar as external bodies that are presented to sense move the will": for example, I see the full moon and decide to enjoy its beauty. The second is "insofar as the organs of

---

6. Lewis (1964).

7. Ibid., 11.

8. Ibid., 96.

9. Ibid., 102–3.

10. Ibid., 103–4.

the sensory powers are subordinate to the movements of heavenly bodies." In **resp. 3** he provides some further details of what he means by this second way: impressions from the heavenly bodies can cause "people to be prone to anger or lust or some other passion." (Consider the words 'mercurial,' 'martial,' 'jovial,' and 'saturnine,' which name traits once thought to derive from the influence of the planets Mercury, Mars, Jupiter [=Jove], and Saturn.)

But can heavenly bodies also move the will to the exercise of its act? No, Aquinas maintains, because the will is immaterial. Aquinas holds that reason, unlike such powers of the soul as vision, hearing, and imagination, is not tied to any bodily organ. (For his reasoning, see I.75.2.) "The will is in reason," as Aquinas likes to quote from *De anima* III, so what is true of reason is true of will: it is a "completely immaterial and non-bodily power." And no material thing can act on an immaterial thing, so no heavenly body can act on the will. But recall that the will can be moved by the sensory appetite, which *is* material. So a heavenly body can move the will indirectly by moving a human body in such a way as to produce a passion in the sensory appetite; this, as we saw earlier, is movement with respect to specification, not with respect to exercise. Such influence from the heavenly bodies is pervasive enough, Aquinas argues (**resp. 3**), to explain why astrologers are frequently able to make correct predictions (though he does not rule out Augustine's view attributing their success to demonic activity). Heavenly bodies produce passions, and most people follow their passions, so it is not surprising that those who understand the influence of the heavenly bodies can predict what most people will do. Only the wise, who are few, resist their passions and live by reason, which (as we have seen) is not within the domain of bodily causes and effects. Thus, as Ptolemy said, "The wise rule the stars": they resist their passions and thereby escape the causal influence of the heavenly bodies.

In I.115.4 Aquinas argues that the heavenly bodies have more influence on the intellect than they do on the will. True, the intellect, like the will, is immaterial, so there can be no direct influence from the heavenly bodies; but they can influence the material powers—the imaginative, cogitative, and memorative powers—that provide the intellect with its input. Given the intellect's dependence on these material powers, if they are disturbed the intellect will inevitably be disturbed as well. But the will is not dependent in the same way on the passions of the sensory appetite: "they have a certain power to incline the will, but the will retains its power either to follow those passions or to resist them." This argument is a particularly striking example of Aquinas's willingness to acknowledge considerable influence from the heavenly bodies while making no room for astrological determinism.

### 9.6. Does only God move the
### will as an external principle?

Answer: With respect to exercise, yes.

I throw a stone up in the air. I thereby move the stone: but this is a violent movement, one that is contrary to the natural inclination of the stone toward the center of the earth. So I can cause a violent movement—can I likewise cause a natural movement? You might think that if I let go of a stone so that it falls to the earth, I have caused its natural movement; but in fact I have merely allowed its natural movement to take place. (In more Aristotelian language, I have removed an impediment to its natural movement.) I did not cause its natural movement; only the one who caused its nature causes its natural movement.

The analogy between the stone and its natural inclination, on the one hand, and a human being and the inclination of the will, on the other, is not exact, and the argument becomes messy at this point. In trying to follow Aquinas's **reply**, it helps to make explicit the distinction between exercise and specification that is implicit in his argument. No such distinction applies to the stone: it can move or not move (exercise), but it cannot move this way or that (specification), because its natural inclination is to one direction only. With that fact in mind, then, we know that when he turns to the will, Aquinas is asking what can move the human will with respect to exercise. Obviously human beings can be moved by external principles with respect to specification, but only what causes the will's natural inclination to what is good can move the will with respect to exercise. Aquinas has two arguments for the claim that only God can be the cause of the will. First, the will is a power of the rational soul, and only God causes the rational soul, which unlike animal souls is not generated through natural processes but is directly created by God (I.90.2 and 3). Second, the will's inclination is to the universal good. No particular good—no particular cause of any kind—can confer a universal inclination; only God, the universal good, can confer such an inclination.

This is why, contrary to **obj. 1 & 2**, angels cannot move the human will to the exercise of its act. Yes, angels are superior to human beings, but not as causes of their very nature (**resp. 1**); and they can move the human will by illuminating the human intellect, but that is movement in terms of specification (**resp. 2**). Elsewhere Aquinas uses the same reasoning to argue that an angel cannot move another angel's will (I.106.2): an exercise of an angelic will is an inclination on the part of the angel's will, and only the one who bestowed on the angel the power to will in the first place can change the inclination of that power. An angel can, of course, propose an object to another angel and thus have a role in moving the other angel in terms of specification, but not exercise. (For example, Aquinas says, "One angel can induce another angel to love God, by way of persuasion" [resp. 2]. One would be interested in knowing how such a conversation might go.) Similarly, the devil (who is, after all, a fallen angel) cannot directly cause a sinful exercise of the human will (I-II.80.1); he can only move the human will by way of specification, by presenting an object or persuading someone that the presented object is in some way desirable. Angels can also rouse passions (I.111.2), which is another way in which they can move the human will by way of specification.[11]

Obj. 3 argues that if only God moved the human will to act, it would never be moved toward anything bad. To this Aquinas replies (**resp. 3**) that God moves the human will as a universal mover. That is, he gives the human will its inclination to the universal good; without that universal inclination the will could not will anything at all. But we determine ourselves to will this or that through reason, and our reason can be mistaken about what is good. That is how the will's God-given inclination to the universal good is consistent with particular instances of bad willing.

Aquinas goes even further in **resp. 3** by saying that in addition to bestowing this universal inclination to the good, God also "sometimes . . . specially moves certain people to will some particular thing that is good, as in people whom he moves by grace." In his discussion of this issue in *DV* 22.8 Aquinas asks whether God's changing the will in this way constitutes *coactio*— coercion or compulsion—and concludes that it does not. God can cause you to want something you did not want before; he can also add an inclination (grace, a virtue) to incline you toward something you were not inclined to before. If the inclination is perfect, as is the perfect charity of those who enjoy the beatific vision, it necessitates in the same way that the natural inclination toward the ultimate end is necessitating; and that, as we saw in 6.4, is not a kind of coercion. By contrast, if the inclination is imperfect, as in the case of those who are still in this present life, it inclines but does not necessitate.

## Question 10: How the Will Is Moved

Q9 was about *what* moves the will; Q10 is about *how* what moves the will moves the will. In particular, it is about whether the will is moved *naturally* or *necessarily*. Those might sound like the same thing, but they are not. "Naturally" is contrasted with "voluntarily" or with "violently"; "necessarily" is contrasted with "contingently" (but also with "voluntarily"). These distinctions can cut across each other. In art. 1 the question is whether the will is moved *toward* anything naturally; in the other articles the question is whether the will is moved *by* various movers necessarily. Basically, art. 1 is asking whether the will is itself a determinate nature, whether it has a built-in dynamism or

---

11. For the way in which the will is moved by passions, see art. 2.

tendency. The answer is yes: the will is not a neutral steering wheel but an inclination toward what is good. Art. 2–4 are asking whether anything necessitates the will. The answer is that (apart from those who are deprived of the use of reason altogether) only an object that appears good no matter how one looks at it moves the will necessarily, and then only with respect to specification, not with respect to exercise.

You might wonder in connection with art. 2–4 exactly how Aquinas understands necessitation. What is his modal theory here—that is, his theory of necessity and possibility? I will take up that crucial question in the commentary on 10.4.

### 10.1. Is the will moved toward anything naturally?

Answer: Yes, the will is moved naturally to the good in general and to the ultimate end, as well as to the goods of powers other than the will.

As the objections make clear, 'nature,' 'natural,' and 'naturally' have a range of meanings and a range of implications. Aquinas's first task in his **reply**, therefore, is to clarify how he understands the word 'naturally' in this question. The sense familiar from Aristotle's *Physics*, in which 'nature' means an internal principle of motion in moveable things, does not apply here. A 'nature' in that sense is either matter or a material form (that is, the form of a material thing), and we already know that the will is in no way material. But there is a broader sense of 'nature' that does apply to the will: "'nature' means any substance, or even any being." (The will is not a substance, because it does not exist in its own right but rather is a power of something that it exists in its own right; it is, however, a being.) In this sense, we say that what is in a nature *per se*—in its own right, rather than through something else—is natural to that thing and is also the principle, the ultimate source or explanation or foundation, for whatever is in the nature and is *not* in it *per se*. "And so," Aquinas concludes, "taking nature in this sense, it must be the case without exception that the principle of whatever characterizes a thing is natural."

This needlessly convoluted argument is made somewhat more straightforward in the second paragraph, when Aquinas returns to his standing analogy between intellect and will. Just as the principles of intellectual cognition are naturally known, the principle of voluntary movements is naturally willed. Note that Aquinas says the *principle*—singular—of voluntary movements, even though he proceeds to list three things: (1) the good in general, which is the will's object; (2) the ultimate end, which (as we have repeatedly seen) plays in the appetitive realm a role analogous to first principles in the cognitive realm; and (3) "in general, all those things that are suitable to those who will in virtue of their nature," which includes the goods of powers other than the will, such as cognition of the truth, being, living, and other aspects of our well-being.

What are we to make of this apparently disparate collection of things we will naturally, all identified as a single principle of voluntary movements? Perhaps nothing much hangs on the fact that 'principle' here is singular, but we can make sense of that fact by focusing on the object of the will, the good in general. In the ultimate end, happiness, the will's object is fully realized, without limitation or deficiency; in other ends, the will's object is realized, not so fully that the will *has* to will any of those things concretely and here and now, but realized to some degree, so that they fall within the scope of the object of the will's natural inclination. (See art. 2 for more on this contrast between the ultimate end, which is willed not only naturally but necessarily, and other goods, which are willed naturally but not necessarily.) Recall also that according to 1.6 non-ultimate ends derive their power to move the will from the ultimate end: they would have no power to move the will at all if the will were not naturally inclined to the ultimate end. By mentioning "all those things that are suitable to those who will in virtue of their nature," Aquinas reminds us that such objects as life, health, and truth move our wills naturally, that is, in accordance with the characteristic inclination that makes the will the kind of thing (nature) it is; but by mentioning the ultimate end and the good in general, he emphasizes that the ultimate source of this variety of motions is in fact a single object, the good in general, which is fully realized in the ultimate end, which in turn serves as the source of the motive power of all other ends.

The objections and responses further clarify what is meant by saying that something is willed naturally. In **resp. 1** Aquinas argues that the contrast between will and nature should not be read as a contrast between two different kinds of agents, as **obj. 1** had argued, but rather between two different ways of causing an act. Nature's distinctive mode of causation is determined to a single outcome, whereas the will's distinctive mode of causation is not so determined; rather, when the will causes in its distinctive way, it is in control of its own act. But the will does not always cause in its distinctive way, because the will is rooted in a nature and therefore also shares ("participates") in nature's way of causing. First the will *is* a certain kind of thing, with a certain inclination that characterizes it as that kind of thing; only then, and as a result of that inclination, can it be in control of the way it acts on that inclination. That is what Aquinas means by the admittedly cryptic phrase, "its being, which is from nature, is prior to its willing, which is from the will."

**Obj. 2** had argued that no movement is natural to the will, because what is natural to a thing is always present in that thing—heat is natural to fire, so fire is always hot—and no movement is always present in the will. Aquinas responds (**resp. 2**) that only what is natural because it follows from the form is always present; what is natural because it follows from the matter is not always present. Form corresponds to actuality: a form, recall, is what makes something what it is. So if some characteristic is a result of the form of the thing, that thing will always have that characteristic. Matter, by contrast, corresponds to potentiality: matter accounts not just for what a thing is but for what it can be. So a characteristic that results from the matter of a thing need not always be present in that thing: in virtue of its matter, fire has the potentiality to move upward. It does not always move upward, however, but only when it is away from its natural place; yet its movement upward is still a natural movement. Now the will is not material, but it does have potentiality; it has to be brought from potentially willing to actually willing. That movement is not always in the will, but like the analogous movement of fire, it is nonetheless a natural movement.

**Resp. 3** further develops the implications of the will's immateriality. The slogan "nature is determined to one" turns out to be misleading, because an immaterial nature corresponds to one *universal*, not to one particular, as the objection assumed. The will corresponds to one universal, the good, just as the intellect corresponds to one universal, the true. That one universal good includes many particular goods, and the will is not determined to any of them, which is how the will is, as the objection correctly said, "open to opposites."

### 10.2. Is the will moved necessarily by its object?

Answer: In terms of exercise, the will is not moved necessarily by any object. In terms of specification, it is moved necessarily only by an object that has no deficiency, namely, happiness.

The question is whether the will is moved necessarily by its object, and since the will is moved in two ways—in terms of exercise and in terms of specification—we must ask about both. Aquinas's treatment of the question here is less thorough than his roughly contemporaneous discussion in *De malo* 6, so I shall use that other discussion to flesh out what is said here. (Both *ST* I-II and *DM* 6 date from Aquinas's second regency at Paris, 1268–1272.)

Aquinas begins his **reply** by arguing that *no* object moves the will necessarily in terms of *exercise*, "because one can just not think about a given object, and consequently one will not actually will it." I do not necessarily will health, because I do not necessarily think about health, and (as we have seen again and again) willing depends on the intellect's presentation of something as good. I do not necessarily will even the ultimate end, because I do not necessarily think about the ultimate end.

Recall that it is not only the object[12] that moves the will to its exercise; the will also moves itself to its exercise (9.3). Aquinas does not ask here whether

---

12. In 9.1 Aquinas says that the object moves the will in terms of *specification*, whereas the *end* is what moves the will in terms of exercise. Is he being inconsistent here? No. An object-presented-as-good is an end—or, to put it in a way that comes closer to Aquinas's own formulation, the end is the object of the will in the same way that sound is the object of hearing.

the will's self-motion is ever necessary, but he does take up that question in *DM* 6. His argument there is that the will moves itself through deliberation. Deliberation is a kind of inquiry, and indeed an inquiry that has no predetermined outcome; "rather," he says, "it offers an open road to opposite destinations."[13] So there is no necessity in the will's self-motion either.

So Aquinas does not recognize any way in which the will is moved necessarily to the *exercise* of its act. He does, however, acknowledge one way in which it is moved necessarily to the *specification* of its act. The will's object is what is good—and here it is particularly important to remember that this means what is good *as presented by the intellect*. So if there is an object "that is not good if you look at it in some particular way," the possibility of not willing that object remains open. The intellect can present such an object as good or as lacking in goodness, and accordingly the will can will it (as good) or not will it (as lacking in goodness). Only if there is some object that is good "no matter how you look at it" does the will necessarily will that object. The only such object is happiness, the total and complete good, which lacks any deficiency.

Now return to the two examples of goods that we used in discussing necessity with respect to exercise: health and happiness. Health is good, and indeed Aquinas said in art. 1 that we will it naturally. We have already seen that we do not will it necessarily, because we do not think about it necessarily. But supposing we do think about it, must we then will it? No, according to Aquinas. For although health is good, it is not good "no matter how you look at it." I might think of health as good in itself, or as pleasant, or as gratifyingly impressive to other people; but I might also think of it as imposing burdensome requirements like exercise and reducing my intake of fried foods. Thus I can regard health as good under certain descriptions but as not-good under other descriptions, and therefore my will can either approve it or reject it accordingly. Why does one description or condition rather than another move the will? In *DM* 6 Aquinas offers three possible explanations:

> In one way, this happens insofar as one condition is [objectively] more important than another. In such a case the will is moved in accordance with reason: for example, when someone chooses what is useful for health in preference to what is useful to the will. It happens in another way insofar as someone thinks about one particular circumstance and not another; this happens quite often because some internal or external prompting brings such a thought to mind. And there is a third way it happens: because of someone's disposition. For according to the Philosopher, "How the end appears to someone depends on what sort of condition he or she is in." This is why the will of someone who is angry is moved differently from the will of someone who is calm.

---

13. That is a somewhat expansive translation of *sed ad opposita viam habens,* "but having a way to opposites."

But what about happiness itself? We do not will it necessarily, because we do not think about it necessarily. But supposing we do think about it, must we then will it? Aquinas does not answer this question here in so many words, but **resp. 3** gives a strong hint that his answer is in fact yes. Happiness is the complete and perfect good; there is nothing about it that lacks goodness, and therefore no description under which the intellect can present it so that the will is not drawn to it. And because "the ultimate end moves the will necessarily," anything that is indispensable for attaining that end will also move the will necessarily. Note, however, that the ultimate end moves the will necessarily only when the intellect *conceives* the ultimate end in its fullness, *as* a complete and perfect good with no deficiency. And such a conception would amount to the vision of God, which no human being in this life possesses (5.3).

### 10.3. Is the will moved necessarily by the lower appetite?

Answer: No. If a passion of the lower appetite is completely in control, reason is incapacitated and so there is no movement of will; if reason is not incapacitated, there is some movement of will, and a passion in the sensory appetite does not move the will necessarily.

In 9.2 Aquinas argued that a passion of the sensory appetite moves the will with respect to specification: "insofar as one is oriented in a certain way by a passion, one judges something to be suitable and good that one would not see as suitable or good if one were not undergoing that passion." The question now is whether a passion moves the will in this way *necessarily*. We saw in art. 2 that reason's ability to consider objects in different ways is what keeps the will from being moved necessarily with respect to specification. So, does reason retain the ability to consider an object in different ways when someone is under the influence of a passion? Maybe, but maybe not, Aquinas says (**reply**). There are cases in which the passion is so overwhelming that reason is simply incapacitated; someone actually goes crazy from lust or anger. Or perhaps the physical disturbance involved in an extreme passion prevents reason from engaging in the kind of thought that would be needed to resist the passion. (You might wonder at this point why Aquinas would think that physical changes could affect thinking, since he has emphasized so strongly that the intellect is not material. But he knows perfectly well that a blow to the head or drunkenness or sleep can interfere with thought, and he has an explanation for this fact: although thinking is not strictly speaking the activity of a material organ, it does require the use of certain resources, called "phantasms," which are provided by a power that *is* dependent on a material organ. See *ST* I.84.7 and 8.) If reason is incapacitated by passion in either of these ways, the passion moves necessarily: but it does not move *the will* necessarily, because there is no movement of will at all. Will is rational appetite, so if there is no movement of reason, there is no movement of will.

The other possibility is that reason is not totally incapacitated by the passion. In that case, the argument of 9.2 applies straightforwardly again here. In my angry condition, lashing out at my colleague seems good and suitable to me; but my reason retains its ability to consider such lashing out not as good and suitable but as wrong or unwise or unworthy of my professional dignity, and so my will does not necessarily act as passion inclines me to act.

In short, if a passion of the sensory appetite moves necessarily, it does so because reason is incapacitated, and so there is no movement of will at all; if reason is not incapacitated, it retains its ability to consider an object in different ways, and so the will is not moved necessarily.

In responding to **obj. 1**, which quotes Paul's famous observation, "the evil that I hate, that is what I do," Aquinas insists (**resp. 1**) that 'do' must mean "desire." That is, Paul may not be able to stop the passion of desire from arising, but he can "will not to have the desire, or not consent to the desire," and therefore his desire will not necessarily move his will. Whether this is a convincing reading of Paul is another question.[14] What matters here is not whether it is at all plausible to suppose that Paul is using 'do' to mean "desire," but how Aquinas understands the relationship between reason and passion. In **resp. 2** Aquinas says that in a virtuous person the sensory part is completely responsive to reason: the virtuous person desires only what it is rational to desire, is angry only about what it is rational to be angry about (and only to the degree that it is rational to be angry), and so forth. In a crazy person the sensory part overwhelms reason. For most people, however, in that very wide and well-populated region between virtue and insanity, passion and reason can be at odds; then there is disharmony within the soul, and one and the same thing appears two different ways to the same person at the same time. **Resp. 3** emphasizes that reason alone can move the will. We do not need a passion to move us, as is "especially clear" in the case of those who experience disharmony within the soul and yet act as reason dictates and resist passion.

---

14. In his commentary on Romans (ch. 7, l.3), Aquinas offers two possible interpretations of "the evil that I hate, that is what I do." If Paul is speaking in the *persona* of a sinner, Aquinas says, the "hate" to which he refers is *incomplete* or *imperfect* hate, "in keeping with the way that all human beings hate evil," whereas "I do" refers to a fully carried-out action. But if he is speaking in the *persona* of someone who is under grace (the interpretation Aquinas prefers), the "hate" is *complete* or *perfect* hate, in which someone persists "to the point of utterly rejecting the evil," and "I do" refers to incomplete or imperfect action, "which consists exclusively in concupiscence on the part of the sensory appetite." The second interpretation is clearly the one that Aquinas adopts here.

## 10.4. Is the will moved necessarily by God?

Answer: No, except with respect to things toward which it is moved naturally. The will is a contingent cause, and God accordingly moves the will in such a way that its movement remains contingent and not necessary.

The case for thinking that the will is moved necessarily by God—assuming that the will is moved by God at all—would seem to be extremely strong. The objections articulate this case unflinchingly. God is infinitely powerful, and infinite power cannot be resisted (**obj. 1**). What God wills for something is natural for that thing, and we already know that the will is moved necessarily toward whatever it wills naturally (**obj. 2**). If the will were not moved necessarily by God, it would be possible for the will not to will something toward which God moved it, which is obviously absurd (**obj. 3**).

Unfortunately, Aquinas's case for holding that the will is *not* moved necessarily by God is far less straightforward. It depends crucially on his modal theory—his understanding of necessity, possibility, and contingency—which is, at the very least, puzzling. In *SCG* I.67 Aquinas says, "what is contingent differs from what is necessary by the way in which they are in their cause: what is contingent is in its cause in such a way that it can exist from that cause and not exist from that cause, whereas what is necessary cannot fail to exist from its cause." In other words, suppose cause $C$ brings about effect $E$. If $E$ cannot fail to come about from $C$, then $E$ is necessary; but if $E$ can fail to come about from $C$, then $E$ is contingent. Now let $E$ be a movement of the will and $C$ be God's causing that movement of the will. Shouldn't that be necessary by this definition? Surely Aquinas would say that what God wills cannot fail to come about.

But this is not how Aquinas reasons. Quoting from pseudo-Dionysius the Areopagite, he says that "The role of divine providence is not to destroy the nature of things but to preserve it." God does not merely move all things; he moves them in the way that is appropriate for their natures. God moves necessary causes in such a way that their effects follow necessarily, and he moves contingent causes in such a way that their effects follow contingently. We already know that the will is a contingent cause: it is open to opposites, not determined necessarily to a single outcome. So, Aquinas says, we can conclude that God moves the will in such a way that the will's effects follow from it contingently, in accordance with its nature, and not necessarily.

If it is not immediately clear why this claim is puzzling, consider an example. Take a particular movement of the will: at 3:30 pm on October 16, 2014, I choose to spend one more hour writing on Aquinas rather than going home early and getting a jump on cocktail hour. Call that movement of the will $M$. Now suppose that God moved my will to $M$. Aquinas is saying that $M$ is contingent, because (1) it is a movement of the will, (2) the will is a contingent cause, and (3) God moves contingent causes in such a way that their effects follow from them contingently. But recall the definition of contingent: what is contingent is in its cause in such a way that it can either exist from that cause or not exist from that cause. If *God* is the cause of M, it is simply not true that M can either exist from that cause or not exist from that cause. Aquinas himself admits in **resp. 3** that "If God moves the will toward something, it is impossible *given this supposition* for the will not to be moved toward it." But he adds that it is "not impossible in an unqualified sense" for M not to exist— that is, it is not impossible, period, just impossible *given that God wills it*—and "so it does not follow that the will is moved by God necessarily." If all it takes to safeguard the claim that M is not necessary is that M could have failed to take place *if God hadn't caused it*, then the claim that M is not necessary is extremely uninteresting.

My example focuses on God's moving a will in some particular way. Certainly Aquinas has that in mind to some extent in this article, since (as we have seen) resp. 3 explicitly considers God's moving the will to some particular thing. But Aquinas's main focus is more likely God's moving the will in a general way, by giving it its nature, its inclination to the good in general, as discussed in 9.6. The claim that God does not necessitate the movement of the will by giving it its general inclination to the good is far more plausible, because (as we have seen) that general inclination to the good leaves it open to many possibilities. Thus Aquinas can say that God "does not determine [the will] necessarily to one outcome" precisely because God determines the will by giving it a general inclination that is not determined necessarily to one outcome. Accordingly, "the will's movement remains contingent and not necessary, except in things toward which it is moved naturally"—that is, in things toward which the natural inclination given by God *does* determine it necessarily to one outcome.

## Question 11: Enjoyment, Which Is an Act of the Will

QQ 8–17 deal with acts of will, which are divided into elicited (interior) acts and commanded (exterior) acts. Elicited acts are in turn divided into those that concern the end and those that concern things that are for the end. There are three acts that concern the end: will, enjoyment, and intention. Having dealt with will in QQ 8–10, Aquinas now turns to the next act concerning the end, which is enjoyment (*fruitio*). The order of presentation is somewhat surprising, since enjoyment is clearly the last of these three acts both temporally and conceptually.[15] There are two plausible reasons, however, that might explain Aquinas's decision to treat enjoyment before intention. First,

---

15. Notwithstanding McInerny and Donagan: see Appendix 1, accounts B and C.

enjoyment is conceptually simpler than intention and accordingly closer to simple willing. Both will and enjoyment concern an end "absolutely," in Aquinas's terminology; that is, they concern an end simply *as an end*. Intention, by contrast, concerns an end *as something to be attained through some intermediate acts*. Thus, enjoyment is the counterpart of simple willing, the perfection and completion of the motion that simple willing inaugurates, and so it makes sense to treat them side by side, as it were. One could even say that enjoyment just *is* a kind of simple willing: it is simple willing of an end that is possessed, whereas *voluntas* is simple willing of an end that is not yet possessed. Second, and following from this first point, it makes sense to discuss intention immediately before discussing acts of will that concern things that are for the end, because intention of an end is precisely the act that occupies the intermediate position between acts of will that concern the end and acts of will that concern things that are for the end.

### 11.1. Is enjoyment an act of an appetitive power?

Answer: Yes.

The Latin verb *frui* is a perfectly ordinary, non-technical word meaning "to enjoy." It becomes something of a technical term in Christian thought through Augustine's famous distinction between *frui* and *uti*. For Augustine, only God is to be enjoyed (*frui*), that is, loved for his own sake; other things are to be used (*uti*), that is, loved for God's sake. (Note that 'used' in this sense does not mean "exploited.") Now the noun form of *frui* is *fruitio*, enjoyment, which unlike *frui* is quite rare in classical Latin and does not even appear in Augustine. Being rare, *fruitio* was particularly well suited to become a technical term, and that is how Aquinas treats it here.

Medieval etymologies are often somewhat fanciful, but Aquinas is at least correct in his **reply** in saying that *fruitio* and *fructus* are related: they come from the same root. Beyond that fact, it would be unwise to put too much weight on the specifics of Aquinas's argument in the reply, which reads like something constructed to fit the conclusion he needed to reach rather than an honest investigation of word origins. (Isidore of Seville's *Etymologies*, an early seventh-century work that was highly influential in the Middle Ages, claims that *fructus* "takes its name from *frumen*, that is, the higher part of the throat, through which we ingest" [342]. This derivation would obviously not have suited Aquinas's purposes.) Ad hoc though it might seem, however, it does rely on well-established principles of Aristotelian philosophy: we name things as we know them, and our knowledge begins with what is evident to the senses and proceeds to things that are more remote from the senses. Accordingly, Aquinas says that it is most likely that fruit was named first and enjoyment derives its name from fruit. Fruit is noteworthy for two things: it is "what we ultimately look for from a tree" and "is perceived with a certain sweetness." Transferring this from the realm of sensation—apples and pears and such—to the realm of human action, we have an account of enjoyment: "the love or delight that someone has in what is ultimately looked for, which is the end."

Enjoyment, then, is love for an end that one already possesses, as distinguished from simple will, which is love for an end that one desires but does not yet possess. I want to play Bach's G-major French Suite reasonably well—say, as well as I did back in high school when I was playing the piano seriously—so I practice hard and, eventually, I can indeed play it well again. (We are speaking theoretically here.) I still *want* to play Bach well, but the wanting has a different character now: an attachment to an ability I have already developed and a contentment or delight in the possession (and, presumably, exercise) of that ability rather than an impetus toward attaining it. The character of this wanting is one reason that "enjoyment," rather than the cognate "fruition," is the best way to translate the Latin *fruitio*: we can use "enjoy" to describe both the possession of an end ("She enjoys good health") and delight or pleasure in something ("He enjoys playing golf"). It is obvious that enjoyment in this sense is an appetitive rather than a cognitive matter—that is, it is not merely a matter of registering or being conscious of a truth, but of being directed in a certain way toward something as a good and an end—and so Aquinas rightly says that "it is evident that enjoyment is an act of an appetitive power." Even so, enjoyment does presuppose an act of a cognitive power, as Aquinas notes in **resp. 3**: if I do not know that I have attained my end, or that what I have attained is good and suitable for me, I will have no pleasure in what I have attained.

**Obj. 1** reminds us that Aquinas has identified the end, happiness, as an activity of the intellect (3.4). So if enjoyment means "getting hold of the fruit," and the ultimate fruit or end is intellectual activity, shouldn't enjoyment belong to the intellect rather than to an appetitive power? Aquinas responds (**resp. 1**) that the ultimate end, the vision of God, belongs to both intellect and will, but in different ways: *as vision* it belongs to the intellect, but *as good and end* it belongs to the will. It is even correct to say that both intellect and will *attain* the end: the intellect as active power, the will as the power that moves one toward the end and enjoys it once it is attained. **Resp. 2** applies similar reasoning to explain why all enjoyment belongs to an appetitive power even though a wide variety of powers have their own proper ends. The object of appetite is what is good, which means that "the perfection and end" of every power, *as good*, is an object of an appetitive power, even though the power that actually achieves that perfection is something other than appetite.

Throughout this question Aquinas has been careful to speak of enjoyment as belonging to "an appetitive power," not (as you might have expected) to "the will." The next article reveals why: Aquinas holds that there is enjoyment in non-rational animals as well. Non-rational animals have appetite—sensory appetite—just not the intellectual appetite that is also called will. Accordingly he speaks of the will in art. 1 only in resp. 1, where the enjoyment of the vision of God, which non-rational animals cannot attain, is at issue.

### 11.2. Does enjoyment belong only to rational creatures or to non-rational animals as well?

Answer: Only rational creatures can have enjoyment in the fullest sense, because only they have perfect cognition of an end; but there is imperfect enjoyment in non-rational creatures, in keeping with their imperfect cognition of an end.

In resp. 1 and resp. 2 of the previous article, Aquinas draws a distinction between two ways in which a power attains an end: an active power actually realizes the end, and an appetitive power moves the active power toward realizing the end and then enjoys the end once it is attained. Aquinas's **reply** in this article develops this distinction further by introducing the notion of *commanding*. Enjoyment, he says, "is not an act of the power that . . . realiz[es] the end" but of "the power that commands its realization." Things that lack cognition do have a power that realizes their end, but they do not have a power that commands its realization. A stone has a power by which it tends downward, but it has no power that commands it to tend downward; the stone's movement is under the sway of "some higher nature" that commands its downward motion. By the argument of this article, of course, that higher nature must be something endowed with cognition; ultimately, it is God who commands the end-achieving motion of all things that lack the cognitive wherewithal to command their own motion. (The idea that all genuinely purposive activity ultimately requires an explanation in terms of the purposes of a cognitive agent is the crucial move in Aquinas's Fifth Way, *ST* I.2.3.) Lacking the power to command the realization of their ends, things without cognition therefore also lack enjoyment.

By contrast, beings that do have cognition of their end have some control over their own motion. The kind of control or command depends on the kind of cognition. Non-rational animals cognize their end, but they do not cognize it *as* an end. That is, they lack the concept of an end—they lack concepts altogether—so although they perceive things that are good for them, they do not desire those things *as* good or *as* end. They cognize the end and the good "in its particularity," as Aquinas puts it in one place in the reply; equivalently, they "cognize the thing that is the end and the good" but not the "universal notion of end and good." This imperfect cognition gives them a kind of command, and therefore a kind of enjoyment; but it is imperfect enjoyment. Full or perfect enjoyment requires full or perfect cognition of the end, and such perfect cognition of an end belongs only to a creature that possesses the universal concepts of *end* and *good*.[16] Only rational creatures can have this sort of cognition, which allows us to command our own actions freely, unlike non-rational animals, which "are moved by natural instinct to the things they apprehend."

Aquinas's reply makes the answers to the first and third objections, as well as to the argument On the contrary, immediately clear. The notion of perfect enjoyment justifies Augustine's restriction of enjoyment to human beings in **obj. 1**; the notion of imperfect enjoyment justifies his extension of enjoyment to non-rational animals in the argument **On the contrary**. And the fact that enjoyment requires cognition of some kind explains why natural appetite is not capable of enjoyment, contrary to **obj. 3**.

**Resp. 2**, however, adds something new, at least in the sense that it makes explicit something that was not stated quite so directly in art. 1 or in the reply in art. 2. The argument of art. 1 that enjoyment is of "what is ultimately looked for," and the occasional focus on the vision of God (art. 1 obj. and resp. 1), might suggest that, as **obj. 2** says, "enjoyment is of the ultimate end." The ultimate end is the vision of God, which non-rational animals cannot attain; so if enjoyment is of the ultimate end, there is no enjoyment in non-rational animals. In resp. 2 Aquinas says that enjoyment need not be of the ultimate end "in an unqualified sense" (the ultimate end, period), but merely of the ultimate end *of a given thing*. Non-rational animals do have their own ultimate ends, even though they cannot attain the vision of God that is the ultimate end, period.

Can one go further, however, and say that there can be enjoyment of ends that are not ultimate even for a given thing? My own example of enjoyment in playing Bach's G-major French Suite was clearly an example of enjoyment of a non-ultimate end. Was this a mistake? Aquinas takes up this question in the next article.

*11.3. Is enjoyment only of the ultimate end?*

Answer: Only the ultimate end is enjoyed in the fullest sense, but other ends are enjoyed in a restricted sense.

---

16. Do not let the word 'perfect' mislead you. Aquinas does not mean that the cognition needs to encompass everything there is to know about a thing, including all the possible ways it does or does not fit into an overall good life, or that it needs to be infallible or unimprovable, or anything of that sort. 'Perfect' just means "complete," in the sense that perfect cognition of an end completely meets the requirements to count as full-blown cognition of an end: knowing the thing that is the end plus knowing what it means for something to be an end. The cognition of an end that non-rational animals have is imperfect, incomplete, because it meets only the first of the two requirements.

The objections all give examples of less-than-ultimate ends that are enjoyed: Paul expresses the desire to enjoy Philemon "in the Lord," even though of course he did not regard a fellow human being as an ultimate end (**obj.** 1); love, joy, and peace are not ultimate ends, but they are called the "fruit of the Spirit," and "Fruit is what someone enjoys" (**obj.** 2); and, in keeping with the general fact that acts of the will are "reflected back on themselves," one can enjoy one's own enjoyment, even though enjoyment is not the ultimate end (**obj.** 3). The argument **On the contrary**, however, speaks decisively for the claim that only the ultimate end is enjoyed. Augustine says that if people will something not for its own sake, but only for the sake of something else, they do not enjoy that thing; and only the ultimate end is willed solely for its own sake and in no way for the sake of anything else. So only the ultimate end is enjoyed.

As was also true in art. 2, Aquinas in his **reply** finds a way to accept the arguments on both sides of the question; and once again he does this by means of a distinction. What is enjoyed (*frui*) is a fruit (*fructus*), and a fruit is what comes last: but there are two ways in which something can come last. Something can be last in particular series, or it can be "unqualifiedly last"—that is, not last in this or that series but last, period. Consider all the things I must do in order to get the G-major French Suite into presentable shape: the slow practice, the work on fingering and ornamentation, the careful study of the best interpretations of the piece, and so on. All these things are directed toward ("referred to" is Aquinas's language) the goal of playing the piece well. I may regard all that work as unpleasant drudgery that I simply have to get through in order to attain my goal—the equivalent of bad-tasting medicine that I take only for the sake of health—and in that case I do not enjoy the work; it "cannot be called a fruit in any way." Playing the piece, though, "has some sort of delightfulness in itself, and prior things"—practice and study—"are referred to it," so my playing can be called a fruit, and I can be said to enjoy it.[17]

My possessing and exercising the ability to play Bach's G-major French Suite well thus comes last in a rather complex series of activities that are directed toward that end. But it is obviously not last altogether. For, as Aquinas puts it, "the will does not rest unqualifiedly except in the ultimate end, since as long as there is anything further to look for, the will's motion remains in an in-between state, even though it has attained something." Playing that

---

17. What if I also take pleasure in the practice and study, and do not regard it as mere drudgery? Can I then be said to enjoy it? The requirement that it have "some sort of delightfulness in itself" is clearly met, but what about the requirement that "prior things [be] referred to it"? I think we can say that the second requirement is met as well, since I must do various things—find an instrument, set aside time, look for videos of András Schiff and Glenn Gould on YouTube, download a metronome app on my cell phone, and so forth—for the sake of study and practice.

piece well is satisfying, and it is the end of a particular series; but in "the full sweep of the motion" toward happiness it is only a resting place on the journey. Only the enjoyment of attaining what is unqualifiedly last, the ultimate end, is enjoyment in the fullest and most proper sense, because it is only in the ultimate end that the will comes to rest, not just for a time or in a particular respect, but altogether.

This distinction between what is last in a particular series, which is enjoyed in a restricted sense, and what is unqualifiedly last, which is enjoyed in the fullest sense, allows Aquinas to answer the first two objections. In **resp.** 1 he agrees that Paul did not regard a fellow human being as an ultimate end. As Augustine comments, the fact that he speaks of enjoying Philemon "in the Lord" indicates that Paul enjoyed Philemon "not as a terminus, but as an intermediate point." **Resp.** 2 actually offers two ways of understanding the fruit of the Spirit, only the second of which depends on the distinction made in the reply. Aquinas first says that in calling love, joy, peace, and the rest "fruit of the Spirit" Paul simply means that they are the effects produced by the Holy Spirit, as fruit is produced by a tree, not that they are fruit in the sense of what we enjoy. Alternatively, he says, we can follow Ambrose in saying that they are fruit "because they should be sought for their own sake," and thus they are enjoyed in exactly the way that intermediate ends are enjoyed, as having "within themselves something that ought to please us" but also as referred to something beyond themselves, namely happiness.

**Resp.** 3 begins with a reminder that we speak of an end in two ways, both as the thing that is the end and as the attainment of that thing. It is one and the same end, however, that we speak of in both ways. What is our ultimate end? God is the thing that is the end, what is ultimately sought; the attainment of God as the end is enjoyment. Since these are not two ends, but one and the same end spoken of in two ways, it follows that God and the enjoyment of God are the same end, and so "our enjoying God is the very same enjoyment as our enjoying the enjoyment of God." (The last step in this argument is perhaps not completely obvious. The idea is that our enjoyment of God *just is* our attaining God, which is our attaining the end: so what would our enjoying the enjoyment of God be? It would be our enjoying attaining God; and enjoying attaining God *just is* enjoyment of the end.) Aquinas adds that the same reasoning can be applied to created or imperfect happiness.

*11.4. Is enjoyment only of an end that is actually possessed?*

Answer: There is perfect enjoyment of an end that is already possessed in reality, imperfect enjoyment of an end that is possessed merely in intention.

Thus far Aquinas has been speaking of enjoyment as the will's delight and rest in an end that is actually possessed. In this article he acknowledges that one can also enjoy an end that is possessed not in reality but in intention. Unfortunately, he does not explain what exactly it means for someone to possess an end "in intention," and we have to try our best to flesh out the notion from the scant indications in this rather short article.

The argument **On the contrary** is a good place to start. Augustine says that to enjoy something is "to cleave with love to [it] for its own sake." This definition reintroduces the close association of enjoyment with simple willing that I discussed in the introduction to this question. I said there that enjoyment is simple willing—what Augustine calls "cleaving with love to some thing for its own sake"—of something already possessed, whereas *voluntas* is simple willing of something not yet possessed. The argument On the contrary says, however, that one can cleave with love for its own sake to something that is not yet possessed, and so by Augustine's definition there can be enjoyment even of an end that is not actually possessed.

Can these two apparently contradictory claims be reconciled? Aquinas reconciles them in his **reply** by describing a way in which an end is possessed imperfectly: "An end is possessed perfectly when it is possessed . . . in fact, whereas it is possessed imperfectly when it is possessed only in intention." In other words, possessing an end in intention counts as possessing it, just imperfectly or incompletely. So Augustine's definition is correct in allowing for enjoyment of an end that is not possessed *in reality*, but the understanding of enjoyment as involving the willing of an end that is possessed is also salvaged, because possession-in-intention is a *kind* of possession, just imperfect possession—or as resp. 3 also puts the same point, it is a *kind* of "getting hold of the fruit." When Augustine (as quoted in **obj.** 1) says that enjoyment means using with joy "no longer in hope, but in actual fact," he is speaking of perfect enjoyment (**resp.** 1); this definition does not exclude the possibility of imperfect enjoyment.

Assuming that Aquinas understands the contrast between "in hope" and "in actual fact" from obj. 1 to be the same as the contrast between "in intention" and "in reality" in his reply, we can get some idea of what imperfect possession of an end is supposed to mean. Begin with a non-ultimate end, my having the ability to play Bach's G-major French Suite reasonably well. As I work toward that goal, I have a kind of enjoyment in the prospect of achieving it. Perhaps I imagine myself sitting down at my 1917 Steinway A and playing the piece rather well, if I do say so myself. And this is not just idle reverie, as it would be if I imagined myself giving my acceptance speech for the nomination of a major party to be their candidate for president of the United States or starring on Broadway as Pippin. Those are scenarios that I am quite sure would never come to pass, whereas it is reasonable to think that, with considerable work, I could play that piece reasonably well on my own piano. On Aquinas's definition, "a future good, difficult but possible to obtain," is the object of hope (I-II.40.1, II-II.17.1), so we can see why he would find it appropriate to say that I possess that intermediate end "in hope," in a way that I clearly do not possess the impossible scenarios I might entertain in a daydream. And I can be said to possess that intermediate end "in intention" because (as we shall see in detail in the next question) to intend an end is to will it as something that can be attained through various intermediate activities. If I am working toward that intermediate end through practice and study—activities animated and driven precisely by my intending the end—then again we can see why Aquinas would find it appropriate to say that I possess that end "in intention."

In **resp.** 2 Aquinas speaks of imperfect enjoyment of the ultimate end. He does not elaborate, but the idea that one can enjoy the ultimate end "in hope" or "in intention" shows that Aquinas does not think that perfect happiness is entirely other-worldly. As he quotes from the Letter to the Hebrews, "we have hope that enters"—meaning "hope that makes us enter"—"within the veil," that is, into the happiness of heaven (II-II.17.2 On the contrary and resp. 1, quoting Hebrews 6:19). That Aquinas allows both imperfect enjoyment of the ultimate end—which is nothing less than the inbreaking of heavenly happiness into this earthly pilgrimage—and the "improper" enjoyment of less-than-ultimate ends goes a long way toward mitigating what one recent commentator calls the "rather grim" idea that "Strictly, *fruitio* comes only when we attain God; nothing else is all that enjoyable."[18]

## Question 12: Intention

### *12.1. Is intention an act of the intellect or of the will?*

Answer: It is an act of the will that presupposes an act of the intellect.

It is not until **resp. 4** that Aquinas tells us what he means by 'intention' or how he distinguishes intention from the other two acts of will that concern the end, will and enjoyment. He says that there are three ways in which the will has to do with an end: absolutely; insofar as someone rests in it; and as the terminus of something ordered to it. These three ways of willing an end correspond to will, enjoyment, and intention, respectively. I *will* health when I simply want it; I *enjoy* health when I delight in possessing it (either in hope or in reality); I *intend* health when I will to attain it through something else.

Aquinas of course has in mind this understanding of intention from the outset of the question, but he does not reach the conclusion that intention is an act of will rather than of intellect by relying on this definition. Instead his **reply** appeals first to the formation of the word *intentio* itself: it indicates tending toward something. Tending-toward is a kind of motion, which means that

18. Pasnau (2002), 251.

it involves both a mover and something moved. The mover is what explains why the thing moved tends toward something, so intention is characteristic of what moves something toward an end. (This understanding of intention, Aquinas argues, is not just a technical notion but corresponds to the way we use the term in ordinary language: "we say that an architect, or anyone in authority, by his command moves others toward the things that he himself intends." We probably would not put it quite that way in contemporary English, but we could certainly say that a building crew carries out the architect's intentions or that a regulatory agency implements what Congress intended, so Aquinas's point still holds.) As we saw in 9.1, the will moves all the powers of the soul (including itself: 9.3), toward an end, so intention is an act of the will.

Aquinas must therefore answer the arguments for holding that intention belongs instead to the intellect. The most important of these is **obj. 3**: "Intention indicates some sort of ordering toward an end, and it is the job of reason to order. Therefore, intention belongs not to the will, but to reason." Aquinas agrees with both premises of the argument—he states in the reply that intention indicates an ordering toward an end, and he acknowledges in resp. 4 that reason, not will, is what orders one thing to another—but in **resp. 3** he rejects the conclusion. The ordering toward an end that intention indicates is reason's ordering, but intention itself is an act of will that presupposes reason's ordering. This understanding of an act of will as presupposing an act of cognition also allows Aquinas to answer **obj. 1**, which quoted Augustine as identifying the "eye" of Matthew 6:22 with intention and argued that the eye, as an instrument of vision, surely signifies an apprehensive rather than an appetitive power. In **resp. 1** Aquinas argues that "Intention is called an eye metaphorically" because it presupposes cognition, not because it belongs to cognition. The eye shows us where we ought to go, but our bodies move us there; analogously, the intellect presents the end, but the will's intention moves us toward it.

### 12.2. Is intention only of the ultimate end?

Answer: Intention is always of an end, but it need not always be of the ultimate end.

Art. 1 established that intention is the willing of an end *as* something to be attained through some intermediate steps, activities, etc. Using the language of motion that has been a crucial analytical tool for Aquinas throughout the Treatise on Human Acts, we could say that intention is by definition motion *toward* an end *through* things that are for the end. In art. 2 Aquinas asks whether this motion must always be toward the ultimate end.

He argues in the **reply** that it need not. In standard Aristotelian terminology, the end-point of a motion—what the motion is motion toward—is called the "terminus" of the motion. Intention has to do with an end as terminus of a motion of the will. But there are two senses of 'terminus': the ultimate terminus, where motion comes to an end and what was moved is now fully at rest; and an intermediate terminus, which is the terminus of one part of the motion but the beginning of another part. If I take a trip from Tampa to Edinburgh with a stop in London, London is an intermediate terminus, Edinburgh the ultimate terminus. There can be intention of either kind of terminus, not only of an ultimate terminus.

This is hardly a surprising conclusion, given that Aquinas has already acknowledged that intermediate ends can be both willed (8.1) and enjoyed (11.3). More surprising at this point is **resp. 3**, in which he says that enjoyment "pertains only to the ultimate end." Despite appearances, this does not contradict his acknowledgment in 11.3 that intermediate ends can also be enjoyed, since he insisted there that such enjoyment is not enjoyment in the proper sense (as opposed to enjoyment of the ultimate end "in intention," which is enjoyment in the proper sense, just imperfect or incomplete enjoyment). His claim that "rest in the end . . . pertains only to the ultimate end" must also be parsed carefully, because Aquinas acknowledges in 11.3 that intermediate ends do "bring the appetite to rest with a certain sweetness or delight"; but such rest is not unqualified or absolute rest, because "the will does not rest unqualifiedly except in the ultimate end, since as long as there is anything further to look for, the will's motion remains in an in-between state, even though it has attained something."

So there is no contradiction between resp. 3 and 11.3, but there is still something quite puzzling about the fact that Aquinas here restricts enjoyment to unqualified rest in what is unqualifiedly last but allows intention of a terminus that is not unqualifiedly last. The explanation given in resp. 3 sheds no light on this: the cases of enjoyment and intention are not parallel, Aquinas says, because enjoyment implies rest in the end, whereas intention implies motion toward the end. How does that help? There can be motion toward an end that is not unqualifiedly last, and there can be rest in an end that is not unqualifiedly last: so far, so parallel. The only difference I can see is that motion toward an end that is not unqualifiedly last is still unqualifiedly motion, whereas rest in an end that is not unqualifiedly last is not unqualifiedly rest.

This seems a very slender difference, and yet it reveals something very important about Aquinas's account of action. Aquinas means to account for and analyze *all* human action, as defined in 1.1; and a great deal of human action is directed at intermediate ends. Yet he is also committed to the view that only the ultimate end can fully satisfy the human will and that it is the goodness of the ultimate end that accounts for all purposive action (1.4). By recognizing intention of intermediate ends, Aquinas can analyze the whole range of human action without having to insist that any of it is somehow not really action; they are all genuine motions, end-directed, purposive, proceeding from "a will that is informed by deliberation" (1.1). But lying behind all these actions, explaining them in just the way that the unmoved mover explains all motion, is the goodness of the ultimate end, in which alone the movement of the human will comes to rest. That there is no genuine rest in intermediate ends—even though the motion toward those ends is genuine motion and the ends are genuine ends—accounts for the restlessness of the human will, for the variability of human action, for the dissatisfaction-in-the-midst-of-satisfaction that characterizes the human condition. Thus, by Aquinas's lights, if we disallow intention of intermediate ends, the purposiveness of every particular action is lost; if we allow unqualified enjoyment of intermediate ends, the full sweep of human action as a whole becomes inexplicable. By upholding this (as it seems at first) very slender difference, Aquinas upholds his aim in the Treatise on Human Acts to account for both particular acts and the larger patterns of human acts.

### 12.3. Can one intend two things at the same time?

Answer: Yes.

Objections 2 and 3 argue from two features of intention that have already been established to the conclusion that the will can intend only one thing at a time. **Obj. 2** begins with the fact that intention is a kind of motion toward a terminus (art. 1, art. 2). A given motion can have only one terminus, and so it would seem that the will can intend only one thing at a time. **Obj. 3** begins with the fact that intention presupposes an act of reason or intellect (art. 1 resp. 1 and resp. 3). Aristotle says that "one . . . cannot understand more than one thing at the same time," and so it would seem that one also cannot intend more than one thing at one time.

Aquinas argues in the **reply**, however, that one can intend more than one thing at one time. This is obvious in a case in which one thing is "ordered to" another. An analogy from motion makes this point clear: if my trip is from Tampa to Edinburgh, connecting through London, both London and Edinburgh are termini of a single motion (cf. **resp. 2**). The same motion that is toward London is at the same time a motion toward Edinburgh through London. Similarly, I intend a proximate end and a more ultimate end at the same time: I intend practicing the piano and mastering a piece of music, attending class and getting a degree, working out and being healthy, at the same time, because the first end in each pair is ordered to the second.

But Aquinas goes further and argues that one can intend two things at the same time even when the two things are *not* ordered to each other. He offers one example in the reply and two more in resp. 2. To flesh out the example in the reply: I can select one car in preference to another both because the one I prefer gets better gas mileage and because it has a better safety rating.

Thus I intend two things at the same time: savings and safety. (Perhaps a third thing as well: environmental responsibility.) In **resp.** 2 he notes the crucial point that intention is directed toward an end *as prescribed by reason*; so when reason regards a plurality of things as one, intention can be directed to that plurality of things. This can happen in two ways: the plurality of things either "come together to make up a whole" or are instances of some more general class. Since Aquinas's example of the first way ("heat and cold in a proper balance come together to produce health") rests on outmoded medical theory, we might substitute this example: I can intend to train in cycling, in running, and in swimming, because those three activities come together to make up a triathlon. (Note, of course, that one intends them all at the same time, not that one intends *to do* them all at the same time.) His example of the second way is straightforward: I can intend both acquiring wine and acquiring clothing at the same time as instances of the more general activity of acquiring wealth.

The fact that a plurality of things can in some way be understood as one also allows Aquinas a quick and simple answer in **resp.** 3: "it is possible to understand more than one thing at the same time insofar as they are in some way one."

### 12.4. Is intention of the end the same act as will of what is for the end?

Answer: Yes.

In the commentary introducing Q8, I noted that most scholarship on the Treatise on Human Acts treats Aquinas as setting forth a sequence of discrete acts or act-stages, whereas I hold that he is simply analyzing the different ways in which the will is related to various objects and to the kinds of purposive activity in which the will allows human beings to engage. One key argument for my interpretation is, in a way, an argument from silence: Aquinas simply does not say the things that the traditional, sequential, multi-act accounts attribute to him. They impose a system, and add a fair amount of content, to produce accounts that contain some material that is genuinely from Aquinas but a great deal more material that derives from the ingenuity of interpreters. But there are also positive arguments, arguments from what he does say, and in art. 4 we find one of the most compelling of them.

It is interesting, first of all, that Aquinas here speaks of "will of what is for the end," when will has been treated as an act concerning the end. This by itself should keep us from insisting on too rigid a definition of the various acts.[19] And here, just as he had in 8.3, Aquinas emphasizes the continuity—indeed,

---

19. But then of course 'will' is ambiguous, as I have noted before (see the commentary introducing Q8); this does not recapitulate the old ambiguity but introduces a new one.

the identity—between acts of will that have been thus far treated separately. The argument of the **reply** is that if the will is drawn to what is for the end *for the sake of the end*, that is the same movement as the will's movement toward the end. In resp. 3 we are told further that will of what is for the end, as ordered to the end, is choice (which will be the topic of Q13). So the upshot of this is to identify choice with intention, when there is choice at all. The last sentence of **resp. 3** is important here: "there can be intention of an end even when one has not yet figured out the things that are for the end, which are the objects of choice." I can intend a good career—remember that intending a good career is more than willing a good career; it is willing a good career *as something to be attained through some intermediate steps*—without yet choosing any particular path toward a good career. Perhaps I have not yet figured out what I have the most aptitude for, or consulted all the people whose advice I trust. In that case there is intention of an end but not yet choice of things that are for the end. When there is choice, however, choice (the will's movement toward things that are for the end) and intention (the will's movement toward the end) are the same movement ("one in subject" is Aquinas's way of saying this) described in two different ways. Described as a movement of the will drawn to what is for the end as ordered to the end, it is called choice; described as a movement of the will drawn to the end by way of things that are for the end, the very same movement is called intention. To use the by now familiar language of motion through an intermediate and to a terminus (On the contrary, reply), intention is movement toward the terminus through the intermediate; choice is movement through the intermediate toward the terminus—obviously just two ways of saying the same thing.

Thus, Aquinas's tendency is to see human action as integrated rather than as fragmented or atomized. This does not mean, however, that he does not recognize distinctions. In the beginning of the reply he makes the important distinction between the will's being drawn to something absolutely, for its own sake, and the will's being drawn to something for the sake of an end. Something that is for the end can be willed in either way: I can will running absolutely, as a good and enjoyable thing in its own right, or for the sake of an end, as something that will help me achieve or maintain health. (Or both, of course: see the commentary on 8.3.) An end can be willed only absolutely; if it is willed for the sake of something else, it is no longer being treated as an end but as something that is for the end. In these cases, then, the difference is not in *what* is willed but in *why* it is willed, that is, on what grounds or under what description. This is exactly what we should expect given that will is intellectual appetite: it is drawn to objects, not as they are in themselves, but as they are apprehended by reason.

This crucial distinction between *what* is willed and *why* it is willed is what allows Aquinas to resist the argument of **obj. 2** that intention of the end and choice of what is for the end must be distinct because the end and what is for the end are distinct objects. In **resp.** 2 he acknowledges that they are distinct objects in terms of *what* is willed but the same object in terms of *why* they are willed. It is the why—the reason for willing—that unifies intention and choice.

### 12.5. Does intention belong to non-rational animals?

Answer: Only in a derivative sense. Intention in its proper and principal sense requires reason.

Why does a dog eat its food? To be healthy, to stay alive. Should we not say, then, that a dog intends health and life? To intend is to tend toward an end, and clearly the dog tends toward the ends of health and life; so it seems we should say that non-rational animals have intention.

In the **reply** Aquinas agrees that intending is tending toward something, but he distinguishes two senses of tending-toward: the sense that character-izes a mover and the sense that characterizes what is moved. A mover tends toward an end by directing some movement—whether that movement belongs to it or to something else—toward an end; only reason can direct movement toward an end. By contrast, what is moved tends toward an end because some-thing else moves it toward that end. It is in this second way that things that lack reason intend an end: things without cognition are moved to their end by God "as an arrow is moved by the archer," and non-rational animals are moved by natural instinct. As Aquinas says in replying to the argument with which we began, "Non-rational animals are not moved to an end as though they were entertaining the thought that by means of some movement they can achieve their end—as is true of someone who properly speaking intends something" (**resp.** 3).

This also explains how non-rational animals can have enjoyment but not intention (**obj. and resp.** 2). Enjoyment is a matter of resting in an end, which requires only the appetitive power along with perception of an end, both of which non-rational animals have (11.2). Intention, by contrast, requires the capacity to cognize an end *as an end* and to direct behavior toward that end; in other words, it requires reason.

### Question 13: Choice, Which Is an Act of Will concerning Things That Are for the End

Aquinas has now finished his account of acts of will that concern the end, con-cluding with intention, an act of willing an end as something to be attained through things that are for the end. The discussion of intention thus natu-rally leads to a discussion of acts of will that have to do with things that are for the end, and first to a discussion of choice (Q13), which as we saw in 12.4 resp. 3 is the same act as intention, just described in a different way. Choice is preceded by deliberation, an act of intellect, which Aquinas discusses after choice (Q14). Then follows a discussion of the two other acts of will concerning things that are for the end: consent (Q15) and use (Q16).

Eleonore Stump rightly argues that "choice" is not a perfectly apt translation of Aquinas's word *electio*:

> '*Electio*' is often translated 'choice', but this is a misleading translation. It suggests that the will is engaged in what is really the intellect's act of ranking alternative possibilities. In the act of *electio*, what the will does is accept the course of action that intellect proposes as the best. Furthermore, 'choice' ranges over cases which include acts of will that Aquinas would classify as simple volition of the end or intention.[20]

Unfortunately, "choice" is the nearest equivalent that English offers, so we are stuck with it; but Stump's caution is a useful corrective and should be kept in mind as the discussion proceeds, lest we import connotations of the English word that are out of place in Aquinas's account.

The discussion of choice, particularly the second paragraph of 13.1 reply, gives us yet another reason to resist the "volley" picture of Aquinas's account of action—act of intellect, act of will, act of intellect, act of will . . . —and note instead that although every component of a fully realized action will be either a desiring or a cognizing, and thus assignable to the will or the intellect respectively, each of the desirings that we are talking about will be informed (in the full-blown sense of "made the kind of thing it is") by reason. Against an overly cooperative Westberg-style reading,[21] though, note that we cannot say the reverse—it is not true that the cognizings will all be informed by appetite, though they will to some extent be shaped by appetite. But how they are shaped is complicated, in ways we have seen and will continue to see. The shaping ranges from a passion's inclining you to attend to a particular feature of a proposed object as especially salient, all the way to the will's directing the intellect to attend to something, either at all or in some particular way.

In any event, choice is a particularly clear case of the general point that desiring is informed by cognizing. Aquinas argues that choice is an act *of the will* (materially) *as formed and directed by reason*. Choice is arguably the central or definitive act in the process of action, for at least three reasons. First, choice is the point at which the internal act is fully baked, so to speak. After choice, what's left is to *realize* or *execute* the choice in external action. This does not mean, however, that there are no further internal acts. The internal acts of use and command come after choice, but they are internal acts that direct the execution of the choice. They are a matter of setting oneself to do

20. Stump (2005), 288–89.
21. For an overview of Westberg's account, see Appendix 1, account D.

what one has chosen to do, whereas until choice, the acts are still about reaching that determination of what, concretely, one is going to do.

Second, Aquinas consistently associates *liberum arbitrium* (translated as "free choice" or "free decision") with choice, not with other acts of will: choice just is the act of *liberum arbitrium*. And that is what you should expect given his positions that (a) we are free because we have deliberation and (b) the act that the will does because deliberation has come to its conclusion is choice.

And third, choice tends to be the locus of moral responsibility. Certainly when Aquinas talks about the moral evaluation of the "internal act," he always means choice.

### 13.1. Is choice an act of will or of reason?

Answer: It is an act of the will formed by reason.

The conclusion defended in this article is clear, but the arguments by which Aquinas reaches that conclusion are somewhat circuitous and difficult. He begins his **reply** by saying that the word 'choice' "implies something that pertains to reason or intellect and something that pertains to will," and in support of this claim he cites Aristotle's dictum that choice is "an appetitive understanding or an intellective appetite." Note that Aristotle seems to leave it open whether choice is a cognizing shaped by desire ("appetitive understanding") or instead a desiring shaped by cognition ("intellective appetite"). Aquinas, never one to leave things open, sets out to determine which of the two choice is.

So we have the idea that choice involves both reason and will, and that it is a single act, not an aggregate of two different acts. One way in which two things come together into a single whole is in a matter-form composite, in which "one of the two is like the formal cause with respect to the other." And according to Nemesius, this is exactly the way in which will and intellect (he says "appetite" and "deliberation") come together as one, just as an animal is neither soul nor body but the two together.[22]

Supposing, then, that choice is a kind of form-matter composite of reason and will, which of the two provides the form and which provides the matter? Aquinas answers this question by appeal to a general principle: in acts of the soul, a higher power or habit that directs a lower power or habit confers the

---

22. The comparison is slightly off, from Aquinas's perspective. Soul is form, but body is not matter; something is not a body (as opposed to a chunk of matter) unless it is informed, and the soul is precisely what informs matter to make it a body. Indeed, for Aquinas, an animal *just is* a living body; and a body is living because it is ensouled. What is not ensouled is not an animal and not a body. But the general point that matter and form come together to make a unified whole is really all Aquinas needs here; that Nemesius really should have spoken of matter and soul rather than body and soul need not detract from that more general point.

form and species on an act that belongs essentially to the lower power. He offers an example: someone performs an act that is materially an act of courage—meaning that it has to do with the matter that falls within the scope of courage, such as standing firm in the face of mortal danger—but does so out of love for God. Such an act is formally an act of charity, the supernaturally granted virtue by which one loves God above all else and for God's own sake. This higher virtue directs the act and makes it what it is, even though an act of facing mortal danger as such belongs to the virtue of courage.

The intellect is a higher power than the will (Aquinas does not argue for that claim here or even state it explicitly; see I.83.3 for the argument), and it directs the act of the will "insofar as the will tends toward its object in accordance with reason's direction, since the apprehensive power is what presents the appetitive power with its object." So, applying the general principle, Aquinas concludes that choice is "materially an act of will but formally an act of reason." And the matter that is formed by the higher power is the substance of the act, so "choice in its substance is not an act of reason but of the will." To use Aristotle's language, it is intellective appetite, a desiring informed by cognition, not appetitive intellect, a cognition shaped by desire.

Accordingly, choice is not the comparison that reason makes, in which one thing is preferred to another (**obj. 1**), or the conclusion of a syllogism that reason formulates in the domain of action (**obj. 2**); it is an appetitive act that presupposes such a comparison (**resp. 1**) and follows from such a conclusion, which is called a determination (*sententia*) or judgment (*iudicium*) (**resp. 2**). As for the argument that there is ignorance in choice (6.8), and ignorance is a cognitive rather than an appetitive matter (**obj. 3**), it depends on a misunderstanding of the terminology. "Ignorance in choice" does not mean that choice itself is a kind of knowledge; it describes a case in which someone is ignorant of what should be chosen (**resp. 3**).

### 13.2. Does choice belong to non-rational animals?

Answer: No.

Given that we already know that choice presupposes reason, which non-rational animals lack, there is really no suspense about what Aquinas's answer will be. What is interesting in this article is how Aquinas develops that answer. Contrary to what one might expect, he does not argue in the **reply** from the dependence of choice on reason but focuses instead on choice as an appetitive act. The crucial difference between the sensory appetite and will is that sensory appetite "is determined to one particular thing according to the order of nature," whereas the will "is indeterminate with respect to particular goods," though of course it is determined to one universal thing, the good. Choice is a matter of accepting one thing in preference to another, so there is room for choice only in an appetite that is open to more than one thing at a time. Consequently, there is no choice in the sensory appetite, which non-rational animals have, but only in the will, the intellectual appetite that human beings have. So choice does not belong to non-rational animals.

The first two objections likewise focus on choice as an appetitive act. **Obj. 1** quotes Aristotle's dictum that choice is "a desire for things on account of an end" and argues that non-rational animals do desire things on account of an end. Aquinas could respond to this by recalling his point in 12.5 resp. 3 that non-rational animals lack the cognitive wherewithal to act on account of an end in the fullest sense, but such a response would not be in keeping with the objection's focus on appetite, so instead he argues in **resp. 1** that animals lack the kind of appetite necessary for choice. Choice is "not just any desire for something on account of an end," but a desire for one thing in preference to something else. So, once again, there is room for choice only in an appetite that is open to more than one thing at a time, as sensory appetite is not. Admittedly, though the focus is on appetite, cognition remains clearly in the background: it is precisely because sensory cognition is determined to one that sensory appetite is determined to one, and there is a hint of this relationship between cognition and appetite in Aquinas's claim that there is choice only when desire "involves some discrimination between one thing and another." "Discrimination" translates '*discretio*,' which could be read as appetitive preference but more naturally suggests cognitive discernment. Non-rational animals lack such cognition and therefore lack the open, indeterminate appetite that goes with it, the kind of appetite necessary for choice.

**Obj. 2** continues the emphasis on appetite by arguing (in effect) that choice is preferential desire, which non-rational animals clearly exhibit: "for example, a sheep eats one plant and spurns another." **Resp. 2** acknowledges that non-rational animals exhibit preferential desire, but only because their appetite is naturally determined to one thing rather than another. There is no more choice in the matter than there is choice in the upward movement of fire.

**Obj. 3**, by contrast, argues that non-rational animals have enough cognitive sophistication to engage in choice. Aristotle says that non-rational animals "have prudence without learning," and prudence is what makes someone "good at choosing things that are for the end"; moreover, observation shows that non-rational animals display "incredible cleverness" in pursuing their ends. In **resp. 3** Aquinas brushes all this aside. Such prudence or cleverness is no more attributable to the animal than the complex (and purposive) movements of clockwork are attributable to the clock. Human ingenuity is responsible for the clock—to take a more up-to-date example, smartphones are not actually smart, but their designers are brilliant—and divine creativity is responsible for giving non-rational animals their "natural inclination to certain highly organized patterns of action." There is no reason or choice in non-rational animals, just natural inclination that is determined to one thing, however complex, at a time.

### 13.3. Is choice only of things that are for the end, or is it sometimes also of the end itself?

Answer: An end as such does not fall within the scope of choice, but an end as directed to some more remote end does.

Aristotle's claim that "will is of the end, whereas choice is of things that are for the end" (**On the contrary**) is practically a matter of definition, and Aquinas does not contest that definition. He does, however, clarify its application in important ways. For whether something is an end is not a fixed or invariable matter: the very same thing that is an end in one context can be something for an end in another context. The **reply** explains how this works. Choice follows a determination or judgment (art. 1 resp. 2), which is like the conclusion of an operative syllogism. Syllogisms proceed from principles to conclusions, and in the domain of action an end is in the position of a principle; that is, one starts from the end and syllogizes (argues) from it, not to it. So an end as such is not subject to choice.

But something that is an end in one piece of practical reasoning can be a conclusion in some other piece of practical reasoning. In the domain of speculative or theoretical reasoning, something that is a principle in one science can be the conclusion of a higher science. Similarly, in the domain of practical reasoning, something that is an end in one piece of practical reasoning can be directed to some higher or more remote end; in that case, it is treated as something that is for an end and is therefore within the scope of choice. Aquinas's example is that the practical reasoning of a doctor takes health as an end. The doctor does not reason about whether to aim at health or at something else instead, and thus what falls within the scope of a doctor's choice is not health itself but only various ways to produce it. But the health of the body is aimed at a further end, the well-being of the soul; and so "for someone who is entrusted with the soul's salvation" the health of the body does fall within the scope of choice. It is important to realize, however, that not every principle in one piece of reasoning can serve as a conclusion in another piece of reasoning. In the domain of speculative reasoning, the very first principles are indemonstrable; they are only principles, never conclusions. Similarly, in the domain of practical reasoning, the ultimate end is the highest end and so by definition cannot be directed toward some further end; consequently, "the ultimate end does not fall within the scope of choice in any way."

### 13.4. Is choice only of things that we do?

Answer: Yes, choice always concerns human acts.

Suppose my end is health. What might I choose for the sake of that end? Certainly there are *acts* that I might choose: running, hiring a personal trainer, selecting steamed vegetables in preference to french fries. But I might also choose *things*: pills to lower my cholesterol, soothing music to calm my overwrought nerves. So it appears that choice can concern either acts or things.

Aquinas's **reply**, however, says in effect that this analysis is too superficial. Ends, too, can be either actions or things; but when they are things, there still needs to be some action that either causes the thing or makes use of it. That health is the doctor's end means that it is for the doctor to *cause* health. That money is the greedy person's end means that it is for the greedy person to *acquire, possess,* or *enjoy* money. And the same thing holds for what is for the end. It can be either an action or a thing, but when it is a thing, there will be some action that either causes the thing or makes use of it. To return to the examples with which I began, my choosing the pills means that I choose to *take* the pills; my choosing the music means that I choose to *play* the music. So choice always concerns some action.

### 13.5. Is choice only of possible things?

Answer: Choice is only of what appears to be possible.

Aquinas begins the **reply** with two quick and easy arguments for the claim that, as Aristotle says, "there is no choice of impossible things" (**On the contrary**). The first argument relies on the conclusion of art. 4. Choice concerns things we do; things we do are possible for us; therefore, choice is of things that are possible for us. The second argument relies on the idea that choice is of something that leads to an end. The "basis for choosing something is that it leads to the end"; one cannot attain an end through something that is impossible; therefore, choice is not of something impossible.

These straightforward arguments for an affirmative answer, however, are a very small part of Aquinas's agenda in this article. The rest of the reply and the responses to the first two objections develop his account of practical reasoning and draw out some new implications of his view of the relationship between intellect and will. As we have already seen, both speculative and practical reasoning proceed from principles to conclusions; in practical reasoning the end serves as a principle and what is for the end, which is the object of choice, serves as a conclusion. Practical reasoning does not even get started if the principle, the end, is impossible; for "no one is moved toward what is impossible," so "no one would tend toward an end unless the end appeared to be possible." Suppose, however, that one is moved toward an end that appears to be possible, but deliberation about how to attain the end reveals that there are no possible actions by which that end can be attained. If indeed there are no possible actions by which the end can be attained, the end itself is impossible; as Aquinas says, "an impossible conclusion does not follow from a possible principle." And in that case, having realized that what appeared to be a possible end is not possible after all, one ceases to will it. One might *wish* it, of course, but there is no will of what is impossible.

**Resp.** 1 explains this fact by appealing to the will's role as "the intermediary between the intellect and external action." The will's movement, as Aquinas puts it somewhat colorfully, "is *from* the soul *toward* the thing." That is, a movement of the will begins from the intellect's apprehension of something as good, and it terminates in some action that is directed toward attaining the good that intellect apprehends. If there is no possible action that can be directed toward attaining that good, the movement of the will is incomplete. Aquinas's terminology here is easy to misunderstand. By "incomplete" here he does not mean that there is an act of will that falls short of its aim, as would happen if, for example, I choose to drive to a philosophy talk but my car breaks down on the way and I end up missing the talk. That is a full-blown act of will—a "complete" act in the sense in which Aquinas means it here—because it extends all the way from the intellect's presentation of a good (attending the talk) to some external action by which that good is to be attained (driving). For that matter, there would still be a complete act of will if, as soon as I chose to drive to the talk, someone tied me up until the talk was over so that I was never able to perform *any* external action directed at attaining my end. The choice itself completes the will's act, because in that choice the will is directed to external action, whether or not any action actually takes place. (This is what is meant by Aquinas's cumbersome formulation, "the termination or completion of the will's act is identified with reference to its ordering toward action, by which someone tends toward attaining the thing." If some actual external action, however minimal, were required for a complete act of will, the words "its ordering toward" would not be there.) Instead, by "incomplete" here he means that the will is not directed toward external action at all. Suppose that instead of a philosophy talk that I can attend if I get in my car and drive to it, I find out that one of my favorite philosophers will be giving a very interesting-sounding talk halfway across the world, and it is scheduled to begin in thirty minutes. Any "will" to attend that talk would be incomplete in Aquinas's sense: I might very much like to go, I might think how lovely it would be if I could go, but I cannot *will* to go, because attending that talk is impossible and so there is no possible ordering to external action by which such attendance might be accomplished. At most we can say that I *would will* to attend the talk if circumstances were more favorable. Some people call this incomplete will "velleity," Aquinas says.[23]

**Resp.** 2 makes explicit what has been implicit in much of the discussion: the object of the will is the good as apprehended. If we apprehend an end as possible, we can will it; if we apprehend an action by which the end is to be attained as possible, we can choose it. We can of course be mistaken, and thus will or choose what is *in fact* impossible; but there can be no will or choice of what is *apprehended* as impossible.

### 13.6. Do human beings choose out of necessity, or freely?

Answer: Freely.

In 10.2 Aquinas asked whether the will is moved necessarily by its object. This article asks a closely related question, and it recapitulates much of that earlier discussion. See the commentary on 10.2 for a fuller account; here I focus on what is distinctive about Aquinas's discussion in this article.

In 10.2 the question was about will in general, whereas here it is about choice in particular. Choice concerns things that are for an end; the end is presupposed. Aquinas argued in 10.2 that the only object that moves the will by necessity is the ultimate end; given that the ultimate end is not an object of choice and thus is not in question here, it is clear that "human beings do not choose out of necessity." This is true both about the exercise of choice (whether we choose or not) and the specification of choice (whether we choose this or that).

The objections offer three initially compelling arguments for the claim that choice is always or at least sometimes necessary. **Obj.** 1 begins with Aquinas's view that ends are to objects of choice what principles are to conclusions and argues that since conclusions follow necessarily from principles, choices must follow necessarily from ends. (If this argument is sound, it would not show that choices are necessary, period, only that they are necessary *given that the will has a particular end.* But since Aquinas does think that there is one end that moves the will necessarily, namely, happiness, the argument would show that choices about how to attain happiness would be necessary, because they

---

23. Aquinas himself uses the word *velleitas* occasionally. It appears eleven other times in his works and always means the incomplete or conditional will that one has toward what one believes to be impossible but *would will* (*vellet*) if it were possible. For some reason, however, commentators on Aquinas often use the word 'velleity' in a quite different way. Thomas Gilby (1970), for example, in his ordered list of what he interprets as a "train of partial acts, according to a succession of before and after," has the following as his second item: "*Wish.* The wanting [an end], a velleity without any effort or advance to realization, sometimes called non-effective volition, *velle*, or *simplex voluntas*" (217). Velleity is not *simplex voluntas* (simple will), nor is it wish.

would follow necessarily from an end that necessarily moves the will.) In **resp.
1** Aquinas responds that conclusions do not in fact always follow from principles by necessity; they follow by necessity "only when the principles cannot be true if the conclusion is not true." Applying this model to the domain of action, suppose someone's end is *E*, and the object of choice, the thing that is for the end, is *C*. Does *E* necessitate *C*? Only if *E* cannot be attained without *C*. (My end is to attend a philosophy talk. Does that necessitate my driving there? No, because I can also walk or take a bus.) And recall that when we are talking about objects of will and choice, what matters is how we *apprehend* the object (art. 5). Even if my *E* cannot be attained without some particular *C*, I am not necessitated to choose *C* unless I cannot fail to apprehend *C* as the sole available way of attaining *E*.

**Obj. 2**, like obj. 1, begins with a view Aquinas has already affirmed: in this case, the view that choice follows reason's judgment [art. 1 resp. 2]. It then argues that reason's judgment is sometimes necessary because its premises are necessary, and so it would seem that in such a case choice, too, will be necessary. In **resp. 2** Aquinas responds that we are talking about the domain of action, which is contingent. Conclusions about contingent things do not follow necessarily from necessary principles, and so the choices that follow such conclusions are not necessary either.

**Obj. 3** argues that choice is necessarily of the best alternative. If there is no best alternative, there is no choice: "if someone who is starving has equally delicious food split into two portions at an equal distance from him, he will not be moved to one any more than to the other." And if there *is* a best alternative, one cannot be moved to any other alternative; the best alternative is chosen by necessity. Therefore, if there is a choice at all, that choice is a matter of necessity. In **resp. 3** Aquinas responds by reminding us yet again that what matters is how the intellect *apprehends* the alternatives: "Even if two things are presented that are equal when viewed in one way, there is nothing to prevent someone from paying attention to some feature in virtue of which one of the two is superior." Indeed, although he does not say so, even if one alternative (call it A) is best *all things considered*, there is nothing to prevent someone from attending to some feature of another alternative in virtue of which it is preferable to A. Presumably, only an alternative that is better than any other alternative *no matter how you look at it* would be chosen by necessity.

## Question 14: Deliberation, Which Precedes Choice

### 14.1. Is deliberation an inquiry?

Answer: Deliberation is an inquiry on the part of reason before it makes a judgment about what should be chosen.

Aquinas begins his **reply** by reminding us of something he had established in the previous question (13.1 resp. 2, 13.3): choice follows the judgment of reason about what should be done. How does reason make such a judgment? If the domain of action were clear cut and certain, reason could make its judgments intuitively; we could just *see* what we ought to choose. But in fact the domain of action is contingent, uncertain, and doubtful. We need to figure things out before we are in a position to make a judgment about how we are to act, about what the best way is to attain our end. This process of figuring things out is a kind of investigation or inquiry; we call it deliberation.

Yet Damascene, one of Aquinas's principal sources in the Treatise on Human Acts, says that "deliberation belongs to desire" (**obj. 1**). How can this be true if deliberation is a kind of inquiry? In **resp.** 1 Aquinas acknowledges that deliberation, though an act of reason, does belong to the will, in two ways. First, the will is the *matter* (or subject matter) of deliberation: deliberation is about things we will to do. Second, the will is the *mover* of deliberation: "it is because one wills the end that one is moved to deliberate about things that are for the end." Damascene himself expresses this by saying that "'deliberation is inquiring desire,' thus showing that deliberation in some way belongs both to the will, which is the subject matter and the mover of the inquiry, and to reason, which conducts the inquiry."

"Deliberation" translates the Latin word *consilium*, which can also mean "plan," "purpose," and "advice," among other things. This breadth of meaning is what gives rise to the other two objections. **Obj. 2** quotes Ephesians 1:11: God "works all things according to the *consilium*"—that is, the plan or purpose—"of his will." Thus *consilium* is ascribed to God, who does not engage in inquiry, because his intellect is not discursive (that is, God does not discover anything by reasoning from one truth to another, but knows everything in a single all-encompassing act). So *consilium* cannot be an inquiry.

Aquinas's response in **resp.** 2 appeals to an important feature of his view about the use of language to describe God. (See I.13 for a full discussion.) We can use our ordinary language to talk about God, but in doing so we must interpret those ordinary words in a way that purges them of any suggestion of limitation or deficiency. We have knowledge (*scientia*) and God has knowledge, but our knowledge involves discursive reasoning from causes to effects, whereas God's knowledge is his "certainty concerning all effects in their first cause"—which is of course God himself—"without any discursive reasoning." We ascribe to God whatever is a matter of perfection in knowledge and deny of him whatever is a matter of imperfection or limitation. In the same way, we have *consilium* and God has *consilium*, but in us *consilium* is a process of inquiry that yields a determination or judgment, whereas in God it is the certainty of his judgment, which requires no inquiry.

**Obj. 3** quotes 1 Corinthians 7:25: "Concerning virgins I have no commandment from the Lord, but I do give *consilium*"—that is, advice. We advise people to do what we are sure is good. Inquiry, by contrast, is for cases in which we are not sure what is good; it "concerns matters that are in doubt." (The claim that *consilium* "is given concerning things that are assuredly good" gets additional force from the medieval understanding of poverty, chastity, and obedience as "evangelical counsels" or "counsels of perfection," good things that are not required of all Christians but are enjoined on those who would aim at Christian perfection. For Aquinas's discussion see especially I-II.108.4.) Aquinas responds in **resp. 3** that counsel is given concerning things that "wise and spiritual men" are sure are good but most people are not certain about.

### 14.2. Is deliberation about the end, or only about things that are for the end?

Answer: Deliberation is not about an end *qua* end, but only about things that are for the end.

We know already that deliberation is closely connected with choice, since deliberation concludes with the judgment that informs choice, so it is not surprising that Aquinas's **reply** to this question about deliberation in very like his reply to the parallel question about choice in 13.3. In practical reasoning the end is the principle: we reason *from* the end, not *to* the end. So in the inquiry that is deliberation, we take the end as a given and investigate how it might be attained. But something that is an end in one inquiry can be ordered to some further end, and then there can be deliberation about it, not as an end, but as something that is for an end.

Accordingly, Aquinas says that "What is taken as an end is already determinate" (**resp. 1**). That is, we investigate *how* to accomplish what we already take as an end. If we are investigating *whether* to accomplish it, we are not yet treating it as an end, but as something that is, or at least could be, directed toward some other end that (at least for the purposes of this particular inquiry) is taken as a given.

### 14.3. Is deliberation only about things that we do?

Answer: Yes.

Nowhere else in Q14, or indeed in the Treatise on Human Acts, does Aquinas suggest that the ordinary process of deliberation—the one that concludes with a judgment or determination and precedes choice—is typically, let alone normatively, collaborative. So it is quite strange that he begins his **reply** by saying that "Deliberation, properly speaking, implies several people conferring." He justifies this claim by appeal to etymology: 'deliberation' (*consilium*) means a sitting-together (*considium*). The etymology is incorrect—the second syllable of *consilium* actually derives from '*calo*,' to call, summon, convoke—but that is neither here nor there. A calling-together implies several people conferring just as much as a sitting-together does, so the proper etymology would not change his conclusion. It is the conclusion itself that is puzzling. Why introduce an etymology to support an understanding of deliberation that (as we shall see) is not consistently adopted even in this question, let alone elsewhere?

And it is not as though the etymology is the only consideration that Aquinas uses here to suggest that deliberation is normatively collaborative. In the reply he notes that in particular contingent matters—which of course include the domain of action—"there are many conditions or circumstances that have to be taken into account if there is to be any certain knowledge." The complexity of human action is precisely why it is best to have a number of people thinking about what should be done, "since one person notices what does not occur to someone else." Necessary and universal matters lack such complexity, "so that one person can be more self-sufficient in carrying out such an investigation." Aquinas concludes that deliberation is therefore an inquiry into the truth about contingent singulars, since those are the objects of investigation that require "several people conferring." And knowing the truth about contingent singulars (unlike knowing the truth about universals and necessary things) is not desirable for its own sake; it is desired only because it gives us guidance about how to act. "And that," Aquinas concludes, "is why we should say that, properly speaking, deliberation is about things that we do."

So Aquinas uses the collaborative character of deliberation in order to argue for the conclusion that he wants, namely, that deliberation is about things that we do. But there are other ways to arrive at that conclusion—Aristotle establishes it in quite a different way, by process of elimination—so surely the fact that Aquinas uses this premise in support of a conclusion he accepts when he does not have to use it to arrive at that conclusion suggests that he really does accept the premise that deliberation is normatively collaborative. And yet there is very little hint elsewhere in the Treatise on Human Acts, or even in the rest of Q14, that this is his understanding of deliberation.

Indeed, the most natural reading even of the claim that deliberation is about things that "we" do is that each of us individually deliberates about his or her own action, not that we collectively deliberate about our collective action. Even **resp. 4**, in which Aquinas argues that "we deliberate about the actions of others insofar as they are in some sense one with us," suggests the idea that deliberation is typically one person's deliberation about how he or she ought to act. For otherwise, why would we need a special argument for the claim that we can deliberate about what other people do? And note that the argument is that we can deliberate about what other people do *precisely to the extent that they are one with us*, which further suggests that normal or standard deliberation is *my* deliberation about what *I* should do, because I can deliberate about what you should do only to the extent that I can count you as being, somehow, me.

I have no theory about why Aquinas here adopts a view of deliberation that is not his usual view.

### 14.4. Is deliberation about all the things that we do?

Answer: No. We do not deliberate about trivial things or about things that have to be done in determinate ways.

We saw in art. 1 and art. 3 that deliberation is needed because the domain of human action is contingent, uncertain, and doubtful. We need a process of investigation to figure out how to navigate those contingencies and uncertainties in such a way as to attain our end. But in the **reply** to art. 4 Aquinas notes two kinds of cases in which the domain of human action is sometimes straightforward enough that deliberation is not needed and would in fact be superfluous. The first kind is found whenever "there are determinate ways to get to determinate ends." Aquinas's example (an interesting one in light of his own notoriously unreadable handwriting) is that someone who is writing does not deliberate about how to form letters, because "that is determined by the skill of writing." He repeats the point in a more general way in **resp. 3**: "when not only the thing but the way of doing it is fixed, there is no need for deliberation." (Skills that require judgment, such as medicine and business, will still require deliberation.) The second kind is found whenever "it does not much matter whether something is done in this way or that way." In these cases, reason can make its judgment about how to attain the end without the preliminary inquiry that is usually necessary (**resp. 1, resp. 2**), and choice then follows that judgment (**resp. 1**).

### 14.5. Does deliberation proceed by analysis?

Answer: Yes. Deliberation begins from the intended aim and continues until one reaches what is to be done right now.

The distinction between proceeding by analysis (*modo resolutorio*: more literally, "by way of breaking things down") and proceeding by synthesis (*modo compositivo*: more literally, "by way of putting things together") is not common in Aquinas, and we have to piece together how he understands the distinction by looking at the few places in which he discusses it. In his *Commentary on Aristotle's Ethics*, Aquinas says that "in every operative science one must proceed by synthesis, whereas in a speculative science one must proceed by analysis, analyzing composites into simple principles" (I.3.4). Speaking in particular of deliberation, he says, "Because one who deliberates inquires analytically (*resolutive*), his inquiry must reach all the way to what is first in activity, because what is last in analysis is first in generation or, in other words, in activity"; taking an example from Aristotle, he likens this kind of reasoning to the analytical procedure of someone performing a geometrical construction, "who analyzes a conclusion into principles until he reaches the first indemonstrable principles" (III.8.4). And in his *Commentary on the Sentences* Aquinas says that someone who proceeds from signs to things signified is proceeding by analysis "because signs are better known to him" (I.1.4.2).

So from those passages we can gather that proceeding by analysis means proceeding (a) from what is better known to what is less well known, (b) from composites to simples, and (c) from conclusions to principles. Proceeding by synthesis means, in each case, the opposite. In the **reply** Aquinas says that proceeding by synthesis is a matter of proceeding from what is both prior in being and simpler: "proceeding from causes to effects is a process of synthesis, because causes are simpler than their effects." Proceeding by analysis is a matter of proceeding from what is posterior in being (and presumably also from what is more complex, though Aquinas does not explicitly say so): "this is how it works when we make judgments about manifest effects by tracing them back to their causes." This characterization of the distinction seems to cohere with (a) and possibly also (b) from the other passages: analysis proceeds (a) from what is first in cognition, the end, to what is more remote from cognition, the means to attain it, and—if we are to accept it as a general rule that causes are simpler than their effects—(b) from the end, which is the effect, to the action that is to be taken in order to attain that end, which is the cause. But what about (c)? Rather than proceeding from conclusion to principle, doesn't deliberation proceed from a principle—the end—to a conclusion about how to attain the end?

It does, but we should not see this as contradicting (c). In one obvious sense, "in every inquiry one has to begin from some principle"—you have to start somewhere, and in practical reasoning the end is where you start. So the sense of 'principle' at work in the distinction between analytical reasoning from conclusions to principles and synthetic reasoning from principles to conclusions must be a sense of 'principle' other than "starting point of an inquiry"; otherwise there would be no such thing as proceeding by analysis, because all reasoning proceeds from principles in that sense. Instead, the sense of 'principle' relevant to this distinction seems to be that a principle is what is prior in being. In proceeding by analysis, one reasons from what is posterior in being to what is prior in being (for example, from effect to cause); in proceeding by synthesis, one reasons from what is prior in being to what is posterior in being (for example, from cause to effect).[24] Deliberation moves

---

24. Aquinas complicates matters here by using 'principle' just to mean "starting point of inquiry" and distinguishing between principles that are prior in both cognition and being and principles that are prior in cognition but posterior in being. In the passages cited from the *Commentary on Aristotle's Ethics* he is using 'principle' for what is prior in being. Sorting out the terminology removes the appearance of inconsistency.

from what is posterior in being, the end, to what is prior in being, "what is to be done right now."

On this analysis, everything Aquinas says about the distinction between analysis and synthesis can be seen to cohere, with one apparent exception: as we have seen, in book I of the *Commentary on Aristotle's Ethics*, he says that "in every operative science one must proceed by synthesis," whereas here he says that deliberation proceeds by analysis. But isn't deliberation a kind of operative science, that is, knowledge concerned with activity? As it turns out, no. The word *scientia* is crucial. *Scientia* in this context is not merely knowledge, but an organized body of knowledge. So when Aquinas speaks of "operative *scientia*," he does not mean just any bit of cognition that is relevant to action; he is thinking of ethics as a whole. This is why Aquinas says in his prologue to the Treatise on Human Acts:

> So, since happiness must be attained through certain acts, we need to inves-
> tigate human acts so that we can know which acts are those through which
> one attains happiness and which acts stand in the way of happiness. Now
> activities and acts concern singulars; it follows, then, that every kind of
> operative *scientia* requires an investigation of the particular in order to be
> complete. Accordingly, moral inquiry, since it concerns human acts, *should
> be carried out first in general and then in particular.*

Deliberation proceeds by analysis, but ethics as a body of knowledge proceeds by synthesis.

## 14.6. Does deliberation go on infinitely?

Answer: Deliberation is potentially infinite but actually finite: it begins from the end and terminates with what is in one's power to do right here and now.

The three objections all make the case that the subject matter of delibera-tion means that deliberation is an inquiry without limit, a kind of shapeless or indefinite process that in principle can never come to an end. **Obj. 1** notes the by now well-established fact that deliberation is about action, and action has to do with particulars; there are indefinitely many particulars, so it would seem that the inquiry into those particulars goes on indefinitely. **Obj. 2** adds a fact about deliberation that has not been stated before: deliberation "includes inquiry not only into what ought to be done but also into how hindrances are to be overcome." And this new fact threatens an infinite regress: every action can be hindered; the hindrance can be overcome through some reasoning; presumably that reasoning will conclude with a judgment about how one should act to overcome the hindrance; but that action can itself be hindered, so one will have to reason about how to overcome *that* hindrance, and on and on. **Obj. 3** draws a contrast with demonstrative reasoning. In a demon-strative science, inquiry does not go on indefinitely; it has to "come to a stop with some self-evident principles that are altogether certain." But there are no such principles, and therefore there is no such certainty, in the domain of action; for action has to do with singular contingents, which are variable and uncertain by their very nature.

The argument **On the contrary** provides the crucial rejoinder: obviously deliberation does not go on infinitely, because if it did, it would be impossible to finish deliberating. And if it were impossible to finish deliberating, no one would start deliberating, since, as Aristotle says, "No one is moved to something that is impossible to attain." But obviously people do start deliberating—and (he could have added) obviously people do finish deliberating as well, because people choose to perform actions on the basis of the judgment that terminates deliberation.

In the **reply** Aquinas argues that deliberation is finite "at both ends": that is, it both starts somewhere and terminates somewhere. It *starts* with two sorts of things: the end and what we might call fixed relevant facts, which can include both particular knowledge ("This is bread." "Flipping this switch will turn on the light.") and universal knowledge ("Adultery is forbidden by God." "Driving under the influence of alcohol or drugs is dangerous."). We do not inquire about either of those, because the end is taken as given for a particular piece of deliberation (recall art. 2) and the fixed relevant facts are just *there*, so to speak, to serve as inputs for deliberation. True, we might inquire into whether adultery is forbidden or drunk driving is dangerous, but such inquiry is not deliberation; it belongs to "another speculative or practical science."

Deliberation *terminates* with "what is in our power to do right here and now." The end is the principle of deliberation and what is done for the sake of the end is a conclusion, so the final conclusion is whatever has to be done first. When my deliberation turns up what I am to do here and now—an action that is directed toward the end and does not have some further action directed toward it—I have reached the terminus of deliberation, and "inquiry comes to a halt."

Aquinas responds to the objections in effect by acknowledging their theoretical force but denying their practical implications. **Resp. 1** agrees that singulars are infinite, but only potentially; they are not actually infinite. There are standard Aristotelian arguments, which Aquinas accepts, for the impossibility of an actual infinity; but one need not know anything about those arguments to understand his point here, which is very down-to-earth and practical (rather than metaphysical): in *theory* there are infinitely many things you could deliberate about, but in practice you have very few attainable ends at a given time, a limited number of ways to attain them, and a manageable range of considerations you need to take into account. Similarly, in **resp. 2** he argues that although it is always possible for an action to be hindered, in any actual case there may well not be a hindrance, and so there will be no need to deliberate about how to overcome it. In **resp. 3** he says that we do in fact achieve a kind of certainty through our deliberation. Granted, we cannot achieve the unqualified certainty of demonstrative science; but we can achieve certainty-for-now, which is all we need as a basis for action.

## Question 15: Consent, Which Is an Act of Will concerning Things That Are for the End

### 15.1. Is consent an act of an appetitive power or of an apprehensive power?

Answer: Consent is an act of an appetitive power.

The key difficulty here, and indeed throughout this question, is the obscurity of the notion of "application." What could the "application of sense to something" (reply) or "the application of an appetitive movement to doing something" (art. 2) possibly mean? Looking at Aquinas's other uses of 'apply' and 'application' (*applicare, applicatio*) helps somewhat. In most cases, when Aquinas speaks of applying something he means making use of it, putting it to work, or bringing it to bear on something. Thus, for example, he speaks of applying a virtue to acting (SCG III.67.4) and of applying cognition to the things we do by judging our past or prospective acts (ST I.79.13, DV 17 passim); the virtue of prudence or practical wisdom is a matter of applying right reason to activity (ST II-II.47 passim). So "an application of sense to something" should mean an act of bringing sense perception to bear on something, and "the application of an appetitive movement to doing something" should mean bringing an appetitive movement to bear on doing something, or putting an appetitive movement to work to do something.

These notions are admittedly still not entirely clear, but perhaps they are enough to go on for now. For although Aquinas begins the **reply** by saying that 'consent' implies an application of sense to something, the emphasis falls on 'sense' rather than on 'application.' Sense, he says, is what cognizes things that are present. It thereby differs both from imagination, which cognizes likenesses of bodily things, "including likenesses of things that are absent," and from intellect, which cognizes universals and can do so whether singulars are present or absent. To put this all more concretely: I can imagine a dog when no dog is present, and I can understand the universal nature of dog (what-it-is-to-be-a-dog, caninity) when no dog is present, but I cannot have sense perception of a dog if there is no dog present for me to sense. This distinctive feature of sense—its being directed toward a particular thing that is present—has an analogue in appetite: "an act of an appetitive power is a certain inclination to the thing itself." So when the appetitive power "cleaves" to a thing—when it is pleased with the thing—it "receives, by a kind of analogy, the name 'sense.'" Just as sense is cognitive experience of a thing, the appetite's taking pleasure in something is a sort of appetitive experience of a thing.[25] This analogy explains how sense, which properly speaking belongs to an apprehensive power, can be attributed to an appetitive power (resp. 2).

In **resp. 3** Aquinas explains the distinction between *assent*, which is something the intellect does, and *consent*, which is something the will does. (He acknowledges, however, that the two words can be used interchangeably; and it would in any case not be wise to put a great deal of weight on his somewhat fanciful etymology.) To assent (*assentire*) is to sense toward something (*ad aliud sentire*); to consent (*consentire*) is to sense together (the prefix 'con' is equivalent to the preposition '*cum*,' "with"). The former implies distance between what gives assent and what is assented to; the latter implies union between what gives consent and what is consented to. Thus consent properly belongs to the will because the will moves toward the thing itself. (Could this not equally serve as a reason to call it assent, given that assent is supposed to mean "sensing toward"? It is hard to overlook the apparently ad hoc character of this explanation.) Assent, by contrast, properly belongs to the intellect because the intellect does not move toward the thing, "but rather the reverse." Aquinas has in mind something akin to what is nowadays called "direction of fit": the intellect is supposed to reflect the way things are (its direction of fit is world-to-mind), whereas the will moves to change the way things are to reflect what one wants (its direction of fit is mind-to-world).

### 15.2. Does consent belong to non-rational animals?

Answer: No, because non-rational animals have no power over the movement of their appetite.

Relying on his previous characterization of consent as "applying an appetitive movement to doing something," Aquinas argues in the **reply** that non-rational animals lack consent because they cannot *apply* an appetitive movement. Application (as we saw in art. 1) implies making use of something, putting something to work, bringing something to bear for some purpose.

---

25. The quotation from Wisdom 1:1 would ordinarily be translated "Set your mind on the Lord in goodness" or "Think of the Lord in goodness." Both of those translations, however, obscure the fact that the passage uses the verb (*sentire*) that is cognate with the noun 'sense' (*sensus*). The connection between Wisdom 1:1 and what precedes is made somewhat clumsily by "That is why" (*unde*), and it may look as if Aquinas means us to understand "sensing" the Lord as something appetitive. But elsewhere when Aquinas quotes the verse (*Comm. 2 Corinth. 11.1, Comm. Philipp. 1.2, Comm. Col. 1.3, Comm. Romans 8.1*) he clearly understands *sentire* as something cognitive. So I take it that his point is that Wisdom 1:1 is right to speak of "sensing" God, even though God is not an object of the senses, because it indicates an experience of God as real and present that is analogous to sense perception.

Accordingly, consent is active, whereas in non-rational animals the appetite is determined passively (**resp. 1**); it results entirely from natural instinct, over which they have no control.

Human beings are (sometimes) like non-rational animals in acting from passion, but there is a crucial difference. Human beings have the power not to follow passion; if they do follow it, it is because they *consent* to it. Non-rational animals have no such power; they cannot consent to, or dissent from, a passion, but act as their natural instinct determines them to act (**resp. 3**). Consent thus precedes action in human beings, but non-rational animals act without consent (**resp. 2**).

### 15.3. Does consent concern the end?

Answer: No. Consent is the application of an appetitive movement to what is determined by deliberation, and deliberation is only about things that are for the end, so consent too is only about things that are for the end.

For the first time in the Treatise on Human Acts Aquinas sets out in his **reply** a clear statement of the "order in the domain of action":

(1) apprehension of an end
(2) desire for the end
(3) deliberation regarding things that are for the end
(4) desire for the things that are for the end.

Note that *will* and *intention* are collapsed into a single item, (2), and *consent* and *choice* are treated as two aspects of (4) that may or may not be separate in reality, depending on the circumstances.

Now consider (1) and (2). If the end in question is the ultimate end, (2) follows naturally and necessarily from (1). Given the way Aquinas has been talking about "application" as implying a kind of control over the appetitive power, we would expect him to say that there is no application of the appetitive power to the ultimate end. Instead, he says that there *is* an application of the appetitive power to the ultimate end, but this "does not count as consent but as simple will," because 'consent' by definition "indicates an application of an appetitive movement to something *that is already in the power of the one who makes the application*." There is clearly a terminological inconsistency here—the way he defines 'consent' in art. 3 makes it equivalent to 'application' as discussed in art. 1 and art. 2, and the implication of control that 'application' had in art. 1 and art. 2 is lost in art. 3—but no more than a terminological inconsistency. The idea remains clear: in the same way that there is no room for consent in non-rational animals because their appetite is always determined, there is no room for consent in human beings when it comes to the ultimate end because, with respect to that object alone, their appetite is determined.

We necessarily will the ultimate end, but we do not necessarily will any particular way of attaining it. So there is room for deliberation about how to attain the ultimate end (note: not *whether* to aim at the ultimate end, but *how* to aim at it), and so anything short of the ultimate end itself "falls within the scope of deliberation" because it can be directed to the ultimate end. Such deliberation can range from a big-picture life-choice question about how to attain the ultimate end itself ("Is the best life for me a career in philosophy or a religious vocation?") all the way down to fairly mundane considerations about how to attain an end quite remote from the ultimate end ("Should I drive to the philosophy talk or take the bus?"). Now where is consent in this? Aquinas began (see 13.2) by defining 'consent' as "an application of an appetitive movement to something that is already in the power of the one who makes the application." This definition does not fit deliberation itself, Aquinas says, because we do not apply an appetitive movement toward deliberation: that is, we do not put our desire for the end to work for the sake of deliberation, but rather we put deliberation to work in the service of our desire for the end. The definition of 'consent' does, however, fit our desire for what is determined by deliberation: we bring our appetite to bear on the things that deliberation reveals as ways of attaining the end that is presupposed in deliberation. And (as the notion of consent requires) we have control over this desire; we can accept or reject what deliberation turns up.

The claim that consent is a matter of "bringing our appetite to bear on the things that deliberation reveals" is admittedly vague; it is a (perhaps slightly more informative) paraphrase of Aquinas's "application of an appetitive movement to what is determined by deliberation." What is that, exactly? **Resp. 3** helps somewhat in the course of laying out the distinction between consent and choice. Both are acts of will that concern what is for the end. They differ in that choice implies preferring one thing to another. If "deliberation turns up a number of ways of attaining the end, and if each of them is pleasing, there can be consent to each of them; but of the many that are pleasing, we choose one in preference to the others." If there is only one way of attaining the end that one finds acceptable, one and the same act will be both consent and choice: "it will be called consent insofar as one finds the prospect of acting in this way pleasing, but choice insofar as one prefers it to other ways that are not pleasing." This discussion tells us that consenting to an act means finding the prospect of performing the act pleasing, where the act in question will be something that deliberation determines is a way of attaining the end that one desires. From earlier discussion in art. 2 as well as here in art. 3 we know that this will not be a purely passive pleasure in the prospect of performing the act but will be to some extent under our control. So where choice is a decision to do x (in preference to y or z) in order to attain one's end, consent is a kind of preliminary volitional endorsement or approval of x, y, and z as acceptable ways of attaining one's end.

### 15.4. Does consent to an act belong
### solely to the higher part of the soul?

Answer: Yes.

The understanding of consent as preliminary volitional endorsement or approval of one or more possible actions as acceptable ways of attaining one's end is what we might call Aquinas's official notion of consent. But there is a more robust notion of consent, inspired particularly by Augustine and prominent in the thought of Peter Abelard, that we sometimes see in the way Aquinas talks about consenting to an act, consenting to a passion, and so forth. This more robust notion is closer to choice or decision. In his commentary *On the Lord's Sermon on the Mount* I.12.34, Augustine says that a sin comes to completion in three stages: suggestion, pleasure, and consent. There is *suggestion* when either thought or perception brings a sinful act to mind, *pleasure* when we take delight in what is brought to mind, and *consent* when we yield to the delightful prospect of sinning. Pleasure by itself does not constitute sin: Augustine quite sensibly points out that if we are fasting and we run across some delicious food, our appetite will be aroused and we will of course experience pleasure. (Whether he means pleasure in the sight and smell of the food or pleasure in the thought of eating it is not altogether clear.) But if we consent to the pleasure, we have sinned, even if no overt act follows. In *On the Trinity* XII.12.17 Augustine makes it clear that this consent means setting oneself to carry out the overt act if the opportunity arises and one has the power to do so; but again, the sin is complete when one consents, whether any overt act follows. If I yield to the delightful prospect of breaking my fast with the marvelously rich food I see before me, I have sinned even if someone whisks the food away before I have a chance to reach for a fork.

The differences between this Augustinian notion of consent and Aquinas's official notion of consent are considerable. Consent in Augustine's view has no necessary relationship to deliberation or to things that are for the end as distinguished from the ends themselves. It is more than a mere endorsement of an act as acceptable; it is a firm purpose, resolution, or decision to perform an act. And whereas Aquinas's official notion allows for multiple consents at a given time to incompatible courses of action, the Augustinian notion does not. Despite these differences, however, the Augustinian notion does sometimes appear in Aquinas:

> Thus a lower appetite is sufficient to produce movement only if the higher capacity consents. (*ST* I.81.3)

> In something done as a result of force, the will does not consent. (*ST* I-II.6.6 resp. 1)

Even if the will cannot stop the movement of desire from arising . . . neverthe-less, the will can will not to have the desire, or not consent to the desire. (*ST* I-II.10.3 resp. 1)

Every sin occurs through the will's consent. (*On Truth* 5 resp. 10)

In fact, the Augustinian notion seems to be dominant everywhere in Aquinas except in I-II.15–16; only in the questions on consent and use does the official notion of consent dominate. And even in these questions the Augustinian notion sometimes comes to the fore, as it certainly seems to do in this article. In the **reply** Aquinas speaks of consent to an act as "the final determination about matters of action," which is true of consent as Augustine understood it but does not reflect the official notion of consent. For according to art. 3 resp. 3, consent (as characterized by the official notion) is not in fact the final determination, at least not when there is consent to more than one possible course of action; consent needs to be followed by choice.

So in order to understand art. 4 it is important to recognize that the question is asking about Augustinian consent, not consent as characterized by the official notion presented in the rest of Q15. We also need to understand the distinction between higher and lower reason. The distinction derives from Augustine's *On the Trinity* XII. Higher reason aims at "contemplating and consulting the eternal"; lower reason is aimed at temporal things. Aquinas insists in I.79.9 (citing Augustine's own words for support) that higher and lower reason are not distinct capacities, just different functions of the same capacity—intellect. Here Aquinas argues that the final determination about a prospective course of action must be made by higher reason, because higher reason has the job of making judgments about everything else. Sensible things are the object of lower reason, but we make judgments about them ultimately by attending to the divine reasons, which are the object of higher reason. In the case of action, then, "so long as it is unclear whether, according to divine reasons, something ought to be resisted or not, no judgment of reason counts as a final determination." Such a final determination in light of the divine reasons has to belong to higher reason, because it is the function of higher reason to contemplate and consult the eternal. And lest we think that "reason" here means intellect rather than will, Aquinas concludes by reassuring us that "consent to an act pertains to higher reason—though in the sense of 'reason' that includes the will."

This argument seems to go even further than Augustinian consent to something one might call hyper-Augustinian consent: Aquinas seems to be saying that "the final determination about matters of action," which he here identifies with "consent to an act," necessarily involves not just a decision to perform the act but a decision *in light of the divine reasons.* Such a definition would mean that whenever we decide to do an action without thinking about God one way or the other—as is surely the case for most actions, for most people

(cf. **obj. 3**)—we would not be consenting to the action; and since "Actions
are called voluntary because we consent to them" (**resp. 2**), that would mean
that such actions—most actions—would not be voluntary. Aquinas deals with
this worry in **resp. 3**. "Higher reason," he says, "is said to consent, not only
because it always moves to action in accordance with eternal reasons, but also
because it does not dissent from acting in accordance with eternal reasons."
That is, higher reason is always *capable* of consenting to action or dissenting
from action in the light of the divine reasons it discerns; so even when it fails
to do so, when people "consent to an act, not on the basis of eternal reasons,
but on the basis of temporal reasons—or even on the basis of certain passions
of the soul," it is correct to say that the final determination lay with higher
reason, because it had the power to do its proper job but failed to do it.

### Question 16: Use, Which Is an Act of Will concerning Things That Are for the End

Choice is not yet action. Having deliberated about how to achieve a satisfying career, I reach the determination or judgment that the best action that I
can take here and now for the sake of my end is to apply to graduate school
in philosophy, and I choose accordingly. But that choice is not yet an action:
choosing to apply is not the same thing as applying. Nor does choice guarantee any action: I could choose to apply but never actually follow through. So
full-blown action requires something further, a process of following through
on what has been chosen, of bringing it to realization. Aquinas sometimes
calls this process of following through "execution," and he identifies a role for
both will and intellect in execution. The act that primarily belongs to will he
calls "use," and the act that primarily belongs to intellect he calls "command."
Q16 examines use, Q17 command.

#### 16.1. Is use an act of the will?

Answer: Use belongs primarily and principally to the will as what initiates
movement, but it belongs to reason as directing action and to other powers
as carrying out action.

"To use something," Aquinas quotes from Augustine (**On the contrary**), "is to
take up something into the power of the will." What Augustine says accords
with what Aquinas has already stated (9.1) about the will: it moves the other
powers of the soul to their acts, or (in other words) the will *uses* those powers
or puts them to use. So it is not surprising to see that Aquinas concludes that
use is an act of the will.

But what *is* use, exactly? The full understanding of use will emerge slowly
over the course of Q16, but in the **reply** to art. 1 we see the most fundamental

aspect of use: it involves applying something to an action. In this broad sense of 'use' we use both "internal principles such as the powers of the soul or the parts of the body, as we apply the intellect to thinking and the eye to seeing, and external things, as we apply a stick to striking." But our use of external things is always mediated by the use of an intrinsic principle: in order to apply a stick to striking I must apply my hand to grasp the stick. And it is the will that initiates the movement of these intrinsic principles, so ultimately it is the will that applies other powers of the soul, the parts of the body, and external things to action; in other words, use is an act of the will. Those other powers, bodily parts, and external things are instruments of the will: the will is the sculptor, they are the chisel. We attribute the sculpture to the sculptor, not to the chisel.

This is not to say that the will's "instruments" are not important or do not contribute to action. (Even an artist's tools, though lacking in any intentionality or motive power of their own, make a contribution: use a different kind of chisel and your sculpture won't look the same.) The will initiates movement—it supplies the dynamism that powers action—but without the intellect, the will's movement would be arbitrary and directionless. (Indeed Aquinas doesn't think the idea of a will unguided by intellect even makes sense.) So because reason directs action, we can say that use is a function of reason as well. Similarly, because other powers carry out the action that the will initiates and reason guides, use can be ascribed to them too. "So it is clear," Aquinas says, "that use belongs primarily and principally to the will as what initiates movement, but to reason as directing action and to other powers as carrying out action."

### 16.2. Does use belong to non-rational animals?

Answer: No.

Aquinas's **reply** offers nothing unexpected; it is roughly parallel to his argument in 15.2 that non-rational animals lack consent. To use, he says here, "is to apply some principle of action to acting." Applying *x* to *y* means "referring" *x* to *y*—that is, in some way bringing *x* to bear on *y* or doing something with *x* for the sake of *y*—so it requires not just a judgment about *x* but a judgment about *x* in light of *y*. Only reason is capable of this kind of judgment, so only an animal that possesses reason is capable of use. Aquinas elaborates on this point in **resp. 2**: animals do walk with their feet and strike with their horns, but they do so by natural instinct and not because they have cognition of the relationship between feet and walking or horns and striking; for that reason, it is not correct to say that animals *use* their feet for walking or their horns for striking.

**Obj. 1** does introduce something new to the discussion: the relative "nobility" of enjoyment and use. The objection argues that enjoyment is nobler (that is, more valuable, of a higher rank or status) than use, because, as Augustine says, we use things for the sake of something that is to be enjoyed. And since non-rational animals are capable of enjoyment (11.2), which ranks higher, it certainly seems that they should be capable of use, which ranks lower. Aquinas responds in **resp. 1** that we need to distinguish between two different ways in which the comparative "nobility" of enjoyment and use can be assessed: in terms of their objects and in terms of the cognition required for them. In terms of their objects, enjoyment is nobler, because the object of enjoyment is something that is desirable for its own sake, whereas the object of use is something that is desirable only for the sake of something else. But precisely because use requires referring one thing to another, it is nobler in terms of the cognition it presupposes, because referring one thing to another is a function of reason; enjoyment merely requires "absolute" cognition (that is, cognition that does not involve referring one thing to another), which even sense can do.

### 16.3. *Can use also concern the ultimate end?*

Answer: In the sense of 'use' that means applying one thing to another, only what is for the end can be used; but there is use of the ultimate end in the sense that one seeks the *attainment* or *possession* of the *thing* that is the ultimate end.

Aquinas's language in this article is uncharacteristically opaque, but his position turns out to be quite straightforward. The best path through the argument is to set aside (for now) the first three sentences of the **reply** and go directly to Aquinas's distinction between the end as "the thing itself" and the end as "the attainment or possession of the thing." We have not heard about this distinction since the Treatise on Happiness, and so we may have forgotten one crucial point about it. When he drew that distinction in the Treatise on Happiness, he typically did not contrast the "thing" with the "attainment or possession" of the thing, but rather with the "use or attainment"—or even "use or enjoyment"—of the thing.[26] Yes, he employs the word 'use' for what he is now calling "possession" and as roughly synonymous with 'enjoyment.'

In the meantime, of course, 'use' has come to have this new, narrower meaning, in which it is contrasted with enjoyment rather than roughly synonymous. But rather than acknowledging straightforwardly that he had employed the word 'use' in a different sense in the Treatise on Happiness from the sense it has in the Treatise on Human Acts, he tries to talk around this fact—a procedure that accounts for the obscurity of some of the discussion here. We can remedy that obscurity by employing "attainment-use" for 'use' in the sense of attainment or possession of the end and "application-use" for 'use' in the

---

26. We find "use or attainment" at 1.8, "use or enjoyment" at 3.1.

sense of applying one thing to another. Aquinas's conclusion is that application-use is only of what is for the end, but attainment-use is of the end, even the ultimate end.

The first part of that conclusion—that application-use is only of what is for the end—is easy to establish. Application-use is applying one thing to another; what is applied to something else (used for the sake of something else) is something that is for the end; therefore, application-use is of something that is for the end. Application-use is the sense of 'use' we have in mind when we call something "useful," meaning that it is suitable for an end; we even sometimes call usefulness itself "use." (This is as true in English as it is in Latin: we can say things like "Ain't no use in complaining when you've got a job to do.")

The second part of the conclusion—that attainment-use is of the end—receives a more complicated argument, although it is not clear that it really requires one. Aquinas introduces a new distinction concerning the ultimate end: we can speak of the ultimate end simply (that is, just *as* the ultimate end) or with respect to a particular person (as *my* ultimate end, *your* ultimate end, *Joe Schmoe's* ultimate end). Aquinas justifies this distinction by appealing to the distinction between end-as-thing and end-as-attainment: if we speak of the ultimate end simply, we are speaking of the end-as-thing; but if we speak of the ultimate end for a particular person, we are speaking of the end-as-attainment. Suppose greedy people are right. Is it better to say that the ultimate end is *money* or *possessing money*? Possessing money is good only because money is good, Aquinas says; so "it is clear that, speaking simply, the ultimate end is the thing itself." (In other words, the goodness of money is what explains the goodness of possessing money, not vice versa; and by definition the ultimate end is the good thing from which any other good things derive their goodness.) But if I am a greedy person, *my* end is the attainment or possession of money; my purpose in dealing with money at all is to have it. I *enjoy* money in the sense that I locate my ultimate end (end-as-thing) in money; I *use* money in the sense that what I "have in view in dealing with money" is possessing it (end-as-attainment).

The distinction between attainment-use and application-use allows Aquinas to agree with Augustine that "everyone who enjoys, uses" (**obj. and resp. 1**) and with Hilary that "use is in the Gift" (**obj. and resp. 3**): both authors are speaking of attainment-use, which is a matter of enjoying—resting in—the ultimate end. It also allows him to interpret Augustine's dictum, "To use is to take something up into the power of the will" (**obj. and resp. 2**). If we interpret 'use' as referring to attainment-use, Augustine's dictum concerns the end, which "is taken up into the power of the will so that the will might come to rest in it." If instead we interpret 'use' as referring to application-use, Augustine's dictum concerns what is for the end, which is taken up into the power of the will so that the will can direct it toward the end in which the will is to come to rest.

### 16.4. Does use precede choice?

Answer: The will's use of reason, referring what is for the end to the end, precedes choice; the will's use of an executive power follows choice.

I want to play Bach's G-major French Suite well. What is the relationship of my wanting to what I want—in Aquinas's vocabulary, what is the relation of my will to what is willed? There is a vague but recognizable sense in which what I want is already *in* me, in my will, simply because I want it; as Aquinas puts it in the **reply**, my will has a "certain proportion or order" to playing that piece. My will is a will-to-play-Bach rather than a will-to-listen-to-Sondheim or a will-to-act-in-a-Shakespeare-play; in that sense what I will is not merely some external thing but something within me, something that characterizes my will. This is the first relation of my will to what is willed. But this is an imperfect way of having the end: I have what I want in a sense, because I have it within me; but I do not yet have it fully, because I am not yet actually playing the piece well. Having what I want in the full sense, as something realized in fact rather than merely as something within me, is the second relation of the will to what is willed.

Aquinas has been talking generally about the relation between the will and what is willed. He now notes that "what is willed" includes both the end and what is for the end; because the question concerns the order of use and choice, both of which have to do with what is for the end, he now turns specifically to a discussion of the will's relation to what is for the end. Choice, he says, is precisely what completes the will's first relation to what is for the end. When I choose one thing that is for the end in preference to other options, that chosen option is fully and completely "in" my will in the sense explored above. But that first relation is imperfect; the will's relation to what is for the end is perfect only when it uses the executive powers to realize in fact what before was merely within the will. Thus choice comes first, and the use of the executive powers follows.

But the executive powers are not the only things that the will uses or moves. As we have seen repeatedly (see especially 9.1 and 16.1), the will also moves reason. In the case of what is for the end, the will uses reason by directing the intellect to consider what is for the end in light of the end and thus to refer it to the end. This sort of use, the will's use of reason, obviously precedes choice.

In **resp. 3** Aquinas makes the striking claim that "in any given act of the will we can find consent and choice and use: we might say that the will consents to its choosing, and consents to its consenting, and uses itself for consenting and choosing." If one understands the Treatise on Human Acts as setting out a determinate sequence of acts (see introduction to Q8), this claim is quite baffling: on that reading consent, choice, and use are supposed to be distinct acts of will occurring in precisely that order in any fully realized and completed human act. But if instead one reads the Treatise on Human Acts as I have proposed—as analyzing the various ways in which the human capacity for intellectual desire is related to possible objects of desire and to the purposive acts that express and realize those desires—then there is nothing at all puzzling about this claim. One and the same act of will can be regarded as an instance of choice, of consent, and of use: choice in that the will is selecting one alternative in preference to others, consent in that this selection does not simply emerge spontaneously and unbidden in the will but is endorsed by the will and under its control,[27] and use in that the will is moving itself toward what is for the end in virtue of its desire for the end (9.3).

### Question 17: Acts Commanded by the Will

At the beginning of Q8 Aquinas distinguished between two kinds of acts of will: the will's own acts, and acts of other powers that are commanded by the will. The will's own acts, called "elicited" acts, belong to the will directly; acts of other powers, called "commanded" acts, belong to the will indirectly, through the mediation of other powers. QQ8–16 were devoted to elicited acts; Q17 examines commanded acts, along with command itself.

### 17.1. Is command an act of the will or of reason?

Answer: Command is an act of reason but presupposes an act of will.

This question is somewhat surprising, given that up to this point Aquinas has spoken consistently of commanded acts as "acts commanded by the will" (Q6 prol., 6.4, 6.5 resp. 1, Q8 prol., Q17 prol.) and never as "acts commanded by reason." If acts are commanded by the will, surely command itself is an act of the will and not of reason. But in his **reply** Aquinas does not see it this way. The will does move other powers to carry out an act, but it does so through a command on the part of reason. The will gives reason its motive force, but reason must direct the executive powers by indicating what is to be done. This indication takes the form of an imperative, "Do this"; reason's issuing such an imperative is the act of command.

Aquinas argues in II-II.47.8 that command is the chief or foremost act of the virtue of prudence or practical wisdom:

> Prudence is correct reason concerning matters of action. . . . Hence it must be the case that the foremost act of prudence is the foremost act of reason concerning matters of action. There are in fact three acts of reason concerning action. The first is deliberation, which pertains to discovery; for to

---

27. The sense of 'consent' here has to be the broader Augustinian sense, not the narrower "official" sense: see commentary on 15.4.

deliberate is to inquire, as I maintained above (I-II.14.1). The second act is judgment concerning what has been discovered; this is as far as speculative reason goes. But practical reason, which is directed toward activity, proceeds further. It has a third act, command; this act consists in applying the results of deliberation and judgment to activity. And because this act is closer to the end of practical reason, it is the chief act of practical reason, and consequently the chief act of prudence.[28]

Failure in the act of command is called "inconstancy," which Aquinas describes in this way:

> Inconstancy implies backsliding from a definite good that one has purposed to bring about. Now this sort of backsliding originates in an appetitive power, because no one goes back on his previous good purpose except because of something that pleases him inordinately. But this backsliding comes to completion only through a failure on the part of reason, which errs by repudiating what it had rightly accepted. And because reason can resist the impulse of passion, reason's failure to resist passion derives from the weakness of reason itself, which does not keep itself firmly fixed on the good it has conceived. . . . Inconstancy concerns the act of command, for someone is called "inconstant" because reason fails in commanding the things that accord with deliberation and judgment.[29]

The possibility of inconstancy indicates that command is not a single, unproblematic act. A lot needs to go right, and accordingly a lot can go wrong, between choice and execution, particularly if the chosen act is in any way complicated. One must overcome obstacles, fight off distractions, and stick to one's purpose even when other prospects arise that please the appetite and arouse passion. Reason has the task of superintending or supervising this process of executing what has been chosen, because reason is what attends (or fails to attend) to what must be done in order to execute the choice, discerns (or fails to discern) obstacles and how to overcome them, and resists (or fails to resist) passion. It is this whole activity of supervision, and not a single decisive act, that Aquinas calls "command." Reason's imperative, "Do this," is not issued a single time and with a single 'this,' but again and again, and with different contents as the process of execution unfolds: "Ignore this distraction," "Attend to this difficulty," "Hold firmly to your purpose," "Do not be seduced by passion."

---

28. Aquinas also identifies virtues that perfect the other two acts of reason: deliberation is perfected by *eubulia*, and judgment is perfected by *synesis* in straightforward matters and *gnome* in exceptional matters.

29. The other two acts of reason likewise have their associated failures: failure in the act of deliberation is *praecipitatio* (undue haste—"jumping the gun" by skipping or shortchanging deliberation), and failure in the act of judgment is *inconsideratio* (lack of consideration, inattention—ignoring or misperceiving relevant evidence).

### 17.2. Does command belong to non-rational animals?

**Answer: No.**

We already know that the answer will be no, given the definition of command in art. 1, and indeed Aquinas needs only a three-sentence **reply** to set out the expected answer. His responses to objections are not quite as predictable. Each objection identifies an aspect of command that can be found in non-rational animals. **Obj. 1** draws on Avicenna's observation that the appetitive power commands movement; of course non-rational animals have an appetitive power. But this is not really command, Aquinas says in **resp. 1**, "unless we take 'command' in a very broad sense as meaning 'move.'" Properly speaking, an "appetitive power is said to command movement insofar as it moves reason, which commands," and so the appetitive power of non-rational animals cannot properly be said to command.

**Obj. 2** draws on Aristotle's analogy between the relation of master to slave and that of body to soul: as a master commands and a slave is commanded, the soul commands and the body is commanded. And of course non-rational animals are composed of soul and body just as human beings are. Aquinas says in **resp. 2** that the soul of a non-rational animal lacks the ability to command because it lacks the ability—the cognitive wherewithal—to give direction. The soul of a non-rational animal *moves* its body but does not *command* its body.

**Obj. 3** argues that "through command a person causes an impetus toward an act." Damascene says that impetus toward an act can be found in non-rational animals, so command should be found in them as well. Aquinas says in **resp. 3** that the impetus found in non-rational animals derives entirely from natural instinct; their appetite is moved naturally. So even if they had the cognitive wherewithal to give themselves direction, there would be no room for such direction; as soon as they perceive something suitable, they pursue it, and as soon as they perceive something unsuitable, they flee from it; they have no options, no possibility of doing otherwise than they in fact do. Human beings, by contrast, not only have options but also have the cognitive wherewithal to direct themselves in pursuing one option or another. It is through this direction or command that human beings bring about an impetus to act. Resp. 3 brings out another facet of something Aquinas said in art. 1 resp. 2: "reason is the root of freedom in the sense that it is the *cause* of freedom." Non-rational animals are not free because they lack reason's capacity to weigh and consider different options, and so their appetite is always determined to a single possibility at a time.

### 17.3. What is the order of command and use?

**Answer:** The will's use of reason, referring what is for the end to the end, precedes command; the will's use of the executive powers follows command.

See 16.4 for more on the two kinds of use. Aquinas concluded there that the will's use of reason, directing the intellect to consider what is for the end in light of the end and thus to refer it to the end, precedes choice; and since choice in turn precedes command, Aquinas concludes here that this kind of use also precedes command (**reply**).

The other kind of use is the will's use of the executive powers. This kind of use follows command. **Resp. 1** gives a clear account of the sequence. Deliberation reaches a conclusion, which is the judgment of reason. Then the will chooses, and "after choice, reason commands the power through which what has been chosen is to be carried out." Only then does the will begin to use something. Use, in fact, is the will's carrying out reason's command; as such, of course it follows command.

**Obj. 3** argues that command itself is a kind of use. How can that be the case? Art. 1 said that command is an act of reason as moved by the will, and we have already seen (16.1) that when the will moves other powers, it is said to use them. So the will's moving reason to command can also be called the will's *using* reason. Thus, command is a kind of use, and since a genus is prior to its species, use is prior to command. In **resp. 3** Aquinas does not really respond to the point about the priority of a genus with respect to its species, and with good reason: that kind of priority—a sort of logical or conceptual priority (think of what could be meant by saying that color is prior to red)—is not the natural or temporal priority he is interested in here. He agrees that the will's use of reason precedes command itself, but presumably he means this in terms of natural (causal) or temporal priority, because he goes on to say that sometimes command precedes use in the same way, "insofar as the acts of these powers are reflected back on each other." That last phrase indicates that just as the will uses reason for commanding, reason commands the will to use. That is, reason directs the will to use reason, and reason's direction can itself be called a command. Remember that the will is intellectual appetite. It has no power of its own to shape human action; instead, whatever it wills—in the broadest possible sense of 'will,' which includes simple will, consent, choice, use, and enjoyment—it wills in accordance with intellect's apprehension of something as good.[30] So the will does not use reason (for commanding or for any other purpose) unless reason apprehends using reason as a good thing and therefore directs or commands the will to use reason.

One might worry, of course, that the reflexivity of acts of reason and will sets up an infinite regress: the will uses reason because reason commands the will to use reason, because the will uses reason to command the will to use

---

30. The claim that the will has no power of its own to shape human action is controversial. See Hause (1997) for a thorough weighing of the arguments, and Williams (2011) for an endorsement of Hause's conclusion in the context of a broader treatment of Aquinas's accounts of action and freedom.

reason, because reason commands the will to use reason to command the will to use reason, and so on, with no end in sight. See 9.4 for how Aquinas stops the regress.

### 17.4. Are command and the commanded act a single act, or distinct acts?

Answer: They are distinct parts of a unified whole; they are related as form and matter.

Command is an act of reason; the commanded act is an act of some power other than reason, whether of the will or of some part of the body. So how can command and the commanded act be one and the same? This is the powerful argument for the distinctness of command and commanded act that is raised in **obj. 1**, and **obj. 2** raises an equally powerful argument: command has to be distinct from the commanded act, because sometimes reason commands but the commanded act does not follow. (See the discussion of inconstancy in the commentary on art. 1 for one explanation of why the commanded act might not follow from command.) It seems obvious that if command and the commanded act were one and the same, it would not be possible for there to be a command without a commanded act. Moreover, as **obj. 3** notes, command is naturally prior to the commanded act; and nothing is naturally prior to itself.

Given the strength of these objections, Aquinas can hardly argue that command and the commanded act are fully and completely one. Instead, he will argue that they are distinct parts of a single whole. Before looking at his arguments, however, it is useful to think about what is at stake in this question. Why would it matter if the commanded act were wholly distinct from the command? The answer is that a commanded act fully separate from command would no longer count as a human act. Recall the definition of a human act: "actions that are properly called human are those that issue from a will that is informed by deliberation. Any other actions that might belong to human beings can of course be called 'actions of a human being,' but they are not properly human actions, because they are not characteristic of human beings precisely *as* human beings" (1.1). A commanded act wholly distinct from the command would have no connection with "a will informed by deliberation"; it would be a mere bodily movement, an action of a human being, rather than a properly human action. And because only properly human acts are voluntary (1.1 resp. 2, 6 prol.), such an act would not be voluntary and would therefore also not be subject to praise or blame (6.2 resp. 3). So in order to secure the claim that commanded acts are fully human, voluntary, and subject to moral evaluation, Aquinas has to argue for a close connection between commanded acts and command.

The first sentence of Aquinas's **reply** quietly concedes that command and the commanded act are distinct in *some* respect but says that this fact does not prevent their being one in some other respect: "It is perfectly possible for things to be many in one respect and one in some other respect." Consider a substance "composed of its integral or essential parts." ("Integral parts" are what we would typically call parts; "essential parts" are the fundamental metaphysical constituents. For example, the heart, lungs, brain, legs, arms, and so on are integral parts of a human being; form and matter are the essential parts.) Though the substance has many parts, it is "one in an unqualified sense" because it is a being in an unqualified sense, and "'one' and 'being' are said in the same way." That is, a substance is a being, period, as opposed to a being-only-in-this-respect; and because unity tracks being—a thing is one in the same way that it is a being—a substance is also one, period, as opposed to one-only-in-this-respect. Of course a substance is also many in some respect: it is many in virtue of having many parts. But its oneness, its unity, is more fundamental than its manyness.

In other cases, manyness is more fundamental than oneness: "things that are distinct according to substance, and one in some accidental way, are distinct in an unqualified sense and one in a certain respect." Many people are one family; many paintings are one exhibit. The manyness is more fundamental than the oneness, which is merely a matter of "composition" or "order." Even oneness in species or genus—a widely recognized type of unity in scholastic thought—is only oneness-in-a-certain respect, because "to be one in genus is to be one as regarded in a certain way by reason." (Just in case you were in danger of thinking that Aquinas is a Platonist.)

Now which kind of oneness characterizes the command and the commanded act? Aquinas says that the command and the commanded act compose a whole analogous to the composite of matter and form. When a higher power moves a lower power, the act of the higher power serves as form and the act of the lower power as matter. Suppose my hand goes upward because I want to ask a question. My hand acts only as an instrument of my will; the hand is *what* my will moves (matter), but my will is what makes the movement of my hand a voluntary act (form) as opposed to a merely physical arm-event, which is why it is so much more natural, and so much more informative, to refer to that movement using the language of human acts ("I raised my hand to ask a question") than the language of mere bodily movement ("My hand went up").

This account of the unity of command and commanded act allows Aquinas to answer the initial objections. Yes, command and the commanded act belong to different powers; but the power that commands moves the power that is commanded, and so their acts are in a sense one (**resp. 1**). Yes, command and the commanded act can be separated. So can the parts of a human being, but body and soul are still one whole (**resp. 2**). (This is somewhat misleadingly put. Saying that they "can be separated" suggests that both body and soul can exist independently, when in fact Aquinas thinks that the human soul can exist apart from the body but the body cannot exist apart from the soul; without a soul, there is no body, just a corpse. And however odd this may sound, Aquinas does not think that a corpse is the same object as the living body, only dead, in the way that when your cup of coffee has cooled, it is the same object as the hot coffee, only cold. The analogy with command and the commanded act is therefore even more exact than Aquinas explicitly says, because the command can exist without the commanded act but the commanded act cannot exist without the command; without the command, any bodily movement is a mere movement, not a human act.) And yes, command is naturally prior to the commanded act; but relations of priority can obtain between parts that make up a whole, as the soul is prior to the body (**resp. 3**).

### *17.5. Is an act of the will commanded?*

Answer: Yes. Reason can direct an act of the will.

Command, Aquinas reminds us, "is nothing other than an act of reason that, presupposing some motion"—motion on the part of the will: see art. 1—"directs something to act." Reason can obviously direct the will to act: it can command the will to will what reason has judged to be good. So an act of the will can be commanded.

But if an act of the will can be commanded, don't we run into an infinite regress? Command is an act of reason that presupposes an act of will, so if an act of will is commanded, we have the sequence *act of will* → *reason's command* → *commanded act of will*. But then that first act of will can also be commanded—has to be commanded, in fact, because the will does only what reason directs it to do—and so we have the sequence *act of will* → *reason's command$_1$* → *commanded act of will$_1$* → *reason's command$_2$* → *commanded act of will$_2$*. But we can't stop there, because the first act of will in this new sequence must also be commanded. And there seems to be no principled way to stop this regress; it has to go to infinity. But "it is absurd for there to be an infinite regress" (**obj. 3**), because one cannot come to the end of an infinite regress; if there were really an infinite regress, then, no one would ever will anything. Clearly, though, we do will things.

Aquinas responds (**resp. 3**) that there *is* after all a principled way to stop the regress. Only acts that can be directed by reason are subject to command, and "the will's first act" is not directed by reason; instead, it is directed "by natural instinct or a higher cause," as he argued in 9.4. The will's fundamental orientation to the-good-as-presented-by-reason is not subject to reason's direction or evaluation; it is built into the nature of the will. Another way to think of this is that for Aquinas the will is by nature dynamic, not static; it does not require direction from reason in order to get moving in the first place, but only in order to be directed to move in one way rather than another.

The second objection and response are particularly important as a warning against a misunderstanding of Aquinas's talk of will and intellect as distinct powers. **Obj.** 2 argues that the will cannot be commanded because it cannot understand a command; the intellect is what understands. Aquinas responds in **resp.** 2 that the intellect "does not understand only for itself, but for all the powers; and the will does not will only for itself, but for all the powers." In fact, if we were to speak properly, we would not say that the intellect does this and the will does that; we would say that a human being does this insofar as he has the power of intellect and a human being does that insofar as he has the power of will. Hence Aquinas concludes his response by saying that "human beings command an act of will for themselves insofar as they have both understanding and will." Speaking of the intellect or the will as if they were agents in their own right is just a kind of shorthand; it should not be taken so literally that we forget that the actual agent is always the human being.

### 17.6. Is an act of reason commanded?

Answer: Yes. The exercise of an act of reason can always be commanded; assent to, or dissent from, what reason apprehends is subject to command in cases in which the intellect does not assent or dissent naturally.

Can reason direct itself? If the question sounds silly, it is probably because we are thinking of reason as an agent in its own right. "It seems absurd for something to command itself," **obj.** 1 argues; the picture of reason as a sort of independent module that issues commands to itself and then obeys those commands does indeed seem absurd, like someone carrying on a conversation with himself. But if we think instead of reason as a *power* by which *a human being* does something, the question is not silly at all: it is asking whether human beings can use their intellectual ability to direct their own thinking, whether the course that our reasoning takes is subject to our own power to reason. That is a perfectly sensible question, and one that needs an affirmative answer: if reason is not subject to command, we lack control over our thinking and therefore over everything we do. Once again, the very possibility of human action is what is at stake: if we lack control over our thinking, nothing we do will count as a properly human action, because "only those actions over which human beings have control are properly called human" (1.1). That this second way of reading the question is the right one is made clear in the argument **On the contrary**, which speaks of what *human beings* do *through* their powers: "What we do by free choice can be done by our command. And acts of reason are carried out through free choice; after all, Damascene says that 'it is by free choice that human beings inquire, examine, judge, and dispose.' Therefore, acts of reason can be commanded."

How does this work? Aquinas notes in the **reply** that reason reflects on itself—I can think about my thinking—and so reason "can direct its own act just as it directs the acts of other powers." It does so in two ways: in terms of the exercise of its act and in terms of the specification of its act ("in terms of the object"). In terms of exercise, "an act of reason can always be commanded, as when someone is instructed to pay attention and use reason." Note that Aquinas's example is most naturally read as involving one person commanding another to pay attention—see art. 3 resp. 1, where Aquinas notes explicitly that commands can be issued both to someone else and to oneself—but it should be read expansively so that it includes commanding oneself to pay attention. Otherwise it skirts the problem raised in obj. 1, and **resp.** 1 makes it clear that Aquinas envisions commanding oneself, for the reasons laid out in the previous paragraph.

As for how reason directs itself in terms of the specification of its act, Aquinas makes a further distinction. With respect to an object, reason has two different acts: apprehending the truth about the object, and assenting to what reason apprehends. What Aquinas means by "apprehending the truth about something" (*veritatem circa aliquid apprehendere*) is somewhat obscure. One would expect it to mean apprehending *that* a statement about something is true, but then it is hard to see how assent to what is apprehended could be a further act (or how dissent from what is apprehended could even be possible—if I apprehend *that something is true* I surely cannot deny that it is true, though I can try to stop thinking about it if I find its truth painful). Generally when Aquinas uses 'apprehend' with 'truth' as a direct object he is speaking of apprehending *a* truth—that is, a statement that is true; he regularly contrasts the way in which angels apprehend truth intuitively, "without investigation," with the way in which human beings apprehend truth discursively, "by proceeding from one thing to another" (*Sent.* II.39.3.1, *ST* I.79.8, I-II.5.1 resp. 1), though human beings do have a share in the angelic kind of intuition insofar as we apprehend first principles intuitively. Now surely when we "apprehend truth" in this sense, whether we apprehend it intuitively or discursively, our assent to the truth is part of that apprehension: it is not merely that we have "A whole is greater than its proper part," which is true, before our mind; we *assent* to "A whole is greater than its proper part." It is not merely that we apprehend it and it is a truth; we apprehend it *as* a truth and thus assent to it.

So what exactly he has in mind when he speaks of "apprehending the truth about something" as something distinct from assenting to it remains obscure. Whatever it is, Aquinas says that it is not in our power: "it comes about through the power of some natural or supernatural light." At the very least it is reasonable to interpret Aquinas as saying here that it is not up to us whether our intellect gets at the truth; whether we succeed or do not succeed in understanding the way things are is not something we can control and therefore not something we command. This does not mean that we bear no responsibility for the success or failure of our thinking—it is up to me whether I am attentive or inattentive, thorough or perfunctory, focused or distractible— but that I do not bring it about that my attentive, thorough, focused thinking gets at the truth. Something beyond my control is responsible for enabling my intellect to grasp truth.

Assent or dissent—affirming or denying some proposition turned up by my thinking—is another matter. There are some things "to which our intellect assents naturally, such as first principles"; assent to them, or dissent from their denials, is not up to us and therefore not subject to command. But some things we apprehend do not overcome or conquer the intellect in the same way that first principles do (the basic meaning of *convinco*, here translated as "are . . . convincing" is "overcome, conquer"). In such cases the intellect can assent for one reason or dissent for another reason, "or at any rate suspend assent or dissent." Such things are the intellectual analogues to partial goods, which can be willed if looked at in one way and not willed if looked at in some other way. For this comparison, see 10.2 reply and resp. 2.

### 17.7. Is an act of the sensory appetite commanded?

Answer: Insofar as an act of the sensory appetite depends on the appetitive power, it is subject to command; insofar as an act of the sensory appetite depends on the condition and disposition of the body, it is not.

Are we in charge of our desires, our fears, our revulsions? It does not seem so. Desires seem to well up even if we do not want to have those desires (**obj. 1**), and desire—sensory desire, as opposed to will—requires an object of sense or imagination to arouse it, and we cannot always control what sense or imagination presents to us (**obj. 3**).

Aquinas argues that we are in fact in charge of acts of the sensory appetite: not always, but under certain conditions and in certain respects. What is subject to command is what is in our power, he says, so we must understand how an act of the sensory appetite is in our power. Well, first, what *is* the sensory appetite? As Anthony Kenny puts it, "the sensory appetite is the capacity for those desires and revulsions which humans and animals have in common."[31] Such appetite, as Robert Pasnau writes, "translates sensory information about the environment into an inclination."[32] Bound up as it is with the senses and with particular information, the sensory appetite is a power of a bodily organ. In this it differs from the will, or intellectual appetite, which takes its information not from the senses but from the intellect; the intellect deals with universals (or deals with particulars in a universal way), and so neither it nor its associated appetite is a power of a bodily organ.

---

31. Kenny (1994), 60.
32. Pasnau (2002), 210.

Because sensory appetite is a power of a bodily organ, its act depends not only on the power itself but also on the condition of that organ. Aquinas offers the example of sight: my seeing depends not only on my power of vision but on the condition of the bodily organ, the eye, of which that power makes use. My power of vision (my capacity for seeing) may be working as well as can be, but if the optometrist has dilated my pupils, the act of that power will obviously be affected by the unusual condition of my eyes. So we have two things to take into account in deciding whether an act of the sensory appetite is subject to the command of reason: the power of sensory appetite itself, and the condition or disposition of the body.

The power of sensory appetite itself follows the apprehension of sense or imagination, which is particular; it is therefore subject to the command of a universal apprehensive power, reason. The condition of the body, by contrast, is not subject to the command of reason. Aquinas does not argue for this point because he does not need to: it is obvious that if my "body is disposed in such a way as to make [me] especially susceptible to this or that passion" (resp. 2), there is nothing I can do about that. Such a disposition might be just a matter of my physical constitution ("from nature"), but it could be the result of a temporary condition that I cannot simply change at will ("from some previous movement that cannot be instantaneously stopped"). As an example of the second situation, imagine that I have not been taking care to get enough sleep, and because I am tired I am susceptible to frustration and grumpiness. I cannot just decide not to be tired, and so I cannot just decide (right then and there) not to be susceptible to frustration and grumpiness,[33] though I can control whether I allow that susceptibility to issue in overt action—that is a matter of commanding the will, not the sensory appetite—and I can also decide to take the steps necessary to get rested and so (eventually) no longer be susceptible to frustration and grumpiness.

The fact that the condition of the body is not subject to command explains why "the movement of the sensory appetite is not totally subject to the command of reason." Aquinas notes two other ways in which an act of the sensory appetite might be beyond the power of reason to command. One is a sudden, unforeseen movement of sensory appetite: out of the blue, imagination or sense apprehends something and incites the appetite, and it is too late for reason to do anything about that, "although reason could have stopped that movement if it had foreseen it." The other is a weakness of the imaginative power. As **obj. 3** noted, sensory appetite requires sense or imagination to arouse it. Aquinas acknowledges in **resp. 3** that it is not in our power to sense something when it is not present. It is, however, in our power to imagine something whether it is present or not, and reason can command the imagination

---

33. "How hard is it just to decide to be in a good mood and then be in a good mood?" "Gee, it's easy." (*Say Anything*)

and thereby the sensory appetite—provided that the object is imaginable[34] and that the imaginative power is sufficiently responsive to reason. It is possible for the imaginative power to be too weak to obey reason's command because of "some indisposition of the organ."

### 17.8. Is an act of the vegetative soul commanded?

Answer: No.

The "vegetative soul" is not a separate or distinct soul; it is the set of capacities of the soul—functions of a living organism—that do not depend on cognition. The heart beats, the digestive system performs its work, the reproductive system generates a new organism, all without input from sense or reason. Aquinas notes in the **reply** that all such functions are appetitive, in the sense that they aim at something: the well-being of the organism and the continuance of its species. But such appetite is natural appetite, which "does not follow from any apprehension." Reason issues commands as an apprehensive power, so reason cannot command the acts of an appetite that in no way depends on apprehension. Therefore, reason can command the acts of animal or sensory appetite (to some extent, as we saw in art. 7) and the acts of intellectual appetite, but it cannot command the acts of natural appetite. So acts of the vegetative soul, such as the functions of generation and nutrition, are not subject to the command of reason.

The most important objection here is **obj. 3**. Praise and blame apply only to acts that are subject to command, because only those acts are free and voluntary. And praise and blame do apply to acts of the nutritive and generative powers: gluttony and lust are blameworthy, reasonable eating and chastity are praiseworthy. So acts of the nutritive and generative powers must be subject to command after all. To this Aquinas responds (**resp. 3**) that what is blameworthy or praiseworthy is not the acts of the nutritive or generative powers themselves—"which are digestion and the forming of a human body"—but acts of the sensory appetite that concern acts of the nutritive or generative power. I am not praised or blamed for the workings of my digestive system or of my reproductive system; I am praised or blamed for the temperate or intemperate character of my desire for the pleasure of eating and drinking or of my desire for the pleasure of sexual relations. Aquinas holds that the vices of lust and gluttony, as well as the virtues of chastity and temperance that are opposed to them, are located in the sensory appetite; they are settled

---

34. Incorporeal things are not imaginable, Aquinas says. This is not quite true. I can imagine angels, even though they are incorporeal; I imagine them in the guise of something corporeal. So can my reason command an act of the sensory appetite regarding angels? I can only report the results of introspection: it appears that it cannot. But perhaps my imaginative power is weak.

dispositions ("habits") of the sensory appetite to accord with right reason. But note that he also says that virtue and vice, praise and blame, apply to acts of "making use of" the desire for sensory pleasure "in the right or wrong way." On Aquinas's view it is the will that uses or "makes use of" other powers in the right or wrong way: does this not suggest that ultimately all virtue and vice resides in the will rather than in sensory appetite? Many thinkers after Aquinas who agree with the claim that it is the will that makes use of the other powers will in fact draw the conclusion that all virtue and vice resides in the will, but Aquinas himself does not.

### 17.9. Is an act of the parts of the body commanded?

Answer: Reason can command the parts of the body that are moved by powers that are themselves subject to reason's command.

We know from experience that (typically) we can control the movement of our hands but not the beating of our hearts; we can turn our head in the direction we want to look but we have no say in what our digestive system does with the food we eat. In other words, we know from experience that we can command the acts of some parts of the body but not those of others. What Aquinas offers in the **reply** is an account that explains why some parts of the body fall into one category and other parts into the other. The parts of the body, he notes, are moved by powers of the soul, so if the act of a given power of the soul is subject to the command of reason, the parts of the body moved by that power will also be subject to reason; and if not, not. As we have seen, the sensory powers are subject to the command of reason; the natural or vegetative powers are not. (And the reason for *that* is that reason commands as an apprehensive power, and acts of the sensory power follow from apprehension whereas acts of the vegetative powers do not.) So the parts of the body that are moved by the sensory powers are subject to the command of reason; the parts of the body that are moved by the vegetative powers (the heart, the digestive and reproductive systems) are not.

Of particular interest here is Aquinas's treatment of Augustine's observations about "the movement of the genital members" (**obj. 3**). For Augustine, the phenomena of spontaneous erections and impotence—those are our words for what he describes rather more circumspectly—are evidence that there is something particularly broken about human sexuality after the fall. As J. M. Rist puts it, "Though [Augustine] normally (but not always) says that our fallen nature is damaged but not wholly corrupt, he seems to think of our proper *libido* as being wholly corrupt, though capable of being put to good use."[35] Aquinas, however, does not quote Augustine in order to argue that

---

35. Rist (1996), 324n.

human sexuality is somehow more thoroughly fallen than other aspects of human nature, but simply as offering one example of a case in which parts of the body do not obey reason. In his response Aquinas quotes Augustine as saying that such disobedience is a punishment for sin: "for its disobedience to God, the soul suffers the punishment of disobedience especially in that part of the body through which original sin is transmitted to one's descendants." (For Aquinas, as for Augustine, original sin is a sexually transmitted disease: "it is through the active power of semen that original sin is transmitted to one's offspring along with human nature" [I-II.83.1].)

In resp. 3 Aquinas does not question Augustine's idea that the genital members' disobedience to reason comes about because of divine punishment for sin, but he argues that we need a further explanation. God's punishment for the primal sin of Adam and Eve was to withdraw supernatural gifts, leaving human nature to itself. So the disobedience of the genital members must have a natural explanation. What is it about human nature that explains "why the movement of these parts in particular does not obey reason"? Aristotle provides an explanation in chapter 11 of *De motu animalium*. Intellect and imagination represent things that arouse passions, and passions in turn produce movements of the heart and the penis. But those movements are not subject to the command of reason, because such movements require physical changes—heating or cooling—that are not subject to the command of reason. Why does this happen in the case of the heart and the penis in particular? Because "both of them are, in a sense, a separate animal, because they are principles of life, and a principle is the whole virtually." The heart is the principle of the senses; and the penis produces semen, which "is the whole animal virtually" and is what transmits the form, the human soul (along with original sin, of course, but Aristotle did not know about that part). As principles, they have their movements naturally—in the sense of 'naturally' that means "without input from cognition," as discussed in art. 8.

## Question 18: The Goodness and Badness of Human Acts in General

As we saw at the outset of Q6, the Treatise on Human Acts is only the first half of Aquinas's discussion of the nature of human acts in general. (The second half is the Treatise on the Passions I-II.22–48.) Q18 kicks off the final section of the Treatise on Human Acts, which examines what makes a human act good or bad. Q18 addresses that subject in general (a subject whose importance is underscored by the fact that it is composed of no fewer than eleven articles, as opposed to the normal eight). QQ19 and 20 address the goodness and badness of interior and exterior acts, respectively, and Q21 wraps up the Treatise on Human Acts with an examination of the implications of the goodness or badness of human acts for an act's sinfulness, praiseworthiness, and/or merit.

Before turning to a discussion of the specific articles in Q18, it's worth spending a moment addressing Aquinas's use of the genus-species-difference approach to classifying moral acts, an approach he picks up from Aristotle's classification of natural things. (Aquinas uses the classification for natural things himself as well, but of course what we're interested in here is why he applies this structure to human acts.) The genus-species-difference distinction is widely accepted in the thirteenth century, but that doesn't itself explain why Aquinas uses it. Aquinas is, after all, willing to modify or jettison traditional approaches. As Mark Jordan notes,[36] the whole structure of the Second Part is a radical revision of standard approaches to the material. Aquinas's use of the genus-species-difference approach here thus indicates that he thinks it is both worthwhile and illuminating in some way.

The general principle behind Aquinas's characterizing human acts in terms of genus, species, and difference is that all natural things can be divided into species, which are set apart by a 'difference' from the other species that belong to the same higher-order category (a genus). Aquinas believes, that is, that the world divides up naturally into certain kinds of things, and that human beings possess the ability to identify these natural classes. The objects in the world don't, for instance, divide up naturally into "wet things," "squeaky things," and "things taller than five feet." They divide up naturally into categories like "cats," "dogs," and "peacocks." These categories or natural kinds are what Aquinas calls species.

Each species is constituted by a genus + a difference (called a "specific difference," where 'specific' here means "species-making"). Human beings, as we saw in the Treatise on Happiness, are defined as 'rational animals.' This can be understood on the genus-species-difference model as follows:

**Human being (*species*) = animal (*genus*) + rational (*difference*)**

"Animal" is the higher-level category that contains relevantly similar natural kinds. Cats, for instance, also belong to the genus "animal," but they are distinguished by the difference "felinity" instead of "rational."

**Cat (*species*) = animal (*genus*) + felinity (*difference*)**

(The identifying characteristics of the difference associated with a particular species are not always obvious; this rubric is used most often in discussions of how human beings differ from other animals and is rarely used to distinguish other species from each other.)

To add confusion to an already-complicated schema, genus and species are also relative terms. That is, in certain circumstances we might consider something a species that for other purposes we would consider a genus. So, for instance, if we're thinking of the genus "plant" because we're trying to

36. See Jordan (1999), 79–100.

explain to a child what all these green, growing things have in common, "tree" would count as a species within that genus, as would "bush." If we're trying to explain to a child what all these tall, leafy things have in common, however, "tree" would function in this context as a genus, with "maple" and "gingko" and "oak" as species. The only exceptions to this sliding rule of genus/species relativity are (1) the most general genera (the ten categories that Aristotle introduces in the *Topics* and which Aquinas accepts: substance, quantity, quality, relation, where, when, being-in-a-position, having, action, and passion), which have no higher categories above them, and (2) the most specific species (*species specialissimae*), which have no subspecies below them, e.g., "short-haired Siamese cat." The only things that fall into the most specific species are individual members of that species—e.g., actual short-haired Siamese cats.

This all might seem a far cry from the account of action that Aquinas has been laying out to this point in the Treatise on Human Acts. Aquinas, however, sees human acts as rooted in and expressing human nature in the same basic way that the movements of natural things and the behavior of non-rational animals are rooted in and express their natures. This is one reason, for instance, that he frequently compares human acts to natural motion in his examples in this treatise. Species and genus talk is going to enter his discussion of human actions when he starts explaining what makes some acts good and other acts bad. There are going to be cases, for example, where Aquinas wants to talk about types of acts being good or bad, and the species language will help him here in distinguishing between individual acts and the type of act that they fall into. As we'll see in the first article of this question, this framework also lets him highlight the relation between human actions and human nature.

### 18.1. Is every human act good?

Answer: every act is good insofar as it exists, but acts are bad insofar as they fall short of what they are meant to be.

The question posed at the outset of this article gets its force from applying Aquinas's basic metaphysics of goodness to his account of human acts. Aquinas, like most medieval philosophers, accepts what's called the 'convertibility' of being and goodness: something is good to the extent that it exists and fulfils its nature. (For discussion of this idea in Aquinas as well as recommendations of some secondary sources, see the commentary on 2.5 in the Treatise on Happiness.) The theory follows from consideration of God's essence, which is identical to his existence. God exists perfectly—there is no "lack" of any kind in God—and thus God is perfectly good. On this theory (famous from earlier treatises such as Augustine's *On Free Choice of the Will*), badness should be understood as privation, or lack of goodness, not as a "thing" in its own metaphysical right.

Aquinas applies this general framework to human acts in the following way: every act is good insofar as it exists (that is, occurs), but individual acts are bad insofar as they fall short in some way of what that kind of act is supposed to be. So, for instance, if I thank someone I should be grateful to, but I do it at the wrong time or in the wrong place or in the wrong manner (too loudly, in a sarcastic voice, etc.), my act falls short of what such an act should be, and to that extent what I do is bad (all the more so if I intentionally mumble my thanks or wait until the person I should thank is out of earshot).

**Obj. and resp. 1.** This objection mentions pseudo-Dionysius's claim that what is bad acts only through the power for what is good—the idea, again, being that everything that exists must come from what is good—but points out that it doesn't look like the power of what is good will actually do anything bad. All human actions should count as good, then.

Aquinas's response draws on the metaphysical framework discussed above; he says that whatever is bad acts through the power of something that is good but deficient in some respect. (Given the context of this discussion, it seems fair to imagine that what is bad here is an act produced by a human being, all of whom are good insofar as they exist but none of whom exist perfectly.) Insofar as it comes from something that is good, Aquinas says, the act is also good—but insofar as it is lacking in some way, it is bad. And since the deficiency is what we're interested in for the purposes of moral inquiry, we can say that the act we're considering is bad in an unqualified sense, even if it is good insofar as it exists. (Note that Aquinas begins his investigation into the goodness and badness of human acts in extremely abstract terms; after he establishes the general metaphysics of good and bad actions, however, he will work his way down to particular actions that take place in particular circumstances.)

**Obj. and resp. 2.** This objection addresses what it means for being and goodness to be convertible: if things are good insofar as they exist and badness is a lack of being, it would seem that actions are good insofar as they exist in actuality and bad insofar as they exist in potentiality. But acts by their very nature involve actualizing potentialities—hence, the name "act." So it seems that every action is good and none is bad. The third objection is similar: it claims that bad things cannot be causes because badness is deficiency (and a lack of something can't cause something else), and thus that every act must be good.

Aquinas's response to the second objection is to remind the reader that things can exist in actuality in one respect while being in potentiality in another. In particular, something can be in actuality and able to act in one respect—as when I actualize my potentiality to move by walking—but can be deprived of actuality in another sense and thus perform an action that is deficient in some way—as when I'm blinded by sunlight on leaving a building and I trip over a curb. The response to the third objection makes the same general point: a bad act causes something insofar as it exists and has goodness, not insofar as it fails to be what it should. Adulterous sex, for instance, doesn't produce a baby because it is *adulterous*. It produces a baby because it is sex.

**Reply.** As discussed in the overview of Q18, the convertibility of being and goodness for *things* carries over to *actions*. In fact, a thing (say, a breadknife) produces the sorts of acts it does (say, cutting bread) precisely because of the kind of thing it is. Each thing has goodness to the extent that it exists fully as a member of its kind. A breadknife, for instance, has goodness to the extent that it conforms to what that sort of knife should be like: sharp, good at slicing crumbly things, etc. We call it a bad knife when it lacks those characteristics. And, Aquinas claims, the same is true for acts. Insofar as the bread knife reduces my loaf of bread into a pile of crumbs instead of cutting through it cleanly, it's doing a bad job of cutting. In the moral realm, of course, this sense of badness takes on additional force, because human beings can bear moral responsibility for the ways in which their acts fall short of what they are meant to be.

### 18.2. Does an action derive its goodness or badness from its object?

Answer: yes, a human act derives a certain sort of goodness or badness from its object.

An act's object—the thing an act is "about"—is what puts an act into a particular species ("homicide," say). Aquinas will discuss in more detail exactly how acts fall into good or bad species in later articles (see art. 5, 6, 8, 10, and 11). For the purposes of this article, it is enough to note that an act's object is going to be related to its goodness or badness, given that the object of an act is what places that act into one species or another. Acts can be good or bad in any number of ways, as Aquinas discusses at rather excruciating length in this article. An act's object is just one of those ways.

**Obj. and resp. 1.** It's hard to make the case that an act's object does not impact the act's goodness or badness; this objection attempts to make that case by maintaining that the object of an action is an external thing and that things are not bad in and of themselves.

Not surprisingly, Aquinas's response is that although external things are good considered in and of themselves, not all things are well-suited to particular actions. And so, considered as objects of a particular act, they can be bad.

**Obj. and resp. 2.** As discussed in the introduction, Aquinas applies not only the species-genus-differentia framework but also his metaphysics of form and matter (called "hylomorphism" from the Greek *hyle*, "matter," and *morphe*, "form") to acts. This objection trades on Aquinas's hylomorphism, claiming that the goodness or badness of an act comes from its form (or actuality) and that the object of an action is its matter (or potentiality).

To respond to this objection, Aquinas distinguishes between matter "from which" (*materia ex qua*) and matter "about which" (*materia circa quam*). Matter "from which" would be the stuff of which a thing is composed: bricks and mortar for a house, say. Matter "about which" is what an act is about—the subject matter of the action. Matter "from which" is what receives a form (as bricks and mortar receive the form of "house"), but matter "about which" is itself the object of an act, which places it in a particular species of action. Species are intrinsically related to form rather than to matter, however, and so in this analogy the object of an action corresponds to form rather than matter.

**Obj. and resp. 3.** This objection delves into the nature of active powers, such as fire's power to heat. The worry here is that the object of an active power—what that power is aimed at, such as heating—is the *effect* rather than the cause of an action. The goodness or badness of a human action depends on its *cause* (what motivates it, etc.), however, not its effect. (It's worth noting that this objection assumes the falsity of consequentialism, an assumption Aquinas shares: see the commentary on 20.5.) Thus, the goodness or badness of a human action won't have to do with its object.

Aquinas denies both of the main presuppositions in this objection. First, he claims that the object of a human act is not always the object of an active power; second, he claims that the objects of active powers are not always effects (as opposed to causes). The example supporting his first claim is appetitive powers (such as the will), which are passive insofar as they respond to what the senses or the intellect presents to them as good, and yet which also serve as a principle of human actions. (See the second half of *ST* I-II for his lengthy discussion of principles of action.) His second example is the relation between food and the nutritive power (which is the power to digest and change food into, say, human flesh). When my lunch has been transmuted by my nutritive power into flesh, that flesh counts as an effect of that power. But when I am still digesting my lunch, the food is the object or matter on which that nutritive power acts. Insofar as an object is an effect of an active power (as my digested lunch is), it is the terminus, or end, of the power's action. Once my lunch has been digested and changed into flesh, the nutritive power has finished its job. And an act gets its form and species (as discussed in resp. 2) from its terminus—that is, what it is aimed at or about. This, of course, is highly relevant to an act's goodness or badness. Thus, the goodness of an object makes the act generically good.

**Reply.** The goodness or badness of an act, Aquinas reminds us, is a matter of the extent to which it fulfils or falls short of the nature of that act—what he here refers to as "fullness or deficiency in being." The role of this and the next two articles is to discuss the three factors that play a role in the extent to which a particular act has fullness or deficiency in being: that act's object, circumstances, and end.

The object of an act—what gives it its species—is what Aquinas says is the "first thing" that determines the extent to which that act has fullness of being. Comparing human acts to both natural things and natural motions (as he likes to do), he states that an action gets its species from its object, just as a natural thing gets its species from its form (for example, a human being falls into the species "human being" because it possesses the substantial form "human being"), and a motion gets its species from its terminus (for example, a stone's falling counts as a descent because the natural motion's terminus is "down").

The first goodness of a natural thing comes from its form: the most basic way in which a cow is good or bad is the extent to which it fully actualizes the natural capacities and potentialities of the form "cow." If, during the process of generation, something goes awry and the result is a three-headed monstrosity, the three-headed thing is "bad" in the sense in which it has not developed into a cow. (It is important to see that this sense is a *non*-moral sense of goodness.)

This suggests that the most basic way in which a moral act is good or bad is the extent to which it fully actualizes the species of action it belongs to. If an act doesn't successfully attain the species-form from its suitable object, it is, in that sense, a bad act. So, to use Aquinas's own example, a suitable or good object for the act of "use" is your own possessions, whereas an inappropriate or bad object for that sort of act would be someone else's stuff. Goodness in genus, or "generic goodness," comes from a moral act's having a suitable object: I'm hungry, and so I take out my lunch and eat it. Badness in genus, or "generic badness," comes from a moral act's having an inappropriate object: I'm hungry, and so I take out *your* lunch and eat it.

### 18.3. Is an action good or bad because of a circumstance?

Answer: yes, the circumstances of an act also have an effect on whether an action is good or bad.

Aquinas has already settled the question of whether circumstances can affect the goodness or badness of human acts (see Q7). He returns to it here, however, to situate the effects that circumstances can have on an action in the broader context of the possible sources of the goodness or badness of a human act (namely, object, circumstance, and end). Having just argued in the previous article that the first basis for evaluation of an act's goodness or badness is its object (which places it in a species of action), Aquinas goes on here to argue that having an appropriate object is not itself enough to make an act good, full-stop. Even acts with appropriate objects can be carried out at the wrong time or the wrong place, in the wrong manner, etc. Thus, circumstances are an important component of what makes an act good or bad.

**Obj. and resp. 1.** This objection is familiar from Q7: circumstances "stand around" an action, as it were. Goodness and badness, by contrast, belong to things in themselves due to the extent to which those things actualize the natural capacities and potentialities of their substantial forms. Circumstances don't seem relevant to this sort of actualization.

Circumstances may not be part of the *essence* of an action, Aquinas responds, and in that sense they may be external to an act—but circumstances are still *accidents* of an action, and in that sense they are involved in the proper or improper actualization of the natural features of a particular species of act. So, for instance, I can use my own laptop and in that way meet the conditions for performing a generically good act, namely, "using one's own possessions," but if I use my laptop to hack into your personal email account and send nasty messages to people I don't like on your behalf, I'm improperly actualizing one of the features of using my own possessions.

**Obj. and resp. 2** are almost identical to the second objection and response in 7.2. In short, the worry is that accidents (such as the fact that daylight saving time began yesterday or that my foot has fallen asleep as I typed this) seem too contingent to affect something as important as the goodness or badness of human actions.

Aquinas's response is, again, to remind the reader that accidents fall into different categories: some of these categories are unimportant for the study of moral inquiry, but others—in particular, accidents that are per se accidents, like the manner in which I apologize to my friend for being late—add to an act's goodness or, if they are inappropriate or missing, detract from that act's goodness and make it bad.

**Obj. and resp. 3** follow immediately on the same theme: goodness and badness belong to an act in virtue of its substance, not its accidents. Aquinas responds that we talk about 'being' in both substances and accidents: we can talk both about how I am a human being, for instance, and how I am cold. Since being and goodness are convertible, as discussed in 18.1, that means that we can also talk about something's being good or bad in virtue of either its substance or its accidents.

**Reply.** In the previous article, Aquinas explained that the first way an act gets its goodness or badness is from its object—what that act is "about" (using my laptop, say)—which places an act in a particular species (for example, using one's own possessions). In this article, he states that the species of an act does not give it *complete* or *perfect* goodness (in the sense of complete and perfect he discusses at length in the Treatise on Happiness). The species of an action simply places it into the category of generic good or bad action.

The circumstances of an act are also part of what completes or perfects that act. In particular, the presence of appropriate circumstances perfects an act and contributes to its goodness, and a lack of such circumstances means that

402      Commentary on the Treatise on Human Acts

an action is deficient in such a way that we call it bad. So, if I use my laptop to answer email that needs answering, and I do so in an appropriate place and at an appropriate time, using an appropriate tone, etc., my act will be good. If, on the other hand, I use my laptop to answer email that needs answering, but I do so in the middle of a lecture that I should be listening to and in the front row of a crowded room (thus distracting people behind me as well), my act is bad because it is performed in the wrong circumstances.

### 18.4. Do goodness and badness in human acts derive from the end?

Answer: yes, human acts derive their goodness or badness from the end of a human act (just as they do from the object and the circumstances of that act).

**Obj. and resp. 1.** Aquinas's account of human action entails that we always act for the perceived good. This objection draws on a quote from pseudo-Dionysius that claims that the end of action is, thus, always good. And if an act got its goodness or badness from its end, there would then never be a bad act, which is clearly false.

Aquinas responds by stressing the '*perceived*' nature of the good in his original claim: we always act for the *perceived* or *apparent* good, but we can be wrong about whether something is a genuine good or if it is only an apparent good. And if an end is just an apparent good rather than a genuine good, the resulting act aimed at that merely apparent good falls short of what it ought to be and so is bad.

**Obj. and resp. 2.** As this objection points out, an end is an extrinsic rather than intrinsic cause of a human act: we act, after all, for an end outside of ourselves. But goodness or badness is not external to a human act, and so not to be found in the end of an action.

Aquinas's response is that although the end itself is extrinsic to an action, having an appropriate *relation* to that end is very much part of the action itself.

**Obj. and resp. 3.** Sometimes people do good things for bad ends (say, giving to charity to receive a tax break or a reputation for philanthropy), and sometimes people do bad things for good ends (say, when Robin Hood steals money from the rich to give to the poor). This makes it seem as though an action is not good or bad from its end, though, since giving to charity is a good act, and stealing money is a bad act, in the "species" sense of goodness discussed in art. 2.

Aquinas reiterates here that a human act must be good in all four of the relevant ways that he lays out in the main body of this article in order to count as fully or completely good. An action such as giving money to charity for the tax break *is* good insofar as it falls in the species "giving to charity," but such an act would be unqualifiedly good only if it were also aimed at the right end and performed in all the right circumstances.

**Reply.** Aquinas returns once more to the convertibility of being and goodness in this reply. Some things—namely, God—have being that does not depend on anything else. But for every other thing, if we're interested in learning more about it, we need to learn about its cause(s). In the case of a natural thing (say, a house), we'd need to learn more about its efficient cause (the agent that is responsible for its coming into being: a carpenter, say, in the case of a house) and its formal cause ("house") to understand its being (and the extent to which it possesses the sort of complete being that also constitutes its complete goodness). In God's case, we don't need to know about anything other than God in order to understand his goodness: God is, after all, identical with perfect goodness. Everything else, however, derives its goodness at least in part from things external to it.

In the case of human actions, these external components include circumstances and—most relevant to this article—the end of the action.

Aquinas concludes this part of Q8 by recapping the four sorts of goodness an action needs to possess in order to count as unqualifiedly or completely good: the act must possess (1) goodness in *genus* (the completely general sort of goodness that an act has simply in virtue of the fact that it exists), (2) goodness in *species* (which requires the act's having an appropriate object), (3) goodness with respect to the *circumstances*, and (4) goodness with respect to the *end* (which requires the act's being related appropriately to the "cause of goodness"—that is, related appropriately to genuinely good ends).

## 18.5. Do good and bad acts differ in species?

Answer: yes, good and bad acts differ in species.

The short answer to this question, as indicated above, is "yes." The long answer is, as it often is for Aquinas, much more complicated. Importantly, the relation that reason or intellect bears to an act's goodness or badness reappears in this article. The good for human beings generally is described as what is "in accordance with reason," whereas what is "opposed to reason" is bad. Aquinas himself doesn't give examples here of what he means by those terms, but it becomes clear as this treatise continues (and throughout the rest of the Second Part of the *Summa*) that one way to understand what's fitting with or opposed to reason is the broadly Aristotelian conception of what would contribute to or detract from one's flourishing.

Moral acts with objects that are suitable to reason are good acts, and they differ in species from moral acts with objects that are opposed to reason and are, thus, bad. The difference between adultery and sex within marriage, for instance, is the difference between a sexual relationship that involves breaking promises and betraying the trust of others and a sexual relationship that expresses love between two people already in a committed partnership. (Whether we find this distinction plausible as a way of distinguishing between species of moral actions is another matter. On the one hand, it's clearly meant to draw on his metaphysics of natural kinds and general account of how human flourishing relates to fulfilling our nature as rational animals. On the other hand, breaking moral acts down into different species depending on whether they get us closer to or farther away from our ultimate end seems rather ad hoc.)

**Obj. and resp. 1.** This objection identifies exactly what seems ad hoc about dividing moral acts into different species based on whether or not they are good or bad—namely, that we don't divide anything else into different species this way. As this objection points out, good and bad human beings both belong to the same species, and Aquinas himself keeps claiming that goodness and badness work the same way in natural things and in action. It seems, then, that it should be possible for there to be good and bad acts within the same species.

Aquinas's response is disappointing, to say the least. It distinguishes between goodness and badness "in accord with nature" and "contrary to nature" and claims that this *does* make for a difference in species, even for natural things. His example, however, is how a living body and a dead body don't belong to the same species. This is a consequence of hylomorphic metaphysics called "homonymy of the body," which holds that a living substance is animated by its substantial form, and that at death, that form is destroyed. (In the case of human beings, what happens is rather more complicated: see the commentary on 4.5 obj. and resp. 2 for the details.)

**Obj. and resp. 2.** This objection is also right on the mark: the convertibility of being and goodness means that evil or badness is, strictly speaking, a privation, or non-being. But privations don't make for species differences: "non-rational animal," for example, is not a species. So dividing moral acts into species by the goodness or badness of their objects seems rather ad hoc.

Aquinas responds to the objection by pointing out that we should think of badness in the case of objects of human acts as a "privation with respect to some particular potentiality." His example is the difference between the act of using one's own possessions (which has a suitable object insofar as it fits with what reason would tell us is appropriate: if we understand what possessions are for, we will understand that we are meant to use them) and the act of taking someone else's possessions (which has an object that goes against reason: if we understand what possessions are for, we will understand that we are meant to use our own possessions, not to take someone else's possessions, which that person is meant to use). If we think not in terms of "failing to use one's own possessions" but instead in terms of "taking someone else's possessions," Aquinas claims, we can see that there is an object for that act that we can classify as bad.

For this to work, it appears that we must accept a rather shaky assumption: we have to think of a general category of action—"use of possessions"— which is divided into different species ("use of one's own possessions" versus "using someone else's possessions") by adding the difference of "one's own" and "someone else's." Suppose that I'm building a bookshelf and realize that I need to use a hammer to pound in some nails. If I use my own hammer for the task, my act will be good insofar as its object is "use of my own possessions"; if I steal your hammer to pound in the nails, however, the object of my act will be bad insofar as its object is "taking someone else's possessions."

**Obj. and resp. 3.** Adultery is a bad act, and sex within marriage is a good act; yet both acts can result in the same effect—namely, a baby. If good acts and bad acts belong to different species, however, they should produce different effects. This is one of the main ways we can tell different species apart from each other, after all: members of different species have different characteristic activities, and thus different effects.

Aquinas's response to this is brief: adultery does not belong to a different species than sex within marriage *in every way*. With respect to baby-making potential, those acts have the same effect. The relevant difference for our purposes is that the two acts have different objects, one of which fits with reason and one of which opposes reason, and thus the two acts have different effects in that sense: sex within marriage deserves praise, whereas adultery deserves blame. ("Being worthy of praise" and "being worthy of blame" are taken as effects here. They seem like rather question-begging effects, however. It would have been more helpful if Aquinas had described their different suitability with respect to reason in terms of resulting in greater closeness, say, or breaking promises.)

**Obj. and resp. 4.** Circumstances can affect whether an act is good or bad, but they don't put acts into different species. So it doesn't look as though being good or bad puts acts into different species.

Aquinas replies that sometimes—in particular, when a circumstance is what determines whether the object of an act is related to reason well or badly—a circumstance does give a moral act its species. Take, for example, a case where my act of answering an important email becomes a bad rather than a good act because I'm doing it when I should be paying attention to a lecture. In this case, Aquinas says, the circumstance is what makes an act bad, because what's appropriate to reason in that situation would be listening to the lecture.

**Reply.** As pointed out in the overview to this question, ***genus + difference = species***. That is, a general kind is divided into more specific kinds by differences that distinguish those kinds from each other. The most famous example of a difference for natural things is "rational," which, added to the genus

"animal," is what results in the species "human being." That is, **animal +
rational = human being.**

In the case of human acts, it will be some difference in the object that
divides a general category of action into different species. What sort of difference? Aquinas says it must be a *per se*, rather than a *per accidens* difference.
This is really just to reiterate, though, that the difference must be the sort of
thing that can divide a genus into species, because *per se* differences—features essential in some way to the thing—just are the sort of differences that
account for differences in species (as opposed to *per accidens* differences,
which distinguish a thing's accidental features from each other—its color,
say, from its size).

As if this distinction weren't enough to absorb on its own, Aquinas goes on
to note that differences in the object of an act can be *per se* for one principle
and *per accidens* for another. The example he gives is "cognizing color and
cognizing sound," which is both essential to sight and what differentiates sight
from hearing. Following Aristotle's theory of sense perception, Aquinas holds
that the proper object of sight is color and that the proper object of hearing
is sound. The difference between cognizing color and sound is thus a *per se*
difference in the object of that activity—one that puts sight into a different
species from hearing. From the perspective of the intellective principle, however, the difference between cognizing color and sound is just a *per accidens*
difference. The intellect's proper object is concepts that express the fundamental nature of things, or "intelligible species."[37] The difference between
color and sound is only accidental to this object.

What does all this have to do with human acts? Aquinas wants to argue
that goodness and badness put moral acts into different species. But, as he's
just pointed out, the same things can be *per se* or *per accidens* in different
respects. So that's where reason comes in—it's the relevant respect in this
case. As Aquinas puts it, "when considered with reference to reason," the difference between good and bad in an object of action is a *per se* difference; it
is enough to place those acts into different species. Things are good and bad
insofar as they aim toward or away from their proper end (like how a knife
is good if it cuts well and bad if it is ineffective in slicing). If the object of an
act is suitable to reason, it's aimed toward the proper end for that sort of act.
(It's using your own possessions, say, rather than taking someone else's to do
a job.) Thus, whether the object of an act is appropriately related to reason
is enough to make goodness and badness be different species in moral acts.

---

37. For a more detailed discussion of Aquinas's account of the intellect and intelligible
species, see MacDonald (1993), 160–95.

### 18.6. Does the goodness or badness that derives from the end make for a difference in species?

Answer: yes, the goodness or badness of an object makes for a difference in species for an act.

The objections and replies to this article focus on the way in which the end of an act is an object. The first one simply reiterates that the end does count as an object. The second and third address the distinction between the interior act of the will and the exterior act.

**Obj. and resp. 2.** Imagine, for instance, that someone makes a large donation to charity simply so that she will gain a reputation for philanthropy. The motivation for making the donation is an accident of the act of donating to charity, and so it might not seem as though it would qualify as the sort of *per se* difference needed to separate acts into different species.

In response, Aquinas draws on the distinction between the interior act of the will and the exterior act to argue that although the object of the exterior act is *donating to charity*, the end or object of the interior act of the will is *gaining an empty reputation for philanthropy*. And that's a *per se* difference in object.

**Obj. and resp. 3.** The difference between interior acts of the will and exterior acts also helps defuse the worry of the third objection and explain how there can be a variety of acts that belong to different species (for example, donating to charity, volunteering at a soup kitchen, and making speeches about social justice) that are all directed toward the same end (for example, gaining an empty reputation). Those *exterior* acts do belong to different species. But insofar as they all share the same end, they have the same interior act of the will and thus belong to the same species in that respect.

**Reply.** Aquinas returns to the distinction between interior acts of the will and exterior acts in this article. As we saw above, properly human acts (that is, voluntary acts) are divided into those two categories—interior acts of the will and exterior acts. The significance for this article is that each of these categories has its own object. The interior act of will has the end as its object; the exterior act has "what the act has to do with" as its object (that is, "object" as it was construed in the previous article).

The end that is the object of the interior act of the will provides the 'form' for the action, because it shapes how we use our bodies in the corresponding exterior action. So, to use Aquinas's own example (modified slightly from Aristotle's in *Nicomachean Ethics* V), if someone (call him Harold) sets having sex with someone else's spouse as his end, then that end—adultery—is the object of the interior act of his will.

408 *Commentary on the Treatise on Human Acts*

To actually perform this action, however, Harold needs to perform certain other preparatory physical acts as well, and that's where the exterior act comes in. For instance, if Harold doesn't have a lot of money but knows that his intended sexual partner is a bit of a gold-digger who is particularly impressed by expensive gifts, he might resort to stealing. If we consider Harold's action at this point, where he is using someone else's credit card to buy his intended expensive gifts, there is a distinction between the object of the interior act of the will (adultery) and the object of the exterior act (someone else's stuff). The species of the human act is, then, *adultery* when considered with respect to its end, and *theft* when considered "materially" (that is, in terms of what the external act is about, in order to support the end of adultery).

The whole point of Aquinas's making this distinction is so that he can explain and defend the claim that the goodness (or badness) of the end of an action makes for a difference in species. Since the end of an action is the object of the interior act of the will, this seems a reasonable extension from the principle defended in art. 5 (namely, that an act gets its species from its object). If goodness or badness in the object puts an act into a particular species with respect to reason in general, it would seem plausible that it would also do so in the particular case of the end of an action—the object of the interior act of the will.

*18.7. Is the species that derives from the end contained in the species that derives from the object, as in a genus, or the reverse?*

Answer: the species derived from the object is contained in the species that derives from the end—that is, the end of an act sets the general goal that the possible objects ordered to that end aim toward.

The first question modern readers unfamiliar with the genus-species distinction are likely to have about this article is what issue, exactly, it's supposed to be addressing. The short answer is that it's continuing Aquinas's discussion of what makes human acts good or bad. More specifically, this article is bringing the previous two articles together. We learned in art. 5 that good and bad acts differ in species, and in art. 6 that a human act can be placed into different species with respect to both (1) the end of that act (the object of the interior act of the will) and (2) the object of the (exterior) act. The motivation for this article, then, is to clarify the relation between (1) and (2). After extensive discussion, Aquinas settles that the object of the exterior act will be contained in the end of that act, the object of the interior act of the will. What this means, however, takes some unpacking (as we'll see in the discussion of the reply below).

**Obj. and resp. 1.** This objection is aimed at the possibility of the end of an action and the object of an action belonging to two different "non-nested" or "non-subordinate" species. (This is like the Robin Hood case, where someone steals in order to give to charity.) The claim is that nothing can belong to more than one species unless one of those species is subordinate to the other. (The reason for this is that species pick out the kind of thing something is, and so you have to get more or less specific within that kind rather than crossing over kinds. You can't have something that's a mammal, say, and also an eagle.)

Aquinas's response is that it's true that a thing can't belong to two different, non-nested species with respect to its substance, or what sort of thing it is essentially. (So you can't have a newt that's also a tree.) But something in the category of substance will also have accidents of various kinds, and it can belong to various non-nested species by virtue of these accidents. A plum, for example, belongs to the species of purple things by virtue of its color and to the species of good-smelling things by virtue of its odor. In this way, you can have a moral act that belongs to two non-subordinate species by virtue of its accidents. My act of thanking someone to whom I owe gratitude, for instance, can belong to the category of "thanking" in virtue of its object (I speak the words, "Thank you!") but to the category of "sarcasm" in virtue of its tone.

**Obj. and resp. 2.** The objection here is that an end has the character of an ultimate, or final, end, because things are done for its sake. So it seems that the species derived from the end will be the most specific species of an act—a category that divides naturally only into individual members of that species, not into further sub-species—and thus must be contained in the species that derives from the object of that act rather than the other way around.

Aquinas replies that the end of an act is final or last in terms of the *execution* of the act (insofar as it is what is ultimately accomplished), but that what counts for determining the species of moral action is the intention of reason (as discussed in art. 5). And the end of an action comes first in terms of reason's intention: it is what provides the form for the exterior act.

**Obj. and resp. 3.** As the overview for Q18 notes, *genus = species + difference*. In hylomorphic terms, the difference (say, 'rational') is the "form" to the "matter" of the genus (say, 'animal') that produces the species. Because the end of an act is more formal than the species that comes from the object (as was discussed in the previous article), it seems that perhaps the species derived from the end would be contained or nested in the genus of the object.

Aquinas's response is to distinguish between different senses in which one thing can be more formal than another. The sense in which a difference is form to the matter of a genus (as in "rational animal") is not one that applies when we're trying to figure out the relation between the end and object of an action. In this case, what's relevant is which one is more "ultimate," in the sense of the previous objection and reply. The end of an action—say, charity—is more absolute and general than the object of that action—taking what belongs to someone else, say, or using one's own possessions—because the exterior act is directed toward accomplishing the end of the action.

**Reply.** This article is meant to clarify the relation between two different ways a human act can be placed into different species: (1) with respect to the end of that act (the object of the interior act of the will) and (2) with respect to the object of the (exterior) act. Aquinas mentions two possibilities at the outset: the object of an exterior act could be intrinsically ordered (in some way or another) to the end of that act (which he refers to here as "the will's end"), or it could just be accidentally related to that end.

To get a sense of what it would mean for the object and the end of an act to be intrinsically related, picture a set of Russian nesting dolls (*matryoshka*), where each doll fits neatly inside the previous, larger doll. If the object and the end are not intrinsically ordered, we're talking about an object and an act that do not belong to the same doll: they won't fit neatly together. If they are intrinsically related, however, one of them will "nest" naturally inside the other.

Aquinas's example of an object and an end that are intrinsically related to each other is how fighting well is intrinsically ordered to victory. If victory is your ultimate goal (the larger doll, so to speak), fighting well is a natural means to achieve that goal, and will "fit" naturally inside it. In contrast, Aquinas gives the example of stealing from someone in order to give to charity as an example of an object and an end that are not intrinsically related to each other. You can, in fact, give money that you stole from someone else to charity—you can even steal that money *in order to* give it to charity. But if you really understand what charity is, you'll understand that taking what belongs to someone else is not an action that fits naturally "inside" that goal.

Aquinas's way of talking about this "fit" is to talk about differences being "intrinsically determinative" of each other. When dividing a genus into species, you have to look for the natural divisions: what Plato called "dividing reality at the joints." So, for example, if someone divided the genus "animal" into "rational" and "non-rational," and then divided "non-rational" into "winged" and "non-winged," that would be an unnatural division, in part because "winged" is not a category that then breaks down into a further series of meaningful sub-categories.[38] When we divide "animal" into "footed" and "non-footed," however, we then have the ability to further sub-divide "footed" into "two-footed," "four-footed," and "many-footed," and in this way end up with a broader range of categories in which to place animals. (See also 19.1,

---

38. Aquinas draws this particular example from Aristotle's discussions of taxonomy in works such as *Posterior Analytics* II and the *Generation of Animals*; see the *Stanford Encyclopedia of Philosophy* (http://plato.stanford.edu/entries/aristotle-biology/) for an excellent discussion of the principles of Aristotle's taxonomy.

where Aquinas talks about 'good' and 'bad' as being intrinsic differences for an act of reason—that is, differences that divide acts of reason into meaningful categories.)

The general point about intrinsic order and determination actually seems clearer in the case of human acts. Sometimes—as in the example from the previous question, where someone commits theft in order to have sex with someone else's spouse—there doesn't seem to be any clear connection between the object of the act (stealing) and the end of the act (adultery). In contrast, we can imagine a case where the object of the act was "securing a private room in a hotel" and the end was "adultery." In this case, the object is intrinsically ordered toward the end: it's easy to see how that act is related to that end.

Bringing all this together with the question of what makes human acts good or bad, Aquinas argues that in some situations, the object of an exterior act is only accidentally ordered to the end of that act—and in these situations, the act falls within two separate species. If you stole money from your roommate because you felt such a strong desire to give to charity, the moral act would count as bad insofar as its object is theft, but good insofar as its end is giving to charity. (Note: Aquinas is not going to claim that the end justifies the means!) If you took what belongs to someone else to commit adultery, however, then you've actually committed two separate moral offenses: theft and adultery, which are different species of bad actions.

In the case of acts in which the object is intrinsically ordered toward the will's end, the original question still remains: is the species derived from the will's end contained in the species derived from the act's object, or vice versa? That is, does the species that comes from the will's end "nest" inside the larger doll of the act's object, or is it the other way around? At this point, it should be fairly clear that the end of the act will be the "larger doll," and that the exterior act directed toward that end will nest inside it. The reason for that is that the end of an act sets the general goal that the possible objects ordered to that end aim toward. Aquinas returns here to his original example of the end of *victory*. That end can be achieved by a variety of different exterior acts (such as marshalling troops, fighting well, etc.), each of which is ordered to victory in the sense that carrying out that act contributes to that end. And the will is like the supreme commander of the army, which moves the other powers of the soul (such as locomotion and imagination) to do the things necessary to achieve the end.

### 18.8. *Is any act indifferent in species?*

Answer: yes, some acts (such as walking through a field or picking up a stick) are indifferent in species.

**Reply.** As Aquinas discussed in art. 2 and 5, moral acts derive their species from their objects *insofar as those objects are related to reason* (the principle of

human acts). Some objects of action—such as helping out someone in need—
are inherently in accord with reason, or ordered toward the good. And those
acts will be good in species. Even if one gives to a charity simply in hopes
of winning the heart of that dreamy guy who works there, the act "giving to
charity" is still good in species. Some objects, by contrast—such as lying or
stealing—go against reason, and the corresponding acts will be bad in species in that respect. Even if the reason someone steals from her roommate is
in order to buy a plane ticket home to see her dying mother, for instance, the
act "taking someone else's possessions" is still bad in species.

Some objects of action aren't inherently related to the order of reason at
all, however. Aquinas's examples are "picking up a stick from the ground" or
"walking through a field." In those cases, we say that this sort of act is *indifferent* in species. As we'll see in the next article, every individual act that is
properly human (that is, voluntary) will be either good or bad, because of its
particular circumstances. But it is possible for an act to be the kind of thing
that isn't itself inherently good or bad. "Looking at someone" or "listening
to music" will count as good or bad acts only because of accidental features
that accrue to that act, such as "in order to annoy your brother" or "to feel
inspired."

**Obj. and resp. 1.** This objection focuses on the definitions of 'good' and 'bad'
that Aquinas provided in the first article of this question. If badness is simply
a privation of goodness, then it seems that all acts will be either good or bad.
There is no middle, "neutral" stage on the sliding scale between absolute
goodness and total privation.

Aquinas's response is (not surprisingly) that privation can be thought of in
more than one way. One way is to think of possession and privation as either/
or opposites, as for instance with the case of dead or alive. There is no intermediate for this sort of privation. Something counts as alive until it becomes
dead. Another way to think of privation, however, is as something that comes
in degrees—partial, rather than complete. The example given here is sickness, which is a partial privation of health. Insofar as someone is still alive,
she still has health. But she can be more or less sick at the same time that she
possesses some degree of health. According to Aquinas, we should think of
goodness and badness in this partial sense. Badness is a partial privation of
goodness, but insofar as the thing exists at all, it retains some goodness. In
the case of human acts, no act can be entirely bad (because that would entail
that it didn't exist). Rather, if we think of a sliding scale between pure goodness and absolute privation, all human acts in this life will possess a blend of
both goodness and badness. And so, Aquinas says, there can be something
intermediate between good and bad.

This response doesn't seem to actually address the original point, however, which allowed for badness and goodness to exist on a sliding scale and

just claimed that there was no intermediate section of the continuum which should be marked "indifferent." And, frankly, the kinds of actions that Aquinas gives as examples of indifferent actions don't seem to help his point out here. "Giving to charity," "walking through a field," and "stealing" are not species of actions that clearly fall along a spectrum from goodness to neutrality to badness as the degree of *privation* involved increases.

**Obj. and resp. 2.** This objection also trades on the original definition of goodness and badness laid out in art. 2 and 5. The first objection points out that every object and end count as either good or bad, insofar as they meet or fall short of being the sort of thing they are meant to be. If I speak too quietly for you to hear my apology, for instance, my apology falls short of what it should be. (The way a thing should be is what's sometimes referred to as a thing's "natural goodness.")

Aquinas's response to this is to say that *natural* goodness doesn't always imply *moral* goodness. Moral goodness or badness derives from how the object of the act relates to reason, and if it's possible for the object of an act to relate indifferently to reason (which it is), then it's possible for an act to be morally indifferent in species. (This, incidentally, seems as though it would have been a much better answer to the first objection than the one Aquinas actually provided.)

This is also related to **obj. and resp. 3**, which is that an act is either good insofar as it has "the appropriate perfection of goodness" or bad, insofar as it falls short of that perfection. Aquinas's reply is that what constitutes an act's having appropriate or complete perfection (that is, goodness) includes more features than just that act's species. In particular, the act can be morally indifferent with respect to its species and have appropriate perfection added via other features (such as circumstances). Take, for example, the species "human being." Individual human beings are neither virtuous nor vicious simply by virtue of being human. They have a certain level of goodness insofar as they exist as a member of that species, but whether an individual human being counts as virtuous or vicious will depend on how she perfects (or fails to perfect) the capacities involved in being human.

### 18.9. Is any individual act indifferent?

Answer: no. Any individual human act, insofar as it is the result of deliberative reason, will be aimed toward a particular end and so either good or bad.

**Reply.** As discussed in the previous article, Aquinas holds that certain types of actions (such as "walking through a field" or "looking across a room") can be morally indifferent (as opposed to the types of action which are inherently good or bad, such as charity or theft). This article argues that no *individual act* can be morally indifferent. So long as it is the result of deliberative reason—the sort of interaction between intellect and will that Aquinas began the Treatise on Happiness by calling a human act, properly speaking (see 1.1)—a particular act will be either good or bad.

In the next article, Aquinas will have more to say about what accounts for the goodness or badness of individual acts that belong to morally neutral species; in this article, he merely points out that individual acts will have particular circumstances that direct them toward good or bad ends—at the very least, the end of an act will either be in accordance with or contrary to reason.

**Obj. and resp. 1.** It seems as though the individual acts that fall into a morally indifferent species would also be indifferent.

Aquinas responds, however, that the objects of a human act can be (and, presumably *are*) always directed toward something that is either good or bad— either through circumstance (as when I use my act of thanking someone as an opportunity to exercise inappropriate sarcasm) or through its end (as when I walk through a field in order to apologize to you for being sarcastic the day before). The individual acts that belong to morally indifferent species of action get their goodness or badness not from the act's object (which determines its morally indifferent species), then, but rather from some other source (the act's circumstances or end), which places the act into the category "good" or "bad."

**Obj. and resp. 2.** The second objection raises an interesting point: according to Aristotle (and Aquinas), we develop dispositions of character by performing individual actions so many times that that sort of act becomes habitual. But there are morally indifferent states of character, such as "being even-tempered" or "being wasteful of one's own resources." This appears to imply that those dispositions are the cumulative result of repeated individual, morally indifferent actions.

Aquinas's response is that calling dispositions such as even-temperedness or wastefulness morally indifferent relies on a particular definition of 'bad' that Aristotle proposes—namely, that a bad person is one who is harmful to other people. That definition of badness is far narrower than the one Aquinas is relying on in this discussion, however, where badness is just whatever is contrary to reason. On Aquinas's definition, every individual act is, all things considered, going to be either contrary to or in accordance with reason.

**Obj. and resp. 3.** The third objection and response also address the relation of individual acts to moral character. The objection states that sometimes people perform acts that are both indifferent in species and also aren't directed toward the end of either a virtue or a vice. I take a stroll on a summer's afternoon, for instance, with no particular goal in mind.

Aquinas simply denies this possibility. Every properly human act, he claims, is directed toward either the goodness of some virtue or the badness of some vice. Take someone who has the virtue of temperance or moderation, for instance. When that person has a glass of wine to unwind at the end of a long day of work, that individual action has an appropriate end and so counts as good. In the same way, when someone with a spiteful personality has a glass of wine in order to empty the bottle and ensure her partner won't be able to have one later, that act is bad. There can be morally indifferent acts on Aquinas's account, but they won't be voluntary actions—they will be the sort of action that Aquinas refers to in 1.1 as "acts of a human being" rather than "human acts": sneezing, or absentmindedly scratching an itch.

### 18.10. Does any circumstance determine the species of a good or bad act?

Answer: yes, the circumstances of an act can place that act into a particular species of good or bad act.

Aquinas has already discussed the role of circumstances in human actions both in Q7 and in several previous articles in Q18. Here he reiterates the main points of those discussions in order to draw the conclusion that certain circumstances can place a moral act into a particular species of good or bad act, if those circumstances play a central role in the act's relation to reason.

**On the contrary.** Take the circumstance of place, for instance. Usually, the location of an action doesn't affect the goodness or badness of an action. It doesn't matter as far as the morality of the act goes, for instance, whether the cash register from which I take all the money is located in a clothing store or in a restaurant. Either way, it's stealing. But there will be situations in which the location of an act does take on special significance. If I steal something from a church, for instance, my act isn't just theft—it's sacrilege, which is a separate species of bad act (namely, "doing something wrong to a sacred place"). In that instance, the place from which I stole something becomes what Aquinas calls a "central feature" of the object of the act, and it gives the act its species. The location of this act is directly relevant to the moral status of that action because reason dictates that we should be especially careful not to do wrong to a sacred place. (In the same way, although there's nothing inherently wrong with shouting, it's considered inappropriate to shout in most sacred places or during certain sorts of events, like funerals.)

**Reply.** Although there is a most specific species (the smallest doll in the set of Russian nesting dolls) for natural things, human reason is able to continue to make divisions long after such natural divisions cease—and so, Aquinas says, we are able to use circumstances as well as objects to place moral acts into different species. Indeed, as Aquinas says in **resp. 1**, there are certain instances in which reason needs to consider the circumstances of an action as essentially a further "difference" in the object of the act. ("Difference" is to be understood, as throughout this question, as what divides a genus into a species.)

Circumstances will place moral acts into particular species of good or bad acts, however, only when they are directly relevant to whether the act is contrary to or in accordance with reason. Not all circumstances will affect the moral status of an act. And, as Aquinas will go on to discuss in the next article, even some circumstances that do affect the moral status of an act don't actually go so far as to place it into a species of good or bad act.

### 18.11. Does every circumstance relevant to goodness or badness give a species to an act?

Answer: no, not every morally relevant circumstance places an act into a particular species.

**Reply.** Aquinas argues that sometimes the circumstances of an act affect its moral status, but not in a way that places it into a particular species of good or bad action. Take, for instance, the difference between my stealing your laptop and my stealing every single thing that you own. Both actions are instances of theft. The fact that I take much more in the second case doesn't change the nature of the act itself (although it does make the sin greater, and so it affects the moral status of the act in that way).

**Obj. and resp. 1.** The first objection argues that anything that makes a difference to the goodness or badness of a moral act changes the act's specific difference and thus places it in another species.

In response, Aquinas points out that increasing or decreasing something's intensity isn't the sort of change in an act that would constitute a specific difference and make the act an entirely different kind of act. In the same way that making something more or less red doesn't put it into a different species of color, making an act of theft more or less intense by stealing more or less doesn't put the act into a different species of action. It just makes the act more or less good or bad.

**Obj. and resp. 3.** The third objection challenges this idea. The worry is that every circumstance that increases an act's badness or goodness adds a separate species of sin or goodness.

Aquinas's reply is that this applies only in cases where the circumstance is adding a new defect in its own right—as would be the case when I thank you for something I owe you gratitude for, but I do it in a sarcastic voice. In that situation, the manner in which I thank you detracts from the goodness of the act sufficiently to place it in a different species of action. In situations where a circumstance is only enhancing the goodness or badness of the overall act, though (as when I thank you in the most sincere voice of which I am capable versus when I thank you with a totally flat affect), that circumstance does not put the moral act into a different species.

## Question 19: The Goodness of the Interior Act of the Will

Now that Aquinas has provided a framework for the general goodness or badness of human acts in Q18, he turns in this question to the goodness and badness of *interior* acts of the will and in the next question to the goodness and badness of *exterior* acts. As the discussion so far in the Treatise on Human Acts has made clear (especially the discussion of the nature of voluntary and involuntary acts in Q6), Aquinas is more interested in the interior act of the will than exterior acts. It's not surprising, then, that Q19 contains ten articles, while Q20 contains only six.

### 19.1. Does the will's goodness depend on the object?

Answer: yes, the will's goodness depends on the object. As we saw in 18.5, an act's object is what puts an act into one species ("good") rather than another ("bad").

Aquinas reminds us at the outset of this question that goodness is the natural object of the will. As a "rational appetite for the good," the will is naturally directed toward the good. In the same way, truth is the natural object of the intellect: the intellect is naturally directed toward the truth. (That is not, of course, to say that we can't believe false things, any more than it is to say that we can't will bad things. We just can't believe or will them *under those descriptions*.) Because truth is the object of the intellect, Aquinas says, the difference between "true" and "false" count as *intrinsic* for an act of reason—they divide opinions or beliefs into different categories. In the same way, "good" and "bad" are intrinsic differences of an act of will—they divide acts of will into different categories. Since an act gets its species (including "good" and "bad") from its object, the will's goodness or badness thus also depends on the object of the act.

In practical terms, this is not new information about the will. Aquinas has already made it clear at this point in the Treatise that goodness and badness depend on the object of the action. Narrowing the focus to the interior act of the will does not change that general point. The primary goal of this article is to re-establish the basic relation between the object of the will's act and the goodness or badness of human actions, and to set the stage for the subsequent discussion of what *else* the will's goodness depends on.

**Obj. and resp. 1.** The first objection starts from Aquinas's definition of the will as a rational appetite for the good and argues that since the will is always aimed at the good, it seems that the object of the will should also always be good; thus, having a bad will should be impossible.

In response, Aquinas makes the same qualification he has made many times in the past: the will naturally desires the good, but there is the *apparent* good and then there is the *genuine* good. The Convertibility Thesis (see the commentary on 18.1) entails that there will always be something good about any object the will could possibly will—but insofar as the will can desire what is only *apparently* good and its object thus fall short of what it should be, the will can will badly.

**Obj. and resp. 2.** The end is what's good; other things get their goodness from the end. Aristotle says that an act can be an end, however, so an act that is an end is a good in its own right, not because of any object.

In response, Aquinas agrees that an act can be an end, but he argues that it can't be just any act that is an end. And act of will can't be an end, for instance, for reasons given in 1.1 resp. 2. In short, willing can't itself be the end of willing. An act of willing has to be for the sake of something beyond itself, and it can't be an ultimate end in its own right.

**Obj. and resp. 3.** The general principle that "things that are F make other things F" (for example, my coffee, which is hot, makes the mug hot) is used by this objection to argue that the goodness inherent in the will's object cannot impart its goodness to the will itself, because we're dealing with two different types of goodness here (an F and a G, so to speak). On the one hand, we have the "goodness of nature" or metaphysical goodness of the object of the will (goodness-F); on the other hand, we have the moral goodness of the will that's the focus of this treatise (goodness-G). If what we want is something that accounts for the will's goodness-G, then the objection says we must look to something that's itself G to explain that.

In his reply, Aquinas claims that the will's object *is* good-G and not merely good-F. The argument he gives for this is that the will's object is something presented to it by the intellect as good—and that insofar as the intellect has judged that object as good, it's done so under the description "should be done" (which is type 'good-G') and thus the object deserves the label 'moral.'

### 19.2. Does the will's goodness depend only on its object?

Answer: yes. Whether an exterior act is good or bad depends on a variety of things, including circumstances (as described in Q18), but the subject of Q19 is the interior act of the will, and the goodness of the will itself comes entirely from its relation to the object—and whether that object is in accordance with reason.

Aquinas claims in this article that the goodness of the will itself (its interior act) comes entirely from whether it is in accordance with right reason. He then spends the rest of the articles in Q19 examining different ways in which the will can be in (or out of) accordance with reason.

**Obj. and resp. 1.** This objection and its response serve primarily to remind us that, when it comes to the interior act of the will, the end and the object of the act are identical. The objection is that goodness comes not just from the object but also from the end of an act; Aquinas's response is that for the purposes of this question, the object and the end are the same thing.

**Obj. and resp. 2.** As we saw in Q18, difference in circumstances can result in an act's being good or bad, and so circumstances appear to affect the goodness or badness of the will. Take, for example, what Aquinas would think of as a newly married couple's appropriate desire to start a family, and then think about the difference between their willing to do so in the privacy of their home and their willing to do so in the check-out lane at the corner grocery store.

Aquinas responds that if the will's object is good, *no* circumstance can make that act of will bad. We should think of the effects of circumstances on acts of the will in two ways: (1) With respect to *what is willed*, where taking the circumstances into account demonstrates that the will's object is actually not good. Willing "to start a family right here in the grocery store" is not an appropriate end. (2) With respect to *the act of willing*, however, it is impossible for someone to will what is good *badly* (say, at the wrong time or in the wrong place). We should always will what is good. What about cases in which we will one good when we should be willing another? I might, for instance, will to watch a movie with my friends instead of spending time with my parents on Christmas. Even in this situation, Aquinas says, it's not bad to will the good, considered as such. What's wrong here is that the person isn't willing the other good, not that they're willing the particular good they're willing. So, in the case of our overly enthusiastic family planners, their act of will is still good insofar as it's a good thing that they're willing.

**Obj. and resp. 3.** This objection returns to the discussion in 6.8 about how ignorance impacts whether an act is voluntary or involuntary. (Aquinas will spend more time spelling out the relation between ignorance and the goodness or badness of the will's act in 19.6.) Because ignorance of certain circumstances can excuse the will's willing something it shouldn't—as when I give someone who is unaware of her own severe strawberry allergy strawberry shortcake, thus causing her to go into anaphylactic shock—the objection argues that circumstances (and not just the object) affect the goodness or badness of the will.

Aquinas points out that in this sort of case, ignorance of the circumstance ("serving strawberry shortcake to someone with a severe strawberry allergy") excuses badness insofar as I'm not actually *willing* the second, bad, part of the circumstance ("with a severe strawberry allergy"), and it's not a circumstance I was morally responsible for having knowledge of.

**Reply.** Aquinas's argument for the claim that the will's goodness depends only on its object (as opposed to the goodness of exterior acts, which depends on other things as well) heads into murky metaphysical territory. It is centered on the claim that the first principle of goodness and badness in human acts is an act of the will. (This is essentially just the point that an act must be voluntary to be good or bad.) The more prior a thing is, though, says Aquinas, the simpler it is. (He appeals to first elements here: the fundamental building blocks of reality are simple and homogenous.) The primary cause of the goodness or badness in an act of will, then, must be singular. It must also be a *per se* cause, Aquinas claims, rather than an accidental cause: if it were accidental, it would depend on something further (and thus not fit the "prior" criterion). Thus, the will's goodness or badness depends entirely on one thing: the act's end or object, which is the *per se* cause of goodness in a human action.

The appeal to first principles here may not seem particularly moving. The idea that the end or object of the action is entirely responsible for the goodness or badness of the will, however, should seem fairly intuitive at this point in the discussion. As we've seen, the will is a rational appetite for the good. It seems fitting, then, that whether it counts as good depends on whether it is appropriately related to its natural object.

### 19.3. Does the will's goodness depend on reason?

Answer: yes, the will's goodness depends on reason.

Aquinas has just spent the last two articles arguing that the will's goodness depends on its object. Will gets that object, however, from reason. On Aquinas's account of action, in order for an act to occur, the intellect must judge a particular object as good and present it to the will to be affirmed or denied (or, depending on your interpretation of Aquinas, ignored). Insofar as the will's goodness depends on the object of the will's act, then, and the will gets that object from reason, the will's goodness depends on reason.

**Obj. and resp. 1.** This objection claims that the goodness of the will doesn't depend on reason because the connection between the will and the good is prior to the connection between the intellect and the good. After all, good is the proper object of the *will*, not of the *intellect*.

In response, Aquinas grants that the will's connection to the good *as such* is fundamentally prior, but he then goes on to argue that, in the series of events that culminates in an act of the will, reason's relation to the good (as true) is prior in relevant ways to the will's relation to the good. In short, the will has to have an object in order to desire the good, and the intellect provides it with that object. (Another way of making this point would be to say that the will's connection to the good is ontologically prior to reason's connection, but that reason's connection to the good is temporally prior in human actions.)

**Obj. and resp. 2.** The practical intellect is often described as the aspect of the intellect responsible for deliberating about things like whether I should have another slice of pie, or whether I should tell a potentially offensive joke. And, as Aristotle comments in *Nicomachean Ethics* VI, what counts as goodness for the practical intellect is judging what is true in accordance with "correct desire"—namely, desires that correspond to what should be done and what should be avoided. But having the right desires requires having a good will. So it looks as though having goodness in practical reason (also called prudence) depends on already having a good will. And this makes goodness in the practical intellect look dependent on goodness in the will, rather than the other way around.

In response, Aquinas clarifies that Aristotle's quote applies to practical reason insofar as it deliberates about things that are for the end—for example, whether having another slice of apple pie is an appropriate way for me to satisfy my appetite, or whether going to bed at 10 pm is an appropriate way for me to meet my goal of being well-rested, given that I have to get up at 6 am. In this sense, it is true that practical reason is good when it conforms to the desire for an appropriate end (judging that I should not have another slice of cake, e.g., or that I should go to bed at 10 pm). But, as Aquinas goes on to point out, the desire for an appropriate end *presupposes* the existence of an appropriate end that is the object of that desire. It's reason that is responsible for correctly judging what the end of our action should be, and so in that sense the goodness of the intellect's act is prior to goodness of the will in a way that makes the goodness of the will possible.

**Obj. and resp. 3.** The will is a mover: it directs both reason (to, say, deliberate about how to achieve its desired end) and other powers (such as locomotion). This objection relies on the principle that a *mover* doesn't depend on what is *moved*, but vice versa. So, for instance, the billiard ball depends on the cue stick in the action of shooting pool, not the cue stick on the billiard ball.

Aquinas responds just as we would expect him to at this point, pointing out that although will moves reason in one way (for example, the will moves reason to deliberate about how to achieve the desired end), reason moves the will in a more fundamental way by presenting it with the potential objects of volition. It is the will's relation to these potential objects of volition—provided to it by the intellect—that its goodness or badness depends on.

**Reply.** Aquinas's main focus in this article is distinguishing between the role of the will (rational appetite) and the role of sensory appetite in human acts. It is the cognized or "understood" good that serves as the object of the will. That is, the will's object is the good that reason has considered and judged to be appropriate. What Aquinas refers to here as "sensible" or "imagined" goods are the sort that the sense appetite naturally responds to. If I smell an apple pie baking and I'm immediately struck by how good it would taste, I'm responding to a particular sensible (and imagined) good. No moral goodness is involved here—whether or not the pie would taste good to me isn't a matter of ethical import. If I start to think about what I should eat today, however, and eventually make the considered judgment that it would be good to have the pie, and then will to eat a slice of it for dessert, I'm responding to the "understood" good that the intellect presented to my will. Whether the will's act is good or bad, then, depends on reason insofar as the intellect is responsible for presenting the end or object to the will in the first place.

### 19.4. Does the goodness of a human will depend on the eternal law?

Answer: yes, the goodness of a human will depends on the eternal law.

The real issue of interest in this article is not whether the goodness of a human will depends on its accordance with the eternal law. Insofar as the eternal law points us toward our highest good (God), and insofar as the will is a rational appetite for the good as such, to that extent the will's goodness of course depends on its relation to the eternal law. The real issue is (as we can see, looking ahead to the next two articles) what we should say about the goodness or badness of the will in cases where human reason and the eternal law come to different conclusions—in short, cases in which human reason screws up. The trajectory of this and the following two questions is to establish the ideal relation between the eternal law, human reason, and the will, and then to examine what happens in situations where human reason goes wrong, as when reason presents an inappropriate object to the will as good, and the will does *not* will it, or when reason presents an inappropriate object to the will as good and the will *does* will it.

**Obj. and resp. 1.** The first objection and reply make this trajectory clear: the objection is that the will has human reason as its "rule." That is, the will's goodness depends on how it relates to (or "measures up to") the judgment of the intellect. Each thing can have only one rule or measure, however, and so the goodness of the will can't depend on how it measures up to both the human intellect *and* the eternal law.

Aquinas's response is that this general principle is true—but only for things on the same level. Because human reason is subordinate to the eternal law, the will's goodness can be measured against its relation to both reason's judgment and the eternal law. Importantly, this twofold means of measuring the goodness of the will also opens up the possibility of reason's judgment and the eternal law differing—precisely the subject of the next two articles.

**Obj. and resp. 2.** This same point comes up again in the second objection. The principle "A measure is homogenous with what it measures" basically boils down to the idea that what's being measured and what's doing the measuring must be the same sort of thing. In this case, the moral status of the human will needs to be measured by something relevantly similar—the human intellect (a fellow rational faculty), say, as opposed to sight.

Aquinas's response is that this is true at the proximate or immediate level. In the case where you have a measure that is subordinate to another measure, however, the higher-level measure does not need to be homogenous with what it's measuring. In short, the eternal law can be the measure of the human will without needing to be on the same level as it.

**Obj. and resp. 3.** The third objection appeals to the inherently unknowable nature of the eternal law. If we don't have access to what the eternal law commands of us, after all, it doesn't seem appropriate to measure the goodness of our wills against it.

Aquinas responds that although we don't have access to the eternal law *as it exists in the mind of God*, we've been given enough access to it through natural reason and special revelation (such as the ten commandments) to make it an appropriate measure of the goodness of the will.

**Reply.** The reply argues that the goodness of our wills depends much more on how our wills measure up to the eternal law than on how they measure up to human reason. Aquinas says that this is because human reason is only the measure of the goodness of the will in the first place because of its relation to the eternal law—which he identifies here as divine reason. According to Aquinas, the eternal law isn't independent from God; it is, in a sense, part of God's absolutely simple nature, and as such it serves as the ultimate measure against which to measure goodness.[39]

Aquinas draws on illumination language to make this point: we have a light of reason in us that allows us to see and judge the truth (much as, four centuries later, Descartes refers to the natural light of reason in his *Meditations*), but this light is itself derived from the light of God's intellect. The eternal law, then, should be understood as the "first cause" with respect to the goodness of the human will, and human reason as the secondary or derivative cause. In situations where the light of human reason falters, Aquinas says, we should turn to eternal reason. So the eternal law is the ultimate measure of the goodness of the will.

But how are we to judge the goodness of the will in situations where its two measures differ—that is, situations where human reason is mistaken? The answer to this question is the topic of the following two articles.

*19.5. Is a will that is out of harmony with mistaken reason bad?*

Answer: yes, every will that is out of harmony with reason is wrong, whether reason is correct or mistaken. (In short, two wrongs don't make a right.)

---

39. For a fuller discussion of this topic, see Aquinas's Treatise on Law I-II.90–108, especially 93.1.

This question gets its main force from the fact that (as we saw in Q1 of the Treatise on Happiness) the will is a rational appetite for the good, and that the intellect is what's responsible for presenting the will with the objects it has judged as good. In cases where that judgment has gone wrong, should the will be inclined towards or against the object the intellect mistakenly presents to it as good?

Aquinas's argument in this article underscores one of the central tenets of his action theory: it is the intellect, not the will, that is responsible for judging whether something is good or bad, to be done or avoided. Insofar as the will is a rational appetite for the good, if the intellect is presenting an object to the will *as good*, it would be wrong for the will to will against that object (again, understood as 'presented to it as a good').

The objections and replies to this article underscore the line Aquinas is holding against those who want to claim that it is appropriate for will to go against mistaken reason.

**Obj. and resp. 1 & 2.** The first objection, for instance, argues that because mistaken reason isn't in line with the eternal law, it's ok for the will not to be in harmony with it—a position that makes sense if you're thinking of the situation from the outside, so to speak.

Aquinas's response emphasizes that he doesn't think this is the appropriate perspective from which to think of the situation. Even if the intellect has judged wrongly about what it presents to the will as to be done or to be avoided, he says, reason still presents that judgment as true and, thus, as derived from God—the source of all truth. That is, the will doesn't "know" that the judgment presented to it is mistaken, and so it is obligated to respond to that judgment as though it is correct.

Aquinas makes much the same point in response to the second objection: the only time you're excused from following the command of a lower power that conflicts with the command of a higher power is when you *know* that there is such a conflict. But the will doesn't *know* anything. Its job is simply to desire the good; it's the job of the intellect to judge what the good is. So even in situations where reason's judgment is mistaken, the will is still bound by the object that reason presents to it as good.

**Obj. and resp. 3.** The third objection argues that there would be no appropriate category of "bad" for the will that went against mistaken reason. After all, if my intellect presents "having sex with anyone who asks me for it" as good, and my will does not desire that object, what species of badness would we put "not willing to fornicate" in?

Aquinas's response is, again, that in the case of actual human acts, we're always talking about particular objects that the intellect has apprehended as good or bad; and the intellect apprehends something as good or bad *for some reason*. If, for instance, reason has judged that having sex with anyone who asks is good because that is what charity requires of me, then the will that does not desire that object is classified as bad insofar as it does not desire what charity requires.

**Reply.** Initially, it might seem reasonable to suppose that the will should reject what reason proposes to it as good in cases where the intellect is mistaken. After all, reason is *wrong*. Are we really supposed to will the *wrong thing?* Aquinas mentions here that some people have argued for this by dividing acts into three sorts: acts that are good in themselves, bad in themselves, and indifferent. Cases of mistaken reason (or conscience) happen when reason (or conscience) (a) commands us to do things that are bad in themselves, (b) forbids things that are good in themselves, or (c) commands or forbids something that is in itself indifferent. So, for example, (a) I might have formed the (false) judgment that I'm obligated to have sex with anyone who asks me to. Or (b) I might have formed the (false) judgment that I'm not ever allowed to have sex with anyone—not even my spouse. Or (c) I might have formed the judgment that the (morally indifferent) act of charging my phone every day is morally forbidden, or (alternatively) that charging my phone daily is morally obligatory.

Aquinas says that there are people who say that in (c)-type situations— where the act being forbidden or commanded is actually morally neutral in itself—the will is obliged to desire the object the intellect presents to it as good. If I've made the mistaken judgment that charging my cell phone every day is forbidden, but there's no moral law that I'm violating with that judgment, my will is good only if it goes along with that judgment of reason.

On the other hand, in (a)- or (b)-type situations—where the action that my intellect has judged as commanded or forbidden is actually in itself bad or good—my will is not obligated to go along with it. That is, my will is not bad if it does not desire having sex with anyone who asks me to, nor is it bad if it does not desire refraining from sex with anyone ever, including my spouse. (Note: this is not the same as saying that my will is *good* if it goes against what my intellect presents to it as commanded or forbidden; the intuition here is just that the will isn't *bad* if it goes against the judgment of reason in these cases.)

Aquinas, however, takes an unequivocal stance on this issue: *every* will that is out of harmony with reason—whether reason is right or wrong—is *bad*. His argument for this relies on one of the central tenets of his action theory: namely, that the goodness of the interior act of the will depends entirely on how it responds to the particular object as presented to it as good by human reason. If reason presents an object (like "charging my phone daily") to the will as bad, and the will is drawn to it, it is drawn to it *under that description*: that is, as something forbidden. And so the will's act in this case is bad. Aquinas's point is that the intellect—*not the will*—is responsible for judging whether something is to be done or avoided. The will's job is simply to respond appropriately to the object presented to it by the intellect: willing those objects presented to it as good and denying those objects presented to it as bad. Thus, although it is objectively speaking a bad thing to have sex with anyone who requests it of you, if the intellect mistakenly apprehends that prospect as good and presents it to the will as such, the will should be drawn to that object *insofar as that object is presented to it as good.*

Our wills do not, on Aquinas's picture, do any judging of good or bad. They function appropriately when they will what the intellect presents to them as good, and they function badly when they will what the intellect presents to them as bad. In fact, Aquinas even goes so far as to say that in the case where reason mistakenly presents 'believing in Christ for your salvation' to the will as bad, the will could only be drawn to that object *as bad*, and thus would be erring.

In short, then, the answer to the question posed at the outset of this article is "yes": will that is out of harmony with a mistaken intellect is bad. Two wrongs don't make a right, and so the fact that reason is mistaken about what should be done doesn't entail that the will's moving against that judgment is right.

### 19.6. Is a will that is in harmony with mistaken reason good?

Answer: no, a will that is in harmony with mistaken reason is not good, although the act of will is morally excused in cases where reason is not culpable for its ignorance.

If it's always bad for the will to be *out* of harmony with mistaken reason, you might think that it would always be good for the will to be *in* harmony with mistaken reason. Yet, as we've seen repeatedly in this treatise, it is much harder to be good than simply not to be bad. In this article, Aquinas draws on the types of ignorance and their effects on the voluntariness and involuntariness of human acts that he discussed in 6.8. He argues that whether or not the will that goes along with mistaken reason is bad depends on the cause of the intellect's ignorance. The will in harmony with mistaken reason will never be *good*, insofar as it will always be willing an inappropriate object, but that will can at least not be *bad*.

The objections and responses to this article further stress the point that it's much harder for an act of will to be good than for it to be bad.

**Obj. and resp. 1.** The first objection is that, if it's always bad for the will to be out of harmony with reason, then it should always be good for it to be *in* harmony with reason.

Aquinas's response is that while all it takes for the will to be bad is for it to be drawn toward something that is either (1) bad by nature or (2) mistakenly apprehended by reason as bad, for the will to be *good*, it must be drawn toward something that is both by nature good *and* correctly apprehended by reason as good.

**Obj. and resp. 3.** The third objection addresses the issue of whether we're trapped in sin once reason makes a mistake. The worry is that if the will that is *out of* harmony with mistaken reason is bad, and the will that is *in* harmony with mistaken reason is bad (in cases where it's willing something bad by nature), then in cases of mistaken reason we're just—so to speak—damned if we do and damned if we don't. As the objection puts it, we'll be trapped in a "state of perplexity and will sin by necessity."

Aquinas grants that there is no way for the will to be good in cases of mistaken reason. He claims that one is not thus trapped in a state of perplexity, however, because he believes that we are always able to correct the original error. This, however, brings up the troubling question of moral luck. What if you're unfortunate enough to be brought up by horrible people—as happens with Cosette in *Les Misérables*—and thus lack the moral resources to correct our errors? Aquinas claims that the natural law and our capacity for reason are, together, enough for us to derive the fundamental moral principles which we are responsible for knowing; at the same time, he grants that it is more difficult for some people than others to gain moral knowledge.

**Reply.** In the reply, Aquinas rephrases the main question as "whether mistaken conscience excuses"; and his answer is that it depends on the cause of the intellect's misjudgment. Aquinas has discussed what types of ignorance cause involuntariness at length in 6.8. Here, he relies on that discussion to argue that whether or not the will that goes along with mistaken reason is good or bad depends on the cause of the intellect's ignorance. As it turns out, the will in harmony with mistaken reason will never be *good*: it will always be willing an inappropriate object. Its willing is morally excused, however, in situations where the mistake arises from reason's ignorance of a particular circumstance (the example given here of such a circumstance involves a rather strange case of potential mistaken identity—namely, "whether the woman I will to have sexual intercourse with is my wife"). Aquinas has classified such actions as involuntary in 6.8; as such, they qualify neither as morally good nor as morally bad.

To run with Aquinas's own example, suppose that, unbeknownst to me, my spouse has an identical evil twin, and it is actually the evil twin in my bed asking me to "pay the marital debt" (that is, have sex: it was standard medieval doctrine that marriage partners owed each other sex at their partner's request, given certain appropriate qualifications and restrictions). The judgment that my intellect presents to my will in this situation is "paying the marital debt is obligatory"; thus, my act of will in this case is aimed at the good of "paying the marital debt." The fact that my desire is misdirected in this instance via a non-culpable mistake of the intellect (namely, judging that the person lying in bed is my spouse and not the identical twin I had no idea my spouse has) is something I'm not blameworthy for, although my willing does not count as *good* in this situation, insofar as it is ultimately aimed at the wrong object. (One might well wonder how common a problem this was in the thirteenth century. The literary source for this particular example, however, may be some of the King Arthur legends which involve cases of people using magic to trick someone else into having sex with them.)

Not all cases of acting from ignorance are situations in which the person is morally excused, however. In his original discussion of ignorance and involuntariness in 6.8, Aquinas focused on the intellect's role—in this article, he explains how the will is involved. In particular, he says, the will can be implicated in the relevant ignorance in two ways: ignorance can be willed *directly* or *indirectly*. These correspond to the two cases of consequent ignorance that Aquinas talks about in 6.8. *Directly willed* ignorance is the same as *affected* ignorance: to use the same example from our discussion of 6.8, if you're at a party, find someone very attractive, and clearly have the chance to hook up with them, and then you actively will *not* to find out whether they are partnered so that you can make out with them guilt-free, you are morally responsible for that act. You know perfectly well that it's bad for people to cheat on their partners, and your will is bad in this case for being drawn toward ignorance of that aspect of your particular situation.

*Indirectly willed* ignorance, on the other hand, involves the cases where you're ignorant of some general principle or rule that you could and should know. In the situation described above, if you're aware that the person you're interested in has a partner, but you go ahead and make out with them anyway because you're totally unaware that it's harmful for people to cheat on their partners, that's a case of indirectly willed ignorance. You could and should know that basic moral fact, and thus your act of will in this case is also bad.

### 19.7. Does the will's goodness depend on the intention of the end?

Answer: yes, the will's goodness depends on its intention of an appropriate end.

For interior acts of the will (which is, after all, the subject of Q19), the object of the act is the same as its end. This article addresses the will's *intention* of the end—that is, the reason why the will desires what it does.

Aquinas says that an intention can either precede or follow the will. If it precedes the will, it is directly relevant to the goodness of the will, because the intention of the end is a "good-making" feature of what is willed (that is, the will's object). Suppose, for example, that my friend and I both choose to go on a fast, but we do so for the sake of pursuing different ends. Perhaps I choose to fast to lose weight for the summer, while my friend chooses to fast in order to develop fasting as a spiritual discipline. When my intention to lose weight causally precedes my willing to fast and is the motivation for my fasting, that intention becomes an aspect of the object of my action and thus affects whether my act of will is good or bad.

On the other hand, sometimes we have intentions that follow the will. A small child might draw a picture, for instance, and then decide that he drew it for his grandfather. Or a quarterback on a college football team might score a touchdown and then afterwards direct that action to God. In these cases, the goodness or badness of the will comes entirely from its original object, not from the intention formed after the act. The subsequent intention only factors into the will's goodness if the original act is repeated (say, the quarterback scores another touchdown), but with the subsequent intention factored in this time (so that the quarterback is scoring the touchdown *for God's sake*).

The objections and replies here all stress the fact that a preceding intention is a good-making (or bad-making) feature of what is willed, and so a will can be called good only if a good intention is the cause of the will's act. In fact, Aquinas ends this article by specifying again what is required for a will to be good: the will must desire what is good *by nature*, and under that description—that is, *because* it is good. Defects in particular aspects of the will's act causes badness; goodness requires a "whole and perfect cause."

### 19.8. Does how good the will is depend on how good the intention is?

Answer: not really. Intensity on the part of an agent's intention can affect the goodness of an act of will, but not in a way that definitively makes that act of will good.

Having now settled the question of the role an intention plays in whether an act of the will is good or bad, Aquinas turns in this article to a discussion of whether the *degree* or *intensity* of the intention makes a difference. Suppose I decide to give money away on a regular basis because I want *very badly* to develop the virtue of generosity. Does the intensity with which I will that end make a difference for how good my will is?

Not surprisingly, Aquinas's answer is quite nuanced. He begins by distinguishing between two ways we can judge the intensity of an act or intention of an end: (1) intensity on the part of the *object*, which is when someone wills or does a greater good, and (2) intensity on the part of the *agent*, which is when someone wills or acts intensely.

Aquinas says that intensity on the part of the object won't impact how good or bad an act is, regardless of whether we're talking about interior acts of the will or exterior acts. For *exterior acts*, intensity won't matter in some cases because things can get in the way of performing the intended act, regardless of how good the intended object is. (Imagine my dying desire to donate my fortune to charity being thwarted by a sudden stock market crash that bankrupts me.) Intensity will also not factor into the goodness or badness of exterior acts in cases where what is done to achieve the intended end is not sufficient (proportionate) to that end. So, for instance, if I intend to kill my philosophical archrival by putting arsenic in his coffee, but I don't put in enough poison to kill him, so that he becomes only mildly ill instead, the object directed toward my intended end is not proportionate to that end. As far as the exterior act goes, I am guilty of making my rival sick, not of killing him.

When it comes to *interior acts* of the will, Aquinas again appeals to the proportionality of object to intended end to defend the claim that the goodness or badness of the act does not depend on how good or bad the intention is. If what I actually will is to give $5 to charity every six months as a way of giving money away on a regular basis, this object is not proportionate to my intended end of acquiring the virtue of generosity. My will, which is drawn to the prospect of giving a mere five dollars every six months, is not as good as my intention of acquiring the virtue of generosity. (Aquinas says that I do get some credit, though, for having the intention of acquiring the virtue, even if I haven't willed an object that would actually achieve that goal. This seems reasonable: it's better for me to want to acquire the virtue of generosity than not to want it, although even better for me actually to *have* the virtue than merely to *want* to have it.)

Aquinas's view on intensity on the part of the agent is less clear. On the one hand, he says that the intensity of the intention overflows into both the interior and exterior acts of the will, because the intention serves as a "formal cause" shaping both sorts of act. If I want very badly to become generous, for instance, this will impact both my acts of will (inclining me toward willing generous acts) and my exterior acts (inclining me toward performing acts I think are generous). On the other hand, the intensity of my intention won't necessarily carry over to my actual interior or exterior acts (what Aquinas here refers to as the "material cause," since those acts are the means necessary for reaching the intended end). I might want very badly to be generous, for instance, but be quite reluctant to actually give my money away. Or, to use Aquinas's example, someone can will to be healthy quite intensely without her willing to take the necessary medicine with the same degree of intensity. All the same, if I want health badly enough, I badly desire to take the necessary medicine as well. So the upshot appears to be that intensity on the part of the agent does carry over to the will in some manner.

Aquinas's final comment on this topic makes his reasons for laying out these detailed scenarios clearer. After presenting all the ways in which the goodness of the will doesn't depend on the goodness of the intention (remember what the road to hell is paved with, after all), he is careful to present one final way in which intensity and intention can be related: the object of intention can actually *be* the intensity with which we will or do something. I can intend to *enjoy* giving money away, for instance, as part of being generous. But that doesn't entail that I will actually manage to do so. And, as Aquinas points out, this is how someone can end up not being as good as she intends to be. Intention isn't sufficient. As Aquinas will go on to discuss in 20.4, merit comes from the intensity of the *actual act*, not from the intensity of the *intention*, even an intention to perform the act with intensity.

The objections and replies to this article stress that, to be good, an act of will must have an object that is both itself good and presented to it by reason as good. Having a good intention is one part of what is required, but it is only one part. An act of will can be bad even if the intention is good.

### 19.9. Does the goodness of a human will depend on its conformity with the divine will?

Answer: yes, the goodness of a human will depends on the extent to which it conforms to the divine will.

It will come as no surprise, given that Aquinas has already argued (in 19.4) that the goodness of a human will depends on the eternal law (which he identified there as divine reason) that he also believes that the goodness of the will depends on its conformity with the divine will. And this is, in fact, the shortest of the articles in Q19.

The main argument here is quite simple: the goodness of a human will depends on its intention of the end. As Aquinas argues at length in the Treatise on Happiness, the final end for the human will is the supreme good (*summum bonum*), or God. For the will to be good, then, it must be directed ultimately toward God. We learned in art. 4 that the eternal law, or divine reason, is the rule or measure of the goodness of the will: it is the standard of truth against which the will is measured. Here Aquinas points out that the divine will is also the measure and standard for all things in the genus of "will." Our wills are good precisely insofar as they conform to the divine will.

The objections and replies for this article are also quite brief. To the objection that we could never hope to have wills that are like the divine will, Aquinas responds that our job is not to attempt equality with God's will, but rather to imitate God's will as far as that is possible. (Conformity here has the same sense as the prologue in I-II, where Aquinas discusses what it means for us to be made in God's image.) In the same way that human knowledge is conformed to God's knowledge when we know what is true, and human action is conformed to God's action when we do what is appropriate for us as agents, our wills are conformed to God's will when we will in accordance with what God wills. This merely requires imitation of, not equality with, God.

### 19.10. Should a human will always be conformed to the divine will in terms of what it wills?

Answer: it's complicated.

At first glance, this article doesn't seem as though it needs to be any longer than the previous article: of course our wills should always conform to God's will, insofar as God's will is the exemplar of perfect goodness. And yet this article is long and complicated. In fact, not only does it have three arguments On the contrary, but Aquinas responds to each of them separately. The reason for the complexity is that we are not God, and so although our wills should always be in line with what God wills, it's not the case that we should always will exactly the same thing that God wills.

The main difference between the subject of this article and the previous one is that the previous article focuses on general conformity, whereas this article distinguishes between particular and general goods. Aquinas sets up this discussion by reminding us that the will can be drawn only to an object *as reason presents it* to the will. So, to use his example, if a judge wills that a robber should be killed because that's the appropriate sentence for someone who committed that crime, the judge wills that under the description "killing someone for the sake of justice." At the same time, it's perfectly possible for the thief's wife to will appropriately that he *not* be killed, insofar as she is focusing on the fact that killing is by nature bad (or how much she will miss him after his death).

This raises an apparent problem. How can two human beings rightly will directly opposing states of affairs? Clearly, both acts of will can't conform with God's act of will here—so how can both of them be good?

Aquinas's answer involves distinguishing between private good and the general or common (*communis*) or universal good. In short, he argues that it can be appropriate for us to will a private good (such as the good of one's family members) even if the same thing shouldn't be willed as a common or universal good. After all, God is concerned about all the creatures in the entire universe. The welfare of everyone else's family members is just as important to God as the welfare of your family members, and so while it may be appropriate for you to will that your thieving spouse not be executed for stealing, it wouldn't be appropriate for God to will the same thing. God needs to will what is best for the universe as a whole, understood as the common or universal good.

We can have directly opposing good human wills, then, when one of those wills is directed toward the private good (which is still in line with the universal good, as it is in the case of the thief's wife, since killing is bad in itself, and it is appropriate not to wish it) and the other is directed toward the common good (as in the case of the judge, who wills for the thief to be killed as part of executing justice as a general good).

Aquinas takes pains to explain that even in cases where the human will doesn't conform to the divine will materially but still wills rightly (as in the case where the thief's wife wishes for him not to be killed because killing is by nature bad), the human will is still in line with the divine will, understood in terms of the ultimate end. That is, the thief's wife is willing that her husband not be killed *because killing is by nature bad*. That's totally in line with God's will. It is, in fact, what God wants her to will in that situation. Willing something out of charity (such as for a person not to be killed) is also what Aquinas calls "formal conformity" with the divine will. God wills that the thief be killed *insofar as that is what justice requires for the common good*, not because killing is itself good. So even in cases of apparent conflict, if two human beings will opposing things rightly, they are both in conformity with God's will.

**Obj. and resp. 1.** The first objection and response return to the question of whether we can have sufficient access to knowledge of God's will to be able to will in conformity with it.

Aquinas's response is that, although we don't in this life know all the particular things that God wills, we know the general shape of what God wills—namely, the good. So any human being who wills things under the aspect of good has a will that harmonizes with God's will in that respect. (And, of course, we have both general and special revelation to help us get a better grasp of what God sees as good and as bad.) Furthermore, Aquinas claims that in the afterlife, we will be able to see how what we will matches up with what God wills. And so our wills will be in both formal conformity (willing the good because it is good) and material conformity (willing the particular goods that God wills) with God's will.

**Obj. and resp. 2 & 3.** The second objection raises the question of hell. On Aquinas's account of foreknowledge, God foreknows who will be saved and who will be damned. The objection states that God thus wills the damnation of those who die in mortal sin, and points out that if we were required to conform our wills in every instance to the divine will, some of us would be willing our own damnation—which seems ridiculous.

Aquinas responds that God doesn't will anyone's damnation under the description "suffering eternally in hell," because God wills that everyone be saved. God wills someone's damnation only under the aspect of justice. And Aquinas says that all we need to will in this case is that God's justice be preserved. We don't have to will anyone's damnation or death as such. (This also takes care of the third objection, which is that if we had to will that our parents or children die when God wills them to die, we would be doing something horribly inappropriate.)

**Responses to the arguments On the contrary.** After he responds to the three objections posed in this article, Aquinas goes on to respond to the three arguments On the contrary that were offered here as well—a fairly unusual move, since normally this would happen only in the scribal report of a "live" disputed question that was happening in the classroom, whereas Aquinas is writing the *Summa theologiae* in his study. This indicates that there are a few issues he would particularly like to address on the other side of the debate: namely, that our wills should always be in conformity with God's will.

The first argument states that we are always obligated to will what God wills. In response, Aquinas nuances this claim, stating that what's most important is to have our wills in conformity with the *reason* for what God wills, not to have it in line with *what* God wills. As he pointed out in the response to the first objection, what's required for conformity with God's will is that we will everything under the aspect of good—the ultimate end of the will. We don't need to will each individual thing that God wills. (And, in fact, as we saw in the responses to objections two and three, for us to will the particular objects that God does would sometimes cause problems.)

The second argument challenges this assumption—namely, that it's not necessary for us to will the particular objects that God wills—on the grounds that the form of an act of will comes from its object. We couldn't have conformity with God's will, then, unless our acts of will had the same object. Aquinas's response is (again) that what's vital for conformity is not material conformity (having exactly the same particular object) but rather having the same species or form (willing something under the aspect of good).

The third argument brings up the case of human beings who will contradictory things (as with the judge and the robber's wife) and claims that both of these acts of will cannot be in conformity with God's will, since they're opposed. Aquinas uses this as a chance to state one final time that the wills of two people who are considering things under different aspects or descriptions ("killing someone for the sake of justice is appropriate" versus "killing is by nature bad," say) are not necessarily incompatible. They would only be incompatible if two people had opposing acts of will *under the same aspect*—as would be the case if the judge and the robber's wife were considering the killing of the thief under the same aspect (say, "killing someone for the sake of justice is appropriate") and had opposing acts of will in this case because the wife is morally opposed to the death penalty.

### Question 20: The Goodness and Badness of Exterior Acts

QQ18 and 19 addressed central features of Aquinas's moral theory, as we can see from looking at their relative lengths (there are twenty-one articles between the two questions, as opposed to the ten articles between QQ20 and 21). After explaining the general causes of goodness and badness of human action in Q18, Aquinas addressed the interior act of the will, which is the primary cause of the goodness or badness of a human act, in Q19. Here, in Q20, he turns to the exterior act of the will—the final aspect of the will's relation to goodness and badness that he will discuss before ending the Treatise on Human Acts with a discussion of the features that human acts have in virtue of their goodness or badness (for example, sinfulness, blameworthiness, and demerit).

Aquinas's main focus in this examination of exterior human acts is the relation between the goodness or badness of interior acts of the will and the goodness or badness of the exterior act. The primary source of the goodness of a human act is the will, in particular, the end which is the object of the interior act of the will. Aquinas spends this question spelling out the ways in which the goodness of the exterior act adds to, influences, or derives from the interior act.

### 20.1. Are goodness and badness primarily in the act of will or in the exterior act?

Answer: goodness and badness exist primarily in the interior act of the will.

We already know that goodness (and badness) exists primarily in the interior act of will, because Aquinas has just told us this in Q19. The purpose of this article, then (as is often the case for the first articles of his questions), is to re-establish the basic framework on which the subsequent articles will expand and develop.

**Reply.** Aquinas describes here two ways in which exterior acts can be called good or bad. The first way is one we're familiar with from the previous question—namely, the way the exterior act is ordered to an end. The end of action is the object of the will's interior act, and the extent to which that end is in accordance with right reason determines whether the will is good or bad. Insofar as the corresponding exterior act is merely a matter of carrying out or fulfilling that end, then, its moral status derives from the goodness or badness of the interior act.

The second way an exterior act can be called good or bad regards what Aquinas calls an act's "matter and circumstances"—basically, what is done and the situation and manner in which it is done. As we saw earlier (18.2), some acts are good or bad according to their genus. Giving to charity is, in itself, a good act. Lying is, in itself, a bad act. (Acts like walking across a field are in themselves morally neutral, but since Aquinas is focused here on the goodness or badness of exterior acts, he doesn't mention such morally neutral acts.) Circumstances come into play here, too, of course: an act is good only if it is performed in appropriate circumstances.

The upshot of these distinctions is that the first way an exterior act can be called good (that is, by its being ordered to a good end) derives from the goodness of the interior act of will—meaning that the goodness is primarily in the will. The second way (matter and circumstances) derives primarily from reason, which judges how appropriate the exterior act would be and presents it to the interior act as to be done or avoided. In that sense, the goodness of the exterior act comes first: reason has to apprehend the exterior act as good and present it to the will as an object. But if the exterior act is evaluated in terms of the order in which an act is actually carried out, its goodness follows the interior act's goodness (since the will is the principle of action and responsible for willing or not willing an object). In terms of moral responsibility, then—which is Aquinas's primary concern in this treatise—the goodness or badness of an act derives primarily from the interior act of the will.

**Obj. and resp. 1.** The first objection and response make the exterior act's relation to the object of action clearer. The objection states that the goodness of the exterior act is primary because the exterior act just *is* the object of the interior act of will. We will what is done (for example, giving to charity or stealing), and that's the object of our action.

In response Aquinas says that the exterior act is the object of the will in the sense that the exterior act is the object that reason presents to the will. In other words, when the intellect apprehends a particular object as good and to be done and presents it to the will as such, what it's presenting as good is a particular exterior act. The will's goodness comes from how it responds to this object. And so, in this sense, the goodness of the will is dependent on the goodness of the exterior act qua object. In terms of the actual human act, however, the exterior act happens after and is posterior to the interior act of will that begins the process. And, given that a human action begins with the movement of the will toward or away from the object presented to it by reason, the will is primarily responsible for the goodness or badness of the act.

**Obj. and resp. 2 & 3.** This also takes care of the second and third objection and response. Goodness comes from the end because, although it is the last thing executed, the end is the first thing willed. That's also how the goodness of an act of will can function as the form of the exterior act: it exists prior to the exterior act and is an important component in shaping that act.

### 20.2. Does the goodness or badness of the exterior act depend wholly on the will?

**Answer:** no, the goodness (or badness) of an exterior act does not depend wholly on the will.

**Reply.** In the same way that we already knew that the goodness of the human act primarily derives from the interior act of the will, we already know at the outset of this article that the goodness of an exterior act does not depend wholly on the will. The central point of this article is to underscore (again) how much harder it is for an act to be good than for it to be bad: everything has to line up correctly for the act to be good, whereas if anything is out of order, the act will be bad.

In particular, Aquinas here is intent on stressing that even if the interior act of the will is good, this is not sufficient for the external act to also be good. The goodness that comes from the exterior act's being ordered to the end of the action depends entirely on the goodness of the will, as we saw in the previous article. But the goodness that comes from having appropriate matter and circumstances depends on reason, not on the will (again, as we saw in the previous article). Reason judges what is to be done and in what circumstances, and it presents that as an object to the will; the will's goodness depends on how it responds to the object.

Complete goodness requires both that the interior act of the will be good and that the object apprehended by reason be good, as well as that the act's circumstances are appropriate. If either the will's intention of the end *or* the actual act willed is bad, *or* the circumstances in which the act is carried out are inappropriate, the exterior act will be bad. (This is the upshot of all three objections and responses, as well.)

### 20.3. Is there one and the same goodness or badness for both the interior and the exterior act?

Answer: sometimes yes and sometimes no.

**Reply.** The interior act of the will and the exterior act are the same qua moral act. They not only share the same end—they are a hylomorphic unity. Yet, as Aquinas has already made abundantly clear, he holds that an act can have more than one aspect of goodness or badness. Going for a run might be good for my health, for instance, but it might also cause me joint pain.

In particular, as Aquinas goes on to comment, the goodness or badness of the interior and exterior acts are interrelated: in his words, they are "ordered to each other," so that if an exterior act is good or bad only because of its relation to the act's end (which is shared by the interior act), then there is one and the same goodness or badness for both acts. The goodness or badness of the interior act of the will "carries over" to the exterior act as well. His example is the case of drinking bitter medicine for the sake of health: the goodness of drinking the bitter medicine (or taking the painful run) is entirely derivative from the goodness of the action's end: health.

There are cases, however, in which an exterior act has its own goodness or badness—as when the medicine you need to drink for your health is independently delicious and something you would happily drink on its own. Aquinas refers to this as deriving from the exterior act's "matter and circumstances" (what is done and the situation and manner in which it is done), which can cause that act to have goodness or badness in its own right. So, for instance,

I might have "apologizing for a wrong I have done" as my end, but then I make the apology too softly to be heard, or I only manage to blurt out, "Ergh, um, well, um . . . ", or I make the apology in a sarcastic voice, and so although my end is good, the exterior act is bad.

**Obj. and resp. 1.** The first objection argues that there can't be one and the same goodness for both the interior act of the will and the exterior act, on the grounds that the two acts stem from different principles. The principle of an interior act of the will is an appetitive power (namely, the will), whereas the principle of an exterior act is the locomotive power (the power responsible for the movement of our bodies). Acts that come from two distinct principles can't share the same goodness, though, because they don't have the same subject.

In response, Aquinas comments that interior and exterior acts are distinct when considered in the "domain of nature"—that is, considered as events in the physical world. Considered in the moral domain, however, the interior and exterior acts together constitute one act (since they share the same end).

**Obj. and resp. 3.** The third objection focuses on the relation between the goodness of the interior and exterior acts. A cause cannot be identical with its effect, but Aquinas has already argued that the cause of the exterior act's goodness is the goodness of the interior act (or vice versa). It looks, then, as though the goodness of the exterior act and the goodness of the interior act must be distinct in order to stand in this relation to each other.

Aquinas replies that cause and effect must be numerically distinct when it comes to a "univocal agent cause," but not when we're speaking of cause and effect in terms of analogy and proportion. In other words, when we're thinking of a case such as when the sun heats water, the cause of the heating (the heat of the sun) and the effect of the heating (the heat of the water) must be numerically distinct. But when we're thinking of a case where cause and effect are more loosely related, they can be the same. The example Aquinas gives is one that goes back to Aristotle: health. We can say that medicine is healthy, we can say that your body is healthy, and we can say that your urine is healthy. In Aquinas's jargon, we're speaking analogically—the sense in which the medicine is healthy is the sense in which it *causes* your body to be healthy, and the sense in which your urine is healthy is the sense in which it is an *effect* of a healthy body. Numerically there is only one thing here: the health of the body that the other two kinds of health derive from. This, Aquinas claims, is the right way to think of the relation between the goodness of the exterior act and the goodness of the interior act of the will. Numerically there is only one thing here: the goodness of the one that the goodness of the other derives from.

## 20.4. Does the exterior act add any goodness or badness beyond that of the interior act?

Answer: only in certain sorts of cases.

**Reply.** Aquinas has already argued that the goodness of the interior and exterior act is one and the same when *regarded as a moral act*. The interior act of the will and the corresponding exterior act are ordered to each other insofar as they share the same end, and their goodness or badness is ordered to each other in the same way. So in that sense, the exterior act adds no goodness to the interior act of the will.

The only exception, says Aquinas, is when "this will itself is made better in those who are good or worse in those who are bad." It is not immediately clear what cases he is thinking of, so it's helpful that he goes on to give three ways that this might happen: *numerically*, with respect to *extension*, and with respect to *intensity*. The first sort of case (*numerical*) is when the interior act of will occurs but (for some reason) the corresponding exterior act does not. I might will to take a swimming class for the sake of my health, for instance, and then fail to sign up for the class during registration. But then the next time the swimming class is offered, I will to take the swimming class and actually sign up and take it. In this case, Aquinas says, my act of will ("taking a swimming class for my health") is repeated, and so there is twice as much goodness involved. My will is itself made better for having willed twice to take the swimming class for the sake of my health.

The second sort of case (*extension*) is when one person who wills to do something for a good or bad end doesn't complete their action because they run into some obstacle, while another person in the same situation pushes through until the deed is complete. Insofar as the second person's will is more persistent, it is better or worse than the first person's will. (Imagine, for example, someone who resolves to hunt down and kill every single family member of the person who shot his father, but then runs into difficulties locating some of the cousins and gives up the quest; that person's will is ultimately less bad than that of his sister, who takes the same vow and refuses to give up the search until she has discovered and killed every last person in that family.)

The third sort of case is simpler: some exterior acts naturally increase or decrease the will to complete the action because those exterior acts are more or less naturally pleasant. The process I have to undergo to get a root canal I require for my dental health, for instance, is excruciating on several levels, and so my will for the root canal will be much less *intense* than my will to, say, reproduce.

Aquinas claims, however, that if we're thinking of an exterior act in terms of its *matter* (namely, what is done) and its *circumstances*, then the goodness or badness of an exterior act definitely adds to the goodness or badness of the will, because the matter and circumstances of the exterior act are the completion and end of the interior act of the will. Suppose that you're furious with one of your friends for telling an embarrassing secret to your other friends, and so you will to tell one of his most closely guarded secrets to them. Your will is not complete until you actually tell one of your friend's secrets to the group. The telling of the secret—and the situation and manner in which you do so—are the matter and circumstances of the exterior act that serve as its terminus.

If you have the chance to tell the secret and you refrain, though, your act is less bad than if you had gone ahead and shared the secret: your will isn't complete because the end isn't fulfilled. On the other hand, if you don't tell your friend's secret only because you don't have the chance to—suppose that particular group of friends doesn't get together again—then your will is complete, because you would tell the secret if you could, and in that case your act has the same degree of badness as if you had told the secret.

**Obj. and resp. 1.** The first objection and response address this same issue: John Chrysostom (Archbishop of Constantinople in the fourth century and an influential early church father) writes that God judges the goodness or badness of our wills, not our deeds; Aquinas responds that Chrysostom is thinking of instances where the act of will is complete and nothing would be added to or subtracted from to the goodness in question by the performance of the exterior act.

**Obj. and resp. 2 & 3.** The second and third objections trade on the sort of goodness the exterior act has in virtue of our willing of the end. In that respect, the goodness of the interior and exterior act are the same. (I will to tell my friend's secret to humiliate him; the badness of my interior act of will, which has as its end my telling the secret, is the same as the badness of my exterior act, which is the telling of the secret.)

Aquinas grants this. He points out, however, that the sort of goodness he's just discussed—the goodness that comes from the matter and circumstances of the exterior act—is distinct from the goodness of the will that comes from the end willed. In fact, as he argued in art. 1 and 2, the matter and circumstances of the exterior act are the ground and the cause of the goodness that the will has in virtue of the act it wills. (So, for example, I will to tell my friend's secret to our mutual group of friends at our annual Christmas party in a loud voice, so that everyone will be paying attention and my friend will be maximally humiliated. The matter and circumstances of the exterior act are what make my will bad in virtue of the act willed.)

### 20.5. Does a consequence add to the goodness or badness of an act?

Answer: Yes. Insofar as we can reasonably foresee a particular consequence, it adds to the exterior act's goodness or badness.

**Reply.** In contemporary ethics, consequentialism is one of the "big three" moral theories (along with virtue ethics—the theory Aquinas advocates—and deontology). Yet at the time Aquinas is writing, the idea that an act's moral status would depend entirely on its consequences is so foreign that he doesn't even consider that possibility, discussing here only whether the consequence of an act adds *anything* to the moral goodness or badness of that act.

Aquinas's answer is that if the consequence is foreseen, then it obviously adds to the act's goodness or badness, insofar as it demonstrates how well- or badly-ordered the person's will is. If you speed down a residential street because you're trying to shake the police officer on your tail, your act is even worse if you realize that the local elementary school is getting out and that you're likely to hit at least one child.

On the other hand, if you don't foresee the consequence of your action, then whether it adds to the goodness or badness of your act depends on whether that consequence usually or always follows from that sort of act (a *per se* consequence), or whether the consequence is accidental or doesn't happen often (a *per accidens* consequence). If the consequence could be easily predicted, then it adds to the goodness or badness of the action whether or not you foresaw that it would occur. After all, if you ask a child to pick up a pan off a stove that you know is hot, it doesn't matter whether you foresaw that the child would burn herself, because picking up pans off stoves is the sort of action that's liable to result in burns. If, on the other hand, you ask a child to pick up a pan off a stove, and she has a severe allergic reaction to the pan's coating, that consequence is accidental and not the sort of thing that follows naturally from that sort of action, and thus it doesn't add to the goodness or badness of the action.

**Obj. and resp. 1–3.** This distinction between *per se* and *per accidens* consequences also features prominently in Aquinas's response to the objections to this article. In response to the first objection—namely, that consequences follow from acts in the same way that effects follow from causes—Aquinas replies that this is true only for *per se* effects and consequences, not the *per accidens* ones. In the same way, Aquinas's response to the second objection—namely, that the good deeds performed by people who hear and are influenced by a preacher add goodness to that act of preaching—is that this is another case of a *per se* consequence that follows naturally from the act of preaching and that does add goodness to the act. The same goes for the third objection: we increase punishment in cases where we think the person should have foreseen and prevented what happened, because what happened was a *per se* consequence of that sort of act and thus does add goodness or badness to the act.

## 20.6. Can one and the same
### exterior act be both good and bad?

Answer: yes, if we're thinking of that exterior act as a natural act rather than a moral act.

**Reply.** Given how many different features of an act can determine whether it is good or bad, it should come as no surprise that Aquinas argues here that the same exterior act can be both good and bad—if we're thinking of the act under the right description. In short, one and the same moral act can't be both good and bad, but one and the same "natural act" (sitting, walking, eating, etc.) can constitute different moral acts with different moral statuses.

    In particular, Aquinas claims that we can think of an act in terms of the "domain of nature" and in terms of the "domain of morals." Take the act of walking across a field without stopping. If we think of it as a "natural" act of continuous walking, it counts as one act. But if we think of it in terms of morality, it can be more than one act. Suppose, for instance, that I start walking across the field to get exercise for the sake of health, but then, as I continue to talk, I start to think about someone I've been having an affair with, and I decide to stop by his house in hopes of getting some action. My one natural act of walking is thus split into two moral acts, one good (exercise for the sake of health) and one bad (walking to my illicit lover's house for the sake of sex). So if we're thinking of an exterior act in the natural domain, one and the same act can be both good and bad.

**Obj. and resp. 1.** The first objection actually gives a good example of the sort of natural action that Aquinas thinks divides into two distinct moral acts: the act is walking to church, first intending to impress others with your piety, but later intending to worship God. As Aquinas points out, this is *one* natural act ("walking") but *two* moral acts ("going to church to impress people" and "going to church to serve God").

**Obj. and resp. 2.** Aquinas also uses the distinction between natural and moral domains in response to the second objection, which says that one and the same moral action can be both good and bad, if we think of it in terms of action (what is being done) and passion (what is being undergone). The example given is more than a little cringe-inducing today: it uses the crucifixion of Christ as an example of one act which is good if thought of in terms of what is being undergone (namely, Christ's suffering for the sake of our redemption) and bad if thought of in terms of what is being done (namely, the Jews putting Christ to death).[40]

---

40. Conditions in Europe for the Jews in the thirteenth and fourteenth century were particularly bad, with the justification for ill treatment often being that they were

Aquinas's response is that action and passion belong to the moral domain only insofar as they are voluntary—that is, although an act of execution might be considered one natural act with two aspects (action and passion), there are two distinct moral acts involved if we think of it from the perspective of the person (or group) willing to perform the execution and from the perspective of the person (or group) willing to undergo the execution.

**Obj. and resp. 3.** The third objection and reply are also rather cringe inducing, for completely different reasons: the example is that of a slave who is considered merely a tool or instrument of his master, and the claim is that if this is the case, an act ordered by the master with a good will (such as building a fire to warm a chilly houseguest) can be carried out with a bad will by the slave (who builds the fire hoping that it burns the guest), and thus one and the same action will be both good and bad.

In response, Aquinas again accepts the problematic underlying assumptions and simply responds that the slave's act does not count as the same act as the master's in terms of what the slave wills. It counts as the same act only in terms of carrying out the act that the master commanded. There are two separate acts of will in this situation, and thus two distinct moral acts.

### Question 21: Features That Accrue to Human Acts

The final question of the Treatise on Human Acts focuses on the further evaluative features that follow on an act's being good or bad. The four features that interest Aquinas here are rightness/sinfulness; praiseworthiness/blameworthiness; merit/demerit in the human realm; and merit/demerit in the eyes of God. Aquinas wraps up the discussion of the ways in which human acts are voluntary—and, therefore, good or bad—by relating that discussion to the features that particularly interest us as human beings. What, for human beings, is the point of knowing whether an act is good or bad? In Aquinas's eyes, it is (at least in large part) so that we know whether that act is sinful or righteous, etc. If we think of the *Summa* as a theological guidebook for Dominican priests,[41] this point becomes even more relevant, and also explains the extreme detail that Aquinas goes into about moral matters in the rest of the *Secunda Pars*. (See the Introduction [pp. xviii–xix, xxv–xxvi] for further discussion of the structure of the *Summa*.)

At the same time, Aquinas must feel that the answers to the questions posed in this Question are fairly self-explanatory, because it is composed of

---

blamed for the death of Christ, rather than, say, the Romans who actually executed him. See Lipton (2014) for further discussion of this troubled history.

41. This is a fairly standard reading of the purpose for the *Summa theologiae*; see Bernard McGinn (2014) for both a history and a defense of this view.

only four articles, all of which are fairly brief. One gets the impression that Aquinas is simply spelling out here conclusions that he expects his readers to have already reached on their own.

### 21.1. Does a human act count as right or sinful simply by being good or bad?

Answer: yes, all human acts count as right or sinful in virtue of their being good or bad.

**Reply.** As Aquinas immediately observes in the body of this article, 'badness' has a broader scope than 'sin.' The Convertibility Thesis (namely, that goodness and being are metaphysically identical) entails that anything that lacks goodness in some respect in which it ought to have it counts as bad. (So, for example, a dull knife that crumbles bread instead of slicing it neatly counts as a bad knife.) Sin, on the other hand, is a term reserved for "an act that is done for the sake of some end," when the act is not related appropriately to the act's end. Why not "an act of will" or "a voluntary act done for the sake of some end"? Because Aquinas is leaving open the space for there to be "natural" sin as well as moral sin. Sin affects all of creation, not just the wills of human beings. Thus, Aquinas says that whenever an act comes from a natural power (as, for example, a puppy's getting larger comes from the natural power of growth) and this happens in line with that thing's natural inclination to an end (the puppy grows into an adult dog), that act has "rightness." But if the act goes wrong in some way (the puppy's cells grow erratically into tumors, for instance, and cancer spreads throughout the puppy's body), Aquinas says that counts as a "natural" sin.

In the case of voluntary actions, however, 'badness' and 'sin' and 'goodness' and 'rightness' have the same scope. The reasons for this are that the will is a natural power, and that human reason and the eternal law provide the rule (proximate rule and supreme rule, respectively) for that power. When the will moves toward an end that is in harmony with reason and the eternal law, it is right, but when the will moves against reason and the eternal law, it sins. In other words, all cases of the will's acting in line with its natural inclination toward the (correctly apprehended) good are instances of right action, and all cases in which the will's acting falls short are instances of sinful action. And so all voluntary acts that count as good or bad count as right or sinful in the same respect.

**Obj. and resp. 1.** The first objection and reply address the issue of monsters, which is Aristotle's term for organisms that develop so differently from how they are supposed to that they can't quite count as members of a particular species. (Think of an "octopus" with only one arm or a three-headed "calf." Can a creature with only one arm even *be* an octopus? Aristotle's response is "No.") In the *Physics*, Aristotle calls monsters "sins in nature"—by which he just means that they are things that develop *outside* the natural order. A human act, however, is *within* the natural order, according to the objection. It doesn't violate the natural order simply by being inordinate or bad.

Aquinas responds very briefly that monsters are called "sins in nature" because they are produced by a defect *in an act* of nature. That is, sin is primarily located in an act and is only derivatively located in things.

**Obj. and resp. 2.** The second objection also references Aristotle's *Physics*, claiming that a sin (in the sense of a deviation from nature) occurs when the intended end is not attained. (For example, when the monster-octopus does not develop eight legs or become a functional member of its species.) But in human acts, badness comes primarily from willing and pursuing an inappropriate end, not from falling short of that end.

Aquinas's reply distinguishes between ultimate and proximate ends, and argues that there is more similarity here than one might think. In a sin of nature (like the monster-pus), the act of generation does indeed fall short of the ultimate end, which is the development and perfection of the thing generated (in this case, a functional adult octopus). But in a sin of the will, the act also falls short of the ultimately intended end, which is happiness. An act of will might achieve its proximate end, but unless it is correctly ordered to the ultimate end of happiness, it falls short of achieving its ultimate end, and counts as sinful.

**Obj. and resp. 3.** The third objection offers a counterexample to the claim that bad acts are always sinful: punishment is bad, but it is not sinful. Aquinas replies that punishment has to do with the person who sins, but is not, considered in itself, bad. Punishment would only be bad, properly speaking, if it were undeserved or improperly carried out. (See Aquinas's discussion of punishment in *ST* I.48.5 resp. 4.)

### 21.2. Is a human act praiseworthy or blameworthy simply because it is good or bad?

Answer: yes, human acts are praiseworthy or blameworthy insofar as they are good or bad.

**Reply.** The question of praise and blame is meant to add a layer of moral responsibility onto the idea of sin, since Aquinas is willing to grant that rocks and trees and koala bears can sin (insofar as acts issuing from the natural powers of these things diverge from their natural inclinations toward their ends). As Aquinas puts it, just as 'badness' is broader than 'sin,' so 'sin' is broader than 'blameworthiness.' In particular, praise and blame are terms reserved for moral agents: they are terms used to indicate or ascribe goodness or badness to the acts that moral agents perform. All voluntary acts are either good or bad, as we saw above (18.9), and so all voluntary acts are praiseworthy or blameworthy in virtue of being good (and right) or bad (and sinful).

**Obj. and resp. 1.** The first objection helps carve out the distinction between 'sinful' and 'blameworthy.' A natural act (such as a puppy's growing) is not under the control of the natural agent (the puppy). To be blameworthy, though, an act has to be under the control of the agent and thus count as voluntary. So, although the puppy's developing cancer counts as a natural sin, the puppy is not blameworthy for developing that cancer. (Again, this underscores the difference between the way we use the term 'sin' and the way Aquinas uses it.)

**Obj. and resp. 2.** The second objection raises a point we haven't seen yet: sin in acts of art—where 'art' refers to areas where human beings direct their acts towards ends relative to a particular craft, such as grammar or medicine—is supposed to be analogous to sin in moral acts. But we don't blame the grammarian or the doctor for writing incorrectly or giving medicine incorrectly, the objection claims, on the grounds that grammarians and doctors have the ability to produce a good or bad result according to their desires. (I can intentionally violate the rules of grammar, for instance, and write, "I speak things real good" to a friend after I've just said something particularly idiotic if I want, and I'm not being sinful. I'm being playful.)

Aquinas's response is (not surprisingly) that art and morality function differently. In the realm of art, "reason is ordered to a particular end, which is something thought up by reason." In other words, in art, I think up the result I want to achieve and then I figure out how to attain it. The only constraint on what I think up is my imagination. In the moral domain, however, "reason is ordered to the general end of the whole of human life." That is to say, as we've seen repeatedly at this point in the Treatise, whether an act is morally good or bad depends on how it relates to the object apprehended as good by reason, and on whether reason has correctly apprehended the good in this case. Whether an action is bad, sinful, or blameworthy depends on whether it diverges from what is required for a well-ordered human life. And if an act is sinful, we are blamed as human beings who are part of the moral community. In contrast, in the case of art, sin can occur when an artist means to produce a good work but actually produces a bad one (as when a carpenter intends to make a lovely bookshelf but actually makes one that collapses the first time books are placed on it), or when the artist means to produce a bad work (perhaps to spite the person who commissioned it) and instead produces a good one (that wins awards for its originality, say). Aquinas also claims that the artist can sin by deceiving someone with her work—as when a counterfeiter successfully produces what passes for currency. In the first case, the artisan should be blamed qua artist (for producing results contrary to what she intended); in the second case, the artisan should be blamed qua human being (for intentionally deceiving someone with her work). In any event, human beings are considered blameworthy for all and only bad and sinful voluntary acts.

**Obj. and resp. 3:** The third objection plays on the relation between badness and weakness or powerlessness. If being and goodness are truly convertible (which Aquinas holds), then the worse something is, the less fully it exists and the weaker or less powerful it is. But we don't blame people for being weak or powerless—in fact, we think that being weak or powerless *diminishes* someone's blameworthiness. (We pity someone who's unable to do what's right because they're not strong enough, but we don't blame them as much as we do someone who's strong enough to do the right thing and simply fails to do it.)

Aquinas's response is simply that when it comes to weakness of will—the relevant sort of weakness or powerlessness—this weakness is in the control of the human agent. If someone is habitually weak-willed, and that is why he fails to get up in time to get to work, that does not excuse him. He is morally responsible for taking the steps necessary for cultivating the habits that would get him up in time for work.

### 21.3. Does a human act count as meritorious or demeritorious simply because it is good or bad?

Answer: yes, human acts count as meritorious or demeritorious in virtue of their being good or bad—that is, there's nothing above and beyond its goodness or badness that an action requires in order to deserve merit or demerit.

**Reply.** Aquinas, having addressed sin and blame, turns in this article to the question of merit and demerit. To modern ears, 'demerit' doesn't mean much (unless you're from the UK, from a former colony, or a fan of British fiction, in which case it makes you think of the system for punishment in the UK public school system). In Aquinas's time, however, 'merit' and 'demerit' were terms that imply that there is another agent in the picture whom the original actor has either helped or harmed, either directly or indirectly (by helping or hurting the community of which both agents are part). And once we're talking about communities and how our acts impact other people, we're in the realm of justice. Thus, the question of whether human acts count as meritorious or demeritorious simply by being good or bad is a question of how justice—and, in particular, recompense (that is, reward or punishment) for actions that affect others—relates to the goodness or badness of our voluntary actions.

In short, the question of this article boils down to whether an action needs to possess some component above and beyond its being good or bad in order to be meritorious (or demeritorious). Aquinas argues that it doesn't. (In fact, building on the previous two articles, he concludes here that good/bad human acts are coextensive with praiseworthy/blameworthy *and* right/sinful, *and* meritorious/demeritorious acts.) The reason for this is that anyone who lives in a society is part of that community, and so the help or harm done to an individual member of that society impacts the society as a whole. Aquinas claims that if someone acts for the good or bad of another person, that act deserves reward or punishment both from the individual who is helped or harmed and from the society as a whole. If I perform CPR on a student who has collapsed on my college campus, for instance, and save his life, my act deserves recompense primarily from the student I've saved but also from the college as a whole. (At the very least, the student should thank me, and the college should officially recognize what I've done for one of its members.) If someone acts directly for the good or bad of the whole society, moreover, as when you intentionally violate its traffic laws, that act deserves punishment primarily from the society as a whole (as enacted by its agents—in this case, traffic cops) and secondarily from the fellow members of that society (who honk and yell as you run yet another red light).

In fact, even when the only person impacted by an act is the agent who performs that act, that act still deserves recompense insofar as it affects the society that agent is part of. So, if you have a backyard garden and grow delicious vegetables for yourself all summer, but there's no one else who lives with you and you don't share the vegetables, your act still deserves reward or blame for how it impacts society as a whole (because of, say, the degree to which you are healthier and happier than you would otherwise have been or because of the impact you have on the local economy, no matter how slight).

In any event, the final upshot of this discussion is that we learn that although the scope of 'good,' 'praiseworthy,' 'right,' and 'meritorious' are identical when it comes to voluntary actions, they count as such for different reasons: a good act counts as *praiseworthy* (or blameworthy) insofar as it is voluntary, as *right* insofar as it is correctly related to an end (and sinful when it diverges from that), and as *meritorious* (or demeritorious) insofar as justice requires recompense toward another agent or society because of it. We attend to the different aspects of moral actions depending on what our particular interests or needs in a situation are.

**Obj. and resp. 1.** The first objection raises the question of the person whose good or bad act affects only them (as in the backyard garden case) and argues that such an act cannot deserve recompense because that term applies only in cases where the act impacts someone else beyond the original agent.

In response, Aquinas claims that sometimes good or bad acts can be ordered to the good or bad of the community as a whole, not just to another particular agent. This seems only partially to respond to the original objection, however, since in the backyard garden case, I have not ordered my action for the good of society—I am just thinking of my eating fresh, tasty vegetables. Aquinas has said in the main reply, though, that even in this case, my act deserves merit or demerit for its effect on the community as a whole, and so we can just pretend that he said that again here, because that actually answers the objection. (The third objection and reply cover this same territory, and there Aquinas actually does make this point—namely, that the good or the bad that people do to themselves carries over into the community as well. As John Donne observed, no man is an island.)

**Obj. and resp. 2.** The second objection is a little quirky: it states that we don't deserve punishment or reward for doing what we like with the things we have control over. If I buy a Prada jacket and then use it to start a fire in my fireplace, for instance, that might be stupid, but I don't deserve punishment for my action. The objection continues, saying that insofar as we have control over our own actions, we don't deserve reward or punishment for them.

Aquinas's response—not surprisingly—is that although our actions are under our own control, insofar as we are members of a society, our actions belong to that society as well as to ourselves, and we deserve merit or demerit insofar as our actions impact that society. Also, he points out that at times we're responsible for using what belongs to us for the sake of the community (for example, if you're a mechanical engineer on a plane that's malfunctioning, you're responsible for using your knowledge for the good of everyone on that plane).

### 21.4. Does a human act count as meritorious or demeritorious before God simply because it is good or bad?

Answer: yes, human acts count as meritorious or demeritorious even before God in virtue of their being good or bad.

**Reply.** Aquinas claimed in the previous article that human acts can be meritorious or demeritorious toward another agent either (1) with respect to that other agent, or (2) with respect to the community that both agents are part of. In this article, he argues that human acts are meritorious (or demeritorious) in God's eyes for both reasons. In other words, one and the same human act will count as (good, right, praiseworthy, and) meritorious in the human realm *and* meritorious in the divine realm. (And vice versa.)

The explanation for how an act that impacts another human agent can count as meritorious or demeritorious before God relies on God's being the ultimate end of all human action. We should direct all our acts to God: if an act toward another human being is in line with that ultimate end (as when I pay my neighbor's electric bill in the winter because I know he is unemployed and is suffering because he can't afford the cost of heating his house), then that act counts as meritorious before God. If I know my neighbor is suffering, though, and instead of helping him out with his heating bill, I use all my excess funds to build an unnecessary addition to my own home, Aquinas says that my action fails to treat God with the honor due to my ultimate end.

At the same time, acts can count as meritorious or demeritorious before God insofar as they affect the society we are all part of—what Aquinas calls "the whole community of the universe." God is in charge of that community, and his primary concern is for the common good of the universe. Insofar as our actions have an impact on the common good, then, God cares about them and sees them as deserving reward or punishment.

**Obj. and resp. 1.** The first objection states that we can't have merit or demerit before God, because that involves helping or harming another agent, and we can't help or harm God. Aquinas responds that although we can't make God himself any better or worse, we can affect the order of the universe that God has created. We count as taking something away from God, then, when we make the created order worse, and we count as giving something to God when we make it better. (If we, say, knowingly pollute the air and rivers around us, we disrupt the order of the world as God created it, and we deserve punishment accordingly.)

**Obj. and resp. 2.** The second objection tries to flip the blame, so that God ends up being responsible for whether our actions are good or bad. Human beings are instruments of the divine power—the Prime Mover—and so how can we deserve merit or demerit for actions that God makes possible in the first place? Aquinas's response is that although God is the ultimate principle of our actions, he doesn't move us in a way that also prevents us from moving ourselves via free choice. (See the discussion of this in 9.6 resp. 3.) To the extent that our actions are voluntary, we are morally responsible for them.

**Obj. and resp. 3.** The third objection claims that not all actions are ordered to God, and so not all actions can be meritorious or demeritorious in his sight. In response, Aquinas points out that the way in which our actions are ordered to God is quite different from the way our actions are ordered to, say, our political community. Our relationship with our political communities does not involve every part of who we are and what we have. Our relationship to God, however, is the relation between us and our ultimate end. Everything we are, everything we can do, and everything we have is directly related to God—our First and Final Cause. Thus, all of our voluntary acts will count as meritorious or demeritorious before God "by the very nature of the act." All our actions inherently aim toward or away from our final end, and so all our actions deserve reward or punishment.

# Appendix 1: Interpretations of the Treatise on Human Acts

## Account A.

Adapted from Gilby (1970, vol. 17, app. 1 "Structure of a Human Act")

HUMAN ACT

| MIND | WILL |
|---|---|
| *immanent activity*<br>*in 'order of intention'* | |
| *about end* | |
| 1. perception of an end as good (8.1, 9.1) | 2. wish, a velleity without effort (8.2) |
| 3. judgment that an end is possible (13.5) | 4. intention to achieve the end (12) |
| *about means* | |
| 5. deliberation about means (14) | 6. consent, approving and promoting the process of deliberation (15) |
| 7. decision about which course is to be taken (13.1 ad 2) | 8. choice of one course (13) |
| *practical action*<br>*in 'order of execution'* | |
| 9. command (17) | 10. application or *usus activus* (16.1) |
| 11. performance or *usus passivus* (16.1) | 12. completion or *fruition* (11) |

Gilby (1966) offers a somewhat different account in vol. 18, Appendix 5, "The Subordination of Morals." He seems to owe his account to Gardeil (1909). The ultimate source of the traditional twelve-step account in modern studies appears to be Billuart (1876).

451

# Account B.

Adapted from McInerny (1992, ch. 3, "The Structure of Human Action")

Acts of intellect are in *italics*; acts of will are in roman type.

## Acts of Will Bearing on the End

*intellect*→will (the simple stirring of the will by thought and image)→enjoyment (an anticipation of the delight of having the object in reality)→intention (tending toward the thing, seeing it as an object of pursuit, as something getting to which may entail doing many as yet unthought-of things)

## Acts of Will Bearing on the Means (presuppose the intention of the end)

*counsel*→consent (the directing of the movement of appetite on something within the power of the one doing)→choice (of one means, if more than one is turned up by counsel)→*command*→use (the will's moving the executive powers)

The basic triad is **intellectual grasp of good/will; counsel/choice; command/use**

McInerny emphasizes that this great variety of acts can best be distinguished by examining acts that are interrupted or left incomplete

# Account C.

Adapted from Donagan (1982)

Acts of intellect are in *italics*; acts of will are in roman type.

## Acts of Will Bearing on the End

*Any intellectual act in which something is affirmed to be an attainable good*→will→enjoyment (every simple act of will has an act of enjoyment as its counterpart)→intention (goes beyond merely willing the end to willing it as an end to which some possible act is ordered—this is what prompts deliberation)

## Acts of Will Bearing on the Means

*deliberation*, terminating in a *judgment/verdict*→consent (is accorded to suitable means to one's ends as soon as they are judged to be such)→choice→*command*→use

Donagan argues that Aquinas should have identified *command* with *judgment* and use with choice. (But see McInerny's response [1992, 178–84]. See also MacIntyre [1988, 190–91].) Like McInerny, Donagan argues that "the components of simple human acts are ascertained, not by introspecting what happens when we perform them, but by examining various cases in which an act is begun but not completed."

## Account D.

Adapted from Westberg (1994, pt. III, "Analysing the Process of Action")

Acts of intellect are in italics; acts of will are in roman type.

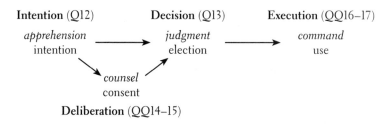

Westberg emphasizes that cognition and volition work concurrently in each of the four stages: in intention (I.79.10 resp. 3), decision (I-II.13.1), deliberation (I-II.14 ad1), and execution (I-II.16.1; 17.1 resp. 2).

# Appendix 2: Being and goodness

ST 1a 5.1, reprinted from Aquinas (2006)

Are good and being identical in reality?

It seems that good differs in reality from being:

1. Boethius says in *On the Hebdomads*: "I see that it is one thing for things to be good and another for things to be." Therefore good and being differ in reality.

2. Nothing gives form to itself. But something is called good through the information of being, according to the commentary on *The Book of Causes*. Therefore good differs in reality from being.

3. Good can be found in degrees of more or less. But existence is not found in degrees of more or less. Therefore good differs in reality from being.

**On the contrary.** Augustine says in *On Christian Doctrine* that "insofar as we are, we are good."

**Reply.** Good and being are identical in reality; they differ only conceptually (*secundum rationem*). This is made clear as follows. The concept of the good consists in this: that something is desirable; hence the Philosopher says in *Nicomachean Ethics* I [1094a3] that "the good is what all things desire." But it is clear that something is desirable insofar as it is perfect, for everything desires its own perfection. Now a thing is perfect insofar as it is actual, from which it is clear that something is good insofar as it exists, since existence is the actuality of every thing, as was shown above [3.4; 4.1 Response to 3]. Hence it is clear that good and being are identical in reality, but that "good" expresses the concept of desirability that is not expressed in "being."

**Response to 1.** Although good and being are identical in reality, nevertheless, since they differ conceptually, something is not said to be unqualifiedly a being and unqualifiedly good in the same way. For "being" properly speaking means that something exists in actuality, and actuality properly speaking has a relation to potentiality; therefore, something is called a being unqualifiedly because of that which first distinguishes it from what is only in potentiality, and this is the substantial existence of a thing. So it is through a thing's substantial existence that we call it a being unqualifiedly. Through additional actualities a thing is said to be in some qualified way, as, for example, "to be white" signifies being in a qualified manner; since to be white does not take something out of absolute potentiality, since it comes to something already actually existing.

Good, on the other hand, implies the character of the perfect, which is the desirable, and so implies the character of the ultimate. Hence what is ultimately perfect is said to be unqualifiedly good. Whatever does not possess the ultimate perfection that it ought to have, even though it has some perfection inasmuch as it is actual, is not said to be unqualifiedly perfect or unqualifiedly good, but rather good only in a qualified way.

To sum up: due to its primary existence, its substantial existence, something is said to be a being unqualifiedly, but good only in a qualified manner, that is, insofar as it is a being. Due to its ultimate actuality, on the other hand, something is called a being in a qualified way and good unqualifiedly. Thus when Boethius says that "it is one thing for things to be good and another for things to be," we should take this to mean being good unqualifiedly and being unqualifiedly, since it is because of a thing's first actuality that it is a being unqualifiedly, while because of its ultimate actuality it is good unqualifiedly. Still, a thing is good in a certain way because of its first actuality, and is a being in a certain way because of its ultimate actuality.

**Response to 2.** Something is called good through information insofar as it receives good unconditionally through its ultimate actualization.

**Response to 3.** Likewise, something is called more or less good because of its further actualization—for instance, because of knowledge or virtue.

# Bibliography

Aquinas, Thomas. *The Treatise on Human Nature: Summa Theologiae 1A, 75–89.* Translated with Commentary by Robert Pasnau. Indianapolis: Hackett Publishing Company, 2002.

Aquinas, Thomas. *The Treatise on the Divine Nature: Summa Theologiae I 1–13.* Translated with Commentary by Brian J. Shanley, O.P. and Introduction by Robert Pasnau. Indianapolis: Hackett Publishing Company, 2006.

Billuart, C.-R. *Summa Sancti Thomae Hodiernis Academiarum Moribus Accommodata.* Paris, 1876.

Boler, John. "The Inclination for Justice." In *The Cambridge History of Medieval Philosophy,* edited by R. Pasnau and C. Van Dyke, 484–92. Cambridge: Cambridge University Press, 2010.

Bradley, Denis. *Aquinas on the Twofold Human Good: Reason and Human Happiness in Aquinas's Moral Science.* Washington, DC: Catholic University of America Press, 1997.

Brower, Jeffrey. *Aquinas's Ontology of the Material World: Change, Hylomorphism, and Material Objects.* Oxford: Oxford University Press, 2014.

DeYoung, Rebecca Konyndyk, Colleen McCluskey, and Christina Van Dyke. *Aquinas's Ethics: Metaphysical Foundations, Moral Theory, and Theological Context.* Notre Dame, IN: University of Notre Dame Press, 2009.

Donagan, Alan. "Thomas Aquinas on Human Action." In *The Cambridge History of Later Medieval Philosophy,* edited by Norman Kretzmann, Anthony Kenny, and Jan Pinborg, 642–54. Cambridge: Cambridge University Press, 1982.

Gardeil, A. "Acte Humain," *Dictionnaire de Théologie Catholique,* vol. 1. Paris: Letouzey et Ané, 1909.

Gilby, Thomas, trans. and ed. *Summa theologiae,* vol. 17. Cambridge: Blackfriars, 1970.

———. *Summa theologiae,* vol. 18. Cambridge: Blackfriars, 1966.

Goris, Harm. "Angelic Knowledge in Aquinas and Bonaventure." In *A Companion to Angels in Medieval Philosophy,* edited by Tobias Hoffmann, 149–86. Leiden: Brill, 2012.

Hause, Jeffrey. "Thomas Aquinas and the Voluntarists," *Medieval Philosophy and Theology* 6 (1997): 167–82.

———. "Aquinas on Non-Voluntary Acts," *International Philosophical Quarterly* 46 (2006): 459–75.

Jordan, Mark. "Ideals of *Scientia moralis* and the Invention of the '*Summa theologiae.*'" In *Aquinas's Moral Theory: Essays in Honor of Norman*

*Kretzmann*, edited by S. MacDonald and E. Stump, 79–100. Ithaca: Cornell University Press, 1999.

———. "The *Summa*'s Reform of Moral Teaching—and Its Failures." In *Contemplating Aquinas: On the Varieties of Interpretation*, edited by F. Kerr, 41–54. London: SCM Press, 2003.

Kenny, Anthony. *Aquinas on Mind*. New York: Routledge, 1994.

Kretzmann, Norman. "A General Problem of Creation: Why Would God Create Anything at All?" In *Being and Goodness*, edited by S. MacDonald, 208–28.

———. *The Metaphysics of Theism: Aquinas's Natural Theology in "Summa Contra Gentiles" I*. Oxford: Clarendon Press, 1997.

Lewis, C. S. *The Discarded Image*. Cambridge: Cambridge University Press, 1964.

Lipton, Sarah. *Dark Mirror: The Medieval Origins of Anti-Jewish Iconography*. New York: Metropolitan Books, 2014.

MacDonald, Scott. "Ultimate Ends in Practical Reasoning: Aquinas's Aristotelian Moral Psychology and Anscombe's Fallacy," *Philosophical Review* 100 (1991): 31–66.

———, ed. *Being and Goodness: The Concept of the Good in Metaphysics and Philosophical Theology*. Ithaca: Cornell University Press, 1991.

———. "Theory of Knowledge." In *The Cambridge Companion to Aquinas*, edited by Norman Kretzmann and Eleonore Stump, 160–95. Cambridge: Cambridge University Press, 1993.

MacIntyre, Alasdair. *Whose Justice? Which Rationality?* Notre Dame, IN: University of Notre Dame Press, 1988.

Marenbon, John. *Medieval Philosophy: An Historical and Philosophical Introduction*. New York: Routledge, 2006.

McDannell, Colleen and Bernhard Lang. *Heaven: A History*, 2nd ed. New Haven: Yale University Press, 2001.

McGinn, Bernard. *Thomas Aquinas's "Summa theologiae": A Biography*. Princeton, NJ: Princeton University Press, 2014.

McInerny, Ralph. *Aquinas on Human Action: A Theory of Practice*. Washington, DC: The Catholic University of America Press, 1992.

Pasnau, Robert. *Thomas Aquinas on Human Nature: A Philosophical Study of* Summa theologiae *1a 75–89*. Cambridge: Cambridge University Press, 2002.

———. "Medieval Social Epistemology: *Scientia* for Mere Mortals," *Episteme* 7 (2010): 23–41.

Pegis, Anton. "The Separated Soul and Its Nature in St Thomas." In *St Thomas Aquinas 1274–1974: Commemorative Studies*, Vol. 1, edited by Armand Maurer, CSB, 131–59. Toronto: Pontifical Institute of Mediaeval Studies, 1974.

Rist, John M. *Augustine: Ancient Thought Baptized*. Cambridge: Cambridge University Press, 1996.

Shields, Christopher. *Order in Multiplicity: Homonymy in the Philosophy of Aristotle*. Oxford: Oxford University Press, 1999.

Stump, Eleonore. *Aquinas*. New York: Routledge, 2005.

Stump, Eleonore and Norman Kretzmann. "Eternity," *The Journal of Philosophy* 78 (1981): 429–58.

Toner, Patrick. "Personhood and Death in St. Thomas Aquinas," *History of Philosophy Quarterly* 26 (2009): 121–38.

Torrell, Jean-Pierre. *Saint Thomas Aquinas, Volume 1: The Person and His Work*. Translated by Robert Royal. Washington, DC: The Catholic University of America Press, 1996.

Van Dyke, Christina. "Not Properly a Person: The Rational Soul and 'Thomistic Substance Dualism,'" *Faith and Philosophy* 26, no. 2 (2009): 186–204.

———. "Aquinas's Shiny Happy People: Perfect Happiness and the Limits of Human Nature," *Oxford Studies in the Philosophy of Religion* 6 (2014a): 269–91.

———. "I See Dead People: Disembodied Souls and Aquinas's 'Two-Person' Problem," *Oxford Studies in Medieval Philosophy* 2 (2014b): 25–45.

Visser, Sandra and Thomas Williams. *Anselm*. Oxford: Oxford University Press, 2009.

Westberg, Daniel. *Right Practical Reason: Aristotle, Action, and Prudence in Aquinas*. Oxford: Clarendon Press, 1994.

Williams, Thomas. "Human Freedom and Agency." In *The Oxford Handbook of Aquinas*, edited by Brian Davies and Eleonore Stump, 199–208. Oxford: Oxford University Press, 2011.

Wippel, John. "Thomas Aquinas on the Separated Soul's Natural Knowledge," In *Thomas Aquinas: Approaches to Truth*, edited by J. McEvoy and M. Dunne, 114–40. Dublin: Four Courts Press, 2002.

———. *The Metaphysical Thought of Thomas Aquinas: From Finite Being to Uncreated Being*. Washington, DC: Catholic University of America Press, 2000.

# Index

Directing (as act of reason), 4, 5, 35, 36, 119, 123, 142, 148, 173, 212, 326, 353, 376, 377, 380, 384

Disposition, 24, 25, 74, 80, 89–90, 121, 142, 154–55, 165, 171, 263, 277, 284, 286, 335, 390–93, 414

Divine simplicity, 160, 231, 241, 279

Domain, 96, 115, 135, 195, 199, 319, 325

Moral, 177, 195, 200, 203, 438, 442, 443, 446

Natural, 151, 195, 200, 203, 438, 442

Of action, 2, 120, 121, 123, 130, 135, 139, 356, 358, 362–63, 365, 366, 369

Dominican Order, xvii–xix, 443

Effect, 4, 8, 40, 85, 107, 112, 129, 134, 159–60, 161–62, 165, 166, 180, 186, 193, 195, 198–99, 209, 213, 239, 299, 311, 314, 325, 329, 338–39, 363, 367, 399, 400, 405, 419, 438, 441. *See also* Cause

End, 104, 124

Appropriate ordering, 45, 46, 63, 164, 172, 179, 201, 261–63, 312, 419, 444

As object of will, 3–7, 11, 13, 26, 90, 91, 96, 167, 169, 192, 212, 259–62, 319–20, 322, 325, 331–34, 341, 353–54, 361, 372, 407–8, 410–11, 420, 435

Attainment, 13, 14, 24–25, 27–28, 33, 40, 44, 56, 63–64, 112, 144, 226, 237, 244, 247–48, 276, 308, 345, 378–79

Final, 208, 213, 216, 226, 238, 263, 450

For human beings, of human life (*see* Happiness)

Intelligible, 33–34, 44

Proximate, 6, 116, 124, 201–2, 350, 445

*See also* Ultimate End

Enjoyment, 27–28, 34, 42, 44, 49, 56, 108–16, 119, 142–44, 240, 247, 255, 256, 258, 276–77, 285, 339–37, 349–50, 353, 377–78, 384, 452. *See also* Delight

Essence, xxii, 22, 28, 40, 46, 48, 51, 163, 236, 325, 401

Divine, xx, 28, 30, 38, 39, 45–46, 47, 49, 54, 57, 59, 61, 63, 65, 223, 231, 240, 241, 244, 246–50, 252, 254–55, 256–59, 263, 266–68, 269, 273, 275–85, 288, 396

Of happiness, 29, 33, 41, 65, 236, 241

Eternal law, 179–80, 183–84, 201, 422–24, 431, 444

As supreme rule, 201, 444

Evil (moral), 19, 79, 80, 83, 105–6, 127, 163, 196, 232, 278, 307, 311, 317, 337, 404

Executive power(s), 141, 142, 145, 149, 380, 381, 383, 384, 452

Fear, 59, 324, 390

As possible cause of involuntariness, 76–79, 301–4, 308

Form, xxii, 4, 5, 6, 8, 21, 23, 29, 37, 45, 48, 63, 64, 86, 87, 88, 102, 103, 121, 151, 158, 161–62, 163, 164, 165, 167, 168, 169, 173, 189, 191, 192, 193, 208, 215, 234, 262–64, 269, 317, 332, 333, 355, 385–86, 394, 398–400, 404, 409

Genus, xxii, 10, 69, 70, 81, 103, 149, 150, 159, 161, 162, 164, 167, 168, 169, 178, 181, 188, 192, 193, 198, 199, 221, 236, 309, 384, 386, 395, 396, 398, 400, 403, 405, 406, 408, 409, 410, 415, 431, 435

Glory, as potential candidate for happiness, 17–18, 38, 52–53, 230–32, 271–72